CW01080410

Written by the Editors at FL Memo with contributions from Philip Fontbin, ACA MBA.

Indicator has joined forces with **FL Memo**

Original edition produced with the input, advice and collaboration of the UK office of

INTERNATIONAL BUSINESS ADVISERS AND ACCOUNTANTS

Important Disclaimer

ISBN: 978-0-9928608-1-3

Indicator - FL Memo Ltd
Calgarth House
39-41 Bank Street
Ashford, Kent TN23 IDQ

Telephone: (020) 7803 4666
Fax: (020) 7803 4699
Email: flm@flmemo.co.uk
Website: www.flmemo.co.uk

Accountancy and Financial Reporting

2014

UK GAAP

Your book is fully updated online. Make sure you have your login details!

Your key benefits

Memo Online – a regularly updated service that features the entire contents of the book:

- fully searchable and always up to date giving you peace of mind

- store information, create notes and set up alerts to suit your own needs

Multi-user version – enabling more than one person to access the service at the same time (option available on request at www.flmemo.co.uk/requestlogin.php)

Email updates – alerting you to the latest news and fully integrated in the online service

Contents

Part 8: Reporting options for smaller entities

Part 9: Group accounts

Part 10: Miscellaneous

Part 11: General information

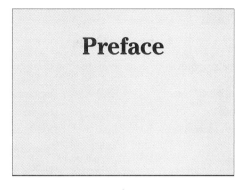

Preface

Accountancy and Financial Reporting 2014 continues to provide clear, concise and accurate guidance on current accounting and financial reporting practice for non-listed companies in the UK. This, the eleventh edition, covers the provisions and requirements of Company Law, the Accounting Standards, UITF Abstracts, and other generally accepted accounting practice, as well as the **new financial reporting framework** currently being developed by the Financial Reporting Council (FRC).

As most readers will know, the FRC is in the process of streamlining the existing system of financial reporting in the UK, in a bid to reduce the regulatory and administrative burden on small and medium-sized companies. However, the **current system of UK GAAP** will continue in force until 1 January 2015, after which the FRSSE will provide the accounting framework for smaller companies, whilst other non-listed entities apply a single financial reporting standard (FRS 102). Listed companies must adopt international financial reporting standards (IFRS) and are beyond the scope of this publication.

Accountancy and Financial Reporting 2014 is an essential reference resource for both experts and non-specialists alike and has been updated and expanded to reflect regulations and practice in force at 31 March 2014. As such, business professionals including practicising accountants, finance managers, tax advisors, financial controllers and management consultants, as well as accountancy students, will find this publication an indispensible reference tool.

Accountancy and Financial Reporting 2014 is based on an internationally successful formula, designed to keep readers abreast of changes affecting accountants in public practice and in industry, and will help guide you through the dynamic reforms currently enveloping UK GAAP. Between editions, readers can monitor regulatory developments by accessing our online updates, via our website at **www.flmemo.co.uk.**

The editors welcome feedback from readers at: accountancy—editors@flmemo.co.uk

Indicator - FL Memo Ltd
March 2014

Abbreviations

The following are the main abbreviations and terms used in this book:

ABI	Association of British Insurers
The Act	Companies Act
ACCA	Association of Chartered Certified Accountants
Accounts	Financial statements
AGM	Annual general meeting
AIM	Alternative Investment Market
ARD	Accounting reference date
ARP	Accounting reference period
ASB	Accounting Standards Board
ASC	Accounting Standards Committee
BIS	Department of Business, Innovation and Skills
Cadbury Code	Code of Best Practice, issued by the Cadbury Committee
Cadbury Committee	Committee on the Financial Aspects of Corporate Governance
CA 1985	Companies Act 1985, as amended
CA 2006	Companies Act 2006
CASE	Committee on Accounting for Smaller Entities, a subcommittee of the ASB
CCAB	Consultative Committee of Accountancy Bodies, consisting of ACCA, CIMA, CIPFA, ICAEW, ICAI and ICAS
CIMA	Chartered Institute of Management Accountants
CIPFA	Chartered Institute of Public Finance and Accountancy
CISCO	City Group for Smaller Companies, now renamed Quoted Companies Alliance (QCA)
Code of Best Practice	Code of Best Practice issued by the Cadbury Committee
Combined Code	Former name of the UK Corporate Governance Code.
DP	Discussion Paper
DRC	Depreciated replacement cost
ED	Exposure Draft
EEA	European Economic Area
EPS/eps	Earnings per share
ESOP	Employee share ownership plan
EU	European Union
EUV	Existing use value
FAS	Financial Accounting Standard (USA)
FASB	Financial Accounting Standards Board (USA)
FIFO	First In, First Out
FRAG	Financial Reporting and Auditing Group
FRC	Financial Reporting Council
FRED	Financial Reporting Exposure Draft
FRRP	Financial Reporting Review Panel
FRS	Financial Reporting Standard
FRSSE	Financial Reporting Standard for Smaller Entities
FSA	Financial Services Authority (Replaced by the Financial Conduct Authority)
FTSE 100	Index: Financial Times Stock Exchange top 100 companies
GAAP	Generally Accepted Accounting Practice
GAAS	Generally Accepted Auditing Standards
GN	Guidance Note (issued by the Institute and Faculty of Actuaries)
Greenbury Committee	Study Group on directors' remuneration
Hampel Committee	Committee on corporate governance
Higgs Report	Review of the role and effectiveness of non-executive directors, by Derek Higgs, January 2003
IAS	International Accounting Standard
IASB	International Accounting Standards Board
IASC	International Accounting Standards Committee
ICAEW	The Institute of Chartered Accountants in England and Wales
ICAI	The Institute of Chartered Accountants in Ireland

ICAS	The Institute of Chartered Accountants of Scotland	**SEC**	Securities and Exchange Commission
		SFA	Securities and Futures Authority
IFRIC	International Financial Reporting Interpretations Committee	**SFAS**	Statement of Financial Accounting Standards
IGU	Income generating unit	**SI**	Statutory Instrument
IPO	Initial public offering	**SME**	Small and/or medium-sized entity
IRR	Internal rate of return	**SORP**	Statement of Recommended Practice (recommendations of accounting practices for specific industries or sectors)
ISA	International Standard on Auditing		
ISAE	International Standard on Assurance Engagements		
ISMA	International Securities Market Association Ltd	**Smith Report**	"Audit Committees; Combined Code Guidance-report and proposed guidance by an FRC-appointed group chaired by Sir Robert Smith"
JANE	Joint arrangement that is not an entity		
LIBOR	London Inter-Bank Offer Rate	**SRO**	Self-regulatory organization
LIFFE	London International Financial Futures and Options Exchange	**SSAP**	Statement of Standard Accounting Practice
LIFO	Last In, First Out	**STRGL**	Statement of total recognised gains and losses
Listed company	A company whose securities have been admitted to the Official List of the UK Listing Authority	**TR**	Technical Release
		TSR	Total shareholder return
LR	Listing rules of the UK Listing Authority	**Turnbull Committee**	The Working Party set up the ICAEW to assist listed companies implement new internal control requirements of the Combined Code
LTIP	Long-term incentive plan		
NASDAQ	National Association of Securities Dealers Automated Quotations		
		UITF	Urgent Issues Task Force of the ASB
NIC	National Insurance contributions	**The UK Corporate Governance Code**	New name (as of 2010) of the Combined Code
OEIC	Open-ended investment company		
P&L	Profit and loss account		
QCA	Quoted Companies Alliance		
RIE	Recognised investment exchange	**VAT**	Value added tax
ROI	Return on investment	**Walker Report**	Sir David Walker's report on the corporate governance of banks and other financial institutions in November 2009
SAS	Statement on Auditing Standards		
Sch	Schedule (to the Companies Act)		

PART 1

General accounting framework and principles

Accounting rules, principles and conventions

This volume is primarily concerned with accounting practice in the United Kingdom for those entities that report under UK GAAP (Generally Accepted Accounting Practice). The accounting principles and conventions currently in force in the UK have developed over many years and from various sources including legislation, accounting standards, and customs practised by accounting professionals. However, as might be expected in a global business world, accounting in the UK is also heavily influenced by worldwide developments in accounting best practice.

1

The Financial Reporting Council (FRC) is the prescribed body for issuing accounting standards, having replaced the Accounting Standards Board in 2012. Essentially, current UK GAAP is to be replaced with a new regime based around the international standard for small and medium-sized entities. A **suite of new standards** has already been issued (FRS 100 – FRS 102) to this effect (¶260) and will be mandatory for accounting periods beginning on or after 1 January 2015, although earlier adoption is permitted. **Small companies** that currently report under the financial reporting standard for smaller entities (FRSSE) can continue to do so.

2

MEMO POINTS   The general framework and sources of authority underpinning UK GAAP are discussed from ¶200.

A. Accounting principles

Both the Act and the accounting standards require company financial statements to be prepared according to the following basic principles:
- true and fair view;
- going concern;
- consistency;
- prudence;

3

- accruals basis;
- separate valuation of assets and liabilities; and
- substance over form (¶100).

As a **general rule**, companies may depart from these principles only if there are special reasons for so doing. In these cases, the notes to the financial statements must give details of the departure, the reasons for it, and its effect on the financial statements.

1. True and fair view

4

For more than 60 years, company law in the UK has required financial statements to present a true and fair view of the reporting entity's financial position and the results of its operations. However, exactly what constitutes such a view is ultimately a matter of professional judgement, because its interpretation is governed by companies' legislation, accounting standards and generally accepted accounting practice. Moreover, "true and fair" is not a static concept, but one that is subject to changes over time. For instance, an accounting treatment that was considered to render a true and fair view as little as 10 years ago may now no longer do so because of changes in business practice or economic realities during the intervening period.

The **principle** that the financial statements present a true and fair view **applies to all companies** regardless of size. Small and medium-sized companies can elect to adopt the FRSSE, which, while it exempts them from the provisions of other accounting standards, still binds them to the requirement of true and fair presentation, irrespective of whether they publish full, shorter-form or abbreviated financial statements.

5

s 393 CA 2006

The **Companies Act** states that the accounts cannot be approved by the directors unless they are satisfied that such financial statements "give a true and fair view of the assets, liabilities, financial position and profit or loss" of the company for the financial year.

For this purpose, accounts are required to comply with the provisions in regard to form and content of the balance sheet, the profit and loss account and any other additional information to be provided. The Act also requires companies to comply with prevailing accounting standards.

However, in **certain circumstances**, strict compliance may result in a situation in which stakeholders are not given adequate information to assess a company's financial statements. In this instance additional information beyond the scope required by the regulations, would be necessary to explain an unusual transaction or to highlight a related party transaction and thereby satisfy the true and fair requirement.

FRS 18, **"Accounting policies"**, also prescribes a reporting entity's duty to ensure that its financial statements present a true and fair view, and adds that the accounting policies it adopts should be consistent with accounting standards, UITF (Urgent Issues Task Force) abstracts and company legislation. Thus, it is generally accepted that true and fair presentation implies compliance with contemporary accounting standards.

> MEMO POINTS This idea was articulated in *Lloyd Cheyham & Co v Littlejohn* [1987] BCLC 303 as follows: "While the Statements of Standard Accounting Practice [SSAP] are not rigid rules, they are strong evidence of what is the proper standard to be adopted and, unless there is some justification, a departure from them will be regarded as a breach of duty."

True and fair view override

6

In special circumstances the accounting treatment required by the Act might not result in a true and fair view even if additional information is given. In these rare instances, the company is obliged to **depart from the relevant provisions** to the extent necessary to give a true and fair view and consequently follow an accounting treatment that is not in accord with the Act. Full details of any departure, including the reasons and the effect, must be given in the notes. This situation, where a company deliberately disregards a Companies Act requirement, is known as the **true and fair override**. The same logic holds for companies in a particular industry, which may be considering issues that are specific to the industry concerned. For example, securities companies "mark to market" their current asset investments and take the resulting gains to the profit and loss account rather than the revaluation reserve, as the Act otherwise requires. This treatment is regarded as acceptable because, owing to the specific nature of the securities business, it gives a better view of such a company's performance. The point to be borne in mind is that before any company can invoke the true and fair override, it must be able to show special circumstances to justify it.

Just as company law recognises a true and fair override, so too does FRS 18. Since all accounting standards have been specifically formulated with the objective of true and fair presentation in mind, departures from accounting standards are permitted only in the most **exceptional circumstances** and only to the extent necessary to give a true and fair view.

8
FRS 18 (15)

Companies that take advantage of the **true and fair override** must follow a certain process. The first step is to determine whether additional disclosure, beyond that ordinarily required under the accounting standards, would provide a true and fair view. Only if it does not should the company, as a last resort, depart from the accounting standards.

Disclosure of true and fair override It is a requirement of the Companies Act that where a company uses the true and fair override, "particulars of any such departure, the reasons for it and the effects must be given in a note to the accounts."

10

This requirement is not exhaustive, but FRS 18 provides greater clarity by requiring:
– a clear and unambiguous statement that there has been a departure from the requirements of an accounting standard, a UITF abstract or companies legislation and that the departure is necessary to give a true and fair view;
– a statement explaining the treatment that otherwise would be required in the circumstances and a description of the treatment actually adopted;
– a statement as to why the "normal" treatment would not give a true and fair view; and
– a description of how the position shown in the financial statements is different as a result of the departure, normally with quantification of the difference (except where this is self-evident or cannot reasonably be made, in which case the circumstances should be explained).

FRS 18 (62)

> EXAMPLE **Unrealised exchange gains**.
>
> In accordance with SSAP 20, exchange gains and losses on the translation of monetary items are taken to the profit and loss for the year. In the case of unrealised exchange gains arising on the translation of unsettled long-term monetary transactions, this treatment represents a departure from the Companies Act, which prescribes that only profits realised at the balance sheet date should be taken to the profit and loss account. However, consistent with SSAP 20, exchange gains on unsettled transactions can be determined at the balance sheet date no less objectively than exchange losses. Therefore, deferring the gains while recognising the losses would in effect deny that any favourable movement in exchange rates had occurred and cloud measurement of the company's performance during the year. Consequently, the directors consider that recognising such unrealised exchange gains is necessary to give a **true and fair view**, as this will increase the profit before taxation by £xxx (previous year £xxx) and increase the value of the asset involved by £xxx (previous year £xxx).

2. Going concern

The preparation of financial statements on the going concern basis can be regarded as a **general rule** automatically followed by all business entities unless there are severe doubts concerning the enterprise's long term ability to continue trading. The importance of this rule is underscored by the Companies Act which states that companies "shall be presumed to be carrying on business as a going concern". Although the Act does not specifically explain the circumstances that might justify a departure from the going concern principle, where the company does prepare its accounts on another basis, the circumstances, reasons and effect must be disclosed in the notes. Again, FRS 18 concurs with this view but is more

20
FRSSE 2.12

explicit. Thus, an entity should always prepare its financial statements on a going concern basis, unless:
– it has ceased trading or is in the process of liquidation; and
– its directors have no realistic alternative but to cease trading or to liquidate the entity.

> ⌐MEMO POINTS⌐ As part of its commitment to improving **risk management and internal controls** in UK companies, the FRC is reviewing its definition of "going concern". The draft guidance sets out board responsibilities concerning the development of a more professional risk assessment culture in organisations, in terms of quantifying and managing the principal risks facing the entity, including solvency and liquidity threats. The "narrow accounting basis" of going concern will be retained but there will be an increased emphasis on identifying and reporting solvency and liquidity issues.

21   **Break-up value** All amounts recognised in financial statements reflect the going concern principle; namely that assets and liabilities are recorded at carrying amounts that are expected to be recovered or discharged in the normal course of business. Only if the **business is no longer a going concern** should the fixed assets be valued at their "break-up" value.

Where these circumstances exist, "the entity may, if appropriate, prepare its financial statements on a basis other than that of a going concern". These financial statements should reflect the amounts recoverable from a quick sale or scrap (i.e. the "break-up" value). As a practical matter, fixed and long-term assets and liabilities should be reclassified as current assets and liabilities, and provisions should be created in respect of anticipated further losses expected to be incurred to the date of termination of business.

⌐EXAMPLE⌐ The details of a manufacturing company's assets are as follows:

		£	£
Factory buildings			
	At cost	800,000	
	Less: accumulated deprecation	100,000	
	Net book value		700,000
Machinery and plant			
	At cost	525,000	
	Less: accumulated deprecation	265,000	
	Net book value		260,000
			960,000

The break-up values of the factory buildings, and the machinery and plant, are £500,000 and £125,000 respectively.

If the company is deemed a going concern, the financial statements will show the fixed assets at their net book value of £960,000. Only if the company could no longer be regarded as a going concern would the fixed assets have to be written down to their break-up value of £625,000.

Significant doubts

22
FRS 18 (23)

Each year, at the time of preparing the financial statements, the board of directors must assess the entity's ability to continue as a going concern. However, even if they believe that there are significant doubts about the entity's ability to continue as a going concern, this does not automatically trigger the requirement to prepare financial statements on a basis other than the going concern basis. In fact, unless the business is actually in the process of being terminated, or where closure cannot realistically be avoided, the financial statements should continue to be prepared on the going concern basis and referred to by the company's auditors in their report.

23
FRS 18 (61)

The following table indicates the disclosures to be made as to a company's ability to continue as a going concern.

Financial statements prepared on going concern basis	Financial statements prepared on a basis other than going concern
Any material uncertainties related to events or conditions that may cast significant doubt upon the entity's ability to continue as a going concern.	The basis on which they have been prepared, and the reason for not regarding the entity as a going concern, should be given in the notes.
Where the foreseeable future considered by the directors is limited to a period of less than 1 year from the date of approval of the financial statements	

> MEMO POINTS   If there is a **fundamental uncertainty** regarding the going concern basis, the company's auditors are obliged to draw attention to the notes to the accounts, where that uncertainty should be explained in detail.

3. Consistency

Accounting **policies** must be applied consistently from one accounting period to another. This requirement facilitates comparison with comparative figures for the previous accounting period. Comparability is essential to help stakeholders understand and evaluate financial performance over time but also with different reporting entities. An important element of consistency is the choice of suitable accounting policies to aid comparability, and include principles, bases, conventions, rules and practices for recognising assets, liabilities, gains, losses and changes to shareholders' funds, including the selection of appropriate measurement bases.

25
FRS 18 (4)

FRS 18 clearly differentiates between accounting policies and **estimation techniques**. Estimation techniques are methods used to make estimates of monetary amounts, under the various bases selected for assets, liabilities, gains, losses and changes in shareholders' funds, when exact values are unknown.

26

Estimation techniques can be used to measure the following:
- depreciation and/or impairment of fixed assets;
- provisions;
- cost of stocks or work-in-progress; and
- turnover and profits attributable to the stage of completion on long-term contracts.

The concept of consistency does not preclude **changes to accounting policies** where changes are appropriate and of benefit to users (e.g., improvements in accounting or introduction of a new accounting standard whose treatment of certain items may differ from those currently employed by the entity). Likewise, the nature of an entity's operations or activities may change, making established accounting policies obsolete. When necessary, new accounting policies or changes to existing policies, should be adopted in accordance with the latest accounting standards.

27

FRS 18 recommends that accounting policies should be **regularly reviewed** and adds that when considering whether a new policy would be more appropriate, account must be taken of the potential effect on comparability, as frequent changes could adversely affect comparability analysis over the long term.

> MEMO POINTS   A **change of accounting policy** requires a **prior year adjustment**, in order to restate the comparative figures for consistency and comparability. A change of estimate affects the current year only and therefore comparative figures are not restated.

Selecting the most appropriate accounting policies

Entities should always choose an accounting policy that is considered most appropriate to "the purpose of giving a true and fair view". Where an accounting standard allows more

28
FRS 18 (17) (35)

than one accounting policy or where a policy is not specified in an accounting standard, the ultimate choice will depend on these considerations, with the most appropriate accounting policies selected on the basis of four **criteria; namely**: relevance, reliability, comparability and understandability.

Criteria	Characteristics
Relevance	Relevant information is information provided in a timely manner to assist stakeholders/investors in evaluating both their previous conclusions and their future decisions.
Reliability	Reliable information that is free from bias or error, is in all material aspects complete and, where conditions are uncertain, is prudent in its assumptions.
Comparability	In selecting appropriate accounting policies, directors should consider whether they are widely used in the industry. If the entity's policies deviate, the directors should be able to explain why this is desirable and results in an enhanced level of presentation.
Understandability	The information provided by financial statements must be capable of being understood by users who have a reasonable knowledge of business, economic activities and accounting.

4. Prudence

30
FRSSE 2.13

Companies are required to use a prudent basis in determining the amount of any item included in its financial statements. Exercising prudence means adopting a degree of caution when making judgements and estimates in periods of uncertainty, so that gains and assets are not overstated and liabilities knowingly understated.

There are two important elements underpinning the concept of prudence; namely:
– the recognition of only **profits** that have been realised at the balance sheet date; and
– all known **liabilities and losses** relating to the current or previous financial years, that have either already arisen or are likely to arise, must be taken into account in the financial statements.
However, it should be noted that the importance of prudence has in recent years been downgraded.

31

Even though realisation is an accounting, rather than a legal, notion, directors must bear in mind their duties under the law. In the first place, **departures from the principle** of recognising realised profits are permitted only where it appears to the directors that there are special reasons justifying this. However, the effect of the departure must be quantified and disclosed. In the second place, directors need to know which profits are realised so that they can determine the amount of profits legally available for distribution.

With regard to the **recognition of all known liabilities**, company law requires that these must be included even if they become apparent during the period between the balance sheet date and the date on which the directors sign the financial statements. It is important to note, however, that this requirement is in respect of losses and liabilities relating to the current and/or previous financial years and is not intended to force directors to anticipate losses and liabilities relating to future years.

5. Accruals basis

35
FRSSE 2.14

It has been a long-accepted accounting principle that revenue and costs should be recognised as they are earned or accrued, rather than when their cash value is received or paid. Income and expenditure should be matched with one another where possible, and reflected in the profit and loss account for the period. If payments are made that partly relate to a future period (e.g. rates), a portion may be carried forward as a current asset (prepayments) and matched to future accounting periods. An accrual represents a current liability in the balance sheet and is charged to the profit and loss account. For example telephone costs may be invoiced on a quarterly basis, so a monthly accrual is credited to a specific accrual account in the balance sheet and reversed when the invoice is received and posted to the profit and loss account.

> MEMO POINTS   **Accruals** are also known as accrued charges, accrued expenses or accrued liabilities an represent an estimate of a liability that is not covered by an invoice when the accounts are prepared. This differs from a **prepayment** which is an advance payment for goods and services, which is accounted for in the balance sheet under debtors.

6. Separate valuation

In determining the aggregate amount of any item, each individual asset or liability making up that item should be determined separately. For example, in calculating the value of "Investments", those investments that are treated as fixed assets should be individually accounted for at cost, less write-downs for any permanent diminution in value. The only **statutory exception** to the separate valuation rule is that in certain circumstances tangible assets, and raw materials and consumables may be included in the financial statements at a fixed quantity and value.   **37**

This should not be confused with the case of **legal right of set-off**, where assets and liabilities could be netted against one another. The reason for this is that in particular circumstances, the assets and liabilities concerned do not constitute separate assets and liabilities.

7. Substance over form

In general, financial statements should give a complete, relevant, and accurate picture of financial transactions and events affecting an entity, and facilitate the users' understanding of the commercial effects of these transactions. "Substance over form" means that information shown in the financial statements should reflect the underlying substance of accounting transactions, rather than just the legal form. In essence, no transaction should be recorded in a manner that hides the true nature or intent of the transaction. This is the principle of substance over form.   **100**
FRS 5 (30-(31)

> MEMO POINTS   **FRS 102** (2.8) contains a similar definition of "substance over form" as set out above.

The key reporting standard for **non-FRSSE companies** is FRS 5, "The substance of transactions", which is designed to encourage greater transparency where companies finance their operations using complex financial/legal arrangements that often results in a deliberate separation of the legal title to an asset from access to its benefits and risks. The effect of this so-called "off-balance sheet accounting" was to not only exclude transactions from the balance sheet but also provide a means of manipulating items in the profit and loss account. For instance, a particular transaction that results in a profit on the sale of an asset might, in reality, be part of a larger transaction whose main purpose is to provide a loan. Common examples of these types arrangements include leases and loans.   **102**

Fortunately, in the majority of cases, substance and form do not differ and as a consequence, **FRS 5 applies only** to those transactions where there is a discrepancy or where the substance is not readily apparent; namely where: **104**
– legal title of assets and their benefits are separated (consignment stock, factored debts, etc.);
– options expected to be exercised, are granted; or
– a series of separate transactions that create a specific commercial effect only when taken as a whole (e.g. securitisations, project financing, circular finance structures).

a. Scope of FRS 5

Entities concerned

115
FRS 5 (13a)

FRS 5 applies to **all reporting entities** whose financial statements are required to give a true and fair view. However, small entities **applying the FRSSE** are exempt from FRS 5 although it should be borne in mind that the principles of FRS 5 are incorporated therein, even if the details are not.

> ⬚ MEMO POINTS **Non-FRSSE companies** may adopt FRS 102 "The Financial Reporting Standard applicable in the UK and Republic of Ireland" which states, that in accounting for its transactions, an entity must reflect the essential substance of the transaction concerned.

Transactions concerned

120

Except for a small number of specific exclusions, **all transactions** fall within the scope of FRS 5. The term "transaction" refers either to a single transaction or a series of legally separate elements that together achieve a particular commercial effect.

The **specific exclusions** are:
– forward contracts and futures (e.g., for foreign currencies or commodities);
– foreign exchange and interest rate swaps;
– contracts under which a net amount will be paid or received based on a movement in a price or specific index;
– expenditure commitments and orders placed, until the earlier of delivery or payment; or
– employment contracts.

If these contracts for future performance were not specifically excluded from the scope of FRS 5, the undesirable result would have been that certain transactions would be recorded at the time of ordering or agreeing to order, rather than at the time of payment or delivery (whichever is first).

121
FRS 5 (13)

FRS 5 combined with other accounting standards   Particular transactions may be subject to various regulations in addition to FRS 5, for example another FRS, SSAP, or specific statute. Where this is the case, the more specific provisions should be followed as illustrated below.

> EXAMPLE Under SSAP 21, "Accounting for Lease and Hire Purchase Contracts", specific rules apply to the measurement and disclosure of leases. In addition the principles set out in FRS 5 are intended to ensure that leases are classified either as finance leases or as operating leases according to their substance, and not only in terms of the 90% test prescribed by SSAP 21 (see ¶3428).

b. Analysing transactions

125

In identifying and recognising assets and liabilities in the financial statements, FRS 5 contains rules that apply both to new transactions and to prior transactions already reflected in the company's books. These are discussed in the paragraphs below.

New transactions

130

It is necessary to fully understand the rationale behind transactions in order to determine whether the provisions of FRS 5 apply to them. This involves the following:
– gaining a realistic appreciation of why a transaction is being entered into and why each party to it is involved;
– examining the transaction in the context of whether it is part of a bigger transaction, including the effect of conditional events such as options or resulting guarantees;
– assessing the outcome of the transaction; and
– identifying which of the parties bears the risks of the transaction.

The commercial effect of **a complex transaction** might change from year to year as the actual economic outcome becomes clearer over time. When the transaction is first entered into, it has to be analysed and the likely outcome determined in the light of prevailing facts (or best estimates). The substance of the transaction is then recorded in the accounts, after which the transaction should be monitored for changes and accounted for accordingly.

Determining the substance: asset or liability In determining the substance of a transaction in order to identify whether it gives rise to an asset or liability that should appear on the balance sheet, the following **aspects of a transaction** should be considered; namely:
– the legal rights of access to benefits and risks rather than the legal form of those rights;
– if the transaction is connected with other transactions the company might be entering into; and
– the options that may be available to the company.

> MEMO POINTS **Assets** are defined as rights or other access to future economic benefits controlled by an entity as a result of past transactions or events. **Liabilities** are defined as an entity's obligations to transfer economic benefits as a result of past transactions or events.

131

Recognition Once an **asset or liability has been identified** it should be recognised in the entity's balance sheet if both of the following conditions are satisfied:
– there is sufficient evidence of the item's existence, and
– the item can be measured at a monetary amount with sufficient reliability.

132
FRS 5 (2)

Separation of title and risks of ownership Complex transactions often include the separation of legal title from the benefits and risks. As such it is possible that the legal title to an asset may remain with a company even if it sells the asset in question.

For example in the case of goods sold under reservation of title,

until payment is received in full, the associated risks, benefits and obligations of ownership pass to the buyer. In this event, the selling company treats the transaction as a sale while the purchaser, recognising the substance of the arrangement, will account for the goods in its own balance sheet (even though strict legal title has not passed to it).

Similarly, where a lessor enters into a finance lease, it retains the legal title to the asset and in reality is merely receiving a lender's return on an investment. The substance of the transaction is such that the asset and related obligation are recorded in the accounts of the lessee. The asset shown in the lessor's books is the amount recoverable under the lease contract rather than the asset itself.

133

Linked transactions Transactions are often linked together in such a way that the commercial effect cannot be appreciated without considering the effect of the various transactions as a whole. For example, a company sells an asset but enters into a separate agreement to repurchase the asset at a future time. The two transactions are inextricably linked and the commercial effect should be considered as if they were a single transaction. Depending on the repurchase conditions, the transactions could be accounted for as a financing arrangement rather than the sale of an asset.

134

Options Simple options such as those to purchase shares can be seen as assets. The asset takes the form of the **right to purchase** the underlying shares at a future date, though not the actual shares themselves. However, more complex transactions often involve options in combination with other elements that give one party access to the future benefits associated with an asset, despite its not necessarily having legal title to the asset.

135

In endeavouring to determine the substance of a transaction that includes options, greater weight must be given to those elements that are more likely to have a **commercial effect**. This involves considering the extent to which there is a genuine commercial possibility that the option will be exercised or not.

FRS 5 (61)

1. Where there is no genuine commercial possibility that the option will be exercised, the option should be ignored.

2. On the other hand, where there is no genuine commercial possibility that an option will not be exercised, its future exercise should be assumed.

3. In less extreme cases, further analysis is required to reveal the true commercial objectives of the parties and the commercial rationale for the inclusion of the options in the transaction, and whether the parties have, in substance, either outright or conditional obligations and access to benefits.

FRS 5 (62)
In these analyses, it should always be assumed that each of the parties will act in accordance with its best economic interests.

EXAMPLE

1. Where the cost of exercising an option is expected to be lower than the benefits to be obtained by exercising it, the option will generally be exercised.

2. If the cost of exercising an option is expected to be higher than the benefits to be obtained in so doing, it can be assumed that the option will not be exercised and, thus, ignored when analysing the transaction.

3. Where the seller of an asset retains a call option over the asset and the buyer retains a put option, it is almost certain that either the seller will call back the asset or the buyer will put it back to the seller. If the asset is sold for £200,000 and the options are both priced at £220,000, then if the value of the asset decreases to £150,000, the buyer will put it back to the seller at £220,000. Conversely, if the value moves up to £250,000, the seller will call back the asset for £220,000. In this case the asset should remain on the seller's balance sheet as a financing arrangement as the seller continues to bear the risks and rewards of ownership.

4. Where the seller of an asset retains a call option over the asset and the buyer does not have an option to put the asset back to the seller, the intentions of the seller and the rationale for including the option will require careful consideration. As in 1. and 2. above, the price of the option might serve as an indicator of whether or not it will be exercised.

Existing assets or liabilities

140
FRS 5 (21) – (22)

Assets that have been **recognised previously** in the financial statements will either:
– continue to be reflected if there has been no significant change in the entity's benefits or risks associated with it, or
– be removed from the balance sheet (derecognised) if a transaction involving the asset has the effect of transferring to another party, all significant rights, benefits or risks. It is also a condition for derecognition that any funds received in respect of the asset should constitute neither a liability nor a form of non-recourse finance that permit linked presentation (¶160).

EXAMPLE   **Recognition**

A Ltd factors its debts in an arrangement with the factor, F Ltd, in terms of which A Ltd is responsible for both slow payment and bad debts.
The asset (debtors) cannot be derecognised because, clearly, A Ltd retains the significant risks associated with the transaction. Even though the legal title to the debts may have passed from A Ltd to F Ltd, in substance the transaction is simply one in which F Ltd supplies finance on which it receives a lender's return.
A Ltd is therefore exposed to the same benefits and risks as it was before the financing. However, it has an additional liability (to repay the finance), which must also be recognised on the balance sheet.

Derecognition

B Ltd sells its debts to F Ltd for a non-refundable amount. This means that F Ltd has no recourse to B Ltd even if the original debtors default on their payments. In this case, the asset (debtors) should be removed from the books of B Ltd.

Derecognition – in part

145

In **special cases**, derecognition is allowed on a partial basis if, in respect of the assets concerned, there has been a significant change in the reporting entity's rights to benefits and exposure to risks. This will apply under three circumstances where the description, classification and amount of a previously recognised asset may change, or where a liability may need to be reorganised and full derecognition is not appropriate.

146

Transfer of part of the asset An asset such as a loan might be transferred to another party either proportionately (i.e. including rights to interest and principal), such that cash flows and profits and losses are shared by the transferee and transferor in fixed proportions or by way of splitting the benefit stream (i.e. one party has the risks and benefits relating to the interest and the other has those relating to the principal).

Where the asset is **split proportionately**, the relevant share transferred should be derecognised.

Where there is a **splitting of the benefit streams**, the party retaining the investment in the principal should derecognise the original asset and in its place recognise a new asset: the investment in the non-interest bearing principal. The original carrying amount should be allocated to the principal and the interest stream to determine the cost element of the interest stream. This is compared with the proceeds, in order to calculate whether there is a profit or loss.

As for the **"new" principal**, it is generally recognised at a different amount than its original carrying value. The amount at which it is recorded should be such that, as it earns interest – which is added to the principal each year and credited to the profit and loss account – it will reach the amount at the end of its term for which it is to be redeemed.

Transfer of asset for part of its life   This arises where a company **sells an asset** reflected   **148**
in its balance sheet, but **agrees to repurchase it** at a future time and at a value that fairly reflects the depreciation and use over the period concerned. The entity now has an interest only in the **residual** but, in addition, a new liability to repurchase the item.

The difference between the proceeds and the old book value is accounted for, at the time of the sale, as a profit or loss. Whether it is appropriate to account for the residual asset and liability depends on the likely commercial outcome of the arrangement. If repurchase is intended or likely, both residual asset and liability should be recognised. Furthermore, if a loss is likely on repurchase, it should be recognised at the start and accounted for by recording a residual liability in excess of a residual asset (i.e. by making a provision against the asset to reduce it to its recoverable amount).

On the other hand, if the company undertakes to **buy back an asset** after a set period but at a price so low that it is more likely that the entity to which it was sold will retain the asset (or sell it elsewhere at a higher price), it would not be appropriate for the company to record a residual asset or liability.

Transfer of asset for all of its life but where some benefit or risk is retained by the   **150**
seller   An example of this situation is **where a subsidiary is sold** but part of the purchase consideration consists of an earn-out arrangement (i.e., an amount related to future earnings of the former subsidiary to be paid at a later date). In this case, the investment in the subsidiary should be derecognised and a new asset (debtor) recorded, reflecting the company's best estimate of the amount to be received.

Another example is where an asset is sold subject to either **a warranty** of its condition at the time of sale, **or a guarantee** in respect of its residual value. Because the selling party has disposed of the benefits and risks associated with the asset, it is permitted to derecognise it; however, it should recognise a liability for any obligation that might arise under the warranty agreement.

c. Specific cases

Offset of assets against liabilities

In general, assets and liabilities may not be offset against one another.   **155**

However, they may be aggregated into a single (net) item where the reporting entity: FRS 5 (29)
– and the other party owe each other **determinable monetary amounts**, denominated in the same currency, or in different but freely convertible currencies for which quoted exchange rates are available in an active market, that can rapidly absorb the amount to be offset without significantly affecting the exchange rate;
– has the ability, **assured beyond doubt**, to insist on a net settlement.

Linked presentation

160   The linked presentation is a specific type of offset and is used in the disclosure of certain transactions in which **non-recourse finance** is received in respect of specific assets and is repayable only out of the proceeds of those assets.

> [EXAMPLE] B Ltd has debtors of £78,500, which it sells for £72,000. The sale is structured such that the proceeds are non-returnable. The linked presentation on the balance sheet will appear as follows:
>
> | | £ |
> |---|---|
> | Debts subject to financing arrangement | 78,500 |
> | Less: non-returnable amounts received | 72,000 |
> | | 6,500 |

162   **Transactions covered**   In general, linked presentation is available in respect of a transac-
FRS 5 (26) – (27) tion that is in substance a financing transaction involving a specific, existing asset (or portfolio of assets) where:
– the finance will be **repaid only from proceeds** generated by the specific item it finances (or by transfer of the item itself) and there is no possibility whatsoever of a claim on the entity being established other than against funds generated by that item (or against the item itself); and
– there must be no provision granting the entity the **right to keep the item** upon repayment of the finance or, where title to the item has been transferred, creating an **obligation to re-acquire** it at any time.

164   **Accounting treatment**   Where the above conditions have been met in respect of the **total finance** received, the linked presentation is permitted.

On the other hand, where these conditions hold for only **part of the finance**, a linked presentation should be used for only that part. In such cases, the amount deducted from the asset on the face of the balance sheet should only cover funds generated by the specific item.

If a **profit has been generated** in respect of an arrangement for which linked presentation is used, it should be recognised only to the extent that the non-returnable proceeds exceed the carrying value of the asset in question. Thereafter, any profit or loss should be recognised in the period in which it arises.

165   **Disclosures**   The following additional disclosures are required in financial statements where the linked presentation is used:
– the directors must state explicitly that the entity is not obliged to support any losses in connection with the transaction; and
– that the provider of the finance has agreed in writing that it will seek repayment of the finance, covers both principal and interest, only to the extent that sufficient funds are generated by the specific item it has financed. The disclosure requirements are treated in greater detail in ¶2508.

Transactions with quasi-subsidiaries

170   In certain situations, a relationship between two entities may exist which, though legally not a parent-subsidiary relationship should, for purposes of "substance over form", be treated as such. In these situations, if a legal parent-subsidiary relationship would have required the preparation of consolidated accounts, these should also be prepared in this case. This type of relationship is referred to as "quasi-subsidiary".

FRS 5 (7) – (8)   To determine whether a reporting entity controls a quasi-subsidiary, the criterion is **control** (i.e. Whether, in practice, it directs the financial and operating policies of the quasi-subsidiary with a view to gaining economic benefit from it). The rules are the same as those in FRS 2, "Accounting for subsidiaries", where control is defined in terms of the ability of a company to direct these elements. The ability to prevent others from deriving any advantage from the quasi-subsidiary's net assets is also evidence of control.

Where these financial and operating policies are predetermined, e.g. by way of a contract, and as a result the reporting entity enjoys benefits arising from its net assets, the other company should be accounted for as a quasi-subsidiary.

> [MEMO POINTS] A **quasi-subsidiary** (Q) is defined as a company, trust or partnership that, though not fulfilling the definition of a subsidiary, is directly or indirectly controlled by another reporting entity (E) and gives rise to benefits for E that are in substance no different from those that would arise if Q were a subsidiary.

Rules for excluding quasi-subsidiaries from consolidation The rules for **excluding** a quasi-subsidiary from consolidation work in the same way as those for normal subsidiaries, are as follows:

172

1. Quasi-subsidiaries need not be consolidated if they are **immaterial or** where the quasi-subsidiary is **held exclusively** with a view to a **subsequent resale** and has not been previously consolidated; or

2. Where there are **severe long-term restrictions** that substantially hinder the exercise of the company's rights over the assets or the management of the other entity, this indicates that the company does not have the requisite control over that other entity for it to be considered a quasi-subsidiary.

> [EXAMPLE]
> **1.** B is a pension fund. Although A is significantly represented on its board of trustees, the benefits of the decisions made accrue to the pension-scheme members and not to A.
>
> **2.** Although A has a participating interest in B, it can be shown that it does not actually exercise a dominant influence over it.

> [MEMO POINTS] The **exceptions from consolidation** given in the Companies Act (i.e. situations where there is (1) disproportionate expense and undue delay, and (2) a significant difference between the activities of the quasi-subsidiary and the rest of the group), cannot be used under FRS 5 to justify the non-consolidation of a quasi-subsidiary, just as they cannot be used under FRS 2 for non-consolidation of legal subsidiaries.

Accounting for quasi-subsidiaries There are two possible ways to account for a quasi-subsidiary:
- consolidation; or
- the linked-presentation basis.

175

Where **consolidation** is used, the quasi-subsidiary should be consolidated into the group's financial statements in the same way as for other subsidiaries. The consolidated financial statements will therefore include the quasi-subsidiary's assets, liabilities, profits, losses and cash flows (after intra-group trading and profits have been eliminated). If a company has **no legal subsidiaries**, it should provide, along with its individual financial statements, consolidated financial statements including the quasi-subsidiary.

FRS 5 (35)

In certain circumstances, a quasi-subsidiary's assets and liabilities may be included in the group's consolidated financial statements using **linked presentation**. This is possible where, for example, a quasi-subsidiary company (B) puts some of its assets into another entity (A) to be financed, and "ring-fences" the transaction. Thus, if there is no recourse to the group's other assets, and the other conditions for linked presentation are met (¶162), the group may account for B in its consolidated financial statements using linked presentation.

176

The presence of quasi-subsidiaries must be disclosed in the financial statements and a summary given of each one in the notes. However, if the reporting entity has more than one quasi-subsidiary of a similar nature, a combined summary may be given. The summarised financial statements should show separately each main heading in the balance sheet, profit and loss account, statement of total recognised gains and losses and cash flow statement for which there is a material item, together with comparative figures.

FRS 5 (38)

d. Disclosure issues

180 The 2006 Companies Act brought about new statutory disclosure requirements for off balance sheet arrangements, and they are expressed differently from those of FRS 5. In general, FRS 5 requires that financial statements should give sufficient detail to allow users to understand the **commercial effects of transactions** irrespective of whether an asset or liability has been recognised (or ceased to be recognised).

181
s 410A CA 2006
Companies Act 2006 requirements The Act's requirements state that if a company has been party to arrangements that are not reflected in the balance sheet, and at the reporting date the risks or benefits arising out of such arrangements are material, the **nature and business purposes** of the arrangement, together with their **financial impact**, must be recorded in the notes. However, this information need be given only to the extent necessary for enabling an assessment of the financial position.

182 **Requirements of FRS 5** While compliance with FRS 5 may not necessarily result in compliance with the Act, in most cases there is sufficient overlap. However, additional disclosure to satisfy company legislation may be required in the following cases:
– where the reporting entity is a party to a transaction that does not give rise to any assets or liabilities being recorded on the balance sheet; or
– where a complex transaction results in assets or liabilities that are different in nature from ones normally included under the relevant statutory balance sheet headings.

B. Accounting conventions

185 The various accounting conventions observed in the preparation of financial statements are made up of different combinations of **basic accounting concepts**.

This is illustrated in the diagram below where the outer circles represent the basic accounting concepts, the nature and operation of which effect the choice of accounting convention adopted.

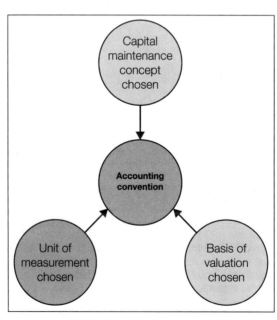

1. Basic accounting concepts

All accounting systems depend on the:
- capital maintenance concept adopted;
- basis used to value assets; and
- unit of measurement used.

186

Capital maintenance concepts

Capital maintenance is concerned with the measurement of accounting profit, which is the difference between a company's capital at the beginning and at the end of a reporting period. For these purposes, distributions from, additions to, and repayments of capital are ignored. There are **two principal forms** of this concept with the

most widely version illustrated in the example below. This methodology seeks to preserve the value of the funds invested in the entity, and expresses it in pure monetary terms.

188

EXAMPLE   In its first accounting period, a dealer in equipment for the construction industry purchases for resale a crane for £50,000, which it sells for £100,000. At the time of the sale, the cost of acquiring an equivalent item is £60,000. Assume there were no other transactions during the accounting period, and no other changes to capital.

	£
Sales	100,000
Cost of sales	50,000
Operating profit	50,000

The accounting profit of £50,000 represents also the amount in excess of the original capital of the business.

Adjusted for the general purchasing-power index   On the other hand, the value of £50,000 could be adjusted by a general purchasing-power index, so that the accounting profit is expressed in terms of its real purchasing power. Although this method is rarely used in statutory reporting and therefore has limited application, the following example explains the effect.

190

EXAMPLE   Assume the same details as in the previous example. However, the factor for inflation between the dates of buying and selling is 5%.

Comparison: monetary capital and general purchasing power capital maintenance concepts		
	Monetary capital (as per previous example)	General purchasing power
	£	£
Sales	100,000	100,000
Cost of sales	50,000	50,000
Operating profit	50,000	50,000
Inflation adjustment – 5%	-	(2,500)
Profit – as adjusted	50,000	47,500

In this case, the inflation adjustment shows the effect of the general increase in prices on the opening financial capital of £50,000. It thereby seeks to ensure that profit is measured only after preserving the opening capital in the business in terms of its purchasing power.

Valuation bases

The basis on which the various assets employed in a business are valued (and revalued, where applicable) depends on the nature of those assets. Bases, such as historical cost,

191

current cost, market value, net realisable value etc, are discussed in the chapters dealing with the different types of assets. For the purpose of this discussion, however, the use of a specific basis and the effect it has on measuring profits or losses, plays a part in the determination of the appropriate accounting convention to be adopted.

Units of measurement

192 The unit of measurement chosen **affects how profit is determined** and reported. Although theoretically amounts can be reported either in units of monetary currency or in units of constant purchasing power, the former is normally selected.

The problem is, however, that over a number of years the financial statements and denominated in the same currency (e.g. sterling), although the purchasing power of these units is not the same, due to the effects of inflation. Nevertheless, this is the basis traditionally used in historical cost accounts prepared under the Companies Act.

2. Common conventions

194 In theory, many different combinations of the options discussed in the section above are possible. However, the historical cost convention is the most widely used with a summary of the less popular options given in the table that follows.

Historical cost convention

195 The historical cost convention uses the following mix of basic accounting concepts:
- assets are valued at historical cost;
- capital maintenance is on the financial basis;
- unit of measurement is historical-cost ($£$ sterling).

Although it is the most common accounting convention, its major limitation is that in times of rising prices, certain values reported in the financial statements may be out-dated. For this reason it is best suited for preparing stewardship accounts and less suitable for investors or potential investors. Furthermore the directors should exercise caution in relying on the historical cost convention for purposes of determining amounts available for distribution. For example, in the example at ¶188, if the directors had distributed the profit of £50,000 there would be insufficient funds remaining to continue trading in the same equipment.

Less common conventions

196

Accounting conventions	Characteristics	Notes
Modified historical cost convention	Uses the following mix of basic accounting concepts: – capital maintenance is on the financial basis; – unit of measurement is generally historical-cost pounds sterling; – certain fixed assets are revalued and shown at an amount above historical cost.	This covention gives a better indication of the value to the business of some of its the assets, not all companies revalue their assets, thereby diminishing comparability between different companies. **Unrealised gains** from the upward revaluation of assets are generally not recognised in the profit and loss account, suggesting that the gain is of a capital nature to be retained within the business in order to ensure that its operating capacity is maintained.
Current purchasing power	Uses the following is the mix of basic accounting concepts: – assets are valued at historical cost; – capital maintenance is on the financial basis; – a unit of constant purchasing power is used instead of historical cost.	All non-monetary items in the financial statements are adjusted by a general price index.

Accounting conventions	Characteristics	Notes
Current cost accounting	Mix of basic accounting concepts is more flexible. While assets are valued at their current value to the business, capital maintenance can be on a **financial basis** with measurement in terms of units of constant purchasing power or an **operating basis**, with measurement units in pounds sterling.	Current cost operating profit shows the entity's current trading margins by charging the costs incurred at prices applying when the sales are actually transacted. This provides an indication the business's ability to generate profits from its current operation.
Fair value accounting	Fair value accounting rules are relatively new and allow certain financial instruments (and other assets, such as investment property) to be carried at fair value, with changes being recorded through the profit and loss account.	Few UK companies have adopted fair value accounting, and as a result these rules are beyond the scope of this book.

C. New UK GAAP – requirements of FRS 102

There are no significant differences between FRS 102 "The Financial Reporting Standard applicable in the UK and the Republic of Ireland" and current UK GAAP. The key accounting concepts and principles are more numerous in FRS 102 (Section 2), as set out below.

198

Key concepts/ principles – FRS 102	Characteristics
Relevance	Information is deemed relevant when it can influence the economic/investing decisions of users.
Reliability	Free from material error.
Comparability	Financial information should be comparable over time and allow users to detect trends and performance between different entities.
Understandability	Information provided in financial statements should be comprehensible to users who have a reasonable knowledge of business/accounting issues. Relevant information should not be omitted on grounds it is too complex.
Materiality	Information is deemed material if its omission or misstatement could influence decisions taken by stakeholders.
Substance over form	Substance of transactions and not merely the legal form.
Completeness	Information should be sufficient given constraints of materiality and cost.
Timeliness	Undue delays reduce the effectiveness of financial information.
Cost versus benefits	Benefits derived from producing financial information should outweigh the costs of producing it.
Prudence	Degree of caution in exercising judgement when making estimates etc.
Going Concern	(Section 3 FRS 102) Entity is deemed a going concern unless management plans to cease trading or has no alternative but to do so. Twelve months from the date the financial statements are signed is the minimum timeframe required for meeting the going concern requirement.

Measurement principles

199   The Statement of Principles under existing UK GAAP includes a dual system of historical cost and current cost for measuring assets and liabilities. Under FRS 102 assets and liabilities should initially be measured at historical cost, unless there is specific requirement to adopt fair value. The treatment of subsequent expenditure is also more varied.

Type of asset	FRS 102 – Valuation approach adopted
Basic financial assets and liabilities	Amortised cost
Other financial assets, liabilities, investment properties, some business combinations (e.g. associates)	Fair value
Stock	Lower of cost or selling price
Tangible fixed assets	Cost model or revaluation model
Intangible fixed assets	Cost model or revaluation model

CHAPTER 2

Regulatory framework for financial reporting

SECTION 1

UK reporting

The system of accounting in the UK has been derived from a number of sources including company law, accounting standards, and precedent/best practice. In addition, accounting in the UK is increasingly being influenced by developments in international financial reporting practice.   **200**

Generally Accepted Accounting Practice (GAAP) is a widely used term that refers to the accounting regime derived from the afore-mentioned sources and components. Given that there are many different classes or kinds of accounting entities, the rules applying to them differ and are derived from mandatory and non-mandatory sources.   **202**

Mandatory sources
Legislation (i.e. company legislation + other rules enacted by law or laid down by regulatory bodies).
Accounting standards comprising: 1. Financial Reporting Standards (FRSs) and Statements of Standard Accounting Practice (SSAPs) issued the FRC (Financial Reporting Council). 2. Abstracts issued by the Urgent Issues Task Force (UITF).
Non-mandatory (advisory) sources
1. Financial Reporting Exposure Drafts (FREDs) issued by the FRC in advance of an FRS for comments from practitioners. FREDs indicate the thinking of the FRC in relation to various areas, and should be followed unless they contradict an existing FRS.

Non-mandatory (advisory) sources
2. The Statement of Principles for Financial Reporting issued by the FRC. This statement, which is not an accounting standard, and does not have the status of one, nevertheless provides a frame of reference (see ¶240).
3. Statements and recommendations from professional or industrial bodies – e.g. Statements of Recommended Practice (SORPs), which suggest accounting practices and policies to be followed by specialised sectors or industries, and ICAEW Technical Releases.
4.The UK Corporate Governance Code and Reports of various committees set up from time to time to report on specific matters.
5. Pronouncements of the International Accounting Standards Board (IASB).
6. Established practice (i.e. practices that are generally accepted, even if they have not been officially codified in the literature).

[MEMO POINTS]   1. **Listed companies**, or those whose shares are traded on the Alternative Investment Market (AIM), adopt the "Listing Rules" issued by the Financial Services Authority (FSA), and the **"AIM Rules"** respectively. The FSA was **abolished** in April 2013 and its responsibilities divided between the Prudential Regulation Authority, the Financial Conduct Authority and the Bank of England.

2. The work of the UITF has now been taken on by the Accounting Council.

3. As a result of the recently issued FRS 102 "The Financial Reporting Standard applicable in the UK and Republic of Ireland" (March 2013), seven of the eight existing **Statements of Recommended Practice (SORPs) are currently being updated** by their respective governing bodies (e.g. The Charity Commission). The remaining SORP, which covers the insurance sector and is issued by the Association of British Insurers, is expected to be withdrawn when FRS 103 "Insurance Contracts" is eventually issued by the FRC. The FRC has also issued a statement relating to the early application of FRS 102 by entities falling within the scope of a SORP. More details can be found on the FRC website.

4. The FRC has published an **updated version of the Financial Reporting Standard for Smaller Entities (FRSSE)**, containing a small number of amendments resulting from the introduction of the revised UK reporting framework set out in FRS 100 and FRS 102. The key amendments cover the removal of references to the old SSAPs and FRSs, the clarification of certain requirements concerning annual impairment reviews and estimates of the useful life of goodwill and intangible assets, and definitions pertaining to related party transactions. The amendments have been issued to ensure the FRSSE remains a one-stop shop for small companies. The amended FRSSE will replace the existing version (effective since 2008) and its adoption is mandatory from 1 January 2015, although earlier application is permitted.

5. The FRC has issued FRED 52 "Draft amendments to the Financial Reporting Standard for Smaller Entities: micro-entities", which aligns UK GAAP with the **new micro-entity reporting regime** developed by the European Union and enshrined in the Small Companies (Micro-Entities' Accounts) Regulations 2013 (SI 2013/3008). The new micro-entity regulations apply to financial years ending on or after 30 September 2013. The exposure draft deals primarily with presentation and disclosure issues, rather than recognition or measurement of items included in the financial statements of micro-entities. The **amendments only apply** to those companies fulfilling the criteria for micro-entity reporting and exclude charities, companies voluntarily preparing group accounts and those included in group accounts.

A. The financial reporting infrastructure

210   The key bodies entrusted with regulating and administering the current financial reporting regime are discussed below.

Financial Reporting Council

212   Established in 1990, the Financial Reporting Council (FRC) is instrumental in:
- setting, monitoring, and enforcing accounting and auditing standards,
- overseeing the regulatory activities of the professional accountancy bodies, and
- promoting high standards of corporate governance.

The FRC's original remit has been extended to include a more proactive role in relation to corporate governance: it seeks a proactive role in relation to compliance with company law and accounting standards, and it has assumed additional responsibilities in relation to audit practice and auditing standards as well as oversight of the professional accountancy bodies (e.g. ICAEW, ACCA).

One of the more **significant roles** of the FRC is to issue accounting standards, which it took over from the ASB in July 2012. The FRC also collaborates with accounting standard-setters from other countries and the International Accounting Standards Board (IASB), to ensure that its standards are developed with due regard to international developments and vice versa.

> ⬚ MEMO POINTS ⬚ The Financial Reporting Council has created the **UK GAAP technical advisory group**, with a remit to provide accounting and related company law advice to the Accounting Council, predominantly concerning small and medium-sized entities applying UK accounting standards. The **advisory group** has been tasked with overseeing the implementation of FRS 102 "The Financial Reporting Standard applicable in the UK and Republic of Ireland", as well as advising on the future of the Financial Reporting Standard for Smaller Entities (FRSSE).

Structure The FRC Board is supported by three Committees; namely: the Codes and Standards Committee, the Executive Committee and the Conduct Committee as follows:

214

1. The **Codes and Standards Committee** advises the FRC Board on issues concerning codes of best practice, standard-setting and policy questions, raised by its Accounting, Actuarial and Audit and Assurance Councils.

2. The **Conduct Committee** advises the FRC Board on matters relating to conduct activities to promote high-quality corporate reporting, including monitoring, oversight, investigative and disciplinary functions, through its Monitoring and Case Management Committee.

3. The **Executive Committee** supports the Board by advising on strategic issues and providing day-to-day oversight of the work of the FRC.

The Executive Committee

The Executive Committee (EC) meets at least eight times a year and only members have the right to attend Committee meetings, with other experts or concerned parties as appropriate. The Chairs of the Conduct Committee and the Codes and Standards Committee are generally invited to attend meetings.

216

The **duties** of the Executive Committee include:
– recommending the strategic direction to the FRC Board and its operational policies;
– providing day to day oversight of the work undertaken by the FRC;
– overseeing the implementation of the FRC business plan;
– advising the FRC Board on its budget, business plan, Board agenda and organisational management;
– debating and resolving issues affecting the Codes and Standards and Conduct divisions; and
– ensuring consistency and connectivity between the Conduct and Codes and Standards Divisions and deciding which part of the FRC should lead.

The Chief Executive reports on the Committee's proceedings at each Board meeting and makes a statement in the FRC Annual Report regarding the Committee's activities including the attendance record of members regarding committee meetings.

217

Codes and Standards Committee

The Codes and Standards Committee (CSC) is tasked with advising the FRC Board on how to produce and maintain an effective framework of UK GAAP, including codes and technical standards for the following disciplines: Corporate Governance, Stewardship, Accounting, Auditing and Assurance.

218

The CSC also exerts an influence on the:
- wider regulatory framework in general;
- FRC's research programme;
- FRC Board regarding the Annual Plan for Codes and Standards work; and
- appointments made to the supporting Councils and their respective work schedules.

219 The CSC also identifies issues covering the range of individual codes and standards, emerging risks, corporate governance questions and other matters delegated by the FRC Board (e.g. international issues). The Committee is made up of FRC Board members plus selected others possessing particular technical expertise, including practising professionals. The FRC Board and the Codes and Standards Committee are advised in turn by three supporting councils covering accounting, audit and assurance and actuarial work.

220 **The Accounting Council**   The Accounting Council (AC) is tasked with providing prompt **strategic advice and guidance** to the FRC and involves consulting with practitioners and users, before advising the FRC Board upon draft codes and standards (or amendments) for tackling emerging issues. Other tasks include advising on proposed developments in relation to international codes and standards and regulations or research proposals and initiatives falling within the FRC's remit.

The Council is made up of a maximum of twelve members, of which half are practising members of the accounting profession. Council members are appointed through an open process overseen by the Chair of the Codes and Standards Committee (CSC), under the guidance of the Nominations Committee of the FRC.

The Accounting Council has also adopted the standards, including 'Statements of Standard Accounting Practice' still in force (SSAPs), that were formerly issued by the now defunct ASB.

> ‎MEMO POINTS‎   The **Urgent Issue Task Force** (UITF) was previously tasked with assisting the FRC in developing accounting standards but was disbanded in July 2012. Their work is now performed by the Accounting Council.

222 **Audit and Assurance Committee**   The Audit and Assurance Council (AAC) has replaced the Audit Practioners Board (APB) and advises the FRC Board and the Codes and Standards Committee on audit and assurance issues, including strategic matters, consultations with practitioners or users, reviewing draft Codes and Standards (or amendments thereto) and proposed developments in relation to international codes, standards and regulations. The AAC also advises on research proposals and other initiatives central to its remit.

224 **The Actuarial Council**   Since July 2012 the FRC has been responsible for overseeing the actuarial profession in general, in addition to developing technical actuarial standards deigned to promote best actuarial practice, competence and transparency. In turn the FRC Board and its Committees are supported and advised by an Actuarial Council, which is comprised of experienced professionals, some of whom have technical expertise, whilst others are from an investor or corporate background. The Council consists of eleven members, half of whom are "practitioners" (current members of the actuarial profession) whilst the remainder represent other stakeholders.

The Conduct Committee

225 The Conduct Committee (CC) as taken on some of the duties of the old Professional Oversight Board, covering corporate reporting, and its key responsibilities include monitoring:
- recognised supervisory and recognised qualifying bodies;
- Audit Quality Reviews;
- Corporate reporting reviews;
- Professional discipline; and
- Oversight of the regulation of accountants and actuaries.

The CC also has a number of **statutory duties** authorised by the Secretary of State under s.457 of the Companies Act 2006 and section 14(2) of the Companies Act (Audit, Investigations and Community Enterprise) 2004. The CC meets monthly and is comprised of FRC Board members and others professionals with a range of relevant skills, experience and technical expertise, including lay members and excludes current practising auditors and representatives of the professional bodies it regulates.

The Conduct Committee is supported by two further committees; namely, the **Monitoring Committee** which is responsible for ensuring the consistency and quality of the FRC's monitoring work and the **Case Management Committee**, which advises on and checks disciplinary cases. Members of these Committees, including the Chairs, sit on the Conduct Committee.

The Conduct Committee does not offer advice on the application of accounting standards or the accounting requirements of the Companies Act 2006.

> ⬚ MEMO POINTS   The **Conduct Committee** has taken on the work formerly carried out by the Financial Reporting Review Panel (FRRP).

Corporate reporting reviews   The Conduct Committee can ask directors to explain any material departures from the accounting standards and if not satisfied by the explanation it receives, can request a more appropriate accounting treatment be adopted. The directors then have the option of revising their accounts voluntarily or the CC can exercise its powers to secure the necessary revision of the accounts using a court order.

Depending on the circumstances, the Conduct Committee may accept another form of remedial action, for example, correction of the comparative figures in the next set of annual financial statements. The Conduct Committee's predecessor was the Financial Reporting Review Panel.

The Conduct Committee attempts to ensure that financial information (e.g. directors' reports and accounts) provided by public and large private companies complies with the relevant reporting requirements and company law. The Conduct Committee's remit and powers in this sphere are provided for in the Companies Act 2006 (CA 2006). Company directors are responsible for the accuracy of the accounts and underlying judgements, whilst the Conduct Committee investigates cases where the legal requirements have not been followed or the directors' report or accounts do not comply with the Act. In undertaking its corporate reporting review functions, the Conduct Committee adopts a cost-benefit analysis in line with operating procedures that chime with those of other international regulators.

The Monitoring Committee   The objective of the Monitoring Committee (MC) is to ensure the consistency and quality of the FRC's monitoring function and its key tasks include:
– agreeing the assessment of the standard of audit work for individual audits reviewed;
– approving summary letters of the key findings from reviews of individual audit engagements;
– agreeing the contents of public reports on individual firms in relation to audit quality;
– determining conditions or sanctions for acceptance by auditors or audit firms and where these are not accepted by the relevant parties, referral to an independent tribunal; and
– referring matters to the Conduct Committee for investigation and possible disciplinary action.

The Case Management Committee   The Case Management Committee provides guidance on the disciplinary process and conduct of hearings/cases. Each case is dealt with by at least three Case Management Committee members, who are required to oversee the conduct of any investigation and/or disciplinary proceeding and the manner in which it is handled by the Executive Counsel.

The Financial Reporting Laboratory   The Financial Reporting Lab (FRL) provides a forum for investors and companies to formulate pragmatic solutions to current reporting

226

227

228

230

232

236

issues. For instance companies can test new reporting formats with investors, who in turn can indicate areas where management can add greater value through the information provided. The objective is to encourage innovative reporting, through collecting and pooling evidence from the market on the value of proposed new reporting formats.

FRC – new organisational structure
238

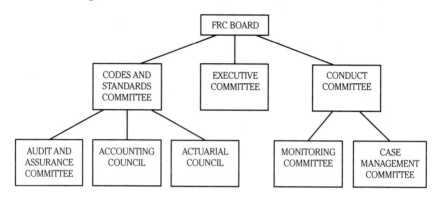

B. The Statement of Principles for Financial Reporting

240   The objective of financial statements is to provide information to various stakeholders about the financial performance of an enterprise. In order to ensure that the financial statements are reliable, basic standards and rules need to be set and observed by all parties.

241   The Statement of Principles for Financial Reporting was first published in December 1999. Its primary purpose is to:
– provide a coherent **framework of reference**;
– clarify the **concepts** underlying specific standards; and,
– ensure **consistency** in the preparation of standards.
The Statement of Principles is not an accounting standard but contains the fundamental principles governing how financial statements should be prepared or presented, whilst meeting the requirements of both company law and the accounting standards. The Statement of Principles for Financial Reporting is based on the IASB framework and stresses the role financial statements play in assessing company management and stewardship, as well providing a useful basis for making economic/investment decisions.

242   The Statement of Principles is not an accounting standard but contains the fundamental principles governing how financial statements should be prepared or presented, whilst meeting the requirements of both company law and the accounting standards. The Statement of Principles for Financial Reporting is based on the IASB framework and stresses the role financial statements play in assessing company management and stewardship, as well providing a useful basis for making economic/investment decisions.

MEMO POINTS   The **Statement's principles** are also applicable to financial statements contained in the interim reports, preliminary announcements and summary financial statements of listed UK companies.

SECTION 2

Reporting frameworks for all entities

243

Type of entity	Reporting Framework 2013/14	Reporting Framework 2015
Micro entities	FRSSE (including amendments 2013)	FRSSE/ EU
Small companies	**Choice of FRSSE, existing suite of FRSs or FRS 102**	**FRSSE or FRS 102**
Medium and large entities (unlisted)	Choice of existing UK GAAP (FRSs), IFRS or FRS 102	FRS 102 or full IFRS
Listed companies	IFRS	No change
Subsidiaries and parent companies	Existing UK GAAP, FRS 101, IFRS	FRS 101, IFRS
Public benefit entities	Choice of Charity SORP or FRS 102	No change

MEMO POINTS   1. The **size of entity** is defined by the Companies Act 2006 (see ¶6017).
2. FRS 102 is based on the IFRS for small companies.
3. Proposals for a separate Financial Reporting Standard for Public Benefit Entities (FRSPBE) have now been shelved as its key elements have been incorporated into FRS 102.
4. The EU and the Department for Business, Innovation and Skills are currently working on a reporting framework for micro-entities.

SECTION 3

Developments in new UK GAAP

260

The Financial Reporting Council has published a suite of new accounting standards to replace the existing UK standards (e.g. FRSs, SSAPs and UITFs) and represents the next stage in the convergence process between UK GAAP with IFRS. Although these new standards represent a change to the current system some entities will continue to have a choice of which accounting framework to adopt. The new standards will be **mandatory from 1 January 2015** and although earlier adoption is permitted, uptake is expected to be minimal. This means that the **first compulsory financial statements** to be prepared under the new reporting regime will be for financial years ending on 31 December 2015, although a comparative balance sheet will be needed for financial years ending on 31 December 2014.

The **new reporting framework** is designed to simplify the existing accounting and reporting requirements for unlisted entities and provide a more streamlined, cost effective reporting framework for all UK companies. The transition process to FRS 102 is supported by a number of clarification statements and staff education notes, issued by the FRC, which are outlined below.

New Standard	Published	Scope
FRS 100 "Application of Financial Reporting Requirements"	November 2012	Sets out the financial reporting requirements/framework for different types (e.g. listed, non-listed), and size of entity (e.g. small, medium-sized).
FRS 101 "Reduced Disclosure Framework"	November 2012	Simplifies the reporting requirements for listed groups – permits subsidiaries and ultimate parents to apply same accounting rules. Reduced disclosure requirements.
FRS 102 "The Financial Reporting Standard applicable in the UK and ROI"	March 2013	Replaces current suite of FRSs with a single financial reporting standard.

MEMO POINTS   The FRC has published **consultation proposals (PN 110)** on updating its new UK GAAP standard on the Reduced Disclosure Framework (FRS 101). This standard substantially reduces the reporting requirements for groups reporting under IFRS by allowing their subsidiaries to use the same accounting standards as adopted in the group accounts whilst permitting reduced disclosures. The FRC aims to review and update the standard on an annual basis in order to ensure that the disclosure framework remains consistent and cost effective. The discussion period closed on 21 March 2014.

261   **Impact of the new reporting framework**   Most of the changes generated by the introduction of FRS 102 only impact on the presentation of the financial statements. However, some changes will influence reported profits, and make them more volatile. This in turn could affect the **calculation of important ratios** that underpin bank covenants, tax payable and the amount of distributable reserves and dividends. Some additional accounting records will also be required such as holiday pay accruals and non-basic financial instruments (e.g. foreign exchange forward contracts).

262   **Clarification Statements**   As the date of migration to FRS 102 "The Financial Reporting Standard applicable in the UK and Republic of Ireland" draws near, the FRC has begun reviewing queries resulting from the implementation process and the possible impact on the new accounting regulations. In response the FRC has issued so-called **Editorial Amendments or Clarification Statements**, as set out in the table below, with the full statements available for download from the FRC website. The **Accounting Council** will continue to monitor developments and issues arising from the implementation of FRS 102, including areas not directly covered by the new standard or where divergence in accounting practice is starting to emerge.

FRS 102	Subject area
Section 1: Scope	The early application of FRS 102 by entities within the scope of a SORP
Section 12: Other Financial Instruments: Issues	Net investment hedges of foreign operations that are branches
Section 29: Income Tax	Deferred tax arising on a business combination

264   **Staff education notes**   The FRC has published **15 staff education notes (SENs)** relating to FRS 102 "The Financial Reporting Standard applicable in the UK and the Republic of Ireland", designed to illustrate some of the more technical aspects of the transition process to new UK GAAP. The education notes cover a number of key subject areas and are seen as a supplement to the new standard without being definitive technical statements in their own right. The full list of SENs is set out below and copies are available for download from the FRC website.

Staff Education Note (SEN)	Title
SEN 01	Cash flow statements
SEN 02	Debt instruments – amortised cost
SEN 03	Impairments to trade debtors
SEN 04	Investment properties
SEN 05	Property, plant and equipment
SEN 06	Leases
SEN 07	Revenue recognition
SEN 08	Government grants
SEN 09	Employee benefits – Short-term employee benefits and termination benefits
SEN 10	Employee benefits – Defined benefit plans
SEN 11	Forward exchange contracts

Staff Education Note (SEN)	Title
SEN 12	Incoming resources from non-exchange transactions
SEN 13	Transition to FRS 102 (updated 8 January 2014)
SEN 14	Illustrative credit union financial statements
SEN 15	Acquisitions and disposals of subsidiaries.

a. Key differences between FRS 102 and existing UK GAAP

FRS 102 "The Financial Reporting Standard applicable in the UK and Republic of Ireland" is based on the international financial reporting standard for smaller entities and includes a number of amendments to incorporate UK company law. The new standard is designed to make compliance and reporting simpler and bring UK regulation more into line with other global reporting systems. By reducing clutter FRS 102 should result in less complex reporting requirements and reduced compliance costs.

265

The **key areas** influenced by the new standard cover recognition, measurement and disclosure. It must be stressed that the FRSSE will still be available for small companies and is in the process of being updated to ensure compatibility with FRS 102.

The key differences between existing UK GAAP and FRS 102 are set out in the table below. For more information on the differences outlined below refer to the individual subject chapter (e.g. cash flow statements ¶4250).

266

Topic	Existing UK GAAP	FRS 102
Financial statements presentation	Balance sheet, Profit and Loss Account, Cash Flow Statement + STRGL	Statement of financial position (Balance Sheet); Income statement (Profit and Loss Account); Statement of Other Comprehensive Income; Cash Flow Statement; Statement of Changes in Equity.
Cash flow statement	Five categories	Three cash flow categories
Financial instruments	Recorded at historical cost unless FRS 26 adopted; Some financial instruments such as derivatives accounted for off balance sheet.	Financial instruments divided into basic (at amortised cost) and other instruments (fair value); Derivatives classified as "other" instruments. Recognised on balance sheet at fair value.
Investments (shares)	Measured at cost or fair value	Fair value used where measurement is reliable
Deferred tax	Based on timing differences	Uses a timing plus approach
Investment properties	Revalued to open market value at end of financial year, with changes recorded in the STRGL.	Revaluation required each year with changes taken to the profit and loss account. The cost less depreciation model is adopted where fair value cannot be accurately measured.
Merger accounting	Merger accounting for business combinations required where certain criteria are met.	Merger accounting only required for group reconstructions and business combinations involving public benefit entities (charities).
Pensions: Defined benefit plans	1. Actuarial gains and losses recognised in the profit and loss. 2. Recognised in group financial statements.	1. Changes in net defined benefit asset or liability taken to other comprehensive income. 2. Surpluses or deficits accounted for in at least one group entity's individual financial statements.

Topic	Existing UK GAAP	FRS 102
Intangible assets and goodwill	1.Useful economic life: maximum 20 years unless a longer asset life can be justified. 2. Business combinations: some intangibles can be included within goodwill.	1. Useful economic life **cannot exceed five years** where reliable estimates not available. An indefinite useful economic life is not permitted. 2. More types of intangibles can be separately recognised in the balance sheet than under existing UK GAAP.
Prior year adjustments	Fundamental errors	Material errors
Holiday pay	Accrual for leave not taken not required	Accrual required at the year end for outstanding staff holidays

b. Developments in micro reporting

270 The European Parliament has adopted a **new accounting directive** designed to reduce the administrative burden for small companies and make it easier to compare accounts across the EU. The new accounting rules permit a small company to just prepare an abridged balance sheet and profit and loss account, with the provision of more information being optional. The new directive also includes **special rules** for "micro-entities"; namely, companies with fewer than ten employees, a turnover of not more than €700,000 and/or a balance sheet total of not more than €350,000.

In short these so called **micro-entities** may prepare very simple balance sheet accounts with hardly any notes. In addition there is a higher audit exemption threshold as the new rules significantly increase the size of companies that EU member states can define as small, and thus be exempt from audit. The new rules allow member states to increase the balance sheet and turnover thresholds to €6 million (approximately £4.89 million) and €12 million (approximately £9.78 million) respectively, although the advantages of savings in audit fees should be weighed against the merits of having audited accounts (e.g. easier to raise finance). Although the new rules may be welcome news for smaller companies, they do not come into force in the UK until ratified by the Government, a process which could take up to two years.

[MEMO POINTS] 1. Currently, **UK small company and audit exemption limits** are aligned with the old EU definition and require companies not to exceed two of the following three criteria: balance sheet of €4 million (£3.26 million); turnover of €8 million (£6.5 million); and average number of employees: 50.
2. The FRC has issued FRED 52 "Draft Amendments to the Financial Reporting Standard for Smaller Entities: Micro-entities" which aligns UK GAAP with the new micro-entity reporting regime developed by the European Union and enshrined in the Small Companies (Micro-Entities' Accounts) Regulations 2013 (SI 2013/3008). The **new micro-entity regulations** apply to financial years ending on or after 30 September 2013. The exposure draft deals primarily with presentation and disclosure issues, rather than recognition or measurement of items included in the financial statements of micro-entities. The amendments only apply to those companies fulfilling the criteria for micro-entity reporting and exclude charities, companies voluntarily preparing group accounts and those included in group accounts.

SECTION 4

Convergence with IFRS

275 Although the subject of international reporting is beyond the scope of this book, some background information giving an overview of the worldwide regulatory framework and its deepening relationship with UK GAAP is given. A major factor driving the development of new accounting standards is the requirement for reporting harmonisation and convergence with International Financial Reporting Standards (IFRS).

In recent years the UK accounting standard setters have worked more closely with the IASB and based UK standards on IFRS where practical and UK standard setting is now firmly anchored within the context of international convergence. Differences between UK standards and IFRS are being whittled away through the FRC's policy of IFRS alignment and the fact that the IASB is currently working extensively with national standard setters to achieve global convergence.

MEMO POINTS The **International Accounting Standards Board** (IASB) is an independent accounting standard setter based in London, composed of the IFRS Foundation (an independent organization comprising the Trustees and the IASB), the IFRS Advisory Council, the Accounting Standards Advisory Forum and the IFRS Interpretations Committee. The IFRS Foundation Trustees appoint the IASB members, exercise oversight and raise the funds needed, whilst the IASB has responsibility for setting International Financial Reporting Standards (IFRS).

PART 2

Profit and loss account

Form and content of the profit and loss account

Every company has an obligation to prepare a profit and loss account that shows a true **350** and fair view of the entity's results for the financial year, although **small companies** filing abbreviated accounts can elect not to publish this. All gains or losses recognised in the financial statements for the period should be accounted for in an entity's profit and loss account, except gains or losses that are required (or permitted) to be taken directly to reserves.

A **small entity adopting the FRSSE** is free to select one of two profit and loss account formats, whilst medium and larger entities can select from four formats contained in the Companies Act. There are a number of **additional key disclosures** required by FRS 3 "Reporting Financial Performance" on the face of the profit and loss account, or in the notes to the accounts.

MEMO POINTS   **FRS 102** "The Financial Reporting Standard applicable in the UK and Republic of Ireland" **will replace current UK GAAP** for non-FRSSE entities for accounting periods beginning on or after January 2015. Although earlier adoption of FRS 102 is permitted the uptake is not expected to be significant.

SECTION 1

Profit and loss formats

352 The **general provisions** and formats for the profit and loss account in the financial statements are laid down in the Companies Act and apply to all companies and have been replicated in the requisite accounting standards. These formats have been further modified by the requirements of FRS 3. In addition specific information must be provided by way of notes to the financial statements. Future adjustments to the formats and content of the financial statements will now be set out in regulations (Schedule 1 SI 2008/410) drafted under the framework of the Companies Act 2006. To-date only a small number of regulations have been issued, that contain only minor adjustments to the formats set out in the Companies Act 1985.

A company has the option of showing any item in the profit and loss account in greater detail than that required by the format and may include an item of income or expenditure, not otherwise covered in the format adopted.

Companies preparing **abbreviated accounts** are not required to produce a profit and loss account.

MEMO POINTS   1. The requirements for **groups** preparing profit and loss accounts are covered in Section 8 of this publication.
2. The profit and loss formats for **entities not adopting the FRSSE** are contained in Schedule 1 SI 2008/410 "The Large and Medium-sized Companies and Groups (Accounts and Reports) Regulations 2008". The profit and loss formats for **FRSSE entities** are contained in SI 2008/409 "The Small Companies and Groups (Accounts and Directors' Report) Regulations 2008".

Choice of Companies Act formats

353

Type of format	Framework	Layout	Reference
Format 1- Analysis of costs by type of operation and function	FRSSE/Sch 4 CA 2006/ SI 2008	Vertical	¶361
Format 2 – Analysis of costs by type of expense	FRSSE/Sch 4 CA 2006/ SI 2008	Vertical	¶516
Format 3 – Analysis of costs by type of operation and function	Sch. 4 CA 2006/SI 2008	Horizontal	¶516
Format 4 – Analysis of costs by type of expense	Sch. 4 CA 2006/SI 2008	Horizontal	¶516

The **choice of format depends on** a number of factors, including the nature of the company's activities and organisation of the accounting system. For example, Format 1 may be chosen by a manufacturing company whose major expenses are the cost of producing its goods, while Format 2 may be suited to a service company whose major expense is its staff costs. Examples of Formats 2, 3 and 4 are shown in section 4.

MEMO POINTS   **Consolidated financial statements** must comply with the provisions of Schedule 6 SI 2008/410 which governs the form and content plus the Companies Act 2006 Section 404 (1).

Analysis of formats Format 1 is the most widely used in practice, and together with Format 3 discloses the entity's cost of sales and gross profit, as well as classifying expenditure in terms of administration and distribution costs. Formats 1 and 3 contain the same headings, in a vertical and horizontal style respectively. Format 1 is the only format that requires gross profit or loss to be shown as a separate item on the face of the profit and loss account. Gross profit or loss can also be derived in Format 3, but is not required to be shown in the profit and loss account.

354

Format 2 does not allow for separate disclosure of cost of sales or gross profit, unless additional information beyond that required by the Companies Act is given. This formats along with **Format 4** tend to be less popular, both in terms of production and presentation. Examples of these formats are reproduced in ¶510.

Change of format The company is required to adopt the same format for its financial statements for each financial year, unless the directors are of the opinion that **special reasons** merit a change. If this is the case, then details of the change and the reasons supporting it should be given in the notes to the accounts.

355
FRSSE 2.17 – 2.18

The following details must be disclosed:
- details of the change in format;
- reasons for the departure; and
- effects on the view given by the financial statements.

FRS 3 requirements FRS 3 has introduced a range of **additional disclosures** within the Companies Act formats, in order to highlight a number of important components of financial performance. Principally, FRS 3 requires every profit and loss account between turnover and operating profit (or loss), to be analysed between **continuing and discontinued operations**, with the results of acquisitions separately disclosed as a part of continuing operations.

360
FRS 3(20)

The **analysis of turnover and operating profit** must be on the face of the profit and loss account while other headings (i.e. cost of sales) can be covered in the notes to the accounts. FRS 3 also requires additional headings (shown in bold in Format 1 below) to be given. FRS 3 requests a sub-total for "operating profits" or "losses" and three additional format headings. FRS 3 stipulates that information be given in respect of any **exceptional transactions** in terms of value or size (see ¶474 for more detail).

Details of exceptional items should also be given, particularly concerning:
- profits or losses on sale or termination of an operation;
- costs of fundamental reorganisation or restructuring; and
- profits or losses on fixed asset disposals.

Format 1

The most common format for **small companies** is set out below. The headings in bold refer to the categories required by FRS 3 "Reporting Financial Performance" and do not apply to companies reporting under the FRSSE.

361

PROFIT AND LOSS ACCOUNT: FORMAT 1	
FRSSE / Companies Act	
1	Turnover
2	Cost of sales (A) **
3	Gross profit or loss
4	Distribution costs (A)
5	Administration costs
6	Other operating income
	Operating profit and loss
	Profits or losses on the sale or termination of an operation
	Cost of a fundamental reorganisation or restructuring

PROFIT AND LOSS ACCOUNT: FORMAT 1	
FRSSE / Companies Act	
	Profits or losses on disposal of fixed assets
7	Income from shares in group undertakings
8	Income from participating interests (B)
9	Income from other fixed asset investments (B)
10	Other interest receivable and similar income (B)
11	Amounts written off investments
12	Interest payable and similar charges (C)
	Profit or loss on ordinary activities before taxation
13	Tax on profit and loss on ordinary activities
14	Profit or loss on ordinary activities after taxation **
15	Minority interests *(D)*
16	*Extraordinary income*
17	*Extraordinary charges*
18	*Extraordinary profit and loss*
19	*Tax on extraordinary profit and loss*
20	*Minority interests (E)*
21	Other taxes not shown under the above items
22	Profit or loss for the financial year
	Dividends paid and proposed (1)
	Amounts set aside or proposed to be set aside to, or withdrawn or proposed to be withdrawn from, reserves (1)

[MEMO POINTS]   1. Headings **in bold type** must be shown on the face of the profit and loss account and are required by FRS 3. Headings in bold italics with number 1 in brackets are not included in the profit and loss formats, although these are required by the Companies Act. Headings 2 and 14 (**) must include provisions for depreciation and write downs of tangible and intangible fixed assets, and must also be separately disclosed in a note to the accounts.
2. Letters in brackets (A-E). For an explanation see ¶512.
3. Headings 16-19 are rarely used.

SECTION 2

Primary disclosures

364   In this section, the key disclosures required on the face of the profit and loss account by the Companies Act and FRS 3 and, to a lesser extent, by FRS 9 "Associates and joint ventures" are reviewed. This section will mirror the **structure of Format 1**, as this is the most common form of presentation adopted. Any detail supporting the key disclosures will normally be given in the notes to the accounts. Small companies adopting the FRSSE need not comply with the disclosures/headings required under FRS 3 which are treated separately.

a. Turnover

368
FRSSE 4.8–4.9
All Companies Act formats require disclosure of turnover, which is defined as amounts derived from the provision of goods and services falling within the company's ordinary activities, after deduction of:
– trade discounts;

- value added tax; and
- other taxes;

and in the case of **consolidated financial** statements:

- intra-group sales; or
- group share of turnover of associates and joint ventures.

Turnover can also include other immaterial income from other sources (see ¶383). There are a number of **different methods for recognising income**. As such, the accounting policy for recognising turnover must be stated in the notes to the accounts. In the majority of cases, a simple statement to the effect that turnover represents the amounts receivable, excluding VAT, in respect of goods and services supplied, has become the norm.

More **specialised businesses** should give additional information on turnover, to enable the reader of the accounts to better understand the nature of the income generated by the business. Examples include house builders, software companies, seasonal industries, or companies providing extended warranties on electronic goods, where the timing of recognition of the turnover is important (see ¶520).

Segmental analysis Where the company has supplied different geographical market **369** segments that, in the opinion of the directors, differ substantially from each other, then the amount of turnover attributable to each such market should be stated in the notes to the accounts. The **same criteria** applies to turnover by type of business activity.

Where classes of business and markets do not differ substantially from each other, the analysis of turnover can be treated as one class. There may be circumstances where, in the opinion of the directors, the disclosure of any information required to be given in respect of geographical and market analysis of turnover would be **seriously prejudicial** to the interests of the company. In such cases, this information need not be disclosed but a note explaining this should be given in the notes to the accounts.

A more detailed treatment of segmental reporting and the requirements of SSAP 25 "Segmental Reporting" is given in ¶750.

Continuing and discontinued operations Turnover should be analysed, on the face of **370** the profit and loss account, between: FRS 3 (14)

- continuing operations;
- acquisitions as a component of continuing operations; and
  - discontinued operations.

The **specific rules** regarding the additional detailed analyses required in relation to continuing and discontinued operations are covered in detail in paragraphs ¶457 to ¶464 below.

Consolidated accounts

Group turnover should include only sales made to external customers and all intra-group **371** sales must be eliminated on consolidation.

Joint ventures In the **consolidated profit and loss account**, the investor's share of its joint **372** venture's turnover should also be shown, but not as part of the group turnover. In the   FRS 9 (21) segmental analysis too, the investor's share of its joint venture's turnover should be distinguished from the turnover for the group itself.

[EXAMPLE] ABC Ltd Consolidated profit and loss account (extract)		
	£m	£m
Turnover: group and share of joint ventures	320	
Less: Share of joint ventures turnover	(120)	
Group turnover		200
Cost of sales		(120)

The topic of joint ventures is covered in greater detail in ¶7410.

373   **Associates** In **consolidated financial statements**, group turnover should not include that of a parent's associates. However, as a memorandum item in the profit and loss account, a total combining the investor's share of its associates' turnover with the rest of the group may be shown, clearly distinguishing between group turnover and that of the associate.

Segmental analysis of turnover and operating profit, if given, should clearly distinguish between that of the group and that of its associates.

Associate undertakings are covered in greater detail in ¶7320.

---

b. Cost of sales

374   The cost of sales be analysed between the same categories as turnover, as set out in ¶370 above.

The costs of sales category **typically includes** the following costs generated from ordinary activities:
- purchases of direct materials;
- direct labour;
- production overheads;
- depreciation or diminution in value of productive assets; and
- research and development costs.

The cost of sales figure is also **subject to adjustments**, in respect of opening and closing stock, work in progress or own work capitalised.

375   **Negative goodwill** Where the amortisation of negative goodwill (¶1062) is material and has been deducted in arriving at the disclosed figure for cost of sales, distribution or administrative costs, it should be analysed separately on the face of the profit and loss account. It is a requirement of the Companies Act that positive and negative goodwill are not offset against each other.

376   **Directors' emoluments** The emoluments paid to directors should be included within the category most closely related to their function within the company. For example, the emoluments of the production director, under Format 1, typically would be included within cost of sales.

---

c. Gross profit or loss

378   Under **Format 1**, gross profit or loss, representing the difference between turnover and the cost of sales, should be shown as a separate category. The gross profit or loss can also be deduced from the information given in Format 3, but is not required to be shown in the profit and loss account. Gross profit should be analysed, between continuing operations, acquisitions (as a component of continuing operations) and discontinued operations, either on the face of the profit and loss account or given in a note to the financial statements.

The manner in which expenditure is analysed under **Formats 2 and 4** makes it difficult to show gross profit or loss, unless additional information to that required by the Companies Act is given.

---

d. Distribution costs

379   Distribution costs generally comprise some or all of the following:
a. Sales related costs
- selling salaries, national insurance, and pension costs;
- sales commissions and other incentives;
- sales promotion costs; and
- cash discounts on sales.

b. Finished goods
- warehousing expenses;
- drivers' wages, national insurance, pension costs and expenses;
- transportation outwards, including vehicle running expenses;
- depreciation of vehicles; and
- repairs and maintenance of relevant premises, vehicles and equipment.

c. Direct overheads
- warehouse rent, rates, light and heat; and
- telephone/internet.

The **inclusion of overhead items** such as printing and stationery, cleaning, staff expenses, and general expenses will depend on the sophistication of the accounting system, in identifying, analysing and allocating these costs to the correct distribution cost centre.

e. Administrative expenses

Examples of administrative costs are as follows:

380

a. Staff costs
- administration salaries;
- national insurance;
- pension costs; and
- other staff costs.

b. Equipment costs
- motor vehicle running expenses;
- hire of office equipment;
- depreciation of vehicles and equipment; and
- repairs and maintenance of relevant premises, vehicles and equipment.

c. Office overheads
- rent, rates, light and heat;
- telephone/internet;
- printing, stationery and postage;
- legal and professional fees; and
- general expenses.

f. Other operating income

Other operating income includes all other income generated from ordinary activities of business, with the exception of income from investments and other income receivable. For the majority of companies this item is often not material and is included as part of turnover. Examples include royalties, commissions and sundry rentals.

383

g. Operating profit or loss (FRS 3)

In addition to the heading required by the Companies Act, FRS 3 requires a sub-total for operating profit, which should be analysed on the face of the profit and loss account, between continuing operations, acquisitions (as a component of continuing operations) and discontinued operations. Where an acquisition has a **material impact** on a major business segment, this should be disclosed and explained.

384
FRS 3 (14)

For most entities, operating profit is normally profit before income from shares in group undertakings. However, income from associated undertakings or from other participating interests may be considered to be part of operating profit (e.g. investment holding companies). In the **consolidated accounts**, the group's share of operating profit of joint ventures and associates must be shown immediately after group operating profit.

h. Profits or losses on sale or termination of an operation (FRS 3)

385

Profits or losses and **any provisions** relating to the sale or termination of an operation should be shown separately on the face of the profit and loss account, after operating profit and before interest, and included under the appropriate heading of discontinued operations. Only profits or losses on a **material disposal** of a business or business segment need be disclosed.

FRS 3 does not provide specific guidance in distinguishing which particular items should be included in the headings covering discontinued operations, as opposed to being presented under the heading of profits and losses on sale or termination of an operation. A practical approach would be to allocate the relevant income and expenses as follows:

a. Operating results of discontinued operations should include trading transactions of the sold or terminated entity up to the date of sale or termination carried out as part of the normal business of the entity (e.g. turnover and cost of sales from routine trading); and

b. Profit or losses on sale or termination of an operation should only include the financial effect of transactions arising as a result of the sale or termination, such as the proceeds on the sale of a part of the business and the legal fees involved in the sale.

386
FRS 3 (41)

Income and costs   Any income and costs associated with a **sale or termination** that has not been completed at the balance sheet date or within three months thereafter, or by the date on which the financial statements are approved, if earlier, should be included in the continuing category. For some entities it might be prudent to disclose separately in a note to the profit and loss account, the results of operations that although ongoing, are in the process of being discontinued.

387
FRS 3 (15)

Material disposals   The profit or loss on each material disposal (or termination) should be disclosed in the financial statements.

There may be circumstances where the **net amount of profits or losses** on the sale or termination of an operation are not material, but the gross profits or losses are material. In such instances, the relevant heading should still appear on the face of the profit and loss account with a reference to a related note analysing the profits and losses.

388
FRS 3 (17)

Reorganisation or restructuring   The restructuring of continuing operations as a consequence of a sale or termination should be accounted for under continuing operations.

390

Profit or loss on part disposal of a subsidiary   Where a company **sells only part of its holding** in a subsidiary, with the retained holding classified as a subsidiary undertaking, a profit or loss on disposal will occur. In the **individual company's accounts**, the determination of the profit or loss will represent the difference between the proceeds received and the carrying value of the shares sold, reflecting the profit or loss on disposal of a fixed asset, which should be recognised on the face of the profit and loss account (see ¶398 below).

In the **consolidated accounts**, the group will still hold a subsidiary as it has not disposed of the operation itself. The operating profit is not affected by the sale as the subsidiary's operating profit will have been wholly reported within the group's operating profit. The issue is whether the profit or loss on disposal should be included before operating profit or treated as an exceptional item.

If the **undertaking is no longer a subsidiary** after the disposal of part of the holding by the parent company, and becomes an associate or simple investment, or where a complete disposal has taken place, then the associated profit or loss arising in the group accounts should be treated as an exceptional item.

i. Costs of a fundamental reorganisation or restructuring (FRS 3)

396
FRS 3 (20)

The costs of a fundamental reorganisation or restructuring should be categorised on the face of the profit and loss account, after operating profit and before interest, under the relevant classification of continuing or discontinued operations.

Where the costs of a fundamental reorganisation or restructuring **are not material**, but the gross profits or losses are, the relevant heading must be included on the face of the profit and loss account, with a reference to a related note detailing the breakdown of the profits or losses.

Where companies have merged, related **merger expenses** should be charged to the profit and loss account of the merged company at the legal merger date, and classed as reorganisation or restructuring expenses.

FRS 6 (19)

j. Profits or losses on disposal of fixed assets (FRS 3)

Profits or losses on disposal of fixed assets should be shown separately on the face of the profit and loss account after operating profit and before interest, and included under the appropriate heading of continuing or discontinued operations.

398

Accounting treatment   1. The **profit or loss on disposal** of an asset should be accounted for in the profit and loss account of the period in which the disposal occurs. This should represent the difference between the net sale proceeds and the net carrying amount, irrespective of whether the asset is carried at historical cost (less any provisions made) or at a valuation.

400
FRS 3 (20-21)
FRSSE 3.7

2. Profit or loss on disposal of **a previously acquired business** should include the attributable amount of purchased goodwill where it has previously been eliminated against reserves as a matter of accounting policy and has not previously been charged in the profit and loss account.

3. **Past revaluation surpluses or deficits** (for temporary diminution in value) in the revaluation reserve, concerning the disposal of a revalued asset, will be treated as realised when the related asset is sold. The appropriate treatment is to make a transfer from revaluation reserve to revenue reserves, which is then disclosed in the notes to the financial statements but not reflected in the statutory profit and loss account for the period (Companies Act formats).

4. **Where the gain is subsequently realised** in a later year, it should not be realised in the profit and loss account as it is not part of the performance of that year, but of a previous year. This is illustrated in the example below.

> EXAMPLE   A company owns an asset which originally cost £200,000, which was revalued upwards to £270,000 in year 2. In year 4 the company sold the asset for £300,000. Depreciation is ignored. The **accounting treatment** is as follows:
> **1.** In year 2 the profit is calculated by reference to the carrying amount of £270,000 and the surplus of £70,000 is credited to the revaluation reserve and presented in the STRGL.
> **2.** In year 4, the asset is sold and profit is calculated as the difference between the sale proceeds and the carrying amount (£300,000-£270,000 = £30,000). The profit is recorded in the profit and loss account as an exceptional item after operating profit and before interest. Under FRS 3, the previous revaluation reserve of £70,000 is taken to the profit and loss account reserve, and only £30,000 is shown in the profit and loss account.
> **3.** If the taxation charge is calculated on the total surplus of £100,000, the charge would be split between the tax due on £30,000 realised in the profit and loss account and the tax due on the £70,000 recorded in the STRGL.

4. A **note of historical profits and losses** for the period should be presented immediately after the profit and loss account, where there is a material difference between the result as disclosed in the profit and loss account and the result on an unmodified historical basis.

> MEMO POINTS   Under FRS 18 "Accounting policies", **entities are prevented** from changing their valuation policies prior to a disposal of an asset from a revaluation basis to a historic cost basis.

k. Other income categories – group accounts

Income from shares in group undertakings   Individual company profit and loss accounts should include dividends received and receivable from subsidiary undertakings and divid-

404

ends from fellow subsidiaries, where a company holds shares in a group undertakings. As intra-group transactions, these dividends will be eliminated on consolidation of the group results. However, dividends received and receivable from **unconsolidated subsidiary undertakings** should be included in the consolidated profit and loss account.

405   **Income from participating interests**   Participating interests are defined as an interest held by an undertaking in the shares of another entity, held on a long-term basis, for the purpose of contributing to the activities of the entity through the exercise of control or influence arising from that shareholding. For **individual companies**, items under this caption in the profit and loss account include dividends received and receivable from participating interests, such as associates and joint ventures.

In **consolidated profit and loss accounts**, joint ventures and associates should be accounted for under the equity method, so this heading must be replaced by the following two items:
– income from interests in associated undertakings; and
– income from other participating interests.

406   The **parent's share of** its **associates' operating results** should be included immediately after group operating result, but after the parent company's share of the results of any joint ventures. Any amortisation or write-down of goodwill arising on acquisition of the associates should be charged at this point and disclosed. In keeping with the general rules, the results of associates should be analysed between continuing operations, acquisitions and discontinued operations.

The **parent company's (investor's) share** of any **exceptional items** relating to an associate, included after operating profit, or of interest should be shown separately from the other exceptional items for the group.

407   **Income from other fixed asset investments**   There should be separate disclosure of income and interest derived from group undertakings, or from other sources.

408   **Other interest receivable and similar income**   As above, income and interest derived from group undertakings must be shown separately from income and interest derived from other sources.

---

l. Amounts written off investments

410   "Amounts written off investments" are disclosed separately between the headings "operating profit" and "profit on ordinary activities before interest".

In situations where a **provision has been made** to write an investment down to below its cost and that provision is subsequently found to be unnecessary and written back, the credit should be disclosed under this heading. Impairments on operating fixed assets are disclosed in the profit and loss account under the same heading as the related depreciation. Impairment losses are covered in greater detail in ¶1550.

---

m. Interest payable and similar charges

412   The **general requirement** is that there must be separate disclosure of interest payable in respect of:
a. the finance cost of borrowing or interest including:
– interest;
– amortisation of discount or premium on the borrowings; and
– amortisation of issue costs;
b. the interest element of finance leases and similar obligations;
c. fees for obtaining credit facilities; and
d. unwinding of the discount on long-term provisions.

It is normal for a single figure to be given on the face of the profit and loss account with a detailed analysis given in the notes to the accounts.

Where **interest or similar charges** are paid to group undertakings, the following disclosures are required analysed between both categories:
- bank loans and overdrafts;
- loans of any other type made to the company; and
- finance leases and similar obligations.

With the **exception of loans** to the company from group undertakings, the disclosure requirements apply to interest and charges on all loans, whether made on the security of debentures or not.

The investor's share of interest in respect of its **joint ventures and associates** should be shown separately from amounts for the group, unless the amounts are immaterial.

Repurchase or early settlement of debt Gains or losses arising from the repurchase or early settlement of debt must be accounted for in the accounting period in which the repurchase or early settlement is made. Disclosure is also required in the profit and loss account as a separate item within interest payable and similar charges.

413
FRS 4 (32)

Long-term provisions included on a discounted basis Provisions relating to cash outflows arising immediately after the balance sheet date are more costly, given the time value of money, than those relating to cash outflows that materialise at a much later date. These provisions are discounted back to the present value of the amount that will be paid at some future date. **Discounting** is only required where its effect is material. The discount rate should be a pre-tax rate that reflects the time value of money and the specific risks attached to the liability.

414
FRS 12 (46)

The **unwinding of the discount** over time should be accounted for as a financial item adjacent to interest, but should be shown separately from other interest either on the face of the profit and loss account or in a note to the financial statements.

FRS 12 (48)

Finance costs

Finance costs **represent the difference between** the net proceeds of a financial instrument and the total payments that the issuer may have to provide in respect of the instrument. Finance costs include interest as well as amortised issue costs or redemption premium.

418
FRS 4 (8)

The **general rule** is that finance costs should be expensed in the profit and loss account. In certain circumstances, finance costs can be capitalised as part the cost of an asset which is achieved by way of a transfer from the profit and loss account. Such transfers should be separately disclosed.

FRS 4 (76)

Finance costs **disclosed under** the heading of **interest payable** and similar charges should be allocated for the period, including interest on finance leases (see also ¶496) and hire purchase contracts that have characteristics similar to finance leases.

The Companies Act permits interest on capital borrowed to finance the production of an asset, to be added to its production cost, during the period of production. **Where interest** on borrowed capital **has been capitalised**, this fact should be disclosed in the financial statements.

> ⌐MEMO POINTS⌐ 1. The requirements of **FRS 29 "Financial Instruments: Disclosures"**, supersedes those of FRS 4 "Capital instruments", and FRS 25 "Financial Instruments: Disclosures and Presentation", except for the material on the measurement of debt and gains or losses on the repurchase of debt. FRS 29 replaces the disclosure requirements in FRS 25.
> 2. **FRS 4 is withdrawn** for entities applying the measurement requirements in FRS 26 "Financial Instruments: Measurement" and hence FRS 25, but remains applicable for other entities.

n. Profit or loss on ordinary activities before taxation

The profit or loss on ordinary activities is a **mandatory disclosure** on the face of the profit and loss account. The figure should include exceptional items (see ¶474) but exclude taxation and extraordinary items.

424

o. Tax on profit or loss on ordinary activities

426   Where applicable the following amounts **should be stated**:
- the charge for corporation tax;
- if the corporation tax charge would have been higher but for double taxation relief, a note of what that higher charge would have been;
- the charge for UK income tax, and;
- the charge for taxation imposed outside the UK on profits, income and capital gains.

These amounts **must be stated separately** in respect of the following items appearing on the profit and loss account; namely:
- tax on profit or loss on ordinary activities; and
- tax on extraordinary profit or loss.

428
FRS 3 (23)   Any **special circumstances** which affect the liability in respect of taxation of profits, income or capital gains for the current financial year, or succeeding financial years, must be disclosed in the notes to the profit and loss account and the financial impact quantified.

p. Profit or loss on ordinary activities after taxation

430   This heading is included in all four Companies Act formats. However, if there are no amounts in respect of the format headings "Minority interests" or "Extraordinary items", in respect of the current or previous year, this heading can be omitted.

q. Minority interests (Non-controlling interests)

431   There is a requirement to show in each of the formats the amount of any profit and loss on ordinary activities attributable to minority interests. This requirement covers shares in subsidiary undertakings included in the consolidation, held by or on behalf of persons other than the parent company and its subsidiary undertakings.

The minority interests charge in the profit and loss account should be analysed between equity and non-equity minority interests. Where there are non-equity minority interests, a description should be given of any rights of holders of the shares against other group companies.

r. Amounts set aside or withdrawn from reserves (FRS 3)

436   The profit and loss account of a company must show separately any amount set aside or proposed to be set aside to, or withdrawn or proposed to be withdrawn from, reserves. This figure is often entitled "Retained profit" or "Transfers to/from reserves".

SECTION 3

Additional disclosures in the notes to the accounts

438   There are a considerable number of disclosures (e.g. depreciation, staff particulars etc.) required in the notes to the accounts by the Companies Act, FRS 3 and other accounting standards and pronouncements.

A. Companies Act disclosures

Depreciation

Formats 1 and 3 do not have a separate heading for depreciation and this item should be disclosed in a note to the financial statements as required by other provisions of the Act. It is a requirement of FRS 15 "Tangible fixed assets" that the depreciation charge in the profit and loss account is based on the carrying value of the asset in the balance sheet, whether it is historical cost or revalued amount. Where **assets are revalued** the amount of depreciation to be shown, irrespective of format, should be based on the revalued amount.

440

$\boxed{\textit{MEMO POINTS}}$ **Format 2**, item 7 (a) and Format 4, item A4 (a) specify the disclosure of depreciation of fixed assets on the face of the Profit and Loss Account.

Provisions for diminution in value of fixed assets

The **following disclosures** are required either on the face of the profit or loss account or in the notes to the accounts:
- provisions for diminutions in value of fixed asset investments;
- provisions for permanent diminutions in value of other fixed assets; and
- previous provisions written back to the profit and loss account.

442

The **general rule** is that a provision for diminution in value should be made in respect of any fixed asset, if the reduction in its value is expected to be permanent, whether its useful economic life is limited or not.

Impairment   An impairment in the value of a fixed asset does not have to be permanent, before it is recognised and charged to the profit and loss account. Impairment losses should be recognised in the profit and loss account within operating profit, under the appropriate statutory heading and disclosed in the notes to the accounts. Where a **provision for diminution** in the value of a fixed asset **ceases to apply**, the Companies Act requires the provision be written back to the profit and loss account. FRS 11 is more detailed and requires that the resulting reversal of the impairment loss be recognised in the current period in the profit and loss account, to the point it matches what the carrying value of the fixed asset would have been had the impairment not occurred, with any balance carried in the STRGL. The topic of impairment is dealt with in greater detail in ¶1550.

443
FRS 11 (56)

Director's remuneration and other emoluments

The Companies Act requires detailed disclosures in respect of director remuneration, pensions, compensation and payments to third parties. This topic is dealt with in greater detail in ¶4800.

448

Staff particulars

The **following particulars must be given** in respect of the employees of the company:
- the average number of persons employed by the company in the financial year, and;
- the average number of persons employed within each category of employee by the company.

449

The **average number of employees** is calculated by dividing the relevant annual number by the number of months in the financial year. The "relevant annual number" is found by adding together the monthly totals of persons employed under contracts of service by the company. Service for part of a month should be taken as being for a full month.

As regards the employees taken into consideration in determining the employee numbers above, the following salary information must also be disclosed in the notes to the accounts:
- wages and salaries paid and payable;

– social security costs incurred by the company; and

– other pension costs incurred.

These items are shown on the face of the profit and loss account for **Formats 2 and 4**.

450   **Social security costs** refers to a contribution by the company to any state social security or pension scheme or fund or arrangement.

Pension costs include any:

– costs incurred by the company in respect of any pension scheme established for the purpose of providing pensions for current and former employees of the company;

– sums set aside for the future payment of pensions made directly by the company to current or former employees; and

– pensions paid to such persons without having first been set aside.

Auditors' remuneration

452   The amount of auditors' remuneration, including sums paid in respect of expenses, must be disclosed in a note in both the individual company and group financial statements. These disclosure requirements include the estimated money value and nature of benefits in kind. Group financial statements are also required to comply with this requirement.

The total audit fees for the group are disclosed in the consolidated financial statements and in addition, it is generally accepted practice to disclose the audit fee for the parent company.

453   **Non-audit fees   Small or medium companies** are exempt from the disclosure requirements in respect of non-audit fees. The auditors of a company have an obligation to furnish the directors of the company with the necessary information regarding the identify of audit associates. For **larger entities**, disclosure in the notes to a company's financial statements regarding the aggregate fees paid to auditors for non-audit work, are required. In practice, this is likely to include fees in respect of tax advice, company secretarial and management consultancy. Such fees apply to services supplied to the company and any UK subsidiaries or associate undertakings audited by the same auditor, or any associates thereof.

Foreign currencies

454   Where sums originally denominated in foreign currencies have been brought into the balance sheet or profit or loss account in sterling, the basis on which those sums have been converted should be stated. This topic is dealt with in greater detail in Part 9, Chapter 3.

B. Required by FRS 3

456   In addition to the changes introduced into the format of the profit and loss account, FRS 3 imposes a number of **additional disclosure requirements** covering continued and discontinued operations, exceptional items, extraordinary items, prior period items and change of accounting policies.

1. Continuing and discontinued operations

457
FRS 3 (38)   Certain items appearing in the profit and loss account should be analysed between continuing and discontinued operations, with the results of acquisitions being shown separately within the continuing category.

The objective of separate reporting of the results of continuing operations, acquisitions as an element of continuing operations and discontinued operations, is to aid stakeholders in judging the financial performance of these elements of the reporting entity's operations and to help assess future income streams.

In order to avoid too much data on the face of the profit and loss account, the **minimum disclosures required** in respect of continuing operations, acquisitions and discontinued operations concern the analysis of turnover and operating profit. The disclosure of the other items, such as cost of sales, gross profit, distribution costs and administration costs, may be given in the notes to the financial statements. FRS 3 (39)

A similar analysis is required of continuing and discontinued operations for all disclosures required in compliance with FRS 3 (see ¶360).

Acquisition and disposal in same financial period

Where the **turnover relates to an acquisition** that is **discontinued in the same period**, this should not be included under continuing operations. Where an acquisition has a material impact on a major business segment, this should be disclosed and explained in the notes.

Where it is not practical to determine the post-acquisition results of an operation to the end of the current period, an indication should be given of the contribution of the acquisition to the turnover of the continuing operations. If an indication of the contribution of an acquisition to the results of the period cannot be given, this fact and the reason should be explained.

458

Discontinued operations

Discontinued operations are those that are sold or terminated and that **satisfy all of the following conditions**:
a. The sale of termination is completed either:
– in the financial period; or
– before the earlier of three months after commencement of the subsequent period, and the date on which the financial statements are approved.
b. When the former activities have ceased permanently (termination).
c. The assets, liabilities and results of operations and activities must be clearly identifiable.
If the results of a operation that has been sold or terminated are **not separately identifiable** or can only be ascertained to a significant extent by making allocations/estimations of income or expenses, then the operation should not be classified as a discontinued operation. For example, a manufacturing facility that is discontinued or mothballed, and for which an external market price for its output cannot be determined, should not be categorised as a discontinued operation.
d. The **sale of termination is material** in terms of its impact on the nature and strategy of the reporting entity's operations and equals a material reduction in its operations, resulting either from:
– its withdrawal from a specific market (i.e. a type of business or geographical segment); or
– a significant reduction in turnover in the reporting entity's continuing markets.
Operations **not meeting all these criteria** should be treated as continuing.
Only income and costs specifically related to discontinued operations should be accounted for under discontinued operations.

459

FRS 3 (4) (17)

Provisions relating to sale or termination

Provisions arising **from a decision to sell or terminate** an operation should cover obligations incurred relating to the said operation that will not be met by the future profits of the business. The provision should only be used to cover the direct costs relating to the sale or termination, and any operating losses incurred up to the sale or termination date. The aggregate expected profit recognised in the profit and loss account from any further trading prior to closure or sale, should be deducted from the provision. These provisions should appear in the continuing operations category, unless the operation qualifies as a discontinued operation in the period under review.

460

FRS 3 (18)

In **subsequent periods**, where the operation qualifies as discontinued, the provisions should be used to offset the results of the operation in the discontinued category. Although FRS 12 "Provisions, contingent liabilities and assets" **prohibits provisions for future operating losses**, the FRS 3 rules cover the situation where provisions relate to a decision to sell or terminate a business. In situations where a provision relating to the costs of terminating a business proved to be materially inaccurate, then an adjustment should be made in the period when the inaccuracy is discovered and should be classified in the profit and loss account as a "non-operating exceptional item".

A **binding contract** entered into after the balance sheet date may provide additional evidence of asset values and commitments at the balance sheet date. In the case of an intended sale for which no legally binding sale agreement exists, no obligation has been agreed by the reporting entity. Accordingly, provisions for the direct costs of the decision to sell and for future operating losses should not be made. In accordance with normal practice, however, any impairment in asset values should be recorded.

The reporting entity should be **"demonstrably committed"** to the sale or termination, as evidence by a binding sale agreement for a sale or in the case of a termination, a detailed formal plan from which the reporting entity cannot realistically withdraw.

> ⌐MEMO POINTS⌐   Provisions are dealt with in FRS 12 "Provisions, contingent liabilities and contingent assets". The **general rule** is where another accounting standard or SSAP with a more specific requirement exists, this should be applied in preference to FRS 12. The requirement in FRS 3 relates specifically to the decision to sell or discontinue an operation.

464   **Disclosure of provisions**   The adoption or release of provisions and the actual profits or losses that occur should be classified into continuing and discontinued operations. For instance, if a company with a June 2013 financial year end was "demonstrably committed" to terminating an operation at that date, but the closure was not affected until December 2013, then the operation should be regarded as continuing in the 2013 accounts and discontinued in the accounts for the following year. The comparative figures should also be restated.

Where **provisions have been utilised** in connection with a sale or termination of an operation, these should be analysed between the operating loss and the loss on sale or discontinuance of the operation. Disclosure should be made on the face of the profit and loss account, below operating profit for continuing operations.

Interest payable

468
FRS 3 (40)   The details regarding continuing operations, acquisitions and discontinued operations is required only down to the heading profit before interest, as interest payable is generally a reflection of a reporting entity's financing policy. This involves both equity and debt funding on a group basis, as opposed to simply combining the particular types of finance allocated to individual operating segments. However allocating interest inevitably involves a considerable level of subjectivity that could undermine the relevance and accuracy of the information.

Where a reporting entity deems it prudent to allocate interest (or tax) between continuing and discontinued operations, the method chosen and underlying assumptions used should be disclosed by way of a note to the accounts.

Comparative figures

470
FRS 3 (30)   Comparative figures should include in the continuing category, only the results operations included in the continuing operations of the current period. No reference need be made to the results of acquisitions reported in the previous period, since they are not required to be presented separately in the current financial year.

The analysis of comparative figures between **continuing and discontinued operations** is not required on the face of the profit and loss account.

The **requirement to restate comparative results** based on the status of an operation in the current period, means that figures for acquisitions made in the prior period, will not be shown separately in the comparative figures given with the results for the year under review. The comparative figures **for discontinued operations** should include the previous period's business segment results that were only discontinued during the current year. These results would in the previous period have been included within continuing operations.

2. Exceptional items

Exceptional items are defined in FRS 3 as material items which:

474
FRS 3 (19) (20)
FRSSE 3.5

a. derive from events or transactions that fall within the ordinary activities of the reporting entity; and

b. individually or, if of a similar type, in aggregate, need to be disclosed by virtue of their size, if the financial statements are to give a true and fair view.

Exceptional items should accounted for in determining the profit or loss on ordinary activities, by including them under the statutory format headings to which they relate.

The effect of any transactions that are exceptional, even where they fall within the ordinary activities of the company, must be disclosed. Exceptional items require separate disclosure in order to explain their nature and impact on the entity's results and future earnings. Exceptional items **of a similar nature** may be grouped together for the purposes of disclosure, except where they relate to discontinued activities, in which case separate disclosure is required.

Examples of exceptional items **include**:

475
FRS 3 (46)

– redundancy and reorganisation costs unrelated to the discontinuance of a business segment;

– abnormal charges for bad debts, stock obsolescence or losses on long-term contracts;

– previously capitalised intangible assets written off other than as part of a process of amortisation;

– surpluses arising on settlement of insurance claims;

– the expropriation of assets;

– amounts received in respect of insurance claims for consequential loss of profits; and

– changes in basis of taxation, or significant change in government fiscal policy.

Separate disclosure compulsory   Separate disclosure is compulsory for:

476
FRS 3 (20)
FRSSE 3.5

– profits or losses on sale or termination of an operation (see ¶385);

– costs of fundamental reorganisation or restructuring (see ¶396);

– profits or losses on disposal of fixed assets (see ¶398).

An adequate description of each exceptional item should be given to enable its nature to be understood and they should be disclosed (where material) after the operating profit for the year.

3. Extraordinary items

Extraordinary items are extremely rare and concern abnormal events or transactions that fall outside the scope of ordinary activities of a reporting entity and which are not expected to recur. Details must be given for any extraordinary income or charges arising in the financial year.

478
FRS 3 (48)

Ordinary activities can be defined as any activities undertaken by an entity as part of its business, and any related activities that furthers or develops from these activities. Ordinary activities include the impact on the reporting entity of events arising in the various environments in which it operates, including the political, regulatory, economic and geographical environments.

FRS 3 (2

480
FRS 3 (22)

Disclosure requirements   An **extraordinary profit or loss** should be shown separately on the face of the profit and loss account, after the profit or loss on ordinary activities after taxation, but before deducting certain commitments (e.g. dividends paid or payable). In the case of consolidated financial statements, it should appear after the figure for minority interests. The amount of **each extraordinary item** should be individually listed, either on the face of the profit and loss account or in a note to the accounts. A detailed description of each extraordinary item should also be given to enable its nature and impact on the results of the reporting entity to be understood.

4. Prior period items and adjustments

488
FRS 3 (60)

In any accounting period, the results will be effected by adjustments required in respect of transactions that were initially recorded in earlier years.

The **majority of these adjustments**:
– arise mainly from the corrections and adjustments which are the natural result of estimates inherent in accounting and more particularly in the periodic preparation of financial statements;
– are dealt with in the profit and loss account of the period in which they are identified and their effect is stated where material; and
– are not exceptional (or extraordinary) merely because they relate to a prior period; their nature will determine their classification.

489

Where adjustments are required, FRS 3 identifies **two specific situations** when adjustments that are required should be treated as "prior period adjustments". These are:
– items arising from changes in accounting policies; or
– from the correction of fundamental errors.

Where either of these two situations arises an entity should reflect the transaction in the results of prior period(s) and not in the current profit and loss account.

Any adjustments involve:
– restating the comparative figures for the preceding period in the primary statements and notes;
– adjusting the opening balance of retained profits or reserves for the cumulative effect; and
– where practicable, disclosing the effect of prior period adjustments on the results for the preceding period.

490

Where the prior period adjustment relates to a transaction that **spanned more than one period** previously and has no impact as such on the operating results for subsequent years, then the comparative figures for the profit and loss account itself will not be adjusted and the prior period adjustment will be reflected through the comparative figures in the balance sheet and, in particular, the accumulated reserves.

5. Change of accounting policies

491

Accounting policies should be **applied consistently** within the same financial statements and from one financial year to the next, although situations may arise when a change in accounting policy is necessary.

However, the Companies Act does allow departure from the principles used in preparing the financial statements in respect of any financial year, if it appears to the directors of the company that there are special reasons. In such cases, disclosure is required in the notes to the financial statements of:
– the particulars of the departure;
– the reasons for the change in accounting policy; and
– its effect on the results for the financial period.

FRS 3 specifies that **a change in accounting policy may only be made** if it can be justified on the grounds that the new policy is preferable to the one it replaces, because it will give a fairer presentation of the result and of the financial position of a reporting entity. It is a characteristic of a change in accounting policy, that it is the result of a choice between two or more accounting methods. Therefore, it does not arise from the adoption or modification of an accounting method, necessitated by transactions or events that are clearly different in substance from those previously occurring.

492
FRS 3 (62)

In those cases where the **effect of the change** on the current year was **either immaterial or similar** to the quantified effect on the prior year, a simple statement confirming this would suffice. Where it is not practicable to give the effect on the current year, that fact, together with the reasons, should be stated.

The **disclosures necessary** when a change of accounting policy is made should include an indication of the effect on the current year's results.

6. Correction of fundamental errors

In exceptional circumstances, it may be found that financial statements of prior periods have been issued containing **significant errors** that call into question the validity of the true and fair view assertion and, in turn, the accuracy of the financial statements. The corrections of such fundamental errors and the cumulative adjustments applicable to prior periods have no bearing on the results of the current period.

493

C. Disclosures required by other accounting standards and abstracts

There are a number of key disclosure requirements dictated by other accounting standards, covering leases, start-up costs, research and development and website development costs. These topics are covered briefly in this section and discussed more fully in the relevant chapters.

495

Leases

The following disclosures are required in the profit and loss account **of the lessee** in relation to operating lease costs:
- rentals charged to the profit and loss account split between plant and machinery and other operating leases;
- aggregate finance charges for finance leases; and
- total depreciation charged for the period under finance leases.

496

The **lessor should disclose** in the notes to the financial statements, the aggregate rentals receivable in the periods in respect of finance leases and operating leases, and details of any operating lease incentives.

Operating lease incentives An example of an **operating lease incentive** is an initial cash payment from a lessor in order to secure a lease contract. Under UITF 28 "Operating lease incentives", a lessee should account for the incentive as a reduction in rentals payable, and allocate this over the term of the lease, or the period before which the market rental will be payable. The **lessor should account** for the incentive given to the lessee as a cost, by reducing the rental income through allocating the cost over the same period, ideally on a straight-line basis unless another allocation method is deemed more appropriate.

497

This topic is treated in greater detail in ¶3400.

Start-up costs

498
UITF 24 (4)

Under FRS 15 it is not permissible to include start-up costs in the cost of a fixed asset. This position is reinforced by UITF Abstract 24 "Accounting for start-up costs", which defines start-up costs as the cost of activities related to the opening of:
- a new business;
- a new production facility;
- a new product or service;
- a new process within an existing facility; or
- relocation or reorganisation of part or all of an entity.

The abstract recommends that costs be expensed in the profit and loss account (i.e. training costs), unless they meet the criteria for recognition as assets under other accounting standards.

Research and development

500
SSAP 13 (21) (31)

The key disclosures required by SSAP 13 "Accounting for research and development" are as follows:

1. The **total amount** of research and development expenditure charged in the profit and loss account, should be analysed between the current year's expenditure and amounts amortised from deferred expenditure.

2. In addition, **movements on deferred development expenditure** and the amount carried forward at the beginning and the end of the period, should be disclosed under intangible fixed assets in the balance sheet.

> ⌐MEMO POINTS⌐ SSAP 13, divides research and development expenditure into the following categories: pure (or basic) research, applied research or development research.

Website development costs

502

The recognition of Website development costs is governed by UITF 29 "Website development costs". Some costs can be capitalised as tangible fixed assets under FRS 15 "Tangible fixed assets", which are subject to depreciation and annual impairment reviews.

Website development costs can be **categorised** as follows:
- planning;
- software costs;
- infrastructure costs; and
- design and content costs.

A **clear distinction** must be drawn between Website planning costs and all other related costs. Website planning costs should be wholly expensed in the profit and loss account and other related costs capitalised, where it can be demonstrated that the entity will derive economic benefits at least equal to the value of the capitalised costs.

For more detail on this topic see ¶1334.

Purchased goodwill

503

FRS 10 "Goodwill and intangible assets" stipulates that financial statements should disclose the profit or loss on each material disposal, of a previously acquired business or business segment.

FRS 10 (71C)

In the reporting period in which the business with which the goodwill was acquired, is **disposed of or closed**:

1. The amount included in the profit and loss account in respect of the profit or loss on disposal or closure should include attributable goodwill, to the extent that it has not previously been charged in the profit and loss account; and

2. The financial statements should disclose, as a component of the profit or loss on disposal or closure, the attributable amount of goodwill so included.

The headings in bold denote the requirements of FRS 3.

PROFIT AND LOSS ACCOUNT FORMAT 3

A	**CHARGES**
1	Cost of sales (A)
2	Distribution costs (A)
3	Administration expenses (A) **Operating profit or loss (1)** **Losses on the sale or termination of an operation (2)** **Cost of a fundamental reorganisation or restructuring (2)** **Losses on disposal of fixed assets (2)**
4	Amounts written off investments
5	Interest payable and similar charges (E) **Profit or loss on ordinary activities before taxation (3)**
6	Tax on profit and loss on ordinary activities
7	Profit or loss on ordinary activities after taxation *Minority interests* (E)
8	Extraordinary charges
9	Tax on extraordinary profit and loss *Minority interests* (E)
10	Other taxes not shown under the above items
11	Profit or loss for the financial year **Dividends paid and proposed (3)** **Amounts set aside or proposed to be set aside to, or withdrawn or proposed to be withdrawn from, reserves (3)**

B	**INCOME**
1	Turnover
2	Other operating income **Operating profit and loss (1)** **Profits on the sale or termination of an operation (2)** **Profits on disposal of fixed assets (2)**
3	Income from shares in group undertakings
4	Income from participating interests (D)
5	Income from other fixed asset investments (B)
6	Other interest receivable and similar income (B) **Profit or loss on ordinary activities before taxation (3)**
7	Profit or loss on ordinary activities after taxation Minority interests (E)
8	Extraordinary income Minority interests (E)
9	Profit or loss for the financial year

PROFIT AND LOSS ACCOUNT FORMAT 4

A	CHARGES
1	Reduction in stocks of finished goods and in work in progress
2	(a) Raw materials and consumables (b) Other external charges
3	Staff costs: (a) Wages and salaries (b) Social security costs (c) Other pension costs
4	(a) Depreciation and other amounts written off tangible and intangible fixed assets; (b) Exceptional amounts written off current assets
5	Other operating charges **Operating profit and loss (1)** **Losses on the sale or termination of an operation (2)** **Cost of a fundamental reorganisation or restructuring (2)**
6	Amounts written off investments
7	Interest payable and other charges
8	Tax on profit or loss on ordinary activities
9	Profit or loss on ordinary activities after taxation
10	Extraordinary charges
11	Tax on extraordinary profit or loss
12	Other taxes not shown under the above items
13	Profit or loss for the financial year

B	INCOME
1	Turnover
2	Increase in stocks of finished goods and in work in progress
3	Own work capitalised **Operating profit and loss** (1) **Profits on the sale or termination of an operation** (2) **Profits on disposal of fixed assets** (2)
4	Other operating income
5	Income from shares in group undertakings
6	Income from participating interests (D)
6	Or group accounts: (a) Income from interests in associated undertakings (a) Income from other participating interests
7	Income from other fixed asset investments
8	Other interest receivable and similar income **Profit or loss on ordinary activities before taxation** (3)
9	Profit and loss on ordinary activities after taxation *Minority interests* (E)
10	Extraordinary income *Minority interests* (E)
11	Profit or loss for the financial year

512

Notes regarding the Schedule 4 profit and loss account formats 1-4

(A)   **Cost of sales: Distribution costs: Administration expenses**
- Format 1: items 2, 4 and 5
- Format 3: items A, 1, 2 and 3

These items must be stated after taking into account any necessary provision for depreciation or diminution in value of assets.

(B)   **Income from other fixed asset investments: Other interest receivable and similar income**
- Format 1: items 9 and 10
- Format 2: items 11 and 12
- Format 3: items B.5, and 6
- Format 4: items B.7 and 8

Income and interest derived from group undertakings must be shown separately from income and interest derived from other sources.

(C)   **Interest payable and similar charges**
- Format 1: item 12
- Format 2: item 14
- Format 3: item A.5
- Format 4: item A.7

The amount payable to group undertakings must be shown separately.

Formats 1 and 3

The amount of any provisions for depreciation and diminution in value of tangible and intangible fixed assets required to be shown under items 7 (a) A.4 (a) respectively in Formats 2 and 4 must be disclosed in a note to the financial statements in any case where the profit and loss account is prepared by reference to Format 1 and Format 3.

(D)   **Income from participating interests**

Sch 4A
para 21 (3)
CA 1985
- Format 1: item 8
- Format 2: item 10
- Format 3: item B.4
- Format 4: item B.6

For consolidated profit and loss accounts, this heading must be replaced by the following two items:
- Income from interests in associated undertakings
- Income from other participating interests

(E)   **Minority interests**

A further item headed "minority interests" must be added:
- In Format 1, between items 14 and 15
- In Format 2, between items 16 and 17
- In Format 3, between items 7 and 8 in both sections A and B; and
- In Format 4, between items 9 and 10 in both sections A and B

(E)   A further item headed "minority interests" must also be added:
- In Format 1, between items 18 and 19
- In Format 2, between items 20 and 21
- In Format 3, between items 9 and 10 in section A and between items 8 and 9 in section B; and
- In Format 4, between items 11 and 12 in both sections A and between items 10 and 11 in section B

Other notes regarding the formats

(1)   Required by FRS 3, paragraph 14.

(2)   Required by FRS 3, paragraph 20. In calculating the profit or loss in respect of these items, consideration should only be given to revenue and costs directly related to the items in question

(3)   Required by Schedule 4, paragraph 3, (6) and (7)

513

Additional disclosures required under Formats 2, 3 and 4	
Category	**Content**
Changes in stocks of finished goods and work in progress	Used by manufacturing companies. Show difference between opening and closing stock of finished goods and work in progress. Finished goods include components purchased as well as manufactured by the company.
Own work capitalised	Includes the value of direct materials and labour and relevant overhead costs relating to the in-house construction of fixed assets are capitalised.
Raw materials and consumables	Purchases of components should be included within the cost of raw materials. Difference between opening and closing stocks of raw materials and consumables is deducted from or added to the total cost of purchases of these items. Companies in the retail trade using this format use another wording for this heading; namely: "Goods for resale".
Other external charges	Includes production costs not included in stock and consumables heading such as: subcontractor's costs, equipment rentals etc.
Staff costs	The formats require a distinction be drawn between wages and salaries, social security costs and other pension costs. The detail classification can be provided in the notes to the accounts.
Depreciation and other amounts written off fixed assets	This information required is dealt with in ¶440.
Exceptional amounts written off current assets	Not often used.
Other operating charges	Other operating charges include selling and administration costs not included under other headings.

SECTION 5

New UK GAAP – requirements of FRS 102

515   FRS 102 "The Financial Reporting Standard applicable in the UK and Republic of Ireland" will replace existing UK GAAP in January 2015, for small and medium sized entities not applying the FRSSE. The new standard contains a **small number of changes** to the presentation of the profit and loss account and there are some differences with FRS 3 "Reporting Financial Performance".

516   The FRS 102 offers **a choice between** either:

1. A **single statement of comprehensive income** for the reporting period containing all income and expenses recognised during the period, including those items recognised in determining profit or loss (which is a subtotal in the statement of comprehensive income) and items of other comprehensive income, or

2. **Two statement approach** comprising a separate income statement and a separate statement of comprehensive income.

Should an entity change from the single statement to the two statement approach or vice versa, this would represent a **change of accounting policy** under FRS 102.

Single statement approach   The single statement comprises two sections. The top part of   **517**
the statement shows the profit for the financial year based on the company law formats detailed in this chapter. The lower (second) part of the statement shows other income and expenses that would previously have been recorded in the STRGL, but are accounted for here under other comprehensive income. An entity should also show, where applicable, any share of profit or loss and other comprehensive income attributable to non-controlling interests and owners of the parent company.

Two statement approach   This option comprises an income statement based on the profit   **518**
and loss and company law formats and a statement of comprehensive income, which more accurately resembles the STRGL. If an entity chooses to present both an income statement and a statement of comprehensive income, the latter begins with profit or loss and then sets out the items of other comprehensive income.

Requirements applicable to both approaches   **519**

Category	Disclosures required
Discontinued operations	Disclosures required on the face of the income statement for total post tax profit or loss and post tax gain/loss attributable to impairment or on disposal of assets/companies comprising discontinued operations. Line by line analysis relating to discontinued operations required.
Material errors/changes	Correction of material errors or resulting from accounting policy changes should be shown as retrospective adjustments to a prior period, rather than in the current period. Further details concerning the nature and amount of material items should also be disclosed.
Analysis of expenses	Classified in the statement of comprehensive income by either the nature (e.g. depreciation, staff costs etc.) or by function (e.g. administrative expenses, cost of sales etc.).

CHAPTER 2

Revenue recognition

The principal accounting standard governing revenue recognition is FRS 5 "Reporting the Substance of Transactions". In addition there are a number of other standards, announcements and additional guidance that reflect developments in this area.

The relationships between the different accounting standards and abstracts often overlap and are set out for easy reference in the table below.

520

Type of company	Standard	Scope
Small entities	FRSSE / FRS 5 / FRS 102	General guidance
Medium and larger companies	1. FRS 5 "Reporting the Substance of Transactions" + Application Note G.	1. Principal standard on revenue recognition. + general principles of revenue recognition relating to the supply of goods and services by a seller to its customers.
	2. SSAP 9 "Stocks and long-term contracts". 3. FRS 102 (see note).	Specific guidance given on revenue recognition on long-term contracts (see ¶2230). Does not amend the requirements of SSAP 9.
Service companies	UITF 40	**Additional guidance** on accounting for revenue on service contracts (see ¶2264).

[MEMO POINTS] The FRC has issued **FRS 102** "The Financial Reporting Standard applicable in the UK and Republic of Ireland" for small and medium sized companies not adopting the FRSSE, which is mandatory for accounting periods beginning on 1 January 2015.

1. Small companies (FRSSE)

The **general rule** is that revenue should be recognised by the seller when they have obtained the right to consideration in exchange for performance of a contract. For **payment in advance** of performance, the seller should recognise a liability equal to the payment received (deferred income), representing its contractual obligation.

522
FRSSE 4.1

As the seller later obtains the right to consideration, the liability should be reduced accordingly. Revenue must be recorded at fair value; namely, the contractual price less discounts,

VAT etc. Where the time effect of money is material, given the length of a contract, the net present value of future contractual payments should be calculated and applied.

2. Other entities

524 Companies not adopting the FRSSE must take account of the specific requirements of FRS 5 "Reporting the Substance of Transactions" and Application Note G.

a. Application Note G - general guidance

525 The Application Note sets out the **basic principles of revenue recognition** to be applied in all instances, with **specific guidance** given for the following types of revenue:
– long-term contracts (¶2200);
– separation and linking of contractual performance;
– bill and hold arrangements;
– sales with right of return; and
– presentation of turnover as principal or agent.

It should be noted that the standard has not been universally welcomed and is the subject of some controversy.

The application note **does not apply to revenues arising** from financial instruments and insurance contracts, issues dealt with more exclusively by FRS 5 or specifically by other accounting standards.

Entities should only report turnover, if they have performed services or supplied goods in accordance with the contractual terms agreed with their customers. Guidance is also given on the measurement of turnover in relation to deferred payments and where significant risks exist concerning payment by debtors.

Examples of sources of revenue covered by the application note:
– barter transactions;
– property sales;
– sale or return;
– software sales;
– interest & dividends;
– royalties, licences, franchise fees;
– insurance recoverable;
– sale of spare capacity;
– warranties; and
– government grants (¶7900).

526

The basic principles of revenue recognition	
Condition	Accounting treatment
1. Revenue recognition- fundamental principle	Seller recognises revenue under a contract with a customer, when it obtains the "right to consideration" (see memo point 3) in exchange for performance of the contract (see memo note 2). At the same time the seller, typically, recognises a new asset, usually a debtor.
2. Recognising contractual performance	1. Goods: delivery terms 2. Services: period over which service(s) is (are) provided (e.g. cleaning contract) Must consider what specific activities constitute performance of a contract.

The basic principles of revenue recognition	
Condition	Accounting treatment
3. Contracts comprising mixture of goods and services	Must consider the terms of the contract. For instance does the performance of the contract consist of clearly identifiable stages? If yes are these stages separable?
4. Contract consists of separable stages	1. Is each stage "an end product"? 2. What benefit does the customer gain at each stage of completion? 3. Where does the balance of risk lie at each stage of the contract?
5. Seller receives payment in advance from customer	The seller should recognise a liability equal to the payment received (deferred income), representing its contractual obligation. When the seller obtains the right to consideration through performance on the contract, the liability should be reduced, with the reduction simultaneously reported as turnover.
6. Seller - partial consideration of contract	The seller should recognise turnover only to the extent that it has obtained the right to consideration through its performance.
7. Fair value	Revenue should be measured at fair value of the right to consideration (see memo note 1 below), normally the contract price, net of discounts, VAT and similar sales taxes.
8. Time-value of money	1. Where material to reported revenue - revenue recognised should be the present value of expected cash inflows. The unwinding of the discount should be credited to finance income as this is a gain from a financing transaction. 2. Subsequent adjustments to a debtor to reflect time-value of money or credit risk should not be included within turnover.

MEMO POINTS **1. Fair value**: The amount at which goods and services can be exchanged in an arm's length transaction, between informed and willing parties. **2. Performance**: The fulfilment of the seller's contractual obligations to the customer through the supply of goods and services. **3. Right to consideration**: A seller's right to the amount received or receivable in exchange for performance of a contract.

b. Specific guidance

Separation and linking of contractual arrangements

A contractual arrangement may require a seller to supply a number of different goods and services, which may not be related but which cannot be sold individually. **530**

On the other hand, the components or goods may be closely related, so that it would be difficult to sell them separately. In this instance, the seller will often sell the goods and services as a package at a discount to the individual prices.

The **issue is to determine**, whether as a result of the performance of the contract:
- the seller should recognise a change in its turnover and assets or liabilities, with regard to its right to consideration on each individual component in the contract (known as "unbundling"); or
- whether two or more components should be combined and turnover recognised on this basis ("bundling").

531   **Accounting treatment**   The accounting treatment for linked contracts is as follows:
– **Unbundled contracts** should be accounted for as two or more separate transactions, where the commercial substance indicates that the individual contract components operate independently of each other (different goods and services).
– **Bundled contracts** are accounted for as a single transaction where indicated by the commercial substance of the contract.

532   **Contracts with multiple components**

Condition	Accounting treatment
Contract components **independent of** each other	1. A **reliable fair value should be assigned** to each component. Recognition of turnover and changes in assets or liabilities is on the basis of each component being accounted for separately. 2. Where **reliable fair values cannot be assigned** to either completed or uncompleted components of the contracts, the seller should recognise turnover and changes in assets or liabilities as a single, bundled contractual arrangement. 3. Where **fair values can only be assigned** to uncompleted components, these fair values should be deducted from the total fair value of the contract, to obtain the turnover for completed components.
Contract components **not independent** of each other (see example below)	The seller should account for components together, to reflect the seller's performance under the contract. Where the contract can be classified (under SSAP 9) as a long-term contract, it should be accounted for in accordance with that standard.

EXAMPLE

1. **Software and related support service - recognition of turnover.**

A customer may purchase a **software package** "off the shelf" from a seller, with or without additional software support and maintenance. In this instance, the seller's performance comprises two components; namely, the software and the support package. The turnover on each part should be recognised separately.

Where a customer purchases **"bespoke" software** such as a management information system, this typically includes a maintenance and support element, needed to ensure continued operation of the system as well as development of the software to meet the specific requirements of the customer. The commercial substance of the arrangement is that the customer is often buying support over a period of time, which is not separable from the rest of the contract as the two elements are closely linked. In this instance, the **turnover should be recognised** on a long-term contractual basis.

2. **Vouchers** Where vouchers for a material amount are supplied with a purchase, a provision should be made to cover the redemption value, with a corresponding reduction in the income recorded. Factors to be taken into account in determining the provision include the range of goods covered by the voucher, redemption date and estimate of expected redemption uptake. If the conclusion is that the fair value of a voucher is not significant, and does not constitute a separable component of the original transaction, no adjustment to revenue is required. At each reporting date the seller should review any voucher scheme to ensure that any estimated liabilities remain realistic in the light of redemption levels or expiry dates. Adjustments to estimates should be included within revenue. Where vouchers are distributed free of charge this does not generate a liability, except if the redemption results in a product being sold at a loss. Should this be the case an onerous contract would be the result and a provision should be made under FRS 12 "Provisions, Contingent Liabilities and Contingent Assets". When the vouchers are redeemed the discount should be deducted from revenue.

Bill and hold arrangements

534   Under a bill and hold arrangement, the seller arranges a contract with a customer to supply goods, where although **legal title** is transferred immediately, physical delivery is deferred to a later date. The issue is whether the seller or purchaser should recognise the goods as assets or can the seller recognise the revenue and the right to consideration in the case where the goods have not been delivered to the buyer.

For the seller to be able to recognise the revenue arising from its **right to consideration** in respect of the bill and hold arrangement, or to continue to recognise the goods as stock, the terms of the contract between the seller and buyer should include all the **following characteristics**:
1. The goods should be complete and ready for delivery to the customer;
2. The seller should have relinquished all significant performance obligations, save safekeeping of the goods;
3. Subject to "Rights of Return", the seller should have gained the right to consideration, regardless of when the goods are subsequently shipped to the customer;
4. The commercial substance of any "Rights of Return" should be examined;
5. The goods should be separately identifiable from other stock held by the seller; and
6. The bill and hold arrangements should be in accordance with the commercial objectives of the buyer not the seller.

Accounting treatment The **accounting treatment** is as follows: **535**
– the seller should recognise the changes in assets or liabilities, and turnover when the "stock" is recognised as an asset by the buyer; and
– where the substance of the transaction indicates that the goods are still an asset of the seller, it should be retained on the seller's balance sheet; any monies received from the customer (payments on account) should be included within creditors.

Principal benefits and risks The **principal benefits** of bill and hold arrangements for the **536**
customer are as follows:
– the right to obtain the goods when required;
– sole rights to the goods in terms of third parties and the associated cash flows; and
– guaranteed prices.

The **principal risks** relate to slow moving stock and the risk of obsolescence.

Sales with a right of return (SOR)

In order to boost the marketing and distribution of certain goods, manufacturers and distribu- **538**
tors often supply goods on a sale or return basis. If the goods are sold to a final customer, the retailer will retain a previously agreed proportion of the selling price. In the event that the goods are not sold, they will be returned to the manufacturer after an agreed time period.

Under the **terms of the contract** a buyer may be permitted to return goods that they have purchased, with the right to a refund or cancellation of an obligation to pay. The existence of "Rights to Return" goods could affect the seller's **"right to consideration"** under the contract and the recognition of revenue thereof. The seller's recognition of its "consideration" and contractual obligation to transfer economic benefits to its customer, in respect of "Rights of Return", are linked transactions. Goods sold on an SOR basis continue to belong to the seller until sold onto customers.

Accounting treatment The **seller's turnover** should exclude the sales value of estimated **540**
returns and only include revenue for items not expected to be returned. Estimates of "returns" should reflect the maximum potential number of returns and other appropriate risks based on historical experience of comparable sales.

Where the risk of returns are significant and effectively all risks associated with the goods are retained by the seller, no turnover or changes in assets or liabilities should be recognised, until such time as:
– the estimated "returns" can be reliably re-measured; or
– any associated time period for the returns has expired.

Any payments received should be included within creditors as payments in advance. **Estimates of returns** should be reviewed at each balance sheet date, taking into account constructive as well as legal obligations.

| EXAMPLE | **Retail operation**

1. A **retailer sells leather shoes** over the internet to customers, who have the right to return the goods within 21 days, provided they are in a resaleable condition. The retailer can estimate the percentage of returns expected (i.e. 25%) based on experience and recognise the appropriate revenue accordingly (i.e. 75%). For each pair of shoes sold, part of the consideration will be recognised as revenue and the remainder as a provision. Cost of sales recognised on each sale should be adjusted for each item returned with a corresponding adjustment to stock. This accounting treatment is in accordance with FRS 12 "Provisions, contingent liabilities and assets".

2. A **book publisher** distributes books to the value of £100,000 on a sale or return basis and estimates that returns (based on experience) will be around 40%. The accounting treatment is as follows:
Stage 1. Debit Sales ledger (trade debtors) £100,000 and credit SOR deferred sales provision £100,000
Stage 2. Make an adjustment to reflect expected sales: Debit SOR deferred sales provision £60,000 and credit sales (P&L) £60,000.
Stage 3. When cash received, debit Bank and credit Sales Ledger. Raise a credit note for value of sales returned (£40,000) with a debit to the SOR deferred sales provision account.
Stage 4. If the company receives more that the £60,000 expected it should debit the SOR deferred sales provision (B/S) and credit the SOR sales account. If the final sales figure is less than £60,000 the company should post the reverse entry: namely credit sales provision and debit the SOR sales account.

Presentation of turnover as principal or as agent

542

A seller acting on its own when contracting with customers for the supply of goods is known as the principal. The seller is an agent where he acts as an intermediary on behalf of a principal in return for a commission.

The **general rule** is that for a seller to account for exchange transactions as a principal, it should have exposure to all **significant benefits and risks** associated with at least one of the following; namely the selling price or in respect of stock (i.e. exposure to risk of damage, slow moving stock). Other indications of principal status are that the seller assumes any credit risk and that the seller retains discretion over the choice of supplier.

Where the **seller acts as an agent**, it will not normally be exposed to the benefits and risks attached to the exchange transaction. Agency arrangements exhibit the following transactions:
– the seller has disclosed that it is acting as an agent; and
– the seller plays no further part in the transaction, once the agent has confirmed the customer's order to the principal;
– the seller's commission is pre-determined;
– the agent bears no credit or stock holding risk.

Summary Condition	Accounting treatment
	Based on substance of transaction
Seller acts as principal	Turnover should be based on gross revenue received or receivable in return for performance of the contract. Seller has exposure to all significant benefits and risks associated with the transaction.
Seller acts as agent	Turnover represents the commission or other amounts received or receivable under the terms of the contract. Amounts received or receivable from the customer that are payable to the principal should not be included in the agent's turnover.

Application Note G gives a number of examples for determining whether the seller is acting as a principal or agent. **543**

> [EXAMPLE]
> **1. Seller acting as the principal** A seller acts a building contractor on the construction of a new office complex. The terms of the seller's contract with its client shows that it includes a negotiated selling price, credit risk for amounts due from the customer, primary responsibility for the construction and quality of the finished building and whether it undertakes the work itself or employs subcontractors to carry out all or part of the construction. In this case the seller is acting as the principal and should account for the gross amount of turnover, irrespective of whether it carries out the work itself or engages sub-contractors to construct part or all of the building.
>
> **2. Seller acting as an agent** A seller operates as an on-line retailer complete with a website advertising holidays. An analysis of the contractual arrangements show the seller is acting as an intermediary between the customers and the ultimate sellers of the holidays and does not set the selling price of the holidays. The seller's terms of business include a rider that it carries no liability once customer and holiday company have been put in touch with one another. The seller receives a fee for each customer that purchases a holiday and has no further involvement in the transaction. In this scenario the seller is acting as an agent and its turnover should only include the fees it receives from the holiday company.

3. Disclosures

Detailed disclosure should be made of revenue recognition policies adopted and for each principal source of revenue the following disclosures should be given: **546**
- the timing of the revenue recognition;
- accounting treatment of discounts;
- measurement of sources of revenue; and
- methods used to allocate revenue in composite transactions where different revenue recognition policies are used.

> [EXAMPLE] Retail
>
> A retailer sells leather shoes over the internet to customers, who have the right to return the goods within 21 days, provided they are unused and in resaleable condition. The retailer can estimate the percentage of returns expected (e.g. 25%) based on experience and recognise the appropriate revenue accordingly (e.g. 75%). For each pair of shoes sold part of the consideration will be recognised as revenue and the remainder as a provision. Cost of sales recognised on each sale should be adjusted for each item returned with a corresponding adjustment to stock. This accounting treatment is in accordance with FRS 12 "Provisions, contingent liabilities and assets".

Barter transactions

The accounting for barter transactions is governed by UITF Abstract 26 "Barter transactions for advertising". This abstract covers transactions, where advertising and related services are provided in exchange for reciprocal marketing services, such as in the internet industry, where advertising space is traded on reciprocal websites. The abstract also covers similar barter transactions involving advertising on television and posters, and in magazines. The abstract **is not mandatory for** other industries although the same principles should apply. **548** UITF 26 (3)

The abstract recommends, that **turnover and related costs** in respect of barter transactions for advertising should not be recognised, unless there is persuasive evidence of its value, i.e. there is evidence of cash revenue being generated from other sales of similar advertising space to other customers.

Contracts for the sale of spare capacity

The **rules governing contracts** for the sale of capacity are covered in UITF 36 "Contracts for sale of capacity". These types of contract are common in the telecommunications and utility **550**

industries such as electricity, where entities buy and sell capacity on their respective networks. The **general rules** are that the seller of the capacity should not account for the sale unless:
- the purchaser has an exclusive and irrevocable right to use of the capacity;
- the asset (or component thereof) is specific and clearly identifiable;
- the seller has no right to substitute for other assets;
- the cost of the capacity can be reliably measured;
- the contract term covers a significant part of the asset's useful economic life; and
- there are no significant risks retained by the seller, such as obsolescence risk or risk of marked change in the value of the asset.

Where the criteria as set out above have been met, then the sale proceeds can be reported as turnover, if the asset was previously classified under the heading of "stock" as "held for resale on acquisition/construction". Otherwise the sale should be reported as a disposal of fixed assets.

The **turnover and profits** on reciprocal contracts, where capacity on one network is exchanged for capacity on the network of another supplier, should only be recognised where the assets or services provided or obtained have a readily ascertainable value. The **substance of each transaction** should be reviewed.

4. New developments in UK GAAP - FRS 102

560   The FRC has issued FRS 102 "The Financial Reporting Standard applicable in the UK and Republic of Ireland", which is mandatory from January 2015 when it will replace the existing UK GAAP (e.g. FRS 5, SSAP 9 and UITF 40). The key elements relating to revenue recognition are set out in the table below.

In addition, the FRC has also issued a **Staff Education Note (SEN 07)** illustrating certain key requirements of FRS 102 relating to revenue recognition, designed to help smooth the transition to the new standard. For the majority of entities, however, there will be no significant change in terms of recognising revenue.

Subject	Accounting treatment under FRS 102
Basic principles – scope, measurement	No key differences in basic recognition and measurement principles.
Discounting	Both FRS 5 and FRS 102 allow discounting, although the former has more detailed requirements regarding the discount rate.
Default risk	Where the risk of default is high and settlement in doubt, revenue should be recognised until receipt is probable. A similar treatment is advocated under current UK GAAP.
Long term contracts	No significant differences with current UK GAAP.
Contracts for multiple services	Under FRS 5 revenue is recognised as each service (or number of services that constitute a single project) is delivered. Under FRS 102 revenue is recognised using a method representing the stage of completion. In practice there is no significant difference in accounting treatment.

CHAPTER 3

Segmental reporting

This chapter provides an overview of some of the general difficulties associated with the compilation of segmental data and the need for consistency in presentation. Entities often conduct a range of different business activities, serve various markets, and operate in more than one geographical location. Each of these business units, irrespective of how they are categorised or organised, have their own unique commercial characteristics, including different rates of profitability, opportunities for growth and degrees of risk.   **750**

As business becomes more globalised and companies grow and diversify their activities, so the users of financial statements need to understand the varying **economic, political and business risks**, as well as opportunities, that exist in the individual segments and the effect they have on overall growth, profitability, and financial well being. In order to provide useful information to the stakeholders most likely to benefit from segmental information (e.g. shareholders, investment analysts and major creditors), the **Companies Act** requires entities, **other than small companies**, to make certain disclosures about the different activities in which they are involved and the various markets in which they operate.

In addition, SSAP 25, "Segmental Reporting", sets out further requirements designed to assist users of financial statements by providing segmental analysis of the information they contain, in particular the disclosure of turnover, results, and net assets by class of business and by geographical sector. The accounting standard seeks to ensure, as far as possible, that segmental information reported is disclosed consistently over time through the adoption of common accounting policies and the treatment of common costs.   **751**

Main categories Two broad categories of segment are distinguished: **business** and **geographical**. SSAP 25 provides guidance on how to determine the segments and what information should be disclosed. The directors can therefore exercise considerable discretion when compiling segmental information.   **752**

If a company operates in two or more significant markets or classes of business, and these differ substantially from one another, it is obliged to comply with the **statutory** disclosure   **753** requirements on segmental reporting contained in the Companies Act. Broadly, these are that the turnover attributable to the different classes and markets should be shown individually in the notes. The regulations to the 2006 Act require that only those classes of business or markets that make a **material** contribution need be disclosed; amounts that are not material may be combined with other classes and markets and shown as such. A **total exemption** from the disclosure requirements of the Companies Act is possible but difficult to justify. One such exemption would be where, in the opinion of the directors, the disclosure of segmental information would be harmful to the company's interests. However, the fact that the information has not been given must be clearly stated.

754   Additional **non-statutory** disclosure requirements are required for certain entities under SSAP 25 and FRS 3 "Reporting financial performance". Further specific disclosure rules apply to certain industries (e.g. Oil and Financial Services), which have issued their own statements of recommended practice (SORPs). Segmental information may also be included in the interim reports published predominantly by listed companies.

As a general rule, the disclosure of segmental information is encouraged even if the entity is able to claim **exemption** from some or all of the additional disclosure requirements of SSAP 25. The majority of companies present their segmental information in the notes to the accounts.

756   **Exempt Companies**   The following entities are specifically exempt from SSAP 25, though not from the Companies Act:
– reporting entities reporting under the dispensation for smaller entities (FRSSE);
– a subsidiary company (that is not a public limited company or a banking or insurance company), where its parent publishes segmental information in compliance with this standard or in accordance with International Accounting Standards; and
– particular types of entity that are subject to different statutory rules and that are outside the scope of this manual (e.g. building societies).

SECTION 1

Determination of significant segments

760   Beyond giving general suggestions for determining classes of business, the Act leaves it to the directors to decide on the matter. Similarly, SSAP 25 identifies a number of factors that the directors might consider when determining what constitutes a significant geographical or business segment.

General factors

762
SSAP 25 (8)

The directors, in trying to identify reporting segments, should consider those operations that have different:
– returns on investment, disproportionate to the rest of the business;
– degrees of risk;
– comparative scales of operation;
– rates of growth; and
– potential for future development.

The **selection of segments** should be based on an assessment of any of these factors. The accounting standard advises that these **criteria** should be reviewed annually and redefined as appropriate because of the likelihood that no single set of characteristics will continue to apply or remain dominant indefinitely. However, as far as is practicable, the directors should maintain consistency of approach so that segmental results will be comparable year on year.

Materiality   A geographical or business segment would also be considered significant if one of the following criteria apply, irrespective of the judgement of the directors:
– its **turnover** is 10% or more of the total turnover (excluding inter-company sales) of the entity;
– the **segmental profit** or loss is 10% or more of the combined results of all the entities' profit or loss making segments; or
– its **net assets** are 10% or more of the total assets of the entity.

763

It is also important to note that additional disclosures are required of **associates and joint ventures** (¶7300) which are triggered at a specific threshold.

Business segments

A business segment is defined as **a separate division** that provides a different product or service and can be **based on** any of the **following criteria**:
– type of the product or service;
– nature of the production process;
– markets in which the products or services are sold;
– distribution channels for the products;
– any particular legislative framework relating to the segment (e.g. bank or insurance company); and
– the manner in which activities are organised.

764
SSAP 25 (12)

The business segments commonly shown in financial statements are shown by way of illustration.

EXAMPLE

Company	Reported business segments
United News and Media	Business services; consumer publishing; broadcasting.
WPP Group plc	Advertising & media planning; information & consultancy; public relations; buying & research.
United Utilities plc	Water and wastewater; electricity distribution; energy supply.

Geographical segments

A geographical segment is generally defined as an area comprising an individual country or group of countries in which an entity either physically operates, or markets and supplies, goods or services. This might also cover a group of countries linked through the adoption of a currency zone such as the euro.

766
SSAP 25 (14)

Geographical segments should reflect the extent to which an entity's operations are affected by:
– the political climate in the country of operations;
– any exchange control regulations; and
– fluctuating exchange rates.

SECTION 2

Compliance

A number of **compulsory disclosures** are prescribed by the Companies Act; additional disclosures are required under SSAP 25, which seeks to ensure consistency of disclosure and presentation of segmental information. The problems inherent in compiling segmental information are also covered.

774

A. Compulsory disclosures required by the Companies Act

776   Under the Companies Act, companies that operate in two or more major markets must provide a **description** of each class of business, as well as an **analysis** of:
– turnover and profit or loss before tax between substantially different classes of business;
– turnover between significant geographical segments; and
– the amount of profit or loss of the company before tax, attributable to each business segment.

In analysing segmental information, the directors must give due consideration as to how the business activities are organised. Furthermore, classes of business or markets that do not differ substantially from each other should be treated as one class, and amounts that are not material may be included in another class of business or market segment.

The Companies Act 2006 **exempts medium-sized companies** from this disclosure.

778   **Exemptions**   An exemption from the Companies Act disclosure requirements is available only where, in the opinion of the directors, the disclosure of information would be **seriously prejudicial** to the interests of the company. An example might be the case of a company that trades with neighbouring countries that are in conflict with each other.

This non-disclosure exemption cannot be used simply to avoid disclosing information that the entity would prefer **competitors** not to know. If the exemption is invoked, this fact must be disclosed in a note to the accounts although the **reasons** need not be given. In practice, the exemption is rarely used.

MEMO POINTS   The **Companies Act** contains provisions exempting banks and insurance companies from the requirement to disclose segmental turnover in certain circumstances. In spite of this, it does not appear that banks enjoy a similar exemption under SSAP 25.

B. Additional disclosures required by SSAP 25

790   SSAP 25 requires the **following entities** to provide additional (mandatory) segmental information to that required by the Companies Act:
a. public limited companies (or companies with a subsidiary that is a public limited company), or
b. banking or insurance companies, or
c. private companies meeting certain criteria.

791   Under SSAP 25, which extends the statutory disclosure requirements, an entity should disclose in its financial statements the **basis** on which it **defines** its geographical and business **segments**. For each segment it should then disclose all of the following information:
– turnover split by group companies, joint ventures and associated companies;
– turnover split by geographical segment but excluding inter-company transactions and VAT;
– turnover analysed by reference to customer location (source) or destination and by its origin;
– operating results after tax, minority interests and extraordinary items; and
– net operating assets.

792
SSAP 25 (18)   **Turnover**   The users of the financial statements should gain a better understanding of the entity's exposure to geographical factors if turnover is disclosed according to the location of both operations and markets.

The **origin** of turnover is the geographical area from which products or services are supplied to a third party or another segment. The **destination** of turnover is the geographical area to which goods and services are delivered. Where there is no material difference between the origin and destination of sales, separate disclosure is not required although a statement to this effect must be provided.

Operating results and net assets   Disclosures relating to segmental results and net assets are generally based on the locations of operation because this will enable the user to match turnover, operating results and net assets on a consistent basis. It will also allow comparisons to be made between the perceived risks and opportunities within each segment.   **796**

Aggregate disclosures   The aggregate figures given for each segment should equal the total as disclosed in the profit and loss account. Where this is not the case, because for example certain common costs have not been apportioned to a particular segment, a **reconciliation** should be provided. The reconciling items should be clearly explained. **Comparative figures** for the previous accounting period should also be disclosed.   **798**

Associate companies   Further disclosure requirements are imposed where an entity has associated entities that form a **material part of the group's results or assets**. These additional disclosures are required where associates account for 20% or more of the total operating results or the total net assets of the group (including the group's share of the associates' results or net assets). The information disclosed should represent the aggregate of all the associate undertakings. The same criteria apply to joint ventures.   **799**

If the **materiality threshold is exceeded**, the entity must supply certain segmental information; namely its share of:
– profits (or losses) before tax, minority interests and extraordinary items; and
– total net assets.
Where practicable, the value of net assets of associates should be restated to incorporate their fair values as at the date the entity acquired its interest in the associate.

C. Disclosures required by FRS 3

Changes to group composition   FRS 3, "Reporting financial performance", requires that when the composition of a group changes through an **acquisition, sale or termination** that has a material effect on a significant business segment, this fact should be disclosed.   **804**
SSAP 25 (34)

The following example illustrates the disclosure of segmental information concerning the termination of a business operation; the discontinued operation is shown as a residual category with continuing operations analysed by segment. This format can be adapted for either a major sale or acquisition requiring disclosure.

EXAMPLE

Discontinued operations	Total £m	UK £m	Europe £m	Americas £m	Pacific £m
Sales	76	35	6	20	15
Trading profit	12	5	1	3	3

Continuing operations – current year	Total £m	UK £m	Europe £m	Americas £m	Pacific £m
Sales:					
Beverages	2500	20	400	1600	480
Confectionary	3000	1000	1000	500	500
Totals	5500	1020	1400	2100	980

D. Difficulties in compiling segmental information

820   A number of difficulties can arise when compiling and presenting segmental information.

Comparative data

822
SSAP 25 (29)

Difficulties comparing similar segments in different entities can result from the:
- **basis** of accounting adopted for inter-segment sales;
- **differences** in accounting policies and standards;
- treatment of common costs being **inconsistent** between entities; or
- **changing** composition of segments.

In order to achieve consistency within a set of accounts, if a company should, e.g. decide to alter the scope of a particular business segment, adopt a new accounting standard, diversify its activities, or isolate an operation previously aggregated within another segment, it should amend the comparative figures for the previous year.

Inter-segment sales

824   SSAP 25 stipulates that turnover should be split between external and internal sales and shown separately with the **geographical analysis** grouped by origin rather than destination. The standard does not require the disclosure of the basis on which inter-segment sales are conducted. Some companies disclose the basis of their transfer pricing; namely whether:
- market price;
- established internal prices; or
- prices derived from arm's length negotiations.

Common costs

826
SSAP 25 (23)

Operating costs that relate to more than one segment should be apportioned by the directors on a basis consistent with their internal reporting structures. **Central administrative overheads** are an example of common costs that should be allocated to business or geographical segments using an acceptable basis such as a proportion of direct costs. However, other methods are acceptable. For instance, a confectionary company stated in its annual report that common or corporate costs were allocated equally between the company's two business segments: beverages and confectionery.

Common costs should not be apportioned over segments if to do so would be misleading. In these cases the cost element that is not apportioned should be deducted from the aggregate of the segment results.

Allocation of interest

828
SSAP 25 (22)

In most companies, different classes of business or geographical segments are financed by different proportions of **interest-bearing debt and equity**. Where all, or a significant part, of the entity's business revenue or costs is interest earned or incurred, or where interest income or expense is central to the business (e.g. the travel industry), interest should be accounted for in arriving at the segmental results. This applies particularly in the case of companies in the financial sector (e.g. loan companies) as well as conglomerates in which some cash-rich divisions finance other businesses within the group.

In the absence of the above situations, the allocation of interest earned or incurred is usually the result of group policy and, consequently, interest is generally excluded from the segmental disclosures so that the net assets of each significant segment should represent the non-interest-bearing operating assets less the non-interest-bearing operating liabilities.

Common assets

Assets or liabilities that do not belong to a specific segment should be allocated on a reasonable basis. The total net assets that cannot be allocated in this manner should be shown as a reconciling item between the total of all segments' net assets and the net asset figure appearing in the balance sheet.

830
SSAP 25 (24)

Net assets

Net assets are not defined in SSAP 25 but are generally considered to be non-interest-bearing operating assets less non-interest-bearing liabilities. Different companies may be justified in interpreting net assets in different ways (as long as the chosen definition is applied consistently). As a result, comparisons between returns on capital employed might have limitations. Operating assets and liabilities may relate to a specific segment or jointly to more than one segment.

832

Change of policy

If segmental definitions or reporting policies have changed, the nature of the change, its effect, and the reasons, must be stated by way of the notes.

834

E. Small companies adopting the FRSSE

The FRSSE requirements relating to segmental reporting for small entities are minimal. If the company has supplied **markets outside the UK** during the financial year, it must disclose separately the percentage of turnover that is attributable to those markets. In analysing the source of turnover, account must be taken of the manner in which the company's activities are organised.

835
FRSSE 3.4

PART 3

Balance sheet – Fixed assets

The Companies Act details the form and content of the balance sheet with additional require- **960** ments contained in the accounting standards. The balance sheet formats for small and medium sized companies are more condensed than those for large and medium-sized enti- ties, reflecting the requirement for reduced disclosures.

A **choice between** two balance sheet formats is permitted, although the most common **962** presentation is format 1 in which the balance sheet headings are presented vertically. Under format 2, the presentation is horizontal with assets on one side and liabilities, capital and reserves on the other. The formats for **group companies** are broadly similar.

There are also a number of rules governing the classification of assets and liabilities and valuation of assets

> _MEMO POINTS_   1. The **formats and content** of the financial statements will now be set out in regulations drafted under the framework of the Companies Act 2006. Two sets of regulations have been issued; one set being exclusively for small companies (SI 2008/409) whilst the other covers large and medium-sized companies and groups (SI 2008/410). The main difference is that the small company regulations include simplified sub-headings.
> 2. **Minority interests** are also known as non-controlling interests (NCIs).
> 3. The requirements for **dormant companies** are covered in ¶6400.
> 4. No significant changes to formats are proposed under **FRS 102** "The Financial Reporting Stan- dard applicable in the UK and Republic of Ireland". Under FRS 102 the balance sheet is known as the **Statement of Financial Position**.

A. Classification of assets and liabilities.

The **definition of fixed and current assets** is based on the intended use of the asset in the **970** business. The distinction is that fixed assets are intended to be used on a continuing basis, whilst current assets are not.

All assets must be classified under the headings of "Fixed assets" or "Current assets", except for the following which can either be shown separately as a main heading (i.e. one that is assigned a letter) in the formats or as subheadings (i.e. one that is assigned an Arabic numeral); namely:
- Debtors;
- Prepayments and accrued income; and
- Called-up share capital not paid.

There is **no statutory requirement** to classify current assets into those realisable within one year or after more than one year.

> MEMO POINTS In the formats laid down by the Companies Act, each major classification of asset, liability and capital and reserves is assigned a balance sheet heading, which in turn is assigned either a **letter or a Roman numeral**. The headings must be presented in the order in which they appear in the formats given in the Act. Under each major classification are various sub-headings, (accompanied by Arabic numerals) which can be adapted to meet the requirements of particular companies. In practice, these items are not usually shown on the face of the balance sheet, but are instead aggregated under the relevant asset heading, with a more detailed breakdown of individual items included in the notes to the financial statements.

972   **Current liabilities** are split into two categories in the formats dependant upon when the liability falls due for payment. The two categories are Creditors; "amounts falling due within one year" and "Creditors and amounts falling due after more than one year".

"Accrual and deferred income" may be shown separately as a main heading or as a sub-heading under one of the two "Creditor headings".

> MEMO POINTS Liabilities are **defined in FRS 5** as "obligations of an entity to transfer economic benefits as a result of past transactions or events".

974   **Net current assets or liabilities** is a subtotal for current assets and liabilities under format 1, which must include "Prepayments and accrued income", even where this item is shown under a separate heading from current assets.

B. Rules for valuing assets

976   The rules for valuing assets are set out in the Companies Act, and are generally consistent with the requirements of the accounting standards. A distinction is drawn between the **historical cost accounting rules** and the **alternative accounting rules**, which permits for certain asset categories the revaluation of assets or the use of current cost in statutory financial statements. A mixture of both sets of rules (i.e. cost and valuation) is permitted although certain restrictions have been imposed by FRS 15 "Tangible fixed assets", where consistency of accounting treatment by class of asset is required.

The **general valuation rules** are set out in the table below along with the respective chapter references.

Overview of asset valuation rules		
	Historical cost	Alternative accounting rules
Cost	Purchase or production cost	Separate requirements: 1. **Tangible fixed assets**: – market value at last valuation date or at current cost (see ¶1200). 2. **Intangible assets** (excluding goodwill) – at current cost (see ¶1000). 3. **Fixed asset investments**: – market value at last valuation date or directors valuation (see ¶1750). 4. **Current asset investments**: – current cost (¶2700). 5. **Stocks**: – current cost (see ¶2000).
Depreciation	Carrying amount of asset is written down to residual value over useful economic life through provisions for depreciation	As under **historical cost**

Overview of asset valuation rules		
	Historical cost	Alternative accounting rules
Impairment – fixed assets (see ¶1550)	Provision required if reduction is permanent (assets recoverable amount falls below carrying value)	1. Assets carried at market value – as under historical cost. 2. Assets carried at current cost each year. Provision required for any diminution in value if current cost falls. 3. Fixed asset investments – provision for diminution in value. 4. Current assets – written down to net realisable value if lower than cost or alternative valuation.

C. Companies Act formats

The formats and content of the financial statements will now be set out in regulations drafted under the framework of the Companies Act 2006. Two sets of regulations have been issued; one set being exclusively for **small companies** (SI 2008/409) whilst the other covers **large and medium-sized companies and groups** (SI 2008/410). The main difference is that the small company regulations include simplified sub-headings. The balance sheet formats for small companies preparing abbreviated accounts are set out in the chapter on SME's (¶6281).

984

1. Small companies

General rules and key disclosures

The directors of the company must use the **same formats** for preparing their financial statements year on year, unless there are special reasons for changing the presentation. Where this is the case the reasons for the change must be disclosed in a note to the balance sheet. Headings can be excluded where there are no transactions for the financial year. Where information provided in the accounts in insufficient to give a true and fair view of the entity's position, additional information should be given in the notes to the financial statements.

985
FRSSE 2.16-26

Corresponding amounts should be shown for each amount included in the balance sheet but are not required for notes to the accounts regarding tangible fixed assets (e.g. additions, disposals, revaluations, cumulative depreciation), transfers to or from reserves, details of subsidiary undertakings, joint ventures etc. For creditors details should be given of all amounts due after five years from the end of the current financial year, including details of any security given by the company to underwrite the debts.

The following disclosures are required for **each reserve** in the notes for:
– the balance at the beginning and end of the financial year;
– details on sums transferred from/to reserves; and
– source and application of funds transferred.

986
FRSSE 2.27

The format for small companies is set out below.

Small companies and groups (Format per SI 2008 No. 409)	
A	**Called up share capital not paid**
B	**Fixed assets**
B-I	Intangible assets 1. Goodwill 2. Other intangible assets
B-II	Tangible assets 1. Land and buildings 2. Plant and machinery, etc.
B-III	Investments 1. Shares in group undertakings and participating interests 2. Loans to group undertakings and undertakings in which the company has a participating interest 3. Other investments other than loans 4. Other investments
C	**Current assets**
C-I	Stocks 1. Stocks 2. Payments on account
C-II	Debtors 1. Trade debtors (See Note 1) 2. Amounts owed by group undertakings and undertakings in which the company has a participating interest 3. Other debtors
C-III	Investments 1. Shares in group undertakings 2. Other investments
C-IV	Cash at bank and in hand
D	**Prepayments and accrued income**
E	**Creditors: amounts falling due within one year** 1. Bank loans and overdrafts 2. Trade creditors 3. Amounts owed to group undertakings and undertakings in which the company has a participating interest 4. Other creditors
F	**Net current assets (liabilities)**
G	**Total assets less current liabilities**
H	**Creditors: amounts falling due after one year** 1. Bank loans and overdrafts 2. Trade creditors 3. Amounts owed to group undertakings and undertakings in which the company has a participating interest 4. Other creditors
I	**Provisions for liabilities and charges**
J	**Accruals and deferred income**

Small companies and groups (Format per SI 2008 No. 409)	
K	**Capital and reserves**
K-I	Called up share capital
K-II	Share premium account
K-III	Revaluation reserve
K-IV	Other reserves
K-V	Profit and loss account

2. Large and medium sized companies

A **choice between** two balance sheet formats is permitted, although the most common presentation is format 1 in which the balance sheet headings are presented vertically in the following order: Assets, Liabilities, and Capital and Reserves. Under format 2, the presentation is horizontal with assets on one side and liabilities, capital and reserves on the other. Also no distinction is made

988

between creditors due within one year and after more than one year. The disclosures required in the notes to the accounts as similar to those set out for small companies but will be more detailed as they reflect the size of the company.

Format 1 (Format per SI 2008 No. 410)	
A	**Called up share capital not paid** (1)
B	**Fixed assets**
B-I	Intangible assets 1. Development costs 2. Concessions, patents, licences…etc. (2) 3. Goodwill (3) 4. Payments on account
B-II	Tangible assets 1. Land and buildings 2. Plant and machinery 3. Fixtures, fittings… 4. Payments on account and assets in the course of construction
B-III	Investments 1. Shares in group undertakings 2. Loans to group undertakings 3. Participating interests (13) 4. Loans to undertakings in which the company has a participating interest 5. Other investments other than loans 6. Other loans 7. Own shares (4)
C	**Current assets**
C-I	Stocks 1. Raw materials, etc. 2. Work in progress 3. Finished goods/goods for resale 4. Payments on account
C-II	Debtors (5)1. Trade debtors 2. Amounts owed by group undertakings 3. Amounts owed by undertakings in which the company has a participating interest 4. Other debtors

Format 1 (Format per SI 2008 No. 410)	
	5. Called up share capital not paid (1) 6. Prepayments and accrued income (6)
C-III	Investments 1. Shares in group undertakings 2. Own shares (4) 3. Other investments
C-IV	Cash at bank and in hand
D	**Prepayments and accrued income**
E	**Creditors: amounts falling due within one year** 1. Debenture loans (7) 2. Bank loans and overdrafts 3. Payments received on account (8) 4. Trade creditors 5. Bills of exchange payable 6. Amounts owed to group undertakings 7. Amounts owed to undertakings in which the company has a participating interest 8. Other creditors including taxation and social security (9) 9. Accruals and deferred income (10)
F	**Net current assets (liabilities)** (11)
G	**Total assets less current liabilities**
H	**Creditors amounts falling due after one year** 1. Debenture loans (7) 2. Bank loans and overdrafts 3. Payments received on account (8) 4. Trade creditors 5. Bills on exchange payable 6. Amounts owed to group undertakings 7. Amounts owed to undertakings in which the company has a participating interest 8. Other creditors including taxation and social security (9) 9. Accruals and deferred income (10)
I	**Provision for liabilities and charges** 1. Pensions and similar obligations 2. Taxation, etc. 3. Other provisions
J	**Accruals and deferred income (10)**
K	**Capital and reserves**
K-I	Called up share capital (1)
K-II	Share premium account
K-III	Revaluation reserve
K-IV	Other reserves 1. Capital redemption reserve 2. Reserve for own shares 3. Reserves provided for by articles 4. Other reserves
K-V	Profit and loss account
M	**Minority interests** (alternative position – before K) (14)

Format 2 (Format per SI 2008 No. 410)	
Assets	
A	**Called up share capital not paid** (1)
B	**Fixed assets**
B-I	Intangible assets 1. Development costs 2. Concessions, patents, licences...etc. (2) 3. Goodwill (3) 4. Payments on account
B-II	Tangible assets 1. Land and buildings 2. Plant and machinery 3. Fixtures, fittings... 4. Payments on account and assets in the course of construction
B-III	Investments 1. Shares in group undertakings 2. Loans to group undertakings 3. Participating interests (13) 4. Loans to undertakings in which the company has a participating interest 5. Other investments other than loans 6. Other loans 7. Own shares (4)
C	**Current assets**
C-I	Stocks 1. Raw materials, etc. 2. Work in progress 3. Finished goods/goods for resale 4. Payments on account
C-II	Debtors (5)1. Trade debtors 2. Amounts owed by group undertakings 3. Amounts owed by undertakings in which the company has a participating interest 4. Other debtors 5. Called up share capital not paid (1) 6. Prepayments and accrued income (6)
C-III	Investments 1. Shares in group undertakings 2. Own shares (4) 3. Other investments
C-IV	Cash at bank and in hand
D	**Prepayments and accrued income**
	Liabilities
A	**Capital and reserves**
I	Called up share capital (1)
II	Share premium account
III	Revaluation reserve

Format 2 (Format per SI 2008 No. 410)	
Assets	
IV	Other reserves 1. Capital redemption reserve 2. Reserve for own shares 3. Reserves provided for by articles 4. Other reserves
V	Profit and loss account
	Minority interests
B	**Provision for liabilities and charges** 1. Pensions and similar obligations 2. Taxation, etc. 3. Other provisions
C	**Creditors** 1. Debenture loans (7) 2. Bank loans and overdrafts 3. Payments received on account (8) 4. Trade creditors 5. Bills on exchange payable 6. Amounts owed to group undertakings 7. Amounts owed to undertakings in which the company has a participating interest 8. Other creditors including taxation and social security (9) 9. Accruals and deferred income (10)
D	**Accruals and deferred income** (10)

990

Notes to the balance sheet formats
1. Called-up share capital not paid may be shown in either of the two positions shown in Formats 1 and 2.
2. Concessions, patents, licences, trade marks and similar rights and assets should only be included in the company's balance sheet under this heading if:
a. the assets were acquired for a valuable consideration and not required to be shown under goodwill; or
b. the assets were created internally by the company.
3. Goodwill should only be included if acquired for a valuable consideration.
4. Own shares The nominal value of the shares should be shown separately.
5. Debtors falling due after more than one year should be shown separately for each item under debtors.
6. Prepayments and accrued income can be shown in either of the two positions shown in Formats 1 and 2.
7. Debenture loans The amount of any convertible loans should be shown separately.
8. Payments received on account of orders should be shown for each item were not shown as a deduction form stocks.
9. Other creditors The amount for creditors in respect of taxation and social security shall be shown separately from the amount for other creditors.
10. Accruals and deferred income The two positions in Format 1 at E9 and H9 are an alternative to the heading under position J. In Format 2 the two positions given are alternatives.
11. Net current assets (liabilities) should include amounts shown under 'prepayments and accrued Income'.
12. Creditors falling due after more than one year should be shown separately for each item under creditors.
13. Participating interests should in group accounts be replaced by "interests in associated undertakings" and "Other participating interests".
14. Minority interests only arises in group accounts. The two positions given in Format 1 are alternatives.

D. Consolidated formats

Parent companies preparing consolidated financial statements must comply with the provisions of the Companies Act, on the basis of the group being a single company. In addition, the parent company must also satisfy the provisions of the Act in terms of their own form and content.   **992**

The format selected by the parent company for its individual balance sheet, will usually be adopted for the consolidated balance sheet.

The **following headings** can be shown in alternative places in the consolidated formats:
- Called-up share capital not paid (A and C.II.5);
- Prepayments and accrued income (C.II.6 and D);
- Accruals and deferred income (E9, H9 and J); and
- Minority interests (before K and M).

For **group accounts**, a category of "Interests in group undertakings" can be inserted after "loans to group undertakings".

E. New UK GAAP

Under FRS 102 "The Financial Reporting Standard applicable in the UK and Republic of Ireland" the balance sheet is referred to as the Statement of Financial Position. The formats are the same as set out in the Companies Act 2006 and the associated regulations drafted under the framework of the Act. Section 4 of FRS 102 details the related **disclosure requirements** for entities reporting under this standard.   **996**

MEMO POINTS   1.**Two sets of regulations** have been issued; one set being exclusively for **small companies** (SI 2008/409) whilst the other covers large and medium-sized companies and groups (SI 2008/410). The main difference is that the small company regulations include simplified subheadings.(¶962).

2. The requirements for banks, insurance companies and LLPs are beyond the scope of this book.

CHAPTER 2

Intangible assets and goodwill

Intangible assets are defined as identifiable assets that do not have a physical substance, but where the controlling entity has access to future economic benefits generated by the asset, either through custody or legal protection of the asset. Examples include trademarks, franchises and copyrights.

1000
FRS 10 (2)

Intangible assets can either be **purchased separately** as part of a business acquisition, **or developed internally** by the business. Intangible assets range from those that are readily available and can be measured separately from goodwill to those that are similar in substance to goodwill. However, only intangible assets capable of **separate recognition** can be capitalised. **Revaluation** under the alternative accounting rules is permitted, although strict criteria must be met.

Goodwill may be purchased or generated internally. **Purchased goodwill** is defined as the difference between the cost of an acquired entity and the aggregate fair values attributed to the individual identifiable assets and liabilities acquired. Purchased goodwill can be capitalised whereas internally generated goodwill may not.

1001

Regulatory framework The **statutory requirements** and principal accounting requirements relating to accounting for intangible assets and goodwill are covered in the Companies Act 2006, FRS 10 "Goodwill and Intangible Assets" and the FRSSE. Intangible assets and goodwill were covered in the same accounting standard, as the basic principles covering initial recognition, amortisation and impairment of intangible assets are similar to goodwill. **Smaller entities applying the FRSSE** are exempt from applying FRS 10, although this standard must be applied where small companies prepare consolidated financial statements. The requirements of the FRSSE are broadly similar to FRS 10 with the principle differences relating to the level of disclosures required, as set out in ¶1127.

1002

The **objective of FRS 10** is to ensure that intangible assets and purchased goodwill are charged to the profit and loss account, for the periods in which they are depleted, and that sufficient information is disclosed in the financial statements to enable users to determine the impact of intangible assets and goodwill on the financial position of the reporting entity. The requirements of FRS 10 apply to all intangible assets (and goodwill), except where specifically addressed by another accounting standard.

> ⬚ *MEMO POINTS*   The **impairment** of intangible fixed assets and goodwill is covered by FRS 11, which although touched on briefly in this chapter, is covered in greater detail in ¶1550.

1003   The Financial Reporting Council (FRC) has published **FRS 102** "The financial reporting standard applicable in the UK and Republic of Ireland" for non-FRSSE entities, which will replace the existing UK GAAP from January 2015. The **key differences** between the new standard and current UK GAAP are set out in ¶1128.

A. Intangibles other than goodwill

1010   This section covers the initial recognition and treatment of intangible assets and the problems inherent in their valuation.

1012   ## Types of intangible assets

Definitions	
Franchise	A franchise is a concession or rights granted to a party to sell a company's goods or services in a particular area, usually to an agreed format, covering corporate style or branding. Examples include car dealerships and fast food outlets.
Licences	A licence is a contract, in which a company enters into an agreement with another party, concerning a particular trading arrangement. Examples include brewers who obtain a licence to brew a beer from another manufacturer and licence agreements for the use of software and computer technology produced by a third party.
Copyrights (intellectual property – see R&D)	Copyrights are designed to protect the holder's exclusive right for a specified period of time to produce copies or control a piece of artistic work, including, for example, film, fashion, computer gaming, original music or literature. Publishing companies often control the rights to exclusively print the works of an author, in the expectation of future income streams from those works.
Patents	Patents are granted by the government to an inventor protecting his sole right to produce, use and sell the invention for a specified period of time.
Trademarks	Trademarks are used to differentiate the products of competing manufacturers and protect the investments made by companies in their brands.
Internet domain names	Internet domain names are hostnames that help identify a computer on the internet.
Emissions allowances	Granted by the government in form of licences with emission limits pre-determined.

> ⬚ *MEMO POINTS*   **Accounting practice** on emissions allowances varies considerably. Some entities classify emissions allowances purchased from the government as intangibles assets and account for them "at cost". Allowances gifted by the government are recorded at nil cost. For emissions allowances accounted for at "fair value", the difference between fair value and cost is recognised as a government grant and classified as deferred income in the balance sheet.

1. Initial recognition

The **general rules** for the recognition of intangible assets are set out in the table below.

1018
FRS 10 (9)

Intangible assets	Accounting treatment – initial recognition
1. Purchased separately	Capitalised at cost.
2. Business acquisitions	Where intangible assets can be separately identifiable from goodwill – record at fair value.
3. Internally generated	Not capitalised. Exception is where they have a readily ascertainable market value such as brands or products.

Each of these situations is discussed in more detail below. In addition, an **alternative treatment** is permissible under the Companies Act, where intangible assets, except goodwill, can be included in the balance sheet at **current cost**.

Intangible assets purchased separately

An intangible asset should initially be capitalised and recorded at cost.

1020
FRS 10 (9)

Once intangible assets have been **capitalised**, they should be dealt with in the same manner as goodwill and amortised over their useful economic lives.

Under FRS 10 there is a **rebuttable presumption** that the useful economic life of goodwill and intangibles will not exceed 20 years. However, when **certain conditions are met**, a longer economic life may be used. The amortisation of intangibles and goodwill is discussed more fully in ¶1086.

Control of access to economic benefits may also be obtained through custody; namely the protection of technical or intellectual knowledge. Where control over the expected future benefits from intangible assets is insufficient due to the absence of legal rights or custody rights, they should not be recognised as assets.

1021

Business acquisitions

The **identifiable assets** of an acquired undertaking should be included in the consolidated balance sheet at "fair value" at the acquisition date, including intangibles such as purchased brands or publishing titles.

1022
FRS 10 (10)

The **exception** is where the asset does not have a readily ascertainable market value. In this instance, the fair value should be limited to an amount that does not create or increase any negative goodwill (¶1058) arising on the acquisition.

1023

There are a **number of specific problems** inherent in valuing certain intangible assets obtained through a business acquisition, which are outlined in ¶1035 below.

MEMO POINTS   1. An **identifiable asset** is defined by companies legislation as one that can be separately identified and sold off without having to dispose of the entire business. If an asset can be sold only as part of the revenue generating activity of which it forms a part, it is deemed to be indistinguishable from the goodwill relating to that activity and accounted for as such.
2. FRS 7 "Fair values in acquisition accounting" **stipulates that** "fair values" should be placed on identifiable assets and liabilities, in allocating the purchase consideration for a business to its separable net assets. Any balance should be attributable to goodwill. The fair value should be based on the estimated market value and be capable of reliable measurement.

Internally developed intangible assets

The **general rule** is that the cost of developing intangible assets internally should not be capitalised, but charged as an expense as they are incurred. The **exceptions** are intangible assets that are clearly identifiable and have a readily ascertainable market value.

1026
FRS 10 (14)

Brands created internally and other unique intangible assets   Although the Companies Act allows the production cost of intangibles to be included in the balance sheet, this treatment is prohibited by FRS 10 in relation to brands and publishing titles created internally.

1028

. The reason is that internally generated goodwill **may only be capitalised if** it has a readily ascertainable market value, and as intangibles such as publishing titles are unique, their market value is not readily ascertainable.

2. Difficulties in valuing intangibles

1035 Where intangible assets are **purchased separately**, valuation is generally not an issue as there is a purchase price that is used for initial recognition. However, where intangible assets are purchased as part of a **business acquisition** or are **generated internally**, they can be much more difficult to value.

1036
FRS 10 (2)

The **principal difficulty** is establishing a **readily ascertainable market value** at which the asset could be exchanged in an arm's length transaction.

The standard requires that the value of an intangible fixed asset could be established by reference to a market for a similar intangible asset or group of assets, that are equivalent in all material aspects and where there is an active market for that group of assets. Intangible fixed assets fitting this definition include licences, quotas or franchises.

> EXAMPLE Readily ascertainable market.
>
> 1. **Taxi licences** granted within a city limit may give identical rights to each licence holder. As such, the licences are traded actively at all times and there is a defined market price and a readily ascertainable market value.
> 2. The **cable television licence** for each region in the UK is different. The population demographics are different and as such the value of the licences will vary. The cable broadcasting licence for a rural area, for instance, will have a different cost structure from that of a more densely populated urban area. As such, these licences are unlikely to have a readily ascertainable market value.

Determining the initial value of intangible assets

1038 **Initial recognition** The rules governing **acquisition accounting** (¶6890) require that the fair value of an intangible asset, when recognised, should normally be based on its replacement cost; this is predominately the asset's estimated market value.

FRS 10 (12-13)

Difficulties in determining initial value In certain industries or entities, methods for determining the market value of intangible assets have been developed, which can be used for the initial recognition of such assets at the time of purchase. These are set out in the table below.

Where the **initial value** of an intangible asset purchased as part of the acquisition of a business **cannot be measured reliably**, it should be subsumed within the portion of the purchase price attributed to goodwill.

Valuation methods

1044 Valuation methods are many and varied and it is beyond the scope of this book to discuss their respective merits and suitability of the values they produce for inclusion in financial statements. However, a small number of the more common valuation methods used for intangibles are summarised below.

Valuation methods	Characteristics
Royalty method	This method is used to determine the value that could be obtained by licensing out the right to exploit the intangible asset, or to estimate the royalties the owner of the licence does not have to pay to a third party. A **notional royalty rate** is calculated as a percentage of the projected revenues, with the resulting royalty revenue stream capitalised by discounting at a risk adjusted market rate, to arrive at an estimated market value.
Premium profits method	This method is used to determine the value of an intangible asset by capitalising the additional profits attributable to it, such as a market leading brand, and deducting the profits earned by comparable unbranded competitor products. The estimated profits are then discounted using a risk adjusted market rate to arrive at an estimated market value.

Valuation methods	Characteristics
Capitalisation of earnings method	This method is used to estimate the sustainable earnings expected from the intangible asset. A capitalisation factor or multiple of earnings is then applied to the earnings, adjusted for future prospects and risk.

A **number of factors** must also be considered, when **determining risk** and valuing intangible   **1049**
assets such as brands using the above methods, including:
- the market sector;
- customer loyalty;
- market share;
- export markets;
- marketing support;
- competition;
- changes to legislation; and
- technological changes.

Revaluation

The **general rule** is that intangible assets **cannot be revalued** after having initially been   **1050**
recognised at cost or fair value on acquisition. The **exceptions are** intangible assets that
have a readily ascertainable market value.

These intangible assets can be included in the balance sheet at market value, provided that:
- all intangible assets in the same class are revalued; and
- regular revaluations are conducted to ensure that the carrying value is the same as the
market value at the balance sheet date.

Where an intangible fixed asset is valued at current cost, the **depreciation rules** are different. The
amortisation charge should be based on the balance sheet value and not the historical cost.

B. Goodwill

Goodwill **may be purchased or generated internally**. In some cases purchased goodwill   **1054**
can have a negative value, whilst internally generated goodwill is generally not recognised.
In this section, the initial recognition and accounting requirements for goodwill (purchased/-
negative) are considered along with the rules governing determination of the useful economic life, the amortisation of goodwill and the requirements for impairment reviews. An
overview of the most common valuation methods is also given.

Goodwill	Definition	Accounting treatment
1. Purchased	**Purchased goodwill** is the difference between the cost of an investment, as shown in the purchaser's own financial statements and the values attributed to the acquired assets and liabilities in the consolidated statements of the purchaser.	Classified as an intangible asset and capitalised as part of a business combination.
2. Internally generated	**Internally developed goodwill** is generated through the interaction of numerous transactions/business processes (e.g. advertising, staff training, stakeholders, service etc). It is intrinsic to the business as it cannot be sold as a separate asset, its value is subjective and can fluctuate widely according to internal and external circumstances.	Generally not recognised or capitalised (some exceptions).

1055   Goodwill **is distinguished from other assets** because of the following characteristics:
– valuations of goodwill are subjective;
– goodwill cannot be sold as an asset separately from the rest of the business; and
– there is no reliable correlation between goodwill and the costs incurred in creating it.
Goodwill is generated through the interaction of **a number of factors**, such as the expertise of the workforce, product reputation, or location. The factors that generate goodwill also make it difficult to value objectively. For this reason, the Companies Act contains a provision that **goodwill may only be recognised** as an intangible fixed asset, if acquired for a valuable consideration as part of the purchase of a business or business segment.

Purchased goodwill

1056
FRS 10 (7)
Purchased goodwill is created when the cost of an acquired entity exceeds the aggregate fair values attributable to the identifiable assets and liabilities acquired. The Companies Act requires that goodwill be classified and capitalised as an intangible fixed asset and amortised over the appropriate period. The **most common instance** of purchased goodwill is that arising on consolidation by a parent undertaking of an acquired subsidiary, but also involves investments such as associates and joint ventures accounted for using the equity method.

1057   Although purchased goodwill **is not in itself recognised as an asset** in an individual entity's accounts, it is included in consolidated intangible fixed assets, rather than as a deduction from shareholders' equity. This treatment is, in recognition of the fact that goodwill is part of a larger group of assets represented by the acquired business. Goodwill is unique in the sense that it is incapable of being recognised without selling the whole business or business segment.

Purchased goodwill diminishes over time as the factors generating it change and it is replaced by internally generated goodwill. However, where goodwill is capable of continued measurement, it can in some very limited circumstances be retained indefinitely in the balance sheet.

EXAMPLE   **MNO Plc – Annual report and accounts**
Notes to the balance sheet

Purchased goodwill

The acquisition of the shares of Bunting Defence Systems in June 20XX was for a consideration of £16m. The table below sets out the fair value of the identifiable assets and liabilities of Bunting at the date of its acquisition by MNO plc. The goodwill is capable of continued measurement and will be amortised over a useful economic life of 15 years.

	£'000
Tangible fixed assets	2,003
Stocks and work in progress	236
Debtors	7,881
Cash in bank	740
Creditors: amounts falling due within one year	(585)
Bank overdrafts	(250)
Bank loans	(125)
Finance lease obligations	(200)
Other creditors	(6,500)
Net assets	**3,200**
Cash	13,000
Costs	3,000
Total consideration paid	**16,000**
Goodwill arising	**12,800**

Amortisation £16M – £12,8m/ 15 = £853,333 per annum.

Negative goodwill

Negative goodwill **occurs when the consideration paid** is less than the fair value of the identifiable assets because, either:
- the seller requires a quick sale and has sold at a "bargain" price;
- the purchase price has been reduced to take account of future expected costs (e.g. reorganisation costs); or
- the seller decides to divest of a business that no longer fits with the strategic direction of the company.

Negative goodwill **can also arise** where an acquired business is expected to generate losses in the immediate future. In these circumstances, it is expected that the value of the net assets of the business will fall as the losses are incurred. However, the requirement to perform **impairment reviews** (¶1550) will eliminate much of the negative goodwill that would otherwise be attributed to future costs or losses.

1058

General rules   Negative goodwill **usually relates** to valuation differences in respect of **non-monetary assets** and FRS 10 seeks to limit situations where negative goodwill is recognised through applying the following rules:

1059
FRS 10 (48)

Intangible assets	General rules
Impairment	In situations where an acquisition appears to generate negative goodwill, the fair value of the acquired assets and liabilities should be tested for understatement or impairment.
Single transaction	Purchased goodwill resulting from a single transaction that contains both positive and negative goodwill should not be divided into the two categories. Negative goodwill and intangible assets should not be recognised in respect of a single transaction.
Fair values	Negative goodwill, up to the fair values of the non-monetary assets acquired, should be accounted for in the profit and loss account in the periods (through depreciation or sale) that are expected to benefit from that negative goodwill, as illustrated in the example below.

EXAMPLE   **Negative goodwill**
Accounting treatment – charge to the profit and loss account.
A company that has net assets with a **fair value** of £30m is purchased for £27 million. The negative goodwill is £3m. The non-monetary assets at the acquisition date total £25m, comprising stocks of £5m and £20m of tangible fixed assets. In the year following acquisition, all the stocks were sold and £5m depreciation was charged on the tangible fixed assets.
Therefore, of the **non-monetary assets** of £25m at the date of purchase, £10m was recognised in the profit and loss account in the year following the purchase of the business. As a result, negative goodwill of £1.2m should be written back to the profit and loss account. The £1.2m is calculated as follows:
£10m [assets acquired now recognised in the profit and loss account in the year] /
£25m [total assets acquired] × £3m [total negative goodwill arising on the original acquisition].

Disclosure   Where negative goodwill is recognised, it should be shown on the face of the balance sheet, immediately below the heading for goodwill. Where both positive and negative goodwill from different acquisitions are shown in the balance sheet, a sub-total showing the net goodwill figure should be added.

1060

Valuation methods

There are a number of techniques for valuing goodwill, the most common of which are set out in the table below.

1061

Valuation methods	General characteristics
Whole company method	Company is valued then a deduction for tangible and other assets is made: = goodwill. Valuation based on a multiple (Price/Earnings (P/E) Ratio) of gross profits. Where valuation is greater than adjusted net asset values, excess deemed to be goodwill. P/E ratios vary for each industry and for individual companies.
Simple multiple approach	A simple but subjective multiple is applied to profits. Multiple depends on quality of clients: estimated growth and expected margins.
Turnover approach	Turnover based valuation focuses on regular fee income rather than overall turnover and is typically used in professional practices (e.g. accountants, surveyors). Typical multiples range from 0.5 to 1.5, but can be higher. The multiples are subjective and reflect changing business conditions such as growth prospects and expected margins (see example).
Discounted cash flow method	This approach is typically employed in the hotel industry or catering where cash flow is a key factor.

EXAMPLE 1. **Whole company approach**. A medium sized furniture company with a wide range of customers, stable turnover of £10m, growing at around 5% per annum: profit after tax of £500k. Net assets £500k and property valued in the books at £250k now has a market value of £750k. The P/E ratio for the industry is 4. Other factors to be considered include adjustments for assets not directly contributing to business profitability, income from non-trading activities, etc. Valuation: £500k × 4 = £2m: less net assets of £500k and asset (property) revaluation of £500k, gives a goodwill valuation of £1m.

2. **Simple multiple approach** A small limited company selling footwear products on-line, with a stable customer base growing at 10% per annum. The business operates from a small rented office and the principal assets are computer equipment valued at 40k. Turnover is £3m and pre-tax profits of 75k after directors' fees of 75k. Valuation: £75k + £75k = £150k. Based on a multiple of 1 indicates goodwill of £150k and a business valuation of 190k, giving a P/E ratio of 3 + based on after-tax profits of 60k (£75k less tax at 20%).This P/E ratio should be measured against the average for this industry.

3. **Turnover approach**. A small, well established architects practice with a turnover of £1m, with loyal customer base in the house building industry. The practice is run by two key individuals and makes industry standard profit margins. Valuation. Turnover of £1m x by P/E ratio of 2 (adjusted from 2.4 industry standard because of reliance on key individuals and dependence on Government house building and planning policy), equals goodwill of £1m.

1062   **Mix of personal and corporate goodwill**   Where the goodwill is attached to the owner of a business such as the creative director of an advertising agency or the chef in a small restaurant, the goodwill will often be extinguished when there is a change of owner. Here any goodwill transferred or sold on will be monitored by HMRC (e.g. valuation methods and key assumptions used).

Taxation issues

1063   There are a number of tax issues involving the valuation of goodwill which have recently been highlighted by HMRC. An overview of one of the most topical issues is given below; for more detail refer to *Corporation tax memo or tax memo*.

1065   **Trade related properties**   HMRC has issued guidance on the **apportionment of goodwill** for transactions involving the sale of a business run from **trade related premises**, such as public houses, cinemas, restaurants, care homes, petrol stations or hotels. When a business operated from a trade related property is sold as a going concern, the sale price usually includes an element of goodwill. The relevant question is what is the value of that goodwill?

The answer will depend on the facts of each individual case. In some cases the value of the goodwill may be nominal but in others it may be substantial. Therefore a distinction must be made between businesses that rely on a particular property and those that do not.

HMRC has deliberated on how the consideration received should be apportioned between goodwill and other assets. This represents a **change of policy**, which was previously based on the assumption that there is unlikely to be any significant element of goodwill, because the occupation of a particular building was deemed essential to the functioning of the business and its revenue generation. However, it is now recognised that when a business is sold as a going concern the price will include an element of goodwill to reflect the combined value of the tangible assets along with the benefit generated by other business assets such as contracts with customers, staff, and suppliers; this enhanced value may not be realised if assets are split up and sold separately.

In general, companies are now being advised to take an accounting based approach when calculating goodwill, as opposed to simply interpreting previous legal rulings. HMRC has also simplified its **classification system** for goodwill.

<u>MEMO POINTS</u>   **HMRC and the Valuation Office Agency (VOA)** have issued guidance on how one can apportion the price paid for a business as a going concern between goodwill and other assets included in the sale, based on the profit making potential of the premises. For more information on this topic see *tax memo.*

C. Useful economic life

As with other fixed assets, the **cost of intangibles** (less their expected residual value), and goodwill should be amortised over their expected useful economic lives, including intangible assets valued at current cost (i.e. the most recent production cost or valuation).

1066
FRS 10 (19, 28)

The **basic premise** set out in FRS 10, is that goodwill and intangible assets have a useful economic life of not more than 20 years. This **presumption can be rebutted** in certain circumstances, which along with the criteria permitting this accounting treatment are set out below. Intangible assets or goodwill should be subject to an annual impairment review. **No residual value** may be assigned to goodwill.

1. Determining useful economic lives

The UEL of intangible assets represents the period over which the owner expects to derive economic benefits from the use of an asset. The useful economic life (UEL) of purchased goodwill represents the period over which the value of an acquired business is expected to exceed the values of its identifiable assets and liabilities.

1070

In addition **economic and legal factors** can influence the UEL of an asset. Economic factors (e.g. technological progress) can affect the period over which the expected future economic benefits will arise, whilst legal factors could restrict the period over which the entity can control the benefits. The UEL is usually finite, but can, if certain conditions are met, be indefinite.

Finite useful economic life

The **general rule** is that the useful economic lives of purchased goodwill and intangible assets should not exceed 20 years from the date of acquisition. The belief is that the premium paid on acquiring a business over its net asset value will not be maintained indefinitely. The cost of the licences, copyrights and patents should be amortised over the period of the agreement. Where the **licences** have been acquired as part of a business acquisition, they should be capitalised separately from goodwill where they can be reliably measured and amortised over the expected useful economic life.

1074
FRS 10 (19)

Legal factors   Where access to the economic benefits derived from an intangible asset are governed by legal rights granted for a finite period, the useful economic life of the asset may extend beyond the end of that finite period, if the legal rights can be renewed or extended

1076
FRS 10 (24)

and are assured. Any costs incurred in extending the legal protection or rights should be excluded from the value of the asset amortised.

In terms of intangible assets, **legal protection** takes the form of:
- a franchise;
- time related protection through licence, quotas, or copyright; or
- a patent or trademark restricting access to others.

Indefinite useful economic life

1078   Where goodwill and intangible assets are deemed to have indefinite useful economic lives they should not be amortised.

FRS 10 (18)   The **non-amortisation** of goodwill constitutes a departure from the companies' legislation requirement to depreciate the value of goodwill over a its useful economic life. This treatment reflects the depletion of purchased goodwill over time and its replacement by internally generated goodwill.

A policy of non-amortisation is only permitted only in **special circumstances**, where following the normal rules of amortisation would not give a true and fair view. The "override" cannot be applied freely and must be considered on an acquisition by acquisition basis and not as a general accounting policy.

1080   **Special circumstances**   The **general rule may be rebutted** and the useful economic life extended indefinitely where all of the following conditions apply:
- the durability of the acquired business or intangible asset can be determined so justifying the extension for a period exceeding 20 years;
- the goodwill or intangible asset is capable of continued measurement; and
- it is possible to conduct annual impairment reviews.

1081   In some circumstances, the **durability** of the premium or goodwill paid for an acquired business can be maintained over **a period exceeding 20 years**, depending on:

FRS 10 (20)   - the nature of the business;
- the stability of the industry in which the acquisition operates;
- the lifecycle of the products to which the goodwill relates;
- where the acquisition scales market barriers to entry that persist; and
- the expected future impact of competition.

> EXAMPLE **Blackstones Brewing Plc**
> Annual report and accounts
> Note. Intangible assets
>
> The Kroppenborg brand was initially recognised at its fair value on acquisition. The brand has a long history in an established industry and enjoys a significant share of the UK beer market. The brand receives continued marketing support in all regions. These factors together with the scale of the business contribute to the durability of the brand. As such, the directors are of the opinion that the useful economic life is indefinite and therefore no annual amortisation is provided. The carrying value of the brand is subject to an annual impairment review.

1082   **Continued measurement**   The useful economic lives of goodwill and intangible fixed assets should be reviewed at the end of each reporting period and any revisions made and reflected in the carrying value of goodwill or intangible asset should be amortised over the remaining useful economic life.

1083   Where the **cost of continued measurement** of goodwill and intangible assets is unjustifiably
FRS 10 (23)   high, ongoing measurement may not be possible, which could mean that UEL's in excess of 20 years will not be permitted. Circumstances where this can arise include the following:
- where the amounts involved are immaterial and do not justify annual impairment reviews;
- the management information systems cannot identify and allocate cash flows at an income generating level; or
- where acquired businesses are merged with existing businesses in such a way that the associated goodwill cannot be tracked.

EXAMPLE **Wrightsbury Publishing Plc**
Annual report and accounts
Note. Intangible assets

The goodwill in the Company arose as a result of the transfer of assets, liabilities and trade of Grant Rollins Publishing Limited to Wrightsbury Publishing Limited, at market value on 30 April 20XX. Since the acquisition, the business acquired has been fully integrated into the operations of the Company, making it difficult to identify the ongoing value of associated goodwill. The Company has taken the view that it is appropriate to write off goodwill to the profit and loss account during the year and this policy has increased the charge to the profit and loss account by £550,000.

Summary

1085

Intangible assets/goodwill:	Accounting treatment
Finite useful economic lives	Intangible assets should be amortised on a systematic basis over life of asset, so recognising the reduction in value of the goodwill over time.
Indefinite useful economic lives	1. The **general rule** is that assets with indefinite UEL's should not be amortised. 2. Where a company **adopts a policy of non-amortisation**, this must be justified in terms of presenting a true and fair view, with disclosure of the reasons for and effect of such a policy. It must also subject the carrying value of any goodwill to an impairment review each year.
Residual value (RV)	1. No residual value may be assigned to **goodwill**. 2. **Amortising an intangible asset**: RV may be attributed to the asset only if it can be measured accurately. The residual value of an intangible asset is often negligible and **only likely to be material** when: – there is a legal or contractual right to receive a certain sum at the end of the period of use of the intangible asset; or – there is a readily ascertainable market value for the residual asset.
Where **continued measurement** of goodwill is not possible	It's depletion should be recognised over a prudent time period.

2. Methods of amortisation

Although the method of amortisation selected should reflect the pattern of depletion of the goodwill or intangible asset, the **straight-line method** of depreciation must be used except where it can be shown that another method is more appropriate.

1086
FRS 10 (30)

An **alternative method** of amortisation that may sometimes be appropriate is the unit of production method. This method could be used where, for example, a licence permits the production of a finite quantity of a product. However, this method should not be used if it proves less conservative than the straight-line method.

MEMO POINTS   FRS 10 **forbids the use of** amortisation methods that aim to produce a constant rate of return on the carrying value of an intangible asset, such as the annuity method. The reverse **"sum of digits"** method is also prohibited, as it effectively transfers the amortisation charge to later periods and is not related to depletion of the goodwill.

3. Impairment of intangible assets and goodwill

Impairment reviews should be conducted to ensure that intangible assets and goodwill are not carried at values exceeding their recoverable amount. An asset is recognised as being impaired, if the **recoverable amount** (the higher of net realisable value and value in use (i.e. income stream) falls below its carrying value.

1090

Systematic amortisation should ensure that the carrying value of an asset is reduced to reflect the reduction in the recoverable amount of the asset over its useful economic life. Therefore, the asset is less likely to be materially impaired, unless the valuation on initial recognition was erroneous or where subsequent events have resulted in a sudden fall in the estimate of the recoverable amount. Subsequent measurement can indicate an increase in the value of an intangible asset (revaluation) but this is not permitted for goodwill. The rules covering revaluations and restoration of past impairment losses are outlined below.

The **impairment process** can be complex and subjective and is dealt with in greater detail in ¶1550, with the specific requirements of FRS 10 considered below.

Useful economic life less than 20 years

1092
FRS 10 (34)

Impairment reviews should only be conducted on intangible assets and goodwill, with a UEL amortised over a period not exceeding 20 years from the date of acquisition:
– at the end of the first full accounting period following the date of acquisition; and
– thereafter, when events or changes in circumstances indicate that the carrying values may not be recoverable.

1093

End of first full accounting period   If, at the end of the first full accounting period following acquisition, there are **no indicators of impairment**, no additional work is required and the carrying values of intangible assets are unaffected.

Where an **acquisition takes place part way through an accounting period**, the impairment review does not have to be undertaken at the end of that period but at the end of the subsequent period, that being the first full accounting period after acquisition.

The **requirement to perform an impairment review**, at the end of the first full financial year after the initial recognition of an intangible asset or goodwill, ensures that any impairment arising on acquisition is recognised as a loss at the time, rather than amortised over the life of the asset.

1094

Subsequent impairment reviews   Impairment reviews should be performed in accordance with the requirements of FRS 11 (see ¶1550).

The **exception is** that the first year impairment review for goodwill and other intangible assets may be performed in two stages; namely:

FRS 10 (40)

1. Identify any possible impairment by comparing post-acquisition performance in the first year with pre-acquisition forecasts used to support the purchase price.
2. **Perform a full impairment review** in accordance with the requirements of FRS 11, **only if the initial review indicates** that the post-acquisition performance has failed to meet pre-acquisition expectations or if any unforeseen events indicate that the carrying value may not be recoverable.

Where an **impairment is identified** at the end of the first full accounting period, this will result from one of the following circumstances:
– an overpayment;
– an event that occurred between acquisition and the first year review; or
– depletion of the acquired goodwill or intangible asset between the acquisition date and the first year review that exceeds the value recognised through amortisation.

1095

A **number of indicators** that could underpin the circumstances outlined above are:
– operating losses or net cash outflows resulting from, such as a decline in market share or profit margins, increased competition, or increased marketing support to sustain present market share;
– the loss of key employees;
– adverse changes in the regulatory market; or
– adverse changes to any of the factors affecting fair values of intangible assets on acquisition.

Where any factors exist that indicate that the carrying amount of an intangible asset may not be recoverable, a full impairment review should be undertaken. Where **impairment in value is confirmed**, then the asset should be written down to its recoverable amount.

EXAMPLE **Dundee Marketing International**
Report and accounts
Note. **Amortisation of goodwill – factors indicating that the carrying amount is not recoverable**

Goodwill in respect of subsidiary companies and associated undertakings of £235.2m (20X9: £265.3m) is subject to amortisation over periods of up to 20 years. The group **tests annually** the carrying values of indefinite life goodwill and other intangible assets for impairment. Goodwill subject to periodic amortisation is tested for impairment if there is a change in circumstances that suggests that the carrying value may not be recoverable.

The 20XX **impairment review** was completed in December and assessed whether the carrying value of goodwill was supported by the net present value of future cash flows derived from assets using a projection period of up to 5 years for each income generating unit (IGU). After the projection period, growth rates of nominal GDP have been assumed for each IGU.

The **estimates and assumptions** made in connection with impairment testing could differ from actual results of operations and cash flows. Further, future events could result in the Company concluding that impairment indicators exist and that the certain asset values have become impaired. Any resulting impairment loss could have a material impact on the Company's financial position. The carrying value of goodwill and other intangibles will continue to be reviewed annually for impairment and adjusted to the recoverable amount where necessary.

Useful economic life exceeding 20 years or non-amortisation

Intangible assets and goodwill amortised over a period exceeding 20 years from the acquisition date, or that are not amortised, should be viewed for impairment at the end of each reporting period. **1096**

The reason that **annual impairment reviews** are required where the amortisation period exceeds 20 years, is that the longer the UEL assigned to intangible assets and goodwill, the higher the risk that the recoverable amount will fall below the carrying value as time progresses.

Impairment losses

Impairment losses **must be recognised by** reference to the expected future cash flows. Any assumption that it might not be possible measure the future value of goodwill will not in itself justify the goodwill balance being written off at the first impairment review. **1098**
FRS 10 (36)

The **first impairment review** should be based on updating initial investment appraisal calculations, with the remaining carrying value amortised over a period not exceeding 20 years.

Where an **impairment loss is confirmed**, the impairment should be recognised immediately through a charge to the profit and loss account. The revised net book value should be amortised over the estimated remaining UEL of the asset.

Revaluation and restoration of past losses   The **general rule** is that goodwill and intangible assets should not be revalued, either to increase the carrying value above original cost or to reverse prior period losses arising from impairment or amortisation. Revaluation has the effect of recognising values that have been developed internally. **1100**

However, intangible assets with readily ascertainable market values may be revalued by reference to those market values. **1102**
FRS 10 (43-44)

If one intangible asset is revalued, then all other capitalised intangible assets in the same class should be revalued. After an intangible asset has been revalued, further revaluations should then be carried out annually to ensure that the carrying value does not differ greatly from the market value at the balance sheet date.

The **amortisation charge** for revalued assets should be based on the revalued amounts and the remaining useful economic lives of the assets. Amortisation charged before the revaluation should not be written back to the profit and loss account.

Where previously an impairment loss has been recognised as a result of an external event and that **impairment has now reversed**, as a result of other external events that were not foreseen in the original impairment calculations, that reversal should be recognised in the current period.

Past impairment losses may not be reversed when the restoration in value is generated internally.

D. Disclosures

Small companies

1116 Small companies **adopting the FRSSE** have **minimal disclosure requirements** covering the amount of negative goodwill in the balance sheet and the period(s) in which it is being written off. For large and medium-sized entities a significant number of disclosures are required by FRS 10, covering recognition, amortisation and revaluation of intangible fixed assets and goodwill.

1117 The **standard classifications** of intangible assets for small companies are contained in Sch.1 to The Small Companies and Groups (Accounts and Reports) Regulations 2008 (SI 2008/409).

> EXAMPLE **B.1 Fixed assets** (extract)
>
> Intangible assets
> 1. Goodwill
> 2. Other intangible assets

Medium and larger companies

1118
FRS 10 (53)

The **standard classifications** for medium-sized and large companies are included in the Large and Medium-sized Companies and Groups (Accounts and Reports) Regulations 2008 (SI 2008/410).

> EXAMPLE **B.1 Fixed assets** (extract)
>
> Intangible assets
> 1. Development costs (¶1150)
> 2. Concessions, patents, licences, trademarks and similar rights and assets
> 3. Goodwill
> 4. Payments on account

Assets included under the category of "Concessions, patents, licences, trademarks and similar rights and assets" **can only be shown** if they:
– were acquired for a valuable consideration; and; or
– are not required to be shown under goodwill or the assets were created internally.

Further **sub-divisions** of intangible assets are permissible where, for example, different types of licence have different functions within the business segments or divisions.

Key disclosure requirements for medium and large entities

1119 The following information should be disclosed separately for **positive and negative goodwill** as well as for each class of intangible asset recorded in the balance sheet; namely:
– the **cost or revalued amount** at the beginning of the financial period and at the balance sheet date;
– the **cumulative provisions** for amortisation or impairment at the beginning of the financial period and at the balance sheet date;
– a **reconciliation of the movements**, with separate disclosures for additions, disposals, revaluations, transfers, amortisation, impairment losses, reversals of past impairment losses and amounts of negative goodwill written back in the financial period;
– the **net carrying amount** at the balance sheet date; and
– the profit or loss on any **material disposal** of a previously acquired business or business segment.

1120 In respect of **negative goodwill** the following should also be disclosed:
– the period(s) in which negative goodwill is being written back to the profit and loss account; and
– where negative goodwill exceeds the fair values of the non-monetary assets, the amount and source of the "excess" negative goodwill and the periods in which it is to be written back should be given.

Amortisation disclosures The following disclosures are required covering the amortisation of goodwill and intangible assets: **1122** FRS 10 (56)

a. The **methods and periods** of amortisation of goodwill and intangible assets and the reasons for choosing these time periods.

b. Where there has been a **change in the method** of amortisation used, the reason and the effect if material.

c. If the **amortisation period is changed** following a review of the useful economic life of any goodwill or intangible assets, the reason and any material effect.

d. Where goodwill or intangible assets are amortised **over a period greater than 20 years**, the grounds for rebutting the 20 year rule should be given, and the particular circumstances supporting the durability of the acquired business or intangible asset.

e. Where **goodwill** in the financial statements **is not amortised**, a note to this effect should be given, stating that the company has departed from the specific requirement of the companies legislation to amortise goodwill over a finite period, in order to give a true and fair view. The specific reasons for the departure and its effect should be disclosed.

Accounting policies FRS 18 "Accounting policies" specifies that disclosures are required to provide the user of financial statements with a clear account of the **reasons for any departure from a statutory requirement**, including when it is not possible to quantify the effect of the departure. **1124** FRS 10 (60) FRS 18 (62)

The following disclosures are required where the "**true and fair view override**" is invoked; namely:

– a statement that the financial statements depart from the specific requirements of the Companies Act to amortise goodwill over the estimated useful economic life;

– details of the accounting treatment actually adopted and reasons why departure from the Companies Act is necessary; and

– a description of the specific factors supporting the durability of the acquired business.

EXAMPLE **Slangram Plc – Annual report and accounts**
Notes to the accounts (extract)

Accounting policies (extract) – amortisation of intangible fixed assets and goodwill
Brands are valued independently as part of the fair value of assets acquired from third parties where the brand has a value which is substantial and long term and where brands can be sold separately from the rest of the business acquired. Brands are amortised on a straight-line basis over the estimated useful economic lives, although no longer than 20 years, except where it is not possible to estimate the useful economic life of the brand.

Goodwill capitalised relating to other group acquisitions is based on a useful economic life of 20 years.
The goodwill arising on the acquisition of Tallydrum Ltd, amounting to £124.2m, has, in the opinion of the directors, an indefinite useful economic life. As such, amortisation is not provided. The Company's main operations are in the UK market, where barriers to entry are high and the company has exclusive rights of operation under ownership rights in perpetuity. As a consequence, the goodwill element is deemed to be durable and there are no plans to merge this business with the existing business as it is deemed capable of **continued measurement** (FRS 10).
As required under FRS 10, an impairment review was carried out in February 20XX, which confirmed that the value of goodwill does not exceed its **recoverable amount**. The accounting treatment is a departure from the requirements of the Companies Act and is adopted in order to present a **true and fair view** of the Group's results. If the goodwill had been amortised over 20 years, the amortisation charge for the year to June 20XX would have been £3.2m and the net book value of goodwill equals £121m.

Revaluation (alternative accounting rules) The **following disclosures** are required in the financial statements where a class of assets has been revalued, namely: **1126** FRS 10 (61)

– the year the assets were valued, the values and the valuation bases;

– the original costs, or fair value, of the assets and any provision for amortisation that would have been recognised had the assets been valued at their original cost;

– the difference between the historical cost amount and the value stated in the balance sheet;

– where any asset has been revalued during the year, the name and qualification of the valuer and reason for revaluing the intangible asset and quantification; and
– a statement of the treatment usually adopted.

E. Small companies – key requirements

1127 An overview of the key requirements for intangible assets and goodwill for small companies is given in the table below.

Topic	Accounting treatment under FRSSE	Accounting treatment under FRS 10
Purchased goodwill/intangibles	Intangibles recognised separately from Goodwill	As for FRSSE
Internally generated goodwill/Intangibles	Not capitalised	As for FRSSE
Depreciation	1. Intangibles – Straight line basis used 2. Goodwill – period chosen must be disclosed + reasoning.	Choice of numerous methods
Residual value	1. Goodwill – RV must be zero. 2. Intangibles – RV must be reliably established.	1& 2. As for FRSSE
Useful economic life (UEL)	Reviewed at end of accounting period – carrying amount depreciated over remaining UEL (Max. 20 years).	As for the FRSSE but permits indefinite UEL if certain conditions met.
Negative goodwill	1. Fair value should be checked to see if assets/liabilities have not been understated. 2. The negative goodwill up to the FV of non-monetary assets should be released to the profit and loss a/c over the lives of the assets. 3. Additional negative goodwill should be taken to the P&L over the period expected to benefit from it. 4. Amount of negative goodwill carried in the balance sheet must be disclosed.	see ¶1058
Revaluation	Revaluation of goodwill and intangibles not permitted	Not permitted under FRS 10 but is under the Companies Act (alternative accounting rules).
Disclosures	Limited to negative goodwill	Extensive disclosure requirements

F. New UK GAAP – FRS 102

1128 Intangible assets are defined in FRS 102 "The financial reporting standard applicable in the UK and Republic of Ireland", as a separately identifiable non-monetary asset lacking in physical substance, as opposed to a tangible fixed asset. FRS 102 proposes a **small number of changes** to current UK GAAP which it formally replaces in January 2015, as set out in the table below.

Topic	FRS 102: Key requirements
Recognition	Intangible assets recognised only if its cost/value can be reliably measured and the estimated economic benefits will be harnessed by the entity as they arise from legal or contractual rights.
Intangibles: Useful economic life (UEL)	All intangibles should have a finite life. If no reliable estimate can be made, the UEL should not exceed 5 years.
Goodwill: Useful economic life (UEL)	The UEL is deemed to be 5 years or less.
Measurement	1. Initial measurement: Intangibles to be measured at cost less accumulated amortisation and impairment losses. 2. Cost of intangible assets arising from a business combination = fair value at acquisition date. 3. Internally generated intangibles: total costs incurred up to stage the recognition criteria are met. 4. Internal goodwill not recognised. 5. Intangibles measured using the cost model or revaluation model (fair value determined with reference to an active market).
Revaluation	**Revaluation gains** taken to other comprehensive income (OCI), or to profit where this reverses a previously recognised revaluation loss. **Revaluation losses** are taken to profit and loss when it arises from a permanent impairment or diminution in value. Otherwise the loss should be recorded in OCI, with any excess then netted against profit when this exceeds a revaluation gain previously recognised in OCI (for a specific asset).
Residual value	Of intangibles deemed to be zero unless a third party buyer for the asset at the end of its UEL has been found and a price contractually agreed, or where the market for the asset is expected to remain strong.
Amortisation	Intangibles should be amortised over their UEL with the charge taken to the profit and loss account, unless relating to inventories, investment properties, plant and equipment where it should be treated as part of the asset's cost.

Disclosure checklist

The key disclosure requirements are set out in the table below.   **1130**

Topic	FRS 102: Key requirements
Presentation (Companies Act)	**Main heading**: Intangible assets *Sub-headings:* Concessions, patents, licences, trademarks etc, Development costs Goodwill Payments on account.
Key information for each class of intangibles	Details of carrying amounts at beginning and end of the financial period of additions, disposals, amortisation, impairment losses, acquisitions as part of a business combination, UELs, amortisation methods used. Other disclosures are required for research and development expenditure capitalised plus intangible assets acquired with government grants.
Revaluation	Details of when the assets were revalued and the valuers names and valuation basis used.

Transitional provisions

1135   In general entities **adopting FRS 102 for the first time** should prepare financial statements on the basis that the new standard has always applied. There are a however, a small number of exemptions relating to intangible assets on transition, covering recognition and valuation issues as well as the permitted useful economic life.

CHAPTER 3

Research and development

The costs of research and development (R&D) can be distinguished from other non-research   **1150**
expenditure due the presence or absence of an appreciable element of innovation. The key
reporting standard is SSAP 13 "Accounting for research and development". **Small companies**
applying the Financial Reporting Standard for Smaller Entities (FRSSE) are subject to the
same accounting requirements as those stipulated in SSAP 13, although the disclosure
requirements are less detailed. There are **no key differences** in the accounting treatment of
R&D between current UK GAAP and FRS 102 "The Financial Reporting Standard applicable
in England and Ireland", which will replace the existing regulatory requirements from
January 2015.

A. Classification

Research and development expenditure can be defined and grouped as follows: **1152**
SSAP 13 (21)

Research classification	Characteristics
Pure research	Pure research is **experimental or theoretical work** undertaken primarily to acquire new scientific or technical knowledge for its own sake as opposed to research directed towards a specific aim.
Applied research	Applied research is an **original or critical investigation** undertaken to obtain new scientific or technical knowledge or develop existing knowledge directed towards a specific commercial objective.
Development costs	Development costs are the costs of using **scientific or technical knowledge** in order to: – produce new or improved materials, products or services; – install new processes or systems prior to the commencement of commercial production or commercial applications; – design, construct and test pre-production prototypes, pilot plants, models and development batches; – design and test products, services, processes or systems involving new technologies or that substantially improve those already produced or installed; or – that substantially improve existing processes or systems - development of new surveying methods and techniques. - fixed assets constructed or acquired to provide facilities for R&D activities spanning a number of accounting periods.

1154
SSAP 13 (7)

Exclusions   The **costs of the following activities** should not be classified as research and development expenditure:
– testing analysis either of equipment or product for purposes of quality or quality control;
– periodic alterations to existing products, services or processes;
– operational research not directly linked to a specific research objective;
– repairs and renewals expenditure relating to processes during normal commercial production;
– legal and administrative work connected with patent applications, records and litigation or the sale or licensing of patents;
– market research;
– design or construction engineering relating to the construction, relocation, rearrangement or start-up of facilities or equipment not directly connected to any particular research activity;
- expenditure related to the actual exploration of oil, gas and mineral deposits in the extractive industries.

B. Accounting treatment

1158   The **general rule** is that research and development expenditure should be expensed as incurred, although certain development costs can be deferred if strict criteria are met. The accounting policies for research and development expenditure are based on the "accruals concept", by which revenue and costs are accrued, matched and dealt with in the period to which they relate. Research and development costs must not be carried forward indefinitely.

1. Small companies

1160
FRSSE 6.3 – 6.10

The **cost** of **fixed assets acquired or constructed** in order to provide facilities for research and development activities over a number of accounting periods should be capitalised and written off over their useful lives through the profit and loss account.

Expenditure on pure and applied research should be charged to the profit and loss account in the year incurred.

1162   Expenditure on **development** should generally be written off **in the year incurred**. Where the development expenditure may be **deferred** to future periods (to the extent that its recovery is assured), it should be amortised commencing with commercial production or application of the relevant product, service, process or system. Deferral is appropriate when:
a) there is a **clearly defined project**;
b) the related expenditure is **separately identifiable**; and
– the outcome of such a project has been assessed with reasonable certainty as to its technical feasibility and its ultimate commercial viability;
– the aggregate of the deferred development costs, any further development costs, and related production, selling and administration costs is reasonably expected to be exceeded by related future sales or other revenues; and
– adequate resources already exist or are reasonably expected to be available to enable the project to be completed and to provide any consequential increases in working capital.

1163   **Deferral**   If a policy of **deferral** is adopted, it must be applied to all development projects. At the end of each accounting period, deferred development expenditure for each product should be **reviewed**. If the circumstances that originally justified the deferral of expenditure no longer apply, or are considered doubtful, the expenditure should be written off.

1164   **Disclosures**   The amount of deferred development expenditure carried forward at the beginning and end of the period should be disclosed under **intangible assets** in the balance sheet or in the notes to the balance sheet. Disclosure must also be made of the **reason for capitalising** these costs as well as the period over which they are being depreciated.

Where development costs are not treated as a realised loss or realised revenue loss this must be stated together with an explanation of the circumstances relied upon by the directors to justify this decision.

2. Medium and larger companies (non FRSSE)

a. Pure and applied research

Expenditure on pure and applied research should be considered part of the continuing operations required to maintain the competitive position of the company. These costs should be expensed in the profit and loss account as incurred.

1165
SSAP 13 (8)

b. Development costs

Expenditure on development should be commissioned with the expectation of commercial success and future benefits from revenues and related profits or reduced costs. To the extent that this type of expenditure meets the capitalisation criteria below, it may be deferred and then expensed against future revenues.

1166

Capitalisation criteria

If an **entity wishes to defer** development expenditure it must be able to demonstrate in respect of the costs to be deferred that:
a. there is a clearly defined project;
b. the related expenditure is separately identifiable;
c. development costs including related production, selling and administrative costs incurred on a project are expected to be covered by future revenues;
d. adequate resources exist, or are reasonably expected to be available, to enable the project to be completed; and
e. the project is deemed technically feasible and commercially viable depending on:
– likely market conditions, including competing products and services;
– public opinion; or
– consumer and environmental legislation.

1167

Application of criteria

Where some of the capitalisation **criteria have not been met**, or have ceased to apply, then the development expenditure should be expensed in the profit and loss account. Where all the **criteria** for recognition **have been met**, development expenditure can be deferred instead of be written off as incurred.

1168

A number of other factors should be considered including the treatment of tangible fixed assets (e.g. amortisation policy), annual reviews for impairment, the complexities of third party contracts and the difficulties involved in forecasting profitability.

Tangible fixed assets   The use of tangible fixed assets acquired, or constructed, to provide facilities for research and development activities normally extends over a number of accounting periods; accordingly, the costs should be deferred and written off over their useful economic lives.

1169

The directors should be realistic in their assessment of the period over which development expenditure should be taken to the profit and loss account, and whether the benefits will accrue evenly. The amounts amortised should commence with the commercial production or application of the product, service, process or system. The **straight-line method** of depreciation is often used but other methods can often be more appropriate.

> EXAMPLE A new hi-technology product may have an estimated life span of three years – but with 50% of sales anticipated in year 1, 35% in year 2 and 15% in year three. Half a million pounds in development expenditure has been deferred in respect of the product. In this case it would be inappropriate to use the straight-line method and the amortisation of the deferred development costs should match the anticipated sales profile. This would therefore result in depreciation of £250,000 in year 1, £175,000 in year 2 and £75,000 in year 3.

1170   **Impairment**   A company must review the development expenditure it has deferred at the end of each financial year. If the circumstances that underpinned the original deferral of development costs no longer apply, or are considered doubtful, then to the extent that unamortised expenditure is considered irrecoverable, it should be charged to the profit and loss account in the accounting period concerned. Deferred development costs fall within the scope of FRS 11 "Impairment of fixed assets and goodwill".

1171   **Reinstatement of development expenditure**   SSAP 13 is silent on the question of reinstating development expenditure that has been written-off, should circumstances change and the criteria set out in the standard be satisfied. Whilst it is theoretically possible to reinstate the costs previously written-off, this is not regarded as best practice and is not recommended.

This does not, however, preclude the deferral of **additional expenditure** incurred from the point at which the relevant criteria are satisfied.

1174   **Third party contracts**   Where companies enter into a firm contract to undertake development work on behalf of third parties, any expenditure not reimbursed at the balance sheet date will usually, depending on the nature and length of the contract, be accounted for in accordance with the provisions of SSAP 9 in respect of **long-term contract** work in progress.

Where the development **costs are fully reimbursed** or there is an agreement to develop and manufacture at an agreed price calculated to reimburse expenditure on development and on manufacture, then these costs should not be deferred and should also be dealt with as contract work in progress.

Complexities arise where there is "**risk-sharing**" within a development contract with third parties. In this case it is necessary to:
– examine the element of cost retained within the company and assess to what it relates to;
– determine whether it qualifies as development expenditure; and
– whether it satisfies the SSAP 13 criteria for carrying it forward.

This may be difficult to justify where the final commercial development of a product being developed lies with another entity.

1175   **Forecasting profitability**   A **specific problem** with the recognition criteria is that companies have to justify the commercial profitability of a project before capitalisation of the costs is permitted, as revenue must exceed costs. For some projects, this could involve revenue projections covering a considerable number of years. As such, the longer the forecast, the more subjective the assumptions are likely to be.

C. Taxation

1176   Any **capital expenditure** incurred on research and development could qualify for allowances with the exception of expenditure on land and buildings. Revenue expenditure may be deducted as an expense of the trade. An overview of the principal tax issues relating to research and development expenditure is given below in order to support the correct classification and accounting treatment of these costs.

HMRC operates separate R&D tax relief schemes for SMEs and large companies and although the types of relief are similar, the scales are different. Specific tax reliefs have been introduced for **intellectual property**.

Qualifying expenditure   For R&D expenditure to qualify it must be related to a trade that   **1178**
the company carries on, or plans to undertake and covers research which leads to an extension of that trade. For example, medical research linked to the welfare of workers employed in a given sector, such as research into an occupational disease, would qualify. On the other hand, if the medical research is undertaken for the benefit of the community as a whole this would not be covered, although it may still qualify as R&D at a later date, if it subsequently leads to or facilitates an extension of the trade undertaken by the host company.

Furthermore, the carrying out of R&D is not necessarily a trade in itself as a person must enter into contracts to provide goods or services to another person for trading to exist. R&D carried out **prior to a company commencing to trade** (pre-trading) may also qualify if the R&D is intended to be relevant to its trade. More information regarding pre-trading expenditure for SMEs (and large companies), as well as guidance on whether activities amount to a trade, can be found on the HMRC website.

A detailed analysis of the tax treatment of research and development expenditure can also be found in *tax memo*.

The following **types of expenditure** could typically qualify for R&D relief: **1179**
- staffing costs including directors, external workers etc;
- payments to volunteers (e.g. clinical trials);
- subcontracted R&D costs;
- software or consumable items (e.g. materials); or
- where the **funding is provided by government** (national, local & EU) in the form of grants or subsidies.

The **staff costs** that can be attributed to R&D differ according to the nature of the research. For instance, the costs of directors and staff (e.g. salaries, pension costs, NI contributions) actively engaged in research projects can be claimed. Where the directors or staff are not 100% engaged in research the costs must be apportioned on a "just and reasonable" basis. For **external workers** (non subcontractor) used on research projects, there are limits (set by HMRC) to the amount of these costs that can be attributed to R&D expenditure. Different rules apply where the company supplying the external workers is a connected (related) company.

Intellectual property   Intellectual property (IP) is defined here as any industrial informa-   **1182**
tion or techniques likely to assist in the manufacture or processing of goods or materials, or
- the working of (and access to) a mine, oil well, or other source of mineral deposits, or
- the winning of access to them, or
- any patent, trade mark, registered design, copyright, design right or plant breeder's right. (CTA09/S1139).

Small and medium-sized entities can claiming tax relief on research and development (R&D) expenditure, where they do not own the intellectual property rights (IPRs).

However, **for expenditure to qualify for R&D tax relief** it is a requirement that any intellectual property created as a result of the R&D costs is, or will be, vested in the host company. The condition needs to be fulfilled at the time the IP is created, and not at a later date. For IP to vest in a company it must have the potential to exploit the IP if it has use or value. This criteria means that IP held by one company for a period of time before transferred to another owner would not qualify.

In practice, there are **many different forms of IP** and attempting to identify all of them and the attached legal rights is difficult. Therefore, it is generally accepted that so long as the claimant company has a real and material interest in any IP that has arisen, then the test is satisfied. But where there is an agreement recording that all IP is created belongs to another party, this would indicate that the test has not been met. HMRC accepts that where the terms of R&D require that the IP is to be placed in the public domain then the key condition would have been satisfied.

EXAMPLE Tube Engineering Ltd has an arrangement with its researchers, and a local university to which it sub-contracts part of the work, that patent rights are split equally on any invention that they devise. The R&D project results in an invention that has commercial possibilities. Immediately following the grant of the patent the company transfers its rights to a subsidiary. Although the company holds a part of the rights and held them only for a brief period it meets the requirements of the legislation, because it was not obliged to transfer them by any pre-existing agreement.

MEMO POINTS The Government has introduced a **reduced rate of corporation tax** on profits generated from patented products (so called "**Patent box**"). In addition, the Government plans to include process patents in this system; namely those not incorporated in products directly but in the industrial processes supporting product production, which could have significant implications for a number of industry sectors, including mining, energy, food processing, biotechnology and agriculture. Income generated from the **sale of such patents** will also be covered. The tax relief will be elective and will only apply to companies. In order to qualify, the patents must have been issued by the UK Intellectual Property Office or European Patent Office and the relief applies to worldwide profits arising from the sale of any products within the scope of the patent. Companies must make an election within two years following the end of the accounting period in which the relevant profits and income arise.

D. Disclosures

1185
FRSSE (6.3-6.10)
SSAP 13 (19)

Entity	Disclosure requirements
Small companies	FRSSE requires disclosure of the R&D accounting policy adopted and details of any deferred development expenditure c/fwd at the end of the financial year under intangible assets, in the balance sheet and in the notes to the accounts. The note should include the reasons for capitalising the costs and the period over which the costs will be depreciated. Where development costs are not treated as a realised cost this fact must be disclosed along with an explanation of the circumstances underpinning the directors decision.
Medium & Large companies	The following **key disclosures** are required: 1. the accounting policy adopted; 2. the total research cost charged to the profit and loss account; 3. the period over which development costs originally deferred are to be written off; 4. the reasons for capitalising development costs; 5. the total development cost charged to the profit and loss account, split between: – the current expenditure and the amounts amortised from deferred expenditure; – the movements on deferred development expenditure during the year.

MEMO POINTS The Companies Act requires development costs, carried in a company's balance sheet as an asset, to be treated as a realised revenue loss. If **special circumstances** exist, which the directors believe justify treating these amounts as unrealised losses, then additional disclosures are required in the notes to the financial statements.
The **notes should disclose**:
– the fact the unamortised development expenditure is not to be treated as a realised loss for the purpose of calculating distributable profits; and
– the reasons justifying the directors' decision not to treat the unamortised development expenditure as a realised loss.

The **general disclosure requirements** for medium and larger entities are illustrated in the   **1186**
following examples.

EXAMPLE **X Ltd. – Notes to the financial statements 2013**
Accounting policies (extract)
Research and development: Research expenditure is written off as it is incurred and charged to
the profit and loss account. Development expenditure is written off, except where there is a separate project that is technically, commercially and financially viable. In these cases, the identifiable
expenditure is deferred and amortised over the period the company is expected to derive benefit.
Product T: Development costs are capitalised and carried forward as the product is not yet in
commercial production. The costs are to be amortised over five years from 2012.

EXAMPLE **X Ltd. Notes to the financial statements**
Development costs

	£
Cost	
As at 1 January, 2013	xx, xxx
Additions	x, xxx
Disposals	x, xxx
Exchange adjustments	xx
As at 31 December, 2013	xx, xxx
Aggregate amortisation	
As at 1 January, 2013	x, xxx
Charge for the year	xxx
Impairment losses	xxx
Reversal of past impairment losses	xx
Exchange adjustment	xx
As at 31 December, 2013	x, xxx
Net book value	
As at 31 December, 2013	xx, xxx
As at 31 December, 2012	xx, xxx

Development costs relate to specific projects utilising technical knowledge to increase the
company's range of products. They are capitalised and written off over a period of five years,
commencing in the year of commercial production.
Development costs are capitalised in accordance with SSAP 13 and hence the amount of unamortised development expenditure is not treated as a realised loss for the purposes of calculating
distributable profits.

CHAPTER 4

Tangible fixed assets

Tangible fixed assets **have been defined** as assets that have physical substance and are either held for use: **1200**
FRS 15 (1)
- in the production or supply of goods and services;
- for rental to others; or
- for administrative purposes on a continuing basis in the reporting entity's activities.

Regulatory framework **All reporting entities** are subject to the provisions of FRS 15 **1202** "Tangible Fixed Assets", **except those small companies** applying the Financial Reporting Standard for Smaller Entities (FRSSE). The Companies Act 2006 and FRS 15 contain the principles that must be consistently applied in accounting for the initial **classification, valuation, revaluation and depreciation** of tangible fixed assets. Disclosures sufficient to enable the users of the financial statements to understand the impact of the accounting policies selected in this area should also be given in the notes to the financial statements.

Subsequent expenditure on tangible fixed assets, the accounting treatment of related finance costs and the impact of the alternative accounting rules on the valuation of tangible fixed assets are also covered.

⸻ MEMO POINTS ⸻   1. The **legal framework** now includes the CA 2006; Sch. 1 to The Large and Medium Sized Companies and Groups (Accounts and Reports) Regulations 2008 (SI 2008/410) and Sch. 1 of the Small Companies and Groups (Accounts and Directors' Report) Regulations 2008 (SI 2008/409).
2. The FRC has issued **FRS 102** for small and medium sized entities not adopting the FRSSE, which is mandatory from 1 January 2015 and a number of staff education notes to help the transition to new UK GAAP (¶1535).
3. The **European Commission** is also in the process of developing its own accounting requirements for smaller (micro) entities.

SECTION 1

Initial recognition and classification

1204
FRS 15 (2)

A number of **recognition criteria** must be met before an asset can be classified as a tangible fixed asset as depicted in the flowchart below. Following recognition the asset must be correctly classified in order to apply the correct accounting treatment.

Tangible fixed assets – recognition criteria

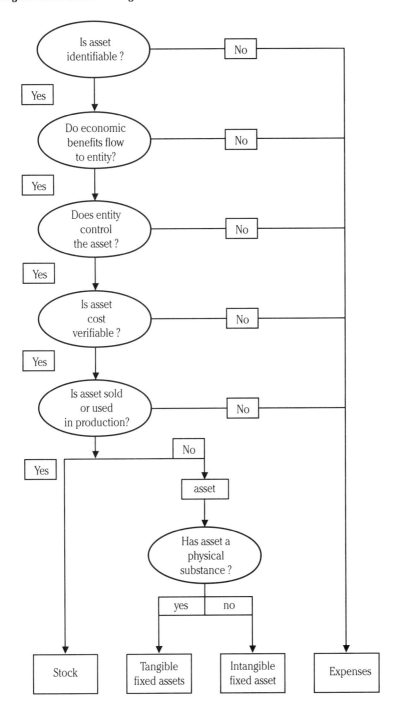

Classification

1210 Tangible fixed assets fall into a variety of categories, each requiring classification in order to determine the appropriate accounting treatment and disclosures.

A classification can be defined as a category of tangible fixed assets having a similar nature, function or use within the business of the entity.

FRS 15 (62) Tangible fixed assets should be classified under the following **broad categories**:
- land and buildings;
- plant and machinery;
- fixtures, fittings, tools and equipment; and
- payments on account and assets in the course of construction.

1212 Within the broad statutory categories, classifications can be narrowed to meet the requirements of **specific industries**. Where it is industry practice to adopt narrower classifications, the disclosures required may be given by **class of asset** and not just the main categories as defined in the Companies Act.

1213 **Land and buildings** Land and buildings which are usually classified as freehold, short or long-leasehold (50 years or more to run at the balance sheet date), and can be **further sub-divided** into specialised properties (see ¶1400) and non-specialised properties (see ¶1388). The issue of **separable assets** and whether they should be classified as land and buildings is covered in ¶1484.

1214 **Plant and machinery** Plant and machinery can be defined as the equipment that enables a business to function. The definition used in the **tax legislation** is that plant and machinery represents whatever apparatus is used by a businessman for the conduct of his business, as opposed to his stock in trade which he buys or makes for resale.

Plant and machinery includes "all goods and chattels, fixed or moveable, live or dead, which the businessman keeps for permanent employment in the business." (*Yarmouth v France 1887*). For example, where fixtures and fittings are immaterial, it may be possible to consolidate them in with plant and machinery, for disclosure purposes.

1216 **Motor vehicles** The Act does not stipulate a separate category for motor vehicles. Therefore, the category in which they should be placed is a matter of judgement. A distinction can be drawn between motor vehicles grouped as production assets (e.g. vans, trucks and cranes), which are typically included within plant and machinery and other vehicles for staff or the sales force, which could be included within fixtures and fittings. If the number of vehicles involved is significant, then a **separate classification** for motor vehicles may be added to the financial statements.

1218 **Fixtures, fittings, tools and equipment** This **group of assets** includes such items as:
- showcases;
- counters;
- shelving;
- display fixtures;
- safes; and
- office equipment and furniture, including computer equipment.

1220 **Tools** are generally divided into two categories: namely machine tools and hand tools. Typically machine tools are expensive and are usually capitalised as fixtures, fittings and equipment, whilst hand tools are normally expensed. Non-production companies often classify all their assets in "other property" under fixtures, fittings, tools and equipment.

1222 **Payments on account and assets under construction** This category includes payments the company has made in relation to assets that are in the process of construction or installation, but that are not in service at the balance sheet date. A company will **not normally**

charge depreciation or impair an asset that is in the course of construction, except in exceptional cases.

Often the amounts involved are immaterial and do not require separate disclosure. However, significant amounts relating to assets under construction (e.g. property) or development should be separately disclosed within fixed assets, until the asset is bought into use, when the costs should be transferred to the appropriate asset categories.

SECTION 2

Initial valuation

This section outlines the **general rules** contained in FRS 15 and the Companies Act for the initial valuation of tangible fixed assets, the recognition of directly attributable costs and the rules governing the capitalisation of finance costs. The rules governing the valuation of specific tangible fixed assets such as donated assets, historical assets, and website development costs are also covered.

1226

A. General rules

A tangible fixed asset is ready for use when its physical construction is complete.

A tangible fixed asset should initially be accounted for at cost irrespective of whether an asset is purchased or produced in-house. **Subsequent valuations** may be carried at market value under the alternative accounting rules as discussed further in ¶1358.

For tangible fixed assets either **purchased or constructed in-house**, there are a number of rules governing the costs that must be capitalised (see ¶1240 and ¶1290) and excluded costs that must be expensed (see ¶1270). The **capitalisation of costs** is only permissible, in respect of the period in which the activities necessary to bring the asset into use are undertaken.

1230
FRS 15 (6) (13)

Initial recognition

1231

Where initial recognition of tangible fixed asset is based on:	
Purchase price	The purchase price of an asset includes the actual price paid plus any expenses directly attributable to its acquisition, in order to bring the asset to its present location and condition.
Production cost	The production cost of an asset includes the purchase price of raw materials and consumables used and other directly attributable costs.

On **initial recognition** the asset should only be **reviewed for impairment** if there is a good indication of a diminution in value or it is specifically required by another accounting standard. This may occur where for instance, there is a sudden slump in demand for a product, that the asset helps produce.

1234
FRS 15 (33)

The **key requirement** is that the value of the tangible fixed asset originally recognised in the accounts, should not exceed the recoverable amount of the asset. Where the capitalisation of directly attributable costs results in the initial cost of the tangible fixed asset, being greater than its recoverable amount, the asset is impaired and should be written down to the lower value. Impairment is treated in greater detail in Part 3 Chapter 5.

1. Attributable costs

1240   The general rules covering attributable costs are set out in the table below.

Directly attributable costs	These costs should be capitalised and can be grouped as either labour or incremental costs.
Labour costs	Only labour costs (e.g. site works, in-house architects, surveyors) arising from the construction, acquisition or installation of the tangible fixed asset should be capitalised.
Costs resulting from potential acquisitions or development that did not proceed	These costs must be excluded. For example, where a company is looking to buy new land, survey costs on land examined but not purchased may not be included within the cost of the land that the company ultimately purchases.

Incremental costs

1242
FRS 15 (9)
Incremental costs can be defined as costs to the entity that would have been avoided if the tangible fixed asset had not been constructed or acquired. Incremental costs include start-up costs, decommissioning provisions and finance costs.

1244
UITF 24 (5)
Start-up costs Start-up costs should be treated in the same way as similar costs incurred by the entity as part of its ongoing activities. The **key issue is whether** specific costs that result from start-up activity should be recognised as an asset or expense when incurred. The Urgent Issues Task Force (UITF) concluded that start-up costs could only be recognised as assets if they meet the **specific recognition criteria**, under a recognised accounting standard such as FRS 15, FRS 10 "Goodwill and intangible assets" or SSAP 13 "Accounting for research and development".

Start-up **costs not meeting** the asset recognition criteria should be expensed in the profit and loss account. Start-up costs that meet the definition of an exceptional item under FRS 3 should be disclosed separately in accordance with the requirements of that standard.

1246

UITF 24 (4)
The following are some examples of activities that **generate start-up costs**:
– the opening of a new facility;
– starting of a new operation;
– initiation of a new process in an existing facility;
– the introduction of a new product or service;
– development of new business in a new territory; and
– relocation or reorganisation of all or part of the entity.

1248   **Examples of start-up costs** include:
– costs of site clearance and preparation;
– initial delivery and handling costs;
– installation costs;
– acquisition costs (import duties, stamp duty); or
– professional fees (legal, architect, engineers etc.).

1250
FRS 15 (14)
Specific costs associated with a **start-up or commissioning period** before an asset is bought into use, should only be included in the cost of the tangible fixed asset, when the asset is available for use but incapable of operating at normal levels, without such a period of commissioning. For instance, costs incurred during a commissioning period required to test a machine, in order to ensure it works to a particular specification and is capable of normal use, could be capitalised even though it is physically incomplete.

1252   **Commissioning costs** should be distinguished from the costs of an initial operating period, in which a tangible fixed asset is not used to full capacity because demand for its output is not yet sufficiently high. For example, a new hotel will normally take a period of time to build up occupancy levels. Insufficient demand in itself is not an acceptable reason for treating operating costs as start-up costs and capitalising them.

Provision for decommissioning costs

Decommissioning costs include the **dismantling and removal** of a facility and the restoration of a site arising from the construction or acquisition of an asset.   **1260**
FRS 12 (66)

If any anticipated costs qualify as a provision before they are actually incurred, then they can be capitalised as a directly attributable cost of the relevant asset on **initial valuation** and depreciated over the life of the asset.

A provision should only be recognised and capitalised when the **obligation incurred** is deemed to give access to future economic benefits.

Even where expenditure of this type emerges only some time after the original capitalisation of the asset, this may not prevent its capitalisation.

Examples of decommissioning costs that may be capitalised as part of the cost of the tangible fixed asset are: **1262**
- removal of machinery;
- abandonment costs in mining and other extraction industries;
- restoration of sites (e.g. landfill, mines); and
- environmental clean up costs.

Where an **obligation arises later in the life of an asset** as a result of legislative, obsolescence or technological change, then any original provision should be adjusted.   **1264**

> EXAMPLE   A **number of provisions** relating to the decommissioning of an asset with a useful economic life of 20 years were capitalised at the time of construction. However, legislative changes after 5 years meant that further obligations totalling £500,000 arose in respect of decommissioning costs. Further provisions were made to cover the additional obligations.
> **Accounting treatment:** The **provision** should be capitalised in full as an addition to the original costs of the tangible fixed asset and depreciated over the remaining useful economic life of 15 years.

2. Excluded costs (non-direct)

All **costs not classified as directly attributable** should be excluded from the capitalised cost of the asset and include the following: **1270**
- trade discounts or rebates;
- employee costs not directly related to the specific asset (initial site selection costs);
- administration costs;
- obligations arising from damage through use that do not meet the criteria discussed above under decommissioning costs;
- indirect production overhead included in cost of stock transferred to fixed assets;
- operating losses resulting from the suspension of revenue generating activities during construction of an asset, not directly connected to bringing the asset into use;
- other general overheads; and
- abnormal costs (e.g. design errors, idle capacity, waste materials or labour or other resources and production delays).

Indirect production overheads   When an item of stock is transferred to fixed assets (from current assets), the indirect production costs previously included in the cost of stock, that do not meet the criteria laid down in FRS 15 for inclusion in the cost of the tangible fixed asset, should be expensed in the profit and loss account at the time the transfer is made.   **1274**

3. Capitalisation of finance costs

Both FRS 15 and the Companies Act permit companies to capitalise finance costs incurred during the production of a fixed asset, where they can be specifically identified. Finance costs relating to **leased tangible fixed assets** should be accounted for in accordance with   **1280**
FRS 15 (19)

SSAP 21 "Leases and Hire Purchase contracts". The process for determining the capitalisation rate is considered in ¶1310 whilst the disclosures required are outlined in ¶1512.

1281 Where a property company constructs its own investment properties, the **capitalisation rules** in FRS 15 must be applied during the construction phase.

Finance costs can be defined as the costs of procuring and servicing the funds for construction of tangible fixed assets. This definition has been widened by the accounting standards to mean "the difference between the net proceeds of an instrument and the total number of payments that the issuer may be required to make in respect of the instrument."

Directly attributable finance costs

1282
FRS 15 (20)

Directly attributable finance costs are those costs that would have been avoided, had the borrowings to fund the asset not been required or if the funds tied up in the asset were used to repay existing loans.

Finance costs are incurred on either:
– specific external borrowings to fund the construction of a particular tangible fixed asset; or
– on funds allocated from the general external borrowings of the company, in which case FRS 15 requires that a calculation be performed to determine the appropriate amount to be capitalised. This is discussed in ¶1306 below.

1284 An **entity has the option** of capitalising directly attributable finance costs or it can choose to write them off immediately. If an entity chooses to capitalise finance costs this policy should be applied on a consistent basis to all tangible fixed assets, where finance costs apply.

Capitalisation is not confined to interest alone but covers all the finance costs associated with the relevant borrowings. The justification for capitalising finance costs is that they are an integral part of the cost which should be reflected in the market price of the asset.

General rules

1290
FRS 15 (25-26)

1. **The capitalisation of finance costs** should start when finance costs are actually being incurred and other expenditures and activities that are necessary to prepare the asset for general use are also in progress.

2. Where **specific funding costs** are being capitalised, the company must ensure that it can adequately record the timing of activity and expenditures involved in the construction of the tangible fixed asset. The activities necessary to bring the asset into general use include, in addition to its physical construction, certain technical or administrative work (i.e. permits) undertaken prior to construction.

3. **Time-span** Finance costs should be capitalised only for the period in which the activities necessary to prepare the asset for use, are in progress. Costs incurred after the asset is in use should generally be expensed in the profit and loss account.

4. **Assets constructed in stages** Where a tangible fixed asset is constructed in stages and each part is capable of being used independently, and construction continues on the remainder of the asset, then the capitalisation of finance costs relating to any completed part should cease. This requirement is intended to prevent companies including costs for periods in which the asset was available for use, but was not actually being utilised.

FRS 15 (29)

EXAMPLE An example of an asset that can be divided into component parts is a business park comprising several buildings, each of which can be used individually. Some units can be operable while others are still under construction. In this instance, the capitalisation of directly attributable costs on the completed units should cease.

5. **Cessation** The capitalisation of directly attributable costs should cease when the asset is brought into use or when its physical construction is complete.

6. **Alterations to assets** Where an asset is purchased and then altered to meet the specific requirements, any borrowing costs incurred should be capitalised, but only on the borrow-

ings incurred to make the alterations and not on the initial purchase cost. Furthermore, where companies hold assets for alterations but are not actually altering them, then any related borrowings should not be capitalised.

EXAMPLE Finance costs incurred while the land is under development may be capitalised. However, finance costs incurred while land acquired for building purposes is held without any associated development activity may not be capitalised. Where land has been purchased and the architects have begun the process of drawing up plans and obtaining permits, these are relevant activities for capitalisation purposes.

7. **Maximum amount that can be capitalised**. If the entity has borrowed funds to fund the purchase or construction of a tangible fixed asset, the total of the finance costs is **limited to** the actual costs incurred on the borrowings during the construction period. The total finance costs capitalised during a period should not exceed the total amount of finance costs incurred during that period.
Construction could include either the use of outside contractors or any construction completed by the company itself.

8. **Exchange rate** Differences arising on exchange rates, on funds borrowed to finance the construction or purchase of a tangible fixed asset are deemed to be an adjustment to interest costs. Any exchange rate "losses" should be capitalised as part of finance costs. Exchange gains will reduce the finance costs.

9. **Taxation** Finance costs should be capitalised gross of tax before the deduction of any related tax relief.

10. **Intra-group borrowing**

i. Subsidiaries can capitalise interest in their own financial statements on finance provided by other group companies. However, at a consolidated level, intra-group interest must be eliminated because the group itself has not incurred external interest (only notional interest) on these internal borrowings.

ii. Where the **group borrows finance externally** and lends to another group member, any interest capitalised in the subsidiary's accounts will remain capitalised on consolidation.

iii. However, **where intra-group interest rates** and other finance charges **vary significantly** from the group's weighted average borrowing rate, consolidation adjustments will be required to bring the amount capitalised by the subsidiary into line with that which would be allowed, based on the group's finance rate.

11. **General borrowings** If the funds used to finance the construction of a tangible fixed asset form part of the entity's overall borrowings, the level of finance costs capitalised is determined by applying a weighted average capitalisation rate to the capital expenditure on that asset.

MEMO POINTS There is a **choice of how to calculate the costs** of general borrowing included in the weighted average for a group; either:
- all the borrowings of a parent and its subsidiaries can be included when calculating the weighted average finance cost; or
- where subsidiaries within a group organise their own treasury function, they should calculate their own weighted average cost of capital, applicable to its own borrowings.

The capitalisation rate

The relevant capital expenditure figure is the **weighted average carrying amount** of the asset during the period, including finance costs previously capitalised. The capitalisation rate is based on the weighted average of rates applicable to the entity's general borrowings (the weighted average cost of capital or WACC), outstanding during the period.

1310

The borrowings included in the **weighted average** should be directly attributable to the construction or purchase of the asset. It is important to ascertain a capitalisation rate that is a fair reflection of the costs incurred in the financing of the construction of the asset.

The **method of determining** the capitalisation rate will depend on how the company or group is structured and how its activities are financed. Where **funds are pooled in a group** and finance is considered at the group level, then the capitalisation rate should be determined at group level, as illustrated in the following example.

EXAMPLE **Capitalisation of interest on general borrowings.**

A company with a June 30 financial year-end finances the construction of a tangible fixed asset from its general borrowings. The level of capitalised expenditure is shown in row 1. The amount brought forward from the previous year (including interest) is £7,000.
The company's general borrowings are shown in row 7 (i.e. total £20,000 on 1 July).

		Annual average £	1 July b/fwd. £	Oct. 1 £	Jan. 1 £	April 1 £	June 30 £
1	Capitalised expenditure	13,250	7,000	10,000	15,000	21,000	23,000
2	Weights			0.25	0.25	0.25	0.25
3	Capitalised interest						**1,623**
4	Total						**24,623**
5	Tranches	13,250	7,000	3,000	5,000	6,000	2,000
6	Weights		1	0.75	0.50	0.25	
7	Total borrowings outstanding		20,000	25,000	18,000	25,000	
8	Borrowing costs during the period		2,200	2,500	2,000	4,500	
9	**Capitalisation rate**	**0.1225**	**0.11**	**0.10**	**0.11**	**0.18**	

The **interest costs** for the year total £1,623 and is calculated by multiplying:
a. the annual average balance of expenditure of £13,250 by
b. the annual average capitalisation rate of 0.1225
The costs are then added to the total capitalised expenditure of £23,000 to be carried forward to the following year.

Calculation.
a. The **annual average capitalisation expenditure** (Row 1) is calculated by totalling the borrowings of £53,000 (£7,000 + £10,000 + £15,000 + £21,000) and dividing this figure by 4 (quarters) = £13,250. Each balance of capitalised expenditure lasts for three months and the annual average is the time-weighted average, using the weights in row 2.
b. The **capitalisation rate** (Row 9) is found for each quarter by dividing the borrowing costs by the total outstanding borrowings for each quarter (i.e. Quarter 1 £2,200/£20,000 = 0.11). The quarterly rates are then totalled and averaged using the weights given in row 2 of the table (0.11 + 0.10 + 0.11 + 0.18/4 = 0.1225).

Prohibited finance costs

1314   Certain types of finance costs are prohibited from being capitalised, such as:
– notional finance costs, such as interest foregone on cash deposits used to finance the purchase or construction of the tangible fixed asset; or
– for the purpose of capitalisation, any interest earned on borrowed funds temporarily re-invested should not be offset against finance costs incurred.

1316
FRS 15 (27)
Suspension Finance costs incurred during a period in which the activities required to prepare any asset for use are suspended, do not qualify for capitalisation as they relate to the cost of holding partially completed assets. **Development** of a tangible fixed asset may be suspended, where a company discontinues or mothballs development in the face of falling demand projections or other external constraints such as government policy.

B. Initial valuation of specific types of tangible fixed assets

1324   Particular types of tangible fixed asset such as donated assets, historic assets and websites require special consideration in terms of their initial valuation.

Motor vehicles

The **purchase price** of the majority of tangible fixed assets will normally be capitalised   **1325**
exclusive of VAT. Motor cars are an exception and should be capitalised at the invoice price
inclusive of VAT as the input tax on cars cannot usually be reclaimed by the company.

Low value assets retained at a fixed amount

Certain types of tangible fixed assets can be valued at a fixed amount (initial measurement)   **1326**
provided that they:
– are not material in value;
– are constantly being replaced; and
– are not subject to material fluctuations in terms of value, quantity or composition.
Examples of this type of asset include low value, short-life assets such as small tools.

Donated assets

Tangible fixed assets by charities received as **gifts** or **donations** should initially be carried   **1327**
at the current value of the assets, at the date they are received. Where the asset is deemed   FRS 15 (17)
to be impaired, the current value should be the replacement cost. Any gain on the recognition of a donated asset should be recognised in the financial statements.
Problems can arise when these assets:
– cannot be disposed of without external consent;
– the assets are of a particular historic, scientific or artistic importance; or
– when conventional valuations are not sufficiently reliable.
Further guidance on these issues is given in the SORP for the charity sector issued by the
Charities Commission (see ¶9500).

Heritage assets

Heritage assets are defined as assets of historical, artistic or scientific value, held to further   **1330**
the preservation, conservation and educational activities of charities, and include land, buil-   FRS 15 (18)
dings, collections, exhibits or artefacts.
The **normal cost rules** apply to historic assets owned by companies.
Historic and similar tangible fixed assets **owned by a charity** should be carried in the
balance sheet where:
– the assets give rise to future economic benefits;
– the entity has stewardship of the assets; and
– the owner may have invested funds in the acquisition, maintenance and restoration of the
assets.
However, for assets that were not previously capitalised or which were donated, **the costs
of obtaining a valuation** may outweigh the benefits. In these instances the appropriate
disclosures should be made in the notes to the accounts. Further guidance can be found in
the relevant sector guidance notes or SORPs. The accounting treatment will be as for
donated assets.
    MEMO POINTS   FRS 30 "Heritage Assets" covers the accounting and disclosure requirements for
heritage assets (¶9586).

Asset purchases with a foreign currency

Where an asset is purchased with a foreign currency, it is the **exchange rate** at the date on   **1332**
which the transaction is originally recorded (historic rate), that should be used for calculating the cost of the asset. If the exchange rate on this date differs from the rate prevailing on
the invoice date, the exchange gain or loss should be taken directly to the profit and loss
account.

Websites

1334
UITF 29 (3)

Companies that have established a website may have incurred significant costs in the process. The **general rule** is that a distinction must be drawn between planning costs (expenses) and development costs (capitalised).

Planning costs comprise the costs of feasibility studies to determine the objectives for the website as well as identifying hardware and software needs. Planning costs should be expensed in the profit and loss account.

1336

Development costs Development costs include the costs associated with the following:
– purchasing specialist hardware;
– purchasing or designing specialist software;
– creative design and graphics;
– content of web pages;
– registration of domain names; and
– other infrastructure costs such as E-commerce systems and encryption software.

1337

Recognition criteria The **key requirement** is that in order **to capitalise** development costs a direct link must be established between the website and any revenues generated. In addition, website development expenditure **can only be capitalised if** the following criteria are also met; namely:
– the expenditure should be separately identifiable;
– the technical and commercial viability of the website should have been established with reasonable certainty;
– the website is expected to generate sales or revenues directly through orders placed or payments made via the website or from selling advertising space; and
– that adequate resources exist to complete, launch and maintain the website.

1338
UITF 29 (17)

Accounting treatment   **Expenditure to maintain or operate** a website once it has been developed and constructed should be charged to the profit and loss account as incurred, in accordance with the requirements of FRS 15.

Where capitalisation of website development costs **is justified**, the following accounting treatments apply:

1. The asset should be **amortised** over its estimated useful economic life (which may well be short given the pace of technological change), which should be reviewed at the end of each accounting period and revised if appropriate.
2. **If the design or content** of the website **is changed frequently**, a different (shorter) depreciation charge should apply to these costs rather than the rest of the asset (see ¶1484).
3. The asset should be **reviewed regularly** for impairment. For instance, if the website is "refreshed", any new design and content costs may be capitalised. However, any design or content costs previously capitalised and not yet written-off should be reviewed for impairment.

1340

Where the website is used only for **promotional purposes** and as a database for customers or the general public, it may be difficult to prove conclusively that sales or revenue are generated direct from the website. In these situations all design and content costs should be written off to the profit and loss account.

Revenues generated from the development of a website, **that previously flowed from other tangible assets**, may mean that these assets have become impaired as a result. Where website development costs **are reclassified from** intangible assets to tangible fixed assets, this represents a change in accounting policy.

SECTION 3

Revaluation

This section covers the rules governing the revaluation of tangible fixed assets (principally property), the revaluation process and selection of valuation bases, the treatment of depreciation as well and the accounting treatment of revaluation gains and losses. **Special revaluation rules** apply to non-specialised properties. The revaluation policy for **charities** and other not-for-profit organisations, which are beyond the scope of this book are treated in the relevant sector guidance notes or SORPs.

1348

The **majority of revaluations** involve property although the process involved is applicable to other tangible fixed assets.

Overview of revaluation policy

Tangible fixed assets are **more likely to be revalued** in times where asset values rise sharply or where a company may wish to strengthen the appearance of its balance sheet. Whilst the Companies Act permits the revaluation of an entity's fixed assets under the **alternative accounting rules**, the detailed rules governing the revaluation process are set out in the provisions of FRS 15.

1350

MEMO POINTS   The term "revaluation" does not cover the **write-down** of the carrying amount of a tangible fixed asset held at historical cost for an impairment, or the determination of the cost of an asset acquired as a result of a **business combination** stated at its fair value at the date of acquisition, in accordance with FRS 7 "Fair Values in Acquisition Accounting".

General rules

1352

FRS 15 (100)

	Revaluation rules
Initial measurement	Tangible fixed assets **should initially be measured** at historical cost and **only revalued** when the entity adopts a formal policy of revaluation. Such a policy is optional for all companies.
Subsequent revaluations	Applied to all assets within that class of assets. Individual assets cannot be selected or "cherry-picked" for revaluation purposes, as the aim is to reduce the scope for selecting individual assets for revaluation that have increased in value.
Specific industries	An entity may, depending on the requirements of a particular industry, **adopt other narrower classes of assets**, provided they meet the definition of a category of tangible fixed asset having a similar nature, function or use in the business of the entity. For example, land and buildings can be sub-divided into specialised properties, non-specialist properties and short-leasehold properties. Separate disclosures are required for each class of asset.
Where a realistic market value cannot be obtained	For particular assets within a **specific class** that is being revalued, i.e. if the asset is located overseas, it may be excluded from the valuation, although the carrying amount and the fact that it has not been revalued should be stated in the notes to the accounts.
Impairment indicated	An **impairment review** should be carried out in accordance with the requirements of FRS 11. The asset should be recorded at the lower of the revalued amount and the recoverable amount; namely the higher of net realisable value and value in use.

MEMO POINTS   **Alternative accounting rules**: The alternative accounting rules in the Companies Act permit tangible fixed assets to be valued at market rate, determined as at the date of their last valuation or at their current cost. However, this policy could lead to a **mix of assets** carried at historical cost and others at market value. There is also no requirement under the alternative accounting rules for the revaluations that are performed to be kept up to date. Therefore, to help introduce an element of consistency, FRS 15 sets out the conditions that must exist in order for the alternative accounting rules to be adopted, covering which types of tangible fixed asset should be revalued and when, the valuation bases that may used and who is permitted to revalue assets. It should be noted that there is **no obligation** under either FRS 15 or the Companies Act for an entity to revalue its tangible fixed assets. They merely set out the rules that have to be followed if an entity should chose to revalue them. In general, the only widespread use of the alternative accounting rules is for the valuation of **freehold and leasehold properties**.

A. Frequency

1364
FRS 15 (43)

Where a tangible fixed asset is revalued its **carrying amount** should represent the current value at the balance sheet date. In order to satisfy this requirement, a full valuation of previously revalued assets should be conducted at least every 5 years, with a formal interim valuation after 3 years.

FRS 15 (45)

In addition to the two aforementioned mandatory revaluations, **interim valuations** in years 1, 2 and 4 should be carried out, where it is likely there has been a material change in value. All valuations should be carried out as close to the financial year-end as possible.

The accounting standard does not insist on **annual revaluations**, although the objective of revaluation policy is to replace the current valuation at the balance sheet date.

1367
FRS 15 (52)

Material changes in value   Valuations must be updated where there is perceived to be a material change in value, which is defined in the standard as "a change in value that would reasonably influence the decisions of as user of the accounts." In determining whether a material change in value is likely, the combined impact of all relevant factors should be considered. Situations that may give rise to a material change in value, include physical deterioration in the property or a general movement in market prices.

1370
FRS 15 (46)

Non-specialist properties   An exception to the general rules set out above exists for non-specialised properties, where an annual valuation may be completed on only a part of the property portfolio. Non-specialised properties should be the subject of a full valuation on a **rolling basis**, designed to cover the entire portfolio over a five-year cycle, together with an interim valuation on the remaining portfolio every year, where a material change in value is deemed likely.

1372

This approach is appropriate where the property portfolio consists of a number of **broadly similar properties** impacted by the same market factors, that can easily be divided into groups.

For instance, a portfolio comprising of sports clubs, hotels and restaurants could be divided into the following classifications:
– business units;
– regions; or
– groupings by size.

B. Revaluation process

1374
FRS 15 (47)

Although the majority of revaluations involve **property** the process involved is applicable to other tangible fixed assets.

A formal revaluation should be carried out at both the interim and full five yearly valuation, and normally involves the following stages:
– a detailed inspection of the property;

- inspection of the locality;
- enquiries of local planning and similar authorities (legal rights, planning permission etc); and
- research on market prices or trends for similar properties.

Full valuation   The full valuation should be conducted by a qualified external valuer with   **1376**
no financial interest in the entity.

A **qualified valuer** is defined as a person who: FRS 15 (48)
- holds a relevant professional qualification;
- has recent post-qualification experience; and
- knows the market, location and category of tangible fixed asset concerned.

An **external review** often involves the valuation of a sample of the entity's properties by the   **1377**
external valuer, for comparison with the internal valuer's figures. The external valuer must
be satisfied that the sample represents a genuine cross-section of the entity's property portfolio. An external valuer cannot be a director, officer or employee of the company.

Interim valuation   An interim valuation should be conducted by a qualified internal (or   **1378**
external valuer) involving essentially the same process as the full valuation. The **main
difference** in the requirements of a full and interim valuation, is that where the interim
valuation is performed by a qualified internal valuer, there is no requirement for it to then
be reviewed by an external qualified valuer.

> ⌐MEMO POINTS⌐   The revaluation process at the **interim date** is also less rigorous and consists of
> the following:
> 1. Research into market transactions involving similar properties, analyses of market trends and
> application thereof, to determine the value of the property.
> 2. A physical inspection of the property and locality by the valuer; and confirmation that:
> - the property has not been radically altered;
> - legal rights and obligations are unchanged; or
> - local planning regulations have not been infringed.

Tangible fixed assets other than properties

For tangible fixed assets other than properties, where an active second-hand market exists   **1380**
as evidenced by frequent activity, or where there are appropriate measurement indices that   FRS 15 (50)
allow the value of an asset to be ascertained with reasonable certainty, then an annual
valuation conducted by the directors may be sufficient (as opposed to using a qualified
external surveyor). Examples include company cars and office equipment.

The **indices** must be appropriate to the class of asset to which it is applied, as well as to the
asset's location and condition and have a proven record of publication and use.

If the **directors are not able** to obtain a reasonable valuation on an annual basis because   **1382**
an active second hand market or indices do not exist, then they must commission a full or
interim valuation. It is the **directors' responsibility** to ensure that the carrying values are
accurately described as current at the end of each financial year.

C. Valuation bases

Different valuation bases **must be applied** to the revaluation of properties, and the revalua-   **1384**
tion of other tangible fixed assets. A company that has revalued its fixed assets must maintain   FRS 15 (53)
records of both historical costs and revaluation of fixed assets, and calculate depreciation
on both historical cost and revaluation.

Type of tangible fixed asset	Valuation base	Notes
Non-specialised properties	Existing use value (EUV) (¶1390)	Include notional directly attributable acquisition costs.
Specialised properties	Depreciated replacement cost (DRC) (¶1404)	
Surplus properties	Open market value (OMV) (¶1390)	After deducting material directly attributable selling costs.
Non-property tangible fixed assets	OMV or depreciated replacement cost where market value not available.	Include notional directly attributable acquisition costs.

1. Non-specialised properties

1388 Non-specialised properties **are defined as** all properties, for which there is a general demand, with or without adaptation, and which are generally bought, sold or leased on the open market for their existing or similar uses, either with vacant possession for occupation or as investments or for development.

FRS 15 (Appendix I) **Examples** of non-specialised properties include:
- residential properties;
- shops and offices;
- industrial and warehouse buildings;
- petrol stations;
- hotels;
- cinemas, pubs, theatres and gaming clubs;
- private hospitals and nursing homes; and
- sports and leisure facilities.

Existing use value

1390
FRS 15 (56) The **general rule** is that non-specialised properties should be valued on the basis of existing use value (EUV), with the addition of notional directly attributable acquisition costs; namely dealing costs such as professional fees and non-recoverable taxes and duties. In practical terms, EUV will typically correspond to Open Market Value (OMV). Where the EUV **differs materially** from the OMV, the EUV and reasons for the difference should be disclosed.

The existing use value of a property takes account of its current function rather than the potential it has to be used in a more beneficial way. For example, a site that is used as an office block may also have planning permission for use as luxury housing. On an EUV basis it will be valued as an office block which may be materially different to the OMV if it were sold, potentially, for redevelopment as houses.

> [MEMO POINTS]   The **open market value** is defined as the best price at which the sale of an interest in a property or tangible fixed asset would be completed, for cash at the valuation date. OMV is the only basis that is appropriate for investment properties surplus to the company's requirements.

1393 The existing use value is the best price at which the **sale of an interest in property** would have been completed for cash on the date of valuation assuming that there is a willing seller, and that:
- the state of the market, level of values and other circumstances were, on any earlier assumed date of exchange of contracts, the same as on the date of valuation;
- both parties conducted the transaction at arm's length;
- the property can be used for the foreseeable future only for the existing use; and
- vacant possession is provided on completion of the sale of all parts of the property occupied by the business.

Certain types of non-specialised properties can be valued separately as businesses on the basis of their existing use value (EUV).

1394
FRS 15 (Appendix I)

The EUV of a property valued as an **operational entity** takes account of the trading potential of the property. **Personal goodwill** created in the business by the present owners, that is not expected to remain in the business when the property is sold, is excluded. The EUV reflects the **service potential** that is used by the owner rather than the alternative uses to which the building may be put.

In the majority of cases where a non-specialised property is being utilised for its most beneficial use, the EUV should equal the OMV (with vacant possession). The EUV generally will not exceed the open market value (OMV), as the latter reflects the additional possible uses ignored in arriving at EUV. For instance, a factory located on the edge of a town may have a greater value as a residential site than as an industrial site.

Where EUV exceeds OMV   EUV will exceed OMV where for instance:

1396
FRS 15 (Appendix
IV.22)

– planning consent is personal to the present occupier;
– there are restrictive alienation clauses in the head leases; or
– there is known contamination that does not affect the existing use of the non-specialised building.

All these examples would result in a lower OMV but would be disregarded in determining EUV, as they do not affect the cost of a replacement. Further information concerning the OMV should be disclosed in the notes to the accounts, where OMV materially exceeds the EUV.

Excluded costs   Expenditure for **enhancing the value** of a site such as costs associated with planning applications, site preparation and clearance and other costs already reflected in the existing use value (EUV) should be excluded. In practical terms, notional acquisition costs that are not material should be ignored.

1397
FRS 15 (57)

2. Specialised properties

Specialised properties are defined in FRS 15, as properties of a specialist nature that are **rarely sold on the open market**, for single occupation for a continuation of their existing use, except as part of a sale of a larger business operation.

1400
FRS 15 (57)

The specialised nature of these properties may arise from the construction, arrangement, size or location of the property, or a combination of these factors. It may also be due to the nature of the plant and machinery and items of equipment that the buildings are designed to house, or the function or purpose for which the buildings are provided.

Specialised properties include the following:

FRS 15 (Appendix I)

– oil refineries and chemical works;
– power installations;
– docks;
– schools, colleges, and universities;
– hospitals and other specialist health care institutions;
– museums, libraries, and other similar premises; and
– standard properties in particular geographical areas (i.e. remote areas), located there for specific business reasons.

Depreciated replacement cost

Specialised properties are primarily valued using depreciated replacement cost (DRC), where the OMV is not available due to the specialised nature of the properties.

1404

However, in certain other cases specialised properties may be valued as **fully operational entities**, given their own trading potential (e.g. docks). If this basis for valuation is adopted this should be disclosed in the financial statements.

The DRC of property is defined as the total amount of the value of the land for the existing use or a notional replacement site in the same locality, and the gross replacement cost of the buildings and other site works from which appropriate deductions may be made.

All of these factors might result in the existing property being worth less to the undertaking in occupation than a new replacement building.

1406　The costs **directly attributable** to bringing the property into working condition for its intended use are included in the depreciated replacement cost. Examples include the costs of:

- installation (e.g. water, electricity);
- commissioning;
- consultants fees; and
- non-recoverable taxes and duties.

1407　In calculating DRC, the **deductions from gross replacement cost** should cover:

- the age and condition of the asset;
- economic and functional obsolescence; and
- environmental and other factors.

---

3. Surplus properties

1410　**Properties surplus to requirements** should be valued by taking the open market value (OMV) (see ¶1390) less any material directly attributed selling costs. Selling costs are deducted to reflect the net realisable value of the asset to the entity. Similar valuation bases are used for tangible fixed assets other than properties.

The OMV is **defined** as the best price at which the sale of an interest in a property or tangible fixed asset would be completed, for cash at the valuation date. OMV is the only basis that is appropriate for investment properties surplus to the company's requirements.

1412　The **criteria that apply** to determining the open market value are the same as those for EUV, except that two conditions do not apply; namely that the property:

FRS 15 (Appendix 1)　– will only be used for the same purpose for the foreseeable future; and

- that it will be sold with vacant possession.

---

4. Non-property assets

1414　Tangible fixed assets other than properties that are used in a business should be valued
FRS 15 (59)　using the **open market value base**; namely what it would cost the entity to replace the asset.

Notional directly attributable acquisitions costs such as professional fees, non-recoverable taxes and duties, should be added to market value where material.

Where market value is not obtainable, assets should be valued on the basis of **depreciated replacement cost**, as determined by a qualified valuer or on the basis of an appropriate index. The cost of replacing an existing asset with a similar new asset with similar production or service capacity is depreciated to reflect the value of an existing remaining useful economic life.

1415　The **value of non-property plant and machinery** to the business is defined (in FRS 15), as the price at which an interest in the plant or machinery would have been transferred at the date of valuation given:

- that the plant and machinery will continue in its present uses in the business;
- the continuing viability or profitability of the undertaking having due regard to the value of the total assets employed and the nature of the operation; and
- the transfer is part of an "arm's length sale" of a business.

MEMO POINTS   An "**arm's length transaction**" is defined as an agreement entered into by unrelated parties, each acting in their own interests in paying or charging prices based on fair market values. This may not be the case with companies belonging to the same group, who may transact with each other for taxation or other reasons.

---

5. Treatment of revaluation gains and losses

This section covers the accounting treatment for revaluation gains and losses and the possible impact of deferred taxation.   **1418**

MEMO POINTS   Depreciation of **revalued** tangible fixed assets is covered in ¶1482 and disclosures in ¶1418.

Revaluation gains

A revaluation gain is the positive difference between the revalued amount and the carrying   **1420**
amount of the tangible fixed asset, net of cumulative depreciation.

General rules   1. **All revaluation gains** on tangible fixed assets should be recognised in   **1421**
the STRGL, as they generally represent gains from rising prices and are valuation adjustments   FRS 15 (63)
and not realised profits, as illustrated in the example below.

EXAMPLE   An entity has a tangible fixed asset that cost £15,000 at the start of year 1; it has a useful economic life of 10 years, a residual value of £3,000 and is being depreciated on a straight-line basis. At the end of year one, the asset was revalued upwards to £17,500.

Accounting treatment Year	Year 1 £
Cost of the asset	15,000
Depreciation charge	(1,200)
Adjusted book amount	13,800
Gain on revaluation	3,700
Closing book amount	**17,500**

The revaluation gain of £3,700 should be reflected in the STRGL.
The **initial depreciation charge** is credited to reserves and the asset depreciated over the remaining useful life of the asset.

Accounting entries

	Dr.	Cr.
Fixed assets – cost	2,500	
Revaluation reserve		2,500
Fixed asset – depreciation	1,200	
Revaluation reserve		1,200

2. Revaluation gains should only be recognised in the profit and loss account (net of the impact of depreciation that would have been charged to the profit and loss account had the property not previously have been revalued downwards), to the extent that they **reverse revaluation losses** on the same asset, previously recognised in the profit and loss account.

3. Any **gain is reduced by** the same depreciation charge that would have been levied had   FRS 15 (64)
the loss previously taken to the profit and loss account not been initially recognised, as
illustrated in the example below.

4. On revaluation, **material gains (or losses)** on individual assets in a class should not be   FRS 15 (67)
aggregated.

MEMO POINTS   For a discussion of the accounting treatment regarding the profit (or loss) on the
disposal of fixed assets – see ¶398.

EXAMPLE   An asset costs £15,000 at the start of year 1; it has a useful economic life of 10 years, a residual value of £3,000 and is being depreciated on a straight-line basis. At the end of year one the asset was revalued downwards to £10,500 (the recoverable amount). In year two the asset has been revalued upwards to £17,500. The accounting treatment is as follows:

Accounting treatment	Yr 1 £	Yr 2 £
Cost/valuation brought forward	15,000	10,500
Depreciation charge	(1,200)	(833)
Adjusted book amount	13,800	9,667
Gain (loss) on revaluation	(3,300)	7,833
Closing book amount	10,500	17,500

Year 1
The revaluation loss of **£3,300** should be reflected in the profit and loss account, because it represents the fall in value below depreciated historical cost.

Year 2
The revaluation gain of **£7,833** should be accounted for as follows:
- **£2,933** (£3,300-£367) should reverse the loss posted to the profit and loss account at the end of year 1. The figure of £367 represents the additional depreciation charge that would have been taken in year 2 had the opening balance been £13,800 and the loss not been recognised.
- **£4,900** should be accounted for in the revaluation reserve and disclosed in the STRGL.

Accounting entries

	Dr.	Cr.
Fixed assets	£7,833	
Profit and loss account		£2,933
Revaluation reserve		£4,900

Revaluation losses

1426

FRS 15 (69)

A revaluation loss is defined as the negative difference between the revalued amount of the tangible fixed asset and the net book value of the asset. A revaluation loss may result from:
- a consumption of economic benefits, as evidenced by a decline in service provided by the asset or the physical destruction of the asset (impairment);
- a result of a general fall in the level of prices; or
- a combination of a fall in prices or consumption in economic benefits.

1427   ## Accounting treatment

Revaluation losses: causes	Accounting treatment
Resulting from a clear **consumption of economic benefits** (impairment)	Revaluation losses should be recognised in the profit and loss account, in line with the requirements of FRS 11. Losses cannot be netted off against gains arising on other assets.
Other general revaluation losses	The revenue loss should be recognised in the STRGL until the carrying amount reaches its depreciated historical cost; and thereafter, in the profit and loss account, unless it can be demonstrated that the recoverable amount of the asset is greater than its revalued amount. In this case the loss should be recognised in the STRGL, to the extent that the recoverable amount of the asset is greater than its revalued amount.

1428

FRS 15 (65)

1. **Where the reason** for the **fall in value of the asset is not clear**, then splitting the revaluation loss between the STRGL and the profit and loss account is an arbitrary allocation, because it depends whether the fall in value is above or below depreciated historical cost.

FRS 15 (66)

2. However, **where** it can be demonstrated that **the recoverable amount is greater than its revalued amount**, the loss should be recognised in the STRGL, to the extent that the recoverable amount of the asset is greater than its revalued amount. The recoverable amount of the asset should be calculated in accordance with the requirements of FRS 11.

3. Where there is **difficulty in allocating an impairment loss**, it is assumed that the fall in value from the previous carrying value of the asset to the depreciated historical cost is due

to a general fall in prices, which should be accounted for in the STRGL as a valuation adjustment.

4. Thereafter, a **further fall in value** from depreciated historical cost to **revalued amount** is due to the consumption of economic benefits and the impairment should be recognised in the profit and loss account.

Revaluation gain followed by a revaluation loss

The example below illustrates the **recognition and accounting treatment** of a revaluation gain followed by a revaluation loss.

1436

EXAMPLE   A **non-specialist property** costs £1m, has a useful economic life of 10 years and no residual value. The company's policy is to depreciate buildings on a straight-line basis and revalue the property annually.
Depreciation is calculated based on the opening book amount. At the end of years 1 and 2 the asset has a EUV of £1,080,000 and £700,000 respectively.
At the end of year 2, the **recoverable amount** of the asset is £760,000 and its depreciated historical cost is £800,000. There is no obvious consumption of economic benefits in year 2, other than that allowed for in the normal depreciation charge.

Scenario A – Accounting treatment under historical cost

	Year 1 £'000	Year 2 £'000
Opening book value	1,000	1,080
Depreciation	(100)	(120)
Adjusted book amount	900	960
Revaluation gain (loss)		
– recognised in the STRGL	180	(220)
– recognised in the profit and loss account	-	(40)
Closing book value (EUV)	1,080	700

Year 1. Revaluation gain
After a depreciation charge of £100,000, a revaluation gain of £180,000 is recognised in the STRGL.

Year 2 Revaluation loss
After a **depreciation charge** of £120,000, the revaluation loss on the property totals £260,000. As this has not resulted from the clear consumption of economic benefits but a fall in prices, revaluation losses should be recognised in the STRGL until the carrying amount reaches the level of its depreciated historical cost. As a consequence, the fall in value from the adjusted book amount (£960,000) to the depreciated historical cost (£800,000) of £160,000 is recognised in the STRGL.
The **depreciated historical cost** of £800,000 represents the opening book amount minus two years depreciation charge (2 x £100,000).
The remainder of the **revaluation loss** of £100,000 (resulting from the fall in value from depreciated historical cost £800,000 to **revalued amount** £700,000) should be recognised in the profit and loss account.

Limitations on use of a revaluation reserve

Once a **revaluation has taken place**, the use of a revaluation reserve is limited. An amount may be transferred from the revaluation reserve to the profit and loss account, only if the amount:

1437

– was previously charged to the profit and loss account;
– represents realised profit;
– is applied in paying up (wholly or in part) unissued shares in the company (this is often referred to as capitalisation); or
– is in respect of taxation relating to a surplus credited to the revaluation reserve.

The revaluation reserve must be disclosed on the face of the balance sheet as a separate amount.

Deferred taxation (timing differences)

1438
FRS 19 (2)

Deferred taxation results from timing differences between capital allowances and the depreciation charge. The revaluation of an asset will generate a deferred tax timing difference insofar as the profit or loss that would result from the asset's realisation at the revalued amount is taxable at that later date, rather than at the point of revaluation. Where a **deferred taxation liability** is recognised the revaluation surplus should be reduced by that amount. The deferred tax is not therefore recognised in the profit and loss but in the STRGL.

It should be noted, however, that under FRS 19, entities should not usually recognise within its deferred tax provision, the potential tax that will arise on revaluation surpluses. The revaluation reserve will not normally be reduced by the potential tax payable. The company is obliged to disclose the **taxation effect** of the revaluation in its financial statements.

Deferred taxation is discussed more fully in ¶9000.

SECTION 4

Depreciation

1444
FRS 15 (81)

This section details the various **methods of depreciation** and the concepts that underpin them as well as the special rules that apply to the provision of depreciation in relation to revalued tangible fixed assets, subsequent expenditure and separable assets.

1445

The general disclosure requirements covering depreciation are covered in ¶1510. For depreciation of **specific categories** of tangible fixed assets covered by other reporting standards such as investment properties or leases, refer to the specific chapters covering these topics.

1446

The **concept of depreciation** is defined in the accounting standards as the cost resulting from the wear and tear, consumption or other reduction in the useful economic life of a tangible fixed asset, whether arising from use, passage of time or obsolescence through technological change.

The **purpose of depreciation** is to charge to the profit and loss account a notional sum that reflects on a consistent basis the costs of using tangible fixed assets during a particular financial period. Depreciation is also a measurement of the loss in value of tangible fixed assets over a given time period.

1448

The **general rule** is that all tangible fixed assets with the exception of freehold land have a finite life not exceeding 50 years. Tangible fixed assets should be depreciated according to an appropriate method, which is underpinned by the concepts of useful economic life, materiality and residual value.

The implications for companies who **choose not to depreciate** an asset or select a depreciation period in excess of 50 years are dealt with below (see ¶1488).

A. Concepts

1450

The concepts of materiality, useful economic life and residual value are inter-linked but not necessarily inter-dependent, as they are based on individual judgements and are therefore subjective by nature.

However, **changing the parameters and assumptions** underlying an assessment of either materiality, useful economic life or residual value will probably impact on one or more of the other concepts. For instance, if an entity chooses to increase the useful economic life of one of its tangible fixed assets, this could in turn reduce its residual value and increase the total depreciation charged albeit over a longer period of time.

Materiality

An asset and related depreciation charge would be deemed material, if its omission from the financial statements would be misleading for users of the accounts. Materiality is in turn, **based on an assessment** of a number of primary factors including the asset's useful economic life and estimated residual value.

1452

When an entity seeks not to depreciate an asset on the grounds that that of immateriality, it must be able to justify that the omitted charge for the year and accumulated depreciation is not significant for an appreciation of both the results for the year and the financial position shown by the balance sheet. As a consequence, it would be difficult for an entity to defend a policy of non-depreciation on an expensive asset.

Residual value

The residual value of an asset is the **expected disposal proceeds** from the sale of an asset (net of costs), at the end of its useful economic life and should be deducted from the cost of the fixed asset when determining the appropriate depreciation charge. It should be noted that when assessing residual values, they should be based on prices prevailing at the time the asset is purchased. An assessment of residual value should not take into account anticipated price increases over the life of the asset.

1453

The residual value of an asset can be **influenced by a number of factors** including its useful economic life or second hand market value. Any material change in the estimated residual value should be accounted for through the depreciation charge over the remaining useful life of the asset.

High residual value In terms of a high residual value, the depreciation charge may be deemed insignificant as a result of one or more of the following:
– the asset is immune to economic or technological obsolescence resulting from changes in demand patterns;
– the entity has a policy of disposing of similar assets, with high residual values well before the end of their useful economic lives;
– where the disposal proceeds of similar assets are not significantly less than their carrying value; or
– a policy of regular maintenance and repair (charged to the profit & loss) that sustains previously assessed performance levels and useful economic lives.

1454

> EXAMPLE   A hotel group does not provide for depreciation in respect of freehold hotels, as it is considered that the useful economic lives and residual values of these buildings are such that any depreciation charge would be immaterial. The logic supporting this decision is that the hotel group regularly refurbishes its hotels, thereby extending the useful economic lives more or less indefinitely and preserving the residual values of the group's assets.

Where the residual value is revised it should where possible be restated in terms of the price that prevailed when the asset was purchased or revalued. If this is neither possible nor practicable, the residual value should be restated in terms of current values only where the residual value at current prices is below the original estimate of residual value. Events or changes in circumstances that **result in a fall in the residual value** may indicate the asset is impaired, in which case an impairment review should be conducted in accordance with the requirements of FRS 11.

1455
FRS 15 (96)

Useful economic life

Initial recognition   The **general rule** is that the useful economic life of an asset is determined when the asset is either purchased or (if self-constructed), commissioned for use and represents the period over which the owner will derive economic benefits from its use. The assessment should, where appropriate take into account the following:

1456
FRS 15 (93)

– contractual or legal restrictions, as in the case of a lease or its covenants; or
– consumption or extraction, which in turn is restricted by capacity or identifiable reserves (e.g. a mine or oil field).

A projection of the useful economic life of a tangible fixed asset should also include an estimate of the impact of such factors as repair costs and the cost of replacement assets. High repair costs may shorten the useful economic life as can the falling cost of replacement assets.

1458   **Revisions**   **Where material in value**, the estimates of useful economic lives should be renewed and revised if appropriate (particularly where a policy of non-depreciation is followed).

1. The useful economic life **can be revised** on an on-going basis reflecting any:
– deterioration in the physical characteristics of the asset through use or the passage of time, which may result from the entity's asset maintenance programme; or
– economic or technological obsolescence resulting from improved technology or changes in market demand for the product or service.

2. **If the useful economic life** of a tangible fixed asset **is revised**, the carrying value at the date should be depreciated (after allowing for any impairment that may have occurred) over the remaining useful economic life of the asset. It should be noted that a change of estimated useful life does not automatically represent a change of accounting policy or give rise to a prior period adjustment.

> EXAMPLE ABC plc owns a paint spray machine which originally cost £200k in January 20X2. The useful economic life of the asset was estimated at 10 years with a residual value of £10k. Annual depreciation was calculated at £19k p.a. on a straight-line basis (£200k-£10k/ 10 years. However after two years, a reassessment of the useful economic life highlighted the fact that changes in technology had **reduced the residual value** to zero and the useful economic life of the asset to 7 yrs, of which five years remained. The revised annual depreciation charge was determined as follows:
> The net book value at January 20X4 was £162k (£200k- £38k (2 years depreciation charge)). This should now be depreciated over 5 years (7-2) giving an annual depreciation charge of £32.4.
> The issue of subsequent expenditure and the possible impact on the UEL of an asset is discussed in ¶1498.

B. Methods

1459   The entity can select from a number of different methods of **calculating depreciation** over the life of the asset, although the straight-line and the reducing balance methods are the most common.

The **choice of method** (and related assumptions of useful economic life and residual value) can have a significant impact on reported profits and asset values in the balance sheet. Furthermore, two companies operating in the same industry can depreciate similar assets differently, thus making comparisons between them difficult.

The **depreciation method adopted is** largely dependent upon the type of asset and its function within the entity and should reflect a realistic, phased charge that matches the consumption of the economic benefits derived from the asset.

1460   A **change from one method** to another is only permissible if it provides a better reflection of the way in which the economic benefits associated with an asset are consumed. However, the use of a **different depreciation method** does not constitute a change in accounting policy, but is simply a change in estimate. The carrying amount of the tangible fixed asset will simply be depreciated using the new depreciation method over the remaining useful economic life of the asset, beginning in the period that the change is made.

If the change in the method of depreciation **has a material effect** on the reported profit for the year, this must be disclosed in the financial statements.

<hr>

1. Principal methods

Straight-line method

The straight-line method **is defined as** the original cost of the asset less its residual value, divided by the estimated number of years comprising its useful economic life. The asset is written off in equal instalments, based on the assumption, that the economic benefits derived from it are consumed evenly over the useful life of the asset.

1462

> EXAMPLE An asset such as a motor vehicle with a useful economic life of 5 years, costing £25,000 and with a residual value of £5,000 would result in an annual depreciation charge of £4000 per annum (25,000-5,000/5).

Although this method is the simplest to apply and is very widely used, it may not be the most appropriate as it is most suited to assets with a short but fixed working life e.g. leasehold property, or plant and equipment including computers. The disadvantage of this method is that an average annual depreciation charge may not reflect the actual consumption of economic benefits derived from the asset.

Reducing balance method

This is a method by which the **annual depreciation charge** diminishes as the asset ages. The depreciation charge is calculated by determining a fixed percentage annual rate, which is applied to the net book value of the asset at the beginning of the period, to arrive at the depreciation charge for the ensuing period.

1463

This **method is designed to** reflect the theory that the consumption of economic benefits derived from the asset reduces as it gets older. Therefore, depreciation is higher in the early years of the asset's life and lower in subsequent years.

Higher initial depreciation charges are offset by low maintenance costs, the reverse of which applies as the asset ages. **Certain assets may become obsolete** quickly and therefore the reducing balance method may be more appropriate.

This method is often used for motor vehicles, in order to match the net book values (NBV) of second hand vehicles to their market values.

The **disadvantages of this method** are:

1464

– that the depreciation charge in the early years can be very high and that it is more complicated to calculate an appropriate depreciation rate; and
– that it will ensure the asset is written down to its residual value by the end of its useful economic life.

> EXAMPLE If a reducing balance rate of 27.5% is applied to a motor vehicle costing £25k with a useful economic life of 5 years and a residual value of £5k, the following depreciation charges will arise.
>
> | Year | NBV Start of year £ | Depreciation charge (27.5%) £ | Closing NBV £ |
> |------|---------------------|-------------------------------|---------------|
> | 1 | 25000 | 6875 | 18125 |
> | 2 | 18125 | 4984 | 13141 |
> | 3 | 13141 | 3614 | 9527 |
> | 4 | 9257 | 2620 | 6907 |
> | 5 | 6907 | 1907[1] | 5000 (RV) |
>
> 1. Rounding

Except for assets that will be sold before the end of their economic life and are expected to have a material residual value, there is some doubt as to whether this is an appropriate method to use.

The sum-of-the-digits method

1466   This method of calculating depreciation is **similar to the reducing balance method**. The estimated life of the asset is first expressed in terms of years, which are then allocated a digit. If an asset is estimated to have a life of four years, year one will be allocated digit 4, year two – digit 3, etc. The sum of the digits is then 4 + 3 + 2 + 1 = 10.

This method front loads the depreciation charge in the earlier years of the asset's life, where cash flows earned by the tangible fixed asset might be highest or the consumption of economic benefits greatest.

One difference between the sum of the digits and reducing balance, is that after a predetermined period, the net book value under the sum of the digits method could be reduced to nil.

1467   The **proportion of the assets cost** (less the residual value) to be written off as depreciation in a particular year is determined by the number of years remaining before the asset is decommissioned, expressed as a proportion of the sum of the years.

EXAMPLE   For an asset with an estimated economic life of 5 years, the sum of the digits will be 5 + 4 + 3 + 2 + 1 = 15. Therefore, 5/15 of the cost (or valuation) is written off in the first year, 4/15 in the second year, 3/15in year 3 and so on.
If the asset cost £25k and has a residual value of £5k total depreciation of £20,000 is required and the depreciation profile will be as follows:

Year	NBV Start of year £	Sum of digits £	Depreciation charge £	Closing NBV £
1	25000	5/15	6667	18333
2	18333	4/15	5333	13000
3	13000	3/15	4000	9000
4	9000	2/15	2666	6334
5	6334	1/15	1334	5000

Where the economic benefit to be derived from an asset is not expected to reduce in a linear fashion, as assumed in the above example, the "digits" applied to each year of the asset's estimated useful economic life do not have to follow a linear series. It should be noted that this method is not widely used.

---

2. Other methods

Production-unit method (output or usage method)

1468   This method of computing the depreciation charge is appropriate where the economic life of an asset is more linked to consumption or usage than to time, such as certain types of machinery and extractive land (i.e. coal, quarries).

1. An estimate is made of the total number of units to be produced over the estimated useful economic life of the asset.

2. A depreciation rate per production unit is then estimated and applied to the production levels for each year of the asset's life.

EXAMPLE   The **formula** for calculating the depreciation rate per production unit is as follows:
C − R/P = PU
Where: C is the original cost;
R is the estimated residual value;
P is the estimated number of production units; and
PU is the rate per production unit.

If we take the asset profile adopted in the previous example and estimate the total output from the asset as 6000 units analysed over its useful economic life as follows:

Year	Production units (estimate)	Depreciation charge
1	2500	2500/6000 * £20000 = £8333
2	1500	1500/6000 * £20000 = £5000
3	1000	1000/6000 * £20000 = £3333
4	750	750/6000 * £20000 = £2500
5	250	250/6000 * £20000 = £834
Total	6000 units	

EXAMPLE In the extractive industries a **number of variations** on the production unit method are used, where estimates are made of the units mined within the accounting period as a proportion of the total reserves.
a) At RXB Mining plc depreciation on mine development is not charged until full production commences or the assets are utilised. On commencement of full production, depreciation is charged on a tonnage-extracted basis over the estimated useful life of the recoverable reserves.
b) Another variation of this method is utilised by a large public utility company, where depreciation on a landfill site is based on the average cost per cubic metre of landfill space, consumed in a given accounting period.

Care must be taken where the production-unit method of calculating depreciation is used as actual production may vary considerably from that originally anticipated. This can result in significant over or under depreciation provision over the useful economic life of the asset. It is important therefore, that at the end of each accounting period, the estimated total production over the remaining useful economic life of the asset is reassessed and if necessary, a revised depreciation rate per unit of production applied.   **1469**

It should be noted that this method is not widely used.

The **revised depreciation rate** per unit of production should be calculated as follows: **1470**

(Net book value at the date of reassessment – estimated residual value)/ estimated remaining units of production over the remaining useful economic life of the asset.

This does not constitute a change in accounting policy, simply a change in accounting estimate and does not therefore, require a prior-year adjustment.

Less common methods Other less common methods include **renewals accounting**, which is applied to groups of infrastructure assets with finite lives that cannot easily be separately identified and the revaluation method, used where the asset to be depreciated is revalued each year at the end of the accounting period and any fall in its value is reflected in the depreciation charged to the profit and loss account.   **1472**

3. Comparison of methods

The summary table reflects the annual impact of the depreciation charge on profits using the most widely recognised methods.   **1478**

In all cases the asset costs £20,000, the estimated useful economic life is 5 years, and the estimated residual value is nil. The charge for the production unit method is illustrative only and the charge would in practice depend on the actual production profile over the life of the asset.

Summary table comparing depreciation methods						
Method	Depreciation charge by year (£)					
	1	2	3	4	5	Total
Straight-line	4000	4000	4000	4000	4000	20000
Reducing balance	6875	4984	3614	2620	1907	20000
Sum-of digits	6667	5333	4000	2666	1334	20000
Production unit method	8333	5000	3333	2500	834	20000

C. Specific depreciation issues

1480   In this section, the accounting treatments are considered for the calculation of depreciation for the following:
– revalued tangible fixed assets;
– assets which have separable components; and
– assets with useful economic lives exceeding 50 years.
The consequences of adopting a **policy of non-depreciation** are also considered.

Revalued tangible fixed assets

1482   For tangible fixed assets that are **subject to periodic revaluation** there is still a requirement to charge depreciation.

The **general rule** is that depreciation charged must be based on the new valuation (less estimated residual value, divided by the remaining useful economic life), rather than the historical cost and must be debited to the profit and loss account.

> EXAMPLE   At 1.1.20X5, the freehold buildings of ABC Ltd, (acquired on 1.1.20X0) have been recorded in the accounts at historical cost and are being depreciated over 40 years. It is estimated that there will be no residual value.
>
> | | Cost | Accumulated Depreciation | Net Book value |
> |---|---|---|---|
> | | £ | £ | £ |
> | Freehold property | 2,500,000 | 312.500 | 2,187.500 |
>
> The freehold properties were then revalued at £3m.
> A revaluation surplus of £812.5k arises being the difference between the net book value of £2817.5k and the revalued amount of £3000k.
> The revaluation surplus of £812.5k (£3m – £2187.5k) will be accounted for as a credit to the revaluation reserve.
> The **original depreciation charge** was £2.5m/40 = £62.5 p.a. The accumulated depreciation charge at 1.1.20XX was £312.5k covering 5 years. The remaining useful economic life is therefore 35 years (40 – 5). The **revised depreciation charge** based on the revalued amount is £3m/ 35 years = £85.7 p.a.

Where an asset has been revalued and the **depreciation charge** in the profit and loss account is **based on the revalued amount**, then in subsequent years there should be a transfer from the revaluation reserve to the profit and loss account. This transfer should represent the difference between the depreciation charge based on historical cost and the charge based on the revalued amount. This transfer is made as a movement on reserves (and disclosed in the notes to the financial statements) and is not reflected in the entity's profit and loss account.

Separable components

1484
FRS 15 (38)   If a tangible fixed asset comprises **two or more significant components** each with substantially different useful economic lives, then each part should be depreciated separately.

Each component is then depreciated over its useful economic life so that the depreciation profile of the entire asset more accurately reflects the actual consumption of the asset's economic benefits.

Any subsequent expenditure incurred in replacing or renewing the component is accounted for as an addition to the tangible fixed asset and the carrying amount of the replaced component is removed from the balance sheet.

The separation of an asset into its individual component parts (including expenditures on overhauls or inspections) for depreciation purposes and will be **based on a number of factors** including one or more of the following:
– whether the useful economic lives of the components are substantially different from the remainder of the asset;

– the materiality (in terms of cost) in the context of the financial statements;
– the regularity (and type) of expenditure required to maintain the asset in different accounting periods; or
– type of asset component.

> EXAMPLE
>
> **a. Land and buildings**, even if acquired together are treated differently for depreciation purposes. Buildings are deemed to have a finite life and are depreciated, whereas land typically does not require a provision for depreciation, unless for example it is subject to depletion through the extraction of minerals.
>
> **b. Buildings and general fixtures and fittings.**
> A building could be depreciated, for example over 50 yrs on a straight-line method which far exceeds the useful economic life of assets acquired within the building, (e.g. the heating systems or the lifts). The element of the purchase price attributable to the provision of the heating system/lifts should be identified separately and depreciated over their own, shorter, estimated economic life.

> EXAMPLE   **Lofgren Haulage Ltd**
> **Annual report and accounts**
>
> **Accounting policy**
>
> **Depreciation**
> Depreciation is provided on operational assets, with the exception of land, over the useful economic lives of the assets as detailed below:
>
> **Fixed assets**
> | | |
> |---|---|
> | Buildings | 50 yrs |
> | Fixtures and fittings | 7-20 yrs |
> | Plant and equipment | 10 yrs |
> | Office equipment | 5-8 yrs |
> | Motor vehicles | 5 yrs |
> | | |
> | Computers | |
> | – hardware | 4 yrs |
> | – software | 5 yrs |
>
> **Separable assets**
> The company owns a fleet of articulated distribution lorries and applies the following accounting policy with regard to the depreciation of separable assets.
>
> | | |
> |---|---|
> | Cab structures | 5 yrs |
> | Truck containers | 10 yrs |
> | Flat bed trailers | 15 yrs |
> | Air conditioning systems | 5 yrs |
> | Freezer units | 4 yrs |
>
> Maintenance expenditure is charged to the profit and loss account, except where this results in the improvement in the asset's service potential, in which case the cost is capitalised and written-off over the useful economic life of the asset.

Where the **trading potential is inseparable** from a property such as a public house or restaurant it should not be treated as a separate asset.   **1486**

Non-depreciation or depreciation over periods in excess of fifty years

In general, all tangible fixed assets are deemed to have a finite economic life and should be depreciated over a period of not more than 50 years. However, the following tangible fixed assets **are generally not depreciated**:   **1488**
FRS 15 (89)

– freehold land; or
– assets capitalised at a fixed amount.

An entity must be able to justify that a policy of non-depreciation is acceptable on the grounds of immateriality, both in aggregate and in terms of individual assets. Depreciation may be immaterial due to:

– a long useful economic life; or

– high residual value (or both).

1489   A **high estimate of residual value** may be justified on the following grounds:

i. the entity has a policy of regular maintenance and repair (charged to the profit and loss account), so that the asset maintains its performance standards;

ii. the asset is not expected to suffer from economic or technological obsolescence resulting from for example, changes in patterns of demand; or

iii. where estimated residual values are material, because:

– the entity has a policy of disposing of similar assets before the end of their useful economic lives; or

– the disposal proceeds of similar assets have been similar to their carrying amounts.

1490   An **impairment review**, in accordance with FRS 11, must be performed annually on tangible fixed assets (other than non-depreciable land), at the end of each accounting period, where:

– no depreciation is charged as it is deemed immaterial because of the length of the remaining useful economic life or where the estimated residual value is not markedly different from the carrying amount; or

– the tangible fixed asset's estimated useful economic life exceeds 50 years.

If there are **difficulties performing an impairment review** on individual assets then assets may be grouped as income generating units (IGUs) (See ¶1550).

1491   **For all other tangible fixed assets**, an impairment review need only be conducted where:

– expectations of future cash flows or discount rates have changed significantly; or

– there are adverse changes in other key assumptions and variables.

SECTION 5

Subsequent expenditure

1494   Subsequent expenditure on tangible fixed assets can be categorised as either **maintenance or performance enhancing** expenditure, although a precise allocation between the two may sometimes be difficult. The issue of depreciation on subsequent expenditure is considered in ¶1484.

Maintenance expenditure

1495
FRS 15 (34)
Maintenance expenditure will be incurred in maintaining the standard of performance of the asset over its estimated useful economic life. The **general rule is** that this type of subsequent expenditure should be expensed as incurred.

Where tangible fixed assets are accounted for as **several components or one element** of the asset is depreciated over a different time scale from the rest of the asset, the cost of replacing, restoring, overhauling or inspecting the asset, or component parts is not capitalised, but expensed in the profit and loss account.

Examples include the routine overhaul of plant and equipment. Without such expenditure the depreciation charge would increase, because the useful economic life or residual value of the asset would be reduced.

Performance enhancing expenditure

1496   Some tangible fixed assets require, in addition to routine repairs and maintenance, substantial periodic expenditure for refits, refurbishment, replacement or restoration of major components.

The **accounting treatment** for subsequent expenditure should reflect the circumstances accounted for on initial recognition of the asset and the depreciation profile adopted.

Where the **initial rate of depreciation** is based on the asset life assuming no additional expenditure, then any subsequent expenditure which enhances its life beyond that original estimate will be capitalised.

Where the **estimated life has been adjusted** to the extended life expectancy, the additional expenditure should be treated as maintenance required to achieve the original estimated life expectancy and written-off immediately to the profit and loss account.

Capitalisation of subsequent expenditure   Subsequent expenditure on a tangible fixed asset can also be recognised as an addition to the asset, and capitalised where:

1497
FRS 15 (36)

– it enhances **the economic benefits** derived from the asset in excess of the previously assessed standard of performance;

– a **component** part of a tangible fixed asset has been **treated separately** for depreciation purposes and depreciated over its useful economic life is replaced or restored; or

– it relates to a **major inspection or overhaul** of a tangible fixed asset that restores the economic benefits of the asset consumed by the entity and reflected in its depreciation charge.

Examples of subsequent expenditure that enhances the economic benefits derived from a tangible fixed asset, include the modification of a plant to increase its capacity or extend its useful economic life or the upgrading of machine parts, in order to improve the quality of outputs or reduce the operating costs of the asset.

Revision of useful economic life   Subsequent expenditure that enhances the economic benefits of an asset could lead to a revision in the estimate of the asset's useful economic life, residual value or the depreciation method adopted.

1498

The **capitalisation of further expenditure** should depend on the revised assessment of the standard of performance of the asset. For instance, the cost of converting storage space into retail space to increase sales capacity should be capitalised. Although this type of subsequent expenditure does not extend the useful economic life of an asset, it may impact on its residual value.

Certain types of subsequent expenditure may impact on either the useful economic life or residual value. For instance, technical developments may result in subsequent expenditure that triggers a revision of the originally assessed standard of performance of a tangible fixed asset, affecting either the useful economic life, residual value or impairment of the carrying value.

Euro conversion costs

The **general rule** is that all conversion costs relating to **modifying systems** to deal with the introduction of the Euro, should be expensed or possibly treated as exceptional items. The exceptions to the rule are where the company has a policy of capitalising software and system costs and that the asset's useful economic lives have been enhanced beyond the previously assessed limit, rather than merely maintaining its current service potential.

1499

Other examples of conversion costs include:

– administrative and planning costs;

– staff training; or

– the adaptation of relevant hardware such as vending machines, cash registers etc.

MEMO POINTS   **UITF 21** "Accounting issues arising from the euro" addresses the issue of subsequent expenditure needed to enhance or maintain existing accounting systems in order to cope with the introduction of the euro.

Gains and losses on disposal

1500
FRS 15 (Appendix IV)

Profits or losses on disposal of tangible fixed assets should be treated in accordance with FRS 3 (the rules of which are repeated in FRS 15) and accounted for in the profit and loss account for the period in which the disposal occurs (see ¶398).

The profit or loss on the disposal of a tangible fixed asset represents the difference between the net sale proceeds and the carrying amount, whether carried at historical cost or at a valuation.

It should be noted that this is inconsistent with the treatment for revaluation gains and losses, which are carried in the STRGL, even though it is the result of the same factors; namely rising prices.

EXAMPLE Replacement asset

Gain on disposal

A new tangible fixed asset valued at £100,000 was acquired from insurance proceeds after a previously held asset was destroyed by fire.
The carrying amount of the destroyed asset was £85,000, which was then removed from the balance sheet and the resulting gain on disposal of £15,000, representing the difference between the insurance proceeds and the carrying amount, was recognised in the profit and loss account.
The new tangible fixed asset should be recorded at replacement cost.

Replacement asset Where an asset (or component of an asset) is replaced, its carrying amount is removed from the balance sheet by eliminating its cost (or revalued amount) and related accumulated depreciation. The resulting gain or loss on disposal is accounted for in the profit and loss account.

Anticipated sale of assets

1502

If a company wishes to dispose of a fixed asset, then the asset is no longer intended for use on a continuing basis in the business. The asset can either be reclassified under a separate subheading under fixed assets of "assets held for resale" or reclassified as a current asset.

Within **current asset investments** only stocks and current asset investments can be revalued under the alternative accounting rules.

Furthermore, a decision to dispose of an asset may trigger an **impairment review**. If a loss is identified, it must be determined whether this is the result of the decision to sell the asset, in which case it should be treated as a loss on disposal, or whether it results from other events.

Disclosures

1508

This section covers the general disclosures for tangible fixed assets required under FRS 15 and the Companies Act, as well as the specific disclosure requirements relating to any revaluation and subsequent expenditure on tangible fixed assets, and the capitalisation of finance costs and leased assets held under finance lease or hire purchase agreements.

General disclosures

1510

FRS 15 requires, that adequate information be disclosed in the financial statements, to enable the user to understand the impact of the entity's accounting policies for the initial measurement, valuation and depreciation of tangible fixed assets on the financial performance on the entity.

There are **extensive disclosures required** in the financial statements for **each category** of tangible fixed asset.   FRS 15 (100)

The following **cumulative disclosures** are required:

1. Cost or revalued amount at the beginning and end of the financial year;
2. Total depreciation charged for the period;
3. Cumulative depreciation charge (or impairment) at the beginning and end of the financial period;
4. Carrying amount (net book amount) at the beginning and end of the financial year;
5. Methods of depreciation adopted;
6. Useful economic lives or the depreciation rates used;
7. The financial effect of a material change in either estimate of useful economic lives or residual values;
8. A reconciliation of the movements on depreciation with separate disclosures for additions, disposals, impairment losses, leases, revaluations, and transfers;
9. Any change in the depreciation method or policy adopted as well as the reason for the change;
10. The amount of any interest capitalised; and
11. The difference between the carrying amount and market value of interests in land, where in the opinion of the directors the difference is significant. This disclosure should be given in the directors' report.

EXAMPLE ABC Ltd
Report and Accounts
31 December 2013

Notes to the accounts	Tangible fixed assets				
	Freehold £m	Long lease £m	Short lease £m	Plant & machinery £m	Total £m
Cost					
Balance as at 1.1.2013	9.8	3.5	2.4	76.6	92.3
Additions	4.7	0.1	0.4	9.4	14.6
Disposals	(3.2)	-	(1.7)	(10.2)	(15.1)
Transfers	-	-	-	(5.0)	(5.0)
Balance as at 31.12.2013	**11.3**	**3.6**	**1.1**	**70.8**	**86.8**
Depreciation at 31.01.2013	0.1	-	0.6	49.6	50.3
Charge for year	0.3	0.1	0.5	8.9	9.8
Disposals	(0.1)	-	(0.7)	(9.0)	(9.8)
Transfers	-	-	-	1.5	1.5
Total depreciation	0.3	0.1	0.4	51.0	51.8
NBV as at 31.12.2013	**10.8**	**3.5**	**0.7**	**19.8**	**35.0**

Example of an accounting policy note.

Depreciation is based on historic cost or revaluation, less the estimated residual values, and the estimated economic lives of the assets concerned. Freehold land is not depreciated. Other tangible fixed assets are depreciated in equal annual instalments (straight-line method) over the period of their useful economic lives. Allowance has been made for technological and commercial obsolescence.

Freehold land and buildings	2%
Short and long lease properties	Period of lease
Equipment:	20%
Furniture, fixtures and fittings	10%
Motor vehicles	25%

Capitalisation of finance cost disclosures

1512
FRS 15(31)

If a policy of capitalisation of finance costs **is adopted**, then the financial statements should disclose the following:
- accounting policy adopted;
- aggregate amount of finance costs included in the cost of tangible fixed assets;
- total finance costs capitalised during the period;
- total of the finance costs recognised in the profit and loss account during the period; and
- capitalisation rate used to determine the total finance costs capitalised during the period.

1514

The disclosures required by FRS 15 governing the capitalisation of finance costs are similar to the requirements of the Companies Acts. **Companies must disclose** in the notes to the accounts, that the interest is included in determining the production costs of particular assets and the amount of interest.

Where finance costs are capitalised by way of simultaneous transfer from the profit and loss account, they should be separately disclosed. The **interest charge** in the profit and loss account will be the net amount, but in the notes to the accounts this should be expanded to show the gross figure with the amount capitalised deducted.

Revaluation disclosures

1518

There are a **number of general disclosures** required for revalued tangible fixed assets and for each class of tangible fixed asset, both under FRS 15 and under the alternative accounting rules in the Companies Act. The **principal disclosures** cover the accounting policies adopted by the company regarding revaluation, and include details on depreciation and any diminution in value of the assets.

1519
FRS 15(74)

Where any **class of tangible fixed assets** of an entity have been revalued, the following disclosures are required for each class of asset, per the balance sheet formats set out in the Companies Act; namely:
- name and qualifications of the valuer(s) or organisation;
- valuation bases adopted (including whether notional directly attributable acquisition costs have been included or selling costs deducted);
- the date and amounts of the valuations;
- whether the valuation is internal or external;
- the date of the previous valuation;
- the cumulative historical cost by class of asset; and
- carrying value including cumulative provisions for depreciation or diminution in value.

These disclosures are given in the notes to the accounts.

1520

Valuation policy A concession is permitted upon the **first application** of FRS 15, allowing an entity to retain previously revalued assets at carrying value. When this policy is adopted, the following disclosures are required up until the date of any disposal:
- that the transitional rules have been adopted;
- that values have not been updated; and
- the date of the last valuation.

This **concession allows** entities to retain any "cherry-picked valuations". However, the above disclosures are required in each year that use has been made of this concession. Likewise, additional disclosures will also be required under the Companies Act.

Where **an entity restates to historical cost** a previously revalued asset, this should be treated as a change in accounting policy, resulting in a prior-year adjustment. Disclosure is required of:
- the reason for the change in accounting policy;
- the cumulative effect on reserves; and
- the impact on profits for the current financial year.

Revalued properties Additional disclosures are required for revalued properties including:

1521
FRS 15 (74b)

– a statement that a property has been revalued as a fully equipped operational entity regarding their trading potential, and the carrying amount of these properties; and
– where material, the total notional directly attributable acquisition costs included in the carrying value.

EXAMPLE **BHI Ltd**
Report and accounts – 31 December 2013
Notes to the accounts (extract)

Movements in cost and depreciation

	Land & buildings	Machinery & plant	Tools & fittings	Assets in course of constr'n	Total
	£'000	£'000	£'000	£'000	£'000
Cost					
Balance as at 1.1.2013	800	350	150	85	1,385
Additions	100	50	25	20	195
Disposals	(15)	(22)	-	-	(37)
Transfers	-	15		(15)	-
Revaluation	65	-	-	-	65
Balance as at 31.12.2013	**950**	**393**	**175**	**90**	**1,608**
Depreciation:					
Balance as at 1.1.2013	120	210	70	-	400
Charge for the year	40	53	15	-	108
Eliminated on disposal	(15)	(18)	-	-	(33)
Revaluation	(55)	-	-	-	(55)
Balance as at 31.12.2013	**90**	**245**	**85**	-	**420**
Net book value:					
At 31.12. 2013	860	148	90	-	1,188
At 31.12.2012	740	140	15	90	985

Report and accounts – 31 December 2013
Notes to the accounts (extract)

5. Land and buildings

Revaluation policy
During each of the last 5 yrs a sample of the freehold and long-leasehold properties owned by the Group's property subsidiary, Rappur Properties, have been valued by external qualified valuers (R. Bittan, C. Clemons & partners). The sample taken on 30 June 2013 has been valued by the external valuers which then formed the basis of the internal valuations performed on the remainder of the group's property valuers by the group qualified internal valuers.

Properties occupied by the Group are valued on an **existing use basis (EUV)**, whilst properties not occupied by Group companies are valued on the basis of **open market (OMV)**. These valuations comply with the RICS Appraisal and Valuation Manual. There is no material difference between the existing use value and open market value. In the opinion of the Directors, there would be no tax payable if all the properties were realised at these values.
The relevant revaluation adjustments have been taken to the revaluation reserve, a surplus totalling £28m (2012 £19m).

Assets held under hire purchase and finance lease agreements

The **following disclosures** are required of tangible fixed assets held under finance leases or hire purchase agreements:

1525
SSAP 21 (49)

– the gross amounts of assets held under finance leases;
– related accumulated depreciation by major class of asset; and
– the total depreciation allocated for the period by major class of asset.

1526   This information may be shown separately from that concerning owned assets or integrated with the total for each major class of owned assets.

For a more detailed review of the disclosure requirements concerning hire purchase agreements and finance lease arrangements see ¶3400.

Small companies

1530

FRSSE 6.19-29
FRSSE 6.1-2

The FRSSE incorporates a simplified version of the requirements of FRS 15 relating to tangible fixed assets and a summary of the main provisions is given in the table below.

Accounting task	Accounting treatment
Valuation	Tangible fixed assets should initially be valued at cost, then written down to their recoverable amount.
Attributable costs	1. Only costs **directly attributable** to bring the tangible fixed asset into use should be included in the cost of the asset. (see also ¶1240) 2. The FRSSE does not contain detailed rules covering costs to be included (or excluded) in the cost of the tangible fixed asset.
Capitalisation of costs	1. Capitalisation of **finance costs** directly related to the cost of the asset is permitted; no guidance given on treatment of specific or general borrowings or the use of a capitalisation rate. The finance costs capitalised should not exceed the total finance costs incurred in the same accounting period. 2. The FRSSE requires that the **capitalisation of directly attributable costs** including finance costs, should be suspended during extended periods where active development is interrupted. Capitalisation should cease when the tangible fixed asset is essentially ready for use. 3. **Disclosure** of finance costs capitalised is required. (see also ¶1280).
Subsequent expenditure	Subsequent expenditure on a tangible fixed asset **should only be capitalised if** it improves the performance/output of a specific tangible fixed asset, or covers costs of restoration or replacement of a component that has been separately depreciated over its useful economic life. In general the FRSSE rules are simpler than those of FRS 15 regarding subsequent expenditure, as it does not cover the accounting treatment for the costs of major inspections or asset maintenance (see also ¶1494).
Revaluation	1. **Carrying value** at balance sheet date should be market value, or where appropriate, current value (i.e. lower of replacement cost and recoverable value). If a TFA is revalued, all assets of a similar type should be revalued. 2. Valuations should be conducted by **qualified valuers** at least once every 5 years or where a material change in value is suspected. 3. **Revaluation gains:** recognise in the STRGL, except where they reverse revaluation losses on same asset previously recognised in the profit and loss account. The gains and losses must be matched. 4. **Revaluation losses:** recognise in the STRGL until carrying amount matches its depreciated historical cost. Further revaluation losses should be recognised in the profit and loss account. 5. **Disclosure** is required of cost or valuation at the beginning and end of the financial year. Disclosures also required include, the year in which a revaluation took place, the basis for this valuation and details of the valuer (i.e. name, qualifications) responsible for the valuations.

Accounting task	Accounting treatment
Depreciation	1. TFAs (cost less estimated residual value) should be depreciated on a systematic basis over its useful economic life. 2. The deprecation **method adopted** should reflect the pattern of consumption of economic benefits derived from an asset, and the expense should be charged to the profit and loss account. 3. TFAs comprising two or more **significant components** – components should be depreciated separately. 4. **Useful economic lives** + residual values of TFAs should be reviewed/revised on a regular basis with appropriate adjustments made to the depreciation charge and carrying values. 5. **Change in method** of depreciation used. Only allowed if it better reflects the consumption of economic benefits derived from the asset and does not amount to a change in accounting policy. 6. **Disclosures required**. For land & buildings and in aggregate for other TFAs – depreciation methods used, details of useful economic lives or depreciation rates and if material, the impact of changes to estimates of useful economic lives or residual values. Also required are details of cumulative provisions for depreciation/diminutions in value, as at the beginning and end of the financial year.
Impairment	(see¶1550)
Additional disclosures	For all fixed assets and goodwill, the cost or valuation at the beginning and end of the financial year, together with details of the following (if applicable): revaluations, acquisitions, disposals and transfers.

SECTION 9

New UK GAAP – FRS 102

The financial reporting standard for small and medium-sized, non-listed entities (FRS 102) not adopting the FRSSE, contains a **small number of differences** from the accounting requirements embedded in FRS 15. FRS 102 was published in 2013 and its although its application is mandatory for accounting periods beginning on or after 1 January 2015, earlier adoption is permitted.

1535

Accounting issue	Accounting treatment under FRS 102
Recognition	Asset recognised when it is probable future economic benefits will flow to the entity.
Initial measurement	At cost (purchase price + costs of bringing assets to location/condition including capitalised borrowing costs).
Residual values (RV)	Based on prices at the reporting date. RV's for appreciable assets (e.g. property) therefore change over time under FRS 102, which in turn impacts on the depreciation charged.
Capitalisation of borrowing cost	Forbidden under FRS 102 which has implications for companies producing goods or assets with long production times, and where the financing costs and impact on asset values and reported profits could be significant.
Subsequent expenditure	Is not actively addressed by the new standard as it does not distinguish between recognition of initial and subsequent expenditure.
Subsequent measurement	Depreciable amount of a TFA should be allocated over its useful economic life. Where an asset comprises components with different consumption patterns, these should be depreciated separately.
Depreciation	Choice of straight line, diminishing balance or units of production method. Depreciable amount = cost less residual value. Land is not depreciated.

Accounting issue	Accounting treatment under FRS 102
Revaluation	After initial recognition TFA's should be valued using the cost or revaluation model. No detailed advice given on required regularity of valuations under FRS 102. FRS 15 is more prescriptive.
Transitional concerns involving adoption of FRS 102	The FRC has issued a **Staff Education Note (SEN05)** in order to clarify certain requirements of FRS 102 when transferring from current UK GAAP. SEN05 compares the accounting treatment for tangible fixed assets under current UK accounting standards (e.g. FRS 15 "Tangible Fixed Assets" and FRS 5 "Reporting the substance of transactions") and Section 17 Property, Plant and Equipment of FRS 102. However, for the majority of entities there are **no significant differences** in the accounting treatment of tangible fixed assets.

MEMO POINTS   In addition to SEN 05 the FRC has also issued **Staff Education Note 12 (SEN 12)**, that compares the accounting treatment for incoming resources from non-exchange transactions under current UK accounting standards and FRS 102. Incoming resources from non-exchange transactions concern primarily donations of cash, goods and services and legacies, not currently covered in existing UK GAAP, other than in relation to gifts or donations received by charities which fall within the scope of FRS 15 Tangible Fixed Assets and the Charity SORP. The SEN highlights key areas of consideration when transitioning to FRS 102.

CHAPTER 5

Impairment of fixed assets and goodwill

Impairment is defined as a reduction in the recoverable amount of a fixed asset or goodwill below its carrying value in the balance sheet. An impairment charge is in addition to normal depreciation. The **principles of accounting** for the impairment of tangible and intangible fixed assets (including fixed asset investments) and purchased goodwill are contained in FRS 11 "Impairment of fixed assets and goodwill".

1550
FRS 11 (2)

The **general rule** is that fixed assets and goodwill are tested for impairment, only if **a number of indicators** suggest a fixed asset (or goodwill), or the environment in which the asset operates, might be impaired. However, in certain circumstances fixed assets and purchased goodwill automatically require annual impairment reviews irrespective of whether an impairment is suspected or not.

A number of other related topics such as the impairment of financial instruments are addressed by other accounting standards and abstracts (see table in ¶1572). The impairment rules for **smaller entities** are less complex.

Small and medium-sized entities not adopting the FRSSE or FRS 11 can also elect to voluntarily adopt FRS 102 "The Financial Reporting Standard applicable in the UK and Republic of Ireland", before it becomes mandatory in January 2015.

SECTION 1
Small companies adopting the FRSSE

1552
FRSSE 6.44-6.49

All **reporting entities** are subject to the provisions of FRS 11, except those smaller entities applying the Financial Reporting Standard for Smaller Entities (FRSSE). For individual company accounts, the FRSSE incorporates the key elements and definitions of FRS 11, including the accounting treatment and recognition criteria for impairment losses and reversals, but does not contain the same level of detail (e.g. disclosure requirements). Small companies preparing **consolidated financial statements** should apply FRS 11 where required to do so by the FRSSE and in full to purchased goodwill arising on consolidation.

> ⌐MEMO POINTS¬ The **terms** impairment and impairment losses are more or less synonymous. For other key definitions relating to impairment see memo point 2 ¶1562.

1553

Accounting issues – individual companies	FRSSE – requirements
Treatment of fixed assets (TFAs) & goodwill	Recorded in balance sheet at no more than recoverable amount (see memo point 2 ¶1562).
Requirement for impairment reviews	Does not specify when an impairment review should be undertaken – but gives situations (e.g. obsolesence) when a review might be triggered. Residual values and estimates of useful economic lives are required on a regular but not annual basis, as in FRS 11.
Impairment losses	Contains main recognition requirements/accounting treatment embodied in FRS 11 (see ¶1670-¶1694); namely that value of TFA should be written down to estimated recoverable amount and depreciated over the remaining useful economic life. Impairment losses (write downs) and any subsequent reversals should be taken to the profit and loss account in the period concerned.
Tangible fixed assets: Reversal of impairment losses due to changes in use or improved economic conditions	If the recoverable amount subsequently increases – the asset's value use should be adjusted to reflect the lower of the revised recoverable amount or the value of the asset had the write-down (impairment) not taken place.Reversal of **write downs** should be taken the profit and loss account. The **exception** is where the original impairment reverses previous revaluation gains resulting from changing market prices, which should instead be carried in the STRGL to the extent that the carrying amount exceeds its depreciated historical cost.
Intangible fixed assets and goodwill capitalised: Reversal of impairment losses due to changes in use or improved economic conditions	If the recoverable amount subsequently increases, a write back to the previous net book value (NBV) is only permitted if the original impairment resulted from an external event that has clearly been reversed but that was not predicted at the outset. For additional details concerning restrictions on reversals of impairment losses on intangible assets and goodwill (see ¶1098).
Disclosures	Restricted to details concerning assets whose value has been reviewed but not changed as outlined below.

The FRSSE does not contain any provisions or guidance covering **capitalisation** of finance costs, the piecemeal construction of fixed assets, costs of inspections and overhauls, classification of start-up or commissioning costs, income-generating units (IGUs), or estimating the recoverable amount.

1554   **Disclosures** Details must be disclosed of any fixed assets that have been **reviewed but not revalued** by the directors and confirmation given of the fact that:

– the directors are satisfied that the stated aggregate value of fixed assets are accurate and that at no time during the financial year did their value fall below that stated; and
– any assets affected are being carried in the financial statements on the basis of a revaluation of the entity's fixed assets that took place at that time.

SECTION 2

Entities adopting FRS 11

Accounting framework

Entities that elect not to adopt the FRSSE must apply FRS 11, the objective of which is to ensure that tangible and intangible fixed assets and goodwill are not carried in the financial statements at more than their recoverable amount, and that:
– any resulting impairment is recognised and measured on a consistent basis; and
– sufficient information be disclosed in the financial statements to enable a proper understanding of the impact of the impairment on the entity's performance.

1555
FRS 11 (1)

Under FRS 11, all diminutions in value, whether temporary and permanent, should be recognised immediately. Impairment losses should be recognised in the profit and loss account, unless they represent the reversal of a previously recognised revaluation surplus that has been credited to a revaluation reserve, in which case the impairment should pass through the STRGL with the revaluation reserve being reduced. The **general rules** underpinning impairment reviews, treatment of impairment losses, reversal of past impairment losses and disclosure requirements are covered in Sections 2-5.

> MEMO POINTS   The financial reporting standard for non FRSSE entities (FRS 102) has now been published and will be mandatory from 1 January 2015. **Earlier adoption** of this new standard is permitted, although the requirements covering impairment are broadly similar to FRS 11, they are less detailed and crucially, there is no requirement to hold annual impairment reviews.

Impairment reviews – overview

The main accounting issues relating to impairment include how to identify an impairment loss and measure the recoverable amount of an asset. An **automatic impairment review** may be required each year or only where certain factors indicate that an impairment has occurred; namely that the carrying value of a fixed asset or goodwill may not be recoverable.

1558

Impairment in relation to **certain fixed assets** and goodwill are addressed by other accounting standards (see table in ¶1572). Irrespective of where another primary accounting standard stipulates that an impairment review is required, the review itself should be conducted within the guidelines of FRS 11.

Measurement of impairment

The **recoverable amount** of an individual fixed asset or **Income Generating Unit (IGU)** will be determined by reference to the higher of net realisable value (NRV) and **value in use**. If the **carrying value** of the asset exceeds its recoverable amount, it is impaired and should be written down to the recoverable amount.

1560

As an assessment of recoverable amount is to look at the higher of NRV and value in use. It is common to look initially at an **estimate of the NRV** of the fixed asset or goodwill. This figure can often be derived relatively easily if there is an active market for the sale of the type of asset under review.

1562
FRS 11 (22) (25)

If this estimate of NRV **proves inconclusive** or turns out to be less than the carrying value, then it will be necessary to perform a more detailed calculation of value in use in order to determine whether an impairment has occurred.

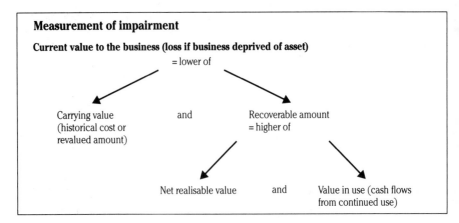

⬚ *MEMO POINTS*   1. The **carrying value** is defined as the value at which an asset (or liability) is recorded in the balance sheet. For example, a fixed asset such as a building will be shown at historical cost less accumulated depreciation to-date. Under the alternative accounting rules the carrying amount is the revalued amount less accumulated depreciation.
2. The **recoverable amount** is defined as the higher of the cash flows generated by the fixed asset or income generating unit either through a sale (net realisable value) or by continued use (value in use).
3. **Net realisable value (NRV)** is defined as the estimated net sale proceeds from a sale of a fixed asset or IGU.(¶1576).
4. **Value in use** is defined as the discounted present value of future cash flows (i.e. income stream) obtainable as a result of an asset's continued use, including those resulting from its ultimate disposal (¶1582).

Impairment indicators

1564   A review may not necessarily be required every year, as the systematic charging of depreciation should ensure that the carrying amount of the fixed asset or goodwill is reduced throughout its useful economic life, so reflecting the reduction in the recoverable amount of the asset, arising from the consumption of economic benefits.

FRS 11 (8)   A **review for impairment** of a fixed asset or goodwill **should only be undertaken** if events or changes in circumstances indicate, that the carrying value of an individual fixed asset (or IGU) (see ¶1590), or goodwill may not be recoverable. Impairment occurs when something happens to affect the value of the fixed asset itself or has altered the environment in which it operates.

1566   **Events indicating impairment**   Common events that indicate impairment include the following:
– a current operating loss or net cash outflow from operating activities;
– expectations of continuing operating losses or net cash outflow from operating activities;
– evidence of physical damage or obsolescence;
– a reorganisation or restructuring of the business; or
– the company has suffered a loss of key employees.

Other **less common indicators of impairment** indicators of impairment are:
1. A significant increase in market interest rates or other market rates of return that are expected to materially affect the assets recoverable amount.
2. There are significant adverse changes in any of the following:
– developments in the market or business segment in which the company operates (i.e. new competitors, new products);
– the regulatory environment governing the business;
– any indicator of value such as multiples of turnover, used to measure the fair value of a fixed asset on acquisition; or
– a significant devaluation of a currency in which the entity denotes its cash flow.
3. The decision to dispose of an under-performing business unit where an analysis of asset values indicates impairment.

Less common indicators of impairment Other less common indicators of impairment   **1567**
indicators of impairment are:
1. A significant increase in market interest rates or other market rates of return that are
expected to materially affect the assets recoverable amount.
2. There are significant adverse changes in any of the following:
– developments in the market or business segment in which the company operates (i.e. new
competitors, new products);
– the regulatory environment governing the business;
– any indicator of value such as multiples of turnover, used to measure the fair value of a
fixed asset on acquisition; or
– a significant devaluation of a currency in which the entity denotes its cash flow.
3. The decision to dispose of an under-performing business unit where an analysis of asset
values indicates impairment.

Automatic impairment reviews

Although automatic annual impairment reviews **are not required** under FRS 11, except   **1568**
where there is an indication that assets might be impaired, they could be required under
other accounting standards as detailed in the table below.

Specific impairment of fixed assets and goodwill not primarily governed by FRS 11	Accounting standard	Reference
1. Intangible assets and goodwill		
a. Requirement for **annual impairment reviews** – on intangible assets and goodwill amortised over a period of 20 years or more or with indefinite useful economic lives.	FRS 10 "Goodwill and intangible assets"	¶1090
b. **Purchased goodwill** written off to reserves under the transitional arrangements.	FRS 10 "Goodwill and intangible assets"	¶1090
c. A **special first year** impairment review (end of first year) for goodwill and intangible assets relating to **new acquisitions**.	FRS 7 "Fair values in acquisition accounting"	¶6864
2. Tangible fixed assets		
a. Tangible fixed assets **other than non-depreciable land**, should be reviewed at the end of each financial year: – when either no depreciation is charged (deemed immaterial); or – the asset's useful economic life exceeds 50 years.	FRS 10 "Tangible fixed assets"	¶1490
b. Impairment resulting from **a fair value exercise** on new acquisitions.	FRS 7 "Fair values in acquisition accounting"	¶6864

Specialist areas covered by other accounting standards

There are a number of specialist areas **exempt from the requirements** of FRS 11, which are   **1572**
covered by other accounting standards.

Specialist areas dealt with by other accounting standards or pronouncements	Reference
1. Financial assets/instruments (FRS 13, FRS 25) Financial assets such as investments in equity and non-equity shares and debt instruments.	¶3400
2. Investment properties (SSAP 19, FRSSE)	¶1900
3. ESOP Trusts Entity's own shares held in an Employee stock option plan (ESOP) and carried as a fixed asset.	¶1780

SECTION 3

Impairment review process

1574   Impairment reviews are a detailed assessment of whether the present value of future cash flows justifies the carrying value of the fixed assets or goodwill. It should be noted that as the underlying cash flow assumptions supporting asset valuations are subjective in nature as they are based on estimates of future events, any impairment write-downs can only reflect broad estimates of impairment losses.

1. The **initial stage** of the impairment review is to estimate the net realisable value of the individual asset or group of assets (IGU).

2. **If this initial review** indicates that the NRV is lower than the carrying value of the individual asset or IGU or that no reliable estimate of NRV is available, then the **value in use** should be calculated.

3. Initially, an estimate of value in use at a post-tax level can be used, although **if this is inconclusive or indicates impairment** then a more detailed calculation (pre-tax level) of value in use is required, involving the calculation of discounted future cash flows (DCFs).

1575

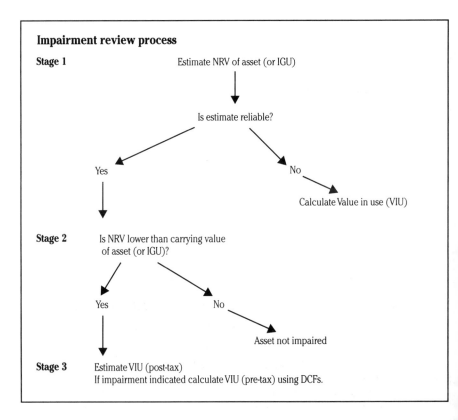

Impairment review process

Stage 1 — Estimate NRV of asset (or IGU)

Is estimate reliable?

Yes / No → Calculate Value in use (VIU)

Stage 2 — Is NRV lower than carrying value of asset (or IGU)?

Yes / No → Asset not impaired

Stage 3 — Estimate VIU (post-tax)
If impairment indicated calculate VIU (pre-tax) using DCFs.

A. Estimating net realisable value

Initial estimate (Stage 1)

1576

NRV of:	Based on
Tangible fixed assets	Market value (e.g. commercial vehicles, computers, plant and machinery).
Other tangible assets – e.g. specialist plant and machinery or buildings	Benchmark may not be available-valuation based on experience or negotiation.
Intangible fixed assets	Difficult to determine where no comparative market exists. For some intangibles such as brands sophisticated valuation techniques have been developed.

1. Where **an asset is being sold**, the expected sale proceeds (less direct selling costs) should equal a reliable estimate of NRV.

2. Where a **business is being sold** subject to a binding contract, the expected sale proceeds may reflect the NRV of the net assets and goodwill.

In determining net realisable value, **selling costs directly related** to the disposal of the asset (e.g. legal costs, commissions) or business should be deducted from the expected disposal proceeds.

1580

Costs or provisions associated with **reducing or reorganising the business**, including redundancy, prior to a sale are not deemed direct selling costs, and so should not be deducted in calculating net realisable value. Provisions for certain costs of re-organisation can be recognised as liabilities, if certain criteria in FRS 12 "Provisions, contingent liabilities and contingent assets" are met; namely, where a company has a constructive obligation to undertake the re-organisation. If the obligation does not exist at the time of the impairment review, no provision should be set aside.

Having determined NRV (Stages 2 and 3)

Where the NRV has been determined, **one of three conditions** applies as illustrated in the table below.

1581

Estimated net realisable value Condition	Accounting treatment
1. If the NRV is **higher** than the carrying amount of the asset.	The asset is not impaired and no further investigation is required.
2. If the NRV is **lower** than the carrying amount of the asset.	Estimate the value in use to determine whether the it is higher or lower than NRV (see table conditions 2 & 3. ¶1584). If NRV **is below the carrying amount** of the asset it should not automatically be written down to this value. This is because, although some assets could only be sold for this lower amount, their value in use may be higher – so this should be calculated.
3. No **reliable estimate** of NRV available.	The recoverable amount should be based on value in use except for specific tangible fixed assets (e.g. fixed asset investments).

FRS 11 (15)

[EXAMPLE] **Based on the conditions stated in the table above.**
Net realisable value

Condition 1 – NRV higher than carrying amount
Company X estimates the value of a tangible fixed asset to be £75,000 less direct selling costs of £5,000, resulting in estimated net sale proceeds (NRV) of £70,000. The carrying value of the asset is £60,000. As the NRV is higher than the carrying amount there is no impairment and no further action is required.

Condition 2 – NRV lower than carrying amount
If the carrying value of the tangible fixed asset were £80,000, so exceeding the NRV of £70,000 Company X would be required to calculate the value in use to determine whether this is higher of lower than NRV.

[MEMO POINTS]   In determining whether the recoverable amount should be based on value in use, or net realisable value, the **deferred tax** (¶9000) that would arise on the potential disposal of each asset should also be considered.

B. Calculating value in use

1582   Value in use is calculated where:
– it has not been possible to measure accurately the net realisable value of an asset or group of assets. As such the only means of determining the recoverable amount is by estimating its value in use; or
– the NRV is lower than the carrying value of asset. In this latter case, value in use will be taken as the recoverable amount where it is greater than the NRV.

FRS 11 (25)   The **general rule** is that the value in use should be calculated for individual assets wherever possible. Where this is not the case, the value in use of an Income Generating Unit (IGU) will suffice.

In reality, it is **often difficult to calculate** the value in use of a single fixed asset as it is the use of groups of assets (and liabilities), together with associated goodwill that generate cash flows. As such, value in use is often determined in total for groups of assets or groups of IGU's, where only material impairments need identification.

1. Quick estimate of value in use (post-tax)

1584   The **carrying value** of each asset or IGU reviewed should be compared with the higher of its value in use or the NRV of the asset or IGU. The possible outcomes are set out in the table below.

It may be possible to dispense with the additional work involved in grossing up a post-tax rate to a pre-tax discount rate, by determining whether an asset is impaired at a post-tax level. Companies need only transfer to a **pre-tax analysis** if impairment is indicated and more detailed calculations are required, as shown by conditions 2 and 3 in the table below.

Estimated value in use	
Condition	Accounting treatment after determining value in use
1. Where estimated value in use is higher than the carrying value.	No impairment has occurred and no further testing is required.
2. If estimated value in use is lower than the carrying value but higher than NRV.	Impairment has occurred but the impairment charge will be based on the difference between carrying value and value in use.
3. Where estimated value in use is lower than net realisable value.	Impairment is measured by reference to net realisable value and not value in use.

> EXAMPLE **Based on the conditions stated in the table above**
> **Value in use**
>
> **Condition 1** If the value in use of a tangible fixed asset is £65,000 and the carrying value is £60,000 then no impairment has occurred.
>
> **Condition 2** If the value in use is £65,000, the carrying value £80,000 and the NRV of £60,000 then the impairment charge should be calculated with reference to the value in use and not the net realisable value (£80,000-£65,000 = £15,000).

2. Detailed calculation of value in use (pre-tax)

Where a **post-tax analysis indicates impairment** then a more detailed calculation of value in use is required, to determine the pre-tax discount rate (see ¶1638) and the pre-tax value in use of the asset or IGU, from which the impairment loss and related deferred tax effects can be calculated.

1586

Where a detailed calculation of value in use **is required**, a number of steps should be followed as set out in the table below. This process is the same for individual assets or groups of assets.

1588

Determination of value in use and comparison with carrying value	Reference
a. Identify the **individual assets or income generating units** (individual or group of assets) comprising net assets and allocated goodwill.	¶1590
b. Estimate the expected **future cash flows** for an asset/IGU (recoverable amount)	¶1614
c. Determine the **pre-tax discount rate** and discount the **future cash flows** of an asset/ IGU to determine the value in use.	¶1638
d. **Compare the value in use** of the discounted cash flows **with the carrying value** of the individual asset or net assets attributable to the IGU (comprising fixed assets and goodwill) and allocate any impairment.	¶1656

a. Identification of individual assets or IGU's

An income generating unit (IGU) **is generally defined** as a group of assets, liabilities and associated goodwill that generates income largely independent of the reporting entity's other income streams. An IGU could also represent a single asset such as a brand. **Examples include** major products or services.

1590
FRS 11 (30)

Assets tested individually   Wherever possible, **assets should be tested individually** when there is an indication that impairment has arisen. In some cases however, impairment may be tested only for **groups of assets** because the cash flows supporting the calculation do not arise from a single asset, but from groups of assets (and liabilities). In these instances, impairment is measured for the smallest group of assets deemed to produce an independent income streams; namely an IGU.

1591

The **IGU's** will generally mirror the structure of the business and its products and services. Income-generating units **can be identified by** dividing the total income of the entity into as many independent income streams as reasonably practical and that are capable of separate measurement.

Level of aggregation   However, the higher the **level of aggregation** of assets and liabilities, the greater the risk that impairment losses on some assets may be obscured by increases in the value of other assets. However, it is possible to aggregate the IGU's for the purpose of calculating value in use, provided that the level of aggregation is reasonable in the circumstances of the impairment review.

1592

MEMO POINTS   Impairment of **fixed asset investments** such as subsidiaries, associates and joint ventures (¶7300) fall within the compass of FRS 11. As their respective cash flows can be measured individually, their value in use should be based on the future net cash flows of the underlying entities that are attributable to the group, rather than on dividend flows. In the case of **associates and joint ventures** the carrying value of the group's interest reflects two elements; namely the group's share of net assets and any purchased goodwill. Any impairments in the underlying fixed assets should have been accounted for in the financial statements of the associate or joint-venture.

Allocation of assets to income-generating units

1594   The assets (and liabilities) allocated to IGU's could include:
- those assets **directly involved** in generating the income:
- an appropriate proportion of those **central assets** used to generate more than one income stream; and
- **purchased goodwill** which if present, should also be apportioned across the IGU's.

The form and content of an income generating unit will vary from industry to industry, as illustrated in the following examples.

EXAMPLE   **Types of income generating-units**

1. Bus company
A long-distance bus company operates a travel network comprising a number of **major routes fed by subsidiary routes**. Decisions about adding or closing any of the subsidiary or feeder routes, are based on the revenues generated by the contribution they make to the revenues derived from the trunk routes; the revenues are not considered in isolation. Each main route and associated subsidiary routes comprise an IGU as the cash flows generated by the major routes are not independent of the subsidiary routes.

2. Brewer-continuous production
A company produces different quantities of beer at a **number of different sites**, not all of which are used to full capacity. In this scenario there is not enough surplus capacity to enable one site to be closed. The cash flows generated by one site will be dependant on the allocation of production across the other breweries. The IGU will therefore, comprise all the sites at which the product can be made.

3. A chain of restaurants
A nationwide chain of restaurants with a large number of outlets can be separated into individual (and small) IGU's. The **cash inflows of each restaurant** can be monitored individually and a sensible allocation of central costs made to each restaurant. Any material impairment is only likely to occur when a number of restaurants within the chain are affected by the same economic factors. In this case it might be possible to group a number of restaurants together in one IGU, such as on a regional basis. However, individual restaurants can also be affected by local factors such as planning, in which case specific restaurants could be accounted for as independent IGU's.

4. Furniture manufacturer
An entity comprises **three stages of production** encompassing the growing and felling of trees, the production of furniture parts and their assembly into finished furniture goods. The output from the first stage is partly transferred to the production of semi-finished goods and partly sold on the open market. The output from the production of semi-finished goods has no external market and is passed in its entirety to the production of semi-finished goods.
The first stage forms an IGU as its cash flows can be separately identified; namely sales to the open market and the transfer price to the second production stage. The second and third stages of production comprises one IGU as there is no external market for the production from the second stage.

Excluded assets and liabilities

1596   All the assets and liabilities of the entity, should be allocated to the IGU's, **except for** the following:
- deferred tax balances;
- interest-bearing debt;
- dividends payable;
- other items relating to financing; and
- disposal of a fixed asset (¶1686).

In addition, where the **disposal of a fixed asset** is planned, the income stream from such an asset should be determined and excluded from the cash flows generated by the IGU. Where the asset is an independent IGU this does not represent a problem, but where the asset is part of a larger IGU, revenues and associated costs must be apportioned.

These assets and liabilities are excluded because the **related cash flows** are also excluded from the impairment calculation, but are taken into account when determining the appropriate discount rate used to discount future operational cash flows in calculating value in use.

Treatment of central assets in relation to IGU's

Central assets such as group or regional head offices, working capital, or computer and research centres, should be identified and apportioned across the IGU's in a logical and consistent manner, so that the total value of the IGU's is equal to the total carrying value of the net assets of the entity. Central assets are included in the IGU's because they are expected to generate sufficient cash flows to recover the carrying amounts of all the entity's assets.

1600

The **non-allocation** of central assets to IGU's, could result in impairment losses on some assets being obscured by other more profitable IGU's. This is because at a combined level there is no impairment of the central assets, as long as the combined assets in aggregate earn a market related return on the carrying values of all assets.

Apportionment of capitalised goodwill

Capitalised goodwill should be attributed to (or apportioned between) IGU's or groups of similar units. There is little guidance in FRS 10 and FRS 11 on how to allocate any purchased goodwill to different business units, except that impairment in goodwill in one business cannot be offset against an increase in value in another dissimilar business acquired subsequently.

1607
FRS 11 (34)

Apportioning goodwill **is difficult in complex group structures**, especially where business are merged with existing operations or are restructured, as FRS 10 does not permit the division of purchased goodwill into positive and negative amounts and FRS 7 requires any impairment be reflected by reducing the fair values of assets on acquisition.

Group companies should keep detailed records of the composition of any purchased goodwill, in order that it can later be allocated (if required) to individual IGU's if required by an impairment review, and for:
– tracking elements of goodwill with different useful economic lives; and
– allocating goodwill to business units subsequently disposed of.

    MEMO POINTS   A **number of methods** have been devised to apportion goodwill to different IGU's on acquisition, the choice of which should reflect the basis on which the business was valued by the market at the time of acquisition. **Earnings-based methods** are appropriate for businesses acquired for their future profit flows whilst asset based methods are more appropriate for asset-based acquisitions such as property companies. A detailed review of these methods is beyond the scope of this book.

Recoverability   Where IGU's are combined for the purpose of testing goodwill, a **two tier review process** is required similar to that used for central assets.

1610

1. Impairment reviews for fixed assets require a **lower level of aggregation** at the level of the IGU to be tested for impairment. A lower level of aggregation means that fixed assets are reviewed at the level of individual IGU's.

2. A **higher level of aggregation** for goodwill is allowed, providing the combined IGU's were acquired as part of the same investment and constitute similar segments of the business. A higher level of aggregation refers to groups of IGU's summed together for the purpose of allocating goodwill.

b. Estimating future cash flows (recoverable amount)

The expected future cash flows of an individual tangible fixed asset or IGU subject to an impairment review, including any allocation of central overheads, should be based on realistic assumptions encompassing the latest budgets or plans.

1614
FRS 11 (36)

There are a **number of constraints** applicable to initial cash flow forecasting for IGU's and **special rules** that apply to the forecasting of cash flows for newly acquired IGU's. The impact of taxation must also be taken into consideration.

Component cash flows

1616   Where the **recoverable amount** of an asset is based on value in use, the asset will be impaired if it does not generate sufficient cash to recover its carrying value including where appropriate, its cost of capital. If interest rates rise, the asset will need to generate higher cash flows to cover financing costs, as such this could trigger a further impairment review.

The cash flows used to estimate value in use **should include the following**:
– cash inflows from the asset or IGU;
– cash outlays directly attributable to the asset or IGU;
– allocation of any overheads attributable to central overheads;
– net cash inflows from disposal of the assets or IGU's subject to the impairment review; and
– cash outflows to maintain operating capacity of existing fixed assets.

Specific exclusions

1618
FRS 11 (38)

Future cash flows **should only be estimated** for IGU's or individual fixed assets in their current condition and with the exception of newly acquired assets or IGU's, should not include:
a. cash outflows or related cost savings such as reducing the number of employees, or benefits that are expected to arise from a future reorganisation for which provision has not yet been made.
b. capital expenditure that will improve the IGU's or assets in excess of their planned or budgeted standard of performance or enhance the future benefits derived from this expenditure.

[EXAMPLE]   **Capital expenditure included within (excluded from) the cash flow forecasts**

The assets comprising an IGU comprise a factory and plant and machinery. The factory is expected to last 50 years, but will need a new roof in 30 years, whilst the machinery needs to be replaced every 10 years. The company expects to be in a position to reduce unit costs of production by extending the factory in order to double production in two year's time.
The replacement expenditure for the 50 years (i.e. for the machinery and roof) should be included in cash flows, but neither the expenditure on factory expansion nor the additional income and revenue expenditure derived from that expansion should be included.

Constraints on forecasting

1624   Forecasts of future cash flows used as a basis for determining value in use of a business are subjective by nature. In order to reduce the risk of over-optimistic forecasting being used to in order to disguise impairment losses and to ensure the reliability of cash flow forecasting, FRS 11 incorporates **two important controls**; namely:
– constraints on the level of **growth rates** used in forecasting; and
– the **requirement to subsequently monitor** the cash flow projections for five years following an impairment review.

1625
FRS 11 (37)

Growth rates   **a.** Longer-term cash flow projections should not assume a rate of growth that normally exceeds the **long-term average** growth rate for the country in which the entity operates.

b. Higher rates can be used in forecasts covering a shorter period, but only in **exceptional cases** can higher rates be used in forecasts exceeding five years, principally where:
– the long-term growth rate for the relevant industry (the industry growth rate) is expected to be higher than the average growth rate for the country; and
– the business concerned is expected to grow in line with projected industry growth, even allowing for the possibility of new entrants.

c. Where an industry growth rate for a **period exceeding five years** has been used, this fact should be disclosed in the notes to the accounts.

d. Furthermore, although the long-term average growth rates in specific industries may exceed the average growth rates for the country, this does not mean that all entities within an industry will grow at the same rate. Progressive industries often attract new entrants so reducing the opportunities for high growth rates for existing businesses.

e. The period before a **steady or declining** growth rate is used should not be longer than five years.

Subsequent monitoring   The **second principal constraint** on estimates of future cash flow projections is the need to monitor the accuracy of cash flow forecasts, for the five years following an impairment review.

Certain **specific issues** are required to be addressed where relevant.

Issue	Accounting treatment
1. Where the actual cash flows are found to be in line with estimates	- no further action is required.
2. Where cash flows are lower than estimated	- an additional impairment loss may need to be provided for in the current period's profit and loss account.
3. Where cash flows are higher than forecast	- a reversal of the original impairment (if recognised) could be permitted.
4. If the monitoring process identifies impairments that would have been recognised in previous years but which have since been reversed	- then the non-recognition of this impairment from a previous year must be disclosed, in order to deter management from building its forecasts on unrealistic assumptions.
5. Where any planned investments or reorganisation assumed at the time of acquisition do not materialise	- the cash flow projections should be revised and any associated benefits embedded in the forecast removed from forecasts used to support future impairment reviews.

Effects of taxation

The standard identifies **two situations** in an impairment review where taxation needs to be considered.

1. **The first of these is** where value in use and net realisable are compared to determine which should be taken as the recoverable amount of a fixed asset or goodwill.

In this situation, the standard requires that the deferred tax balances that would arise on both the value in use and the net realisable value be calculated and then deducted from the gross amount. It is the net value arising in each case which should then be compared to determine which is the recoverable amount.

EXAMPLE   **Impact of deferred taxation on recoverable amount of asset or IGU.**

If the net realisable value of a IGU is £110 and gives rise to a deferred tax liability of £45 and the value in use £100 and gives rise to a deferred tax liability of £30, then the recoverable amount should be based on value in use as follows:

	NRV	Value in use
	£	£
Asset value	110	100
Tax	(45)	(30)
Net	65	70

At first, NRV appears to be higher than Value in use (£110 v £100), but after the tax effects are taken into account, one can see that the recoverable amount should be based on Value in use (£70) and not NRV (£65).

2. The **second situation** relates to the cash flows used in order to arrive at the value in use of an IGU. The accounting standard requires that the discounted cash flows are pre-tax cash flows and the discount rate should be a pre-tax discount rate. Once the impairment process

1626

1628

has been completed and, for example, any provisions for impairment losses made then the extant standards relating to tax should be applied to the resulting financial statements and thus the tax effects of the impairment, if any, will be taken into account.

c. Determining pre-tax discount rates

1638   The discount rate is defined as the rate of interest or cost of capital used in discounted cash flow appraisal calculations and is used to estimate:
- the time value of money;
- the effect of risk in the valuation of a stream of future cash flows; and
- reflects the rate of return an entity requires on its assets.

1639   **Estimating pre-tax discount rate**   The discount rate should be calculated on a **pre-tax basis**. The required pre-tax rate of return is that, which after tax has been deducted gives the required post-tax rate of return.
1. The pre-tax rate is estimated by grossing-up the post tax discount rate to reflect the effective rate of corporation tax levied on the operating profits of the particular asset or IGU.
2. The estimated pre-tax rate should then be adjusted to allow for any **special factors** that might distort the relationship between the post-tax and pre-tax discount rate, such as the timing of cash flows due to accelerated capital allowances.
3. The estimated **pre-tax cash flows** expected from the asset or IGU are then discounted by the estimated pre-tax discount rate, to give an estimated value in use, which should then be compared with the carrying value.
4. Where the impairment loss is estimated on a pre-tax basis, the **deferred tax effect** can be calculated by applying the current tax rate to the impairment loss.

1640   The pre-tax rate can be derived from the post-tax rate and the post-tax cash flows as illustrated in the following example.

> EXAMPLE   **Calculation of pre-tax rate of return and value in use**
> An asset is required to generate a post-tax return of 14%. Therefore, if the asset cost £100, it would be expected to generate post-tax cash flows of £114. The tax rate is 30%.
>
> | | £ |
> |---------------------------------|-----|
> | Pre-tax cash flows | 114 |
> | "tax value" of capital allowances | 30 |
> | net post tax cash flows | 84 |
>
> This £84 is then grossed up to determine the pre-tax cash flows that would be required to leave post tax cash flows of 114.
> Therefore £84 × £100/£70 = £120
> The **required pre-tax cash flows** would be £120, and the pre tax rate of return would be 20%.
> Assuming pre tax cash flows of £120 and post tax cash flows of £114 the value in use assigned to the asset would be £100, irrespective of whether it was calculated by discounting the pre-tax cash flows of £120 by:
> 1. The pre-tax cash required discount rate (20 %); or
> 2. By discounting post-tax cash flows of £114 by the post-tax required rate of return of 14%.
> It should be noted that in this example it has been assumed that the cost of the asset is fully deductible for tax purposes, due to the capital allowances of 100% that are available and, therefore, there are no deferred tax considerations. There is therefore a £30 "tax credit" in effect in respect of these capital allowances which is taken into account in determining the pre-tax cash flow required.

Discount rate adjusted for risk

1644
FRS 11 (Appendix I)
The discount rate should be adjusted to reflect specific risks associated with the entity or industry in which it operates. The purpose is to calculate the value in use of a tangible fixed asset or IGU, by discounting the cash flows derived from their use, at the rate of return the market would expect from a similar asset.

Estimating the market rate – three options	Accounting treatment
1. The weighted average cost of capital (WACC) for the entity adjusted for the specific risks associated with the IGU;	Where the **first option** is selected, the following conditions are of note: 1. Where the cash flow forecasts assume a growth rate that exceeds the long-term average growth rate for more than five years, the discount rate should be increased to reflect the higher level of risk. 2. The discount rates applied to individual IGUs should, when aggregated, equal the entity's overall WACC.
2. The current WACC of a listed company whose cash flows are of a similar risk profile to those of the IGU; or	The **second option** is restricted in use as there will be few listed companies that offer a useful comparison, because they generally have a wider product or service base, larger markets and, potentially, a lower risk profile.
3. The market rate used in transactions of similar assets.	The **third option** is seldom used due to the unique nature of these types of transactions.

1645
FRS 11 (42)

Whichever method of determining the market rate is adopted it must be disclosed in the notes to the accounts.

Cash flows adjusted for risk

As an alternative to using the market rate, the cash flows can be adjusted for risk and then discounted at a risk-free discount rate. Where a risk-free discount rate is used, an indication of the risk adjustments made to the cash flows should be disclosed in the financial statements along with details of the **underlying assumptions** on which they were based.

1654

The discount rate should exclude the effect of any risks for which the cash flows have already been adjusted.

d. Discounting future cash flows to determine value in use

After a stream of future cash flows has been calculated for an individual asset or group of assets, they must be discounted at the agreed pre-tax discount rate, in order to determine the value in use as illustrated in the following example. The value in use is then compared with the carrying value to assess the extent (if any) of the impairment.

1656
FRS 11 (41)

EXAMPLE   **Discounting future cash flows to determine the value in use.**

XYZ Ltd. comprises two IGU's for which the cash flow projections for the next six years have been made. The cash flows have been discounted as follows: The **discount rate** is assumed to be 10% for IGU 1 and 12% for IGU 2.
The **net realisable value** of the assets of IGU 1 and IGU 2 are £5 million and £7 million respectively. The **discounted cash flows** are then totalled to determine the present value in use (i.e. £3,940.5 for IGU 1 and £9,359.7 for IGU 2). These figures are then compared with the carrying value in order to determine whether the IGU has suffered impairment.
The **carrying value** of IGU 1 and 2 is £6m and £8.5m respectively.

	IGU 1 Cash flows: £000	Discount Rate 10%	**Present value £000**	IGU 2 Cash flows: £000	Discount Rate 12%	**Present value £000**
Year 1	800	0.909	**727.2**	2,000	0.893	**1,736.0**
Year 2	600	0.826	**495.6**	2,200	0.797	**1,753.4**
Year 3	900	0.751	**675.9**	2,700	0.712	**1,922.4**
Year 4	1000	0.683	**683.0**	2,400	0.636	**1,526.4**
Year 5	1100	0.620	**682.0**	1,500	0.567	**850.5**
Year 6	1200	0.564	**676.8**	3,000	0.507	**1,521.0**
Value in use			3,940.5			9,359.7
NRV			5,000.0			7,000.0
Recoverable amount [greater of Value in use and NRV]			5,000.0			9,359.7

In **IGU 1**, the value in use of £3,940.5m is less than the NRV, so **recoverable amount** is based on NRV of £5m. The carrying value of the IGU is £6m so the impairment loss is £1m.
In **IGU 2**, the recoverable amount of £9,3597m based on value in use exceeds the NRV of £7m. The recoverable amount of £9,3597m exceeds the carrying amount of £8.5m so there is **no impairment loss**. The entity may be able under the alternative accounting rules and FRS 15 to revalue the asset to reflect the higher value in use.

SECTION 4

Treatment of impairment losses

1670
FRS 11 (21)

The **general rule** is that where an impairment loss on a fixed asset or goodwill is recognised, for instance through physical damage or deterioration in the quality of service provided, the remaining useful economic life and residual value should also be reviewed and where appropriate revised. The new carrying amount should be depreciated over the revised estimate of the asset's useful economic life.

FRS 11 (Appendix II)

Where a **fixed asset or IGU is impaired** it will always be the case that both the value in use and the NRV will be below carrying value. Although this does not mean that a loss is permanent, it is prudent in relation to fixed assets held at depreciated historical cost, that this be regarded as permanent and charged to the profit and loss account.

Particular care should be taken regarding impairment relating to acquisitions, mergers, asset disposals and revaluations. The reversal of impairment losses also requires special consideration.

General rules

1674
FRS 11 (49)

A number of general rules apply as detailed below.

a. A tangible asset with a net realisable value that can be **measured reliably** should not be written down below this value.

b. The **carrying amount** of an IGU that is reviewed for impairment should be calculated as the net of the carrying amounts of the assets, liabilities and goodwill allocated to the unit.

c. The **IGU is impaired where** the carrying amount of the IGU exceeds its recoverable amount, and the extent of the impairment reflects this difference in value.

i. Where there is **obvious impairment of specific assets** then the impairment loss should be allocated against these assets first (Part A of Table below).

ii. Where there is **no impairment of specific assets** then the aim in allocating an impairment loss, is to write down the assets with the most subjective valuation first (Part B of Table below).

Allocation of impairment losses within an income generating unit	
A) Obvious impairment of specific assets	B) No obvious impairment of specific assets
	(Most subjective valuations first)
The impairment should be initially allocated to the specific assets in the IGU, and thereafter: – to any capitalised goodwill asset within the IGU; and – thereafter to any tangible assets in the IGU on a pro-rata basis.	The impairment should be allocated initially to any goodwill in the unit, and thereafter on a pro-rata basis to: – any intangible asset within the IGU; and – any tangible assets in the IGU on a pro-rata basis.
This process is illustrated in scenario 1 below.	This process is illustrated in scenario 2 below.

EXAMPLE **Scenario 1**
Impairment of specific assets

Comparison of value in use to carrying value
An impairment loss of £60 million has been identified and allocated first against specific tangible fixed assets in IGU B, where total carrying value exceeds value in use. The remaining £50 million

has been allocated against capitalised goodwill of £40 million with the balance (£10m) allocated against head office assets.

Income-generating unit:	A	B	Unallocated central assets and cash flows		Sub Total	Impairment	Total
Carrying values:							
Direct net assets	£100m	£150m	(i)		£250m	(£10m)	£240m
Goodwill			£90m	(ii)	£90m	(£40m)	£50m
Head office assets			£40m	(iii)	£40m	(£10m)	£30m
Total carrying value	**£100m**	**£150m**	**£130m**		**£380**	**(£60m)**	**£320m**
Value in use	**£200m**	**£140m**					

Summary
A total **impairment of £60 million** (£10m direct assets, £10m head office assets and £40 goodwill) has been identified is allocated as follows:
1. IGU A. No action required as value in use exceeds carrying value.
2. IGU B plus central assets and overheads:
i) £10 million apportioned against specific assets in IGU B; assuming no intangibles carried.
ii) £40 million is allocated to capitalised goodwill.
iii) £10 million is allocated to head office assets.
If head office assets were carried at NRV, then the £10 million would be allocated between assets in the IGU's on a pro-rata basis.

Scenario 2
No obvious impairment of specific assets – allocate to assets whose recoverable amount is most subjective first.

Calculation of an impairment loss and subsequent allocation
In this example the comparison of carrying value with recoverable amount means that **IGU 1** has suffered no impairment.
In the case of **IGU 2** there is an impairment of £6,140.3 allocated between the different asset categories as illustrated below.
The **carrying value** of the assets in IGU 1 and IGU 2 are as follows:

	IGU 1 £'000	IGU 2 £'000
Goodwill	–	2,100
Trademarks	1,000	400
Tangible fixed assets	1,600	10,700
Stocks	2,200	2,300
Carrying amount	**4,800**	**15,500.0**
Recoverable amount	5,000	9,359.7
Lower of carrying value and recoverable amount	4,800	9,359.7
Impairment loss	**0**	**6,140.3**

Allocation of the impairment loss – IGU 2

		Impairment loss	Recoverable amount
Goodwill		2,100.0	0
Trademarks		400.0	0
Tangible fixed assets	(1)	2,996.2	7,703.8 (3)
Stocks	(2)	644.1	1,655.9 (4)
Total		**6,140.3**	**9,359.7**

Notes
(1) Tangible fixed assets – impairment: £6,140.3 – £2,500 (£2,100 + £400: goodwill + trademarks) = £3,640.3 × (£10,700/£13,000 = tangible fixed assets + stocks)) = £2,996.2
(2) Stocks – impairment £3,640.3 × (£2,300/ £13,000) = £644.1
(3) Tangible fixed assets revised carrying value – £10,700/£13,000 × £9,359.7 = £7,703.8
(4) Stocks revised carrying value – £2,300/£13,000 × £9,359.7 = £1,655.9

a. Allocation of impairment when acquired businesses are merged with existing operations

1680 There are **specific requirements** regarding the measurement of an impairment arising after a purchased business has been merged with existing operations.
1. A single IGU that results from the merger of an acquired operation with an existing operation includes assets and liabilities of both acquired and existing business, will also combine both purchased and internally generated goodwill arising from previous operations.
2. If an impairment review of the combined IGU is later required, its value in use will be compared with the carrying value. The value in use of the IGU will comprise:
– carrying values of the recognised net assets of the acquired and existing businesses; and
– the carrying value of the purchased goodwill relating to the acquired business.

Notional carrying amount

1682
FRS 11 (51)
Any **future impairment of the combined business** will need to be apportioned between the purchased and internally generated goodwill, by notionally adjusting the carrying amount of the IGU, to take account of the internally generated goodwill of the existing operation at the date the businesses are merged.

Even **where an impairment review is not required** at the point of the "merging" of the two elements of the business the distinction should still be drawn between internal and purchased goodwill, in order to provide an accurate basis for any future impairment reviews that might be required.

Notional carrying value of a combined IGU.		
	Net Assets	Goodwill
Acquisition	Fair value	Purchased
Existing businesses	Carrying value	Internally generated
		Purchased (i.e. earlier acquisitions)
		Purchased (previously written-off to reserves under FRS 10 transition rules).

1683
FRS 11 (52)
Notional value of internally generated goodwill 1. The notional carrying amount of the internally generated goodwill is first estimated, by deducting the fair value of the net assets and purchased goodwill within the existing IGU, from its estimated value in use before the businesses are combined.

2. The notional value of internally generated goodwill of the existing business is added to the carrying amount of the newly combined IGU for the purpose of performing an impairment review on that combined IGU. The notional goodwill is assumed to be depreciated on the same basis as purchased goodwill, even though it is not recognised in the financial statements.

Initial recognition of impairment

1684
FRS 11 (50)
At the date an acquired businesses is merged with an existing business, and the **aggregate carrying value** of the net assets and goodwill, (including the notional internally generated goodwill) exceeds the **recoverable amount** of the IGU, the resulting impairment should recognised as follows:

Any impairment should **first be allocated** entirely to the purchased goodwill within the newly acquired business and recognised in the consolidated profit and loss account. The logic for this is that any impairment relating to notional internally generated goodwill will have been identified when the fair value exercise was undertaken on acquisition. Therefore, any further impairment identified must relate to the purchased goodwill of the acquired business.

Subsequent impairments

Subsequent impairments should be allocated pro-rata reflecting the current carrying values, **1685**
between the goodwill of the acquired business and the existing business;

1. the impairment allocated to the existing business should be first apportioned to the internally generated goodwill; and

2. only the impairments allocated to purchased goodwill (or recognised intangible or tangible assets) should be recognised in the profit and loss account.

EXAMPLE **Where an acquired operation is merged with existing operations – allocation of**   FRS 11 (53)
impairment losses

Initial allocation
1. An entity acquires a business for £60 million with net assets with a total fair value of £80 million, resulting in **purchased goodwill** of £20 million. The acquired business is merged with an existing operation that has net assets with a fair value of £100 million and a carrying amount of £70 million. Purchased goodwill is amortised over ten years.
The **value in use** of the existing operation at the time of the acquisition is £150 million, resulting in internally generated goodwill of £50 million. The comparison with the value in use may have resulted in the recognition of any impairment of the existing business at the time it was merged with the acquired operation.

2. **Subsequent impairments** must be attributed between the internal goodwill and the purchased goodwill on a pro-rata basis reflecting their current carrying values.

3. After five years
The carrying amount of the net assets of the combined IGU is £105 million and the carrying amount of the purchased goodwill is £10 million. Value in use is calculated at £119 million. There is no reliable estimate of net realisable value.

4. Calculation of the impairment loss	£m
Carrying amount of acquired assets	105
Carrying amount of goodwill	10
Notional carrying amount of the internally Generated goodwill at acquisition date – calculated on same basis as purchased goodwill.	25

i.e. The purchased goodwill has been amortised by 50% therefore for the purposes of the impairment review so too should the notional internally generated goodwill identified at the date of the merger.

Total	140
Value in use	119
Impairment	21

Accounting treatment

Scenario A) The impairment of £21 million should be **allocated** on a pro-rata basis as follows:
– purchased goodwill £10 million (10/25 = 2/7) = £6m
– internally generated goodwill £25 million (25/35 = 5/7) = £15m
Purchased goodwill should be written down to £4 million (£10m – £6m).
(£21m x 2/7 = £4m).
Internally generated goodwill should notionally be "written down" to £10 million (25m -£15m)
(£21m x 5/7).
But as the internally generated goodwill is not recognised in the financial statements this aspect of the impairment is entirely notional and does not impact upon those financial statements.

Scenario B) If the **value in use** were calculated at £98 million, the resulting impairment loss of £42 million would be allocated as follows:
– first against purchased goodwill and notional internally generated goodwill) £35 million,
– then to any intangible assets,
– then any tangible fixed assets in the IGU.

The resulting impairment loss of £42 million (£140m – £98m) should be recognised as follows:
– a write down of purchased goodwill of £10 million.
– a notional write down of internally generated goodwill of £25 million.
– a write down of intangible and tangible assets of £7 million.

b. Disposal of assets

1686
FRS 11 (31)

Where an asset is to be disposed of it should be regarded as an IGU in its own right and not part of any other IGU. The **estimated disposal proceeds** should be factored into the calculation of its recoverable amount as opposed to using cash flows from continued use. If the carrying amount of the asset for sale exceeds the recoverable amount, the asset is impaired.

Impairment losses arising on the intended disposal of an asset should be recognised as soon as a decision to dispose of an asset has been taken.

> MEMO POINTS   FRS 12 "Provisions and liabilities" forbids the recognition of provisions for liabilities in respect of the sale of a business or disposal of an asset, unless:
> – there is binding contract for sale; or
> – a constructive obligation to transfer resources has been incurred.

EXAMPLE **Disposal of a group of assets**

XYZ Ltd. intends to dispose of a group of assets whose recoverable amount of £95,000 is below their carrying values of £140,000. The recoverable amount of £95,00 is the value in use to the group. This results in an estimated loss of £45,000 which should be taken to the current period profit and loss account.

c. Revalued fixed assets

1690
FRS 11 (63)

Impairment losses arise on revalued fixed assets when the asset's recoverable amount falls below its carrying amount.

The **general rules** are as follows:
1. An impairment loss on a revalued fixed asset should be recognised in the profit and loss account where it is caused by a clear **consumption of economic benefits**, such as physical damage or a decline in the quality of service provided by the asset.
2. Other impairments of revalued fixed assets caused by **a general fall in market prices** should be recognised in the STRGL until the carrying amount reaches its depreciated historical cost, and thereafter in the profit and loss account.
3. Where an **impairment loss has been recognised** it is important that detailed records are kept, in order that any reversal (see ¶1694) of an impairment loss can be substantiated and recognised in later years.
4. Where **assets are revalued upwards,** the historic cost is adjusted to reflect the revalued amount.

The accounting treatment for any impairment in subsequent years is illustrated in the following example.

EXAMPLE **Impairment loss on a revalued fixed asset – accounting treatment**

A **fixed asset** costs £3 million and has a useful economic life of 10 years with no residual value. It is depreciated on a straight-line basis and **revalued annually**. At the end of years 1 and 2 the asset is revalued and has a market value of £3.6 million and £2.1 million respectively. The historical costs are shown for comparison.

	Historical cost £	Revaluation £
Year 1		
Opening carrying value	3,000,000	3,000,000
Depreciation	(300,000)	(300,000)
Revaluation surplus		900,000
Closing carrying value	**2,700,000**	**3,600,000**

Year 2

Opening carrying value	2,700,000	3,600,000
Depreciation	(300,000)	(400,000)
Impairment loss		(1,100,000)
Closing carrying value	**2,400,000**	**2,100,000**

Depreciation on historical cost is calculated £3.6m/10 years = £300,000 per annum. After revaluation the new carrying value of £3,600,000 is depreciated over its remaining useful economic life of nine years.

The resulting impairment loss of £1.1 million should be recognised in year 2. The accounting treatment will depend on the reason the impairment arose.
a. If the impairment was due to the consumption of economic benefits, such as physical damage, then the loss of £1.1 million should be charged to the profit and loss account.
b. In other circumstances the carrying amount based on the revaluation policy immediately before impairment, needs to be compared with what the depreciated historical cost would have been immediately before impairment:

	£	
Carrying amount based on revaluation	3,200,000	(£3.6m-£400,000)
Depreciated historical cost	(2,400,000)	(£2.7m- £300,000)
Total	800,000	

£800,000 of the impairment can be deducted from the **revaluation reserve**, leaving £300,000 (Impairment loss of £1.1 million – £800,000) to be charged to the profit and loss account. £300,000 equals the loss where the asset to be carried at historical cost.

---

d. Reversal of impairment losses

FRS 11 contains different rules covering the recognition and reversal of an impairment loss for tangible fixed assets and investments, and for intangible assets and goodwill.   **1694**

Tangible fixed assets and investments

The reversal of past impairment losses can be recognised, when the recoverable amount of   **1696**
a tangible fixed asset (or investment in a subsidiary, an associate or joint-venture) has increased because of a change in economic conditions or in the expected use of the asset. This will normally be the reverse of the economic conditions that triggered the original impairment.

General rules	
1. A **reversal** of an impairment loss should be recognised in the profit and loss account	- to the extent that it increases the carrying amount of the asset up to the amount at which it would currently be carried, had the original impairment not been recognised. This is after taking into account the annual depreciation charges that would have arisen between the date of the impairment and the date of the reversal.
2. Any **balance remaining** of the reversal of impairment	- should be recognised in the Statement of Total Recognised Gains and Losses (STRGL).
3. Provisions for **diminutions in value**	- must be written back if the reasons for the impairment provision cease to apply. There may be practical problems in applying these rules as it may be difficult to distinguish between increases in the value of a fixed asset or IGU, because the reasons for the impairment no longer apply or as a result of increases in value through other reasons.
4. The **reason** an impairment loss has been recognised	- should be disclosed in the accounts (see Table B ¶1710).

1700   **Exceptions**   The **general rules** outlined above **do not apply to the following**:
a. Where the asset was previously revalued in which case the reversal should be accounted for as stated in ¶1690.
b. The recognition of an increase in the recoverable amount of a tangible fixed asset, above the amount that its carrying amount would have been had the original impairment not occurred, is a revaluation and not a reversal of an impairment.
c. Increases in value in use should not be recognised as reversals of impairment losses if they:
i. reflect the passage of time (increases in the discounted value of future cash flows as they become closer) rate; or
ii. the occurrence of forecast cash outflows which once they have happened no longer form part of the value in use calculation and as a result, the value in use increases.
In such cases, the increases in value should be treated as revaluation surpluses and taken to the revaluation reserve.

Intangible assets and goodwill

1704   The accounting treatment under FRS 11 regarding intangible fixed assets is consistent with principles laid down in FRS 10 "Goodwill and intangible assets"; namely that the revaluation of goodwill is prohibited, but that the revaluation of intangible assets is permitted in certain circumstances. Increases in the value of internally generated intangible assets should not be recognised.

1705
FRS 11 (60)

The **general principle** is that the reversal of an impairment loss relating to goodwill or intangible assets, resulting in an increase in the recoverable amount, should be recognised in the current period only if:
a. An **external event** caused the recognition of the impairment loss in previous periods, and subsequent events clearly reverse the effects of the original event, in a way that was not foreseen in the original impairment forecast (as with tangible fixed assets); or
b. The impairment loss arose on an intangible asset with a readily ascertainable market value and net realisable value based on that market value, has increased above the assets impaired carrying amount.

Where an **impairment loss (recognised) has been reversed**, the carrying amount of the asset should be increased up to the pre-impairment level (after adjusting for depreciation), and an increase recognised in excess of this level is regarded as a revaluation and may not be recognised unless it satisfies the conditions set out in FRS 10.

EXAMPLE **Impairment losses – allocation and subsequent reversal**

An IGU consisting of a factory, plant and equipment and purchased goodwill becomes impaired, because the products it manufactures have become outdated compared with a competitors product.
The recoverable amount of the IGU falls to £60 million, with an impairment loss of £80 million recognised, but not attributable to identifiable tangible fixed assets.

	Carrying amounts Before impairment £m	Impairment £m	Carrying amounts after impairment £m
Goodwill	40	(40)	-
Patent – no market value	20	(20)	-
Tangible fixed assets	80	(20)	60
Total	140	(80)	60

The impairment loss is first allocated to goodwill (£40m), then other intangibles (£20m) with the balance of £20m set against tangible fixed assets.
After four years the entity makes its own technological breakthrough and the recoverable amount of the IGU increases to £90 million. The carrying amount of the tangible fixed assets had the impairment not occurred would have been £70 million (£80m – £10m depreciation charge).

Reversal of impairment and allocation
1. The impairment loss is reversed to the extent that the carrying amount of the tangible fixed asset is increased to the **pre-impairment value**, i.e. a reversal of £10 million of the original impairment loss of £20 million is recognised (the other £10 million represents depreciation) and the tangible fixed

assets written back to £70 million which is what their carrying value would have been had their not been an impairment recognised in the first place.

2. Reversal of the impairment is not recognised **in respect of** the goodwill and patent, because the event causing the reversal was not reversed; the original product has still been overtaken by a superior model and the original goodwill and patent is still therefore impaired. As such £20m of the £30m revaluation is not recognised.

SECTION 5

Disclosures

Impairment losses recognised in the profit and loss account should be included within operating profit under the appropriate statutory heading and disclosed as an **exceptional item** if appropriate.

1710
FRS 11 (67)

Impairment losses recognised in the STRGL must be disclosed separately on the face on that statement.

Table A	
Presentation and disclosures for impairment losses arising on revalued fixed assets	
1. Assets carried on a **historical cost basis**.	Impairment loss included within cumulative depreciation. The cost of the asset should not be reduced.
2. Revalued assets held at **market value** (e.g. existing use or open market value).	Impairment loss included within the revalued carrying amount.
3. Revalued assets held at **depreciated replacement cost**.	**a.** Impairment loss charged to profit and loss account should be included within cumulative depreciation. The carrying amount of the asset should not be reduced. **b.** An impairment loss charged to the STRGL should be deducted from the carrying amount of the asset.

FRS 11 (68)

Table B	Additional disclosures concerning impairment losses
Discount rate	Where the impairment loss is measured with reference to the value in use of a fixed asset or IGU, then the discount rate applied to the cash flows should be disclosed. If a risk-free discount rate is used a note of the adjustments made to the risk profile of the cash flows should be given.
Value in use-measurement	Where the period before a steady or declining long-term growth rate has been assumed, extends to more than five years, the longer period adopted and the reasons justifying it should be given.
Recognition in previous period	Where an impairment loss would have been recognised in a previous period if the forecasts of future cash flows had been more accurate, but the impairment has reversed and recognition of the reversal is permitted, the impairment loss now identified and its subsequent reversal should be disclosed.
Reversal of impairment loss	Where an impairment loss recognised in a previous period is reversed in the current financial period, then the reasons for so doing should be disclosed, including the revised assumptions upon which the new calculation of recoverable amount is based.
Forecasting	Where the long-term growth rate used in the measurement of value in use exceeds the long-term average growth rate for the country or countries in which the entity operates, disclosure is required of the assumed growth rates and the reasons for their selection.

FRS 11 (69)

SECTION 6

New UK GAAP – FRS 102 provisions

1720
FRS 102 (27)

The FRC has published FRS 102 "The Financial Reporting Standard applicable in the UK and the Republic of Ireland", applicable to **smaller entities** not adopting the FRSSE. Application of the new standard is mandatory from 1 January 2015. The key elements of the new standard concerning impairment are set out in the table below. There are **no significant differences** in the treatment of impairment between old UK GAAP (FRS 11) and new UK GAAP under FRS 102.

Topic	Overview of FRS 102 – Impairment of assets other than inventories
Principle	Impairment review required where there are indicators of impairment; namely the recoverable amount of the asset is lower than the carrying value. The recoverable amount is the higher of an asset's far value (less selling costs) and its value in use. Value in use equals the present value of future cash flows generated by the asset.
CGU's – allocation impairment losses	Loss matched first against any goodwill and then against other assets in the cash generating unit (CGU).
Reversal of impairment losses	Only permitted if the reasons for the impairment loss are no longer valid. Individual assets- reversal taken to the profit and loss account up to the pre-impairment level. For a CGU any reversal is apportioned against assets in the unit on a pro-rata basis.
Goodwill – impairment review	Goodwill acquired as part of a business combination should include goodwill attributable to non controlling interests (NCI).
Transition phase to FRS 102	First accounts produced under FRS 102 – No exemptions relating to impairment available. Accounts prepared on the basis that FRS 102 requirements have always applied. Amounts recorded under old UK GAAP will be carried forward in the opening FRS 102 balance sheet (Statement of Financial Position).

[*MEMO POINTS*]   1. The **accounting treatment** relating to the impairment of construction contracts, stocks, deferred tax assets, financial assets and investment properties are covered in the respective chapters dedicated to these topics.

2. The FRC has issued **Staff Education Note 3: "Impairment of trade debtors"** (SEN 03) detailing the requirements for the impairment of financial assets measured at cost or amortised cost. There are some differences in the degree of guidance provided for identifying and measuring impairments. The SEN is designed to help the transition phase to new UK GAAP and the adoption of FRS 102.

CHAPTER 6

Fixed asset investments

Fixed asset investments **are defined as** assets which are intended for use on a continuing basis in the company's activities; thereby distinguishing them from current asset investments (¶2700) which are held for the short-term. There is no specific UK accounting standard that deals with fixed asset investments, although there is a choice of measurement (valuation) bases. For **companies applying** the **FRSSE** the accounting requirements are the same.

1750

A. Small companies adopting the FRSSE

Initially, fixed asset investments should be **measured at cost**. Alternatively, they may be measured at a market value determined as at the date of their last valuation or on any other value determined by the directors to be appropriate. In this event, the method of valuation adopted and the reasons for adopting it should be disclosed by way of a note to the accounts. Gains and losses must be recognised in the profit and loss account or STRGL using the same basis applied to tangible fixed assets.

1751

Revaluation   Where fixed asset investments have been revalued, either the **comparable amounts** determined under the historical cost accounting rules (i.e. the aggregate historical cost amount that would have been included had the assets not been revalued, reflecting any write-downs to recoverable amount that would have been necessary) or the differences between those amounts and the corresponding amounts actually shown in the balance sheet should be shown separately in the balance sheet or in a note to the accounts.

1752
FRSSE 6.31

Disclosures   The key disclosure requirements for fixed asset investments include the aggregate amount of **listed investments** included under each item of investments in the balance sheet. For each investment the following must be disclosed:
– the aggregate market value of the listed investments differs from the amount at which they are shown in the balance sheet;
– both the market value and the stock exchange value, where the market value is deemed higher than the stock exchange value.

1753
FRSSE 6.32

1754
FRSSE 6.33

If a company has at the end of the financial year a **significant holding in an undertaking** that is not a subsidiary and the holding represents either 20% or more of the nominal value of any class of shares in the undertaking, or more than 20% of the book value of the investing company's total assets, it must disclose the following:
- the name of the undertaking;
- if incorporated outside Great Britain, the country in which it is incorporated;
- if unincorporated, the address of its principal place of business;
- the identity and proportion of the nominal value of each class of shares held;
- the aggregate amount of the capital and reserves of the undertaking as at the end of the most recent financial year ending with or before that of the investing company; and
- its profit or loss for that year.

B. Medium and larger entities

1. Classification

1755

Investments should be classified as fixed where the company can demonstrate that it intends to hold them on a **long-term basis**, depending on:
- the nature of the investment;
- the investment strategy of the company; and
- whether there are restrictions on the investor's ability to dispose of the investment.

1756

Investments that are **not intended to be held for the long-term**, should be classified as current asset investments. If the value of the investments held by a company is material, the accounting policies should provide details of the criteria applied in determining whether or not an investment is a fixed asset. Investments is a **main heading** which appears on the face of the balance sheet under fixed assets. A number of subheadings are required for fixed asset investments as set out in the Companies Acts, with different requirements for small companies.

Balance Sheet formats (extract)	
Small Companies (FRSSE)	**Large & medium-sized companies**
B Fixed Asset Investment	**B Fixed Assets**
III Investments	**III Investments**
– Shares in group undertakings and participating interests – Loans to group undertakings and participating interests – Other investments (non-loans) – Own shares	– Shares in group undertakings (subsidiaries) – Shares in participating interests (Associates, Joint-ventures, Qualifying Partnerships) – Loans to participating interests – Loans to group undertakings – Other loans – Other investments (non-loans) – Own shares

Shares in group undertakings

1760

Shares in group undertakings are investments by a parent company (be it the ultimate or the intermediate parent within a group) in a subsidiary undertaking.

Shares in participating interests

1762
FRSSE 6.33

A participating interest is defined in the Companies Act as an interest in the shares of another undertaking that are intended to be **held on a long-term basis**, for the purpose of seeking to **exercise control** or influence the activities of the entity. Participating interests include holdings in qualifying partnerships, unlimited companies and associates and joint-ventures, but exclude interests in subsidiary undertakings.

MEMO POINTS   A **qualifying partnership** or **unlimited company** is an entity governed by the laws of the United Kingdom, each of whose members are a limited company or another unlimited company, whose members are a limited company.

Holdings of 20% or more   A participating interest is deemed to be a **holding of 20% or more** of the nominal value of share capital or where the value carried in the investing company's accounts exceeds one-fifth of the assets of the investing company. Where the investing company **does not prepare consolidated financial statements**, but holds a 20% or more shareholding in another entity, that investment should be shown as a participating interest. This category also includes interests in associates and joint ventures.   **1763**

Where the investment is included in the consolidated balance sheet, any shareholding in excess of 20% should be shown under a sub-heading of fixed asset investments, termed "interests in associated undertakings" or "interests in joint-ventures". If the shareholding relates to **non-voting shares** then the investment should be classified under "other participating interests".

Holdings of less than 20%   A holding of less than 20% is considered to a participating interest if the investor exerts considerable influence over the strategic policies of the company. An interest includes any convertible rights and options or interests held on behalf of the company.   **1764**

Loans to group undertakings and participating interests

The balance sheet formats include categories for amounts owed to and from group undertakings. The **classification of loans** to group and participating undertakings will depend on the terms of each loan agreement and in particular the repayment terms of the loan.   **1770**

Group undertakings   Many types of loan between companies in a group are often not governed by a formal agreement, having been made on an informal basis, with no agreed repayment terms. These loans may be intended to meet the capital requirements of various group companies and are often **long-term in nature**, representing investments that will be used on a continuing basis in the group. If that is the intention they should be classified as fixed asset investments. Loans made to group undertakings on a **short-term basis** and routine trading balances should be classified as current asset investments and shown under debtors.   **1772**

Where a **parent company has loans both to and from** its subsidiary companies, it may not offset these loans against each other in arriving at the amounts to be disclosed in the parent's balance sheet.   FRS 5 (29)

The loans to and from each group undertaking should be considered separately and classified appropriately, according to their terms.

Loans to 3rd parties

Loans to third parties should be classified as fixed asset investments if: **1776**
– the term of the loan would be regarded as long term; or
– they are related to the company's activities such as establishing a new trading venture with a partner or supplier.
These types of loans should be covered by a **formal agreement** stipulating payment dates and interest arrangements. Other types of loan that are **less than 12 months** or are unrelated to the company's activities should be included in debtors.

MEMO POINTS   Determining whether a loan is long-term or not is somewhat of a grey area and therefore, the **purpose behind the loan** is as important as the length of the loan period.

Other investments (non-loans)

Fixed asset investments other than group undertakings and participating interests can include: **1778**
– listed and unlisted shares;
– time deposits with banks and building societies;

– life insurance policies; and
– unusual investments (e.g. debenture holdings, entitling the holder to tickets at a major sports grounds).

The **classification** of other investments as either a fixed or current asset investment will depend on the rationale behind making the investment.

"Own shares"

1780 The **general rule** is that a company (including a subsidiary company) is not permitted to own its own shares, except where it is acting as a personal representative for a third party or trustee, and where either the holding company or subsidiary has no beneficial interest.

1782 Under UK legislation, there are a number of instances where **shares can legally be held by a subsidiary in a parent**. These include situations where shares in the parent were acquired:
– by forfeiture, surrender or way of a gift;
– by a company before it became a subsidiary of that parent; or
– where a subsidiary company has held the shares since prior to the Companies Act 1948.
The rules governing the accounting treatment and disclosure requirements of different types of "own shares" are dealt with in share capital and reserves (¶3600).

1784 Where a company owns shares in **an entity that subsequently purchases it**, then any shares so held will not carry voting rights at company meetings. If the shares are held for the continuing benefit of the sponsoring company, they must be accounted for as "own shares" within fixed assets or as current assets.

---

2. Measurement

1785 Fixed asset investments can be recorded in the financial statements using different valuation regimes as set out in the table below.

Regime choice – initial recognition	Regulation
Historical cost	Companies Act (SI 2008/410 Sch 17); FRSSE
Alternative accounting rules (Market valuation)	Companies Act (SI 2008/410 1 Sch. 32 (3))
Statement at fair value (Listed companies only/ IFRS)	Companies Act + FRS 26/FRS 29 (some exceptions)

---

a. Historical cost

1786
FRSSE 6.30

The **general rule** is that fixed asset investments are initially measured at historical purchased cost. **Alternatively**, fixed asset investments can be valued at market value (alternative accounting rules) based on the last valuation or other basis deemed appropriate by the directors, with the relevant disclosures regarding method adopted and accompanying reasons given in the notes to the accounts. **Revaluation gains and losses** should be taken to the profit and loss account or STRGL depending on circumstances (see ¶2754).

Shares in group undertakings that are retained as fixed asset investments should be recorded in the investing company's balance sheet at historical cost less provision for any permanent diminution in value. **Shares in participating interests** include associates and joint-ventures carried in the company's own balance sheet at historical cost, less any provision for permanent diminution in value (equity method).

1789 **Expenses** In determining the cost of an investment, any **expenses incidental to its acquisition**, such as stamp duty and broking fees, can be added to the purchase cost as long as this does not result in a value that exceeds the value of the investment. In some instances, the incidental costs of purchase can be significant as with the purchase of an investment in a subsidiary, where the costs incurred in issuing shares, or other capital instruments, due diligence and legal costs, need to be considered. **Excluded costs** However, depending upon the nature and structure of the purchase, some costs, such as issue costs related to capital instruments used to finance the purchase of the investment, should be excluded. Issue costs should be deducted from the proceeds of the debt instrument or for share issues written off to the share premium account or other reserve.

Provisions for a diminution in value   Fixed asset investments should initially be measured   **1791**
at historical purchased cost. Where there is a subsequent diminution in value of a fixed asset investment, a provision may be made against the carrying value which should be charged to the profit and loss account. The Act does not make the creation of a provision compulsory, except where the diminution is considered to be permanent. There is therefore, considerable judgement to be applied when assessing the nature of a diminution in value and the appropriate accounting treatment. When the **reasons for the provision no longer apply** it should be written back to, and separately disclosed in, the profit and loss account and in the notes to the accounts. In determining the need for any provisions each investment should be valued separately.

Further guidance is provided by FRS 11, which does not distinguish between a temporary   **1792**
and permanent diminution in the value of fixed assets, but adopts a single approach to   FRS 11 (5)
measuring the value of fixed assets, with **some exceptions**; namely:
– investment companies permitted to take a permanent diminution in the value of tangible fixed assets to the revaluation reserve;
– "own shares" held in ESOP trusts and investments;
– investments that fall within the jurisdiction of FRS 13 "Derivatives and other financial instruments"; and
– investments that fall within the scope of FRS 25 "Financial instruments: measurement" (e.g. investments covered by FRS 13 plus contracts that can be settled by an entity's own equity instruments (FRS 25 (11)).

b. Alternative accounting rules

Under the alternative accounting rules, investments **classified as fixed assets** may be valued   **1794**
either:
– at market value at the date of the most recent valuation (marking to market); or
– at a more appropriate value as determined by the directors.

Directors' valuation   The provision in the Companies Act to allow a directors' valuation   **1795**
does not give guidance on permitted valuation bases. Considerable flexibility is allowed in the valuation of investments and it may be the case that the valuation derived by the directors, may be neither the historic cost nor the current value, but some intermediate value.

The Act does, however, require that the reasons for adopting a directors' valuation and the valuation bases used must be disclosed in a note to the accounts.

Revaluation   A profit (or loss) arising on revaluation under the alternative accounting   **1796**
rules must be credited (or debited) to the revaluation reserve, after which the normal rules regarding that reserve apply. The **exception is investment companies** which take revaluation gains or losses to another reserve. In addition, investment companies can also take permanent diminutions in the value of fixed asset investments to that same reserve, whilst **other companies** must take such diminutions to the profit and loss account.

Statement at fair value (marking to market)

Listed companies are now required to adopt FRS 26 "Financial Instruments: measurement".   **1798**
The standard **is also compulsory for** all other **entities that elect to adopt** fair value accounting (now incorporated into the Companies Acts) and state fixed asset investments at fair

value. However, as not many UK companies adopt these rules, only a brief summary of the recognition and subsequent measurement requirements is given here. Also under FRS 26, **an exception** is permitted; namely that **unquoted equity investments** whose fair value cannot be measured reliably, can be stated at cost less impairment.

1799
FRS 26 (45-46)

Initial recognition and subsequent measurement   Financial assets are initially recognised at fair value and fall into **four main classifications** as set out in the note below.

> MEMO POINTS   1. Accounting standards necessitate that companies classify any investments in debt or equity securities when they are purchased as either: held to maturity, held for trading or available for sale. **Held for trading (HFT)**, or simply trading securities, are typically short-term in nature and are revalued at fair value at the end of the financial year (e.g. derivatives) and represent debt and equity investments purchased with the intent of their being sold within a short period of time (usually less than one year). Gains and losses resulting from changes in the investment's value are recorded as gains and losses on an income statement.
> 2. **Held for maturity (HTM)**: Investments with fixed payments and maturity dates are held at amortised cost. The difference between original cost and maturity value is amortised to the profit and loss account over the life of the asset. If impaired, assets should be written down.
> 3. **Originated loans and receivables (OLR)**: Accounted for as HTM assets except where they are not of fixed maturity, in which case they are measured at amortised cost and written down if impaired.
> 4. **Available-for-sale (AFS)**: Available-for-sale securities are debt or equity investments that are held for an indefinite period of time without any intention to resell for profit. They are not trading assets, as in the case of short-term assets held for speculation, nor are they acquired with an intention to hold till maturity. AFSs are initially stated at fair value and revalued at the end of each financial reporting period, with changes in value taken either to reserves or the income statement.

1800

Reclassification   1. Fixed assets cannot be reclassified in and out of the "fair value" regime through the profit and loss account.
2. Reclassification within the "fair value" regime is permitted. For example, an asset originally classified as HTM can be redesignated as AFS.
3. Where as asset formerly stated at fair value is restated at amortised cost, the previous fair value becomes its deemed cost.
4. For HTM assets, any gain or loss previously accounted for in equity is released to the profit and loss account over the period to maturity. For other assets, gains or losses remain in equity until the asset is disposed of.
5. An asset originally stated at cost because no reliable valuation measure was available, but which should be valued at fair value, must be restated if and when an accurate valuation becomes possible.

---

c. Gains or losses on disposal

1804

The profit or loss on the disposal of an asset should be accounted for in the profit and loss account in the period, in which the disposal takes place. The gain (or loss) should represent the difference between the net sale proceeds and the net carrying amount of the investment at the date of disposal; namely historical cost less any provisions for impairment valuation. **Surpluses on revaluation** previously credited to the revaluation reserve do not therefore flow through the profit and loss account when the asset is subsequently sold. However, the amount held in the revaluation reserve in respect of that investment should be treated as a movement on reserves.

1806

Individual shares or similar types of investment **may not be easily identifiable**; therefore, a basis for identifying the cost of particular holdings is required for part-disposals. In the example of a company in which a shareholding is managed through **piecemeal acquisition and disposal**, the following methods can be used for determining the cost of the investment at any particular time:
– first in first out (FIFO); or
– weighted average.
These valuation methods are described in greater detail in the chapter on inventories.

Smaller companies

For smaller entities the FRSSE requires that gains and losses should be recorded in the profit and loss account or STRGL depending on the underlying reason for the change in value. **Revaluation losses** resulting from changing prices should be recorded in the STRGL until the carrying amount matches the depreciated historical cost, **Other losses** resulting from a revaluation should be treated in the P&L account. **Revaluation gains** should be recorded in the STRGL, except where they reverse revaluation losses on the same asset recorded in the P&L account, in which case they should be matched. **Gains and losses** arising from the revaluation of assets that have been recorded in the STRGL must be credited or debited to a separate revaluation reserve.

1807

Summary

1808

Initial recognition	Revaluation	Gain/loss on disposal
Historical cost	Diminution in value – provision charged to P&L Increase in value – release to P&L as movement on reserves.	Charge to P&L
Alternative accounting rules	Cr (Dr) to revaluation reserve. Some exceptions permitted	Cr (Dr) to P&L Amounts previously held in revaluation reserve – to P&L (movement on reserve)
Fair value	Cr (Dr) to P&L	Dr. (Cr) – P&L. Exception is AFS assets – STRGL

3. Disclosures.

There are a number of general disclosures that are required for all investments (including those investments valued under the alternative accounting rules), in respect of their cost and any diminution in the value recorded. There are also additional disclosure requirements relating to listed investments, subsidiaries, participating interests, qualifying partnerships and "own shares". The disclosure requirements are more comprehensive for listed companies and are detailed below. Companies listed on the Alternative Investment Market (AIM) are not listed companies for the purpose of this classification.

1810

a. General disclosures

The Companies Act model formats for the balance sheet include headings for investments under the general heading of both fixed and current assets. Where an entity has a holding or more than 20% or more of the nominal value of any type of share, or the book value of the investing company's total assets, at the end of the financial year, then the following disclosures are required:
- the name of the entity;
- country of incorporation if not the UK;
- if unincorporated the address of the principal business operation;
- name and nominal value of the type/class of shares involved;
- profit & loss for the financial year ending with or before that of the investing company; and
- aggregate value of capital and reserves at end of most recent financial year.

1811

Medium and larger entities

Under each **sub-heading** of fixed asset investments, the following information should be disclosed either on the face of the balance sheet or, more usually, in the notes to the accounts:

1813

- the balances at the beginning and end of the financial year;
- any revaluation revisions made during the year;
- acquisitions and disposals during the year;
- details of any provisions made in respect of fixed asset investments;
- transfers of assets to or from fixed asset investments; and
- details of listed investments.

Permanent diminution in value

1814   Where there is a permanent diminution in value, the following disclosures are required in the notes to the accounts:
- the balances at the beginning and end of the year;
- provisions made during the year;
- adjustments from provisions arising from disposals; and
- other adjustments made in respect of provisions during the financial year.

Comparative figures for the preceding year are not required.

If a **diminution in value is temporary** then a provision may be made at the discretion of the directors. This fact must be disclosed in the notes to the financial statements.

The disclosure requirements are more comprehensive for **listed companies** and are detailed below. Companies listed on the Alternative Investment Market (AIM) are not listed companies for the purpose of this classification.

---

b. Additional disclosure requirements

Listed investments

1816
FRSSE 6.32

Listed investments refer to any investment that is quoted either on all "recognised" **investment exchanges in the UK** and certain other countries or only the stock exchanges of repute in specific other countries (see table). All other investments are regarded as unlisted and no additional disclosures are required.

> ⸻ MEMO POINTS ⸻   1. There is **no legal definition** of a "stock exchange of repute" in the Financial Services and Markets Act (FSMA) 2000 (Part 18), as this will depend on the status of an individual stock exchange within its own country. A recognised investment exchange as defined by the FSMA 2000, is one in which a recognition order is in place. This definition is also addressed in The Large and Medium-sized Companies and Groups (Accounts and Reports) Regulations 2008 (SI 2008/410, Para 8, Sch 10) and The Small Companies and Groups (Accounts and Director's Report) Regulations 2008 (SI 2008/409, Para 5. Sch 8).
> 2. **The Alternative Investment Market (AIM)** is a subsidiary of the London Stock Exchange that provides small companies with access to capital and a market for the trading of their shares without the expense and restrictions of a full stock exchange listing.
> 3. List of recognised investment exchanges.

Table 1 Designated UK Investment exchanges	All official exchanges in the following countries	Specific Overseas Stock Exchanges
London Stock Exchange (inc. AIM)	The European Union; USA; Switzerland; Japan & Norway	Canada
London Securities and Derivatives Exchange Ltd.		New Zealand
The London Metal Exchanges (LME)		Australia
ICE Futures and OTC energy market		Hong Kong
The London International Financial Futures Exchange (LIFFE)		South Africa

The **following information** regarding listed investments is required in the notes to the accounts: **1818**
- the total carrying value of listed investments included in each subheading;
- the aggregate market value of listed investments, where this differs from the amount stated in the financial statements; and
- details of any differences between the market value and the stock exchange value, where for instance, a sizeable shareholding could be deemed more valuable than a smaller shareholding.

EXAMPLE **XYZ Ltd.**
Notes to the accounts (extract)
Listed investments

	Company	Balance Sheet Value £'000	Market Value £'000	Stock Exchange Value £'000
Listed on the London	F	130	220	285
Stock Exchange	G	210	175	175
	I	50	60	60
		390	455	520
Listed on the Frankfurt	A	100	120	140
Stock Exchange	B	75	45	45
		175	165	185

Subsidiaries

Holdings in subsidiary undertakings should distinguish separately holdings by the parent   **1820**
company and by the group (if different). Where a company **does not prepare consolidated accounts**, but has subsidiary companies, then certain disclosures are required in the financial statements of the investing company. In addition, a company is required to state why it is not required to prepare consolidated financial statements.

MEMO POINTS   A company may not be required to prepare **consolidated financial statements** because its subsidiaries come within the scope of the exclusions from consolidation provided in the Companies Act 2006. The precise reason for the exclusion should be disclosed for each subsidiary.

The disclosures are required for **each individual subsidiary** company and include: **1821**
- the name of each subsidiary;
- its place (country) of incorporation;
- if unincorporated, the address of its principal place of business;
- the identity and proportion of the nominal value of each class of shares held;
- the profit and loss for the year; and
- the aggregate amount of the capital and reserves of the undertaking as at the end of the financial year.

The above disclosures are also required for **investments held by subsidiary companies**. As   **1824**
such the identity and number of shares in each class held by the investing company and its subsidiaries in a subsidiary undertaking must be disclosed, and classified between those shares held by the investing company and those held by any of its subsidiaries.

Additional disclosures are required under FRS 2, for each subsidiary company whose results   **1826**
or financial position substantially affect the figures in the consolidated financial statements.   FRS 2 (33)
The disclosures required include the:
- nature of the business;
- number of shares that the subsidiaries or their nominees hold;
- proportion of voting rights held by the parents and its subsidiaries; and
- details of own shares held by the subsidiary or held in the parent company.

1830   **Exemptions**   Some companies are exempt from the disclosure requirements outlined above; where:
– where the company is exempt due to sections 399-402 of the Companies Act 2006 from preparing group accounts (parent company included in the accounts of a larger group);
– the investment is accounted for by way of the equity method and is shown in aggregate in the notes to the accounts;
– the undertaking is not required by the Act to deliver a copy of (or publish) its balance sheet in Great Britain or elsewhere; and
– the shareholdings to be disclosed are immaterial.

> MEMO POINTS   Section 399 CA 2006 concerns the requirements and exemptions from requirements in relation to **group accounts**. Parent companies **not subject to the small companies regime** have a duty to prepare consolidated accounts unless exempt from having to do so under sections 400 to 402. Section 400 provides an exemption from preparing group accounts for companies included in EEA group accounts of a larger group. Section 401 provides such an exemption for companies included in non-EEA group accounts of a larger group, and section 402 provides an exemption when all the company's subsidiary undertakings could be excluded from consolidation in Companies Act group accounts.

1832
SI 1996/189   Furthermore, information on own shares is not required where the subsidiary holds the shares as a **personal representative** or as **trustee**. If the company or any of its subsidiaries is a beneficiary under the trust, then this exemption is not available for a subsidiary acting as a trustee, unless the beneficial interest is a security for a normal business transaction such as a loan.

1834   If the **number of undertakings** involved **are numerous**, then the directors need only give the information for undertakings which materially affect the figures shown in the individual or group accounts and undertakings which have been excluded from consolidation. A note to this effect should be given.

Significant interests

1836   If a company has significant interests through exercising **considerable influence but owns less than 20%** of the share capital of the undertakings concerned, then no additional disclosure beyond the separate categorisation of the investment and income is required. **Where the company owns 20% or more** of the share capital of a significant interest, the disclosures required in respect of each undertaking, in the notes to the accounts, are as set out in ¶1832.

1840   **Shares held** by the company **on behalf of a third party** should not be attributed to the company for disclosure purposes, but shares held by third parties on behalf of the company should be disclosed.

1842   The following **additional disclosures** are also required in the notes to the financial statements for amounts:
– owed by undertakings in which the company has a significant interest should be disclosed under debtors; and
– owed to undertakings in which the company has a significant interest should be disclosed under creditors.

Separate figures are required in both cases, for amounts due for payment after more than one year.

Qualifying companies

1844   Where a company **holds a material interest in a qualifying company** or partnership [an undertaking] at the end of the financial year, the disclosures required in the notes to the company or group accounts are:
– the name and legal form of the undertaking; and
– the registered office, or if not applicable, the head office.

Exemption   A company need not provide the disclosures listed above, if it has taken advantage of the exemption permitted under The Partnerships and Unlimited Companies Regulations 2008.

> MEMO POINTS   Exemptions will continue to apply to a **partnership** forming part of a group which is consolidated in group accounts prepared under the European Community Accounting Directives, or in accordance with international accounting standards. A European Economic Area (EEA) member of the qualifying partnership or the EEA parent of such a member must prepare group accounts.

1846

Own shares

Where a company owns its own shares or shares in its parent, the number and nominal values of the shares, the subsidiaries or their nominees hold and the carrying amount or value must be disclosed in the notes to the accounts.

1848

EXAMPLE   **XYZ Group Plc**
Notes to the financial statements 20XX
Fixed asset investments

Own shares Cost and net book value	Group £'000	Company £'000
As at January 20XX	485.0	346.0
Additions	10.0	
Disposals	(145)	-
As at December 20XX	350.0	346.0

The number of own shares totals 250,000 with a nominal value of £100,000.

---

c. Alternative accounting rules

Where fixed asset investments are valued in accordance with the alternative accounting rules, the following disclosures are required in the notes to the accounts:
a. the investments concerned and the valuation bases.
b. for fixed asset investments excluding listed investments:
– the name of the valuers and their qualifications; and

– the values and basis of the valuation. If any valuation base other than market value is used the reason for adopting the alternative valuation must be given.
c. the comparable historical cost for those investments and any provision for any diminution in value that would have been made under the historical cost convention, or the difference between these amounts and the alternative valuation.

1850

Investment properties

Investment properties are **defined as** an interest in land and or buildings on which construction or development work has been completed and which is being held for its investment potential, with any rental income being negotiated on an arm's length basis.

1900
SSAP 19 (7)

Investment properties may be held by all companies, but are typically held by an entity that specialises in this type of asset, such as an investment trust or property investment company.

Exclusions A property which is **owned and occupied** by a company **for its own purpose** is not an investment property, as is a property let and occupied by another group company, except where rent is determined on an arm's length basis and charged accordingly. **Partial owner-occupation** of an investment property is not addressed in SSAP 19, although a significant level of occupation will prevent the assets classification as an investment property.

1901

Regulatory framework The **principles of accounting** for investment properties are contained in SSAP 19 "Accounting for investment properties". The application of this standard represents a departure from the requirement of the Companies Act to give a true and fair view, arising from the non-provision of depreciation on a fixed asset with a useful economic life. **Small companies** applying the Financial Reporting Standard for Smaller Entities (FRSSE) are exempt from this accounting standard, although it contains similar provisions to those contained in SSAP 19.

1902

Classification	Reporting regime
Small companies	Choice of adopting FRSSE; SSAP 19; or FRS 102
Medium and large companies	Choice of SSAP 19, FRS 102,
Listed companies	IAS 40 (Beyond scope of this book)

MEMO POINTS   The FRC has published FRS 102 "The Financial Reporting Standard applicable in the UK and Republic of Ireland", applicable to smaller entities not adopting the FRSSE. **Adoption** of the new standard is mandatory from 1 January 2015 (¶1935).

1. Accounting treatment

The **general rule** for investment properties is that they should be recorded in the balance sheet at their **open market value (OMV)**, at the balance sheet date. This contrasts with **property owned by an entity**, that is held as a fixed asset, and recorded in the financial statements at cost, or valuation, and that is subject to an annual depreciation charge that reflects the loss of value, arising from use, passage of time or technological or market changes.

1904
SSAP 19 (11)

SSAP 19 (2)
FRSSE 6.50-53
Investment properties **are not subject to** an annual depreciation charge, except where the property is a leasehold property, with less than 20 years to run. The rationale for this, is that a **different treatment** is called for where a significant proportion of an entity's fixed assets are held as investments and not for use within the operations of the business, and where the disposal of such assets would not materially affect the trading position of the entity. In these circumstances, the current value of these investments and changes in current value are more relevant, than the calculation of an annual depreciation charge. **Leased properties** can be classified as investment properties if let to unrelated third parties.

1905
SSAP 19 (10)
Short leasehold properties There is an important **exception to the rule** that investment properties should not be subject to depreciation charges; namely, properties held on a lease with a term of 20 years or less. It is necessary in such cases to recognise the annual depreciation charge in the financial statements, to prevent the scenario whereby a short lease is amortised against the investment revaluation reserve, whilst the rental income is taken to the profit and loss account.

The **problem of** accounting for property **leases originally in excess of 20 years**, but which still have 20 years to run from the current accounting period, is not covered by SSAP 19.

1906   **Reclassification** Where an investment property loses its status the balance on the investment revaluation reserve should be transferred to the revaluation reserve for non-investment properties.

Recognition of gains and losses

1909   The determination of whether a **deficit is permanent or temporary** may not be so obvious. For a diminution in value to be deemed temporary there must be a reasonable expectation that the value will reverse in the near future. **Each investment property** must be judged on its individual circumstances. For instance deficits arising from structural damage, obsolescence, or changes to local infrastructure, that render the property unattractive, should be deemed permanent. Deficits that arise from short term fluctuations in market sentiment or that arise from damage that is repairable, should be regarded as temporary.

Temporary changes in market value of investment properties from one balance sheet date to the next, should be taken to the statement of total recognised gains and losses (STRGL), and not the profit and loss account, as this represents a movement on an investment revaluation reserve. The amount taken to the **revaluation reserve** will ordinarily be the gross revaluation surplus, without a deduction for any potential deferred tax liability that might arise on that surplus.

EXAMPLE Annual report and accounts Statement of total recognised gains and losses Year ended 30 September 2013						
		2013			2012	
	Group	Associated undertakings	Total	Group	Associated undertakings	Total
	£m	£m	£m	£m	£m	£m
Profit on ordinary after taxation	195.2	4.5	199.7	165.2	6.2	171.4
Revaluation of properties	(0.3)	(1.0)	(1.3)	–	–	–
Currency translation differences	(20.2)	–	(20.2)	(10.5)	–	(10.5)
Total recognised gains and losses for the year	174.7	3.5	178.2	154.7	6.2	160.9

1910   **Permanent changes in value** Where a **deficit (or reversal of a deficit)** on an individual investment property is expected to be **permanent**, it should be charged (or credited) to the profit and loss account for the financial period in question.

MEMO POINTS   Investment properties are exempt from the requirements of FRS 11 "Impairment of fixed assets".

Exceptions However, the above requirement does not apply to:
- insurance companies and groups (and consolidated financial statements incorporating these entities) where changes in the market value of investment properties are carried in the profit and loss account;
- pension funds where changes in the market value of investment properties are included in the relevant fund account; and
- investment companies and property unit trusts as valuation deficits are shown in the STRGL.

1912
SSAP 19 (14)

Status of Valuer

SSAP 19 does not require the valuation of investment properties to be made by a qualified or independent valuer, although certain disclosures are required in the financial statements. However, where investment properties represent a **substantial proportion of the assets** of the entity, a valuation should be:
- undertaken annually by suitably professionally qualified persons with recent post-qualification experience in the location and type of properties concerned; and
- at least every five years by an external valuer.

1916
SSAP 19 (6)

Development costs

Investment properties cover buildings in which development and construction work has been completed. As such when a property company or group constructs its own investment properties, the capitalisation rules set out in FRS 15 "Tangible Fixed Assets" apply, as the buildings can not classified as investment properties until completed.

1917

Sale of investment property

The general rule is that when an asset that has previously been revalued is sold, the resulting gain or loss, which has now been crystalised, is based on the net carrying amount (rather than historical cost), and should be taken to the profit and loss account.

1918

Taxation

Where investment properties are reclassified as non-investment properties (or vice versa), there may be capital gains tax implications, particularly concerning rollover reliefs.

1919

---

2. Disclosures

Key disclosures include:
- details of the valuers including names, qualifications and bases of valuation;
- the valuation bases;
- where the valuation is conducted by an employee or officer of the company or group that owns the property, this fact should be disclosed in the financial statements; and
- the carrying value of investment properties and the **investment revaluation reserve** should be prominently displayed in the financial statements.

1920
SSAP 19 (12)

EXAMPLE **Example**
ABC Group Ltd
Annual Report and Accounts – September 2013
Tangible fixed assets (extract)

Land and buildings including investment properties	Group £m	Company £m
Valuation as **at 1 October 2012**	120.7	105.3
Additions	25.0	22.0
Reclassification	(3.0)	(3.0)
Revaluation surplus	(15.0)	(13.0)
As at 30 September 2013	127.7	111.3

Investment properties were valued on the basis of open market value (OMV) as at 30 September 2013 by the group's internal qualified personnel. In accordance with SSAP 19, no depreciation is charged in respect of investment properties. This policy represents a departure from the requirements of the Companies Act 2006, to provide systematic annual depreciation for fixed assets. However, as these properties are held for investment and not consumption, the directors consider the adoption of this policy necessary to give a true and fair view.

EXAMPLE **Example**
XYZ Groupl Ltd
Annual report and accounts – September 2013
Investment revaluation reserve

	Group £m	Company £m
As at 1 October 2012	270.5	170.3
Currency exchange differences	(20.2)	
Revaluation of property	(1.3)	(0.3)
Revaluation surplus realised on disposal	(45.3)	(15.0)
As at 30 September 2013	203.7	(155.0)

---

3. Small companies adopting FRSSE

1925
FRSSE 6.50 – 6.53
Investment properties should **not** be **subject to** periodic **depreciation** charges unless they are held on lease and the lease has an unexpired term of less than 20 years.

1926
Investment properties should be disclosed in the balance sheet at their **open market value**. The carrying value should be stated prominently on the face of the balance sheet or in the notes. **Changes in market value** should be taken to the STRGL and not the profit and loss account. Where a deficit, or its reversal, on an individual property is expected to be permanent, it should be taken to the profit and loss account.

1928
The names of the persons undertaking the valuations or particulars of their qualifications, together with their **bases of valuation** and, if relevant, the fact that they are an employee or officer of the company or group, should be disclosed.

---

4. New UK GAAP – FRS 102

1935
The FRC has published FRS 102 "The Financial Reporting Standard applicable in the UK and the Republic of Ireland", applicable to smaller entities not adopting the FRSSE. Adoption of the new standard is mandatory from 1 January 2015. The key elements of the new standard concerning investment properties, plus additional advice included in a staff education note published by the FRC, are set out in the table below.

MEMO POINTS **Staff Education Note (SEN 04)** compares the accounting treatment for investment properties under current UK GAAP (SSAP 19 "Accounting for Investment Properties") and FRS 102 (Section 16). This SEN has been published in order to highlight key areas concerning the transition to FRS 102.

Topic	FRS 102
Definition/classification	1. Property (land or a building, or part of a building, or both) held by the owner or by the lessee under a finance lease to earn rentals or for capital appreciation or both. 2. Properties held under an operating lease (SSAP 19 gives no guidance) can be classified as investment properties if the value of the property can be calculated in a cost effective manner, based on the fair value of the lease, on an ongoing basis. 3. Mixed use property can be separated into an investment property and a tangible fixed asset.

Topic	FRS 102
Exclusions	FRS 102 does not exclude investment properties let to and occupied by group companies, which are recognised as investment properties in individual financial statements of the lessor. In the group accounts such properties would be accounted for as part of property, plant and equipment.
Initial recognition	Investment Property should be recorded in the balance sheet at its fair value at each reporting date. Changes in fair value are taken to the profit or loss (rather than to a revaluation reserve under SSAP 19).
Subsequent recognition/revaluation	A property can be measured at fair value where this determined without undue cost or effort. Changes in fair value are recognised in profit or loss as opposed to a property revaluation reserve.All other investment property is accounted for as property, plant and equipment (using the cost model). If a reliable, cost effective fair value cannot be determined the property should be held at cost and depreciated. There are some presentational changes.
Revaluation gains/losses	The profit on revaluation of investment property does not represent a realised profit available for distribution. An entity can elect to transfer such gains and losses to a non-distributable reserve. Under the FRSSE, reporting entities will continue to use the revaluation reserve and report fair value changes through the statement of total recognised gains and losses (as per paragraph 6.53). However, if a deficit (or a reversal of a deficit) on an individual investment property is expected to be permanent, then it will be charged to the P&L account in the period the impairment or reversal arises.
Transfers to and from investment properties	1. Transfers to/from investment property recorded when the property first meets, or ceases to meet, the definition of investment property (FRS 102 paragraph 16.9). 2. A transfer also permissible where a reliable measure of fair value is no longer available without undue cost or effort for an investment property measured using the fair value model. However, application is unlikely to change as fair values can normally be obtained without undue cost or effort.
Disclosure/presentation	1. Under FRS 102 (Section 16), investment property is required to be carried in the balance sheet at its fair value at each reporting date. Changes in fair value are taken through profit or loss (rather than directly to a revaluation reserve as is the case under SSAP 19). 2. The presentation of capital and reserves may be different on application of FRS 102 as amounts that would previously have been shown in a revaluation reserve will now form part of the accumulated profit and loss account. 3. An entity choosing not to show a separate revaluation reserve may wish to make disclosure regarding distributable and non-distributable profits.

PART 4

Balance sheet – Current assets

Stock (Inventories)

This chapter sets out the **general guidelines** and rules for determining the valuation of stock, including the determination of historical cost, net realisable value and the replacement cost of stocks. **All reporting entities**, except unincorporated entities, are subject to the provisions of SSAP 9 "Stocks and long-term contracts" and the Companies Acts. Companies applying the Financial Reporting Standard for Smaller Entities (FRSSE) benefit from reduced disclosure requirements.

2000

The FRC has now issued FRS 102, applicable to non-listed entities that choose not to apply the FRSSE. The new standard is mandatory from 1 January 2015 and requires no major adjustments to the accounting treatment for stocks and work in progress. There are, however, some small differences in terminology.

> MEMO POINTS   The terms **stock** and **inventories** are interchangeable. "Stock" is the terminology used in the Companies Act and SSAP 9, while "inventories" is used in international accounting standards.

2001
SSAP 9 (1)

It is a key principle that the revenues generated from sales are matched with the related costs incurred in earning them. Therefore, the **costs of unsold or unconsumed stocks** at the end of one financial year should be carried forward into the next financial period and matched with the revenue recognised on their future sale. Furthermore, the **choice of stock valuation method** can have a significant impact on the entity's reported profit for the period. Fewer disclosures are required from small companies, including those who elect to submit shorter-form or abbreviated accounts. The detailed treatment of **consignment stock** and the **sale and repurchase** of stock agreements is covered in this chapter, based on the provisions of FRS 5 "Reporting the substance of transactions". However, the procedures that have evolved for the costing and valuation of stock in **specialist industries**, such as agriculture, are beyond the scope of this book.

SECTION 1

Classification

2005
SSAP 9 (16)

Stock is classified in SSAP 9 as set out in the table below.

Classification	Examples
Consumable stores	Consumables are materials used in the production process that do not form part of direct material cost. Examples of direct consumables include the cooling fluids and lubricating oils used for production machinery and items of small value such as nails, nuts and bolts.
Raw materials and components	Purchased for incorporation into finished goods. Raw materials are direct materials used in the production process which are at a low level of completion, relative to the final product (e.g. steel plate, wood, chemicals).
Semi-finished goods (Work in progress)	Includes products and services in the intermediate stages of completion.
Finished goods	Represent products that have completed the manufacturing process and are available for distribution or sale.
Goods or other assets purchased for resale	Includes trading stock, which covers products available for sale that have either been produced in-house or purchased externally.
Long-term contracts (¶2200)	Defined as a contract that falls into two or more accounting periods and are commonplace in the construction industry.

A company may hold a combination of the stock classifications listed above, each potentially **2006** requiring different valuation methods. In their disclosures in the accounts, companies can adopt the standard classifications, if this provides a better understanding of the type of stock they hold (see ¶2113). Alternatively, the standard classifications can be supplemented with additional categories that fit the profile of the industry in which the reporting entity operates.

SECTION 2

Valuation

Stock valuation is a subjective exercise which has resulted in a **number of valuation** **2012** **methods** (¶2064) being adopted. The statutory regulations embodied in the Companies Act and SSAP 9 are designed to promote uniformity in the valuation methods used and in their disclosure in the financial statements prepared under the historic cost convention. The **key** **valuation issues** are set out in the table below:

Valuation issues	Accounting treatment
Historical cost	Stocks are valued for inclusion in the balance sheet at historical cost (¶2015), namely the purchase price or production cost.
Net realisable value **(NRV)**	If, however, the net realisable value (NRV) (see ¶2090) is less than historical cost, the stock should be written down to (and stated at) the net realisable value. The comparison of cost with net realisable value should be completed for each line of stock individually and not in aggregate.
Replacement cost	Stock may also be stated in the financial statements at replacement cost (see ¶2108) but only where this is lower than the net realisable value; this approach is not often adopted in practice.
Transfers of assets	Adjustments may be required in respect of stock items where there are transfers of assets (¶2085) from fixed assets to stock or vice versa and also on the cessation of a trade.
Tax issues	There are also a number of important areas that must be considered when adjusting accounting profits for tax issues (see ¶2122), namely trading stock, appropriations of stock and cessation of trade.

MEMO POINTS   1. The **NRV** is defined as the actual or estimated net selling price (net of trade but excluding settlement discounts) less additional costs to completion and marketing, distribution and selling costs.
2. Where a company adopts the **alternative accounting rules**, stock may be stated at the lower of current replacement cost or net realisable value, with any permanent diminution in value (i.e. obsolete) provided for. However, this method is not often used in practice.

There are a **number of methods for valuing closing stock** which impact on the reported **2014** profit for the year, so care must be taken not to over- or undervalue the stock. Stocks meet SSAP 9(4) the definition of assets as the entity holding any unsold stocks at the year end will expect to earn revenues from them at some future date.

A. Historical cost

2015
SSAP 9 (17)

Cost is defined in relation to the different categories of stocks as expenditure incurred in the normal course of business and required to bring the product or service to its present location and condition. The cost should include the purchase cost plus an appropriate proportion of any conversion costs.

The **value of stocks carried forward** represents the expenditure incurred in purchasing or producing the goods. In many cases, it will be difficult to identify the exact production or purchase cost for each item held in stock at the year end and, in reality, an element of averaging, costing and allocation of overheads will be required to determine the "cost" of stock.

2017

The **cost of trading stock** is simple where goods are purchased for resale in the same condition, such as where a wholesaler buys goods in bulk and then divides the stock for further distribution to smaller retail or production outlets. The cost is the price of the goods purchased plus the additional costs of bringing the goods to market. For **other types of stock**, the valuation may be more complex, especially in a complicated industrial process involving conversion costs and apportionment of both direct and indirect overheads. Production costs that do not relate to "normal" levels of activity, such as **abnormal costs**, should be excluded from the stock valuation figure.

1. Cost categories

2022

On a **historical cost basis**, the cost of the different categories of stocks includes various elements of expenditure incurred in bringing the product or service to its present location and condition.

The **calculation of the costs** of stock for a company involves **two principal stages**, namely:
– an assessment of the material and direct costs (e.g. labour) attributable to each item of stock; and
– the calculation of the proportion of total direct overhead costs attributable to that item.

Calculation of attributable overhead is an important element of cost especially when the stock item is generated through a complex manufacturing process.

Direct material cost

2025

Direct material costs consist of the actual invoice price of material purchased plus any additional charges such as:
– import duties;
– transport; and
– handling and other amounts directly attributable to the acquisition of the direct materials.

Trade discounts, rebates and other subsidies should be deducted.

2026

Other related costs include the costs of normal levels of scrap and wastage where these are unavoidably incurred as part of the production process, and may be included either as part of the material cost or treated as an overhead.

Conversion costs

2028
SSAP 9 (19)

Conversion costs (direct costs) consist of expenses that are **specifically attributable** to units of production:
– direct labour;
– direct expenses and sub-contracted work;
– direct production overheads; and
– indirect (other) overheads incurred in bringing the product to its present location and condition.

Costs of **direct labour** should be allocated to production based on normal operating conditions.

Direct production overheads Production overheads **are costs based on** "normal levels of activity" incurred in respect of materials, labour or services for production and will vary with the level of production.   **2030**

The **general principle** is that production overheads should be included in the cost of stock but only where they are directly related to the process of generating stock. As such, general company overheads should be excluded from the cost of stock. The allocation of overheads is not a precise exercise and inevitably involves a degree of subjectivity or judgement.

In determining what is deemed "normal", the **following factors** should be considered for the financial year in question: **2032**
- production capacity (volume);
- budgeted level of activity; and
- actual level of activity.

Some of these overhead costs, e.g. depreciation of manufacturing plant and equipment, are included even though they may accrue wholly or partly on a time basis. **Temporary changes in activity** may be ignored but persistent variations should result in a revision of any overhead allocation.

The **allocation of overhead costs** must be based on the level of activity, and so enable the costs of excessive wastage, inefficiency or idle time to be written off in the current period and not carried forward to future years in the stock valuation.

Other (indirect) overhead costs Overhead costs comprise the total cost of indirect materials, labour and expenses (e.g. rent, rates, insurance). Only those overhead costs that arise from the "normal commercial activity" of the entity can be included in the cost of stock, except in special circumstances as outlined below.   **2034**

Overheads **not directly attributable** to a specific product or service are not normally included in the costs of stocks. If, however, firm sales contracts have been entered into for goods or services made to customers' specifications, **overheads incurred before the manufacturing process** begins can be included, if they relate to the following: **2036**
- design;
- administration (e.g. central administrative departments);
- marketing; or
- selling costs.

Only where **central administrative costs** can be **reasonably apportioned** to production should they be included in the cost of conversion.   **2037**

Central service departments, such as accounting, usually support the following functions:
- production (paying salaries, controlling purchases, and preparing financial analysis for the production units);
- general administration (preparing management accounts and annual financial statements or preparing budgets, controlling cash resources and planning investments); or
- marketing and distribution (analysing and controlling sales).

The **costs of general management** are not directly related to current production and should be excluded from the cost of conversion, except in smaller organisations, where the separation of duties between production and administration is not so clearly defined. Where management is involved in the daily supervision of various functions, it may be permissible to allocate these costs using appropriate bases.   **2038**

Absorption bases for apportioning general overheads There are a **number of methods** of apportioning overheads to production. The method selected should be appropriate to the nature of both the product and the process of production and include: **2040**
- by labour hour or machine hour rate;
- as a proportion of direct labour costs;
- as a proportion of material costs; and
- by unit of production (possible only if a single product is produced in the relevant cost centre).

Whichever **allocation method** is selected, the overheads should be applied on the basis of the company's usual level of production activity.

A detailed treatment of these absorption bases is beyond the scope of this book.

Production costs excluded from stock valuation

2044
There are a number of production costs that should be excluded from the stock valuation figure where they do not relate to "normal" levels of activity.

1. **Abnormal costs** generated from spare capacity, exceptional spillage or other losses, other than normal loss.

2. Labour costs resulting from **operating inefficiencies** such as abnormal idle capacity, spoilage or rectification work.

3. **Distribution costs** from the sales point to the customer should not be included in the production cost. **Exception**: Distribution costs relating to the transfer of goods from the factory to the sales depot represent costs incurred in bringing the product to its present location, and are included in cost.

4. As a general rule, **interest is not included** in the costing of stock because capital is usually borrowed to finance the activities of the enterprise as a whole. **Exception**: In the rare situation where borrowed capital can be identified as financing specific stocks, the interest payable during the period can be charged to these contracts as a direct expense. An example is the whisky distilling industry, where stocks often include a classification for "maturing whisky stocks", to cover units that are neither work in progress or ready for resale. The interest charges involved in holding this stock can be included in the valuation.

Summary

2045

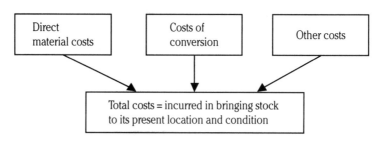

---

2. Methods of overhead cost allocation

2046
SSAP 9 (Appendix 1.11)
The **costing methods** adopted by an entity are designed to capture, and charge on a reasonable basis, overhead costs for the purposes of valuing stock.

The main costing methods in **general use** include:
– job (contract) costing;
– batch costing;
– process costing;
– standard costing; and
– other variations on the above.

2047
Often it is not practical to relate expenditure to **individual units of stock**. Therefore, the use of costing methods often requires judgements to be made to ensure that the method selected provides the fairest approximation to cost. **Once a method has been adopted**, the company must be consistent in its application from one accounting period to the next. If an entity adopts a different method, this must be stated in the note on accounting policies adopted in the financial statements. Also, **where a change in methodology** is implemented, consideration needs to be given to the impact of the change.

The choice of the most **appropriate costing system** will depend on the nature of the company's product or service or the volume of the goods produced. A general outline is provided of each of the principle cost allocation methods.

2048

Where possible, stocks should be valued by attributing costs to specific units of production using either the **job costing**, **contract costing** or **batch costing** methods. This requires the identification of each stock item referenced to a particular purchase invoice or specific costs of production. Standard costing can be used, especially where costs are relatively constant and the standard cost is therefore likely to be a close approximation to actual costs.

Where individual **stock identification is not practicable** or a number of similar items have been purchased or form part of a continuous process, then costs can be determined and allocated by using process costing.

Job costing

A job costing system can be used to collect costs on **specific jobs or individual units of stock** being produced. It is adopted in organisations producing different products or making bespoke items to order and in service companies, in order to cost each service provided.

2050

An **effective job costing system** requires:
– identifiable cost centres;
– detailed documentation for materials or stores issues;
– detailed labour analysis;
– a method of catching time costs; and
– appropriate absorption bases for overheads.

As the "job" progresses through a number of stages and departments (cost centres), costs are collected. Materials requested from stock are costed to the "job card", along with the cost of labour and the related overheads.

> MEMO POINTS   A **job card** is a computerised or manual record of all the costs posted to a particular job or project.

The **accounting treatment** is to debit the work in progress account with the cost of direct materials, as raw material stock is being converted into work in progress (stock), and credit the stores ledger control account. In addition to these entries in the **control accounts**, individual jobs should be charged with the cost of materials issued, so that job costs can be calculated. Indirect costs such as factory overheads are collected and pooled before being transferred to the stores ledger control account.

2051

In **service industries**, many job cards do not generally show an overhead absorption rate but an inflated labour rate, which includes both the direct labour costs plus an allocation for the production overhead and the profit margin. However, it should be noted that this "inflated labour cost" method is only appropriate where there is a close correlation between labour costs and the production overhead.

Contract costing   Contract costing is a form of job costing, often large scale, long-term in nature and undertaken to meet specific customer requirements. Examples include large civil engineering projects (e.g. motorways or bridges), shipbuilding and aircraft manufacture. This subject is dealt with in greater detail in the chapter on long-term contracts (see ¶2200).

2052

Batch costing

Batch costing is more appropriate to production processes that produce a large number of identical units or **"fungible items"**, which are defined as being indistinguishable from each other, such as stocks of nuts, bolts, pens and pencils. Batch costing is used extensively in the printing, packaging, clothing and building products industries.

2054

This method **differs from job costing** in that production costs are charged to one production order which covers a quantity of cost units. When the batch is complete, the unit cost is found by dividing the quantity produced into the total batch cost.

2055   The **key principle** is that the longer the production run, the lower the unit costs, although the risk of obsolescence is greater. There are a number of considerations involved in the determining the size of a batch, namely:
– the financing of the stock, including interest;
– demand for the product; and
– other production demands and competition for resources.

Process costing

2057   Process costing is a method of cost accounting used by companies whose production consists of **continuous or operational stages, or processes** such as those used in the chemical and oil industries. The costs are accumulated for the whole production cycle and the average unit production costs are computed for each stage.

Special rules are applied in process costing to the valuation of work in progress, normal losses and abnormal losses. It is also common to distinguish between the main product of the process, by-products and joint products.

Joint products are defined as two or more products separated in the course of processing, each having a sufficiently high saleable value to merit recognition as a main product in its own right. Any costs incurred need to be identified and matched with revenues.

Standard costing

2059   Standard costs are **pre-determined estimates** based on expected levels of costs, production and efficiency. Standard costs are based on "normal levels of production" and should be reviewed on a regular basis to ensure that they reflect current prices, while any abnormal costs or costs arising from inefficiencies should be written off in the period. Also, standards should be adjusted for new products in order to take account of new production techniques.

Standard costing **is often used for internal purposes** such as stock valuation for management accounting purposes. It can also be the basis for stock valuation in published financial statements where the standard cost provides a close approximation to actual costs.

2060   **Accounting treatment**   Where purchases are valued at standard cost, any difference between the standard and actual cost is written off to the profit and loss account. All issues from stores are at the same standard price.

The table below illustrates the management accounting treatment for materials received, materials variance and issues from stores.

Table	Debit	Credit
Materials received	Stock a/c at standard cost	Purchase ledger at cost
Materials variance	Debit variance posted to manufacturing profit/loss.	Credit variance posted to manufacturing profit/loss.
Issue of materials	Work in progress at standard cost	Stock a/c at standard cost

Where the materials variance is significant this may indicate that the standard cost is not sufficiently accurate to form an acceptable basis for use in published financial statements.

2061   **Specialist industries**   In certain industries such as farming, specialist **valuation techniques** have been devised for valuing stock. For instance, it can be difficult to determine the true cost of livestock and the stock valuation is generally derived by taking the market price less estimated profit. Owing to the varying methods applied and their limited application, a detailed review of valuation methods for specialist industries is beyond the remit of this book.

---

3. Methods of valuing stock

2064   There are **two principal methods** of valuing stock: the first in first out (FIFO) and the weighted average price method. There are also a **number of other methods** whose usage is restricted. When selecting a method for valuing stock, the directors must ensure that it provides the fairest approximation to "actual cost".

Whichever method has been adopted requires a disclosure to this effect to be given in the notes to the accounts. The method selected could impact on trading profit, as illustrated in the following examples.

a. Principal valuation methods

First in first out (FIFO)

Under the first in first out (FIFO) method, stocks at the end of the financial period are recorded at the most recent purchase price or cost of production. The logic is that the method reflects the **physical flow of goods** from production or purchase to sale; it assumes that the goods purchased or produced first will have been used first and that the remaining stock at the period end will represent the latest purchases or production.

2066

The **profit and loss account** should then provide a close approximation to the actual costs incurred in the production or purchase of each unit of sales. This method is the most widely used.

EXAMPLE **Scenario 1**
In this example closing stocks total 300 units. The FIFO method assumes that the stock is appropriated from the **most recent stock purchase**, which was at £36 per unit.
The total value of the stock will be 300 × £36 = £10,800.

Gross profit (extract)	£	£
Turnover		108,500
Purchases	90,000	
Less: closing stock	10,800	
Cost of sales		79,200
Gross profit		**29,300**

Scenario 2
The second scenario illustrates how the FIFO method is applied to **multiple stock purchases** throughout the financial year.

Date	Quantity Units	Price per tonne £	Value £
25 May	500	41.00	20,500
18 June	500	32.00	16,000
7 August	800	34.00	27,200
19 September	500	38.00	19,000
3 November	200	36.50	7,300
Total	**2,500**		**90,000**

At the end of the accounting period on 30 October, the entity has 300 units of raw material in stock.
Using a FIFO basis, the year-end stocks are assumed to relate to the latest purchases and will be valued as follows:

200 units [purchased on 3 November] at £36.50 =	£7,300
100 units [out of the batch of 500 units purchased on 19 September at £38] =	£3,800
Totals 300 units	**£11,100**

Profit and loss account (extract)

Gross profit	£	£
Turnover		108,500
Purchases	90,000	
Less: closing stock	11,100	
Cost of sales		78,900
Gross profit		**29,600**

2067 The **advantages** of the FIFO method are as follows:
- the oldest items are issued from stock first;
- closing stock should represent the current value of stock (matches pricing); and
- this valuation method is accepted by the inland revenue.

The **principal disadvantage** of the FIFO method is that the issue price may not reflect current economic values.

Weighted average price

2070 Under the weighted average price method, the cost is determined by dividing the total cost of the units by their number. This price may be arrived at through a continuous, periodic or a moving average.

The weighted average method does not reflect the costs incurred in the production of individual stock units. However, in many instances the differences are unlikely to be significant. Situations where the use of weighted average is unlikely to be appropriate include times of high inflation or where, for example, purchases are made in foreign currencies with fluctuating exchange rates.

2071 The **advantages** of the weighted average method are:
- issue prices from stores need only be computed on the receipt of new deliveries and not with each issue, as required by FIFO;
- receipts tend to be less frequent than issues, so the method is less cumbersome to operate;
- price fluctuations are "ironed out" over time; and
- the costs computed will be somewhere between the figures derived from the LIFO and FIFO methods.

The **disadvantage** is that issues from stock may be priced at a level different from current economic value or prices. The required accounting entries are illustrated in the example.

EXAMPLE As with the example used in the FIFO method, the closing stock is 300 units and the financial year end is 31 October 20X3.

Date of purchase	Quantity	Price per tonne	Total cost	
	Units	£	£	
25 May	500	41.00	20,500	
18 June	500	32.00	16,000	
7 August	800	34.00	27,200	
19 September	500	38.00	19,000	
3 October	200	36.50	7,300	see 1.
	2,500		**90,000**	

The **average cost** should be based on normal stockholding and usage patterns. In this example, the total cost is divided by the total units (£90,000/2,500 = £36.00) to determine the average price. Another time period (i.e. the latest quarter or half year) can also be selected. The average price for the year or the last quarter can be applied to the year end stock holding.

Profit and loss account (extract)
Gross profit

	Dr	Cr
	£	£
Turnover		108,500
Purchases	90,000	
Less: closing stock (300 x £36)	10,800	
Cost of sales		79,200
Gross profit		**29,300**

Summary of primary valuation methods

2075

£	FIFO	Weighted average
Turnover	108,500	108,500
Purchases	90,000	90,000
Closing stock	11,100	10,800
Cost of sales	78,900	79,200
Gross profit	**29,600**	**29,300**

b. Other valuation methods

Unit production cost method   The unit production cost of each item in stock is the actual cost of its production. Unit cost is a practical method of calculating cost used by retailers and wholesalers who specialise in low-volume, high-value goods (e.g. jewellery manufacture), where the allocation of overheads is relatively straightforward and is likely to be an immaterial part of the overall cost.

2076

The **method is not suitable** for most types of manufacturing companies where the costs of collecting the relevant information may often be prohibitive. Where there are high levels of production it will be difficult and costly to determine the costs of each production unit.

Retail method   Under this method, the total stock in hand is valued at current selling price which is then adjusted to an approximate purchase cost by deducting the gross margin. For example, this method is sometimes used in department stores, where a large number of different stock lines can be identified and adjusted for any difference in gross profit margins.

2077

> EXAMPLE   **DEF Ltd – Annual report and accounts**
> **Accounting policies** (extracts)
> **Stocks – Retail method**
>
> Stocks comprise goods held for resale and are valued at lower of cost and net realisable value. Stocks in stores are calculated at retail prices and reduced by appropriate margins to the lower of cost and net realisable value.

Fixed amount method   The Companies Act allows items to be included in stocks of raw materials at a fixed quantity if the value is immaterial or if the quantity, valuation and composition are not subject to material variation.

2078

The cost of the stocks are calculated on the basis of a fixed unit value ascribed to a predetermined number of units of stock. Any excess number over above this stock quantity is valued on the basis of one of the other methods.

Marginal costing   Marginal costing may be used as a basis of stock valuation for management accounting purposes only, by adding a proportion of production overhead not already included in marginal cost. For financial accounting purposes, the method is deemed unacceptable under SSAP 9.

2080

Base stock method   This is similar to the fixed amount method but is generally discouraged. The problem with this method is that it often results in stocks being stated in the balance sheet at amounts that are very different to current prices. The method relies on a buffer stock that does not change and which is accounted for in the stock-take at its original purchase price.

2081

Latest invoice price method   Under this method the latest invoice price is applied to the number of items in retained stock. The problem is that this is not necessarily the same as

2082

the actual cost of previously acquired stock, and in times of rising prices will result in "unrealised" profits being taken. In addition, closing stock valuations will be higher, resulting in higher gross profits. The **exception** is if price fluctuations during the period have been insignificant and the calculated value is a reasonable approximation of cost.

4. Transfers from current to fixed assets

2085   There are **different rules** for valuing fixed assets and stocks. Fixed assets are valued at cost less depreciation and provisions for permanent diminution in values. Current assets are carried at the lower of historical cost or net realisable value. Companies could, theoretically, avoid charging write downs to the profit and loss account on **unsold trading assets** by transferring them to fixed assets at a figure exceeding net realisable value. However, situations do arise where such transfers are legitimate, as in the example below.

2086   **Accounting treatment**   FRS 5 requires an entity to account for stock under the current asset accounting rules, up to the effective date the asset is transferred, at the lower of cost or net realisable value. Any **diminution in value** up to that date should be charged to the profit and loss account, covering the loss to the entity while the asset is held as a current asset. Accurate records should be kept of any transfers and external valuations should be undertaken for material items which should be disclosed in the notes to the accounts.

> EXAMPLE   A property company constructed an office block with the intention of selling it on the open market. However, due to the expansion of its own operations it decided to use the building for its own headquarters and not sell it. The building cost £1.5m and the NRV was £1.2m. The transfer from current to fixed assets should be at the NRV of £1.2m, with the diminution in value charged to the profit and loss account.

> MEMO POINTS   UITF 5 "Transfers from current assets to fixed assets" covers current assets included in the balance sheet at the lower of cost or net realisable value. The abstract does not apply to assets accounted for under the **alternative accounting rules**.

B. Net realisable value (NRV)

2090
SSAP 9 (5)   The net realisable value or "market value" is the estimated proceeds from the sale of stock items minus all further costs to completion, including the costs of marketing, distribution and selling. Where the net realisable value of the stock is less than cost, the stock should be written-down to that value.

In assessing NRV, there may be a **number of specific issues** to consider such as provisions, stocks of spare parts, post-balance sheet events, group stocks or by-products.

2091   **NRV below cost**   The net realisable value is likely to be less than the cost, where one or more of the following events has occurred:
– an increase in costs;
– a fall in selling price;
– physical deterioration of stocks;
– product obsolescence;
– a strategic decision to produce goods at a loss; or
– production or purchasing errors.

2092   In addition, **when excess stocks are held** which are unlikely to be sold within the current period, the impending delay in converting stocks to sales could result in one or more of the situations listed above becoming significant.

Where materials are purchased for use in the **production of a larger product** that is to be sold (e.g. the cost of a radio to be included within a new car), the NRV of that item on a standalone basis may be less than its cost. However, no reduction need be made to the cost of that individual component, provided that the goods into which the materials are to be incorporated can still be sold at a profit after incorporating the material at cost price.

If there is **no reasonable expectation** that retained stocks will be able to generate sufficient revenue to cover the costs incurred in purchasing or manufacturing, then these costs, to the extent that they are irrecoverable, should be written-off in the current year.

Provisions

If a provision is required to **reduce the value of finished goods** below cost, the stocks of parts and "sub-assemblies" comprising such goods, together with committed orders for stocks, should also be reviewed.

2094

Even if a company uses a pre-determined formula (see example below) to determine the value of its stocks, the calculation of provisions to reduce stocks from cost to net realisable value must take account of the following:

SSAP 9 (Appendix 1.16)

- age of the stock;
- expected future stock movements; or
- estimated scrap values.

Consideration must be given to other **any special factors** that may influence the value of the stock.

If **stocks in hand** have **previously been written down** to net realisable value, but in the current period it is determined that the reasons for doing so no longer apply (whether in full or in part), then that part of the provision should be written back through the profit and loss account.

> EXAMPLE **Basis of the provision for slow-moving goods (predetermined formula based on the frequency of stock usage)**
> Company X calculates on the basis of experience that the following year-end provision is required for slow-moving goods.
>
> | Last movement | Provision (%) |
> |---|---|
> | Goods that have not moved in the last: | |
> | – 3 months | nil |
> | – 6 months | 15% |
> | – 9 months | 30% |
> | – 12 months | 50% |
> | – Over 12 months | 100% |

Stocks of spare parts

Where stocks of spares are held for resale, **special consideration** of the factors listed in ¶2094 is required in the context of the:

2098

- number of units sold to which stock is applicable;
- estimated frequency with which replacement spares are required; or
- estimated useful life of the unit of production to which the stock applies.

The demand for spares is strongly correlated to the demand for the underlying product and so should be considered when calculating the net realisable value for the stock.

> EXAMPLE Motor vehicle dealerships generally incorporate a spare-parts department that holds large stocks of car parts. There is generally a high turnover of general parts such as air filters, or spark plugs or other components that fit a range of cars across the fleet. These stocks are usually replenished on a frequent basis to meet the demand for servicing, MOTs etc.

Consumable stores and other stocks not intended for resale must be stated at lower of cost or net realisable value. As there is often no anticipated net realisable value they will often be written off as purchased.

Stock write-offs – post balance sheet

2100   Events that occur between the financial year end and the signing of the financial statements, when considering net realisable values at the balance sheet date, should be considered.

> EXAMPLE   The company estimated future demand for product X as 50,000 units per annum at £10 per unit. At the year end 40,000 units were still in stock at a cost of £5 per unit. Initially, no provision against the carrying value was considered necessary.
>
> Following the year end, a large contract of 30,000 units per annum was lost and the company does not anticipate finding a replacement customer. Therefore, based on revised sales forecasts, 20,000 units have been deemed surplus to requirements and will be scrapped for nil consideration. As such, a provision of £100,000 [20,000 units at a cost of £5 per unit] has been made in the financial statements.

Groups of stock items

2102   Ideally, the comparison of cost with net realisable value should be made on an item-by-item basis. However, this is usually not practicable and in such cases it is permissible to consider groups of similar items together.

> EXAMPLE   **Trading stock**
>
> A company holding trading stock in a warehouse suffered some damage from flooding. Although the stock had deteriorated it was deemed saleable through discount channels. The stock was originally valued at £100,000, but is now deemed to have a net realisable value of £25,000.

By-products

2104
SSAP 9 (Appendix 1.15)

By-products are recovered incidentally from the materials used in the manufacture of the main products or may be further processed to create joint products. In industries **where the cost** of minor or by-products **is not separable** from the cost of the principal products, stocks of such by-products may be stated in the financial statements at net realisable value. The cost of the main product is then calculated after deduction of the NRV of the by-product.

> EXAMPLE   **Refining Plc – Annual report and accounts**
> **Accounting policies** (extract)
> **By-products**
>
> The company produces by-products from its refining process. The costs incurred in processing prior to the separation of the products are known as joint costs. The proceeds from the sale of the by-product are treated as pure profit and stocks held are stated at net realisable value; namely selling price less marketing, selling and distribution costs.

C. Replacement cost

2108
SSAP 9 (6)

Replacement cost is the cost of replacing stock at current prices, whether this be purchase or production cost. The use of replacement cost **is not acceptable where** the effect is to take account of a loss greater than that originally expected. The **estimated replacement value** of stock may be used in certain circumstances where the replacement cost is below net realisable value. For example, in the case of materials whose prices are fluctuating and which have not formed part of sales contracts agreed at the date the financial statements are prepared, the replacement cost may be the best measure of net realisable value. It is the responsibility of the directors to determine whether replacement cost is the best measure.

If the value of stocks reflected in the accounts at historical cost **differs materially** from the replacement cost, that difference must be disclosed in a note to the accounts. Where the actual purchase price or production cost of stock items has been calculated on an individual basis and not using one of the stock valuation methods, then this disclosure need not be given.

EXAMPLE **Disclosure of replacement cost**
Notes to the accounts (extract)

When the replacement cost of stocks is materially greater than the historical cost at which they are stated:
Included in the amount shown for stocks of raw materials are items valued at cost on a first in, first out basis (FIFO). The replacement cost of these items at 31 December 20X3 exceeds by £225,000 (20X2 – £180,000), the amount at which they are included in the financial statements.

MEMO POINTS   Also, where a company adopts the **alternative accounting rules** as permitted under the Companies Act, items of stock may be stated at the lower of current replacement cost and net realisable value. Any permanent diminution in value should be provided for. However, it may be difficult to estimate the cost if the asset in question cannot be replaced.

SECTION 3

Disclosure framework

"Stocks" is a main heading under current assets and must be shown on the face of the balance sheet. Additional disclosures are required under the Companies Act of various sub-categories of stock. The **accounting policies** adopted with regard to stocks should also be disclosed. The disclosure requirements for all stock classifications are the same.

2112

Formats – small companies

The stock categories for small companies, as required by the Companies Act (SI 2008/409), are:
– stocks; and
– payments on account.
These details can be given either on the face of the balance sheet or in the notes to the accounts.

2113

Accounting requirements   The accounting requirements for small companies electing to adopt the FRSSE are set out in the table below. If the FRSSE is not adopted then the requirements of SSAP 9 apply. Should a company decide to **file abbreviated accounts**, then only the total (combined) stock figure need be disclosed. Any difference between the stock figure disclosed in the accounts and the replacement cost of the stock need not be disclosed.

2115

General rule	Stocks should be stated at lower of cost and net realisable value.
Finance cost	Directly attributable finance costs (e.g. interest) relating to acquisition, production or construction of stock can be included in cost. Disclosure of finance costs is also required in the notes to the accounts.
Distribution costs	Must be excluded from production costs of stock.
Replacement stocks	If value of replacement stocks is not material to gauging the company's health and their quality, value or composition are not subject to considerable variation, they should be included at a fixed quantity/value.

MEMO POINTS   Small companies are not required to give a sub-classification of stock, except to distinguish between stocks and payments on account. Schedule 8 to the Companies Act 1985 has been replaced by Schedule 1 to the Small Companies and Groups (Accounts and Director's Reports) Regulations 2008/SI 2008/409.

Formats – medium and larger companies

2116   As required by the Companies Act, the stock categories listed in ¶2005 should be grouped and disclosed under the following sub-categories of "stocks":
– raw material and consumables;
– work in progress;
– finished goods and goods for resale; and
– payments on account.
These details can be given either on the face of the balance sheet or in the notes to the accounts. In certain circumstances, the **special nature** of a company's business will mean that the formats adopted in the company's financial statements may need to be amended.

> ⌐MEMO POINTS⌐   Schedule 4 of the Companies Act has now been **replaced by Schedule 1** to the Large and Medium-sized Companies and Groups (Accounts and Reports) 2008/SI 2008/410.

Accounting policies

2119
SSAP 9 (32)
It is a further requirement of the Companies Act that accounting policies for stocks (and long-term contracts) and the method of calculating turnover and attributable profit be disclosed and applied consistently within the business from year to year. If **different bases** have been adopted for valuing different types of stock, this fact must be disclosed as illustrated in the following example.

> ⌐EXAMPLE⌐ **Notes to the accounts** (extract)
> **15. Disclosure of general accounting policies**
>
> **Weighted average cost**
>
> Stocks are valued at the lower of weighted average cost or estimated net realisable value.
> Cost comprises direct material and labour costs together with relevant factory overheads (including depreciation) on the basis of normal activity levels. The cost of cocoa also reflects the use of the futures market on the basis of forecast physical requirements.
> The following are examples of different accounting policy notes that highlight that at different stages of production, different valuation methods are appropriate for explaining the **treatment and valuation** of stocks:
> 1. **Stocks and work in progress** are stated at the lower of cost and net realisable value.
> 2. **Finished goods and goods for resale** are stated at the lower of cost, including appropriate production overheads, and net realisable value. Distribution and administrative expenses are not included in the stock valuation.
> 3. **Work in progress** is valued at cost of materials plus manufacturing labour and overheads.
> 4. **Raw materials** are valued at purchase price but reduced to net replacement cost if this is lower.
> 5. Provision is made for **slow moving or obsolete** items.

Hedging of stock transactions in foreign currencies

2120   Once a foreign exchange transaction has been recorded, the gain or loss should be disclosed at the rate specified in the forward contract used to hedge the stock items.

The **deferred gain or loss** should be calculated by re-translating the stock at the spot rate at the transaction date and comparing the value to the carrying amount. The recognition of the deferred gain or loss will depend on stock utilisation through the production process or its subsequent resale.

SECTION 4

Taxation

2122   In general the requirements of HMRC regarding the **valuation of stock** are aligned with those of SSAP 9, with a small number of exceptions as set out in the table below. The treatment of depreciation is also considered.

Discontinued business	Unsold stock and work in progress is included in taxable trading profit, as if sold at market value on the date the business ceases trading.
Stock sold to connected persons	If the seller and buyer are connected persons (e.g. family members) the stock must be valued at the prevailing market price, as if the sale had been made at arm's length.
Stock sold to another trader who continues with the business	Where the stock is sold to another trader who will continue the business, the stock should be valued in the final accounts at the agreed consideration for the sale.
Appropriations of trading stock for private use	Market value should be used for tax purposes rather than cost, where stock is appropriated for private use. This requirement is based on case law (Sharkey v Wherner [1955]), which was subsequently codified in the Finance Acts.

MEMO POINTS   **Special rules exist** for certain trades or industries such as motor dealers or farming. HMRC issues regular tax bulletins updating its guidance in these areas.

Depreciation   For financial statements to accurately reflect business costs they should include a cost element covering the reduction ("wear and tear") in the useful economic life of fixed assets (depreciation ¶1444). The depreciation charge for each period is recognised as an expense in the profit and loss account for the period. This depletion charge against income should be added back in the tax computation.

2123

The **determination of profit** for an accounting period **requires the matching of costs** with related revenues and, as such, a business should ensure that it has appropriate mechanisms in place to ensure that depreciation is added back in the computation for each year/period of disposal of stock.

Where there are only a **small number of relatively large items in stock**, it is easier to track the depreciation within stock and so ensure that on the disposal of the stock in question, the relevant depreciation is correctly included in the tax computation.

Where the stock comprises a **large number of individual items each of relatively modest value**, the record-keeping requirements for depreciation in stock are rather more burdensome.

The relationship between the accounting treatment for depreciation and the requirements of tax law is encapsulated in a ruling handed down by the House of Lords, and provides guidance for companies in this area.

MEMO POINTS   A **ruling in the House of Lords** dated 28 March 2007 in the case involving joint appeals by Mars UK Ltd. and William Grant & Sons Distillers Ltd. was based on the generally accepted accounting practice that costs be matched with related revenue. The costs of stock may have been incurred in the year in question, or in earlier years and carried forward in accordance with the general principle that they be matched with the related sales when they occur. The Judge concluded that both Mars and Grant had prepared their accounts in accordance with SSAP 9.

SECTION 5

Consignment stocks

Consignment stocks are a **type of stock-financing arrangement** predominately used by car manufacturers and dealers, although it does apply to other industries. Application Note A to FRS 5 "Reporting the substance of transactions" details how the principle of recognising assets and liabilities should be applied to these arrangements.

2126

2127
FRS 5 (A1)
Consignment stock is held by one party (the "dealer") **whilst still the legal property** of another (the "manufacturer") on terms that give the dealer the right to sell the stock in the normal course of its business, or to return it unsold, without penalty, to the legal owner. Consignment stock may be physically located on the premises of the dealer or held at another site.

This type of arrangement can provide the following **commercial advantages** to both parties, namely:
- the dealer can hold or have quicker access to a larger range of stock;
- the manufacturer can avoid stock building up on its premises by moving it closer to the customer; and
- the sales potential of the product may be enhanced.

2128
The **terms of consignment agreements** can vary considerably concerning key aspects such as:
- the right of return by the dealer (¶2135);
- determination of the sale (transfer) price; or
- the deposit terms required by the manufacturer of the dealer.

Characteristics of consignment stock arrangements

2129
FRS 5 (A2)
FRSSE 8.9
The **main features** of a consignment stock arrangement are as follows:
1. The **manufacturer** passes goods to the dealer but **retains legal title** to the stock until one of a number of events takes place:
- the dealer sells the goods to a third party;
- a specified time period elapses triggering the return of the goods; or
- the dealer uses the goods as demonstration models.

Until such a qualifying event occurs, the dealer is entitled to return the goods to the manufacturer or the manufacturer is able to require their return or insist that they are passed to another dealer.

2. As soon as the **legal title** to the goods **passes**, the transfer price becomes payable by the dealer. The price may:
- be fixed at the date the goods are delivered to the dealer;
- vary with the period between delivery and transfer of title; or
- be the manufacturer's list price at the date of transfer of title.

3. The **dealer may** be required to **pay a deposit, display or financing charge** to the manufacturer, which may be fixed for a period and may bear interest. In other cases, a finance company will pay the deposit or charge to the manufacturer and will charge interest when recharging the dealer.

4. **Other items** include inspection rights or insurance for loss or damage.

A. Benefits and risks

2130
The **substance of each agreement** should be determined to see where the principal risks and benefits lie by examining all commercial aspects of the agreement. The **general rule** is that the stock should appear on the dealer's balance sheet when they have access to its principle benefits, whilst at the same time carrying the principal risks inherent in these types of transaction. The aim is to determine whether, at any given time, the **dealer has acquired an asset** in the form of stock and a corresponding liability to the manufacturer, where the legal title has passed to the manufacturer.

2132
FRS 5 (A3)
The **principal benefits** of consignment stocks for **dealers** are:
- the future cash flows from a sale to a third party and the right to retain the items of stock in order to achieve such a sale;

- insulation from changes to the transfer price charged by the manufacturer for its stock; and
- the right to use the stock (e.g. as a demonstration model).

The **principal risks** are being compelled to retain stock that is not readily saleable or obsolete and the risk of slow movement, resulting in increased financing costs and possible write downs.

The accounting standard identifies **four principal sources** of benefits and risks associated with consignment stocks:
- the manufacturer's right of return;
- the dealer's right of return;
- the stock transfer price; and
- the dealer's right to use stock.

2133

Manufacturer's right to demand the return of stock

The **dealer's access** to the benefits of the stock will be restricted if the manufacturer can demand the return of the goods or their transfer to another dealer. If, for instance, a high proportion of the stock meets this definition, this indicates that the stock remains an asset of the manufacturer.

2134
FRS 5 (A5)

Alternatively, if the dealer is not obliged to comply with the request of the manufacturer to return stock, this would indicate that the stock is an asset of the dealer. A number of different scenarios are considered in the table below.

Asset of the manufacturer	Deemed an asset of the dealer
Manufacturer can require the dealer to return or transfer stock without compensation	Manufacturer cannot demand the dealer return or transfer the stock
Manufacturer can levy penalties on a dealer for non-return or transfer of stock at the manufacturers request	Financial incentives provided to persuade the dealer to return or transfer stock

Dealer's right of return

Where the dealer has a right to return stock **without penalty**, it does not bear any obsolescence risk, thereby indicating that the dealer has neither the asset "stock" nor the liability (to the manufacturer). The **commercial effect** of this arrangement should be considered. For instance, if the right of return is exercised frequently or the manufacturer provides an incentive such as price discounts, in order to persuade the dealer to retain the stock, this would indicate that the stock is in substance, not an asset of the dealer.

2135
FRS 5 (A6)

Conversely, if the **dealer has no right to return the stock** or is charged a penalty for so doing, this would indicate that the dealer bears significant commercial risks regarding the stock; thus making the stock an asset. The dealer also has a corresponding liability to the manufacturer to pay for the stock.

Dealer's right of return	
Dealer has unfettered right to return stock to the manufacturer without penalty and actually exercises the right to practice	**Dealer has no right to return stock** or is commercially compelled not to exercise its right of return
Manufacturer bears obsolescence risk, e.g. – obsolete stock is returned to the manufacturer without penalty; or – financial incentives given by manufacturers to prevent stock being returned to it (e.g. model change or if it becomes obsolete)	**Dealer bears obsolescence risk**, e.g. – penalty charged if dealer returns stock to manufacturer; or – obsolete stock cannot be returned to the manufacturer and no compensation is paid by the manufacturer for losses due to obsolescence

Stock transfer price and deposits

2136
FRS 5 (A7)

Where the stock transfer price is the manufacturer's list price at delivery, then the dealer is protected from any price changes imposed by the manufacturer. This would indicate that the stock is an **asset of the dealer** at the delivery date.

Alternatively, if the price charged to the dealer is the manufacturer's list price at the date the legal transfer of the goods take place, this could indicate that the stock is an asset for the manufacturer, until such a transfer takes place.

2137

Slow movement risk   The price at which the stock is transferred may also affect who absorbs the slow payment risk and the financing costs until the stock is sold. The **manufacturer bears** the slow payment risk when there is no deposit and the charge to the dealer is simply the list price, payable when legal title is transferred.

Conversely, the **dealer bears the slow payment risk** whenever the transfer price is determined by the length of time for which the stock is held. For instance, the arrangement may include a clause that the price to the dealer increases over the time the stock is held, or where the transfer price is the list price at the transfer of the legal title and not simply the delivery date.

2138

Where a **deposit is provided by the dealer** to the manufacturer, the question arises as to whether the dealer bears any variations in stock financing costs due to slow movement, such as where a large interest-free deposit is related to stock levels held by the dealer. Alternatively, a finance company could provide a deposit to the manufacture and charge interest to the dealer.

FRS 5 (A8)

EXAMPLE

Stock transfer price	
Asset of the manufacturer	**Asset of the dealer**
Stock transfer price charged by the manufacturer is based on the manufacturer's list price at date of transfer of legal title	Stock transfer price charged by manufacturer is based on manufacturer's list price at date of delivery
Manufacturer bears slow movement risk, e.g. transfer price set independently of time for which dealer holds stock, and there is no deposit	**Dealer bears slow movement risk** – dealer is effectively charged interest as transfer price or other payments to manufacturer vary with time for which the dealer holds stock; or – dealer makes substantial interest free deposits that vary with the levels of stock held

Dealer's right to use the stock

2140
FRS 5 (A10)

Where the dealer exercises a right to use the consignment stock in its business, this will usually make it an asset of the dealer; the legal title will be transferred to the dealer and give rise to an obligation to pay the manufacturer.

B. General accounting treatment

2142
FRS 5 (A12)

Varying treatments in respect of the same transaction are possible depending on the terms underlying the transaction.

Where the **substance of the transaction** indicates that the **stock is an asset of the dealer**, the stock should be recognised on the dealer's balance sheet, together with the corresponding liability.

Any **deposit should be deducted** from the liability to the supplier. The notes to the financial statements should detail:
- the nature of the arrangement;
- the value of the consignment stock included in the balance sheet; and
- the main terms, under which the stock is held, including the terms of any deposits.

Where the **substance of the transaction indicates** that the **stock is not an asset of the dealer**, the stock should not be included on the dealer's balance sheet until the transfer of title has crystallised. Any deposit paid by the dealer to the manufacturer should be classified under "other debtors". The notes to the financial statements should include information similar to that required where the stock is deemed to be an asset of the dealer.

A **typical consignment arrangement** is illustrated in the example below.

2145

EXAMPLE **Consignment stock**

Terms and conditions, accounting treatment and disclosure requirements.
A motor manufacturer may conclude an agreement with its dealer network to consign stock to them. These agreements are often very detailed; a typical consignment agreement will consist of some of the following **terms and conditions**:
1. The dealer is **allocated stock** by the manufacturer which is to be stored at the dealer's premises.
2. The manufacturer can **reward or penalise** the dealer through the allocation of consignment stock, with preferred dealers gaining favourable access to new models etc.
3. **Legal title** to the stock does not pass until the dealer has paid for the stock, which for example could be the earlier of:
- the date of sale of a vehicle to the custom;
- the date the stock is appropriated for demonstration purposes; or
- 90 days.
4. The manufacturer and dealer may conclude a deal with a third-party finance house to finance the vehicles consigned to a dealer, who pays a **finance cost** based on the value of the consignment. The manufacturer receives a payment from the finance house for all the vehicles consigned to the dealer.
5. Until the dealer **sells or adopts the stock** with the agreed time limit (e.g. 90 days), the stock may be returned to the manufacturer, exchanged or transferred to another dealer in the network. This increases the stock availability to the dealer.
6. Where a particular model is slow moving and is approaching the limit of the agreed time period, the dealer has the **following options**:
- exchange or transfer the vehicle to another dealer;
- negotiate an extension of the consignment deal; and
- provide incentives to generate sales.
7. The stock **transfer price** is based on the manufacturer's list price.

Accounting treatment for the dealer
The **agreement** should be assessed to ascertain where the **principle risks and benefits of ownership** lie. In this example the manufacturer appears to carry the risk of obsolescence, with the risk of slow payment falling on the dealer after the free stocking period has expired.
The dealer should recognise the **obligation** (equal to the principal on which interest is paid) in its balance sheet at the end of the free stocking period. The **related asset** of similar value should be accounted for as an "interest in consignment stock". At the point the stock is adopted by the dealer for either sale or demonstration, it should be recorded as stock of the dealer.
In this example, the **interest payments payable** by the dealer to the finance house represent an obligation to transfer economic benefits; namely a liability in the form of a loan.
Revenue recognition In this example **the manufacturer** recognises revenue at the date the consignment stock is adopted; namely, at the point all the risks and rewards of ownership are transferred. In the free stocking period the manufacturer still holds the stock and the dealer does not recognise the asset. In the period between the end of the free stocking period and adoption of the stock, the manufacturer will continue to hold the stock whilst the dealer also holds an "interest" in the consignment stock.

Disclosure requirements
Year-ended 30 June 20X3
Accounting policies (extract)

Stocks of motor vehicles have been valued at the lower of cost or net realisable value. Part stocks are valued at cost on a weighted average or first-in first out basis (FIFO). Provisions have also been made against slow-moving, obsolete and surplus stock. **Consignment stocks** from manufacturers that are the subject of interest or other charges are included at cost. Vehicles subject to repurchase agreements are included at the contracted repurchase price. In both cases, the associated liability is accounted for in creditors.

Stocks

	20X3 £	20X2 £
Goods for resale	2,750,000	1,620,000
Repurchase agreements	150,000	105,000
Consignment vehicles (interest bearing)	98,000	65,000
Total	**2,998,000**	**1,790,000**

Accounting treatment for the manufacturer

2146   In relation to the example above, the accounting treatment for the manufacturer is not discussed in FRS 5. Whereas the dealer might register an "interest in the consignment stock" on its balance sheet, the manufacturer could register the **physical stock** in its balance sheet. Also, the manufacturer is not required to make any specific disclosures in its financial statements other than the need to provide sufficient information on the commercial effect of the transaction.

Under a typical agreement there are **three possible dates** on which a sale might be registered:
– the date the stock is assigned to the dealer;
– the date from which interest is payable by the dealer under a related financing arrangement; or
– the date the dealer adopts or sells the stock.

The most appropriate date for the purposes of **derecognition** is the latter option.

Disclosure requirements

2147   In general, the FRS 5 criteria permitting a **linked presentation** will not be satisfied where the terms of the consignment agreement allow for the vehicle to be retained by the dealer.

C. Sale and repurchase of stocks

2150   Stock is sometimes sold with an **option to buy it back** at a later date. Options have different terms and conditions and run for different time periods, during which time the company that sold the stock uses the sale proceeds as a form of finance.

2151   The **substance of each option** must be examined and the accounting treatment will be dependent upon where the risks and benefits associated with the stock lie. For example, **options may be structured** so that the purchaser agrees with the lender for them to buy back the stock at the original sale price, without genuine exposure to, or benefit from, changes in the value of underlying assets. Such an agreement should be accounted for as a financing arrangement not as the sale of an asset.

> EXAMPLE Company A agrees to sell stock for £50,000 to Company B, with whom Company A enters into an agreement to buy back the stock ten months later for £55,000. The additional £5,000 should be accounted for as the finance cost or interest and not as part of the cost of the stock, and should be charged to the profit and loss account of Company B.
> The **substance of this agreement** is that of a secured loan that requires the presentation of the original asset (stock) at an agreed future date. The receipt of £50,000 should be accounted for by Company A on its balance sheet as a finance liability. For the ten-month period the stock should be carried on the balance sheet of Company B.

Goods with reservation of title

Companies may sell goods to other companies with reservation clauses included in the sale **2160**
contracts enabling the seller to retain ownership of those goods until the debtor is settled.
These clauses are sometimes referred to as **"Romalpa clauses"**.

The **principal advantage** of trading with reservation of title is that if the purchaser becomes
insolvent, a creditor may be able to reclaim the stock from their insolvent customer. In
practice, it has been shown to be difficult to enforce these "reservation of title clauses" and
they no longer have the prominence that they once had.

> MEMO POINTS   The case of *Aluminium Industrie Vaassen B.V. v Romalpa Aluminium Limited* (1976) gave rise
> to what is known as the "Romalpa clauses", which govern contractual relationships.

Accounting treatment   These **legal clauses only come into effect** when a company   **2162**
becomes insolvent and, as accounts are prepared on a going concern basis, the **general
rule** is that the purchaser recognises the stock and the corresponding liability in its balance
sheet, even though the supplier usually retains legal title to the goods. This is consistent with
FRS 5, as it is the purchaser who bears the risks and enjoys the benefits from the asset. A
note to this effect should be given in the financial statements. Disclosure will be necessary
where there are doubts as to the going concern status of the purchaser.

> EXAMPLE   **ABC Ltd – Annual report and accounts**
> **September 20X3**
> **Notes to the accounts**
>
> **Creditors – amounts falling due within one year (extract)**
> Trade Creditors includes a sum of approximately £30,000, which is secured by the reservation to
> the supplier of a legal title to goods supplied and the proceeds from their sale. However, the
> amount secured in this manner depends on the legal interpretation of individual contracts and so
> cannot be determined exactly.

Accounting requirements for small companies

Companies adopting FRSSE

Stocks are stated in the financial statements at the lower of cost and net realisable value.   **2170**
This amount must be given in respect of **separate** items of stock or of **groups** of similar   FRSSE 8.1 – 8.5
items. If there is **no record** of the purchase price or production cost of stock, the earliest
available record of its value must be used (and this fact disclosed in the first year it applies).

Finance costs (such as interest) that are directly attributable to the acquisition, construction
or production of stock may be included as part of the cost. By way of note, the fact that
finance costs are included in determining the cost of the asset, and the amount, must be
disclosed.

Where **stocks are constantly being replaced** and their value is not material to assessing the
company's state of affairs and their quantity, value and composition are not subject to
material variation, they may be included at a fixed quantity and value. **Distribution costs**
may not be included in the production costs of stocks.

> MEMO POINTS   The accounting treatment for **consignment stocks** for small companies is covered
> in section 5.

SECTION 8

New UK GAAP – FRS 102

Outline

2175   The requirements of FRS 102 regarding stocks are similar to current UK GAAP in terms of measurement and costs that can be included in the valuation of stock (e.g. purchase cost, conversion costs, apportionment of production overheads). The techniques employed for measuring cost (e.g. standard cost, retail method, most recent purchase price etc) are the same. However, there are some **small differences** in terms of terminology used.

CHAPTER 2

Long-term contracts

This chapter sets out the general guidelines, rules and principles governing the determination of turnover and profit on long-term contracts, as well as the disclosures required.

2200
SSAP 9 (22)

A long-term contract **is defined as** a contract that typically falls into two or more accounting periods, for the construction of a substantial asset or provision of a service. The test is whether the reported turnover and profits represent a true and fair view of the contract activity in the relevant accounting period. The **choice of accounting treatment** for long-term contracts will have a significant impact on the entity's reported results for the period.

In addition to the Companies Acts, the accounting treatment and disclosure requirements for long-term contracts is principally covered in the FRSSE and SSAP 9 "Stocks and long-term contracts", supported by other standards and abstracts. Small and medium-sized companies **not applying the FRSSE** will have to apply **FRS 102** "The financial reporting standard applicable in the UK and Republic of Ireland" from January 2015, when it will replace the existing accounting standards and abstracts.

However, long-term contracts are not specifically covered in FRS 102, but are briefly mentioned in the section on revenue recognition. Given the **lack of specific guidance** on this topic the likelihood is that accounting practice will continue to follow existing UK GAAP.

SECTION 1

Types of long-term contract

The **main types** of long-term contracts include:
– the design, manufacture or construction of a single asset (e.g. civil engineering projects);

2206

– the provision of a service (e.g. catering contracts); or

– a combination of assets and services that make up a single project (e.g. refurbishment of a chain of retail outlets).

2208   A **distinction needs to be drawn** between long-term work in progress for a third party and that for the contracting company itself. For example, a company building an office block for sale to a third party will, assuming the relevant criteria are met, account for it as a long-term contract. A company building the same office block for its own use will treat the partly completed building as an asset in the course of construction and include it within fixed assets at cost.

SSAP 9 **does not specify** particular types of contract. The **most common types** of long-term contracts are fixed-price or cost-plus contracts.

Fixed-price contracts

2210   Under fixed-price contracts, the **computation** of the amount **of turnover** is quite independent of the issue of how much profit should be taken. This is because even if a contract is loss making the turnover will still be generated. The amount of the profit or loss to be recognised will then be a function of the level of turnover recognised and the level of actual costs to date and anticipated costs to completion of the contract. There are numerous types of fixed-price contract, each with different penalty regimes or cost escalation clauses.

> EXAMPLE An engineering company agreed a fixed-price contract to upgrade track and signalling on a small section of the national rail network. The contract price agreed was in the region of £2.5m, but delays and cost overruns have forced the company to revise its cost estimates for the project to around £3m. Under the terms of the contract the contractor is liable for any excess costs, which should be provided for when recognised.

Cost-plus contracts

2212   After all legitimate costs have been authorised, an **agreed profit percentage** is applied to determine the appropriate turnover figure. All the costs that have been incurred, including those that are not approved, should be included in the cost of sales figure to derive the profit or loss to date on the contract. Provisions should be made for known **additional costs** not yet incurred that will not be approved under the contract.

SECTION 2

Accounting treatment

A. Overview

2214
SSAP 9 (28)

This section covers the accounting treatment for long-term contracts including recognition of turnover, identifying profit, loss-making contracts, treatment of legal claims and pre-contract expenses. On long-term contracts in progress, it is appropriate to take credit for ascertainable turnover, associated costs and profit, in keeping with the requirement for financial statements to present a true and fair view. **A separate contract account** should be opened for each long-term contract although different treatments may apply to different parts of the contract. As a result, individual contracts may be treated differently regarding the timing of the recognition of revenue, costs and profits. Once **a particular accounting treatment** has been adopted it must be applied consistently to each individual contract from one accounting period to the next. Some **contracts lasting less than one year** should also be accounted for as long-term contracts, if they are material to the activity of the accounting period and the omission of turnover and the related costs in respect of those contracts could impair the truth and fairness of the financial statements.

In addition to the Companies Acts, the accounting treatment and disclosure requirements for long-term contracts are covered in the following accounting standards:
– FRSSE;
– SSAP 9 "Stocks and long-term contracts";
– FRS 5 "Reporting the substance of transactions (Application Note G)"; and
– UITF 40 "Revenue recognition and long-term contracts".
SSAP 9 gives specific guidance on the accounting treatment for all aspects of long-term contracts. Application Note G (FRS 5) deals with the general principles of revenue recognition while UITF 40 is narrower in scope, providing additional guidance for accounting for revenue on service contracts. These standards will be replaced by **FRS 102** "The financial reporting standard applicable in the UK and Republic of Ireland" (mandatory from January 2015), although earlier adoption is permitted. Small companies can continue to apply the FRSSE.

2215

MEMO POINTS   Long-term contracts are not specifically covered in FRS 102 but are briefly mentioned in the section on revenue recognition. Given the **lack of specific guidance** on this topic, the likelihood is that accounting practice will mirror existing UK GAAP.

General rules

2218

Scenario	Accounting treatment
Outcome of contract can be assessed with reasonable certainty even though it is not complete	The part of the profit attributable to the work performed at the accounting date should be included in the profit and loss account for the year.
Outcome of the project is uncertain in terms of profitability or losses are envisaged	Turnover and costs recognised should be equal and a profit should not be recognised. It is relatively common, therefore, not to recognise profits in the early stages of long, complex projects.
Project will be loss making	The costs recognised should include full provision for that future loss.
Estimates for projects spanning several accounting periods	As estimates vary so should the relevant provisions and profit estimates.

As the **estimated outcome** of a contract that extends over **several accounting periods** could vary with changes in circumstances, then the results for the year will not necessarily represent the proportion of total profit on the contract, appropriate to the amount of work actually carried out in a relevant accounting period, as they will also incorporate the impact of adjustments made to profits recognised in previous periods, as a result of any revision to estimated profits. However, by recognising the proportion of each contract attributable to the accounting period, the costs and revenues generated can be matched more accurately.

2219

B. Guidance for small companies (FRSSE)

The accounting guidance given in the FRSSE is similar to that contained in SSAP 9, namely that long-term contracts should be assessed on a contract-by-contract basis and reflected in the profit and loss account by recording turnover and related costs as contract activity progresses. Turnover is ascertained in a manner appropriate to the stage of completion of the contract, the business, and the industry in which it operates. Where it is considered that the outcome of a long-term contract can be assessed with reasonable certainty, attributable profit should be calculated on a prudent basis and recognised in the profit and loss account as the difference between turnover and related costs for that contract.

2220
FRSSE 8.6–8.7

C. Guidance for non-FRSSE companies

2230
SSAP 9 (7)

The **general rule** under which turnover and profit are recognised on the sale of goods and services is that the seller's full performance under the terms of the contract must have been completed when the turnover is recognised. Where that stage has not been reached, the cost of work completed to date is included in work in progress and no turnover recognised.

However, simply applying the above rule to businesses that enter into long-term contracts would not necessarily result in a fair presentation of the level of activity in the year.

2232

Basis of recognition The basis on which turnover and costs are recognised should be appropriate to the nature of the particular contract. A **common approach** is to assess the percentage of work completed to date and apply that to the total value of the contract in order to determine the cumulative value of the turnover on that contract. This is then matched against the costs incurred to date to assess the profit that should be recognised.

In order to determine the amounts at which long-term contracts should be included in the financial statements, the following accounting treatment for the recognition of turnover, costs and profit (or loss) should be applied.

Recognition	
Category	Accounting treatment
Turnover to date	% of contract completed based on valuation or estimate (¶2248)
Cost of sales	Costs transferred from work in progress (¶2266)
Profit – indentifiable	Prudent (matching) (¶2276)
Profit – unidentifiable	No profit recognised (¶2284)
Loss – realised or anticipated	Full loss taken to P & L (¶2310)

1. Turnover

2240
SSAP 9 (9)

SSAP 9 does not give a definition of turnover in view of the different methods of determining it. The turnover on long-term contracts taken to the profit and loss account in an accounting period must relate to either **separate or measurable parts** of the contract completed in that period.

SSAP 9 (23)

Companies should **calculate turnover** on long-term contracts in a way that is **appropriate to**:
– the stage of completion of the contract (e.g. 30%);
– the nature of the contractual relationship with the client; and
– the particular business and industry concerned (e.g. construction).
FRS 5 "Reporting the substance of transactions: revenue recognition" and UITF Abstract 40 provide **additional guidance** on the recognition of turnover derived from long-term contracts (¶2262).

a. Stage of completion

2242

The determination of the stage of completion can be derived from:
– an actual valuation of the contract work carried out to date;
– an estimate of contract completion; and
– values attributable to specific stages or agreed dates (multi-stage) as specified in the contract.

2244

In some contracts **interim payments** are agreed on certain dates or at certain points in the contract (or milestones as they are termed). These payments are not necessarily related to the value of work completed when a milestone is reached, so care must be taken not to simply accept the value of payments received as being a fair reflection of the value of the turnover to be recognised.

Actual valuation

On certain contracts, particularly in construction, valuations are prepared by **independent surveyors**. However, the accounting standard does not specify that an independent valuation be undertaken, although the use of appropriately qualified individuals is recommended as best practice. Accounts prepared by the construction agent and agreed by the client or their advisors form the basis of the turnover recognised on the contract.

2248

EXAMPLE A long-term contract worth £300,000 has been independently valued as 45% complete at the end of the first accounting period. Assuming the value of turnover accrues evenly throughout the contract, the recorded turnover should be £130,500.

If the valuation is conducted some time **prior to the financial year end** an adjustment reflecting additional turnover on work completed should be made.

Certification   Remuneration for the building contractor is usually based on architects' certificates or an engineer's certificate for engineering contracts. Work certified will usually include a figure for retentions, which represent monies withheld until rectification work has been completed. The value of turnover recognised should therefore be the gross figure before any deductions for retentions.

2250

EXAMPLE The value of work on a long-term contract was assessed at £350,000 with a figure of 10% for retentions. The payments to date total £300,000 with the outstanding debtor balance of £35,000 representing the retention fee.

Estimates

In some cases it is not possible to conduct an independent valuation or it is not required under the terms of the contract. The entity therefore estimates the **value of the work completed** by reference to milestones in the contract or the judgement of the directors, and calculates the **percentage completion** achieved to date before multiplying this figure by the contract value to ascertain the turnover.

2252

This **method is only appropriate** where:
– costs are incurred evenly over the life of the contract; and
– there is a strong correlation between costs incurred to date and the stage of completion of the contract.

Percentage cost completion method   The following **formula** should be used to **determine turnover** on long-term contracts:

2253

$$\frac{\text{costs incurred}}{\text{total expected costs}} \times \text{estimated contract value}$$

EXAMPLE On a contract worth £35,000 the company has incurred actual costs of £15,000 and estimates further costs of £10,000 to completion of the contract. Using the above formula would result in turnover of £21,000 being recognised:

$$= \frac{\text{£15,000 (costs incurred to-date)}}{\text{£15,000 + £10,000 (costs to-date + additional costs expected)}} \times \text{£35,000 (contract value)}$$

$$= \text{£21,000}$$

EXAMPLE This example illustrates a single contract that spans three financial years using the percentage cost completion method. The costs of £10,464 in year one represent 24% of the total estimated costs of £43,600. The cost percentage is then applied at the end of each accounting period to the total contract turnover to derive the profit for the period.

Contract – Alpha	Yr. 1 £ 20X1	Yr. 2 £ 20X2	Yr. 3 £ 20X3
Turnover per contract	55,000	55,000	55,000
Costs incurred to date	10,464	30,520	43,600
Costs to complete	33,136	13,080	0
Total estimated costs	43,600	43,600	43,600
Total estimated profit	**11,400**	**11,400**	**11,400**
Stage of completion (%)	24%	70%	100%

The profit and loss account for the three financial years 20X1-20X3 are shown below.

Contract – Alpha Profit and loss account	Cumulative profit £	Profit previous year £	Profit current Year £
Year 1 20X1 (cumulative)			
Turnover (£55,000 × 24%)	13,200		13,200
Costs (£43,600 × 24%)	10,464		10,464
Profit	2,736		2,736
Year 2 20X2 (cumulative)			
Turnover (£55,000 × 70%)	38,500	13,200	25,300
Costs (£43,600 × 70%)	30,520	10,464	20,056
Profit	7,980	2,736	5,244
Year 3 20X3 (cumulative)			
Turnover (£55,000 × 100%)	55,000	38,500	16,500
Costs (£43,600 × 100%)	43,600	30,520	13,080
Profit	11,400	7,980	3,420

Multi-stage contracts

2258 On some long-term contracts, for example the construction and delivery of a number of large capital items, the contract price may be determined and invoiced according to separate parts (or performance) of the contract (e.g. the number of aircraft or trains delivered). The most **appropriate method** of accounting for this type of contract is to match the costs of each distinct part of the contract with the corresponding sales value.

---

b. Cumulative turnover

2260 The cumulative turnover on the contract recorded in the profit and loss account for all accounting periods is compared with the total payments on account. If **turnover exceeds** "payments received on account", then an "amount recoverable on contracts" is determined and separately disclosed within debtors. For example, if the cumulative turnover over three accounting periods is £60 million and the payments on account total £45 million, then the balance of £15 million should be accounted for as "amounts recoverable on contracts".

2261 Where **payments on account** exceed turnover, the excess is classified as a deduction from the contract balance in long-term contract balances, if the contract is still work in progress. **If the contract is complete**, then **any residual balance** in excess of cost should be accounted for in creditors.

---

c. Additional guidance

2262 SSAP 9 gives specific guidance on the accounting treatment for all aspects of long-term contracts. Application Note G deals with the general principles of revenue recognition, while UITF 40 is narrower in scope providing additional guidance for accounting for revenue on service contracts.

Application Note G (AN G)

The application note to FRS 5 sets out the **principles of revenue recognition** to be applied in specific areas such as long-term contracts but does not amend the requirements of SSAP 9.

Under SSAP 9, the seller recognises turnover as the contract progresses where the value can be assessed with reasonable certainty. The seller should recognise changes in its assets or liabilities and turnover that reflect the accrual (of the right to consideration) over the term of the contract.

The **right to consideration** is, in turn, derived from an assessment of the fair value of the goods or services provided to date under the contract as a percentage of the total contract value. The fair values should be determined using the prices in force at the beginning of the contract unless the contractual terms allow for price changes to be passed on to the customer.

The **guiding principle** for all contracts is to determine the stage of completion of each project, in order to determine the seller's right to consideration. A consequence of this is that profitability may vary for different stages of a project.

It should be noted, however, that even with the introduction of Application Note G, there is still no single universally applied (or agreed) method of determining turnover on long-term contracts. The **most acceptable methods** are those based on calculating cumulative turnover by multiplying an estimated percentage of completion by the agreed value of the contract (see ¶2294).

UITF 40 (service contracts)

UITF 40 "Revenue recognition and service contracts" was issued to support the interpretation of FRS 5 AN G, and applies to all entities including those adopting the FRSSE.

The **principles** contained in the Abstract **apply to all contracts for services**, including those rendered by professional service firms such as accountants, solicitors and estate agents.

UITF 40 addresses the issue of whether SSAP 9 or AN G requires or permits revenue to be recognised as contract activity progresses or only on completion of the contract. As the terms and commercial substance of service contracts vary considerably, it is difficult to provide specific guidance for all types of contract. Each company will be required to develop an appropriate income recognition policy, taking into consideration the requirements of SSAP 9, AN G or UITF 40.

Companies may be **required to recognise profits** on contracts at an earlier stage. There is also a related tax issue in terms of the possible impact on taxable profits and the timing of the related tax charge.

UITF 40 reinforces the general principles contained in AN G, namely that there is no difference between the accounting treatment required for long-term contracts and other contracts for services. The **prime consideration** is whether the seller has performed, or partially performed, its contractual obligations. If the seller has performed some, but not all, of its contractual obligations, it is required to recognise revenue only to the extent that it has obtained the "right to consideration" through performance.

> MEMO POINTS   **Work in progress** is valued on the basis of the lower of cost and net realisable value (NRV). This principle applies to incomplete service contracts with the consequence that a profit or loss is not recognised for tax purposes until all the relevant contract obligations have been fulfilled.

Key elements   The principle elements of UITF 40 are as follows:

1. The Abstract **applies to** all contracts for services.
2. Where a single contract may be divided into **separate clearly identifiable stages**, it may be appropriate to account for them as separate transactions.
3. Where a contract for services falls into **separate accounting periods** and is deemed material it should be accounted for as a long-term contract. Where a number of such contracts exist, the aggregate effect should be assessed in relation to their impact on the financial statements.
4. Where the **substance of a contract** is that the seller's obligations are performed over time, revenue should be recognised as contract activity progresses, to reflect the seller's partial

performance of the contract. The revenue recognised should reflect the accrual of the "right to consideration" as the contract activity progresses.

5. Where the substance of the contract is that a **"right to consideration"** does not arise until a critical event has occurred (or condition fulfilled), then revenue should not be recognised until such time.

6. The **accounting policy** should be applied consistently to all similar contracts and from one accounting year to the next.

2. Cost of sales

2266 The costs associated with the turnover recorded in the profit and loss account should be deducted from the total costs incurred on the contract to date (under work in progress) and charged to the profit and loss account. The costs of sales relate directly to the **performance of the contract** and include:
– construction material costs;
– labour costs;
– transport costs for plant and equipment;
– depreciation of plant and machinery;
– design and technical costs;
– rectification and guarantee costs; and
– miscellaneous costs (e.g. insurance, general overheads).

2268 Traditionally, the cost of sales is matched with turnover with the balance representing profit. However, where the **recognition of profit** is uncertain, the cost of sales could represent the balancing figure after turnover and profit are calculated at the end of each financial period prior to completion of the contract.

The costs expensed should accurately reflect that part of the contract completed at the accounting date, and should be transferred from total contract costs incurred to cost of sales in the profit and loss account. If **format 2** of the balance sheet **is adopted**, then the cost transfer should be to the more detailed but appropriate headings.

2270 **Cost overruns** should be expensed in the relevant accounting period. In considering future costs, it is necessary to take account of likely increases in wages and salaries, and the price of raw materials and general overheads that are not recoverable.

2272 **Allocation of overheads** Administration overhead expenses that are not directly traceable to a specific contract are often split on an arbitrary basis and charged to each contract. The **alternative approach** is to omit these costs from the contract accounts and offset them against the total contribution to profit from contracts.

3. Identifiable profit

2276
SSAP 9 (23) Identifiable profit is the total profit estimated to arise over the **duration of the contract**, after allowing for:
– estimated remedial and maintenance costs; and
– increases in costs that are not recoverable under the terms of the contract.

The overall profit calculation may be independent of the valuation of turnover allocated to different accounting periods on a long-term contract. SSAP 9 aims to prevent the **arbitrary allocation** of profits between accounting periods.

Reasonable certainty

2278 The **overriding principle** is that profit cannot be attributable until the profitable outcome of the contract can be assessed with reasonable certainty. SSAP 9 does not give any guidance on how to determine reasonable certainty, and a contract completion figure of 30% may generally be regarded as the earliest point at which profit should be recognised. The general rules for identifying profit and appropriate accounting treatment are as set out in the following table.

General rules	
Scenario	**Accounting treatment**
When the outcome of long-term contracts can be assessed with reasonable certainty	The identifiable profit should be calculated on a **prudent basis** and included in the results of the period under review.
Recognising profit	It is necessary to determine the earliest point for each contract at which **profit** should be taken.
Specific nature/characteristics of the contract	In deciding whether a **stage in the contract** has been reached, at which it is appropriate to take profit (as with turnover), account should be taken of the nature of the business concerned.
Matching costs and revenues	The profit should not only reflect the proportion of the work completed at the accounting date but also take into account any known **inequalities in profitability** over the various stages of a contract's life cycle, thus resulting in a better match of costs and revenues.
Estimating profit	If the contract **is not split into stages or** where the **costs attributable to certified work** are not readily identifiable, then the profit attributable to completed work can only be estimated.

Profit uncertainty If the outcome of a long-term contract cannot be assessed with **reasonable certainty**, then no profit should be reflected in the accounts. Nevertheless, as long as it can be reasonably assumed that no loss will arise, it may be appropriate to show a proportion of the total contract value as turnover, using a zero estimate of profit.

2284
SSAP 9 (10)

> EXAMPLE If a zero profit (or loss) is expected on a long-term contract with a projected value of £200,000 that is 80% complete, it may be appropriate to reflect £160,000 as turnover. The transfer to cost of sales will equal the amount recorded as turnover.

Methods for determining identifiable profit

The two main methods for determining identifiable profit are:
– the percentage cost completion method; and
– valuation of the work authorised at the balance sheet date.

In addition, there are a **number of variations** on these methods that may be used to arrive at identifiable profit.

2290

The **choice of method** will depend on the difficulty of ascertaining costs and the type and scale of the project. The method selected should:
– be appropriate to the nature of the contract;
– be used consistently; and
– accord with the methods adopted by other companies within the industry.

2292

Percentage cost completion method   Under this method, the **cost of the work** completed to date is determined and then compared to the total estimated costs of the project. The total anticipated profit to completion is then calculated by multiplying the budgeted contract profit by the percentage of completed costs, as illustrated in the example below.

2294

A **variation** on the completion method is illustrated in the subsequent example, where the turnover is calculated by comparing actual costs to an agreed "bill of materials", derived from the contractor's project costings.

> EXAMPLE **Completion method – percentage cost basis**
>
> An aircraft manufacturer has agreed a fixed-price contract for £5m to supply components to a large commercial airline. The contract is for two years and the total estimated costs are £3.8m. The contractor ascertains the **stage of completion** of the contract by measuring the costs of work to date with the estimated total costs. The turnover was determined through an external valuation.

	Year 1	Year 2 Cum
	£m	£m
Turnover	3.0	5.0
Costs to date	1.5	3.0
Balance on costs	2.3	0.8
Total estimated costs	3.8	3.8
Estimated profit	1.2	1.2
Completion	**39%**	**100%**

The **completion rate** of 39% is derived by dividing costs to date by total estimated costs (£1.5m/£3.8m = 39%). A profit of £468,000 would be taken in year one (estimated profit of £1.2m × 39%) with the balance in year two. These figures can be presented as follows:

		£
Turnover in year 1		**3,000,000**
Less:		
costs to date	1,500,000	
cost provisions (balancing figure)	1,032,000	
Total cost		**2,532,000**
Profit		**468,000**

The cost provisions are found by deducting costs to date and profit from turnover.

An example of the **alternative cost completion method** based on budgeted costs is given below.

EXAMPLE   **Alternative cost completion method – based on budgeted costs**

A construction company that has a contract to refurbish a number of car showrooms with new branded elements including signage and entrance facia has agreed to invoice the client on a completion-based method. At the year end the costs for each site are computed and compared with the agreed "bill of materials" for each showroom. For instance, the costs incurred for showroom 1 total 75% of the budgeted costs which represents the turnover billed.

Under this contract the **profit element** (cost plus) for the contractor **is invoiced separately** on the basis of an agreed percentage fee for each completed showroom.

	Showrooms			
	1	2	3	4
Budgeted costs (£000's)	100	250	165	312
Actual costs to date (£000's)	75	158	122	200
Completion (%)	75	63	74	64
Turnover billed (£m)	75	158	122	200

2300   **Valuation method**   The valuation method may be based on either an independent **external valuation** or on **internal costings** prepared by the company. The procedure adopted will depend on the nature of the contract and the terms agreed with the client. Profit is recognised by taking an agreed proportion of the total contract value as turnover and using the formula stated in the example immediately below.

However, **profits may fluctuate considerably** over the life of a project (see example in ¶2302), thus requiring a different treatment. The valuation should also incorporate any known contingencies such as legal claims as illustrated in the example in ¶2306.

Care needs to be taken that the estimated profit is based on current levels of expenditure and not simply on initial profit estimates.

EXAMPLE   **Valuation method**

Formula

$$\frac{\text{External (internal) surveyor's valuation}}{\text{Total estimated contract value} \times \text{estimated profit}}$$

A company has a three-year contract valued at £500,000 with current estimated profits of £75,000. The recognition of turnover and profits is calculated using an **external** valuation at the end of each accounting period.

At the **end of the first accounting** period the external valuation of the contract is agreed at £258,750 (52% complete). A profit of £39,000 is determined as follows:

$$\frac{£258,750}{£500,000 \times £75,000} = £39,000 \text{ (approx)}$$

The cost of sales totals £219,750 with the balance of total costs of £55,250 (£275,000-£219,750) representing work in progress. In **year 2** the project is 80% complete with cumulative turnover of £400,000. Profits of £60,000 are recognised.

Contract – Beta	Year 1 £	Year 2 £	Year 3 £
External valuation of turnover (cumulative)	258,750	400,000	500,000
Percentage completion	52%	80%	100%
Profit taken (cumulative)	39,000	60,000	75,000
Costs to date (WIP)	275,000	385,000	425,000
Costs transferred to cost of sales	219,750	340,000	425,000
Work in progress	55,250	45,000	0

All **direct costs** are debited to the contract account, as are overheads, which are apportioned using one of a number of costing methods (¶2040). **Revenues** are credited to the contract account which is effectively a trading profit and loss account. As contracts usually span a number of accounting periods, the turnover and profit attributable to each financial year must be apportioned as illustrated in the following example.

2302

EXAMPLE **Gamma Construction Ltd.**

A construction contract valued at £250,000 is expected to take two years to complete, yielding a profit of £30,000. The contract accounts for the two years are as follows. Certified revenues totalled £120,000 in year 1.

For the purpose of the annual accounts the **depreciation charge** for plant was calculated (using the straight-line method) with reference to the expected value of the plant when the contract is complete. The estimated cost of the plant over two years is £16,000 (£18,000 – a residual value of £2,000). The **stocks** of materials on site, not utilised at the year end, were carried forward to year 2 at cost price. Costs not transferred to cost of sales form **work in progress** balances transferred to the profit and loss in year 2.

Credit is taken in year 1 for part of the estimated total profit on the completed contract (see note 2).

Gamma Construction Ltd.				
	Dr. £			Cr. £
Plant purchased	18,000	Certified work (see 1 below)		120,000
Materials purchased	47,950	Plant c/d		10,000
Plant hire	8,500	Stock c/d		2,000
Materials issued from stores	12,500	Work in progress c/d		27,181
Wages	32,045			
Subcontractors	10,000			
Direct expenses	15,786			
Gross profit – transferred to p/l	**14,400**	(See 2 below)		
	159,181			**159,181**
Year 2				
Plant b/d	10,000	Work certified		130,000
Stock b/d	2,000	Sale of plant		2,000
Work in progress b/d	27,181			
Materials purchased	44,691			
Wages	17,960			
Direct expenses	14,568			
Gross profit – to p/l	**15,600**	(See 2 below)		
Totals	**132,000**			**132,000**

1. Valuation of turnover
Year 1 The work completed to date was certified at £120,000.
Year 2 The contract was completed in year 2 and the balance of the contract's value (£130,000) was certified and invoiced. A retention fee of 5% (£15,000) was withheld at the year end and is reflected in debtors.

2. Calculation of profits (Valuation method)
Year 1
Work certified / total contract price × total estimated profit
£120,000 / £250,000 × £30,000 = 14,400

The contract is 48% complete so it is reasonable to take an element of profit in year one.
Year 2
£130,000 / £250,000 × £30,000 = 15,600

Fluctuating profits

2304 Profits may not be generated evenly over the life of a project, for instance where the project is divided into a number of distinct stages, each generating different levels of profit. The **relationship between costs and profit** in the valuation method is not based on a fixed percentage. Profits generated over the life of a contract may be uneven due to unexpected variations in cost and should reflect the activity undertaken in the period. Factors other than the percentage of contract completion, such as contract variations or legal claims, should also be considered.

EXAMPLE **Fluctuating profits**
This example illustrates a contract in which the **level of profits** varies over the life of the contract, without profit smoothing. A contract spanning three years has a value of £350,000 and a profit of £70,000. The **profits are not recognised** in proportion to costs but are based on an external valuation, with the costs matched subsequently. For instance in year one, the costs total 41% of the total costs although only 34% of the contract was valued as complete.

	Year 1 £	Year 2 £	Year 3 £	Totals £
External valuation (cum)	120,000	275,000	350,000	350,000
Turnover recorded	120,000	155,000	75,000	350,000
% of total contract turnover	34%	45%	21%	
Costs (actual) – by period	115,000	105,000	60,000	280,000
% of total costs	41%	38%	21%	
Profit by period	5,000	50,000	15,000	70,000
% of total contract profit	7%	71%	22%	

Adjustments to valuation

2306 The profit recorded in an accounting period should incorporate any variations in the estimated profitability of the contract and not just factors relevant to the period in question.

EXAMPLE A contract worth £500,000 spanning two years was expected to yield a profit of £50,000. At the commencement of the project the profit was estimated to accrue evenly over the life of the project.
After the first year, the project was 60% complete with an estimated profit of £30,000. However, due to expected cost overruns resulting from legal claims, the cumulative profit on the project has been downgraded to £30,000. As a result, the profit for year 1 should be reduced to £18,000.

Conversely, the profits calculated at previous accounting year ends may have been formulated on expectations of **cost overruns** that subsequently did not materialise, thus requiring an adjustment to the initial valuation.
Other factors that can affect the profits from a contract are considered in ¶2320 to ¶2328.

4. Contract losses

Foreseeable losses are those losses that are estimated to arise after the commencement of a contract after allowing for all remedial and maintenance work and cost overruns not recoverable under the terms of the contract. An **estimate is required** for foreseeable losses irrespective of:
2310
SSAP 9 (24)
– whether or not work has yet commenced on such contracts;
– the proportion of work completed at the accounting date; or
– the level of profits expected to be generated from other contracts with the same client.

If the outcome of a long-term contract is expected to be a loss, then the full loss should be taken in the accounting period in which it first becomes apparent.
SSAP 9 (11)

The foreseeable loss should be deducted from the work in progress figure of the relevant contract, thus reducing it to the net realisable value.

Any loss in excess of the work in progress figure should be classified as an accrual within **"Creditors"** or under **"Provisions for liabilities and charges"**, depending on the circumstances.

However, the accounting standard is not clear as to the exact nature of these circumstances. One interpretation could be that if a loss arose on a long-term contract because of an event that had already occurred, such as an overrun on material costs, then this would represent an accrual. If, however, the loss was estimated based on forecast levels of costs and remedial work, then a provision would be more appropriate, as set out in the following example:

EXAMPLE	**Loss recognised in full in the profit and loss account**		
The estimated loss for **Project Z** is as follows:			
			£
Value of work done and recognised as turnover			200,000
Total direct costs incurred			250,000
Total contract value			320,000
Expected total costs (including administrative overheads of £20k)			380,000
Estimated loss			60,000
The amount shown as a provision for foreseeable losses is:			
			£
Actual costs incurred			250,000
Less: Transferred to cost of sales		250,000	
Foreseeable loss on contract as a whole		**60,000**	
Total costs			310,000
Classified as: Provision for foreseeable losses			**60,000**

Where the **expected loss** on a contract is of such a magnitude that it will utilise a considerable part of company resources for a substantial period, any related administrative overheads incurred during the period to completion of the project should be included in the calculation of the provision for the losses.

5. Miscellaneous issues

Treatment of interest

In determining the value of long-term contracts it is not normally appropriate to include interest payable on borrowed money as this is charged separately to the profit and loss account. Financing is often agreed in tranches and may not be project specific. In circumstances where the finance procured can be identified as contract specific, a proportion of the related interest may be included in cost. The disclosure requirements are as for stocks.
2320

Contract variations

Examples of variations to long-term contracts include changes to:
– the scope or design requirements;
2322

- the contractual completion period; or
- legal requirements (e.g. health and safety).

Where **approved variations** have been made to a contract in the course of its execution and the amount receivable in lieu of the alterations is material, it is necessary to make a conservative estimate of the revenue which should be included in the total sales. Alternatively, provision should be made for any foreseen losses or penalties arising out of delays in completion or from other sources.

Legal claims

2324   The settlement of claims arising from circumstances not foreseen in the **original contract** or that result from approved variations can result in a high level of uncertainty. It is generally prudent to recognise receipts in respect of such claims only when:
- negotiations are at an advanced stage; and
- the value of the claims have been agreed.

2326   Where **additional contract costs** are expected to be incurred as a result of a dispute or losing a legal case, then the normal recognition of liabilities under FRS 12 apply. If the liability is recognised then this should be added to the contract costs and the estimated profit revisited. Where the **potential loss is considerable** it may be prudent not to recognise further profit until any dispute or legal claim is resolved.

Pre-contract costs

2327
UITF 34 (15)

Companies bidding for contracts can incur significant costs before the contract is secured. The issue is whether these costs should be expensed in the profit and loss account or recognised as an asset and charged to expenses over the term of the contract. The **general rule** is that directly attributable pre-contract costs should be recognised as an asset only when it is sufficiently certain that the contract has been secured.

> ⌐MEMO POINTS⌐   **UITF 34** covers the accounting treatment of pre-contract costs, namely expenses incurred in tendering for contracts to supply goods and services. The Abstract discusses which pre-contract costs should be recognised as an asset.

2328   **Directly attributable costs** should be interpreted as the range of costs that can be included in the cost of a tangible fixed asset under FRS 15 "Tangible fixed assets". Pre-contract costs incurred during the competitive tendering stage, up to the point at which it becomes reasonably certain that the contract has been secured, should be recognised as expenses and not subsequently reinstated as an asset. Further pre-contract costs are then recognised as an asset (within debtors) and charged as an expense over the period of the contract.

Amounts recovered in respect of **costs written off** are deferred and amortised over the life of the contract.

> ⌐EXAMPLE⌐   A marketing services company incurred considerable cost in tendering for a multinational services account. The costs incurred covered creative design and management time and were expensed as incurred.
> From the time the company expects to win the contract, costs incurred (e.g. management time, additional creative work, production materials and market research) can be recognised as an asset under work in progress (stocks) and later transferred to cost of sales.

SECTION 3

Disclosure requirements

2334   The requirements of the Companies Act and the accounting standards cover the general accounting policies to be disclosed, as well as the specific disclosures relating to key aspects of the accounting treatment for long-term contracts. Long-term contract balances are disclosed under the balance sheet heading of "Stocks".

---

1. Small companies

Long-term contracts must be accounted for on an individual contract basis, with turnover and associated costs included in the profit and loss account that reflects the progress on contract activity. Turnover is calculated after considering the stage of contract completion and the criteria applicable to the entity's particular industry. Where the outcome of a long-term contract can be assessed with reasonable certainty, attributable profit can be calculated on a prudent basis and included in the profit and loss account, representing the difference between turnover and related costs.

2335
FRSSE 8.6

The table below **summarises the key classifications** and balance sheet locations for disclosure requirements relating to long-term contracts. For companies undertaking many long-term contracts, the appropriate balance sheet disclosures should be determined contract by contract and not on an aggregate basis.

Key classifications	Key disclosures under FRSSE
Amounts "recoverable on contracts" (see also ¶2344)	Represents the amount recorded as turnover less amounts paid and should be disclosed separately in Debtors.
Payments on account (see ¶2348)	Disclosed separately in creditors.
Long-term contract balances (see ¶2356)	Represents costs incurred, less amounts transferred to cost of sales, after allowing for foreseeable losses & payments on a/c not matched with turnover. Disclose separately in balance sheet under stocks. In a note to the balance sheet the following balances should be given where appropriate: – net costs less foreseeable losses; and – applicable payments on accounts.
Provision for foreseeable losses (see ¶2352)	Represents amount of provision for foreseeable losses that exceeds costs incurred and should be disclosed within either creditors or provisions for liabilities.
Profit and loss disclosures	Turnover, cost of sales or losses.

---

2. Medium-sized and large companies

The principal disclosures are included in SSAP 9, covering accounting policies, payments on accounts and provisions for losses.

2336

---

a. Accounting policies

It is a key requirement of SSAP 9 that accounting policies for long-term contracts and especially **the method** of calculating turnover and identifiable profit (on a prudent basis) are disclosed in a note to the financial statements. The accounting policies must be applied consistently within the business from year to year.

2337
SSAP 9 (32)

Where different bases have been adopted for various types of long-term contracts, the amount included in the financial statements in respect of each type should be stated.

2338
SSAP 9 (14)

The first example below illustrates the general information to be disclosed relating to the valuation and ongoing control or review procedures on long-term contracts. The following examples illustrate accounting policies relating to turnover, profits, and costs.

> **EXAMPLE** **Accounting policies – Valuation policy**
>
> **Valuation** Long-term contract balances are valued at costs incurred on specific contracts, net of amounts transferred to cost of sales in respect of work recorded as turnover, less foreseeable losses and payments on account. If the ultimate profitability of a contract can be assessed with reasonable certainty, after having made prudent allowance for future risks and uncertainties, then profit is recognised in proportion to the contract work completed. Immediate provision is made for all foreseeable losses.

> **EXAMPLE** **Disclosure of accounting policies**
>
> **Turnover.** Contract turnover includes the value of work completed during the financial year, after reference to the total sales value and stage completion of the project and including the settlement of claims arising from previous years.
>
> **Profits** on long-term contracts are calculated in accordance with industry standard accounting practice and do not directly relate to turnover. Profit on current contracts is only taken at the stage near enough to completion for that profit to be reasonably certain. Provision is made for all losses incurred to the accounting date, together with any further losses that are foreseen in bringing contracts to completion.
>
> **Costs** for this purpose include valuation of all work done by subcontractors, whether certified or not, and all overheads other than those relating to the general administration of the relevant companies. For any contracts where receipts exceed the book value of the work done, the excess is included in creditors as payments on account.

b. Other key disclosures

2342 The **key classifications** and balance sheet locations for disclosure requirements relating to long-term contracts for medium-sized and larger entities are set out below and supported by examples modelled on published accounts. For companies undertaking many long-term contracts, the appropriate balance sheet disclosures should be determined contract by contract and not on an aggregate basis.

Amounts "recoverable on contracts"

2344 Amounts "recoverable on contracts" is a classification specific to long-term contracts and represents the amount by which **turnover exceeds payments received on account**; it is shown separately under debtors.

An "amount recoverable on contracts" does not have the contractual status of a debtor in the strict legal form, although it represents accrued income receivable and has all the attributes of a debtor. This is because once a transaction has been recorded as turnover and invoiced to the client, then any amounts remaining unpaid represent debtors and not stock.

2346 The balance may, in effect, include an **element of profit** recognised on contracts still in progress. Therefore, it would be inappropriate to include the balance within stock, which is required by company law and the accounting standards to be shown, normally at the lower of cost and net realisable value. This treatment is well established under the **accrual concept** of cost and revenue recognition and the requirement under FRS 5 to reflect the substance of a transaction.

> **EXAMPLE** **Project X**
>
> | | £ |
> | --- | --- |
> | Turnover recognised | 265,000 |
> | Cumulative payments on account received | 220,000 |
> | **Excess – recoverable on contracts** | **45,000** |
> | – included in Debtors | |
> | Total costs incurred | 230,000 |
> | Costs transferred to cost of sales | 190,000 |
> | **Balance to work in progress** | **40,000** |

The amount to be included under "Amounts recoverable on contracts" in the balance sheet and disclosed separately under debtors is £45,000, being the amount by which turnover of £265,000 exceeds payments on account of £220,000.

The balance of costs not yet transferred to cost of sales is included in work in progress.

Balance sheet (extract)
Note – Debtors Amounts recoverable on contracts

	Group £'000
Amounts falling due within one year	
Trade and other debtors	360
Amounts recoverable on contracts	**45**
Amounts falling due after one year	
Trade and other debtors	35
Contract retentions	25
Totals	**465**

Accounting policy note

Amounts "recoverable on contracts" which are included in **debtors** are stated at cost, plus attributable profit to the extent that this is reasonably certain after making provision for contingencies, less any losses incurred or foreseen in bringing contracts to completion and less amounts received as progress payments.

Payments on account

If payments on account **are greater than** the amount of **turnover recognised**, then the excess balance should initially be offset against the amount disclosed as long-term contract balances under stocks for the project concerned.

If the excess is greater than the contract balance, the residual amount should be shown as "Payments on account" under creditors.

Payments on account may also be listed as "Payments received in advance of turnover".

2348
SSAP 9 (30)

EXAMPLE Assume that payments on account for **Project X** in the example above were £320,000. The result, after deducting the value of work completed of £265,000, is a credit balance of £55,000. This represents the balance of costs not transferred to cost of sales (£40,000) and recorded in Stocks and the £15,000 accounted for as "excess payments on account".

This figure should be set off against the amount carried under stocks for the project and the balance remaining shown separately as "Payments on account" under creditors:

	£	
Value of work completed	265,000	
Total costs incurred	230,000	
Transferred to cost of sales	190,000	
Included under stock	**40,000**	
Offset: excess payments on account	55,000	(320,000 – 265,000)
Included in creditors	**15,000**	(55,000 – 40,000)

Balance sheet (extract)
Note – Creditors

	Group 20X3 £'000	Group 20X2 £'000
Amounts falling due within one year		
Trade and other creditors	180	158
Contracts – payments received on account	**15**	**12**
Amounts falling due after one year		
Trade and other creditors	35	30
Totals	**230**	**190**

Provision for foreseeable losses

2352
SSAP 9 (30)

The amount by which the provision for foreseeable losses exceeds costs incurred (after transfers to cost of sales) must be shown under provisions for "liabilities and charges" or "creditors", as appropriate.

EXAMPLE **Balance sheet**
Provisions for liabilities and charges

	Deferred Tax £m	Losses on contracts £m	Total £m
Group			
Balances at 1 April 20X2	55	15	70
Charged against profit for the year	15	25	40
Total provisions at 31 March 20X3	**70**	**40**	**110**

Long-term contract balances

2356

Long-term contract balances **represent** the cost of works in progress, after deducting any foreseeable losses and payments on account not matched with turnover; they are classified as "long-term contract balances" and disclosed separately under stocks.

SSAP 9 (30)

By **way of note**, the following should be also be **disclosed separately**:
– net cost less foreseeable losses; and
– applicable payments on account.

The first example is of a contract expected to produce a profit whilst the second example illustrates the accounting treatment and disclosures required for a loss-making contract.

EXAMPLE **Profitable contract**

	£
Value of work completed	245,000
Total costs incurred	267,000
Payments received on account	215,000
Contract value	320,000
Estimated total costs	307,000
Estimated profit	13,000

Accounting treatment
Profit and loss account   **20X3**

Turnover	245,000
Cost of sales	(235,050)
Profit	**9,950**

Profit calculated as follows: (245,000/320,000 × 13000)

Balance sheet   **20X3**

Total costs	267,000
less costs transferred to profit and loss	(235,050)
Long-term contract balances	**31,950**

Disclosures
Annual Report and Accounts (extract)
Notes to the accounts – Stocks and long-term contracts

	£'000's
Raw material and consumables	10.0
Long-term contract balances:	
– Net costs less foreseeable losses	246.9
– Applicable payments on account	(215.0)
Total stocks	**41.9**

EXAMPLE **Loss making contract**

Assume the following details for **Project Y**, a long-term contract in progress undertaken by B Ltd. as at 31 December 20X3. The directors are of the opinion that there will be a loss of £25,000 on the contract as a whole.

	£
Value of work done and recognised as turnover	255,000
Payments on account	260,000
Total costs incurred	310,000
Costs transferred to cost of sales	265,000

The amount to be included under long-term contract balances is calculated as follows:

	£
Total costs to date	310,000
Less: transferred to cost of sales	265,000
	45,000
Less: foreseeable losses on contract as a whole	(25,000)
	20,000
Less: Excess payments on account (£260,000 – £255,000)	(5,000)
Long-term contract balances	**15,000**

The notes to the balance sheet must disclose separately:
1. the net cost less foreseeable losses of £275,000 (£255,000 + 25,000 – £5000); and
2. payments on account of £260,000.

Balance sheet extract – B Ltd.
Notes to the accounts – Stocks

	20X3 £m
Raw material and consumables	4
Properties in development	45
Long-term contract balances:	
– Net cost less foreseeable losses	275
– Applicable payments on accounts	(260)

Disclosure of losses in the profit and loss account

Where an **expected loss has crystallised**, the gross loss to be shown in the profit and loss account is the difference between amounts recognised as turnover and the amounts transferred to cost of sales plus provisions for foreseeable losses.

2360

EXAMPLE If, for example, a project is expected to yield a loss of £40,000 and costs of £250,000, then the profit and loss account should be charged with the following:
Profit and loss account

		£
Included in turnover		250,000
Less: Included in cost of sales	250,000	
Foreseeable loss on contract as a whole	40,000	290,000
Loss		**40,000**

CHAPTER 3

Debtors

Debtors **are defined as** monies owed to an organisation for the sales of goods or services and amounts paid to third parties in advance of goods and services.

The classification, accounting treatment and disclosure requirements relating to debtors are contained primarily in the Companies Act although the legislation is supported by a number of accounting standards and pronouncements.

2400

In general, all debtors should be disclosed as current assets, no matter when they fall due. Additional disclosures are also required for **material debtors** due more than one year from the end of the financial period. **Small companies** that adopt the financial reporting standard for smaller entities (FRSSE) are exempt from the reporting requirements of the other accounting standards. **Specific rules** also apply to small companies who elect to submit short-form or abbreviated accounts.

2404

There are no significant differences between current UK GAAP and the new financial reporting standard FRS 102, whose adoption is mandatory from January 2015.

1. Classification

"Debtors" is a **main statutory heading** under current assets and must be shown on the face of the balance sheet. Various sub-categories of debtors are also required to be shown either on the face of the balance sheet or in the notes to the accounts.

2408

Small companies The **statutory sub-categories** of "debtors" for small companies are contained in SI 2008 No.409 as follows:
– Trade debtors;
– Amounts owed by group undertakings and undertakings in which the company has a participating interest; and
– Other debtors.

2410

Medium-sized and large entities The classification and sub-categories for medium-sized and large entities are contained in SI 2008 No. 410 as follows:
– Trade debtors;
– Amounts owed by group undertakings;
– Amounts owed by undertakings in which the company has a participating interest;
– Other debtors;

2412

- Called up share capital not paid; and
- Prepayments and accrued income.

2413   Further items **not covered** by the statutory format but which are covered by financial reporting standards may be shown separately in the financial statements and include amounts:
- Receivable in respect of finance leases;
- Receivable in respect of hire purchase contracts;
- Factored debts; and
- Recoverable on contracts (e.g. long-term contracts).

---

2. Accounting treatment

2416   The Companies Act **requires all debtors** to be stated at the lower of cost and net realisable value, after deducting any provision for doubtful or bad debts. The accounting treatment for the different categories of debtors is outlined in this section.

---

a. Statutory categories

Trade debtors

2420   Trade debtors represents the aggregate of amounts due from customers in respect of goods and services supplied, but not yet paid for. It will also include the **VAT payable** by customers on invoices raised but not yet paid.

The category "trade debtors" typically consists of:
- amounts invoiced to customers;
- goods delivered but not yet invoiced;
- retentions on contracts; and
- suppliers debit balances.

2422   Each individual **sales ledger account** records sales, cash received, discounts given and details of goods returned. The totals of the individual debtor balances should be reconciled to the debtors ledger control account.

If the **net realisable value** of the total debtors is likely to be less than the amount recorded in the company's accounts, a provision should be made against the carrying value of the debt to reduce it to the estimated realisable value.

Provisions

2426   Such provisions made are needed in respect of the following:
- bad and doubtful debts;
- credit notes issued for returns/credit balances; or
- settlement discounts.

2427   **Bad debts**   All debtors balances should be assessed prior to the finalisation of the annual statutory accounts, in order to determine the "recoverability" of each debt. Particular attention should be paid to debtors outstanding **in excess of the current credit terms**. Where a debtor is not expected to pay either in whole or in part, a specific provision should be made against the balance to cover the anticipated shortfall. **General provisions** as a percentage of the total outstanding debtor balance may also be provided based on past experience. Such general provisions may not, however, attract tax relief.

2428   **Credit notes and credit balances**   Provision should be made for any credit notes issued after the year end (post-balance sheet) in respect of invoices included in end of year balances, as the debtors figure in the balance sheet will not be fully realised. If a material credit balance arises on a debtor account, for instance where a customer has paid an invoice twice, then this amount should be transferred to creditors.

Settlement discounts   A company may give a discount to customers for prompt payment   **2432**
of invoices. The discount is deducted from the payment remitted and must be removed from
trade debtors and charged to the profit and loss account.

Amounts owed by group undertakings

All amounts owed by group members, namely the **parent, subsidiary and fellow subsidiary**   **2436**
undertakings, are required to be shown separately under debtors, as amounts due from
group undertakings. These amounts include:
– loans;
– current accounts; and
– dividends receivable.

Inter-company balances due from one group undertaking should not be set off against those   **2438**
due to another group undertaking, unless a legal right of set-off exists. For example, if
Company A has a debtor balance of £30,000, due from a subsidiary company with whom it
also has a creditor balance of £25,000, but no legal right of set-off, then it cannot offset one
account against the other.

The **disclosure requirements** for group undertakings and participating interests are illustrated in the example below.

EXAMPLE   A Ltd – Annual report and accounts 20X3
Notes to the accounts (extract)

Debtors

	20X3 £'000	20X2 £'000
Due within one year		
Trade debtors	56,500	48,750
Amounts recoverable on contracts	15,785	11,786
Amounts owed by subsidiaries	**5,785**	**1,567**
Amounts owed by associated undertakings	**2,789**	-
Amounts owed by joint ventures	**3,568**	**1,256**
Prepayments	687	2,568
Other debtors	1,473	899
	86,587	66,826
Due after one year		
Trade debtors	5,786	2,457
Amounts owed by joint ventures	-	**287**
Prepayments	2,023	1,602
	7,809	4,346
Totals	**94,396**	**71,172**

Amounts owed by participating interests

Participating interests include any **associates or joint ventures** of the company. Under FRS   **2444**
9, amounts owed by participating interests should be analysed between amounts relating to
loans and amounts consisting of trade balances.

Called-up share capital not paid

Any amounts outstanding at the balance sheet date in respect of called-up share capital can   **2450**
be shown either as a **sub-category** of debtors or as a **main heading** in the balance sheet
before fixed assets. It is usual for an explanation to be given in the share capital
note concerning the amounts outstanding.

EXAMPLE   Company A has a called-up share capital of £6m of which £4.5m has been paid in two
stages. The balance outstanding as at 30 June 2013 of £1.5m was stated in its financial statements
under debtors and represents the following:

– £0.5m called-up share capital not paid from the second "call"; and
– £1m representing the third and final call in respect of the original flotation terms.

Prepayments and accrued income

2452   Prepayments and accrued income may be disclosed as a sub-category of debtors or under a separate heading on the face of the balance sheet. Factors that will influence how they are disclosed include the materiality of the amounts concerned and whether they fall due after more than one year.

When determining profit or loss for a period, it is important that revenues earned are matched against the costs incurred in earning them. Therefore, any costs incurred in respect of future revenue streams should be disclosed as prepayments.

2454   In order to **carry forward expenditure** as a prepayment, the **following criteria** should be satisfied:
a. the expenditure should not relate to income that has been included in the profit and loss account;
b. the expenditure should generate future revenues sufficient to cover the amortisation of these costs (otherwise they will result in losses that should be recognised immediately);
c. the period during which the expenses should be amortised should be short enough to allow for reasonable certainty of recovery; and
d. prepayments should be subject to continuous review and written off immediately their "recoverability" becomes doubtful.

2455   **Examples of prepayments** include:
– rent paid in advance;
– unexpired portion of insurance premiums;
– unexpired portion of interest payments; and
– advertising costs paid in advance (but only if the specific campaign has not commenced at the accounting date).

In practice, if the enterprise is deemed to be a going concern and the element prepaid is not in respect of an onerous contract, for example, rent not paid on a factory that is no longer operational, it is usual to assume that the necessary conditions have been met.

EXAMPLE   **C. Ltd – Annual report and accounts**
Notes to the financial statements 20X3 (extract)

Debtors

	20X3 £000's	20X2 £000's
Due within one year		
Trade debtors	589	478
Other debtors	399	153
Prepayments	**40**	**41**
	1028	672
Due after more than one year		
Amounts recoverable on contracts	530	125
Pension prepayment	28	
	558	125
Totals	**1586**	**797**

The prepayments of £68,000 include a payment in advance for materials under a ten year agreement which was signed this year, totalling £40,000 and £28,000 for a receivable due after more than one year resulting from a bond posted in the US in lieu of litigation.

2456   **Exemptions and exclusions**   UITF Abstract 24 "Accounting for start-up costs" **specifically prohibits** the treatment of certain start-up activities as prepayments, except where similar costs as part of a company's ongoing activities would also be deferred.

Start-up costs cover costs relating to:
- the establishment of a new entity;
- a new operation within an existing business; or
- the launching of new products or the reorganisation of all or part of an enterprise.

Accrued income includes amounts earned at the end of the accounting period but which   **2458**
the reporting entity has not yet invoiced or received. Examples are rental income, interest
and goods despatched but not invoiced. Goods despatched but not invoiced are usually
included in trade debtors, since the transaction has legally taken place although the invoice
has yet to be raised.

Other debtors

Other debtors that result from **non-trading activities** include: **2459**
- amounts due from the sale of fixed assets (e.g. sale of building, land);
- insurance claims (e.g. fire, theft);
- refundable deposits (e.g. land purchase);
- tax balances; or
- loans to finance the acquisition of the company's own shares.

Although principally trading related, this category also includes advances or partial payments
for the construction of stocks or fixed assets (e.g. long-term contracts).

Tax balances   Tax balances listed under other debtors include VAT repayments or recover-   **2460**
able corporation tax.

Debtor tax balances do not need to be shown separately, except where they are material to
an appreciation of the balance sheet. It should be noted that deferred tax assets, which are
not netted off against deferred tax liabilities, should also be included within debtors and
shown separately if material.

EXAMPLE B Ltd – Annual report and accounts – 20X3		
Notes to the financial statements (extract)		
Debtors		
	20X3	20X2
	£'000	£'000
Trade debtors	499	353
Other debtors	366	153
Corporation tax	**49**	**21**
Other taxes and social security	**15**	**10**
Advance corporation tax recoverable	**12**	
Prepayments	32	26
Totals	**973**	**563**

Loans to finance acquisition of shares   If a company has provided loan capital to fund   **2461**
the purchase of its own shares, the aggregate amount of such loans should be disclosed in
the notes to the accounts. The degree to which a company can provide loans for the acquisition of its own shares is limited and there are specific conditions that must be satisfied before
they are permitted. The **relevant rules** are discussed in greater detail in part 5 chapter 5.

The following are examples of the **types of loans** made by a company to finance the acquisition of its own shares:

a. financial assistance to an **employee share scheme** or to facilitate transactions in the
company's shares between employees, former employees, their spouses, infant children or
stepchildren;

b. loans to **bona fide employees** to enable them to purchase shares in the company or its
holding company to be held by them by way of beneficial ownership; and

c. loans made by a **private company** to acquire its own shares or those of its holding
company, or to reduce any liability incurred as a result of acquiring these shares.

b. Non-statutory categories

Amounts recoverable on contracts

2470   Enterprises engaged in **long-term contracts** are required by SSAP 9 "Stocks and long-term contract" to include turnover within debtors as "Amounts recoverable on contracts" where turnover exceeds payments on account. SSAP 9 requires that these amounts be disclosed separately within debtors as an additional heading to those normally required by the Companies Act.

Any amounts actually invoiced to customers, including requests for progress payments are included under trade debtors.

Finance leases

2472   Where a finance lease is in place, SSAP 21 "Lease and Hire Purchase Contracts" requires that the lessor follows "substance over form". Therefore, instead of showing an asset which is the subject of the lease within fixed assets, the lessor includes a "debtor" in their balance sheet, representing the net investment in the lease; namely, the fair value of the asset at the beginning of the agreement less the present value of the lease payments received.

2473   The **lease rental payments** representing the income stream over the life of the agreement must be apportioned between:
– the repayment of the principal capital; and
– the interest element on the outstanding finance provided.

2474   The **lease debtor** should not include any unearned interest, leaving only the principal balance to be disclosed. In the case of finance leases, the lessor's net investment in the lease is recorded under debtors as an additional heading "Amounts receivable under finance leases". This heading is in addition to those required by the Companies Act.

2476   The **net investment** in finance leases should be disclosed separately under "amounts receivable under finance leases", within debtors.

The figures should also be analysed between amounts due within one year and after one year.

EXAMPLE   **D. Ltd – Annual report and accounts 20X3**
Notes to the financial statements (extract)

Finance leases

	20X3 £'000	20X2 £'000
Amounts due within one year		
Trade debtors	652	385
Capital grants receivable	285	178
Other debtors	199	93
Prepayments	27	31
Net investment in finance leases	14	13
	1,177	**700**
Amounts due after more than one year		
Other debtors	18	20
Net investment in finance leases	53	68
	71	**88**
Totals	**1,248**	**788**
Net investment in finance leases comprises		
Total lease payments receivable	96	116
Less finance charges allocated to future periods	(43)	(48)
Totals	**53**	**68**

Hire purchase agreements

Hire purchase agreements are similar in nature to finance leases and are therefore accounted for in the same way.   **2478**

Under a hire purchase agreement, the buyer takes possession of the goods, usually following the payment of an initial deposit, and ownership is obtained when all the agreed number of subsequent installments have been paid. Hire purchase agreements often involve a finance company as a third party. The manufacturer of the goods often sells them to a finance company which then enters into a hire purchase agreement with the customer.

Where **hire purchase agreements** have also been agreed, these should be disclosed separately under a subheading, detailing:
– the outstanding lease payments due under the terms of the agreement; and
– the residual values of "leased" assets.
The figures should also be analysed between amounts due within one year and after one year.

2479

EXAMPLE **D. Ltd – Annual report and accounts**
Notes to the financial statements 20X3 (extract)

Hire purchase debtors

	20X3 £m	Due after more than one year £m
Amounts due within one year		
Installments and hire purchase debtors	999.7	203.6
Provision for unearned finance charges	(60.1)	(17.2)
Other debtors	380.0	25.2
Total trade debtors	**1,319.6**	**211.6**
Book value of finance leases in lessor subsidiaries	16.5	15.2
Prepayment and accrued income	120.5	18.2
	1,456.6	**245.0**

3. Debt factoring

Debt factoring comes in many guises but typically **allows companies to** convert debtors into cash quickly and can help mitigate the risk of slow payment or bad debts. However, in most cases it is the company entering the factoring arrangement, and not the debt factor, that is still exposed to the risk of bad debts. In general, therefore, applying the principles inherent in FRS 5, "Substance of transactions", means factored debts are usually accounted for as trade debtors, although the presentation will differ depending on the type of debt or agreement.   **2480**

FRS 5 gives guidance in Application Note C on the applicable accounting treatment and disclosure requirements for debtors.

a. Overview

Debt factoring is a popular method of raising funds from the **sale of debtor balances** to a third party, before the debts are collected. The transactions can take many forms, with the simplest involving a clear sale at a fixed price without recourse or where the factor takes over the administration of the sales ledger and collects the debts on behalf of the company.   **2482**
FRS 5 (C1)
FRSSE 8.10

In **more complicated arrangements**, the buyer (factor) may have recourse to the seller in the event of non-payment and, in addition, the price received for the debts may vary depending upon how long they remain unpaid, to reflect any possible slow payment risk. Under these types of arrangement, where the seller retains a significant economic interest in the   **2483** underlying debts, they should be accounted for as financing arrangements, with the debtors remaining on the balance sheet.

2484   **Debt factoring agreements may require** different accounting treatments as dictated by the terms of each individual agreement, the main characteristics of which are usually as follows:
a. a company sells or assigns specific debts to the factor;
b. the factor provides finance to the company selling the debt based on a percentage of the value of the debt transferred; and
c. the factor will charge for the factoring services which may be a fixed amount, or based on actual sums collected from the debtors. Alternatively, it could represent an amount based on the sum advanced and the time taken to collect from the debtor.

b. Principal factoring methods

2486

FRS 5 (C3)

There are **three principal accounting treatments** for companies factoring their debtors:
– derecognition;
– separate presentation; or
– linked presentation
Each of these options is discussed below.

A detailed understanding of the **commercial terms** (as well as the practical and theoretical detail) of each factoring agreement is necessary in order to determine which of the accounting treatments is most suitable. It is **important to ascertain**:
– which party retains the benefits and risks of each agreement; and
– the basis of the factoring charges.

2488   **Benefits**   The benefits of the agreement include future cash flows derived from the settlement of monies due by the debtors and the risks will be of default or slow payment. It will often be **the nature of the risk** that determines the appropriate accounting treatment.

Summary table	
Accounting treatment	**Characteristics**
Derecognition	No significant risks/benefits retained.
	Factor has no recourse to the company.
Separate presentation	Factored debts and related finance shown separately (not linked) on balance sheet where a company retains significant risks/benefits. Conditions for linked presentation not met.
Linked presentation	Company retains significant benefits/risks. Exposure to losses restricted to a fixed amount.

Derecognition

2490

FRS 5 (C11)

An entity may only use this accounting treatment where all the **following criteria** exist:
– a sale of the debtors to the factor at arm's length;
– the company receives fixed, non-returnable funds from the factor for the debts;
– there is no recourse to the company selling the debt (in terms of slow payment or bad debts); or
– the company will not benefit or suffer in any way if the debts perform better or worse than expected.

2492   Where **debts are sold without recourse** and all further risks to the seller are effectively eliminated, the accounting treatment is termed "derecognition". The debts can be credited with the sale proceeds and the effect is the same as if the respective debtors had settled the debts themselves. These debtors are then removed from the balance sheet and no liability to the factor is recorded.

However, an entity would be required to record a loss on the disposal of the debts which represents the difference between the face value of the debts and the payment received from the factor. Where **any of these features is not present**, this means the seller has retained the risks and benefits relating to factored debts and either a separate or linked presentation should be used.

> [EXAMPLE] **Wortley Ltd**
> **Notes to the accounts**
> **Derecognition**
>
> A company opts to factor debtors valued at £300,000 for £270,000. No further sum is receivable from the factor company who in turn has no recourse to the company for bad debts or slow payment. In this instance, the company has sold the debtors for a fixed sum and does not retain the right to any benefits from the payments made by the debtors or bear any further risk in relation to the debts.
> The entity will be required to post a charge of £30,000 to the profit and loss account representing the factor's fee for purchasing the debtors.

Separate presentation

The **following characteristics** indicate that a separate presentation is the appropriate accounting treatment:

2494
FRS 5 (C17)

- the cost of factoring varies with the speed of payment by the debtors;
- there is full recourse to the seller for losses; and
- the seller is required to repay a fixed amount on a specified date, regardless of timing or debtor balances collected.

In other words, where the seller retains significant benefits and risks relating to debts and conditions for a linked presentation are not met, then separate presentation is required.

Where the company retains **significant risks** in respect of the factored debts, these debts remain under debtors on the balance sheet with the amounts disclosed by way of note. The proceeds received from the factor are reflected as a liability and shown separately as a creditor, as it represents the finance provided by the factor for the debts. The **interest element** of the factor's charges should be charged in the profit and loss account on a basis consistent with the terms of the financing.

2496
FRS 5 (C20)

> [EXAMPLE] **B Ltd – Separate presentation**
>
> Funding from a factoring agent has been arranged totalling £125,000 against a debtors ledger balance of £155,000. These monies are repayable to the factor in three months' time, when any outstanding debtors are transferred back to the company. In this instance the company has retained all the **benefits and risks** in respect of the debts.
>
> **Accounting Treatment** The problem will be if the debtors are slow in paying then the company will have to find alternative funding in order to repay the factoring agent after three months. Furthermore, all potential bad debts will be returned to the company after the agreement has expired.
> The notes to the financial statements should detail the total of the factored debts **discounted with recourse** that are outstanding at the balance sheet date.
>
> **B Ltd – Annual report and accounts – 20X3**
> **Notes to the accounts (extract)**
> **10. Debtors**
> Following the adoption of FRS 5, "Reporting the Substance of Transactions", trade debtors and bank loans and overdrafts as at 30 June 20X3 include £125,000 of invoices discounted with recourse.

Linked presentation

A linked presentation **is defined** as the presentation in the balance sheet of an asset that is in substance a financing arrangement. The asset can be shown gross on the face of the balance sheet with the finance liability deducted from the same asset caption.

2498
FRS 5 (C15)

2500 A linked presentation will be appropriate where, although the seller has **retained significant benefits and risks** concerning the factored debts, there is no doubt that the exposure to a loss is limited to a fixed monetary amount. A linked presentation **should only be used where** there is no doubt that the factor's claim extends solely to collections from the factored debts and no provision exists for the seller to reacquire the debts in the future.

Where the company **retains significant risks and benefits** in respect of the factored debts but the downside exposure to losses are limited to a fixed amount, the debts concerned may be recorded as a linked presentation.

2502 However, in order that a linked presentation may be adopted, **the following criteria must be met**:

FRS 5 (27)   1. The financing (principal and interest) must be repaid from the proceeds of the item.
2. The entity should not have the option of retaining the title to the asset on repayment of the financing or be able to reacquire the item at some point in the future.
3. The entity does not have the right to retain the item upon repayment of the finance or to re-acquire it at any time.
4. The finance relates to a specific item and, in the case of a loan, is secured on that item and not on any other asset.
5. The finance provider has no recourse to the other assets of the entity for losses and the entity has no obligation to make good the losses.
6. The directors of the entity must disclose in the financial statements that where a linked presentation has been adopted, the entity is not required to make good any losses incurred by the finance provider.
7. If the revenues generated by the item are insufficient to repay the finance provider, this does not constitute a default by the entity.
8. Where all of the above conditions hold for only a part of the finance, a linked presentation should be used only for that part.

2504 **Accounting treatment** The **following conditions** also apply when considering the **accounting treatment** of a financing arrangement as a linked presentation:
– a linked presentation should not be used where the debts that have been factored cannot be separately identified; and
– the factor agrees in writing that there is no recourse, and such an agreement is noted in the financial statements.

FRS 5 (C16)   Where debts are **factored on an ongoing basis**, the arrangements for terminating the agreement must be scrutinised to ensure that the conditions for a linked presentation are met. It is a requirement that, although it does not take on further debts, the factor continues to bear the risk of any losses on debts already factored and is not able to transfer them back to the seller. Where this is not the case, the factor may have the option of returning the debts that it suspects will be bad, by terminating the factoring arrangement. In this situation the seller's exposure is not limited and a linked presentation inappropriate.

The mechanics of linked presentation are illustrated in the examples below.

2506 **Profit recognition** Where a **linked presentation** is adopted, profit should be recognised only to the extent that the non-returnable proceeds received exceed the previous carrying value of the item. Thereafter, any profit or loss arising from the item should be recognised in the period in which it relates. The net profit or loss recognised should be included in the profit and loss account with separate disclosure of its gross components given in the notes to the accounts.

2508 **Disclosures** Under the linked presentation, the company continues to reflect its factored
FRS 5 (27)   debts (after deducting the finance element and providing for bad debts) on the balance sheet. In addition, the **notes to the financial statements** should include the following:
– the main terms of the agreement;
– the gross amount of the outstanding factored debts;
– the factoring charges recognised during the period (analysed as to interest and other charges);

– a statement that the company is not obliged to support, or intends to support, losses beyond the specified recourse in respect of specific debts under the arrangement; and
– confirmation that the factor has agreed, in writing, to seek recourse to interest and principal only to the extent that sufficient funds are generated by the specific debts it has agreed to finance.

The accounting treatment and key disclosure requirements for two different examples are given below.

EXAMPLE **Linked presentation**
C Ltd has factored debts of £745,000 in return for an initial non-returnable payment from the factor of £520,000, plus further deferred sums, based on the amounts actually collected from the debtors.

Accounting treatment C Ltd has retained:
– some of the benefits of future payments from debtors as further sums will be receivable from the factor, depending on the level of payment by the debtors; and
– a proportion of the risks of non-payments by the debtors.
C Ltd has limited its potential exposure to the risk of slow payment or bad debts to £225,000. The company should adopt a linked presentation in its disclosure in the balance sheet.

EXAMPLE **Linked presentation**
D Ltd enters into a factoring agreement with **F Ltd** under the following terms:
– D will transfer by assignment to F such trade debts as D shall determine, subject only to a credit approval by F who levies a charge of 5% of turnover, payable monthly;
– D will continue to run the sales ledger and handle all aspects of debt collection;
– D may draw up to 75% of the gross debts assigned;
– D assigns and forwards copy invoices as and when they are raised;
– F provides protection from bad debts. Any debts not recovered after 90 days are passed to F. A charge of 1% of the gross value of the debts is levied for this service; and
– F pays the debt less advances, interest and credit protection, 90 days after the date of purchase.

Accounting treatment Although the debts have been legally transferred to F, D continues to bear significant benefits and risks, such as a slow payment risk, as the interest charged by F varies with the speed of debt collection. The gross amount of the debts should be shown on the front of the balance sheet until they are either collected or all of the risks are transferred to F after 90 days. For D, the maximum downside loss is limited since any debts not recovered after 90 days are paid by F which then assumes all slow payment and credit risks. Therefore, a linked presentation should be adopted.

Disclosures The amount deducted on the face of the balance sheet should be the lower of the proceeds received and the gross amount of the debts less all charges to the factor. For example, debtors of £500,000 would be shown less proceeds from the factoring arrangement, credit protection and finance charges.
Assume proceeds of £375,000 and costs of £10,000.

Balance sheet (extract) – 30 June 20X3

	£'000
Current assets	
Stocks	X
Debts factored without recourse:	
Gross debtors after credit protection and accrued interest (£500k-£490k) 490	
Less: non-returnable proceeds (375)	
	115
Other debtors	X
Cash	X
	XX

The non-returnable proceeds of £375,000 would be accounted for in cash and the profit and loss account will be charged with the interest and credit protection expenses of £10,000.

Notes to the accounts
Debtors – linked presentation
Trade debtors **subject to limited recourse financing** represent debts discounted with financial institutions, subject to strictly limited recourse in that the majority of the cash received on discounting is not returnable. The returnable portion of these proceeds is recorded as loans due within one year and more than one year, as appropriate. The company **does not intend to make good any**

losses over the agreed recourse limit and the financial institutions concerned have confirmed their acceptance in writing.

Bills of exchange

2510   A bill of exchange **is defined as** an unconditional order in writing, addressed by one person (drawer) to another (drawee), requiring the drawee to pay on demand or on a fixed date a specified sum of money.

FRS 5 prescribes the treatment and disclosure of bills of exchange received from debtors that have been discounted. Where the bank has full recourse to the company in the event that the bill is not honoured, it is clear that the risks in respect of the underlying debts have remained unchanged. Therefore, following the **treatment of factored debts**, the debtor should remain on the company's balance sheet while the cash received for discounting the "bill" should be shown as an asset with the finance provided shown as a liability.

Bills of exchange can be either short or long term so care must be taken to ensure that the correct debtors classification is applied (i.e. after one year). Furthermore, if the bill of exchange is settled after the year end, this does not constitute a separate post-balance sheet adjusting event.

---

4. Disclosure framework

2520   The **general rule** is that the total debtors figure must be disclosed within current assets on the face of the balance sheet. However, different formats are permitted and more detailed information can be provided in the notes to the accounts. The disclosures required of small companies filing shorter-form or abbreviated accounts can be reduced.

Small companies

2522   **Shorter-form accounts**   Should a company elect to prepare and file shorter-form accounts then it can reduce the level of disclosures in respect of debtors. The only categories required are:
- trade debtors;
- amounts owed by group undertakings;
- amounts owed by participating interests; and
- other debtors.

Disclosure is also required of the aggregate amount of debtors due after more than one year.

2526   **FRSSE**   If a small company chooses to adopt the FRSSE, then it is not bound by either FRS 5 or UITF 4 "Presentation of long-term debtors in current assets". Disclosures required under FRSSE are limited to the categories listed in ¶2410.

2528   **Abbreviated accounts**   Where a company files abbreviated accounts only the aggregate debtors figure need be disclosed. However, called-up share capital not paid and prepayments and accrued income can either be included in debtors or shown as a separate heading on the balance sheet.

If a **small company files** abbreviated accounts, a complete set of accounts or shorter-form accounts must still be presented to the members. These accounts should include a detailed analysis of debtors.

Medium-sized and large entities

2532   **Debtors falling due after one year**   Any amounts in respect of each category of debtors that fall due after one year should be shown separately. The Companies Act 2006 does not require this information to be given on the face of the balance sheet itself, but may be given in the notes to the accounts. In determining whether an amount is due **within or after more than one year**, it is normal practice to take the earliest date at which payment is expected.

It is a requirement of UITF Abstract 4, therefore, that debtors due after more than one year are disclosed on the face of the balance sheet if the amount is material in the context of total net current assets.

UITF 4 (3)

The following are **examples of items** that potentially may fall due after more than one year and which may require separate disclosure:
- amounts due to lessors by lessees under finance leases; and
- deferred payments in respect of the disposal of fixed assets or investments.

2533

EXAMPLE   Alpha Ltd
Annual report and accounts 20X3

Balance sheet (extract)		20X3 £'000		20X2 £'000
Current assets				
Stocks		250		195
Debtors				
Due within one year	125		169	
Due after one year	85	210	71	240
Cash resources		155		85
		615		**520**

Notes to the accounts   The example below illustrate the most common disclosure presentation method adopted in the notes to the accounts.

2536

EXAMPLE   **Presentation of debtors**

Beta Ltd Annual report and accounts 20X3
Notes to the accounts (extract)

	20X3 £'000	20X2 £'000
Debtors		
Due within one year:		
Trade debtors	100	120
Less: Amounts provided for doubtful debts	(11)	(10)
	99	110
Other debtors and prepayments	12	30
	111	140
Due after one year:		
Owing by subsidiary companies	17	12
Other debtors and prepayments	16	-
	33	12
Totals	144	152

5. New UK GAAP – FRS 102

FRS 102 "The Financial Reporting Standard applicable in the UK and the Republic of Ireland" has been published and its adoption is mandatory from January 2015. There are no significant accounting differences between the treatment of debtors under the new standard and existing UK GAAP, including the transition to new UK GAAP.

2540

Under FRS 102 short-term trade receivables (debtors for settlement within one year) are recognised at the transaction price/invoiced price as under current UK GAAP, namely at the undiscounted cash amount or other consideration expected to be received.

MEMO POINTS   The FRC has issued (December 2013) two staff education notes (SENs) covering debtors. **SEN 02 "Debt instruments-amortised costs"** highlights a number of key areas for consideration when transitioning to FRS 102. This Education Note discusses application of the amortised cost measurement requirements in FRS 102 and indicates whether entities should expect accounting differences on transition when applying the new standard for the first time. SEN 03 **"Impairments to trade debtors"** deals with the impairment of financial assets measured at cost or amortised cost, and specifically the impairment of trade debtors, and applies to entities that do not apply FRS 26 (IAS 39) "Financial instruments: recognition and measurement".

Cash

This chapter explains the rules governing the accounting treatment and disclosure of cash at bank and in hand. There are no differences in accounting treatment for small companies. **2600**

Cash is defined in FRS 1 "Cash flow statements" as cash in hand and deposits repayable on demand with any qualifying financial institution, less overdrafts repayable on demand. FRS 1 does not, however, define the accounting treatment of bank and cash balances within the balance sheet, which is addressed to a limited extent by the Companies Act. **2602**
FRS 1 (2)

Classification The term **"cash"** includes the following: **2610**
– legal tender;
– amounts due by banks;
– cheques;
– bank credit card vouchers;
– short-term deposits (up to seven days);
– other demand deposits such as those denominated in foreign currencies;
– overdrafts; and
– short-term loans.

A more **expansive definition** of "cash at bank" includes the total amount of cash on deposit with other financial institutions (e.g. building societies) and term deposit funds. This definition does not restrict cash to demand deposits; the rationale being that cash should include all "monies" available on demand as this gives a better indication of the liquidity of a company. **2614**

Deposits are deemed repayable on demand if they can be withdrawn at any time without notice or penalty, or if a maturity or notice period of not more than 24 hours or one working day has been agreed. Deposits may also be accounted for as investments, depending on the terms attached to each deposit account.

Cash advances to employees on account of expenditure to be incurred are not considered cash and should be shown under debtors. **2616**

1. Accounting treatment

The **two principal** methods of accounting for cash are the cashbook and bank statement methods. According to the circumstances of the company either method could be selected, **2620** although the company should be **consistent in its choice**. In practice, however, the cash book method is almost universally adopted by companies although care needs to be taken that it is not manipulated by delays in despatching cheques. It is not common to see an accounting policy for bank and cash in a set of financial statements, but one should be considered where the statement method is adopted. A **change of method** should be accompanied by a note of the comparative figures in the financial statements and an explanation for the change.

Cash book method

2622   In general, the amount to be shown under "Cash" should be the figure recorded in the company's cash book, including cheques issued and despatched but not yet presented for payment and receipts lodged which have not yet been credited by the bank. This is considered an appropriate treatment which represents the substance of the payment/receipt, with the reverse side of the double entry for the lodgements and issued cheques being reflected in debtors and creditors. Where cheques in settlement of liabilities or cheques received have, at the reporting date, been drawn but not yet despatched, then they should be added back to both the cash balances and the outstanding creditor balances.

Bank statement method

2624   Under this method, the company records the balance as per the bank statement at the end of the reporting period. A company **may adopt this method** where, in practice, a considerable period of time elapses between the date on which cheques are drawn (or received) and posted to the cash book and the date they cleared the company's bank account. The rationale for this method is that the company does not recognise the cash transaction until it is reflected in the bank balance.

2626   A **different accounting treatment** may be appropriate if the sums involved are material, which involves disclosing the transactions as either "Cash in transit" or "Uncleared banking terms". The balance per the bank statement represents the cash balance disclosed in the financial statements, and debtors and creditors are adjusted to incorporate cheques drawn or received prior to the year-end (but not reflected in the bank statement), with the opposite entries being in "Cash in transit" or "Uncleared banking items".

---

2. Set-off of bank balances

2630   It is a **general requirement** of the Companies Act and FRS 25 "Financial instruments: Presentation" that assets may not be offset against liabilities in the financial statements, except when there is a **legally enforceable right** of set-off between the balances.

An agreement can be reached between parties involving the set-off of one debt against another or a loss against a gain. For instance, a bank may match a credit balance with a company on one account against a debit balance on the other, if:
– the accounts are in the same name; and
– denominated in the same currency or in other freely convertible currencies.

2640   **Criteria for set-off**   Offset is permitted only when:
– the entity has a legally enforceable right to set off the asset and liability; and
– the entity intends to settle on a net basis the asset and associated liability simultaneously.

A **net presentation should only be used** if this reflects the future cash flows expected to arise from the settlement of the separate financial instruments. The existence of a legally enforceable right is not enough to justify the use of net presentation in the financial statements. Likewise, the stated intention of two parties to settle on a net basis without a legally enforceable right to do so does not justify use of a net presentation, as the rights and obligations of the underlying financial instruments remain unaffected. Use of net presentation in this case would not be a true reflection of the agreement. **Special care** is needed when preparing consolidated accounts.

Offsetting is **not an appropriate policy, where**:
– financial assets and liabilities arise from financial instruments with the same risk profile but that are comprised of different underlying components;
– financial assets have been pledged as collateral for non-recourse financial liabilities; and
– insurance proceeds are expected to be recovered from a third party that cover related obligations.

3. Restricted funds

2650

Restricted funds in specially designated bank accounts, which may only be used for certain specific or restricted purposes, as is often the case with charities (see ¶9500), should be shown separately.

Examples of restricted funds include:
– monies held in countries whose currency is **subject to exchange regulations** which could delay repatriation; or
– deposits subject to either **a legal assignment** or a charge in favour of a third party.

> EXAMPLE **Alpha Ltd – Report and accounts 31 December 20X3**
> **Notes to the accounts** (extract)
>
> **10. Cash at bank and in hand**
>
> £25m of the cash balances of £65m (20X2 £356m) are held in countries subject to exchange controls which may delay repatriation of these funds. A further £5m represents cash deposits subject to a legal assignment in favour of a third party.

4. Disclosures

2654

The disclosure requirements for cash are set out in the balance sheet formats contained in the Companies Act and illustrated in the following example of a balance sheet extract for current assets, irrespective of size of the company. Additional disclosures are required in the notes to the accounts. Overdrafts and short-term loans are disclosed separately within creditors.

Balance sheet (extract)

2655

> EXAMPLE **Alpha Ltd – Report and accounts**
> **Balance Sheet** (extract)
> **Current assets**

	20X3 £'000	20X2 £'000
Stocks	361.2	102.2
Debtors	568.3	324.5
Investments	145.6	89.0
Cash at bank and in hand	**62.9**	**40.9**
Total current assets	**1138.0**	**556.6**

Notes to the accounts

2656

The first example of a note to the financial statements illustrates cash and a separate category of short-term deposits. The second example shows the option of showing deposits under current asset investments (see ¶2700).

EXAMPLE **Alpha Ltd – Annual report and accounts**
Notes to the accounts (extract)

15. Cash and short-term deposits

	20X3 £'000	20X2 £'000
Cash at the bank	42.9	25.3
Short-term deposits	20.0	15.6
Totals	**62.9**	**40.9**

EXAMPLE **B Ltd – Annual report and accounts**
Notes to the accounts (extract)
Current assets

	Note	20X3 £'000	20X2 £'000
Investments and deposits	5	758.3	589.2
Cash at bank and in hand		18.2	14.1
		776.5	**603.3**

Notes – No 5 Current asset investments

	20X3 £'000	20X2 £'000
Listed investments	587.2	475.5
Short-term deposits	171.11	113.7
	758.3	**589.2**

Current asset investments

This chapter covers the rules determining the classification, accounting treatment and disclosure requirements for current asset investments, which are defined as assets retained by an investor for a short period of time. The reporting framework for companies adopting **historical cost** is governed by the requirements of the Companies Act, whilst entities electing to value current asset investments at **current cost** must adopt FRS 26 "Financial Instruments: Measurement".   **2700**

Small companies applying the FRSSE benefit from reduced disclosure requirements.

A. Classification

Investments can be classified either as fixed assets or as current assets under the Companies   **2704**
Act. Investments are treated as current assets when they are **short-term** in nature and where there are no restrictions on the company's ability to dispose of them. Investments are classified as fixed when the investing company's intention is to hold them on a continuing basis over the longer term.

Statutory headings

The Companies Act formats prescribe certain subheadings for current asset investments,   **2706**
which can be shown either on the face of the balance sheet itself or in the notes to the financial statements.

The **required "subheadings"** for investments under current assets are as follows:
– shares in group undertakings;
– other investments; and
– own shares.

For **small companies** only the first two categories are required.

Shares in group undertakings Shares in group undertakings should be classified as   **2708**
current assets only in exceptional circumstances, for example, if they were acquired for the express purpose of resale.

When an entity or business is **purchased solely for resale**, such as when acquired as part of a larger acquisition, it should be valued at the estimated sale proceeds and included under current asset investments. Depending on the nature of the investment, the interest may also be regarded as a financial asset under FRS 13 "Derivatives and other financial instruments" and therefore subject to additional disclosure requirements.

Investments that satisfy the definition of associated undertakings, partnerships and joint ventures should be treated as **fixed asset investments** (¶1750).

2716   **Other investments**   Other investments include the following:
- bank or building society deposits;
- quoted and unquoted securities; and
- short-term loans to institutions (e.g. banks).

Bank and building society deposits can be disclosed as either current asset investments or as cash in hand, depending on the precise terms attached to the deposits. If the figures involved are material in value, a policy note should detail where the investments have been included in the accounts.

2718   **Quoted investments** are defined in the Companies Act as any investment listed on either:
- a recognised investment exchange other than an overseas investment exchange; or
- any stock exchange of repute outside Great Britain.

>   ⬚ MEMO POINTS ⬚   Recognised investment exchanges in the UK include:
> - The London Stock Exchange PLC;
> - The London Metal Exchange Ltd;
> - LIFFE Administration and Management; and
> - ICE Futures.

B. Accounting treatment

2724   The accounting rules for FRSSE and non-FRSSE companies are the same, with only the level of disclosure reflecting the size of the company.

1. Small companies

2725
FRSSE 8.13

The general rule is that current asset investments should be valued under the historical cost regime and stated at the lower of purchase price or net realisable value. Companies also have the option of valuing current asset investments at current cost (market value).

Gains and losses must be recognised, in the profit and loss account or STRGL, using the same basis adopted for tangible fixed assets.

If listed shares are held as current assets investments, the following disclosures are required:
- the aggregate market value (where it differs from the balance sheet amount); and
- both market value and cost of any investments, where there is a significant difference.

2. Non-FRSSE companies

a. Historical cost

2726   The same accounting treatment applies as for small companies, namely that current asset investments are normally recorded at the lower of their purchase price or net realisable value. The cost of current assets can be calculated using a cost-flow assumption such as FIFO, provided the replacement cost or latest purchase price is disclosed.

Where the **net realisable value (NRV)** of an investment **is lower than its historical cost**, the diminution in value should be debited to the profit and loss account and the carrying value of the investment reduced accordingly.

If, in a subsequent period, any part of this **diminution in value is reversed**, any provision made should be written back to the profit and loss account.

> EXAMPLE **A Ltd – Annual report and accounts**
> **Notes to the financial statements** (extract)
>
> **Current asset investments**
> **A Ltd** had previously made a number of short-term loans to institutions in the construction sector. However, due to difficult trading conditions the prospect of default on the loans became a serious possibility and a provision was made at the end of the financial year 20X2 to reflect the revised estimated net realisable value of the investments. In 20X3, these loans were repaid in full to A Ltd. and the provision released to the profit and loss account.

Companies can **voluntary elect** to disclose the market value of their current asset investments, even where there is no strict requirement for them to do so. The exception is where the cost of a listed investment is less than its market value; in this instance the market value should also be disclosed.

2728

---

b. Current cost

Best practice on revaluation is contained in FRS 15 "Tangible fixed assets", which prohibits the cherry-picking of assets for revaluation. This accounting treatment supports the line taken in the Companies Act, that any surpluses and deficits on the revaluation of assets should be treated line by line and not on a portfolio basis.

2730

A **variation of current cost** is fair value accounting.

> MEMO POINTS   Current cost is the **lower of** net current replacement cost and recoverable amount, which in turn is the **higher of** net realisable value and value in use.

Determining current cost

Market value is often taken as the current cost of current asset investments. However, account should also be taken of other issues that could affect the value of the underlying investment.

2732

Quoted investments   The market value to be used is usually the mid-market share price at the financial year-end, although the directors should adjust the market price to take into account any additional factors that could affect the proceeds from the disposal of the shares.

2736

> EXAMPLE   B Ltd has acquired a large holding of shares in S Ltd but less than the 20% barrier that represents a significant interest. At the end of the accounting period, B Ltd classified its investment in S as a current asset, on the basis that it was a strategic short-term investment. The mid-market price of the shares was £8.50. If the directors of B Ltd were planning to dispose of part of the company's holding in S Ltd (e.g. 5%), this could cause the value of its remaining shareholding to fall. This should be reflected in the valuation of current asset investments at the financial year-end and disclosed by way of a note to the accounts.

Unquoted companies   Where an **investment is not listed** and has no readily ascertainable market value, the directors may determine the value using other methods. The directors are responsible for identifying a suitable basis for identifying the current cost. Where the alternative accounting rules are to be applied to unquoted current asset investments, the company should disclose in the notes to the financial statements details of the basis they have adopted.

2738

The directors may wish to record unquoted investments at a value **other than historical cost** in the financial statements. A commonly used method of determining the market value in these circumstances, is to apply the price-earnings ratio (P/E) of a similar listed company to the company in question. The P/E is often used for valuing small parcels of shares in trading companies.

> EXAMPLE   The **price-earnings ratio** is the current market price of a company share divided by the earnings per share (EPS). The P/E ratio is expressed as a number and reflects the number of years it would take a company to earn profits matching its market value. High multiples are synonymous with growth stocks and low multiples with no-growth stocks. The ratio enables comparisons between companies in the same sector.

A **company** which is listed has made profits of £10m and its shares currently trade at £15. The number of shares in issue is 5 million.
The EPS is calculated as follows: £10m/5m = £2.0
The P/E ratio is therefore: £15/2 = 7.5 times (multiple).

The **unquoted company** can then use this P/E ratio as a benchmark against which to value its unquoted investments after adjusting for any additional factors such as risk, size of holding and, if not quoted, lack of marketability.

MEMO POINTS   **Other valuation methods** can be used to determine current cost, namely the:
- net asset method;
- accounting rate of return;
- dividend yield; or
- discounted cash flow valuations (DCF).

A detailed discussion of these methods is beyond the scope of this book.

Revaluation to current cost

2743   Where a revaluation to current cost is undertaken, the following rules apply:

1. Any **surplus arising** on restating current asset investments to current cost should be taken to the revaluation reserve.

2. Any **subsequent diminution in value** should first be debited against the revaluation reserve, and to the extent that the diminution takes the value below cost, that element should be charged through the profit and loss account.

Fair value accounting

2744   The requirements of the Companies Act have been amended by the EU Fair Value Directive, FRS 25 "Financial Instruments: Disclosure and Presentation" and FRS 26 "Financial Instruments: Measurement", which allow assets to be included in the balance sheet at fair value and any changes in value to be recorded in the profit and loss account. This is a variation on the alternative accounting rules.

These **provisions apply** predominantly to financial instruments, but also permit certain current investments to be carried as "marked to market". The new provisions are optional rather than mandatory. Fair value accounting covers both individual and consolidated accounts and is available to all companies including smaller companies preparing shorter-form accounts.

A number of companies hold considerable portfolios of highly liquid (readily marketable) investments. Under the alternative accounting rules (current cost) all **revaluation gains or losses** must be credited or debited to the revaluation reserve.

However, **some exceptions** are permitted. Companies such as commodity brokers (market makers) can elect to carry their investments at market value where there is a ready or active market for the investments.

The **key difference** is that the investments are considered to be the equivalent of cash with any profit recognised in the profit and loss account.

MEMO POINTS   The **fair value** of an asset represents the amount at which it can currently be bought or sold in a transaction between willing parties.

---

3. Other valuation issues

2754
FRS 3 (21)   **Recognition of gains or losses on disposal**   The profit or loss on disposal of a **revalued current investment** should be accounted for in the profit and loss account for the period in which the disposal occurs and should represent the difference between the net sale proceeds and the net carrying value, whether that be historical cost or revalued cost.

Where an investment that is sold has **previously been revalued**, that element of the revaluation reserve relating to those investments should be released to the profit and loss account as a movement on reserves.

Reclassification of investments   Under Abstract UITF 5 "Transfers from current assets to fixed assets", assets should be accounted for under the relevant rules until the date of the transfer, and transferred at the lower of cost or net realisable value, unless the alternative accounting rules have been applied. This rule is designed to prevent companies avoiding a write-down of current assets to net realisable value, simply by reclassifying them as fixed assets.   **2756**

Composite valuation   If a company has a series of current asset investments resulting from a number of purchases at different prices, it is not necessary for each investment to be recorded at its actual price. One of the methods of valuing stock such as **FIFO or Weighted Average** can be used for the purposes of valuing current asset investments, with the caveat that the replacement cost or most recent purchase price should be disclosed if it is materially different from the figure in the balance sheet.   **2758**

Investments held exclusively for resale   Where an entity is acquired exclusively with the intention of subsequently being disposed of, such as where it forms part of a larger acquisition, then the interest in that investment should be accounted for at fair value (estimated sale proceeds) under the heading of "Investments".   **2760**

Such investments are not excluded (unlike subsidiaries, joint ventures and associates) from the scope of FRS 13 "Derivatives and other financial instruments: disclosures". As such, these investments are categorised as financial assets available-for-sale (AFS) (see ¶1799), which must be revalued at each reporting date at fair value. Any movements in fair value must be accounted for in the profit and loss account or in reserves.

C. Disclosures

The key disclosure requirements for current investments, including the specific disclosures required for **listed investments**, are set out below.   **2764**

Entities adopting **fair value accounting** will be required to adopt FRS 25 "Financial instruments: disclosure and presentation", as FRS 13 will no longer apply to these entities. In addition the disclosure requirements of FRS 25 have now been superseded by FRS 29 "Financial instruments: Disclosures".

MEMO POINTS   **Equity instruments, and other investments** such as bonds, **held by one reporting entity** in another, whether classified as fixed or current assets, are also regarded as financial instruments/financial assets under FRS 13 "Derivatives and other financial instruments: disclosures", thereby triggering additional disclosure requirements. It should be noted that FRS 13 only applies to companies which have one or more of their capital instruments listed or publicly traded on a recognised stock exchange or market.

General disclosures

The examples listed below cover the disclosure requirements for balance sheet extracts, accounting policies and notes to the accounts. "Investments" is a primary heading that should appear on the face of the balance sheet under current assets.   **2766**

EXAMPLE   **Brimar Ltd**
Annual report and accounts
Current assets (extract)

	20X3 £'000	20X2 £'000
Stocks	15.9	9.2
Debtors	353.4	274.2
Investments	690.6	254.3
Cash at bank and in hand	125.4	85.9
Totals	1,185.3	623.6

Details of **accounting policies** relating to current asset investments should also be disclosed, as illustrated in the following example.

EXAMPLE Ashridge Ltd – Annual report and account 31 December 20X3

Accounting policies (extract)
Investments held as current assets are stated at market value at the balance sheet date and the difference between cost and market value is taken to the profit and loss account. This treatment is a departure from UK accounting rules which stipulate that unrealised profits be credited to the revaluation reserve. In the opinion of the directors, this treatment is necessary to adopt a true and fair view.

True and fair override

Marketable securities held as current trading assets are stated at market value. The resulting profits and losses have been accounted for in the profit and loss account. This treatment is not in accordance with the Companies Act, which requires that: (1) these assets be stated at the lower of cost and net realisable value; and (2) any revaluation differences be taken to a reserve account.

The directors consider that these requirements would fail to give a true and fair view of the company's profit during the year because the marketability of the securities in question allows the economic measure of profit to be made by reference to the market values.
The effect of this departure is an increase in profits before taxation of £90,000 (20X2 – £50,000) and an increase in the value of current assert investments of £90,000 (20X2 – £50,000).

2768 **Notes to the accounts** The first example illustrates listed investments included in the balance sheet at cost and market value, whilst the second example illustrates a more detailed accompanying note.

EXAMPLE **Note to the accounts**
Current asset investments – disclosure of market value

	20X3 £'000	20X2 £'000
Listed investments	85	5
Short-term loans to subsidiary undertakings	10	7
Other short-term deposits and investments	245	58
Total current asset investments	**340**	**70**
Market value of listed investments	**90**	**7**

EXAMPLE **Notes to the accounts** (extract)
Current asset investments

Liquid resources comprise treasury investments that are readily convertible into cash close to their carrying value or are traded in an active market. Liquid resources included as current asset investments are stated at the lower of cost and market value.

Investments (extract)

	Note	20X3 £'000	20X2 £'000
Listed:			
– UK		353.3	145.6
– Overseas		78.2	55.6
Other		102.5	85.3
	10	**534.0**	**286.5**

Note 10
Analysis of investments

	20X3 £'000	20X2 £'000
Commercial paper	158.4	87.6
Floating and variable rate notes:		
– issued by banks	75.4	55.3
– issued by building societies	24.3	15.8
– mortgage backed	98.4	36.1
– other asset backed	145.6	48.0
– issued by corporates	15.0	10.0
Term deposits	6.0	15.0
Other	10.9	18.7
	534.0	**286.5**

Specific disclosures for listed investments

Investments in listed companies should be disclosed separately for each subheading. In addition, the following information must be given:

2770

– the **aggregate market value**, if this is different from the amount at which they are stated on the balance sheet; or
– in cases where **the market value** of listed investments is used in the preparation of the financial statements and this value exceeds the stock exchange value, both must be disclosed.

EXAMPLE

	Name of company	Balance sheet value	Market value	Stock Exchange Value
South Downs Ltd				
Annual Report and accounts				
Details of listed investments		£'000	£'000	£'000
Listed on the London Stock Exchange	X Ltd	270	230	230
	Y Ltd	200	275	250
	Z Ltd	110	85	80
		580	590	560
Listed on the New York Stock Exchange	P, Inc.	130	220	210
	Q, Inc.	100	125	120
		230	345	330
		810	935	890

The shareholdings should also be disclosed in summary format.

Listed investments	£'000
Balance sheet value	810
Market value	930

Certain listed investments included in the market value figure above are stated at a value greater than the stock exchange value. The details are as follows:

Market value (£'000)	660
Stock exchange value (£'000)	540

Exemptions

Where the disclosure in respect of current asset investments would be either excessively long or prejudicial to the interest of the company, then a company may take advantage of exemptions from the normal disclosure requirements.

2774

Disclosures of excessive length   If a company **has significant holdings** in a number of undertakings that would result in disclosure requirements of excessive length, the company need not comply with the detailed disclosure requirements. Instead the company can supply, in the notes to the accounts, brief information relating to the undertakings whose results or financial position principally affect the results shown in the company's financial statements.

2776

If the **exemption is invoked**, a statement should be given in the notes to the accounts, explaining that the information provided relates only to those investments that are material in terms of the financial results. In addition, the information that would otherwise have been disclosed must be annexed to the company's next annual return.

2778   **Prejudicial information**   Where disclosures concern investments in undertakings established outside the UK and the directors believe that such disclosures will be seriously prejudicial to the business or any of its subsidiaries, they may apply to the Secretary of State to waive the disclosure requirements. Where the agreement of the Secretary of State has been obtained, this must be stated in the notes to the accounts.

PART 5

Balance sheet – Liabilities

A financial instrument is **defined as** "any contract that gives rise to a financial asset of one entity and a financial liability or equity of another entity."   **3000** FRS 25 (11)

 MEMO POINTS   **Creditors** fall into the general definition of financial liabilities but, as they are treated in the same way by all companies, are discussed in a separate chapter beginning at ¶3200.

The manner in which financial instruments are accounted for differs according to the reporting regime applicable to the entity. If the entity has elected to adopt FRSSE, it is exempt from other Financial Reporting Standards; if not, the applicable rules depend on whether the reporting entity is **listed** or **unlisted**, and whether it has adopted **fair value accounting**.   **3001**

Current UK GAAP will be replaced by a new reporting regime in 2015. The FRSSE will still be available to small entities but other non-listed entities will have to apply FRS 102 "The Financial Reporting Standard applicable to the UK and Republic of Ireland.   **3002**

This chapter is concerned only with (1) **smaller entities** reporting under the FRSSE and (2) **unlisted companies** that do not apply fair value accounting. Other companies, such as listed companies, or unlisted companies that apply fair value accounting, are beyond the scope of this book.   **3003**

 MEMO POINTS   In practice, **most UK companies** have not adopted the fair value rules.

SECTION 1

Companies reporting under FRSSE

The FRSSE gives brief, succinct guidance on the treatment of financial instruments, as follows.   **3005** FRSSE 12.1-6

3007   All financial instruments must be **classified** as a financial asset, a financial liability or an equity instrument in accordance with the **substance** of the contractual arrangement rather than its legal form.

While some financial instruments take the legal form of equity, they may be liabilities in substance, and in that event must be classified as a liability. Others may combine features associated with equity instruments with those associated with financial liabilities and must be classified according to the substance of the contract. For example, a preference share that provides for mandatory redemption by the issuer for a fixed or determinable amount at a fixed or determinable future date, or gives the holder the right to require the issuer to redeem the instrument at or after a particular date for a fixed or determinable amount, is in fact a financial liability despite being called a share and seeming to be an element of equity.

3009   All **finance costs of borrowing** should be charged in the profit and loss account and allocated to periods over the term of the borrowing at a constant rate on the carrying amount.

Where there is an **arrangement fee** and it represents a significant additional cost of finance when compared with the interest payable on the instrument, the same treatment should be followed. However, if the arrangement fee is not material, it should be charged to the profit and loss account.

3010   Any **convertible debt** issued should be disclosed separately from other liabilities. Initially, borrowings should be stated in the balance sheet at the fair value of consideration received. The carrying amount of borrowings should be increased by the finance cost in respect of the reporting period and reduced by payments made in respect of the borrowings in that period.

3011   **Dividends** relating to a financial instrument or a component that is a financial liability must be recognised as expense. Distributions to holders of an equity instrument should be debited by the entity directly to equity, net of any related income tax benefit. If an entity declares dividends after the balance sheet date, the dividends are not recognised as a liability at the balance sheet date.

Disclosures

3012
FRSSE 12.7-8

The required **disclosure in the notes** is the aggregate of dividends:
– paid in the financial year (other than those for which a liability existed at the immediately preceding balance sheet date);
– liable to be paid at the balance sheet date; and
– proposed before the date of approval of the accounts, and not otherwise disclosed above.

In addition, any fixed cumulative dividends on the company's shares that are in arrears (i.e. the amount of the arrears and the period for which each class of dividends is in arrears) must also be disclosed.

SECTION 2

Companies not reporting under FRSSE

3020   Of the companies that do not report under the FRSSE, only those that are **unlisted** companies and that **do not apply fair value rules** are discussed in this chapter. Other companies, such as listed companies, or unlisted companies that apply fair value rules, are beyond the scope of this book.

3021   Unlisted companies that neither report under FRSSE nor apply fair value rules are required to comply with the provisions of:
– FRS 4 (though many of these were withdrawn when FRS 25 was introduced);
– FRS 13; and
– FRS 25 (only the presentation requirements).

Under FRS 4, capital instruments were defined as any instrument issued by a reporting entity "as a means of raising finance, including shares, debentures, loans and debt instruments, options and warrants that give the holder the right to subscribe for or obtain capital instruments." The **important difference** brought about by FRS 25 is that it follows a *substance over form* approach in terms of which items are treated as equity only when there is no obligation on the part of the company to transfer economic resources. In all other cases, items are treated as debt.

A. Debt

1. Types of debt

Financial instruments that are classified as debt, and therefore disclosed as liabilities, can take different forms, ranging from debentures and loans with basic repayment terms, to more complex arrangements such as convertible debt, subordinated debt, or perpetual debt.

3025

Debentures and loans

A debenture is generally taken to refer to a loan carrying a fixed rate of interest and repayable at a fixed date. Under the Companies Act, the term "debenture" includes debenture stock, bonds or any other securities of a company, whether or not constituting a charge on the assets of the company.

3026
s 738 CA 2006

For companies wishing to raise finance, issuing debentures is advantageous. Compared to overdrafts, the interest rates are usually lower and the repayment term much longer.

Convertible debt

Convertible debt confers on the lender the option to convert the loan into shares in the issuing company usually at the end of a specific period. Sometimes, the conversion right is exercisable not at one specific point in time but during a conversion window that could last several months or even several years. In practice, this form of debt carries a lower rate of interest than straight debt, and generally results in cheaper financing. In addition, convertible debt can provide a cash-flow advantage to the issuer, which has the opportunity to increase equity rather than repay cash when the instrument matures.

3028

For **the holder**, convertible debt provides not only a fixed interest rate as well as a fixed repayment at maturity, but also, by electing to convert rather than redeem, the possibility of benefiting from any future appreciation in the value of the company's share price.

If a company has issued any convertible debt that carries a **redemption option**, the company has a contingent liability to transfer economic benefits. The possibility of conversion should not be anticipated. Note 7 to the balance sheet formats requires convertible debt, if material, to be shown separately on the face of the balance sheet within liabilities. Where the amount is not material, it may be shown in the notes.

Bonds with detachable warrants

A bond issued with a warrant attached allows the holder to use the warrant at any time to subscribe for equity shares while still retaining the bond. These compound capital instruments differ from ordinary convertible debt in that, with ordinary convertible debt, the bond has to be surrendered at the time that the option is exercised.

3030

The two constituents of this type of instrument can be independently and separately transferred, cancelled or redeemed. Therefore, when an entity issues this type of warrant, the proceeds are allocated between the debt portion (i.e. included in liabilities) and the warrant portion (i.e. included with shareholders' funds).

Subordinated debt

3032 Subordinated debts are those that are ranked behind other loans and debts for purposes of repayment if the borrowing company is liquidated. Note, however, that holders of such debt rank ahead of shareholders on liquidation. Although holders always retain the right to repayment, these payments may be effectively postponed for the long term. From the company's point of view, its obligation to transfer economic benefits remains in force and, consequently, subordinated debts are classified as part of liabilities.

Perpetual debt

3034 Perpetual debt is debt issued with no redemption date and on which interest payments are made in perpetuity. Clearly this debt contains an ongoing obligation to transfer economic benefits and it must be shown as a liability.

The finance charge for each period will be the actual interest payable and the debt will be carried in the balance sheet at the amount of the net proceeds. Any difference between gross and net proceeds (i.e., discounts on issue or costs of issue) are not amortised, but reflected in the carrying value from period to period. This treatment applies whether the interest is fixed or variable.

---

2. Maturity profile

3040
Sch 4 para 85
CA 1985

Because disclosures given in the financial statements and also the recognition of finance charges associated with the debt are influenced by the date of maturity of that instrument, it is important to correctly establish the maturity profile.

General rule

3041 The maturity date of a loan is the earliest date on which holders are entitled to call for repayment under the rights and options available to them.

Early redemption

3042
FRS 4 (74)

Normally, the term of the debt should be taken as the earliest date that the instrument could be redeemed, unless there is no realistic commercial possibility that the early redemption would be exercised. For instance, if a lender can require early redemption, but, on exercising that right, would receive substantially less than the full redemption value, it is most likely that such a lender would not normally choose to redeem unless the issuer's ability to repay the debt was in question. In such a case, the term of the debt should be taken to extend to its final maturity date because, though this date comes after the theoretical first redemption date, it represents the lender's earliest opportunity to require repayment without suffering a penalty.

Commercial paper arrangements

3046 Under commercial paper arrangements, funds are raised from lenders who are not parties to an agreement providing finance beyond the maturity of existing indebtedness. As these lenders are not the same as the original lenders, the date of maturity of these arrangements should be taken to be the maturity date of the existing debt.

---

3. Carrying amount and allocation of finance costs

3050
FRS 4 (27)

Immediately after issue, debt should be recorded at the amount of net proceeds received (i.e. the fair value after deducting issue costs).

At the end of the year and in respect of subsequent accounting periods, the carrying amount of the debt is increased by the finance costs for the period and reduced by any payments made in respect of the debt (e.g. interest and any capital payments) in that period. Finance costs are discussed together with examples showing how the carrying amount is calculated and disclosed from year to year.

---

a. Issue costs

Issue costs are often incurred specifically in connection with the issue of a capital instrument, and include:
- underwriting fees;
- arrangement and registration fees; and
- certain legal, merchant bank and accounting fees incurred in producing a prospectus in respect of a public offering of shares or in relation to documentation drawn up to cover a debt instrument.

3051
FRS 4 (10)

The costs are accounted for as a reduction in the proceeds of a capital instrument and released into the profit and loss account over the life of the debt as part of the total finance charges. The carrying value of the debt is increased each year by the amount charged to the profit and loss account.

Costs that **do not qualify as issue costs** should be written off immediately to the profit and loss account.

3052

Examples include:
- costs of researching and negotiating sources of finance or of ascertaining the suitability or feasibility of particular instruments;
- allocations of internal costs that would have been incurred irrespective of whether the instrument had been issued (e.g. management time); and
- costs incurred in connection with a financial restructuring or renegotiation.

Where **shares and debt are issued together**, the total issue costs should be apportioned on an appropriate basis (e.g. in proportion to gross proceeds) to the two categories.

Where an entity **issues debt with an indeterminate life**, the issue costs should not be taken to the profit and loss account until the instruments are redeemed or cancelled.

---

b. Finance costs

Definition

Finance costs are defined as the difference between the net proceeds of an instrument and the total amount of the payments (or other transfers of economic benefits) that the issuer may be required to make in respect of the instrument. Finance costs therefore incorporate both interest payments and any costs associated with the issue of the instrument that were not charged immediately to the profit and loss account.

3055
FRS 4 (8)

Allocation

As a general rule, finance costs must be allocated to profit and loss, and included together with interest payable, over the term of the debt at a constant rate of return on the carrying amount.

3056

Term of the debt

In order to properly apportion the finance charges, an accurate determination of the term of the debt instrument must be made.

3057

3058
FRS 4 (16)

The term is defined as the period from the date of issue to the date at which it will expire, be redeemed or cancelled. Thus, the term of a capital instrument is not necessarily the same as its life, and rules for establishing the term are summarised in the following table.

Option	Term of capital instrument is from date of issue to:
If **neither party** has the option to redeem or cancel	date of expiry
If either party has a **genuine option to redeem or cancel** – and it is not certain whether the option will be exercised	the earliest date on which the instrument may be redeemed or cancelled (Note: see ¶3060 and ¶3061 for exemptions)
If either party has the **right to extend the period** of the instrument, and	
• there is a genuine commercial possibility that the period will not be extended; or	the earliest date on which the instrument will expire
• it is certain that the period will be extended	the end of the period of the extension

As the table shows, the term and therefore the carrying value of capital instruments are affected by options that attach to them. Options held by holders and issuers do not always have the same result.

3060
FRS 4 (73)

Holder's option   In general, if the holder has the option to redeem early, the term of the debt should be taken to be the earliest exercise date of the option. An exception to this rule is where there is no commercial possibility that the holder will exercise the option (e.g., if, by doing so, the holder will receive an amount that is disproportionately lower than the redemption value). In such a case the early redemption date is ignored in determining the term of the debt.

3061
UITF 11 (6)

Issuer's option   Where a capital instrument is issued subject to the issuer's option to redeem early on payment of a premium, UITF Abstract 11, "Capital instruments: issuer call options", does not consider it appropriate to account for the premium as a finance charge. Therefore, should the issuer decide to exercise the option, the premium payable will be treated as an elective payment to be reflected as a gain or loss arising on early redemption.

EXAMPLE   C Ltd issues 1,000 £100 bonds at par redeemable in 10 years at a premium of 10%. Issue costs amount to £2,000.
Interest is payable at 5% per annum. C Ltd has the option to redeem the bonds at the end of 5 years at a premium of £15.
Under UITF Abstract 11 (6), the term of the bonds will be taken as 5 years.
If C Ltd redeems the bonds at the end of 5 years, the premium of £15,000 will represent a loss on early settlement.
During the first 5 years, the finance costs to be allocated will be £32,000, i.e.

Interest (5 × £5,000)	£ 25,000
Half of the premium	5,000
Issue costs (in total)	2,000
	£ 32,000

These finance costs must be allocated at a constant rate on the outstanding balance over the period. To achieve this, a rate of 6.36% should be used.

Year	Balance at beginning of year	Finance cost allocated at 6.36%	Cash paid	Balance at end of year
1	98,000	6,233	5,000	99,233
2	99,233	6,311	5,000	100,544
3	100,544	6,395	5,000	101,939
4	101,939	6,483	5,000	103,422
5	103,422	6,578	5,000	105,000
		£ 32,000		

Assuming that at the end of 5 years C Ltd does not exercise its option, for the remainder of the term the interest rate will reduce to 5.61% (because the issue costs will have been fully amortised by year 5).

Year	Balance at beginning of year	Finance cost allocated at 5.61%	Cash paid	Balance at end of year
6	105,000	5,894	5,000	105,894
7	105,894	5,944	5,000	106,837
8	106,837	5,997	5,000	107,834
9	107,834	6,053	5,000	108,887
10	108,887	6,113	*115,000	0
		£30,000		

* This final payment consists of the capital repayment of £100,000 plus premium of £10,000 plus interest for the year of £5,000.

The UITF applies only to genuine options and not to situations where it is clear that the issuer would be **commercially obliged** to exercise the call option.

Constant rate of return

The constant rate of return is the discount rate that equates the present value of the net proceeds of the instrument with the present value of the total amount that will be repaid on the instrument over its term. In practice, it is computed using the internal rate of return function on most spreadsheet programmes or financial calculators.

3064

While this calculation is relatively straightforward when a fixed interest rate is charged over the term of the debt, it becomes more complex when, for instance, **there is an interest-free period** at the start of the term of the debt or where the rate of interest is stepped and changes at predetermined dates over the term of the debt. Further complexities arise when the rate of interest for the term of the **debt is variable over the debt period**, as at any time there will be considerable uncertainty over the total amount of payments to be made. However, even though in cash terms there may be an interest-free period or low-start interest rate attached to the instrument, finance charges should be charged to the profit and loss account from date of inception based on the cost of the borrowing over the life of the debt.

It would therefore generally not be acceptable to use the **straight-line method** to allocate finance costs unless it produced a similar result to that which would be obtained using a constant rate. Only where the two results are essentially the same may the nominal interest rate on the loan be charged to the profit and loss account.

3065
FRS 4 (75)

EXAMPLE A Ltd issues convertible debt on 1 January 20X1 for 5 years, redeemable at £350,000. Interest is payable at £12,000 per annum. Assume that there are no options for early redemption. Total finance charges are:
£12,000 × 5 = £60,000 plus the premium on redemption of £100,000, therefore, a total of £160,000.
Finance charges are required to be allocated at a constant rate on the carrying amount. This can be achieved using a rate of 11.2%. Thus, the carrying value over the term of the debt is as follows:

Year	Balance at beginning of year	Finance cost allocated at 11.2% (rounded)	Cash paid	Balance at end of year
31.12.20X1	250,000	28,000	12,000	266,000
31.12.20X2	266,000	29,700	12,000	283,700
31.12.20X3	283,700	31,775	12,000	303,475
31.12.20X4	303,475	34,000	12,000	325,475
31.12.20X5	325,475	36,525	*362,000	0
		160,000		

* £350,000 on redemption, plus £12,000 interest for the year.

MEMO POINTS   A **nominal interest rate** will not differ materially from the amount computed at a constant rate where:
– issue costs on a debt instrument are immaterial; and
– there is no redemption premium to be accrued over its term.
This is the usual situation in the case of simple bank loans or overdrafts, and the actual charge is taken to the profit and loss account.

Premium or interest subject to contingencies

3066   The payments required under a debt instrument are sometimes linked to **external factors**, such as an interest rate index or the risk of uncertain events. This produces uncertainty over the total future payments that will have to be made over the term of the debt. In these circumstances, the calculation of expected total future payments will be based initially on the information known when the calculation is first performed (e.g. the total estimated interest payable on a variable rate loan will usually be based on the current interest rate). When one of these factors changes, the estimated payments for the whole term of the debt will have to be recalculated.

Charges made in **prior periods** are not recalculated nor is a prior period adjustment made. The changes in total cost arising from the change in a variable factor are in effect therefore absorbed over the period of the debt remaining at the date the change takes place.

EXAMPLE   B Ltd receives a loan of £1,250 on 1 January 20X1 on which interest of 4% is payable (£50). The principal amount repayable on 01.01.20X5, is based on an index.
The balance at the end of each year is calculated by multiplying the original principal amount by the index at the end of the year; the change in the amount is treated as additional finance costs.

Year ending	Balance at beginning of year (A)	Index at end of year (B)	Balance at end of year (C)	Cash paid (interest) (D)	Finance cost for the year [(C) + (D) − (A)]
31.12.20X1	1250	106	1325	50	125
31.12.20X2	1325	110	1375	50	100
31.12.20X3	1375	112	1400	50	75
31.12.20X4	1400	120	1500	50	150
31.12.20X5	1500	130	1625	50	175

B. Presentation and classification

Initial recognition

3072   One of the key requirements of FRS 25 is that the issuer must classify a financial instrument (or its component parts) on initial recognition, in accordance with the substance of the contract, as either:
– a financial asset;
– a financial liability; or
– an equity instrument.

3073   The **substance** of a financial instrument, **rather than its legal form**, governs its classification in the entity's statement of financial position. While substance and legal form are generally consistent with one another, some financial instruments take the legal form of equity but in substance are liabilities. Others may combine features associated with both, namely:

– a **preference share** that provides for mandatory redemption by the issuer for a fixed or determinable amount at a fixed or determinable future date, or gives the holder the right to require the issuer to redeem it at or after a particular date for a fixed or determinable amount, is a financial liability; and

– a financial instrument that gives the holder the right to put it back to the issuer for cash or another financial asset (a "**puttable instrument**") is a financial liability, except for those instruments specifically classified as equity instruments.

Equity instrument

A **financial instrument** is regarded as equity (rather than a financial liability), only if both of the following conditions are satisfied:

3074
FRS 25 (15)

1. The instrument does not include a contractual obligation to:
– deliver cash or another financial asset to another entity; or
– exchange financial assets or financial liabilities with another entity under conditions that are potentially unfavourable to the issuer.

2. If the instrument will, or may, be settled in the issuer's own equity instruments, it is:
– a non-derivative that includes no contractual obligation for the issuer to deliver a variable number of its own equity instruments; or
– a derivative that will be settled only by the issuer exchanging a fixed amount of cash or another financial asset for a fixed number of its own equity instruments.

A **contractual obligation**, including one that arises from a derivative financial instrument, that could result in the future receipt or delivery of the issuer's own equity instruments, but does not meet both of the conditions above, is not an equity instrument.

Entity's own financial instruments   A contract that is to be settled by the entity's delivering (or receiving) a fixed number of its own equity instruments in exchange for a fixed amount of cash, or another financial asset, is regarded as an equity instrument. For example, an **issued share option** that gives the other party the right to purchase a fixed number of the entity's shares for a fixed price or for a fixed principal amount of a bond is an equity instrument. This principle applies also to transactions in foreign currencies.

3079
FRS 25 (21–22)

A contract is not an equity instrument for the sole reason that it may result in the receipt or delivery of the entity's own equity instruments. An entity may have a contractual right or obligation to receive or deliver a variable number of its own shares (or other equity instruments) that varies in such a way that the value equals the amount of the contractual right or obligation. This type of contract is a **financial liability** despite the fact that the entity can or must settle it by delivering its own equity instruments. It is not an equity instrument because the entity uses a variable number of its own equity instruments as a means to settle the contract.

However, if the entity's own equity instruments to be received, or delivered, by the entity upon settlement of contract are financial instruments with all of the associated features and meeting the conditions described in ¶3074, the contract is a deemed either a financial asset or a financial liability.

Contingent settlement provisions   A **financial instrument** may require the entity to deliver cash or another financial asset (or otherwise to settle it in such a way that it would be a financial liability), in the event of the occurrence or non-occurrence of uncertain **future circumstances** that are beyond the control of both the issuer and the holder of the instrument. Examples of these circumstances include a change in a stock market index, consumer price index, interest rate or taxation requirements, or the issuer's future revenues, net income or debt-to-equity ratio.

3080
FRS 25 (25)

Because the issuer of such an instrument does not have the unconditional right to avoid delivering cash or another financial asset (or to settle it in such a way that it would be a financial liability), the instrument is generally a financial liability.

C. Treasury shares

3085
FRS 25 (33)

Where an entity reacquires its own equity instruments ("treasury shares"), these should be deducted from equity. No gain or loss is recognised in profit or loss on the purchase, sale, issue or cancellation of an entity's own equity instruments; consideration paid or received is recognised directly in equity. The amount of treasury shares held is disclosed separately either on the face of the balance sheet or in the notes.

> MEMO POINTS   Where an entity **holds its own equity on behalf of others** (e.g., a financial institution that holds its own equity on a client's behalf) there is an agency relationship in effect and, therefore, these holdings are not included on the entity's balance sheet.

The legal implications surrounding treasury shares are discussed more fully in the chapter on Share Capital and Reserves, from ¶3689.

D. Interest, dividends, losses and gains

3087
FRS 25 (35–36)

Interest, dividends, losses and gains relating to a financial instrument or a component that is a financial liability must be recognised as income or expense. Distributions to holders of an equity instrument must be debited directly to equity, net of any related income tax benefit.

Transaction costs of an equity transaction, other than costs of issuing an equity instrument that are directly attributable to the acquisition of a business, must be deducted from equity, net of any related income tax benefit.

3088

Whether a financial instrument has been classified as a financial liability or an equity instrument determines how interest, dividends, losses and gains relating to it are recognised. Therefore, dividend payments on shares wholly recognised as liabilities are recognised as expenses (i.e. in the same way as interest on a bond). Gains and losses associated with redemptions or refinancings of financial liabilities are recognised in profit or loss, while redemptions or refinancings of equity instruments are recognised as changes in equity.

E. Offsetting

3090

FRS 25 requires an entity to present its financial assets and financial liabilities on a net basis (i.e. offset against one another) if doing so reflects the expected future cash flows from settling two or more separate financial instruments. Where an entity has the right to receive or pay a single net amount, it has in effect, only a single financial asset or financial liability.

3091
FRS 25 (42)

A financial asset and a financial liability may be offset and the net amount presented in the balance sheet when the entity concerned:
– has a legally enforceable right to set off the recognised amounts; and
– intends either to settle on a net basis, or to realise the asset and settle the liability simultaneously.

In other circumstances, financial assets and financial liabilities are presented separately from each other consistently with their characteristics as either resources or obligations of the entity.

F. Developments in UK GAAP – FRS 102

Current UK GAAP will be replaced by a new reporting regime in 2015. Although the FRSSE **3095**
will still be available to small entities other non-listed entities will have to apply FRS 102
"The Financial Reporting Standard applicable to the UK and Republic of Ireland".
A brief overview of the differences between current UK GAAP and FRS 102 is set out below.

Category	FRS 4/FRS 25	FRS 102 (Section 11)
Classification	No clear distinction	Financial instruments divided into "basic" and "other".
Measurement	Usually at historical cost unless FRS 26 "Financial instruments: Recognition and measurement" adopted.	Basic: Usually recorded at amortised cost. Other: Recorded at fair value with movements taken to the profit or loss. Examples include derivatives and complex loan arrangements.

MEMO POINTS   1. The FRC has issued a **staff education note (SEN 02)** covering debt instruments
held at amortised cost. Under section 11 of FRS 102 **basic debt instruments**, which include
simple loans and other receivables and payables, should be measured at amortised cost. The
SEN discusses application of the amortised cost measurement requirements in FRS 102 and highlights some key areas for consideration when transitioning to FRS 102.
2. The FRC has also issued proposals for consultation in the form of **FRED 54**: Draft Amendments
to FRS 102: "Basic financial instruments", which proposes to amend the conditions that determine
whether debt instruments can be measured at amortised cost or fair value under new UK and
Irish GAAP" (FRS 102). The comment period closed on 30 April 2014 and the amendments proposed will, if adopted, be effective from the 1 January 2015.

CHAPTER 2

Creditors

A. Classification and accounting treatment

Creditors are defined as entities or individuals to which an organisation owes money. The amounts can be owing in respect of purchases, loans or any other indebtedness. The accounting treatment for the various types of creditor is discussed below. **Small companies** adopting the FRSSE have reduced disclosure requirements.

3200

MEMO POINTS   The FRC has issued FRS 102 "The Financial Reporting Standard applicable in the UK and Republic of Ireland" for non-listed, non-FRSSE entities, application of which is mandatory for accounting periods beginning on or after 1 January 2015 (see ¶3245).

1. Statutory formats

Creditors is a main statutory heading under both Formats 1 and 2 of the Balance Sheet.

3201

Under Format 1, creditors falling due within one year are set off against "Current assets" in the calculation of "Net current assets", while those due after one year are shown separately after "Total assets less current liabilities".

Under Format 2, creditors are shown on the face of the balance sheet under "Liabilities". For each subheading under "creditors", amounts falling due within one year must be shown separately from amounts falling due after one year.

A company's "net assets" and "shareholders' funds" will be the same irrespective of the balance sheet format it adopts. However, for users of financial statements who may be less sophisticated, the differing presentation of the amount for "creditors" can affect their perception of the apparent overall position. The following example illustrates how the balance sheet of the same company will differ under the two formats.

EXAMPLE Comparison of **Balance Sheet** under **Format 1** and **Format 2** for the current year (20X3) and the previous year (20X2)

Format 1	20X3 £'000	20X2 £'000
Fixed assets		
Tangible assets	12,932	10,221
Investments	1,284	1,190
	14,216	11,411
Current assets		
Stocks	38,540	35,217
Debtors	16,849	18,044
Cash in hand and at bank	27,636	25,625
	83,025	78,886
Creditors due within one year		
Borrowings	(10,000)	–
Other creditors	(29,624)	(23,951)
	(39,624)	(23,951)
Net current assets	43,401	54,935
Total assets less current liabilities	57,617	66,346
Creditors due after more than one year		
Borrowings	(5,000)	(10,000)
Other creditors	(3,547)	(10,386)
Provisions for liabilities and charges	(6,500)	(4,000)
Net assets	42,570	41,960
Capital and reserves		
Called up share capital		
Ordinary shares	21,455	21,455
Preference shares	6,000	6,000
Share premium account	8,500	8,500
Profit and loss account	6,615	6,005
Shareholders' funds	42,570	41,960

2. Sub-categories of creditors

3202 Both Format 1 and Format 2 provide for various sub-categories, which may be shown either on the **face** of the balance sheet or in the **notes** to the accounts. If, however, the individual amounts are not material, they may be added together.

These sub-categories are explained below (except **debenture loans**, which are discussed at ¶3026).

Format 2	20X3 £'000	20X2 £'000
ASSETS		
Fixed assets		
Tangible assets	12,932	10,221
Investments	1,284	1,190
	14,216	11,411
Current assets		
Stocks	38,540	35,217
Debtors	16,849	18,044
Cash in hand and at bank	27,636	25,625
	83,025	78,886
Total assets	97,241	90,297
LIABILITIES		
Capital and reserves		
Called up share capital		
Ordinary shares	21,455	21,455
Non-equity share capital		
Preference shares	6,000	6,000
Equity reserves		
Share premium account	8,500	8,500
Profit and loss account	6,615	6,005
Shareholders' funds	42,570	41,960
Creditors		
Due within one year	39,624	23,951
Due after more than one year	8,547	20,386
Provisions for liabilities and charges	6,500	4,000
Total liabilities	97,241	90,297

a. Bank loans and overdrafts

Most bank loans and overdraft facilities are extended subject to the agreement that the bank has the right to **demand payment in full at any time**. If this is the case, the overdraft should be treated as repayable within one year, even if other arrangements have been made for periodic repayments.

3203

If bank accounts with both debit and credit balances are maintained at the same bank and there is a **right of set-off** (¶2630), the net amount may be shown under current liabilities (or current assets, as the case may be). If there is no right of set-off, the debit and credit balances should be shown in full under respective headings.

3204

b. Payments received on account

Payments received on account represent payments received in advance of work being undertaken (or a service provided) and are therefore accounted for as a liability and not

3206

income of the receiving company. Only when the work has been performed is the creditor released and the income recognised.

In the case of **long-term contracts**, SSAP 9 prescribes that progress payments should be set off against amounts recoverable on the contract concerned included in debtors. Any excess not absorbed should be set off against any balance in stocks relating to the contract. Finally, only if there is a balance remaining should it be included in creditors and shown as payments received on account.

c. Trade creditors

3208   Trade creditors are amounts owed to **suppliers of goods and services**.

Occasionally, suppliers of trade goods try to protect themselves with "reservation of title" clauses as part of their terms and conditions. These clauses seek to establish that the goods remain the property of the seller until paid for in full. Certainly from an accounting point of view, these clauses have no practical effect. Therefore, both the goods, and the liability in respect of amounts owing, should be accounted for in the ordinary way.

3209   Where there are **debit balances** on suppliers' accounts, and these are material, they should be shown instead with debtors.

d. Bills of exchange payable

3210   Bills of exchange normally represent agreements entered into to obtain **extended credit terms** or to facilitate transactions with **overseas-based** suppliers. If material, these should be stated separately.

Where bills of exchange payable and accruals are not material and do not justify being shown separately, they can be included with trade creditors.

e. Amounts owed to group undertakings

3212   Amounts owed to companies within the group, whether trading balances or loans, should be included under this caption. The normal rules apply; therefore these amounts must be analysed between balances falling due within one year and subsequently. One of the characteristics of inter-company indebtedness is that there is often **no formal agreement** concerning the debtor company's right to demand repayment. In such cases, it is usual for the balance to be treated as due within one year in the accounts of the creditor company.

f. Amounts owed to undertakings in which the company has a participating interest

3214
FRS 9 (55)

Where these amounts relate to participating interests in **associated undertakings** or **joint ventures**, FRS 9 requires additional disclosures over and above those prescribed by the Companies Act. The total creditor balance must be analysed between amounts relating to loans and amounts relating to trading balances.

As a matter of good practice, the analysis should be given separately for the amounts due within, and after more than one year, as well as for the total amount.

g. Other creditors including taxation and social security

3216   Note 9 to the balance sheet formats states that "other creditors including taxation and social security" should be analysed between "other creditors", and amounts in respect of "taxation and social security".

Additional items that will be shown as "**other creditors**" include loans (other than debenture loans and bank loans), dividends declared but unpaid, and any other creditor that cannot be appropriately shown elsewhere.

MEMO POINTS   **Dividends** that have been **proposed or recommended** but not yet declared are not a liability in law. It would therefore not be appropriate to include them under this heading. Such dividends, if undeclared at the year end, may be shown instead under "Creditors, amounts falling due within one year".

The following amounts can be aggregated and shown as **taxation and social security**: corporation tax, VAT, PAYE, NI contributions, excise duties, and any other amounts owing to central government.

Deferred tax is excluded from this subheading as the balance sheet formats require it to be disclosed as part of "Taxation, including deferred taxation" under the separate statutory heading "Provisions for liabilities and charges".

h. Accruals and deferred income

The balance sheet formats permit companies to show accruals and deferred income under "Creditors" or a **separate heading** after "Creditors" or "Provisions for liabilities and charges" – depending on the format being used. Where disclosure is made under "Creditors", the amounts that will fall due within one year should be shown separately from amounts that will fall due after one year. However, when disclosure is made under a separate heading, this analysis is not specifically required.

3218

Accruals   In general, accruals consist of items such as estimated liabilities in respect of goods and services for which invoices have not yet been received, unpaid salaries, pension costs, employees' accrued holiday pay, bank interest not yet charged, or royalties due for payment. All such expenses should be included here, except accrued taxes, which should be shown under "taxation and social security" (see ¶3216).

3219

Deferred income   Certain items of income – such as rent, interest or government grants – may have been invoiced and received in advance of the period to which they relate. According to the matching principle, these items should not be recognised as income but disclosed as a liability until they fall due.

3220

B. Disclosure requirements

The general and specific disclosure requirements are outlined below along with the different types of balance sheet layout permissible and forms of presentation used in the notes to the accounts. **Small companies** preparing short-form accounts **are exempt** from certain disclosure requirements.

3222

1. General disclosures

In disclosing "creditors" in the balance sheet, the Companies Act formats must be adopted and an aged analysis of the total debt must be given, specifying amounts falling due as follows:

– within one year or less;
– after one year but not more than two years;
– after two years but not more than five years;
– after five years.

This analysis may be shown on the face of the balance sheet or, as is more usual, in the notes.

3223

3224   When **aggregating** items shown under creditors, the following information must be disclosed:
– debts falling due after five years from the balance sheet date and which are not paid by instalments; and
– where debts are repayable by instalments, the amount of instalments that fall due after five years.

In respect of each debt, the terms of payment and rates of interest payable must be shown. If the number of debts is large, a general indication of the terms and rates of interest may be given.

3225

EXAMPLE Creditors – amounts falling due after one year		
	20X3 £'000	20X2 £'000
9% Debentures (20X3 to 20X9, repayable £60,000 annually)	540	600
Bank loans		
Interest at 0.75% above base lending rate, repayable 20X6	100	100
Interest 1.25% above base lending rate, repayable 20X7	50	50
	690	750
Analysis of repayments:		
Due in 1 year or less	60	60
Due after 1 year but not more than 2 years	120	120
Due after 2 years but not more than 5 years	280	280
Due after more than 5 years	230	230
	690	690
Amounts payable after 5 years		
Debenture loans	180	180
Bank loans	50	50
	230	230

Debentures are secured by a floating charge on all the assets of the company. Bank loans are secured by first mortgages over the company's land and buildings.

---

2. Specific disclosures

3227   In respect of debentures and trade creditors additional disclosure requirements apply.

Debenture loans

3228   Disclosure of the following is required in respect of **issues** of debentures **during the year**:
– the classes of debentures issued; and
– for each class, the amount issued and the consideration received.

3229   The balance sheet formats require that the amount of **convertible debt** (which almost always falls within the definition of debentures) must be shown separately.

FRS 4 (25)   FRS 4 extends this requirement by stating that convertible debt should be stated separately from other liabilities. Generally, it is taken to mean that the disclosure should be made on the face of the balance sheet if material, but allows disclosure in the notes if not material. However, in the latter case, the caption on the face of the balance sheet should make it clear that convertible debt is included.

In either event, the following must be shown in the notes:
– date and amount payable on redemption;
– number, description and class of shares into which the loan is convertible; and
– whether conversion is at the option of the issuer or the holder.

[EXAMPLE] **Extract from financial statements**
Balance Sheet
31 December 20X3

Creditors – amounts falling due after one year

	20X3 £'000	20X2 £'000
9% Debenture loans, including convertible loans (Note 25)	1,350	1,600

Notes

Note 25

Convertible unsecured loans stock may be converted at the company's option into fully paid ordinary shares of £2 each in any year up to and including 20X8 at the rate of one ordinary share for every £5 of convertible loan stock. Full conversion of the outstanding rights will result in the issue of 270,000 ordinary shares. If the company does not exercise the conversion option, it will redeem the loan stock on 1 January 20X9 at a premium of 5%.

Trade creditors

Public companies, and companies that do not qualify as small or medium-sized companies that at any time during the year were part of a group of which the parent company was a public company, are required to state the following in their directors' reports:
– the creditor payment policy; and
– the number of days represented by trade creditors as at the year end.

3230

---

3. Sample disclosure

The following sample disclosure follows Format 1.

3235

[EXAMPLE] **Extracts from financial statements**
Balance Sheet
31 December 20X3

	Note	20X3 £'000	20X2 £'000
Fixed assets	XX	XXX	XXX
Current assets	XX	XXX	XXX
Creditors – amounts falling due within one year	12	523	455
Total assets less current liabilities		XXX	XXX
Creditors – amounts falling due after more than one year	13	688	577
Net assets		XXX	XXX

Notes to the Accounts
31 December 20X3

12. Creditors – amounts falling due within one year

Debenture loans (note 21)	-	38
Bank loans and overdrafts (note 21)	169	92
Payments received on account	27	11
Trade creditors	256	207
Other creditors, including taxation and social security	16	27
Proposed dividend	55	80
	£523	£455

13. Creditors – amounts falling after more than one year

Bank loans (note 21)	150	20
Obligations under finance leases (note 21)	475	502
Accruals and deferred income	63	55
	£688	£577

21. **Debenture loans** (3%; 10-year term ending 20X9) are secured by first mortgages over the company's freehold property

Bank loans and overdrafts are secured by first mortgages over the company's freehold property

Obligations under finance leases and hire purchase contracts are secured by related leased assets and bear finance charges ranging from 5% to 10% per annum

Directors' Report
31 December 20X3

Policy on payments to creditors
The Company's policy is to agree payment terms with its suppliers when it enters into binding purchase contracts. The Company seeks to abide by such terms whenever it is satisfied that the supplier has provided the goods or services in accordance with the agreed terms and conditions. The Group seeks to treat all of its suppliers fairly and has a standard dealing specifically with the payment of suppliers.
The Company had 34 days' purchases outstanding at 31 December 20X3 based on the average daily amount invoiced by suppliers during the year then ended.

C. Small companies adopting the FRSSE

3240

Sch 4 para 8 (1–2)
SI 2008/409

For all items shown under creditors the following **aggregate figures** must be stated:
– creditors payable otherwise than in instalments and falling due for payment more than five years after the balance sheet date; and
– any creditors payable by instalments and the amount of any instalments that fall due more than five years after the balance sheet date.

In respect of each item shown under creditors in a small company's **abbreviated balance sheet**, the aggregate of any debts included under that item for which the company has given any security must be disclosed.

If any **fixed cumulative dividends** of a small company are in arrears, the following must be shown:
– the amount of the arrears; and
– the period for which the dividend or (if there is more than one class of share) for each class is in arrears.

D. New UK GAAP – requirements of FRS 102

3245

The accounting requirements for creditors under FRS 102 are broadly similar to existing UK GAAP, with only a couple of areas requiring particular attention as set out in the table below.

FRS 102 requirements concerning:	
Bank debt	Loan documentation must be checked to establish whether loan should be recorded at fair value. Problem areas could include interest rate changes prompted by share price movements, cap or collar arrangements, currency options, etc.
Intercompany loans	Loans to/from group companies = classified as financial instruments within section 11/12 of FRS 102. These loans are usually held at amortised cost with any finance charges recognised. For non-interest bearing loans a similar market interest rate should be used to discount the carrying amount to its present value, with interest charges accrued over the term of the loan. This treatment differs from current UK GAAP where non-interest bearing debt is usually recorded at face value until settlement.

CHAPTER 3

Provisions and contingencies

Regulatory framework

An entity's balance sheet reflects all the assets and liabilities that are known to exist at the balance sheet date. However, there are circumstances in which, for various reasons, it may **be unclear whether an obligation actually exists**. Moreover, even where the existence of an obligation is known, there may still be some uncertainty regarding the amount or the timing of the payment required to discharge it. **3250**

In these cases, the obligation should be classified as either a provision or a contingency, depending on the circumstances. The accounting treatment of both of these sub-categories of liability is covered in the Companies Act and by FRS 12, "Provisions, contingent liabilities and assets". **3251**

Entities that report under the **FRSSE** are exempt from FRS 12. However, the FRSSE's rules for provisions and contingencies, though more succinct than those under FRS 12, replicate most of its key provisions.

Liabilities and losses that have arisen or are likely to arise in respect of the financial year, including those that become apparent between the balance sheet date and the date on which it is signed, should be taken into account.

3252
FRS 12 (64)

Provisions should be used only for expenditures in respect of which they were originally created. Where the purpose for which the provision was created no longer exists, it should be eliminated. Provisions that are no longer required should not be used to absorb other unrelated, possibly unexpected, expenditure.

3253

Introduction of FRS 102 – New UK GAAP   There are **no major differences** between the recognition and treatment of provisions and contingent assets and liabilities under FRS 12 and FRS 102 "The Financial Reporting Standard applicable in the UK and Republic of Ireland", which officially replaces the current guidance (UK GAAP) from January 2015.

Exclusions

3254
FRS 12 (3)

The FRS applies to all provisions and contingencies, except those:
- in respect of **financial instruments** that are **carried at fair value** (FRS 12 applies to instruments, e.g. guarantees, that are not carried at fair value);
- resulting from **executory contracts** (unless the contract is onerous, see ¶3275);
- in the case of insurance entities, arising from **contracts with policy-holders**; or
- covered specifically by another FRS or a SSAP (e.g. FRS 7 "Fair Values in Acquisition Accounting", FRS 17 "Retirement Benefits").

> MEMO POINTS   An **executory contract** is one under which (i) neither party has performed any of its obligations or (ii) both parties have partially performed their obligations to an equal extent (e.g, contracts with employees in respect of continuing employment, obligations to pay council taxes and levies, supplier purchase contracts or capital commitments).

SECTION 2

Provisions

Definition

3255
FRS 12 (2)

The word "provision" as used in FRS 12 has a narrower meaning than is ascribed to it by normal, everyday usage, even among accountants. Provisions are defined as liabilities "of uncertain timing or amount." Liabilities are defined as obligations of an entity to transfer economic benefits as a result of past transactions or events. Though the FRS clearly regards provisions as a type of liability, it considers them separately from other liabilities because of the element of uncertainty as to their timing and/or amount.

> MEMO POINTS   **Provisions for liabilities** does not apply to items that arise in the context of **adjustments to the carrying amounts of assets**, which are sometimes referred to as provisions (e.g. provisions for depreciation, impairment, bad debts, stock write-downs).

3256

Comparison with liabilities and accruals   In the case of "strict" **liabilities**, such as creditors, the reporting entity will have received goods or services at the balance sheet date and can therefore easily determine the amount required to settle the obligation. In addition, because payment terms will most likely have been agreed in advance, the timing is also known.

In the case of **accruals**, the underlying goods or services will have been supplied, but not invoiced, at the balance sheet date. Therefore, in the absence of an invoice, the reporting entity may have to make an estimate of the amount. While this treatment may be similar to that of provisions, there is much less uncertainty in the case of accruals.

> MEMO POINTS   In practice, the difference between **provisions and other liabilities** is not always clear and reclassification from "provisions" to other classes of liabilities is not uncommon.

A. Criteria for recognition

A provision **must be recognised** in the financial statements when all three of the following criteria are met:
- an entity has a present obligation (legal or constructive) as a result of a past event;
- it is probable that a transfer of economic benefits will be required to settle the obligation; and
- a reliable estimate can be made of the amount of the obligation.

If all of these are **not met**, the provision should not be brought into the accounts. However, it is still possible that the obligation is a **contingent liability**, depending on its characteristics (see ¶3280).

3260
FRS 12 (14-19)

Present obligation

Before a present obligation can exist, an **obligating event** must have taken place. An obligating event is one that results in the entity's having no realistic alternative but to settle the obligation created. The obligations will be **legal** (i.e. enforceable by law) or **constructive** (i.e. it creates a valid expectation in the other party that the entity will settle the obligation).

It is not always immediately clear whether a particular event is an obligating event. In practice, it may become apparent only after some time has passed that the event was, in fact, the obligating event. For example, a legal claim might be received after the balance sheet date alleging damage as a result of an event that occurred during the financial year. At the time, though, the damage had not manifested itself.

3261

Past event

Only those obligations **arising from past events** and **existing independently** of an entity's future actions are recognised as provisions. For example, penalties or clean-up costs for unlawful environmental damage caused before the balance sheet date will lead to a transfer of economic benefits in settlement regardless of the future actions of the entity. On the other hand, the situation is different where, as a result of commercial pressures or legal requirements, an entity may need to incur expenditure to **operate in a particular way in the future**. An example of this might be a new law requiring the installation of health or safety equipment in factories where specified manufacturing processes are to be undertaken in the future. Because it is theoretically possible for the company to avoid the future expenditure by its future actions (for instance by changing its method of operation), it has no present obligation for that future expenditure. Where this is the case, no provision should be recognised.

3263

Probable transfer of economic benefits

The obligation to transfer economic benefits is an integral component of the definition of a liability. Similarly, in determining whether a provision in respect of a liability should be recognised, there must be a probability that such a transfer will take place. For the purpose of the Standard, an occurrence is regarded as "probable" if it is more likely than not to occur (i.e. a probability greater than 50%).

3265
FRS 12 (23)

Where an entity has a **number of similar obligations** (e.g. in respect of product warranties) the probability that a transfer will be required in settlement is determined by considering the class of obligations as a whole. Although the likelihood of outflow for any one item may be small, it may be probable that some transfer of economic benefits will be needed to settle the class of obligations as a whole. Where this is the case, and the other recognition criteria are also met, the entity should recognise a provision.

3266

Reliable estimate

The use of estimates is an essential part of the preparation of financial statements. Provisions, by their nature, are more uncertain than most other balance sheet items. Entities are normally

3268

able, in respect of likely situations, to determine a range of possible outcomes and make a sufficiently reliable estimate of the obligation that will arise. Instances in which a liability is known to exist but no reliable estimate can be made are unusual. However, where this does happen, the liability cannot be recognised as a provision but, instead, must be disclosed as a contingent liability (see ¶3325).

B. Application of criteria to specific cases

a. Future operating losses

3270
FRS 12 (68)

Provisions should not be recognised in respect of future operating losses because there is no present obligation, and therefore no liability, existing at the balance sheet date.

There is also a specific prohibition against recognising future operating losses up to the date of a **restructuring** unless the losses relate to an onerous contract.

b. Onerous contracts

3275
FRS 12 (71))

If an entity is a party to an onerous contract, the present obligation under the contract should be recognised and measured as a provision.

An onerous contract is one under which the **economic benefits** to be received are less than:
– the costs of fulfilling it; or
– the penalties arising or compensation owing as a result of failing to fulfil it.

Before a **separate provision** for an onerous contract is established, an entity must recognise any impairment loss that has occurred on assets dedicated to the particular contract.

c. Restructuring programmes

3280

FRS 12 provides specific guidance on how the general recognition criteria for provisions apply to restructuring programmes. The FRS **defines** a restructuring programme as:

"A programme that is planned and controlled by management, and materially changes either:
a) the scope of a business undertaken by an entity; or
b) the manner in which that business is conducted."

FRS 12 (75)

This definition includes events such as:
– the **sale** or **termination** of a line of business;
– the **closure** of business locations in a country or region or the **relocation** of business activities from one country or region to another;
– changes in **management structure** (e.g. eliminating a layer of management); and
– fundamental reorganisations that have a material effect on the **nature and focus** of the entity's operations.

Requirements triggering recognition

3283

Where a provision in respect of restructuring costs falls within the general criteria for provisions (¶3260), it is appropriate to recognise the provision. It is also necessary that at the balance sheet date a **detailed formal plan** for the restructuring was in place, and there is a **valid expectation** that the plan will be implemented.

The following must be specified as part of a detailed formal plan:
– the business or part of a business concerned;
– the principal locations affected;
– the location, function, and approximate number of employees who will be compensated for terminating their services;

– the expenditures that will be undertaken; and
– when the plan will be implemented.

> _MEMO POINTS_   1. A **valid expectation will exist** for those affected either when the company actually begins to implement the plan or announces its main features in a sufficiently detailed manner to make it clear that the company will not be able to withdraw or otherwise fail to move forward with the plan.
> 2. The existence of a valid expectation relates to the situation **at the balance sheet date**. Therefore, if by the balance sheet date no event has taken place to give rise to a valid expectation, then even if the implementation had commenced by the time the financial statements are approved, no provision should be made.
> 3. To constitute a **constructive obligation** there would have to have been, at the balance sheet date, some action such as dismantling of a plant, the sale of assets or a public announcement giving rise to an expectation that the restructuring will be carried out.

No obligation arises for the **sale of an operation** until the entity is committed to the sale by way of a binding sale agreement.

3284

When a sale is only one element of a restructuring, a constructive obligation can arise concerning the other parts of the restructuring before a binding sale agreement exists. Where this is the case, the assets of the operation should also be reviewed for impairment under FRS 11.

Expenditures included in the provision

The standard specifies that only the **direct expenditures** arising from the restructuring may be included in the provision. Such expenditures must be both:
– necessarily entailed by the restructuring; and
– not associated with the entity's ongoing or future activities.

3290
FRS 12 (85)

The following table indicates whether specific expenses can be included within a provision for restructuring.

Expenses that may be included	Expenses that are excluded (as they relate to future activities of the business and are not an obligation arising from a past event).
Costs of making employees redundant	Costs of retraining or relocating continuing staff
Costs of terminating leases and other contracts (where the termination results directly from the restructuring).	Investment in new systems and new distribution networks
Remuneration of staff engaged in dismantling plant	Gains on the expected disposal of assets (even if the sale is part of the restructuring) cannot be taken into account.
Remuneration of staff involved in disposal of surplus stocks	Future operating losses up to the date of restructuring (unless relating to an onerous contract).
	Marketing expenses

> _MEMO POINTS_   Note that the items in the second column are excluded because they **relate to future activities** planned by the business and do not arise as an obligation from a past event.

C. Measurement

1. Best estimate

The amount recognised as a provision should be the best estimate of the expenditure required to settle the present obligation at the balance sheet date.

3295
FRS 12 (36,37)

The best estimate is the amount that an entity would "rationally pay to settle the obligation at the balance sheet date or to transfer it to a third party at that time." Of course, it will often be either impossible or prohibitively expensive to actually settle or transfer the obligation at the balance sheet date; nevertheless this approach gives the best indication under the circumstances.

There are a number of **different methods** for dealing with the uncertainties surrounding the amount to be recognised as a provision, and are set out in the table below.

3296

Methods of measuring uncertainties surrounding recognition of provisions	Characteristics
The **expected value** (i.e. an amount that takes account of all possible outcomes using probabilities as weights).	Where the provision involves a large population of items, the obligation is best estimated using this method, which weights all possible outcomes by their probability of occurring. This method is commonly used.
The **most likely outcome** (i.e. the outcome with the highest probability).	The problem with this method is that it ignores the effects of other possible outcomes and can result in a misstatement of the entity's obligations.
The **maximum amount** (i.e. the highest possible outcome).	The disadvantage of this method is that it can lead to excessive provisions where the likelihood of the outcome is small.
At least the minimum amount (i.e. a value falling between the lowest possible outcome and the highest possible outcome).	This problem here is that the wide range of possible estimates could impair comparability between financial statements.

> EXAMPLE A Ltd sells goods with a warranty under which customers are covered for the cost of repairs of any manufacturing defects arising within the first year after purchase. If minor defects were detected in all products sold, repair costs of £500,000 would result. If major defects were detected in all products sold, repair costs of £2 million. The entity's past experience and future expectations indicate that, for the coming year, 75% of the goods sold will be defect free, 20% of the goods sold will have minor defects and 5% of the goods sold will have major defects.
> The expected value of the cost of repairs is:
> (75% of nil) + (20% x £0.5m) + (5% x £2m)
> = 0 + £100,000 + £100,000
> = £200,000

3297   Alternatively, if a **single obligation** is being measured, the most likely outcome may be the best estimate of the liability. However, the entity should still consider other possible outcomes.

> EXAMPLE B Ltd built a major item of manufacturing plant for a customer. If the company is called upon to rectify a serious fault, the single most likely outcome is that the repair will succeed at the first attempt at a cost of £1 million. However, a larger provision should be made if there is a significant chance that additional attempts will be necessary to solve the problem.

3298   Provisions are measured **before tax**. The consequences, if any, of tax are dealt with in accordance with FRS 19 "Deferred tax" (¶9060).

---

2. Adjustments to amounts

3300   The following factors may also impact on estimates of any provisions required; namely:
- time value of money;
- adjusting for risk;
- future events;
- reimbursement from 3rd parties;
- disposal of assets; and
- changes in provisions.

Time value of money

Where the effect of the time value of money is material, the amount of a provision should be the present value of the future expenditures expected to settle the obligation. The discount rate used should be a pre-tax rate that reflects current market assessments of:
– the time value of money; and
– the risks specific to the liability.

3301
FRS 12 (45)

Adjusting for risk

Inherent in estimating the provisions to be set aside is an element of uncertainty. The effect of adjusting cash outflows for risk is that the provision will be greater than otherwise would have been the case. The FRS states that one way of taking a risk into account is to use a discount rate (e.g. a government bond rate) that reflects current market assessments of the time value of money. The discount rate is then applied to the cashflows in order to determine the net present value of any provisions, which will be lower than the value found using a risk-free rate.

3303

Where the cash flows arising under an obligation are certain in monetary terms, then no element of risk need be incorporated in the discount rate applied.

> EXAMPLE A Ltd is obliged to provide for a liability that is expected to be payable two years after its current financial year. Its best estimate of the amount payable at that time is £20,000, although the actual liability will fall into the range of values between £19,000 and £21,000.
> A) The company has ascertained that it can pass the obligation on to another party for a fixed payment of £20,500 in two years' time. Assuming that a fair, risk-free rate is 4.5%, the fixed cash flow of £20,500 will render a net present value of £18,780.
> B) However, the obligation arising at the balance sheet date for which provision must be made should be the same net present value amount irrespective of whether the best estimate, or the fixed equivalent, is used.
> To arrive at a net present value of £18,780 on the basis of a payment in two years of £20,000, the rate to apply is 3.2% (the calculation is easily done on a financial calculator or PC spreadsheet). This rate therefore represents a risk-adjusted rate.

	Cash flow at end of:		Net present value	Rate
	Year 1	Year 2		
Certain cash flow (i.e. on the fixed amount)	0	20,500	18,780	4.5% (risk-free)
Expected/best-estimate cash flow	0	20,000	18,780	3.2% (risk-adjusted)

Future events

Where future events, such as changes in legislation and technology, are expected to affect the amount required to settle an obligation, the provision should be adjusted to reflect these events. However, this treatment can be applied only if there is sufficient objective evidence that the changes will occur. A key point is that we are considering the impact of future events on conditions that already exist at the balance sheet date and not on conditions arising thereafter.

3305
FRS 12 (51)

For **example**, an entity may believe that the cost of cleaning up a site at the end of its life will be reduced by future changes in technology. The amount recognised should reflect the reasonable expectations of technically qualified personnel as to whether any new technology will be available at the time of the clean-up. Similarly, the expected cost reductions associated with increased experience in applying existing technology, or the expected cost of applying existing technology to a larger or more complex clean-up operation than has previously been carried out, may also be taken into account. However, an entity should not anticipate the development of a completely new technology except where there is sufficient objective evidence to support that view.

Where **new legislation** is certain to be enacted, the effect it is expected to have on an existing obligation should be taken into account. Evidence is required both of what legislation will demand and of when it will be enacted and implemented.

Reimbursements from third parties

3307

Where an entity is able to look to a third party to pay either part or all of the amount required to settle a provision, it should reduce the amount of the provision accordingly, but only if the entity:
– would not be liable for the costs including if the third party failed to pay them; or
– will be liable for the full amount of the costs not reimbursed, although the reimbursement is virtually certain to be received when the entity discharges the obligation.

In the second instance, the reimbursement should be treated as a separate asset with the sum recognised not exceeding the amount of the provision.

Examples of circumstances in which an entity is able to expect a recovery from a third party are **insurance contracts**, **indemnity clauses** and **suppliers' warranties**. It makes no difference whether the third party reimburses amounts paid by the entity or whether it pays the amounts directly.

Disposal of assets

3309
FRS 12 (54)

Gains expected to be made on the disposal of assets should not be taken into account when determining a provision.

The FRS states clearly that no such gains may be recognised even if the expected disposal is closely linked to the event that gives rise to the provision.

Changes in provisions

3311

Existing provisions should be reviewed at each balance sheet date and adjusted to reflect the current best estimate.

Adjustments are usually required as a result of:
– revisions to estimated cash flows;
– changes to present values as a result of the passage of time; and
– revision of discount rates used to bring them in line with current market conditions.

In cases where it appears to be no longer probable that a transfer of economic benefits will be required to settle the obligation, the provision should be reversed.

D. Accounting consequences of recognising provisions

3315

Once it has been established that an entity should recognise a provision, the question that arises is how to treat the other side of the accounting entry (i.e. the debit side). There are two choices: to create an asset account, or to charge the amount to the profit and loss account. The correct treatment will depend upon how probable the access to economic benefits is deemed to be.

3316
FRS 12 (66)

FRS 12 requires that when a provision (or a change in a provision) is recognised, an asset can be recognised if **the obligation incurred** gives access to **future economic benefits**. Where this is not the case and the transfer of economic benefits is merely probable, the provision should be charged to the profit and loss account.

In the majority of cases the debit entry will be a charge to the profit and loss account and only occasionally will it give rise to the creation of an asset, such as where the provision is in respect of costs relating to the purchase of a fixed asset.

For **example**, in the oil and gas industry, an obligation for decommissioning costs arises as a consequence of commissioning an oil rig. The commissioning of the rig also gives access to an income stream from oil reserves over the years that the rig operates. Therefore, it would be appropriate to recognise the decommissioning costs as part of the total cost of the rig and capitalise them to the asset account. They would then be amortised over the useful life of the rig.

Another reason to create an asset rather than make a charge to the profit and loss account might be where an insurance recovery may be possible. This situation could arise where a provision is made in respect of injury to an employee covered by an insurance policy.

E. Disclosure requirements

The sources of the rules relating to the disclosure of provisions are the Companies Act and FRS 12. The Act requires that all liabilities and losses that either have already arisen or are likely to arise in respect of the accounting period under review (or a previous year, if appropriate) must be taken into account.

3318

For **each class of provision** recognised by the company, the following must be disclosed:
– a brief description of the nature of the obligation, and the expected timing of any resulting transfers of economic benefits;
– an indication of the uncertainties about the amount or timing of those transfers of economic benefits and, where necessary to provide adequate information, details of the major assumptions made concerning future events;
– the amount of any expected reimbursement, stating the amount of any asset that has been recognised for that expected reimbursement; and
– particulars of any material provision included in "other provisions".

3319
FRS 12 (90)

The following table indicates the information to be provided when a **transfer is made** to or from a provision.

3320

	Authority: FRS 12 ¶
The carrying amount at the beginning and end of the period	89 (a)
Additional provisions made in the period, including increases to existing provisions	89 (b)
Amounts used (i.e. incurred and charged against the provision) during the period	89 (c)
Unused amounts reversed during the period	89 (d)
The increase during the period in the discounted amount arising from the passage of time and the effect of any change in the discount rate	89 (a)
The source and application of funds transferred	–
Note: Comparative figures are not required by either the Companies Act or FRS 12.	

The principal disclosure requirements are usually satisfied by way of a summary of movements in the notes to the accounts in a format similar to the following.

3321

Summary of movements	Pensions	Deferred taxation	Other	Total
	£	£	£	£
Balance at beginning of year	50,000	22,000	4,000	76,000
Used during the year	(9,000)	–	–	(9,000)
Reversed during the year	–	(4,500)	–	(4,500)
Provided during the year and charged to profit and loss			1,000	1,000
Balance at end of year	**£ 41,000**	**£ 17,500**	**£ 5,000**	**£ 63,500**
Note that the number of columns required depends on whether items need to be separately disclosed or whether they can be grouped together by class.				

SECTION 3

Contingent liabilities

Definition

3325
FRS 12 (2)

The FRS differentiates between "provisions" (which are liabilities) and "contingent liabilities" (which are not).

Contingent liabilities are:

1) possible obligations that cannot be recognised as liabilities because they have not **yet come into existence** – and may never do so unless some future event takes place; and

2) obligations that have **arisen** from past events but cannot be recognised because either the **amount cannot be measured** or there is **little probability that a transfer of economic benefits** will settle them.

Contingent liabilities are therefore potential liabilities that do not meet the **recognition criteria** for provisions. The question then is whether the users of the entity's financial statements should be made aware of them by way of **disclosure in the notes**. The answer to this will depend on the circumstances, as discussed below.

A. Criteria for disclosure

3327

Contingent liabilities should be disclosed in the notes to the accounts **unless the probability of a transfer** of economic benefits is **remote**.

FRS 12 (29)

In certain circumstances, an entity might be **jointly and severally liable** for an obligation (such as may arise in joint venture arrangements). The portion of the obligation for which the entity itself may be liable should be recognised as a provision or disclosed as a contingency depending on whether the transfer of economic benefits is probable (i.e. according to the general rules). The part of the obligation that the entity expects the **other parties** to meet should be treated as a contingent liability and disclosed if appropriate.

3328
FRS 12 (30)

From **year to year**, the status of contingent liabilities should be monitored for any changes that may require their being recognised as provisions instead. Should it become probable that a transfer of future economic benefits will be made in respect of an item previously treated as a contingent liability, a provision should be recognised in the financial statements relating to the period in which the **change in probability** occurs. The exceptions to this rule are those cases in which it is not possible to make a reliable estimate.

Conversely, where the likelihood of a transfer of economic benefits becomes remote, it may no longer be necessary to disclose the contingency at all.

3329

The following table summarises the possible outcomes of reviewing annually any amounts previously disclosed in the financial statements as contingent liabilities.

If the outcome of the future event giving rise to the contingency is:	Contingent liabilities should:
virtually certain	be recognised
probable	be recognised
possible	be disclosed by way of note
remote	not be disclosed

B. Disclosure requirements

FRS 12 states that unless the possibility of a transfer in settlement is remote, for each class of contingent liability an entity should disclose a brief description and, if practicable, the following:
- an estimate of its financial effect;
- an indication of the uncertainties as to amount or timing; and
- the possibility, if any, of reimbursement.

3330

The **Companies Act** requires disclosure of:
- the amount (or estimated amount) of any contingent liability,
- its legal nature; and
- whether any security has been provided in connection with it and, if so, the nature of the security.

3331

Where there has been a charge on the assets of the company to secure the liabilities of any other person, details should be given. However, this requirement will not be necessary if the existence of the charge creates a contingent liability that will in any event have to be disclosed.

Guarantees and other financial commitments (e.g. bills discounted) undertaken on behalf of:
- the parent or fellow subsidiary undertakings; or
- any subsidiary

of the company, should be disclosed separately.

SECTION 4

Contingent assets

In general, entities should choose not to recognise contingent assets in their financial statements. The reason is simple: recognising such assets could result, in turn, in the recognition of profits that may never be realised. However, in situations where it is **virtually certain** that the profit will arise, then the related asset is not a contingent asset, but in fact a real one – and its **recognition is appropriate**.

3333
FRS 12 (31-33)

Contingent assets generally come about from unplanned or other unexpected events that give rise to the possibility of an inflow of economic benefits to the entity. Where such an inflow of economic benefits is **probable**, an entity should **disclose the nature of the contingent asset** at the balance sheet date and, if practicable, an estimate of its financial effect.

3334

Disclosure

Where an inflow of economic benefits is probable, a brief description of the nature of the contingent assets at the balance sheet date should be given together with an estimate of their financial effect, if practicable.

3335

Care should be taken that disclosures for contingent assets do not give a misleading indication of the likelihood that a profit may arise from contingent assets.

As in the case of contingent liabilities, if any of the disclosures relating to contingent assets are not made because it is not practicable to do so, that fact should be stated.

Schematic summary

3340   The following diagram, adapted from Appendix II to FRS 12, illustrates the steps to be taken in deciding whether an obligating event gives rise to a provision or a contingent liability, or whether neither provision nor disclosure should be made.

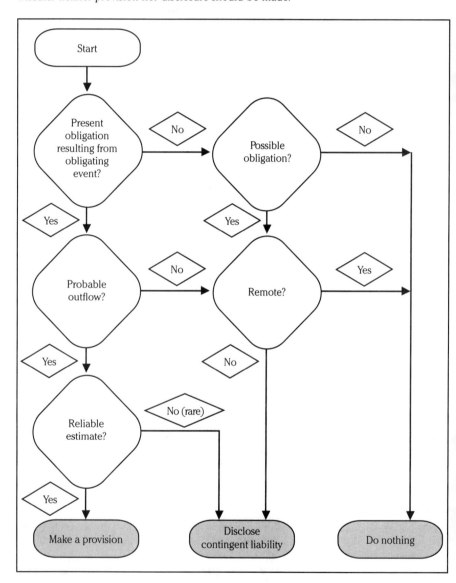

SECTION 6

Small companies adopting FRSSE

The requirements under this heading do not apply to leases, deferred tax, and retirement benefits, for which there are specific requirements covered in the respective chapters on these topics.

3350

A provision should be recognised only where it is more likely than not that a present obligation exists as a result of a past event, and that it will require a transfer of economic benefits in settlement that can be estimated reliably. The amount recognised as a provision should be the best estimate of the **expenditure required to settle the obligation** at the balance sheet date. Where the effect of the time value of money is material, the amount of a provision should be the present value of the expenditures expected to be required to settle the obligation. Where discounting is used, the unwinding of the discount should be shown as "other finance costs" adjacent to interest.

3351
FRSSE 11.2

Where some or all of the expenditure required to settle a provision may be **reimbursed by another party** (for instance, resulting from an insurance claim), the reimbursement should be recognised as a separate asset only if it is virtually certain to be received. In the profit and loss account, the expense relating to the provision may be presented net of the recovery. Gains from the expected disposal of assets should be excluded from the measurement of a provision.

3352
FRSSE 11.3 - 11.5

Provisions should be **reviewed** at each balance sheet date and adjusted to reflect the current best estimate. They should be used only in respect of expenditures for which the provision was **originally recognised**.

For **each class of provision** the following must be disclosed:
– the amount of the provision at the beginning and the end of the financial year;
– amounts transferred to or from the provision during the year;
– the source and application of the amounts transferred; and
– particulars of each material provision included under "other provisions" in the company's balance sheet in any case where the amount of that provision is material.

3353

> MEMO POINTS   The above **disclosures are not required where** the movement consists of the application of a provision for the purpose for which it was established.

Contingent liabilities and contingent assets should not be recognised in the accounts but the following should (unless, in the case of contingent liabilities, where their existence is remote) be disclosed in the notes:
– a brief description of the nature of the contingent item;
– where practicable, an estimate of its financial effect; and
– its legal nature.

3355

Where any **significant security** has been provided by the company in connection with a contingent liability, details must be disclosed.

3356

Where practicable, the aggregate amount, or estimated amount, of contracts for capital expenditure not provided for must be disclosed. Details of any other **financial commitments** not provided for, which are relevant to assessing the company's financial position, must also be disclosed.

Particulars must be disclosed relating to any **charge on the assets** of the company to secure the liabilities of another person, including the amount secured.

CHAPTER 4

Leasing and hire purchase contracts

Leases and hire purchase contracts are a major source of finance for businesses in the UK and provide companies with a means of obtaining the **right to use** assets or acquire them without compromising their liquidity. A lease can be defined as a contract between the owner of a specific asset (the "lessor") and another party (the "lessee"), which allows the latter to use the asset in question. A lease can be classified as either an **operating or finance** lease, with another variant being a **hire purchase contract**.   **3400**

All leases transfer some of the **risks and rewards of ownership** to the lessee, and the distinction between an operating lease and a finance lease is essentially one of degree, as discerned from the **terms of the contract** between the lessor and lessee. Assets held under both finance leases and operating leases are not legally owned by the lessee because the rights granted relate to use, and not ownership. The lessor generally retains the right of ownership but whilst the lessee obtains use of the asset for a specific period of time in return for agreed rental payments.   **3401**

Hire purchase contracts are structured in a similar way to leasing arrangements. However, there is one fundamental difference: at the end of the contract there is a further payment by the hirer, sometimes optional and often for a notional amount, which the hirer pays to acquire ownership of the asset they have "hiring". In spite of this, the accounting for hire purchase contracts is essentially the same as for leases.   **3402**

3403   **Regulatory framework**   The accounting requirements for **small companies** regarding leases are covered in the FRSSE, and for **medium and larger entities** by SSAP 21 "Accounting for leases and hire purchase contracts". SSAP 21 draws a distinction between hire purchase contracts, finance leases and operating leases and codifies the **principles to be applied** in accounting for leases and hire purchase contracts. In addition the standard specifies standard accounting practice through a comprehensive series of guidance notes and sets out the disclosures required in addition to those specified under company law.

SSAP 21 will be replaced in January 2015 by **FRS 102** "The Financial Reporting Standard applicable in the UK and Republic of Ireland".

3404   In **accounting for leases**, one must determine whether the lease in question is, in the context of the life of the asset, a short-term hire contract with most risks associated with the asset remaining with the lessor and with rentals charged to the profit and loss account (operating lease), or whether it is a financing arrangement for the use of fixed assets (finance lease), where the accounting requirements are based on the **substance of the transaction**.

> ◻ MEMO POINTS ◻   The Finance and Leasing Association (FLA) endorses the requirements of **FRS 5** "Reporting the Substance of Transactions" and **SSAP 21**, in that lease transactions should be accounted for in accordance with the substance of the transaction and not simply their legal form. Under FRS 5, the classification of a SSAP 21 transaction can be challenged if the resulting treatment contradicts the substance of the transaction.

SECTION 1

Classifications and terminology

3405   SSAP 21 provides a detailed list of definitions and terminology relating to the accounting for leases and hire purchase agreements, which are set out in the table below and the notes that follow.

3406
SSAP 21 (19)

Classification	Characteristics
Finance lease	A lease that transfers substantially all the risks and rewards of ownership of an asset to the lessee. Finance leases are recorded on the balance sheet.
Operating lease	A lease other than a finance lease, which usually involves the lessee paying a rental for the hire of an asset for a period of time, normally substantially less than its useful economic life. Operating lease payments are recognised as an expense over the lease term.
Hire purchase contract	A method of buying goods where the purchaser takes immediate possession on payment of an initial instalment of the price (deposit). Legal title passes to purchaser when all instalments have been paid.
Sale and leaseback transaction	A sale and leaseback transaction is a linked arrangement (¶3485), typically involving a property, in which the owner of the asset sells that asset and then leases it back from the purchaser.

3407   **Terminology**

Terminology	Definition
Lease	A contract between a lessor and a lessee for the use of a specific asset for a specified period of time, in return for a stream of rental payments. Legal title to the asset remains with the lessor.
Lessor	The entity holding the legal title to an asset that it leases to another entity.
Lessee	A party who leases an asset from a lessor.

Terminology	Definition
Lease term	The period for which the lessee has contracted to lease the asset and any further terms for which the lessee has the option to continue to lease the asset (secondary lease period, with or without further payment). It should be reasonably certain at the inception of the lease that the lessee will exercise the option if that period is to be included in the lease term for the purposes of assessing the nature of the lease.
Present value	The present value of a leased asset should be calculated using the interest rate implicit in the lease.
The interest rate implicit in a lease	Represents the discount rate that at the inception of a lease, when applied to the amounts that the lessor expects to receive and retain, produces an amount (i.e. the present value) equal to the fair value of the leased asset. The amounts the lessor expects to receive and retain consist of: **a.** the minimum lease payments to the lessor, as defined above, *plus* **b.** any residual value not guaranteed, *minus* **c.** any part of (a) and (b) for which the lessor will be accountable to the lessee. If the interest rate implicit in the lease is not determinable, it should be estimated by reference to the rate that a lessee would be expected to pay on a similar lease.
Minimum lease payments	Classified as the minimum payments over the remaining part of the lease term, excluding charges for services and taxes to be paid by the lessor, and: – in the case of the **lessee**, any residual amounts guaranteed by him or by a party related to them, or; – in the case of the **lessor**, any residual amounts guaranteed by the lessee or by an independent third party.
Early termination penalties	Where the lease contains an option for early termination, any calculation of the minimum lease payments that accounts for the exercise of the option should also include any penalty payments attached to the termination.
Finance charge	The amount borne by the lessee over the lease term, representing the difference between the total of the minimum lease payments, including any residual amounts guaranteed, and the amount at which the leased asset is recorded in the balance sheet at the inception of the lease.
The gross investment in a lease	Represents the total of the lease payments and any residual value (not guaranteed) accruing to the lessor.
Net investment in a lease	Comprises the gross investment in a lease less gross earnings allocated to future periods.
Net cash investment in a lease	Equals the total funds invested in a lease by the lessor, including the cost of the asset plus or minus the following payments and receipts: – grants towards the purchase price of the asset; – rentals receivable; – taxation payments and receipts (including capital allowances); – residual values at the end of the lease term; – interest payments on loans to finance asset purchases; – interest receivable on cash surpluses; and – profit extracted from the lease.

SECTION 2

Accounting: Lessees

This section covers the accounting treatment for hire purchase contracts, operating leases and finance leases.

3417

SSAP 21 requires **assets held under finance leases** and the related leasing obligations to be capitalised on the lessee's balance sheet. A hire purchase is normally accounted for in a

SSAP 21 (10)

similar way. However, under an **operating lease**, the lessee accounts only for the rental as a charge to the profit and loss account.

3418   **Non-material leases** that would otherwise be accounted for as finance leases may be accounted for as **operating leases**. The size criteria for a lease, or aggregate of a number of leases, is in relation to:
- total fixed assets;
- total borrowings;
- the gearing ratio; and
- the profit or loss for the year.

> MEMO POINTS   **Gearing ratios** express a company's capital gearing. There are a number of ratios that can be calculated from the balance sheet or profit and loss account. Ratios based on the balance sheet usually express debt as a percentage of equity, or a percentage of debt plus equity.

3419   When **assessing materiality**, a lessee should assess the lease both individually and in aggregate with other similar leases. For example, where a company leases a single computer on a finance lease, this would not be deemed material. However, if that company leases 100 individual computers on finance leases, then their treatment as operating leases could be said to materially distort the balance sheet and in this case the finance lease rules should be applied.

A. Operating leases

3420
SSAP 21 (8)
An operating lease is a **lease other than a finance lease**, which usually involves the lessee's paying a rental charge for the hire of an asset for a period of time, normally substantially less than its useful economic life. The lessor retains most of the risks and rewards of ownership of an asset in the case of an operating lease.

3421   **Basis for allocating rentals**   The rentals under an operating lease should be charged as an **expense** on a straight-line basis over the lease term, even if the payments are for differing amounts, unless another basis is more appropriate, such as where the rentals of an asset are based on:
- the actual usage of that asset;
- periodic revisions that reflect market rates (e.g. property leases); or
- the efficiency of the asset.

3422   **Property leases**   A **lessee** may be offered various incentives, for instance a rent-free period, as an inducement to enter into a new lease transaction (see also ¶3466). Other incentives include contributions to service costs, relocation costs or refurbishment. UITF 28 requires that any lease benefits or inducements should be accounted for as a reduction in rental costs. The **value of the benefits** should be allocated on a straight-line basis over the shorter of the lease term or the period to the first rent review date.

B. Finance leases

3424
SSAP 21 (8)
A finance lease is a lease that transfers substantially all the **risks and rewards of ownership** of an asset to the lessee. A finance lease usually involves payment by a lessee to a lessor of the full cost of the asset together with a return for the finance provided by the lessor. It is the transfer of risk that distinguishes the finance lease from an operating lease.

Assets held under a finance lease should be recognised on the balance sheet of the lessee **3425** as both an **asset** and an **obligation (liability)** to pay future rentals. Such assets should be described as "leased assets" in order to distinguish them from owned assets and they should be **depreciated** over the shorter of the lease term or their useful economic life.

The **terms and conditions** attached to each lease agreement must be reviewed to determine **3426** whether it is a finance lease, and in particular a test (see ¶3428) should be applied to determine the net present value (NPV) of the minimum lease payments relative to the fair value of the leased asset. SSAP 21 uses this assessment of the NPV of minimum lease payment as a benchmark in determining whether substantially all the risk and rewards of ownership have been transferred to the lessee.

At the **inception of the lease**, the sum to be recorded as an asset should be the present value of the minimum lease payments, derived by discounting them at the rate of interest implicit in the lease. The lease is deemed to start at the earlier of:
– the date on which the asset is first used by the lessee; or
– the date from which lease rentals first accrue.

For **example**, if a lease provides for an initial rent-free period at the start of the lease term, the lessee should adopt, as the inception date, the date on which it first used the property.

Rationale for capitalisation

If a company were to **lease an asset** in preference to purchasing it outright and not capitalise **3427** it and its associated obligations, then potentially large off-balance sheet liabilities could be accumulated of which a user of the accounts would be unaware. In addition, the leased assets employed would not be reflected on the balance sheet, which could mislead external users of a company's accounts when making investment or credit decisions.

The capitalisation of assets held under finance leases means that the company's assets and obligations are more readily apparent than if leased assets and obligations are not recognised.

The 90% test

There is a presumption that if the net present value of minimum lease payments exceeds **3428** 90% of the fair value of a leased asset, the lease is a finance lease (see ¶3444 below).

Further, the presumption is that a **transfer of risks and rewards** occurs if – at the inception of a lease – the present value of the minimum lease payments, including any initial payment, amounts to substantially all (i.e. 90% or more) of the fair value of the leased asset.

Rebuttal of presumption   In **exceptional circumstances**, this presumption may be rebut- **3429** ted if it can be clearly demonstrated that although the lease in question exceeds the 90% threshold test, it does not transfer substantially all the risks and rewards of ownership, other than legal title to the lessee, as other factors may indicate otherwise.

Likewise, **where the threshold is not met** the lease could still be classified as a finance lease if other terms and conditions of the lease support this. However, SSAP 21 does not state that a minimum value less than 90% automatically represents an operating lease as greater emphasis may need to be placed on other factors.

Other factors   The classification of a lease should be based on the most likely course of **3430** events. Therefore, **evaluation of a lease** requires an examination of the **lease agreement** including supporting schedules, covering rental payments, and rebates to which the 90% test can be applied and arrangements applicable if the lease runs its full term; namely the inclusion of:
– options;
– balloon payments;
– guarantees;

– process of disposal of asset;
– break clauses with the option to return equipment and cancel further rentals; and
– the useful economic life of the asset relative to the term of the lease.

Other relevant clauses cover insurance, maintenance procedures, and insolvency. For instance, with property leases, the present values of rentals often exceed 90% of the fair value of the property.

However, they are often not classified as finance leases but operating leases, because:
– the useful economic life of the asset is expected to be considerably longer than the term of the lease; and
– the lessor retains the right (reward) to raise rents (rent review) during the term of the lease.
The financial consequences of **terminating a lease contract** must be taken into account.

3431
SSAP 21 (34)

Impact of grants and capital allowances   The benefit to a lessor of regional development and other grants together with capital allowances (which reduce tax liabilities) may enable the minimum lease payments under a finance lease to be reduced to a total that is less than the fair value of the asset. In these circumstances, the amount to be capitalised and depreciated should be restricted to the minimum lease payments. A **negative finance charge** should not be shown.

Apportioning rentals between capital repayments and finance charges

3435   Rental payments should be apportioned between the finance charge and a reduction of the outstanding obligation for future amounts payable.

The **total finance charge** under a finance lease should be allocated to accounting periods during the lease term so as to produce a constant (or a reasonable approximation) periodic rate of charge on the remaining balance of the lease obligation for each accounting period.

3436   **Methods of apportioning rentals**   The table below illustrates the **main methods** used by lessees for apportioning the rental payments between the finance charge and capital obligation under a **finance lease**. The methods of apportioning rentals under other types of leases are shown for comparison.

As will be seen in the examples below, the different methods can produce significantly different results; care must therefore be taken when selecting the method.

Type of lease	Method of apportioning rentals
Finance lease	**Straight-line method**: Writes off finance charges evenly over the lease term and as such does not take into account the reductions on the outstanding obligation for future amounts payable. **Sum-of-the-digits method**: Writes off finance charges over the lease term approximately in proportion to the reducing obligation for future amounts payable. **Actuarial method**: Writes off the finance charges over the lease term based on the actual interest payable on the outstanding obligation for future amounts payable. This is based on the internal rate of return that will effectively discount the minimum lease payments to the carrying cost at which the asset is recorded.
Hire purchase contracts (¶3447)	As for finance leases
Sale and leaseback (¶3485)	Depends on whether classified as finance or operating lease
Operating leases (¶3420)	Straight-line method

Of these methods, the **actuarial method** most closely accords with the objectives and requirements of SSAP 21.

The first part of the example below illustrates the method of determining whether the minimum lease payments equate to or exceed 90% of the fair value of the asset. The second part then compares the way the rentals would be apportioned under each of the methods outlined above.

EXAMPLE **Finance lease – allocation of finance costs**
A quarrying company leased a cement mixer truck on 1 January 20X3 under the following terms:
- **Annual rental** of £10,000, for 4 years, first payment due on 31 December 20X3.
- **Cash price** is £28,550.
- The lease can be **extended indefinitely** after the primary period, at a nominal rental.
- The lessee is required to **maintain and insure** the mixer.
- The **interest rate** implicit in the lease is 15%.

Stage 1: 90% test for finance lease
1. Minimum lease payments = £10,000 × 4 = £40,000.
2. Present value of minimum lease payment, using 15% (interest rate): £10,000 × 2.855 (derived from discount tables) = £28,550.
3. Fair value, taken as cash price = £28,550.
As the rentals in the **secondary period** are purely nominal, they are unlikely to have a material impact on the calculation; as such, they have not been taken into account. If the secondary rentals were set at a more commercial level (but sufficiently beneficial to the lessee) to make it probable that the option for the secondary rental period would be taken up, they should be brought into the calculation.
Given that the present value of minimum lease payments of £40,000 is greater than 90% of the fair value of the asset, this arrangement should be treated as a **finance lease**.

Stage 2: Allocation of rental payment between finance charge and capital repayment
The total rental charge to the profit and loss account over the term of the lease will be the same for all three methods. The difference lies in the **spread of the payments** over the term of the lease.

a) Straight-line method (Most commonly used)

	£
Total minimum lease payments	40,000
Fair value of truck	28,550
Total finance charges over 4 years	11,450
Finance charges per annum	2,862.50

The **charge to the profit and loss account** under the straight-line method is **spread evenly** over the term of the lease as follows:

Instalment	Annual rental repayment	Finance charge	Repayment of obligation
Year ended	£	£	£
31 December 20X3	10,000	2,863	7,137
31 December 20X4	10,000	2,862	7,138
31 December 20X5	10,000	2,863	7,137
31 December 20X6	10,000	2,862	7,138
Total	40,000	11,450	28,550

b) Sum-of-the-digits method
The sum of the digits is calculated as follows:

Instalment	Digit	Relevant fraction	Total finance charges	Annual finance charge
Year ended	£	£	£	£
31 December 20X3	4	4/10	11,450	4,580
31 December 20X4	3	3/10	11,450	3,435
31 December 20X5	2	2/10	11,450	2,290
31 December 20X6	1	1/10	11,450	1,145
Total	10	10/10		11,450

The charge to the profit and loss account and reduction of the obligation under this method results in **higher charges in the earlier years** of the lease term as follows:

Instalment	Annual rental repayment	Finance charge	Repayment of obligation
Year ended	£	£	£
31 December 20X3	10,000	4,580	5,420
31 December 20X4	10,000	3,435	6,565
31 December 20X5	10,000	2,290	7,710
31 December 20X6	10,000	1,145	8,855
Total	40,000	11,450	28,550

c) Actuarial method

Instalment	Obligation at beginning of year	Finance charge at 15%	Subtotal	Annual repayment	Obligation at end of year
Year ended	£	£	£	£	£
31 December 20X3	28,550	4,282	32,832	10,000	22,832
31 December 20X4	22,832	3,425	26,257	10,000	16,257
31 December 20X5	16,257	2,439	18,696	10,000	8,696
31 December 20X6	8,696	1,304	10,000	10,000	– 0 –
Total		11,450		40,000	

Under the actuarial method, the charge to the profit and loss account is **higher in the early years** of the lease. The reduction in the outstanding lease obligation is loaded towards the end of the lease term, as follows:

Instalment	Annual repayment	Finance charge	Repayment of obligation
Year ended	£	£	£
31 December 20X3	10,000	4,282	5,718
31 December 20X4	10,000	3,425	6,575
31 December 20X5	10,000	2,439	7,561
31 December 20X6	10,000	1,304	8,696
Total	40,000	11,450	28,550

The relevant obligation in the balance sheet would be as follows:

Instalment	Total obligation	Non-current obligation	Current obligation
Year ended	£	£	£
31 December 20X3	22,832	16,257	6,575
31 December 20X4	16,257	8,686	7,561
31 December 20X5	8,696	-	8,696
31 December 20X6			

Summary

The following table summarises the profile of finance charges over the three available methods.

Method	Year ended 31 December				
	20X3	20X4	20X5	20X6	TOTAL
	£	£	£	£	£
Straight-line	2,863	2,863	2,863	2,863	11,450
Sum-of-the-digits	4,580	3,435	2,290	1,145	11,450
Actuarial	4,282	3,425	2,439	1,304	11,450

3445   As this example demonstrates, the **straight-line method** produces a significantly different spread of finance charges to the sum-of-the-digits and the actuarial methods. This is generally the case in actual lease situations.

In practice, while it is the **actuarial method** that is theoretically most pure, the **sum-of-the-digits** method will often produce a spread of finance charges over the life of the lease that is sufficiently close to the actuarial method to be acceptable. The increasingly sophisticated computer programs now available to lessees means the actuarial methodology is increasingly being adopted.

C. Hire purchase contracts

A hire purchase contract has **similar features to a lease**, except that the hirer may acquire **legal title** by exercising an option to purchase the asset upon fulfilment of certain conditions (most commonly the payment of an agreed number of instalments). A hire purchase agreement often involves a finance company as a third party; the seller sells the goods to the finance company, which in turn enters into a hire purchase agreement with the hirer.

3447
SSAP 21 (1)

Purchase options

Purchase options at a favourable price are often included in hire purchase contract agreements. Where it is certain at the inception of the lease that the lessee will take up the option, it is therefore expected that the depreciable economic life of the asset will extend beyond the current term of the contract. While leased assets are depreciated over the period of the lease, assets held under hire purchase agreements will normally be depreciated over the full expected life of the asset. Except for the principal difference, that accounting requirements for hire purchase contracts is to all intents and purposes the same as that for leases.

3448

Assets held under hire purchase contracts should be recognised on the balance sheet of the hirer of the asset and this is reconfirmed in SSAP 21. Assets leased under hire purchase contracts displaying the character of finance leases should be depreciated over their useful economic lives.

D. Summary

The table below summarises the key requirements for accounting for finance leases and operating leases (lessees) and for hire purchase contracts (hirers).

3450

Finance lease	
	BALANCE SHEET
Inception of the lease	**Leased asset and related lease obligation** capitalised where the net present value of minimum lease payments exceeds 90% of the fair value of the asset. This presumption is **rebutted** if other terms and conditions of the lease contradict this.
Leased assets	Describe as "**leased assets**" to distinguish them from owned assets.
Depreciation	1. Leased assets should be **depreciated** over the shorter of the lease term (including secondary lease periods), and their useful life. 2. In respect of a hire purchase contract that has the **characteristics of a finance lease**, the asset should be depreciated over its useful life.
Effect of government grants or capital allowances	The receipt of grants or capital allowances could mean that an asset is available on a finance lease such that the **minimum lease payments** are less than the fair value of the asset. Consequently, the leased asset and related lease obligations should be recorded at inception of the lease at the total of the minimum lease payments.

Finance lease	
Rental variation clauses	**Rentals** are adjusted to reflect movements in interest rates or changes in taxation rates. Any increase or reduction in rentals should be accounted for first as an increase or reduction in finance charges; further reductions in excess of the finance charge should be reflected in the depreciation charge.
	PROFIT AND LOSS ACCOUNT
Charge to profit and loss account	1. The difference between total minimum lease payments and their present value at inception of the lease represents the finance charge to be allocated to accounting periods over the term of the lease. 2. Any difference between planned rentals at inception of lease and actual rental payments is charged to profit and loss account.
Operating lease	
Inception of the lease	Lessee pays a rental for hire of asset for a specific period of time. Lessee retains risks and rewards of asset ownership.
Allocation of rentals	Rentals should be allocated on a straight-line basis over term of the lease, unless another basis is more appropriate.
Hire purchase contract	
Inception of the HP contract	HP contracts are similar to leases, except where the hirer may acquire legal title through exercising an option to purchase the asset. HP agreements often involve third party finance.
Depreciation	Assets held under HP contracts should be recognised on the balance sheet of the hirer and depreciated over the full economic life of the asset.

SECTION 3

Accounting: Lessors

3460 This section covers the accounting treatment required of lessors for leases and hire purchase contracts.

SSAP 21 (4) Lessors fall into three broad categories, namely entities (including banks and finance houses) that:

– **provide finance** under lease contracts to enable a single customer to acquire the use of an asset for the greater part of its useful life;

– operate a business that involves the **renting out of assets** for varying periods and probably to more than one customer; or

– are **manufacturers or dealer lessors** and who use leasing as a means of marketing their products, which involves leasing a product to one customer or to several customers.

3462 **Classification of leases** As with lessee accounting, a lessor should classify a lease as operating or finance depending upon the risks passed to the lessee. It can happen that the same lease may be classified as a finance lease by the lessor but as an operating lease by the lessee. This might result from differences in cash flows and the fact that in calculating the minimum lease payments, the lessor accounts for third-party income (e.g. grants, residual values) whereas the lessee accounts only for payments made.

Operating leases

3463 For **operating leases**, the lessor treats the leased asset as a fixed asset and **depreciates** it
SSAP 21 (43) over its useful life. Rental income from an operating lease, excluding charges for services

such as insurance and maintenance, should be recognised on a **straight-line basis** over the lease period.

Depreciation   The depreciation method adopted should reflect the usage pattern of the asset. Typically, the **straight-line method** is used especially where the use of the asset over its useful economic life takes place evenly.   **3464**

In order to smooth profit over the term of the lease, the Finance and Leasing Association permits the use of the **annuity method** for operating leases provided the following conditions are applicable:
– the asset is leased for a considerable part of its useful economic life;
– the lease terms protect the lessor against early termination of the lease; and
– sufficient income is retained in the lease to cover projected realisable values.

The annuity method better reflects the **time value of money** and results in a lower depreciation charge in the early years of the lease, and more even net profit after interest.

[MEMO POINTS]   The Finance and Leasing Association has issued a SORP covering the use of the **annuity method** for operating leases.

Rental incentives   A lessor may grant a rent-free period or an up-front cash payment or   **3466**
contribution to costs, as an incentive to encourage a prospective tenant to take up a lease (see also ¶3422). These incentives should be accounted for by reducing the lease income. UITF Abstract 28 requires that **reimbursement of expenditure** that does not relate solely to the lessee's use of the property, but enhances the value of the property (from which the lessor will benefit beyond the term of the lease), should not be classified as a lease incentive.

Initial direct costs such as commissions, or legal costs incurred by a lessor in arranging a lease, may be apportioned over the period of the lease on a systematic basis.

Finance leases

A lessor generates **two types of income** from a finance lease: namely, the finance income   **3470**
generated by the lease and any profit on the "sale" of the asset. In accounting for **finance leases** the lessor should recognise the substance of the transaction, namely that the lessor is supplying finance to enable the lessee to use a specific asset. It is the rental income due under the finance lease that should be recognised as an asset in the balance sheet, rather than the asset itself.

In the balance sheet of a lessor this should be shown as a debtor at the amount of the net investment in the lease (¶3407) after making provisions for items such as bad and doubtful rentals receivable.

Lessor rentals   The rentals received by the lessor should be apportioned between finance   **3471**
income to the lessor and repayment of the debtor balance, so reducing the net investment in the lease by the lessor over the term of the lease. Over the period of the lease the finance income represents the gross earnings. **Total gross earnings** under a finance lease should normally be allocated to accounting periods to give a constant periodic rate of return to the lessor's net cash investment in the lease in each period.

Methods of allocating rental payments   The guidance notes in SSAP 21 advocate two   **3472**
methods by which lessors allocate gross earnings on finance leases, namely:
– the actuarial method; and
– the investment period method.

The latter method is deemed the more prudent although both methods require complex calculations.

Hire purchase contracts

A hire purchase contract with **characteristics similar to those of a finance lease** should be   **3475**
accounted for on a similar basis to that used for finance leases as set out in ¶3470 above.   SSAP 21 (31)

Other hire purchase contracts should be accounted for on a similar basis to that adopted for operating leases as covered in ¶3463.

The allocation of gross earnings so as to give a constant periodic rate of return on the finance company's net investment, will in most cases, be an approximation to an allocation based on the net cash investment. This is because the **capital allowances** under a hire purchase contract are claimed by the lessee and therefore the lessor's net cash investment will not be significantly different from its net investment.

The **guidance notes** in SSAP 21 give examples of two methods applicable to hire purchase contracts, namely:
– the actuarial method; and
– the sum-of-the-digits method.

The detail behind these methods is beyond the scope of this book.

3476   As an **alternative treatment**, an allocation may first be made out of gross earnings of an amount equal to the lessor's estimated cost of finance included in the net cash investment calculation, with the balance being recognised on a systematic basis.

SECTION 4

Sale and leaseback transactions

3485
SSAP 21 (46–47)   Where a company owns an asset but subsequently sells that asset to a third party, typically a finance company, and then leases that asset back, the accounting treatment of the sale will depend upon whether the leaseback has the characteristics of a finance lease or an operating lease. The leaseback itself will then be accounted for in accordance with the rules for operating and finance leases outlined above.

Where a sale and leaseback transaction results in a **finance lease**, any apparent profit or loss (i.e. the difference between the sale price and the previous carrying value of the asset) should be deferred and amortised in the financial statements of the seller/lessee over the shorter of:
– the lease term; and
– the useful life of the asset.

An example of a sale and leaseback transaction that should be classified as a finance lease is a long lease on a property at a fixed rental.

3486   Where the leaseback arrangement is an **operating lease**, (i.e. where significant risks and rewards of ownership have been transferred to the purchaser), the fair value of the asset should be determined and compared with the price of the sale contract. Any differences are accounted for as follows:

Condition If:	Accounting treatment
a. Sale price is equal to the fair value but above book value	Any profit or loss on the sale should be recognised immediately.
b. Sale price is below fair value	No action is required.
c. Sale price exceeds fair value	The difference between the book value and the fair value should be taken to the profit and loss account. Any excess of the sale price over fair value should be deferred and amortised over the shorter of the remainder of the lease term and the period to the next rent review, if any.
d. Sale price is also below the book value	The shortfall resulting from lower lease rental income should be carried forward and charged to the profit and loss account over the period to the next rent review, or end of the lease period.

EXAMPLE **a. Sale price is EQUAL TO fair value**

	£
Book value	350
Fair value	400
Sale price	400
Profit to be recognised	**50**
Profit deferred	-

b. Sale price is BELOW fair value

	£
Book value	350
Fair value	400
Sale price	370
Profit to be recognised	**20**
Profit deferred	-

c. Sale price is HIGHER THAN fair value

	£
Book value	350
Fair value	400
Sale price	450
Profit to be recognised	**50**
Profit deferred	**50**

The deferred profit of £50 is deferred and spread over the remaining period of the lease.

SECTION 5

Disclosures

The principal disclosures required by both lessees and lessors for companies not adopting the FRSSE, for hire purchase contracts and the different types of lease, are set out below. For lessees/lessors reporting under FRSSE see ¶3520.

3490

A. Disclosures required of lessees

The accounting policies adopted by lessees for operating leases, finance leases and hire purchase contracts should be disclosed.

3491

Finance leases

A finance lease should be shown in the lessee's balance sheet as both an **asset** and a corresponding **obligation**. At the inception of the lease these figures will be the same, but may well differ in subsequent years as, for example, the lease obligation is reduced on an actuarial basis whilst the asset may be amortised on a straight-line basis.

3492
SSAP 21 (48)

There are two principal forms of disclosure for fixed assets held under finance leases – namely, class of asset and cumulative disclosure.

Class of asset For each class of asset the following disclosures in respect of finance leases are required:
- the gross amounts of assets;
- related accumulated depreciation; and
- the total depreciation allocated for the period in respect of assets held under finance leases for each major class of asset.

3493

EXAMPLE **Finance leases**
Extract from balance sheet of D Limited at 31 December 20X4

	£
Fixed assets	
Plant and equipment under finance leases	28,550
Less: Accumulated depreciation	3,570
Net book value	24,980

3494
SSAP 21 (50)

Cumulative disclosure   The alternative treatment afforded by SSAP 21 is to include the information set out in ¶3492, within the **overall totals of fixed assets**. The totals of
– gross amounts;
– accumulated depreciation;
– net amount; and
– depreciation allocated for the period for each major class of asset
are included with similar amounts in respect of owned fixed assets and not separately disclosed.

Where this **alternative treatment** is adopted, the **net value of assets** held under finance leases included in the overall total should be disclosed. The amount of depreciation allocated for the period in respect of assets held under finance leases included in the overall total should also be separately disclosed. This latter treatment is widely adopted in practice.

3495

Net obligations   The amounts of obligations related to finance leases, net of finance charges allocated to future periods, should:
a. be disclosed separately from other obligations on the face of the balance sheet or in the notes to the accounts; or
b. where the total of these items is combined on the balance sheet with other obligations and liabilities, give the equivalent analysis of the total in which it is included.

Net obligations under finance leases should be **analysed between**:
– amounts payable in the next year;
– amounts payable in the second to fifth years inclusive from the balance sheet date; and
SSAP 21 (52)   – the aggregate amounts payable thereafter.

If the analysis is presented according to (a) above, a lessee may, as an alternative to analysing the net obligations, analyse the gross obligations, with future finance charges being separately deducted from the total.

EXAMPLE **Finance lease – disclosure of lease obligations**
X Limited
Balance sheet (extract) at 31 December 20X3

Liabilities	£
Current obligations under finance leases	6,575
Non-current obligations under finance leases	16,257
	22,832

Notes to the accounts
The company's commitments at 31 December 20X3 to future **minimum lease payments** are as follows:

Finance charges	£
Amounts payable within 1 year	10,000
Amounts payable in the second to fifth years	20,000
Amounts payable after 5 years	-
	30,000
Less: Finance charges allocated to future periods	7,168
	22,832

Alternative disclosure – Notes to the accounts
The company's commitments at 31 December 20X3 in respect of **future net obligations** are as follows:

	£
Amounts payable within 1 year	6,575
Amounts payable in second to fifth years	16,257
	22,832

Aggregate finance charges allocated for the period in respect of finance leases should be disclosed, as should the amount of any commitments existing at the balance sheet date in respect of finance leases which have been entered into but whose inception occurs after the year-end.

3497

> EXAMPLE **ABC Group Ltd**
> **Notes to the accounts 31 December 20X3**
>
> **15. Finance leases**
> The Group has contracted to lease an asset under a finance lease, under which the asset will be supplied and rental obligations incurred from April 20X4. The minimum payments under the lease amount to £18,000 over a period of three years.

The Companies Act require that particulars should be given of any financial commitments that have not been provided for and that are relevant to assessing the company's state of affairs. While finance leases are capitalised by lessees, the obligations under finance leases should be provided for in the accounts. The Regulations also require disclosure of the amount charged to revenue in respect of sums payable for the hire of plant and machinery.

3500

The **balance sheet formats** require that:
– creditors falling due within one year should be shown separately from creditors falling due after more than one year; and
– amounts falling due after more than one year shall be shown separately from each item included under debtors. This is relevant to the disclosure of amounts receivable by a lessor.

Operating leases

The total of **operating lease rentals** charged as an expense in the profit and loss account should be disclosed, and analysed between amounts payable in respect of (1) hire of plant and (2) other operating leases.

3504
SSAP 21 (55)

The lessee should disclose the payments it is committed to make during the next year regarding operating leases, and analyse between those in which the commitment expires:
– within that year;
– in the second to fifth years inclusive, and;
– more than five years from the balance sheet date.

3506

It should be noted that this disclosure is of the amount payable in the next year and not the cumulative amount payable over the remaining lives of those leases.

Commitments should be shown separately in respect of leases of land and buildings and other operating leases

> EXAMPLE **ABC Group Ltd**
> **Notes to the accounts (extract)**
> At 31 December 20X3, the company had annual commitments in respect of **operating leases** as follows:
>
> | | Land and buildings £ | Other assets £ |
> | --- | --- | --- |
> | **Operating leases** that expire: | | |
> | – Within 1 year | - | 5,000 |
> | – In the second to fifth years inclusive | 50,000 | 7,000 |
> | – Later than 5 years | 30,000 | - |
> | Total annual commitment at 31 December 20X3 | 80,000 | 12,000 |

B. Disclosures required of lessors

Finance leases and hire purchase contracts

3510
SSAP 21 (58)

The following key disclosures are required:
1. The net investment in finance leases, and hire purchase contracts, at each balance sheet date should be disclosed under debtors as "Amounts receivable under finance leases (and hire purchase contracts)". This is an additional sub-heading over and above that required by the Act.
2. The cost of assets acquired, whether by purchase or finance lease, for the purpose of letting under finance leases.

Operating leases

3512

The gross values of assets held for use in operating leases and the related accumulated depreciation charges should be disclosed.

3514

Other disclosures should also be made of:
1. the **accounting policy** adopted for operating leases and finance leases and, in detail, the policy for accounting for finance lease income.
2. the **aggregate rentals receivable** in respect of an accounting period in relation to finance leases, and operating leases; and
3. the **cost of assets acquired**, whether by purchase or finance lease, for the purpose of letting under finance leases.

> EXAMPLE **Annual Report and Accounts – (extract)**
> **Q Ltd**
> **Accounting policies**
>
> **Finance leases** Assets obtained under finance leases are included in tangible fixed assets at cost and are depreciated over their useful economic lives, or the term of their lease, whichever is the shorter. Future instalments under such leases, net of finance charges, are included within creditors. Rental payments are apportioned between the financial element, which is charged to the profit and loss account, and the capital element, which reduces the outstanding obligation for future instalments, so as to give a constant rate of charge on the outstanding obligation.
> **Hire purchase transactions** are treated similarly, except that the assets are depreciated over their useful economic lives.
> **Operating leases** Rental payments under operating leases are charged to the profit and loss account on a straight-line basis over the term of the lease, even if the payments are not made on such a basis. Assets held for leasing under operating leases are included in tangible fixed assets at cost less accumulated depreciation.

SECTION 6

Small companies reporting under FRSSE

a. Accounting by lessees

3520
FRSSE 7.2 – 7.5

A finance lease should be recorded in the balance sheet of a lessee both as an **asset** and as an **obligation** to pay future rentals. In other words, at inception, the fair value of the asset should be recorded both as an asset and a liability. This represents a difference to SSAP 21, which requires the value of the asset and liability to be recorded initially at the present value of the minimum lease payments. However, where the **fair value** of the asset does not give a realistic estimate of the cost of the asset and the value of the obligation entered into, a more reliable estimate should be made. For example, if the lessee has benefited from grants and capital allowances such that the minimum lease payments can be adjusted to an amount less than the fair value of the asset, discounting the lease payments at the interest rate implicit in the lease would provide a more suitable estimate. A **negative finance charge** should not be shown.

The **total finance charge** under a finance lease should be allocated to accounting periods during the lease term so as to produce a constant periodic rate of charge on the remaining balance. The straight-line method may provide such a reasonable approximation.

3522

The **rental under an operating lease** should be charged on a straight-line basis over the lease term even if the payments are not made on that basis, unless another basis is more appropriate.

3524

Incentives to sign a lease, in whatever form they may take, should be spread over the lease term on a straight-line basis. If these are shorter than the full lease term, they should be spread over the period to the review date on which the rent is first expected to be adjusted to the prevailing market rate.

An **asset leased under a finance lease** should be depreciated over the shorter of the lease term and its useful life. However, in the case of a hire purchase contract that has the characteristics of a finance lease, the asset should be depreciated over its useful life.

b. Accounting by lessors

The amount due from a lessee under a finance lease should be recorded in the lessor's balance sheet as a debtor at the amount of the **net investment** (i.e., after providing for items such as bad and doubtful rentals receivable) in the lease.

3526
FRSSE 7.8 – 7.11

The **total gross earnings** under finance leases should be recognised on a systematic and rational basis – such as a constant periodic rate of return on the lessor's net investment.

Rental income from an operating lease should be recognised on a straight-line basis over the period of the lease, even if the payments are not made on that basis, unless another basis is more representative of the time pattern in which the benefit from the leased asset is receivable.

3528

An asset held for use in operating leases by a lessor should be recorded as a fixed asset and depreciated over its useful life.

A lessor that is a **manufacturer or dealer** should not recognise a selling profit under an **operating lease**. Under a **finance lease**, the selling profit should be restricted to the excess of the fair value of the asset over the cost to the manufacturer/dealer less any grants towards the purchase, construction or use of the asset.

3530

c. Sale and leaseback transactions

In a sale and leaseback transaction that results in a **finance lease**, any apparent profit or loss (i.e., the difference between the sale price and the previous carrying value) should be **deferred and amortised** in the financial statements of the seller/lessee over the shorter of the lease term and the useful life of the asset.

3534
FRSSE 7.13 – 7.14

In the case of an **operating lease**, any profit or loss should be **recognised immediately** provided it is clear that the transaction is established at fair value. However, if the sale price is not at fair value, two possibilities exist:
– if the sale price is **below fair value**, any profit or loss should be recognised immediately, except that if the apparent loss is compensated for by future rentals at below market price

3536

it should to that extent be deferred and amortised over the remainder of the lease term (or, if shorter, the period during which the reduced rentals are chargeable); or

– if the sale price is **above fair value**, the excess over fair value should be deferred and amortised over the shorter of the remainder of the lease term and the period to the next rent review (if any).

Disclosure by lessees

3538

Category	Disclosure requirements
Assets held under finance leases	The gross amounts of assets held under finance leases together with the related accumulated depreciation and analysed into "land and buildings" and "other fixed assets" in aggregate; or, alternatively, leased assets may be aggregated with owned fixed assets provided that there is separate disclosure of the net amount of assets held under finance leases and the amount of depreciation for the period attributable to them.
Obligations related to finance leases (net of finance charges allocated to future periods)	1. The amounts of obligations related to finance leases (net of finance charges allocated to future periods). These should be disclosed separately from other obligations and liabilities, either on the face of the balance sheet or in the notes to the accounts. 2. The amount of any commitments existing at the balance sheet date in respect of finance leases entered into but whose inception occurs after the year end.
Commitments in respect of operating leases	The amount of commitments in respect of operating leases for the next year, analysed into those in which the commitment expires within that year, those expiring in two to five years, and those expiring more than five years after the balance sheet date. There is no requirement, as there is under SSAP 21, to analyse these commitments into those relating to land and buildings, and all other operating leases.

Disclosure by lessors

3540
FRSSE 7.18

Disclosure should include the following:

– the gross amounts of assets held for use in operating leases and the related accumulated depreciation;

– the cost of assets acquired, whether by purchase or finance lease, for the purpose of letting under finance leases; and

– the net investment in finance leases and in hire purchase contracts at balance sheet date.

SECTION 7

New UK GAAP – FRS 102

3550

The FRC has issued a Staff Education Note (SEN 06) to help smooth the transition from existing UK GAAP to the new financial reporting standard FRS 102 "The Financial Reporting Standard applicable in the UK and Republic of Ireland".

The SEN compares the **accounting treatment for leases** using existing accounting standards (e.g. SSAP 21 "Accounting for leases and hire purchase contracts", FRS 5 "Reporting the substance of transactions" and UITF abstract 28 "Operating lease incentives" and the requirements of Section 20 of FRS 102.

Although the two accounting frameworks are similar there are some small **differences in terms of application** that are highlighted in this SEN and set out in the table below. Application of FRS 102 is mandatory for non-FRSSE, non-listed entities for accounting periods beginning on or after 1 January 2015.

Category	FRS 102 requirements (SEN 06)
Classification	FRS 102 + SSAP 21 seek to identify contracts where substantially all the **risks and rewards of ownership** of an asset are held by a lessee, although the former uses different specific tests or indicators. It's unlikely many lease classifications will change after applying FRS 102.
Determining whether an arrangement contains a lease	Some arrangements **do not take the legal form of a lease** but convey rights to use assets, often together with related services, in return for payments (e.g. outsourcing arrangements, telecommunication contracts that provide rights to capacity etc.). Determining whether an arrangement is, or contains, a lease shall be based on the substance of the arrangement.
Accounting for finance leases	**Initial recognition**: Under FRS 102 **finance leases** are recorded at the fair value of the leased asset, or if lower, the present value of the minimum lease payments. SSAP 21 requires measurement at the present value of the minimum lease payments, but also permits the use of the fair value of the asset.
Accounting for operating leases	**Operating lease incentives**: Lease incentives are recognised on a straight line basis unless another measurement basis is more representative. The key difference is at the period over which operating lease incentives can be recognised may be longer under FRS 102.
Disclosures	Companies (other than those subject to the small companies' regime) are required to comply with Companies Act 2006 s410A, concerning disclosure of **material arrangements** that are not reflected in the balance sheet, including the nature and business purpose of the arrangements; and the financial impact of the arrangements on the company. Disclosure of **operating leases** will be different under FRS 102 and covers the total future minimum lease payments due within each of the required periods, rather than the annual amount due to expire in the relevant year.

CHAPTER 5

Share capital and reserves

This chapter summarises the legal issues surrounding share capital and reserves and the general requirements covering their recognition, calculation and disclosure in the financial statements. The objectives of the Companies Act in relation to share capital and reserves are twofold; namely:
– **recording their issue** and the consideration received, the **maintenance** of share capital and reserves, and the protection of the rights of shareholders and creditors; and
– providing a framework for the **presentation** of information concerning share capital and reserves.

3600

Initial issue of share capital

A. Types of shares

3602   Shares can be of various types and classes, including:
– ordinary shares;
– preference shares;
– redeemable shares; and
– non-voting shares.
The **differences between each type** depend on the rights they confer on their holders.

3603   Companies are, in general, free to issue the types and classes of shares in the numbers and ratios they choose but may issue redeemable shares only if:
– they are authorised to do so in the Articles of association;
– there are also non-redeemable shares in issue at the time when the redeemable shares are issued; and
– the shares can be redeemed only when they are fully paid and where payment is made on redemption.
The members may, however, restrict or prohibit the company's ability to issue redeemable shares by including a provision to this effect in the Articles.

Distinction between equity and financial liabilities under FRS 25

3604   FRS 25, "Financial Instruments: Disclosure and Presentation", has the effect of **withdrawing FRS 4** (except in relation to the measurement of debt and gains and losses on the repurchase of debt) for all entities applying the measurement requirements of FRS 26.

FRS 25 requires all financial instruments to be classified as equity, financial liabilities, or financial assets and therefore FRS 4's distinction between equity and non-equity falls away and becomes instead a distinction between equity and financial liabilities. As a result, some shares are no longer classified as share capital but as financial liabilities instead, even though their legal status remains the same as before. These requirements correspond with the amendments to the Companies Act that also require the classification of items on the balance sheet to follow the approach of substance over form.

3605   **Equity: definition**   Equity is defined in FRS 25 as "any contract that evidences a residual interest in the assets of an entity after deducting all of its liabilities".

3606   **Liabilities: definition**   A **financial liability is defined** as any liability that is:
a. a contractual obligation to deliver cash or another financial asset to another entity, or to exchange financial assets or financial liabilities with another entity under conditions that are potentially unfavourable to the entity; or
b. a contract that will or may be settled in the entity's own equity instruments and is either a non-derivative for which the entity is or may be obliged to deliver a variable number of the entity's own equity instruments, or a derivative that will or may be settled other than by the exchange of a fixed amount of cash or another financial asset for a fixed number of the entity's own equity instruments.
As an **exception**, certain puttable financial instruments and certain instruments that impose on the entity to deliver to another party a pro rata share of the net assets of the entity only on liquidation are classified as equity instruments despite meeting the definitions of a financial liability.

B. Payments for shares

1. Issue price

Companies may issue shares either at nominal value or at a premium.

3609

At nominal value   When shares are issued at an **amount equal to the nominal value** (also called "par value"), the amount received must be recorded in the balance sheet as "called up" or "issued" share capital.

At a premium   Shares can be issued by the company at a **price that is higher** than their nominal value. Again, the nominal value will be shown as explained, but the excess over nominal value is usually credited to a separate **share premium** account.

Matters relating to shares issued at a premium are discussed in further detail at ¶3745.

Shares may not be allotted at a discount, meaning that they cannot be issued as **fully paid** for an amount less than their nominal value.

s 580 CA 2006

2. Payment terms

In the majority of cases in the UK, shares are paid for **in full** when issued. However, the Act does allow shares to be issued partly paid. Similarly, the issue price is usually settled in **cash**, but non-cash considerations are possible. These points are discussed below.

3610

Partly paid shares

It is not obligatory that shares are paid for in full (i.e. the amount of the nominal value) at the time of issue. They may be paid for in part but the shareholder will be liable to settle the balance later when it is called up.

3611
s 581 CA 2006

In the case of **private companies**, there are no rules that stipulate the minimum amount that has to be paid in respect of each share at the time of issue.

For **public companies**, there are two possibilities:
– Issue of shares to the subscribers to the Memorandum of Association. In this case, these shares must be paid in full.
– Other issues of new shares. In these cases, payments must be equal to **at least** 25% of the nominal value **plus** 100% of any share premium.

Any amounts owing from shareholders should be recorded as, and shown together with, assets in the balance sheet.

> EXAMPLE   **B Ltd** plans to issue shares with a nominal value of £1 at a premium of 50p. The company intends asking shareholders to pay 60p per share. Whether this is acceptable will depend on the company's status as either private or public, as follows.
>
> If **B Ltd** is a **private company**, there is no minimum amount of consideration imposed by the Act and the arrangement will be acceptable.
>
> On the other hand, if **B Ltd** is a **public company**, and the share issue is not to subscribers to the Memorandum, the Act requires that at least 25% of the nominal value (i.e., 25p) plus the full amount of the premium (i.e. 50p, making a total of 75p) must be paid and allocated to share capital and share premium accordingly. Unless the potential shareholders are willing to pay this amount, the company may not go ahead with the issue.

Considerations not in cash

In general, companies may accept payment for shares (including any share premium) either in the form of cash or in the form of assets other than cash. Non-cash payments can be tangible, such as assets or shares, or intangible, such as goodwill or services.

3612

For **private companies** there are no restrictions on this rule.

For **public companies**, the following restrictions apply as set out in the table below.

3613

Form	Restrictions
For services	An undertaking for services to be performed is not permitted as a form of non-cash payment.
Payment resulting from a long-term undertaking	If the consideration for the allotment of shares includes an undertaking which is to be, or may be, performed more than 5 years after the date of allotment, the consideration must be in the form of cash.
In respect of a valuation	To be acceptable as payment for shares, a non-cash consideration must be independently valued within the 6-month period before allotment. This valuation must be made by a person qualified to be the company's auditor (who may rely on the valuation of an independent expert). A copy of the valuer's report must be given to the proposed allottee.
Circumstances where a valuation is not required	A valuation is not required where shares are issued: – as a **bonus issue** and the company uses any balance on an appropriate reserve account to transfer to share capital and share premium; – in connection with a **takeover** or **merger**; or – as payment for the **transfer** or **cancellation** of shares in another company – provided the arrangement is open to all the shareholders of the same class of shares in the other company.

C. Share capital denominated in foreign currencies

3614
s 763 CA 2006

UK companies are permitted to issue share capital denominated in foreign currencies. **Public companies** are required by the Act to have an authorised minimum allotted share capital of 50,000 in pounds sterling or the prescribed euro equivalent. Once a company has obtained a trading certificate, there is no requirement for the authorised minimum to remain denominated in sterling or euros and, if it wishes, a public company may subsequently redenominate all of its share capital. **Private companies** are not restricted and may issue any amount of shares in foreign currencies.

Difficulties are sometimes encountered when companies that have previously issued share capital in foreign currencies wish to purchase, redeem or cancel them, assuming that they have fulfilled all the necessary conditions.

D. Financial assistance for the acquisition of own shares

3617

The Companies Act 2006 repealed the prohibition against **private companies** giving direct or indirect financial assistance to any entity for the purpose of acquiring its own shares or those of its holding company.

3618

In the case of **groups**, where a private company takes advantage of the exceptions in order to give assistance in connection with the acquisition of shares in its **parent**, the following rules apply:
– the parent must also be a private company;
– a private company (A) may not give assistance for the acquisition of shares in its private parent (B) if B has a subsidiary that is a public company (C) and C is a parent of A; and
– special resolutions and statutory declarations are required from the company giving the assistance, the company whose shares are the subject of the financial assistance, and any other company that is an intermediate holding company of the company giving the assistance.

SECTION 2

Increases in share capital

Share capital can be increased in various ways including: **3622**
- issuing additional shares for cash or other consideration;
- converting loan capital into share capital;
- using reserves to make bonus issues of additional shares to existing holders; and
- various combinations of the above.

A. Issue of new shares

The rules that apply to the initial issue of shares also apply to subsequent issues. However,   **3623**
additional factors must be taken into account.

Pre-emption rights

When a company **wishes to allot** additional ordinary shares (or securities that are convert-   **3624**
ible into ordinary shares) for cash, it must first offer them to **existing holders** of the same
class of shares or securities on terms that are either similar to, or more favourable than, the
terms being offered to outsiders. These are called pre-emption rights.

Private companies are permitted to dispense with pre-emption rights entirely by means of a
provision in the Articles of the company. **Public** companies can, by **special resolution**,
authorise directors to issue shares without regard to pre-emption rights.

Warrants and options

Warrants and options are securities that give their owners the right to subscribe for ordinary   **3625**
shares in the company at a fixed future time and usually at a fixed price.

When a company issues warrants or options, the proceeds are treated as shareholders' funds
and allocated as equity or non-equity according to the rights that attach to the underlying
shares. Thereafter, the accounting depends on whether the warrants or options are exercised.

If exercised, the amount of the proceeds should include both the amount previously recognised when they were issued and the additional consideration received at the time of exercise.

Both warrants and options can lapse **if** their holders choose **not** to exercise them. This will
represent a realised gain to the company and should be reflected in the STRGL (¶4300).

B. Utilisation of reserves to finance new issues

Bonus shares   Companies may use the **available balances on reserves**, such as distributable   **3630**
profits, share premium, revaluation reserve or capital redemption reserve, out of which to issue
additional shares to existing members. These are called **bonus shares**. Where the profit and
loss account is used, the company is in reality reallocating some of its distributable profits to
the capital base. Similarly, where the share premium or capital redemption reserve is used,
the company is effectively exchanging one set of non-distributable reserves for another.

Scrip dividends   Sometimes companies offer **additional shares** to shareholders **in place of**   **3631**
a cash dividend. This is called a **scrip dividend**. The consideration to be used in recording
the transaction is the value of the cash alternative (i.e. the cash dividend that could have
been taken) and is treated as an appropriation of profit. To the extent that the total consider-

ation for the shares (in other words, the dividend foregone) exceeds the par value of the shares issued in lieu thereof, the excess should be credited to the share premium account.

Scrip dividends are often treated for legal purposes as bonus issues. In this case the appropriation of profit should be written back as a movement on reserves and a transfer made from distributable profits to share capital (for the nominal value of the shares issued) and to share premium (for any excess).

If a company has offered a scrip dividend and is preparing annual financial statements before it knows the extent to which shareholders will take them up, it should treat the whole amount as a liability to pay a cash dividend. In the next accounting period it will effectively treat any amount of scrip dividend as a conversion of debt.

MEMO POINTS   When debt is converted into shares, the **carrying amount** of the debt at the date of conversion is treated as the consideration received for the shares (see ¶3805).

SECTION 3

Reduction of share capital

3635 Companies may for various reasons **choose** to reduce their issued share capital. There are different ways in which they can do this: by a reduction of capital, by redeeming redeemable shares, or by purchasing non-redeemable shares, usually on the open market. Redemption and acquisitions of shares are discussed in the next section (¶3645).

In some cases, reductions in share capital can result from transactions the company enters into with the co-operation of members and creditors. These are discussed in this section.

3636 A reduction of capital is most commonly undertaken where the company's:
– **share capital exceeds the fair value of its underlying assets**. In this situation, it would be to the company's benefit to reduce the share capital to more closely represent the employment of its capital; or
– has **liquid assets that may be partially surplus to its needs**. Typically, in situations where a company has excess cash or other liquid resources, it may be appropriate to reduce its capital by returning these excess funds to shareholders.
The freedom of a company to reduce its capital depends on its status as either **limited** or **unlimited**.

3637 **Unlimited companies** In general, **unlimited** companies are free to make distributions of capital to members. For **limited** companies, however, the **principle of capital maintenance** requires that, if any part of the permanent capital base is repaid to members, it must be:
– replenished by a transfer out of profits; or
– replaced by new capital.

3638 **Limited companies** A limited company having a share capital may reduce its share capital:
s 641 CA 2006 **a.** in the case of a private company limited by shares, by special resolution supported by a solvency statement; or
b. in any case, by special resolution confirmed by the court.

A company may not reduce its share capital by special resolution supported by a solvency statement if as a result of the reduction there would no longer be any member of the company holding shares other than redeemable shares.

Reduction of capital supported by solvency statement

3639 The directors of the company must make a statement of the solvency of the company not more than 15 days before the date on which the resolution is passed and the resolution, solvency statement and a statement of capital must be delivered to the registrar within 15 days of the resolution being passed. The solvency statement must be made available to the company's members when they vote on the resolution to reduce capital. In making the solvency statement, the directors have to form the opinion: that at the date of the statement there are no grounds on which the company could later be found to be unable to discharge its debts; that in the event of any winding-up within the following 12 months the company will be able to pay its debts in full within 12 months of the commencement of the winding-up, and that in any other case the company will be able to pay its debts as they fall due during the 12 months following the date of the statement. In doing so, the directors are required to take account of all of the company's liabilities.

Registration of resolution and supporting documents

Within 15 days after the resolution for reducing share capital is passed the company must deliver to the registrar a copy of the solvency statement and a statement of capital. The statement of capital must state with respect to the company's share capital as reduced by the resolution:

3640

a. the total number of shares of the company;

b. the aggregate nominal value of those shares;

c. for each class of shares:

– prescribed particulars of the rights attached to the shares;

– the total number of shares of that class; and

– the aggregate nominal value of shares of that class; and

d. the amount paid up and the amount (if any) unpaid on each share (whether on account of the nominal value of the share or by way of premium).

Reduction of capital confirmed by the court

Where a company has passed a resolution for reducing share capital, it may apply to the Court for an order confirming the reduction. Before the Court will confirm the transaction, it must first consider whether the cancellation or reduction of capital would prejudice the **rights of creditors**, who are normally entitled to look to the share capital in the event that debts owing to them are not paid. The Court will usually require an undertaking from the company that it will not distribute the special reserve until all creditors outstanding at the time of the transaction have been settled. Alternatively, if new capital is being raised, the special reserve may be distributed on a pound-for-pound basis with the new issue.

3641

Co-operation with members and creditors

The following are **examples** of transactions that, while not setting out specifically to bring about a reduction in the share capital, may nevertheless have that result:

3642

– the **transfer** of a going-concern business (i.e. its assets and liabilities) to one or more companies followed by the dissolution of the transferor company without a winding up,

– the **variation** of shareholders' rights including the consolidation or division of shares into other classes, and

– the **cancellation** of one class of shares and replacing it with new shares.

The mechanism by which these transactions are completed often requires the company to obtain the agreement not only of the shareholders, but also of creditors before the court will sanction the capital reduction. Where three quarters of shareholders and creditors vote in favour of any such scheme, the court will usually direct that it is binding on them all.

SECTION 4

Acquisitions of own shares

Transactions authorised

In general, the Companies Act does not permit a limited company to acquire its own shares, whether by purchase, subscription or otherwise. In contrast, **unlimited companies** are not subject to these restrictions and may purchase their own shares as long as their Articles of Association do not preclude it.

3645
s 658 CA 2006

However, the general prohibition on limited companies is not absolute, and if the proposed transaction falls within one of the following **exceptions** specifically provided for, it will be allowed:
– the redemption of redeemable shares;
– the acquisition of shares under an authorised reduction of capital;
– the purchase of shares is made under a court order, such as in a reconstruction;
– the purchase of qualifying shares to be held as treasury shares (see ¶3689);
– specific shares are forfeited or surrendered as a result of calls on them not having been paid;
– the shares are acquired by way of a gift or bequest without the payment of a consideration (e.g. to nominees to hold on trust for the company).

An **unlawful acquisition** (i.e. one that is not covered by the above exceptions) is void and will be considered not to have taken place. The company and its officers are liable to criminal sanctions.

> MEMO POINTS   The most common reasons for a company to find it desirable to acquire its own shares include:
> – to allow shareholders of shares that are **restricted** as to their transfer to other shareholders to sell them to the company instead;
> – to **return surplus funds** to shareholders;
> – to **increase earnings** or **net asset value** per share.

Legal conditions

3646
s 690 CA 2006

Private companies will be permitted to purchase any of their own shares (including redeemable shares that have not yet reached redemption date) if the following conditions can be satisfied; namely:
– there are no prohibitions in the company's **Articles of Association**;
– where there are **restrictions on transfers** of shares (in practice, a situation that arises mainly in the case of private companies), the specific consent of shareholders will be required before the transaction can be entered into;
– after the purchase or redemption of its own shares, the company must have at least one other non-redeemable share in issue; and
– the company cannot purchase or redeem any of its own shares that are not fully paid.

The legal requirements and procedures are discussed at ¶3670.

Funding conditions

3647

A purchase or redemption can be made only out of:
– distributable profits;
– proceeds of a fresh issue of shares – but only up to the nominal value of the shares being purchased;
– share premium (where there is a fresh issue at a premium and the shares being purchased were also issued at a premium);
– capital (but only once the above three sources have been exhausted) (see ¶3661).

> MEMO POINTS   1. **Distributable profits** are those profits out of which a company would be lawfully able to make a distribution equal in value to the payment.
> 2. A company may **purchase or redeem its own shares** only out of distributable profits or the proceeds of a fresh issue of shares made for that purpose. Further, any premium payable on the transaction must be paid out of the company's distributable profits, unless the premium arose on the original issue of the shares now being acquired, in which case it may be funded out of a fresh issue of shares made for that purpose.
> 3. A **private company** may, only if the total of distributable profits and the proceeds of any fresh issue do not cover the purchase or redemption price, make up the shortfall by a payment from capital.

Payment of consideration

3649

The consideration for a company's own shares must be paid in cash at the time of purchase and cannot be paid for by instalments or by way of a loan extended by the seller to the buyer. In addition, the payment cannot be in the form of an asset other than cash (e.g. land).

Impact on existing shareholders

If a company intends purchasing its own shares but this is not done in proportion to existing shareholdings, there may be unexpected or undesired effects for the remaining shareholders. As an example, a particular shareholder or group of shareholders may, as a result of their shareholding becoming proportionately larger, be in a position to control the voting in a way that they could not before.

3650

As soon as a company purchases or redeems any of its shares, it must treat them as cancelled. They will not be able to be reissued in the future. The effect will be to permanently reduce the issued share capital by the nominal amount of the shares purchased, though the authorised share capital will not be affected. If, however, the company is not willing to see this permanent reduction, at the time that it is about to purchase or redeem its own shares, it has a special power to issue shares up to the nominal value of the shares about to be purchased. In practice this could mean that for a short period (i.e. between the issue of the new shares and the cancellation of the purchased shares) the authorised share capital is exceeded, but this is specifically permitted in the circumstances.

3651
s 688,s 706
CA 2006

1. Accounting procedures

Acquisition out of distributable profits

The following example explains the steps that must be taken in a typical case of an acquisition by a **private company** of its own shares out of distributable profits.

3652

EXAMPLE Mr A is the chairman and a shareholder of A Ltd. As he is approaching retirement age, he wishes to sell his shares in the company. He originally paid £20,000 for his 20% stake in the company's authorised and issued share capital of £100,000.
The other directors (who between them own all the other shares in A Ltd) have agreed that the company will purchase Mr A's shares for £250,000. The company will make the payment out of distributable profits.
The transaction will be reflected in the books by way of the following entries:

Dr: Share capital	20,000	
Dr: Distributable profits	230,000	
Cr: Cash		250,000
Purchase of 20,000 £1 shares at a premium of £230,000		

Dr: Distributable profits	20,000	
Cr: Capital redemption reserve		20,000
Transfer to maintain the capital of the company		

Balance sheet	Before transaction	Purchase of own shares	Transfers to maintain capital	After transaction
	£'000	£'000	£'000	£'000
Share capital	100	(20)		80
Capital redemption reserve	-		20	20
Capital	100	(20)	20	100
Distributable reserves	300	(230)	(20)	50
	400	(250)	-	150

Thus the company's capital remains £100,000.

The accounting for the debit to **distributable reserves** will depend on how the shares had been presented in the balance sheet immediately before the purchase took place.

3653

If the shares are regarded as **debt** (by FRS 25), the loss on the repurchase of the shares should be recognised in the profit or loss for the period. On the other hand, if the shares meet the definition of **equity**, the loss should be taken directly to reserves and shown in the reconciliation of movements in shareholders' funds.

Acquisition at a premium out of fresh issue

3654
s 692 CA 2006

The **nominal value** of the shares being acquired can be funded out of the proceeds of a fresh issue of shares made for the specific purpose. In addition, if the shares had originally been issued at a premium, any premium now being paid on the reacquisition may, subject to the following limitation, also be funded out of the proceeds of a fresh issue.

The amount of premium that can be met by the fresh issue is the lower of:
– the aggregate of the premiums the company received when it first issued the shares it is now purchasing; and
– the amount of the company's share premium account after crediting the premium, if any, on the new issue of shares it makes to fund the purchase or redemption.

EXAMPLE   The following is an extract from the balance sheet of B Ltd, which intends to purchase the 10% shareholding (i.e., 20,000 shares) of Mr B, at a premium of 50p.

Ordinary shares of £1	200,000
Preference shares of £1	100,000
Share premium	80,000

Additional information
The preference shares and share premium arose as a result of a fresh issue that was intended to fund the purchase of Mr B's 20,000 ordinary shares.
The following two cases will be considered:
Case (a) – the shares, when originally issued, were issued at nominal value; and
Case (b) – the shares were originally issued at a premium of 5p but the resulting share premium was later used in full to make a bonus issue to existing shareholders.

Determination of how the purchase will be funded	Case (a)		Case (b)	
From the proceeds of the fresh issue of shares: **Nominal value** shares to be purchased		20,000		20,000
Premium on purchase: The lower of:				
– balance on share premium account; or	80,000		80,000	
– initial premium on issue of the shares now being purchased (20,000 at 5p)	N/A	–	1,000	1,000
Amount that can be funded from fresh issue		20,000		21,000
Total amount payable on purchase		30,000		30,000
Therefore, balance to be funded out of distributable profits		£10,000		£9,000

The transaction will be reflected in the books by way of the following entries:

	Case (a)		Case (b)	
	Dr	Cr	Dr	Cr
Dr: Cash	180,000		180,000	
Cr: Preference share capital		100,000		100,000
Cr: Share premium		80,000		80,000
Issue of 100,000 £1 preference shares at a premium of £80,000				

	Case (a)		Case (b)	
	Dr	**Cr**	**Dr**	**Cr**
Dr: Share capital	20,000		20,000	
Dr: Share premium			1,000	
Dr: Distributable profits	10,000		9,000	
Cr: Cash		30,000		30,000
Purchase of 20,000 £1 shares at a premium of £10,000				

Note that there is no transfer to capital redemption reserve because the nominal value of the shares purchased (£20,000) is less than the proceeds of the fresh issue. Therefore, the company's capital has been maintained and there is no need for a transfer.

Capital maintenance   Except in the case of a private company making an acquisition of its own shares out of capital, in all other situations companies are required to **maintain their capital** before and after the acquisition of shares. This generally requires the company to transfer to a capital redemption reserve an amount that is equal to the nominal value of the shares that it acquires, or on cancellation of shares held as treasury shares.

3656

The reason for the capital maintenance rule is to safeguard the interests of creditors and others by ensuring that the company's legal capital is maintained.

Where, however, the acquisition is funded wholly or partly by a **fresh issue of shares**, the amount to be transferred to the capital redemption reserve is the difference between the proceeds of the fresh issue and the nominal value of the shares being purchased. The reason is that the company's share capital is being maintained (even though some of the capital before the transaction is now represented in part by share premium and the amount that was transferred to the capital redemption reserve).

3657

Capital redemption reserve   The capital redemption reserve is restricted in much the same ways as to its use as share capital, though with some exceptions. For instance, it can be used to pay up unissued shares allotted as fully paid bonus shares. Also, in certain circumstances, a private company may be able to use its capital redemption reserve to fund the purchase or redemption of shares.

3658

The following table summarises the rules for public and private companies:

Circumstances surrounding purchase, cancellation or redemption of shares	Transfer to capital redemption reserve that must be made
Company purchases or redeems shares wholly out of **distributable profits**	An amount equivalent to the nominal value of the shares it purchased. In addition, it must reduce the issued share capital by the nominal value of the shares purchased.
Company purchases or redeems shares wholly or partly out of a **fresh issue** with no payment being made out of capital, where the nominal value of the shares purchased or redeemed exceeds the amount of the proceeds of the fresh issue.	The difference between the nominal value of the shares purchased/redeemed and the proceeds of the fresh issue (see example, immediately below).
Company cancels shares held as **treasury shares**	An amount equivalent to the nominal value of the shares cancelled. In addition, the company must reduce the amount of its issued share capital by the nominal value of the shares cancelled.

EXAMPLE   C Ltd purchases 10,000 £1 "A" ordinary shares at a premium of £1.20 partly out of the proceeds of a fresh issue of shares and partly out of distributable reserves. C Ltd issues 5,000 "B" ordinary shares with a nominal value of 20p at a premium of £1.00 (the total proceeds therefore being £6,000).

The amount to be transferred to the capital redemption reserve is:

Nominal value of shares redeemed	10,000
Proceeds of fresh issue	6,000
Transfer to the capital redemption reserve	£4,000

Determination of how the purchase will be funded	
From the proceeds of the fresh issue of shares:	
Nominal value shares to be purchased, limited to the proceeds of the fresh issue	6,000
Total amount payable on purchase	22,000
Therefore, balance to be funded out of distributable profits	£16,000

Acquisitions out of capital

3660   The Companies Act 2006 permits **private companies** to purchase or redeem their own shares out of capital. This means that permission exists unless it has been specifically excluded. Members may, if they wish, restrict or prohibit such transactions by including a provision to this effect in the articles.

3661   The statement required when a company makes a payment out of capital in respect of a redemption or purchase of its own shares must specify the amount of the **permissible capital payment** for the shares in question. It must also state that, having made full inquiry into the affairs and prospects of the company, the directors have formed the opinion that the company will be able to continue to carry on business as a going concern (and will accordingly be able to pay its debts as they fall due) throughout that year. In forming this opinion, the directors must take into account all of the company's liabilities, including any contingent or prospective liabilities.

s 714 CA 2006   The statement must have annexed to it a report addressed to the directors by the company's auditor stating that:
– they have inquired into the company's state of affairs;
– the amount specified in the statement as the permissible capital payment for the shares in question is in his or her view properly determined in accordance with the relevant sections of the Companies Act 2006; and
– they are not aware of anything to indicate that the opinion expressed by the directors in their statement is unreasonable in all the circumstances.

3662   **Permissible capital payment (PCP)**   The maximum amount of payment that may be made out of capital is limited to the "permissible capital payment" or PCP, which is equal to the price of the shares being purchased, less the total of any available profits and proceeds of a fresh issue made to fund the purchase. The effect of this rule is to require a **private company** to use its available profits and any proceeds arising from a new issue before looking to capital. The calculation of the permissible capital payment is represented by the following formula:

PCP = acquisition price – (available profits + proceeds of fresh issue)

MEMO POINTS   **"Available profits"** refer to those that are available for distribution within the meaning of the Companies Act (i.e. its accumulated realised profits, to the extent they have not been used in distributions or capitalisations, less its accumulated realised losses, so far as they have not been previously written off in a reduction or re-organisation of capital).

EXAMPLE   E Ltd has the following balances in its balance sheet:

Share capital	£500,000
Share premium	£200,000
Distributable reserves	£25,000

The company intends to purchase 200,000 £1 shares from one of its shareholders at a premium of £1. (These shares were originally issued at par value.) The company issues 100,000 ordinary

shares of £1 each at a premium of 75p per share for the purposes of purchasing the shares in question.
The PCP is calculated as follows:

200,000 £1 shares at a premium of £1 per share		400,000
Less: Proceeds of fresh issue (100,000 £1 shares at a premium of 75p)	175,000	
Distributable profits	125,000	300,000
PCP		£100,000

The purchase would be made as follows:

Out of the proceeds of the fresh issue:		
(a) Nominal value of shares purchased	200,000	
(b) Share premium account	-	200,000
Out of distributable profits		125,000
		325,000
Total cost of purchase		400,000
Therefore, balance out of capital		£75,000

Transfer to capital redemption reserve

When a **private company** purchases its shares wholly or partially out of capital, a transfer must be made to the capital redemption reserve represented by the following formula:

3663
s 734 (2) CA 2006

Transfer to capital redemption reserve = Nominal value of shares purchased − (payment out of capital + proceeds of fresh issue)

EXAMPLE   X Ltd, Y Ltd, and Z Ltd are private companies. Each purchases 40,000 of their own shares that were originally issued at their nominal value of £1 per share. In each case, a premium of £1.20 per share is payable on purchase. Y Ltd issues 28,000 redeemable preference shares at par and Z Ltd issues 16,000 redeemable preference shares at par. In both cases, the shares are redeemable at par. The companies' retained profits are: X Ltd £64,000; Y Ltd £120,000; and Z Ltd £60,000. The purchase price to be paid is determined as follows:

	X Ltd	Y Ltd	Z Ltd
Out of proceeds of new issue:			
(a) Nominal value of shares purchased – restricted to proceeds of fresh issue	-	28	16
(b) Share premium	-	-	-
	-	28	16
Available from distributable profits	64	60	60
	64	88	76
Therefore, balance out of capital	24	-	12
Total amount to be paid	88	88	88

Amount to be transferred to the capital redemption reserve is as follows:

	X Ltd	Y Ltd	Z Ltd
Nominal value of shares purchased	40	40	40
Less:	24	28	28
Proceeds of fresh issue	-	28	16
Permissible capital payment (PCP)	24	-	12
Transfer to the capital redemption reserve	16	12	12

3664
s 734 (3) CA 2006

When the PCP **exceeds the nominal value of the shares** purchased or redeemed, the company may use the excess to reduce one of the following:
- the capital redemption reserve;
- the share premium account;
- fully paid share capital; or
- the revaluation reserve.

3665

Similarly, where shares are purchased out of the proceeds of a new issue, if the nominal value of the shares being purchased is **less than** the sum of the permissible capital payment and the proceeds of the new issue, the company may use the excess to reduce the above. This is represented by the following formula:

> Debit to reduce capital = (payment out of capital + proceeds of fresh issue) – (nominal value of shares purchased)

> EXAMPLE S Ltd and T Ltd are private companies. They intend to purchase, at a premium of £1.50 per share, 200,000 of their own £1 shares (originally issued at a premium of 20p per share). To help fund the purchase, T Ltd issues 8,000 £1 preference shares at par (redeemable at par). The distributable reserves of S Ltd and T Ltd are £25,000 and £18,000 respectively. The purchases are made as follows:

	S Ltd	T Ltd
Out of proceeds of fresh issue of shares: Nominal value of shares purchased – limited to the proceeds of the fresh issue	-	8,000
Share premium account	-	-
	-	8,000
Out of distributable profits	25,000	18,000
	25,000	26,000
Total cost of purchase	50,000	50,000
Therefore, balance out of capital	£25,000	£24,000

> The amount by which the companies may reduce their capital redemption reserve, the share premium account and/or the fully paid share capital is as follows:

	S Ltd	T Ltd
PCP	25, 000	24,000
Proceeds of new issue	-	8,0004
	25,000	32,000
Nominal value of shares purchased	20,000	20,000
Excess available	£5,000	£12,000

Disclosure requirements

3667

Any company that purchases its own shares during the year must disclose in its financial statements the details of such share purchases during the year, the rights of redemption of any redeemable shares, and the authority under which the company acquired the shares in question.

3668

The directors' report in respect of the year in which the purchase of a company's own shares takes place must include the following:
- the number and nominal value of the shares purchased or redeemed;
- the aggregate consideration paid;
- the reason/s for their purchase;
- the percentage of the called-up share capital that the shares purchased or redeemed represent.

2. Legal procedures

One of the important legal procedures relating to a company's purchasing its own shares is to first determine whether the purchase will be a market purchase or an off-market one.   **3670**

An "**off-market**" purchase is one in which either of the following applies: **3671**
– the shares are not purchased on a recognised investment exchange (such as the Stock Exchange and AIM); or
– the shares are purchased on a recognised investment exchange, but they are not subject to a marketing arrangement on that exchange (in other words, where they are not listed or where they cannot be traded without prior permission for individual transactions and without constraints as to timing).   s 693 CA 2006

Any other purchase is a "**market**" purchase.

Returns and contracts

After a company has purchased its own shares, it is required to submit, no later than 28 days after the delivery of shares to it, a return in the prescribed form to the Registrar of Companies stating: **3678**
– the number and nominal value of the shares purchased; and
– the date they were delivered to the company.

Companies are obliged to keep a copy of each contract they enter into, together with any variations to any such contracts. These documents must be kept at the company's registered office (or elsewhere, as specified in accordance with s.1136 Companies Act 2006), from the date the contracts are concluded until the end of a period of ten years from the date of the purchase to which they relate.   **3680**

The company must make a copy of such a contract available for inspection by any member without charge. Companies must give notices to the registrar of the place where the contract is kept available for inspection.   **3681**

Contingent purchase contracts

A contingent purchase contract is a contract under which a company becomes either entitled or obliged to purchase its own shares. Contingent purchase contracts can be used to give a company the option to purchase its shares. Alternatively they can be used to give a shareholder the right to require the company to purchase the shares – where, for instance, a shareholder is prepared to maintain an investment in a company only if there are arrangements in place that enable them to sell their shares back to the company at some future time.   **3683**

Liability on winding up

Under the Insolvency Act 1986, if a company proves to be **insolvent** and is wound up within a year of making a payment out of capital, both the shareholders whose shares were purchased or redeemed and the directors who signed the statutory declaration will be called upon to contribute to the assets of the company. However, directors will be exempt from such a liability if they can show that there were reasonable grounds for their opinion stated in the statutory declaration.   **3685**

Such a person's liability will be limited to the amount they received out of capital in respect of their shares, and the company's directors are jointly and severally liable with the past shareholder for that amount.

Failure to acquire shares

If a company agrees to purchase or redeem any of its shares but fails to do so, the affected shareholder cannot rely on the courts to order specific performance of the contract,   **3687**   s 735 (2) – (3) CA 2006 especially in a case where the company is not able to meet the costs of purchasing the shares out of distributable profits. Neither can the shareholder sue the company for damages.

s 735 (4) CA 2006 Where, however, the company's failure to perform under the contract happens at the same time as it faces going into liquidation, the terms of the purchase can be enforced, but only if:

– the purchase was to take place before the winding up commenced; and
– there would have been distributable profits equal to the purchase or redemption price.

Treasury shares

3689
s 725 CA 2006
Companies with "qualifying shares" (i.e. those that are listed on the London Stock Exchange or that of another EEA state, or traded on AIM or similar market in an EEA state), may purchase them out of distributable profits and hold them in treasury for resale, transfer, or cancellation at a later date.

Where a company has **only one class of shares**, the aggregate nominal value of shares held as treasury shares may not exceed 10% of the nominal value of the issued share capital. Similarly, if the company has more than one class of shares, the aggregate nominal value of the shares of any class held as treasury shares must not exceed 10% of the nominal value of the issued share capital of the shares in that class at that time.

3691
The company **may not exercise any rights** (including voting rights) over the treasury shares. In addition, it may not pay a dividend or make any other distribution including any distribution of assets to members on a winding up to itself in respect of the treasury shares.

Where shares are held in treasury, the company must be entered in the register of members as the member holding those shares.

3695
Sale   When a company sells treasury shares, if the **proceeds** are **equal to or less than** the **purchase price** paid for the shares, the proceeds are treated as realised profit. If the proceeds **exceed** the purchase price, the excess over the purchase price must be transferred to the share premium account.

The purchase price paid by the company for the shares is determined by the use of a weighted average price method. If the shares were allotted to the company as fully paid bonus shares, the purchase price is deemed to be nil.

3697
Cancellation   If a company cancels shares held as **treasury shares**, it must reduce the amount of its issued share capital by the nominal value of those cancelled shares. If shares held as treasury shares cease to be "qualifying shares" for any reason other than if they are suspended from listing, the company must immediately cancel them.

s 733 (4) CA 2006 The amount by which the company's issued share capital is reduced on the cancellation of treasury shares must be transferred to a capital redemption reserve.

Redeemable shares

3702
The redemption of redeemable shares is one of the **exceptions to the general rule** that a company may not purchase its own shares. Much of the legislation relating to redemptions is similar to the rules for purchases of own shares.

3703
s 685 CA 2006
Private companies no longer require prior authorisation under the articles of association. However, a company's members may, prohibit or restrict the authority of the company to issue redeemable shares by including a provision to this effect in the articles. In addition, the directors are permitted to determine the terms, conditions and manner of a redemption of redeemable shares. The power conferred on the directors requires prior authorisation by the company's members, either by resolution of the company or through the articles. The terms and conditions of the redemption must be stated in the statement of capital. If the directors are not authorised to set the terms of the redemption, then they must be set out in the company's articles.

Distributions

"Distributions" include all **payments to members**, whether in the form of cash or other assets. The following are **not** distributions:
- issues of bonus shares;
- the redemption or purchase of shares out of capital or unrealised profits;
- the reduction of share capital by reducing or extinguishing amounts owed;
- distributions of assets on winding up;
- repayments of loans to members made not in their capacity as members.

3710

1. Profits available for distribution

The amount of profits that are available for distribution depends on the type of company wishing to make the distribution. For companies other than investment/insurance companies, available profits consist of **accumulated realised profits** less **accumulated realised losses**. The origin of these profits can be either capital or revenue.

3711
s 830 CA 2006

Private companies may distribute the whole of their accumulated realised profits not previously distributed or capitalised less any accumulated realised losses not previously written off in a reduction or reorganisation of capital. Private companies are not required by the Act to take unrealised losses into account. However, under common-law principles, the duty of directors to act in the best interests of the company means that in practice unrealised losses cannot simply be ignored if, as a result, the company's financial standing is compromised.

3712

Investment companies   **Investment companies** may distribute only **the excess of their accumulated realised revenue profits** over their accumulated revenue losses (both realised and unrealised). The advantage is that **capital losses** may be ignored when making distributions.

3714

In addition, an investment company must satisfy the following conditions before making a distribution:

a) its assets must be at least equal to 150% of the aggregate of its liabilities, and the distribution will not reduce the company's assets to a level below 150% of the aggregate of its liabilities;

b) the company's shares are listed on a recognised investment exchange other than an overseas investment exchange; and

c) that the company did not, during the preceding accounting period, use any unrealised profits in paying up debentures or any amounts unpaid on any of its issued shares.

2. Reference to financial statements

Before a distribution can be made, the company must first ensure that it is lawful, i.e., that sufficient distributable reserves are available. For this purpose, reference is usually made to the company's most recent audited financial statements.

3717

Audit report   The first step is to examine the audit report on the previous financial statements. An **unqualified audit report** gives rise to the following possibilities:

a) If there are **sufficient distributable profits** to cover the distribution, the distribution can be made.

b) If the last annual accounts show insufficient distributable profits to cover the proposed distribution, **interim accounts** should be prepared. There is no requirement for interim accounts to be audited. If the statements show adequate distributable profits, the company, if a **private** company, can make the distribution.

3718

3719   A **qualified audit report** gives rise to the following possibilities:
a) If the auditors' report stated that **the financial statements do not give a true and fair view**, no distribution may be made.
b) If, in the auditors' opinion, **the financial statements were not properly prepared**, their report will reflect that opinion. In this event, there is a requirement that the auditors state in writing, either at the time of their report or later, whether the qualification is material for purposes of determining the legality of any proposed distribution. If the qualification is not material for these purposes, the next step is to look at the available distributable profits.

3721   **Effect of previous distributions in the current period**   If, since the last financial statements, a company has already made a distribution or has entered into an arrangement such as the purchase or redemption of shares, which may reduce distributable reserves, it may continue to rely on the last annual accounts as long as it takes into account the cumulative effect of such earlier transactions on the available profits.

3723   **Distribution in first accounting period**   Where a company wishes to make a distribution during its first accounting period or before it has prepared its first annual accounts, it must publish **initial accounts** for the purpose of justifying the distribution. These accounts do not have to be audited or filed with the Registrar of Companies (if it is a private company).

---

3. Realised profits and losses

3725
s 853 CA 2006

The Act **defines** realised profits and losses as:

"profits or losses of the company as fall to be treated as realised in accordance with principles generally accepted at the time when the accounts are prepared."

In areas not covered by accounting standards, it may prove difficult to show that any particular treatment is sufficiently generally accepted to ensure compliance. One obvious solution is to look to the **principle of prudence** (see ¶30), in terms of which **profits** should not be anticipated but recognised in the profit and loss account only when realised in the form of cash or, if in the form of other assets, where the realisation of those assets into cash can be assessed with reasonable certainty. **Losses** should be provided for whether the amount is known with certainty or even if it can only be estimated based on available information.

3727   In addition to those situations in which a profit is "readily apparent", the following could **also constitute a realised profit**:
a) the receipt or accrual of investment or other income receivable in the form of qualifying consideration;
b) a gain arising on a return of capital on an investment where the return is in the form of qualifying consideration;
c) a gift (such as a "capital contribution") received in the form of qualifying consideration;
d) the release of a provision for a liability or loss that was treated as a realised loss; and
e) the reversal of a write-down or provision for diminution in value or impairment of an asset that was treated as a realised loss.

3728   Examples of **realised losses** include:
a) a cost or expense (other than one charged to the share premium account) that results in a reduction in recorded net assets;
b) a loss arising on the sale or other disposal or scrapping of an asset;
c) the writing down, or providing for the depreciation, amortisation, diminution in value or impairment, of an asset;
d) the creation of, or increase in, a provision for a liability or loss that results in an overall reduction in recorded net assets. However, when assets are revalued to their fair value, with any unrealised gain being included in the profit and loss account (for instance, by insurance companies), the deferred tax on that gain should be treated as a reduction in that unrealised gain rather than as a realised loss;
e) a gift made by the company (or the release of all or part of a debt due to the company or the assumption of a liability by the company) to the extent that it results in an overall reduction in recorded net assets; and

f) a loss arising from fair value accounting where profits on remeasurement of the same asset or liability would be treated as realised profit.

Asset revaluations

A **surplus on revaluation** of a fixed asset is credited to the **revaluation reserve** and is not distributable.   **3730**

In general, **provisions for depreciation and write-downs** are treated as realised losses, except where a company **revalues all of its fixed assets**, in which case these provisions and write-downs in value of the revalued assets are unrealised.   s 841 CA 2006

However, where only certain classes of assets have been revalued (e.g. properties), **assets that have not been revalued** can be treated as having been revalued if they are worth as least as much as the aggregate amount at which they are stated in the accounts. The effect is to permit a provision for diminution in value of a fixed asset to be treated as an unrealised loss, but only if the directors make the following disclosures in the accounts:
– the directors have considered the value of the fixed assets without revaluing them;
– they are satisfied that the aggregate value of the assets in question is not less than their net book value; and
– they are treating their consideration of the fixed assets as a revaluation.

Where fixed assets have been revalued and the **annual depreciation charge is higher** than it would otherwise have been, an amount equal to the cumulative additional depreciation should be treated as a realised profit. This restores the amount of profits available for distribution as if the assets had not been revalued. This will be effected by making a transfer, as a reserve movement between the revaluation reserve and the profit and loss account, of an amount equal to the increase in the annual depreciation charge resulting from the revaluation.   **3731** s 841 (5) CA 2006

Goodwill

Goodwill **arising on consolidation** does not affect realised (and, therefore, distributable) profits because distributions are made by individual companies and not by the group. However, in the case of purchased goodwill that has been **capitalised** in a company's balance sheet, amortisation charges will reduce distributable profits.   **3734**

Non-cash distributions

Where a company makes a **distribution in the form of an asset** other than cash, any unrealised profit relating to that asset must be treated as realised. Under the Companies Act 2006, a company that has revalued assets showing an unrealised profit in the accounts will be able to treat that profit as a realised profit if it makes a distribution that includes a non-cash asset.   **3735**

4. Transactions between group companies

Although the question of whether a distribution can be made is decided by reference to the distributable profits of individual companies within a group, certain inter-company transactions may have an effect on the distributable reserves of such companies.   **3740**

Great care should be exercised when making distributions based on profits generated through inter-company transactions, for two reasons:
1. the profit, although technically realised, may not be supported by the liquid resources to make the payment of a dividend commercially viable; and
2. intra-group transfers can be used to manipulate profits in individual companies and may not reflect the same results as would have been achieved had the transactions been done on an arm's-length basis.

Sales of fixed assets

There are questions as to how to treat the profit that is made within a group if one company sells an asset to another. The following example illustrates two possible scenarios.   **3741**

EXAMPLE Scenario 1

A Ltd sells an asset to B Ltd, a fellow subsidiary. Although A Ltd had carried the asset in its books below market value, B Ltd bought it at its market value.

The profit should be considered realised or unrealised. The answer will depend on all the circumstances surrounding the transaction itself but also the companies, and legal advice may be needed. If B Ltd has **net liabilities** and the consideration is added to an inter-company account with no realistic possibility of its being settled, it is likely that the profit arising in A Ltd's books should be treated as unrealised. On the other hand, if B Ltd is trading profitably and pays for the asset with cash, there is a strong case for A Ltd to regard the profit as realised.

Scenario 2

S Ltd sells an asset to H Ltd, its holding company. The asset is sold at its book value of £5,000. It has a market value of £12,000. The difference of £7,000 may be deemed to be a dividend from S Ltd to H Ltd. If S Ltd does not have sufficient distributable reserves, the dividend will be a return of capital, which is unlawful.

See also ¶3742 regarding inter-company dividends.

Inter-company dividends

3742   The dividends paid and received within a group can also affect distributable reserves. There are two issues that need to be considered: the **method of payment** and the **timing of recognition** in the receiving company's accounts.

A parent company should regard dividends as realised whether they are paid in cash or passed through a current account – provided that a proper assessment of the realisable value of the current account balance is made.

With regard to the question of timing, dividends receivable from subsidiaries and associates with respect to accounting periods ending on or before that of the parent company are normally **accrued** in the parents' financial statements. This is so even if the dividends are declared after the parent's year end. In other words, while it would not be normal practice for a company to accrue dividends receivable from another company unless they were declared before the receiving company's year end, this rule is not observed in the case of companies within a group.

---

5. Unlawful distributions

3743
s 847 CA 2006   Before a distribution can be made, the company must first ensure that it is lawful, in that sufficient distributable reserves are available. Where an unlawful distribution is made by a company to one of its members who knows, or has reasonable grounds for believing, that it is so made, the member is liable to repay to the company a sum equal to the value of the distribution at that time. This is not applicable in the case of financial assistance given in contravention of the rules governing financial assistance for the acquisition of a company's own shares, or in the case of any payment made by a company in respect of the redemption or purchase by the company of its own shares.

SECTION 6

Reserves

Share premium account

3745   If a company **issues shares for a consideration that exceeds their nominal value**, the difference is accounted for in the share premium account. Where the consideration is paid in cash, this value is easily measured. If the consideration is composed of assets other than cash, the consideration must be valued in order to properly determine the amount, if any, in excess of nominal value that must be credited to the share premium account.

Uses of the share premium account   The share premium account can be used: **3747**
- to issue new fully paid **bonus shares** to members; and   s610 CA 2006
- where, on issuing shares, a company has transferred a sum to the share premium account, to write off the **expenses** or **commission** on the issue of those particular shares.

For purposes of **reducing share capital**, the share premium account is treated as forming part of a company's capital. It can therefore also be used for the following:
- a reduction of capital sanctioned by the court;
- repayment of original share premium to shareholders if there has been a fresh issue of shares; and
- payment of a permissible capital payment (see ¶3662).

Revaluation reserve

A revaluation reserve will arise in a company's books if it revalues any of its assets under the   **3748**
alternative accounting rules. Any profit or loss arising on the revaluation must be credited or   Sch 1 para 32
debited, as the case may be, to the revaluation reserve.   SI 2008/410

An exception to the rule is provided for **investment companies**, which need not transfer the profit or loss to the revaluation reserve.

The **initial surplus** credited to the reserve on revaluation represents the difference between the revalued amount and the previous carrying value of the asset.

> EXAMPLE   The historical cost of an asset was £150,000. Its book value, after accumulated depreciation of £50,000, is £100,000. The asset is revalued at £180,000. The amount to be credited to the revaluation reserve is £80,000.

Uses of the revaluation reserve   The balance on the revaluation reserve represents an   **3749**
unrealised profit and is therefore not distributable. However, the balance on the revaluation reserve may be used for the following purposes:
- wholly or partly paying up unissued shares in the company that will be allotted to members as fully or partly paid shares (e.g. bonus shares);
- recognising taxation relating to any amount credited or debited to the reserve;
- eliminating amounts no longer necessary for the purposes of the valuation method used; and
- transfers to the profit and loss account of amounts either previously charged there or representing realised profits.

Adjustments to the revaluation reserve   Two adjustments are considered: the **adjustment**   **3751**
for depreciation and the **adjustment for impairment losses**.

The **depreciation** charged in the profit and loss account in respect of assets that have been   **3752**
revalued is based on the revalued amount. However, the amount by which this depreciation exceeds the depreciation that would have been charged on the historical cost represents a realised profit. Therefore, the excess should be transferred annually from the revaluation reserve to the profit and loss account, in effect reducing the total depreciation charge to the amount that would have been charged on the asset's historical cost.

> EXAMPLE   An asset with a book value of £16,000 is revalued to £25,000. At the date of revaluation the remaining useful life was estimated at 10 years. The annual depreciation charge based on the revalued amount is therefore £2,500. Assuming that the historical-cost depreciation amounted to £1,600 per annum, the excess, i.e. £900, should be transferred every year from the revaluation reserve.

An **impairment loss** is a permanent diminution in value of an asset. Where the impairment   **3753**
is in respect of an asset that has been revalued upwards, the loss is recognised in both the profit and loss account and the revaluation reserve.

> EXAMPLE   An asset with a cost of £20,000 is revalued to £30,000 when its book value is £16,000. It is estimated that the asset has a useful life of 10 years. Two years later, the asset is deemed to have suffered an impairment. Its carrying value is reduced to £6,000.

Initial amount transferred to revaluation reserve on revaluation (£30,000 – £16,000)	£14,000
Excess annual depreciation charged over the 2 years (2 × £1,400)	2,800
Balance on reserve	£11,200
Carrying value of asset at date of impairment (£30,000 – [2 × £3,000])	£24,000
Transfer from revaluation reserve	11,200
	12.800
Carrying value	6,000
Impairment loss to be recognised in profit and loss account	£6,800

3754   If amounts have been transferred from the revaluation reserve in connection with a **bonus issue** and, later, certain of the assets which had been revalued and which had given rise to the revaluation reserve are sold, the amount to be transferred to the profit and loss account should be limited to the balance remaining on the revaluation surplus in respect of those assets.

Capital redemption reserve

3756   When a company uses **distributable profits** out of which to purchase or redeem its own shares, it is required to transfer to the capital redemption reserve an amount equal to the nominal value of the shares concerned. The capital redemption reserve is specifically required by the Act to be shown under "Other reserves" – either on the face of the balance sheet or in the notes.

3757   If a redemption is **funded in part by a fresh issue** of shares, the amount required to be transferred to the capital redemption reserve is the difference between the nominal value of the shares redeemed and the proceeds of the fresh issue.

The **capital redemption reserve may be used** to pay up fully paid **bonus** shares.

EXAMPLE   Scenario 1 - **No fresh issue of shares**
D Ltd redeems shares with a nominal value of £110,000 (originally issued for £120,000) for £140,000. The journal entries to give effect to the transaction and the requirements of the Act are as follows:

To record the redemption:	Dr.	Cr.
Distributable reserves	140,000	
Cash		140,000
To transfer to the capital redemption reserve:		
Called up share capital	110,000	
Capital redemption reserve		110,000

Scenario 2 – **Fresh issue of shares**
E Ltd makes a fresh issue of ordinary shares to finance the redemption of redeemable shares as follows:

Shares issued
Nominal value	75,000
Issue price	150,000

Shares redeemed

Nominal value of shares	150,000
Originally issued at a premium of	7,000
Premium on redemption	£30,000

Immediately before these transactions took place, the salient balances in the books of E Ltd were:

Issued share capital	£450,000
Share premium (including the original premium on the shares to be redeemed)	35,000
	£485,000
Distributable profits	180,000
	£665,000

Redemption of shares

The total amount to be redeemed is £180,000, being nominal value of £150,000 and premium on redemption of £30,000. The premium on redemption may be funded out of the fresh issue to the extent of the premium originally received (£7,000) or the balance on the share premium account after the new issue (£35,000 + £75,000 = £110,000) – whichever is the lower.

	Nominal value	Premium
Redemption to be financed	150,000	30,000
Premium on redemption – out of fresh issue		7,000
Therefore, amount to finance from distributable profits		£23,000
Proceeds of fresh issue already applied to redemption premium	7,000	
Redemption of nominal value financed by fresh issue	£143,000	

Following a strict interpretation of the Act, there is no difference between the aggregate proceeds of the fresh issue and the nominal value of the shares redeemed. Therefore, no transfer to the capital redemption reserve is required. Thus, the balance sheet after redemption will reflect the following:

Issued share capital	[450,000 – 150,000 + 75,000]	375,000
Share premium	[35,000 – 7,000 + 75,000]	103,000
		478,000
Distributable profits	[180,000 – 23,000]	157,000
		£635,000

The rules can be interpreted another way. The proceeds of the fresh issue used to finance the redemption of the share premium (£143,000) is different from the nominal value of the shares redeemed (£150,000). There is thus an argument that this difference should be transferred to the capital redemption reserve. In this case, the post-redemption balance sheet will appear as follows:

Issued share capital	[450,000 – 150,000 + 75,000]	£375,000
Share premium	[35,000 – 7,000 + 75,000]	103,000
Capital redemption reserve		7,000
		485,000
Distributable profits	[180,000 – 23,000 – 7,000]	150,000
		£635,000

Reserves provided for by the Articles of Association

Reserves under this heading will be those specifically required by the company's Articles of Association. For example, the Articles of an investment trust may require that profits on the sale of investments be transferred to a non-distributable capital reserve.   **3759**

Other reserves

The finance costs in respect of non-equity shares, accrued over the term of such shares, may appear under this heading. Another example may be translation differences arising on the consolidation of foreign subsidiaries.   **3761**

SECTION 7

Disclosure in the accounts

The Companies Act, in particular, the balance sheet formats given in Schedule 1 to SI 2008 No. 410, prescribes the headings that must be shown on the face of the balance sheet under **Capital and reserves**, as follows: **3770**

I	Called up share capital
II	Share premium account
III	Revaluation reserve
IV	Other reserves 1. Capital redemption reserve 2. Reserve for own shares 3. Reserves provided for by the articles of association 4. Other reserves
V	Profit and loss account

Additional disclosure requirements are set out in FRS 4, FRS 25, FRS 29, and the Listing Rules. FRS 29 replaces the disclosure requirements of FRS 25 for all companies applying FRS 26 "Financial instruments: recognition and measurement".

MEMO POINTS   As FRS 4 remains applicable to **unlisted entities** not applying the measurement requirements of FRS 26, references to FRS 4 have been retained in this chapter. While the Act refers specifically to shares and debentures many companies issue other types of capital instruments as a means of raising finance, including loans, other debt instruments, warrants and options.

A. Share capital

1. Under the Companies Act

3775
Sch 1 para 48
SI 2008/410

On the face of the balance sheet, the respective amounts of **allotted** share capital and **called up** share capital that has been paid must be shown separately under "Share capital and reserves". The following disclosures are required in the notes to the financial statements.

3776

Category	Disclosures
Types of shares	– for each **class** of share that has been allotted, the **number** and **nominal value**.
Treasury shares	– the number and aggregate nominal value of the treasury shares and, where shares of more than one class have been allotted, the number and aggregate nominal value of the shares of each class held as treasury shares.
If the allotted capital includes redeemable shares	– the earliest and latest dates on which the company can redeem the shares; – whether the company is obliged to redeem the shares or whether the shares are redeemable at the option of either the company or the shareholders; – whether any premium is payable on redemption and, if so, the amount.
If any shares have been allotted during the current year	– the class of shares allotted; – for each class, the number allotted, their aggregate nominal value and the consideration received; – the reason for making the issue.
If there are options to subscribe for shares or other rights that require the allotment of shares	– the number, description and amount of shares for which the rights are exercisable; – the period during which the rights are exercisable; and – the price to be paid.

2. Under FRS 25

3778   FRS 25 requires all financial instruments – or their component parts – to be classified as equity, financial liabilities, or financial assets. As a result, certain types of shares will no longer be classified under share capital but as financial liabilities. Furthermore, some shares may actually be **compound financial instruments** and, accordingly, must be split into their respective "equity" and "financial liability" components.

Ordinary shares are treated as equity and are disclosed as part of shareholders' funds. Preference shares can either fall into the same category or be classified as a financial liability depending on the rights and characteristics attaching to them. For example, **non-redeemable** preference shares, whose dividends are payable at the **company's option**, are regarded under FRS 25 as equity instruments and would be disclosed together with ordinary shares.

On the other hand, **cumulative preference shares** will be treated differently. Because the dividend accumulates if not paid in any year, they do not fall into the category of dividends payable at the company's option as described above; on the contrary, they remain a liability until paid. Therefore, these financial instruments must be divided into their components so that the **equity component** is shown in the balance sheet under "Shareholders' funds" while the **liability component** would be shown under "Creditors: Amounts payable after more than one year".

---

3. Under FRSSE

The following information must be given regarding a small company's share capital: **3779**
- the number and aggregate nominal value of shares of each class allotted;
- share allotments during the year including the type of shares allotted, their number and aggregate nominal value, the reasons for the allotment, and the consideration received by the company; and
- for redeemable shares, the earliest and latest redemption dates, redemption premiums and details of options held.

---

4. Example

The following serves as an example of prevailing disclosure requirements in respect of share   **3780**
capital in the notes.

20. Share Capital

	Ordinary shares £000	Preference shares £000	Total share capital £000	Share premium £000	Total £000
At 1 January 20X3	100	12	112	10	122
Proceeds from shares issued	10		10	5	15
At 31 December 20X3	110	12	122	15	137
Preference shares reclassified to borrowings	-	(12)	(12)	-	(12)
At 1 January 20X4	110	-	110	15	125
Proceeds from shares issued	20		20	20	40
At 31 December 20X4	130		130	35	165

	20X4		20X3	
	Shares	£000	Shares	£000
Authorised ordinary shares of £1 each	250,000	250	250,000	250

	20X4		20X3	
	Shares	£000	Shares	£000
Allotted, called up and fully paid ordinary shares of £1 each:				
At start of year	110,000	110	100,000	100
Proceeds of issue	20,000	20	10,000	10
At end of year	130,000	130	110,000	110

> During the year, the company issued 20,000 ordinary shares (20X4 – 10,000) at a premium of £1 each (20X4 – 50p)

B. Reserves

1. Disclosure on the face of the balance sheet

3782   Where appropriate, the **following reserves** must be shown on the face of the balance sheet:
- share premium account;
- revaluation reserve (or similar title);
- other reserves; and
- profit and loss account.

Unless the balance sheet is in deficit, the reserves, in aggregate, represent the excess of assets over liabilities after called up share capital has been deducted. The revaluation reserve is the only reserve that companies are allowed to call by another name.

Comparative figures for the preceding year are not required.

3783   The main heading "**other reserves**" has the following constituents, which can be shown on the balance sheet itself or by way of a note:
- capital redemption reserve;
- reserve for own shares;
- reserves provided for by the articles of association; and
- other reserves (realised and unrealised that do not fit elsewhere in the formats).

3784
Sch 1 para 59
SI 2008/410

For each reserve in respect of which there have been **transfers either in or out** during the year, the following must be shown:
- opening and closing balances;
- amounts transferred to or from reserves during the year; and
- the source and application of the amounts transferred.

Companies can provide the required information for each reserve separately or in a combined note, as illustrated below. When there have been transfers between reserves, a combined note will often give readers a clearer view of the overall movements.

2. Statement of movements on reserves

3787   The Companies Act requires companies to reconcile the opening and closing balances of individual reserves. Where the entity's reserves structure is complex, it may be useful to show the information in a statement of movements on reserves.

EXAMPLE **Statement of movements on reserves**

	Profit and loss account	Share premium	Revaluation reserve	Total
	£	£	£	£
At beginning of year	200	120	450	770
Surplus on revaluation of investment properties	-	-	42	42
Decrease in value of trade investment	-	-	-27	-27
Transfer of realised profits	58	-	-58	-
Profit retained for the year	110	-	-	110
At end of year	368	120	407	895

3. Distributable reserves

If, in the context of **group accounts**, there are any significant statutory, contractual or exchange control restrictions on the parent undertaking's access to distributable profits, FRS 2, "Accounting for subsidiary undertakings", requires the consolidated financial statements to disclose both the nature and extent of those restrictions.

3789
FRS 2 (53)

EXAMPLE **Example note envisaged by FRS 2:**

The Group has certain reserves that are not freely distributable and represent amounts of foreign tax exempted under non-UK investment-incentive programmes. These reserves cannot be distributed to shareholders without incurring liability for payment of the previously exempted taxes, interest and penalties. The reserves are currently reinvested in the business and there is no intention to remit them. At 31 December 20X4, these non-distributable reserves amounted to £25 million (20X3: £32 million).

---

4. Items charged or credited direct to reserves

Items should be charged or credited direct to reserves (without going through the profit and loss account) only if:
– it is specifically required by an accounting standard; or
– it is required or permitted by law.

3791

Examples are items charged directly against share premium account (such as issue costs on shares) or **contributions from owners**.

C. Shareholders' funds

Reconciliation of movements in shareholders' funds

FRS 3 prescribes a reconciliation of the opening and closing totals of shareholders' funds to highlight those items that do not appear in the profit and loss account or the **statement of total recognised gains and losses** (STRGL). The reason is to ensure that attention is drawn to matters that are important for a proper appreciation of the company's affairs. These include dividends as a deduction from the year's net profit/loss as well as other movements in shareholders' funds such as goodwill written off and share capital issued or redeemed.

3795
FRS 3 (28), (59)

This reconciliation should, however, be shown separately from the STRGL.

EXAMPLE   The following is an example of a reconciliation of movements in the **STRGL:**

	20X3 £'000	20X2 £'000
Profit for the year	49	41
Dividends	-23	-19
	26	22
Other recognised gains and losses for the year (net)	15	-9
New share capital subscribed	12	0
Net increase in shareholders' funds	53	13
Shareholders' funds at beginning of year	243	230
Shareholders' funds at end of year	396	243

Where only a **small number of movements** on reserves has taken place during the year, it is permissible to combine the statement of movements in shareholders' funds with the statement of movements on reserves.

3796

EXAMPLE Combined Statement of Movements in Shareholders' Funds and Statement of Movements on Reserves

	Profit and loss account	Issued share capital	Share premium account	Revaluation reserve	20X3	20X2
	£	£	£	£	£	£
At beginning of year	200	500	120	450	1270	1195
Profit for the year	112	-	-	-	112	98
Dividends	-56	-	-	-	-56	-43
Surplus on revaluation of investment properties	-	-	-	42	42	-
Increase (decrease) in value of trade investment	-	-	-	-27	-27	20
Capital subscribed	-	20	2	-	22	-
Transfer of realised profits	25	-	-	-25	-	-
At end of year	281	520	122	440	1363	1270

Capital contributions

3798   If a parent makes funds available to a subsidiary in the form of a **non-returnable gift**, the transaction is deemed to be a contribution of capital. The subsidiary has no obligation to transfer economic benefits and the contribution should be taken directly to shareholders' funds. The item should be shown in the reconciliation of movements in shareholders' funds.

As to where, within shareholders' funds, a capital contribution should be shown, the following possibilities exist:
– unless otherwise provided by the Articles of Association, if the contribution was received in cash it can be considered realised and therefore taken to the profit and loss reserve;
– if the contribution was received in a form other than cash, until such other assets have been realised they should not be considered as part of distributable profits. In this case, showing the contribution under "other reserves" is more appropriate.

MEMO POINTS   As to the treatment of the capital contribution by the **parent company** (i.e. the donor), no formal reporting guidance has been given. It is most commonly capitalised as part of the cost of the investment in the subsidiary.

Share issue expenses

3800   When shares are issued, any expenses that can be treated as share issue costs must be taken into account in determining the net proceeds of the issue and shown in the reconciliation of movements in shareholders' funds and not the STRGL.

For **non-equity shares**, the total finance costs recognised in the profit and loss account over the term of the shares must include the share issue expenses.

D. Carrying amounts

3805   The carrying amount is the amount at which shares are stated in the balance sheet and is of particular importance where, for instance, the shares in question are redeemed. The amount at which the transaction is recorded is based on the carrying value of the shares at the time.

Amount recorded on issue

3807   When shares are **first issued**, the net proceeds are reported in the reconciliation of shareholders' funds. The Act requires the nominal value of shares to be shown as share capital and any premium (excess of proceeds over the nominal value) in the share premium account.

The Act prescribes further that the **share premium account** can be used to write off share issue expenses. However, if the amount in the share premium account is insufficient to absorb them, these costs should be taken to an "other" reserve. Although it is also permissible for these share-issue expenses to be taken to the profit and loss account reserve, this is a less desirable option because:

– share issue costs do not represent a realised loss, which means that charging profit and loss reserves could create a potentially misleading view of profits available for distribution; and

– for purposes of establishing legally distributable reserves, separate records will have to be kept of the unrealised loss included within the profit and loss account reserve.

Subsequent adjustments

In the case of **equity shares**, no adjustments are made to the value at which they are carried.   **3809**

The treatment of **non-equity shares** differs in that the carrying value is increased each year by the **finance costs** (¶3055) for the period and reduced by the amount of any dividend or other payment made during the year.

Conversion of debt or non-equity shares to equity share capital

When **debt** is converted to equity share capital, the amount at which to record the new   **3811** issue is the carrying value of the debt at the date of conversion. No gain or loss is recognised.

In cases where **non-equity shares** are converted to equity shares, the conversion can take the following forms:

– the non-equity shares can be cancelled and new equity shares issued in their place; or

– the non-equity shares are not cancelled but the rights attaching to them are altered so that they fall under the definition of equity shares.

Under both methods the net total reserves will remain the same; however, individual reserves may be affected.

EXAMPLE   To raise funds, **C Ltd** issues 1000 redeemable convertible preference shares as follows:

Nominal value	£1
Issue price	£1.40
Dividend rate	8.5%

The issue costs amounted to £270.

The shares can be redeemed at a premium of 30p on the nominal value after 5 years. Alternatively, holders may elect to convert their preference shares into £0.50 ordinary shares in the ratio of 1:1 at any time after the first 2 years.

Finance costs are to be apportioned at a rate of 10% on the carrying amount.

The net proceeds of the issue, £1130, will be recorded as follows:

Share capital	£1000
Share premium (premium of £400 less issue expenses of £270)	£130

Over 5 years, the carrying amount of the shares will accumulate to equal the amount of the redemption payment as follows:

Year	Beginning-of-year balance	Finance Charge	Payments	End-of-year balance (carrying value)
1	1130	113	85	1158
2	1158	115	85	1188
3	1188	119	85	1222
4	1222	122	85	1259
5	1259	126	85	1300
			*1300	0

* Final redemption payment

Annual finance costs in excess of dividends paid should be taken to a separate reserve (£113 – £85 in Year 1; £115 – £85 in Year 2, and so on).

If any of the preference shares are converted before their redemption date, the proceeds of the ordinary shares issued (or their issue price) is the carrying value of the preference shares at the time. This amount will have a nominal value element and a share premium element.

To illustrate, assume that all the shares are converted – into 1000 50p ordinary shares – at the end of year 3, when the carrying value is £1,222. The following journal entries will record the transaction:

	Dr.	Cr.
Preference share capital	1000	
Preference share premium	130	
Other reserves (reserve for premium on redemption)	92	
Ordinary share capital		500
Ordinary share premium		722

E. Finance costs of non-equity shares

3813   The cost of financing non-equity shares is the difference between the net proceeds received by the issuer and any payments it makes to the holders over the term of the shares. Specifically, the financing charge for the company includes all dividend payments and the premium payable on redemption. In addition, any issue costs on converting the non-equity shares to equity shares are included as finance costs.

3814   In general, the total finance costs of non-equity shares should be spread over the term of the shares. The term of the share will end on the earliest date that the provider of the finance (i.e. the shareholder) can demand repayment.

Where **options for early redemption** are available, the term should be taken to the first date at which the option can be exercised. The term should not include any period for which the share may be extended, unless it is known at the time the shares are issued that the term is certain to be extended.

F. Warrants and options

3816   Warrants and options are similar instruments generally requiring the issuer to issue shares but not to transfer economic benefits. Options are usually granted to specific individuals while warrants are generally transferable. Where a company **issues** warrants, the treatment under FRS 4 was that proceeds were credited directly to shareholders' funds. Provided that the purchase relates to equity shares, a similar treatment after 1 January 2005 (the date from which FRS 4 was superseded by FRS 25) should apply.

FRS 25 introduces the requirement that where an entity issues a compound financial instrument, it must account separately for the components that create a **financial liability** and those that grant an option to the holder to convert it into **equity**.

3817   When warrants are **exercised** the net proceeds must be transferred out of shareholders' funds to share capital (and share premium account, if appropriate).

3818   The disclosures required in respect of warrants and options include: the number, description, and amount of shares; the period during which the option is exercisable; and the price to be paid. Where the warrants are convertible into a class of shares not already issued, the rights attaching to them should also be disclosed.

PART 6

Other primary statements

CHAPTER 1

Cash flow statements

There is **no statutory requirement** under the Companies Act for companies to publish a cash flow statement. However, FRS 1 "Cash flow statements", requires that all reporting entities preparing financial statements intended to give a true and fair view include a cash flow statement, unless specifically exempted. The cash flow statement comprises a number of standard classifications, within which the cash inflows and outflows should be shown separately in accordance with the substance of the underlying transactions.

4000
FRS 1 (5)

Although **small companies** are exempt from the requirements of FRS 1 and a cash flow statement is not required by the FRSSE, **voluntary compliance** is encouraged. Medium sized and larger entities are expected to include a cash flow statement in their published financial reports. Where group accounts are prepared these should include a group cash flow statement.

> *MEMO POINTS*   The FRC has published **FRS 102** covering non-FRSSE entities, adoption of which is mandatory for accounting periods beginning on or after 1 January 2015. Earlier adoption is permitted.

4002
FRS 1 (2)

Cash flows are defined as increases or decreases in cash and comprise cash in hand and deposits, or an overdraft repayable on demand at a qualifying financial institution such as a bank, building society or other business that grants credits and receives deposits or other repayable funds.

The **purpose** of the cash flow statement is to:
– report the cash generation and absorption of/by an entity by highlighting the significant components of cash flow; and
– provide information enabling users to assess an entity's liquidity and solvency and hence the financial risk.

A cash flow statement is usually reviewed in conjunction with the profit and loss account and balance sheet and is supported by a number of **key reconciliations** and **disclosures**. Group cash flow statements and foreign currency cash flows require additional disclosures.

> *MEMO POINTS*   **Deposits "repayable on demand"** qualify if they can be withdrawn at any time without penalty, or if a maturity or period of notice of not more than 24 hours or one working day has been agreed. Cash also includes deposits denominated in foreign currencies.

4004

Exemptions   The **following entities are exempt** from the requirements of FRS 1 to produce a cash flow statement; namely:
– companies satisfying the small company criteria under the Companies Act 2006, except for the exemptions listed below;
– subsidiary undertakings where 90% of the voting rights are controlled within the group and consolidated accounts are publicly available; and
– mutual life assurance companies, pension funds and open-ended investment funds.

> *MEMO POINTS*   1. **"Publicly available"** means disclosure in a national registry or national gazette.
> 2. **Exemption is not available** where a small company is a small bank, insurance company, a person authorised under the Financial Services Act 1986 (2010), or a member of a group containing one or more of the above entities.

4010

Small groups may also be excluded from preparing cash flow statements if the parent company qualifies as a small company, and claims exemption from preparing consolidated financial statements. **Medium sized groups** are not entitled to claim exemption under the Companies Act from preparing consolidated financial statements and hence a cash flow statement, unless the parent is itself a small company, in which case it is entitled to exemption in its own right.

SECTION 1

Small companies

4020

Small companies **are exempt** from the requirements of FRS 1 and a cash flow statement is not required by the FRSSE, although **voluntary compliance** is encouraged. The **definition of cash** is simplified to that of "cash at bank and in hand, less overdrafts repayable on demand".

The main elements of the statement are as follows:

1. The **indirect method** (see ¶4134) should be used for calculating cash flows from operating activities, and involves making a number of adjustments to operating profit.

2. The **cash flows from operating activities** should be reconciled to the cash position in the balance sheet.

3. The key headings are:
– cash generated operating activities;
– reconciled to cash generated from operations;
– cash from other sources;
– application of cash;
– net increase in cash; and
– cash at bank and in hand less overdrafts at year end.

An example of the format for a small company cash flow statement is set out below. For consolidated (group) cash flow statements see ¶4180.

MEMO POINTS   1. FRS 1 **widens the definition** to include "deposits or overdrafts with qualifying institutions" and "deposits in foreign currencies".
2. **FRS 102** (see ¶4250) requires a statement of cash flows and has a different layout to that stipulated under FRS 1 as it actually mirrors the format adopted in IAS 7 "Cash flow statements". The main difference is that the FRS format includes, as well as cash, highly liquid cash equivalents such as short-term investments that are readily convertible into cash. The FRS permits use of either the direct or indirect method and the format is divided into three categories: operating, investing and financing.

4022

EXAMPLE **NOP Ltd – 31 December 20X3**
Cash flow statement – Indirect method

	20X3	
	£	£
Cash generated from operating activities (¶4034)		
Operating profit (loss)	25,500	
Reconciled to cash generated from operations:		
Depreciation		
Increase in stocks	(34,000)	
Decrease in trade debtors	72,000	
Decrease in trade creditors	(27,000)	–
Increase in other creditors	26,000	
		62,500
Cash from other sources		–
Interest received (see ¶4050)	1,000	
Issue of shares for cash	20,000	
New long-term borrowings (¶4082)	2,500	
Sale of tangible fixed assets (¶4060)	2,500	–
		26,000
Application of cash		–
Interest paid (see ¶4050)	(3,000)	
Tax paid (see¶4052)	(9,500)	
Dividends paid (see ¶4050)	(10,000)	–
Purchase of fixed assets	(8,500)	
		(31,000)
Net increase in cash		**57,500**
Cash at bank and in hand less overdrafts at beginning of the year		(23,250)
Cash at bank and in hand less overdrafts at end of year		**34,250**

SECTION 2

Medium and larger companies

The accounting standard stipulates how cash flow information should be presented under the following **standard headings** in the order shown below:
– operating activities;

4024

FRS 1 (c)

- dividends from associates and joint ventures;
- returns on investments and servicing of finance;
- taxation;
- capital expenditure and financial investment;
- acquisitions and disposals;
- equity dividends paid;
- management of liquid resources; and
- financing.

4026 The **cash flow classifications** may be further divided into inflows and outflows to provide a more detailed breakdown of the entities' operations. In addition to the standard headings, certain reconciliations, as discussed in section 3 below, must be provided along with other information in the notes to the cash flow statement. There is also a requirement to detail any **exceptional cash flows**.

All the headings should be in the sequence set out above **with the option** of the last two being combined under a single heading, provided that the cash flows pertaining to each are shown individually with sub-totals. The format is the same for both individual company and group cash flow statements. Including **a sub-total** after any of the other standard headings is neither required or prohibited, but is a useful device for highlighting the level of net cash flows under a particular category.

4028
FRS 1 (8)
In general, there is **a degree of flexibility** allowed in the reporting of cash flows. Companies may elect to report all significant gross cash flows on the face of the cash flow statement under the appropriate standard headings, or the information can be detailed in the notes to the cash flow statement, with only the main headings being shown on the face of the cash flow statement itself.

4030 The **standard classifications** are intended to improve the comparability of cash flow statements of different entities. Entities are encouraged to provide further information in the notes to the cash flow statement that better reflect the particular circumstances of their industry. Reporting the division of cash flows between **continued** and **discontinued operations** is also required.

The standard classifications adopted in the FRS **can be changed only** in exceptional circumstances and where failure to do so would mislead readers of the financial statements.

A. Content by classification

4034 The **general rule is** that each individual cash flow should be classified according to the substance of the underlying transaction that gives rise to it. Where the reason for adopting a particular classification is not readily apparent from the nature of the transaction, additional detail should be provided either in the form of notes or a reconciliation.

Operating activities

4036
FRS 1 (11)
Cash flows from operating activities are the cash effects of transactions and other events relating to operating or trading activities, as shown in the profit and loss account in arriving at operating profit. Operating cash flows can be presented by using either the **direct method** or the **indirect method**.

4040
FRS 1 (58)
Direct (gross) method   Under the direct method of preparing a cash flow statement, the operating cash receipts and payments are aggregated to show the net cash flow from operating activities. This method reports individual company cash flows, **based on an analysis** of the cash book and tabulates the actual cash received or remitted, to show the net cash flow from operating activities. This method is considered more costly and time consuming to

prepare. The **principal advantage** of the direct method is that it shows operating cash receipts and payments.

EXAMPLE Direct method
ABC Ltd
Notes to the cash flow statement

Operating activities	£'000
Cash received from customers	28,000
Cash payments to suppliers	(12,000)
Cash paid to employees	(4,000)
Other operating cash payments	(3,000)
Net cash inflow from operating activities	**9,000**

Indirect (net) method The cash flow statement prepared on the basis of the indirect method indicates the relationship between profitability and the cash generating ability of the business. The indirect method arrives at the same net cash flow from operating activities as the direct method, by working back from operating profit in the form of a reconciliation (as illustrated in ¶4134). The **operating profit is adjusted** for charges such as depreciation, amortisation, and profits and losses on the disposal of fixed assets. The reconciliation should also include adjustments for movements in stocks, debtors and creditors.

4042

Dividends from joint ventures and associates

Dividends for joint ventures and associates are shown separately because of the high degree of influence that an investing entity may exercise over joint ventures or associate companies. Also in the **consolidated financial statements**, the dividend received figure for individual companies is not readily apparent from the consolidated profit and loss account.

4044

Cash flows from a group's operating activities are different from the cash flows resulting from returns on its investments and, as such, should be separately identified. FRS 1 intends that although there should be a single heading, this should be analysed further into the two separate categories for associates and joint ventures.

Other cash flows from associates and joint ventures, such as those arising from trading or loan interest, should be included under the appropriate heading in the statement.

EXAMPLE **ABC Ltd**
Notes to the cash flow statement (extract)

	20X3 £m	20X2 £m
Dividends from joint ventures and associates	**10.5**	**6.8**
Dividends received from joint ventures	7.5	4.2
Dividends received from associates	3.0	2.6

Returns on other investments and servicing of finance

Returns on investments and servicing of finance **are receipts resulting from** the ownership of an investment, other than an associate or joint venture and payments to providers of finance, non-equity shareholders (e.g. preference shares) and minority interests. **Dividends paid** to equity shareholders are shown under a separate heading because they are discretionary by nature whereas other finance costs such as interest are contractual.

4046
FRS 1 (13)

Cash inflows include interest received, including any related tax recovered and dividends received.

4050

Cash outflows include:
– interest paid, even if capitalised;
– finance costs, including issue costs on debt and non-equity share capital;
– the interest element on finance lease rental payments;

FRS 1 (15)

– dividends paid on non-equity shares of the entity; and

– dividends paid by subsidiaries to minority interests.

The **capital element on finance lease rental payments** is included under the separate heading of financing.

It is worth noting that because of the method of calculating finance costs under FRS 4, the charge in the profit and loss account may not represent the cash flows actually arising in that year. The amount included within the cash flow statement may well be different from the charge in the profit and loss account.

EXAMPLE **ABC Ltd**
Notes to the cash flow statement (extract)
Returns on investments and servicing of finance

	20X3	20X2
	£m	£m
Interest received	11.0	8.8
Interest paid	(3.5)	(2.7)
Interest element of finance lease rental payments	(1.4)	(1.3)
Dividends received from other investments	5.0	2.0
Dividends paid to minority shareholders	(2.2)	(1.8)
Preference dividends paid	(1.1)	(0.8)
Total	**7.8**	**4.2**

Taxation

4052
FRS 1 (16)

The cash flows under this heading represent taxation on the profits of the entity. Payments in respect of other taxes paid by the entity, such as PAYE, should be shown as part of the cash flow to which the taxation relates.

Cash inflows include tax rebates and returns of overpayments. For **subsidiaries**, payments received from other group companies for group relief, should be included as cash inflows.

Cash outflows cover tax payments and for subsidiary undertakings, payments made to other group companies for group relief.

EXAMPLE **ABC Ltd**
Notes to the cash flow statement (extract)
Taxation

	20X3
	£m
UK Corporation tax paid	(69.0)
Non UK tax paid	(10.2)
Total	**(79.2)**

4058
FRS 1 (39)

Value added tax Cash flows should be shown net of any attributable VAT unless the tax is recovered by the reporting entity. The net movement on the amount payable to, or receivable from, the taxing authority should be allocated to cash flows from operating activities unless a different treatment is more appropriate.

Where **restrictions apply** to the recovery of VAT, the **irrecoverable amount** should be allocated to those expenditures affected by the restrictions. If this is not practicable, the irrecoverable tax should be included under the most appropriate standard heading.

Capital expenditure and financial investment

4060

The cash flows included under this heading relate to the acquisition or disposal of fixed assets (other than those to be disclosed under the heading "acquisitions and disposals"), and current asset investments not regarded as liquid resources.

Cash inflows include receipts from:

– the sales or disposals of property, plant and equipment;

– the repayment of the reporting entity's loans to other entities; and
– sales of debt instruments of other entities.

FRS 1 (20)

Cash outflows include:
– payments to acquire property, plant or equipment;
– loans made by the reporting entity; and
– acquisition of debt instruments.

Also included in this category are cash flows relating to development costs that have been capitalised.

EXAMPLE **ABC Ltd**
Notes to the cash flow statement (extract)
Net cash inflow (outflow) for capital expenditure and financial investment

	20X3 £'000	20X2 £'000
Purchase of intangible fixed assets	(4,208)	(1,710)
Purchase of tangible fixed assets	(4,756)	(2,150)
Sale of tangible fixed assets	440	375
Purchase of fixed asset investments	(93)	(80)
Disposal of fixed asset investments	175	135
Total cash inflow (outflow)	**(8,442)**	**(3,430)**

Assets acquired under finance leases are not shown separately but included in the total **4064** addition to fixed assets figure for the year. However, as the purchase of fixed assets does not involve a cash outlay at the start of the lease, the fair value of the leased asset included in fixed asset additions should be eliminated, in order to reflect the true cash outflow.

The finance lease rental payments should be analysed between interest and capital, and shown under "Returns on investments and servicing of finance" and "financing" respectively.

Acquisition and disposals

Cash inflows comprise receipts from sales of: **4068**
– investments in subsidiary undertakings, associates or joint ventures; and
– minority interests (non-controlling interests).

FRS 1 (22)

– the take up of shares resulting from a rights issue by a subsidiary; or
– a capital contribution from a parent to a subsidiary (non-returnable gift).

For the subsidiary, non-returnable gifts are included in the financing section of the cash flow statement. The parent should treat the gift in its cash flow statement under acquisitions and disposals.

Cash outflows cover payments to acquire:
– investments in subsidiary undertakings, associates and joint ventures; and
– minority interests (non-controlling interests).

EXAMPLE **ABC Ltd**
Notes to the cash flow statement (extract)
Acquisition and disposals

	20X3 £'000	20X2 £'000
Purchase of subsidiary undertakings	(14,450)	(3,605)
Investments in joint ventures	(3,750)	(1,800)
Investments in associates	(5,720)	(3,250)
Repayment of loan to joint venture	(750)	(250)
Disposal of subsidiary undertakings	4,250	1,116
Sale of investments in joint ventures	500	125
Net cash (outflow) for acquisitions and disposals	**(19,920)**	**(7,664)**

The presentation above can be included on the face of the cash flow statement or detailed as **4069** a note to the accounts. Cash flows for any subsidiary disposed of should be added to the cash flow statement for the period its results were included in the group profit and loss account.

Information should also be supplied by way of note, covering net assets acquired and net assets disposed of.

The following information for **disposals** should be given in the notes:
– cash received;
– a summary of the effect of the disposal on each category of asset and liability;
– where material, the effect on the cash flow position of the parent company resulting from the disposal of the subsidiary. Comparative figures for the previous year are not required.

Similar information covering the **impact of any acquisitions** on the group cash flow statement should also be disclosed.

Equity dividends paid

4074
FRS 1 (25)

This classification includes equity dividends paid by the reporting entity or, if part of a group, the parent's equity shares. Dividends paid by subsidiaries to shareholders outside the group (minority shareholders) must be shown under "Returns on investments and servicing of finance".

Management of liquid resources

4076
FRS 1 (26)

This section of the cash flow statement is designed to reflect the profile of a reporting entity's cash and liquidity management. Liquid resources are **current asset investments** (¶2700) held as disposable stores of value readily convertible into cash at, or close to, their carrying amount. An entity is required to detail the investments it has included as liquid resources and any change in accounting policy. **Charges in the market value** of current asset investments included under liquid resources do not have an immediate impact on cash flow but may affect the carrying value of the investment at the balance sheet date.

4077

Unlisted investments held as current assets are unlikely to qualify as liquid resources and are more appropriately included under capital expenditure and financial investment. **Fixed asset investments** (¶1750) do not qualify because they are held as a ready store of value for continuing use in the business and are not readily disposable.

4080

Cash inflows include withdrawals from short-term deposits not qualifying as cash and inflows from disposal or redemption of any other investments held as liquid resources.

Cash outflows cover payments into short-term deposits not qualifying as cash and outflows to acquire other investments held as liquid resources.

FRS 1 (26)

The cash inflows and outflows in this section may be "netted-off" against one another if the following apply:
– the cash flows relate in substance to a single transaction; or
– are due to short maturities and high turnover occurring from the rollover or reissue of short-term deposits. Simply **renewing overnight deposits** with the company's bankers would not be regarded as a separate inflow and outflow of cash.

Unlisted investments held as current assets are unlikely to qualify as liquid resources and are more appropriately included under capital expenditure and financial investments.

EXAMPLE **ABC Ltd**
Notes to the cash flow statement (extract)
Management of liquid resources

	20X3 £'000	20X2 £'000
Purchase of government securities (treasury bills)	(1,555)	(1,023)
Short term deposits over 3 months	(345)	(255)
Sale of government bonds	1,265	952
Withdrawals from short-term deposits	1,002	520
Sale of corporate bonds	50	
Net movement of short-term investments and deposits under 3 months not repayable on demand.	(450)	(390)
Net cash inflow (outflow) from management of liquid resources	**(33)**	**(196)**

Financing

Financing cash flows consist of receipts from or repayment to external providers of finance. Only the principal amounts of finance should be included in this category with any interest element or dividend dealt with under the appropriate category.

4082
FRS 1 (29)

Cash inflows covers receipts from issuing:
- shares or other equity instruments; and
- debentures, loans, notes, and bonds and from other long-term and short-term borrowings (excluding overdrafts).

Cash outflows:
- repayments of amounts borrowed (excluding overdrafts);
- the capital element of finance lease rental payments;
- payments to require or redeem the entity's shares; and
- payments of expenses or commissions on any issue of equity shares.

It should be noted that **because of the basis for recognising capital instruments** under FRS 4, for example showing a debenture in the balance sheet net of issue costs, recognition of amounts in the balance sheet and therefore the profit and loss account, may differ from the cash flows arising. Movements in the amount recorded in financial instruments and other liabilities in the balance sheet may not therefore correspond with the amounts shown in the cash flow statement. This is partly why certain reconciliations (see ¶4128), are required by FRS 1.

4083

EXAMPLE **ABC Ltd**
Cash flow statement (extract)
Financing

	20X3 £'000	20X2 £'000
Issue of ordinary share capital	175	110
Issue of shares to minorities	25	
Issue of debentures	2,000	1,200
New loans	7,500	5,430
Redemption of preference share capital	(350)	(125)
Repayment of secured loans	(2,175)	(1,175)
Net increase (decrease) in short-term borrowings	(2,200)	(1,356)
Repayment of unsecured loans	(125)	(68)
Initial element of finance lease rentals	(1,342)	
Net cash inflow (outflow) from financing	**3,508**	**4,016**

B. Exceptional cash flows

A cash flow may be deemed exceptional due to its value, size or incidence, or it relates to an item treated as exceptional in the profit and loss account. Cash flows deemed exceptional should be shown separately under the relevant standard heading or by way of a note to the accounts. In addition, sufficient information should be provided to allow the users to understand the underlying transactions generating the cash flows.

4085
FRS 1 (37)

Examples of exceptional cash flows include:
a. Cash inflows arising on the sale of fixed assets;
b. Restructuring or reorganisation costs; resulting from:
- the costs of training;
- new systems development;
- the downsizing of operations;
- elimination of product lines; or
- the mothballing or relocation of production facilities.

4086

4088   Exceptional profits or losses from a **sale of operations** should be included under "acquisitions and disposals", whilst proceeds from a **sale of fixed assets** should be categorised under "capital expenditure and financial investment". Where cash flows are exceptional, because of the size or incidence, but are not related to items in the profit and loss account, sufficient disclosure should be given in the notes to explain the cause and the nature of the cash flow.

SECTION 3

Foreign currency cash flows

4090   The accounting treatment of foreign currency activities in cash flow statements is relatively complex and FRS 1 gives minimal guidance on the treatment required. Foreign currency transactions for **individual companies** are dealt with in this section and can be divided into a number of categories. **Group foreign currency cash flows** are covered in ¶4218 whilst for a more detailed review of the accounting treatment for foreign currency transactions, see ¶8000.

Companies may enter directly into business transactions denominated in foreign currencies or conduct foreign currency operations through overseas subsidiaries, associates or branches. A distinction should be drawn between **settled** and **unsettled foreign currency transactions** at the balance sheet date. **Special rules** exist for non-operational transactions and hedging transactions.

> MEMO POINTS   The financial reporting standard for **non-FRSSE, non-listed entities** (FRS 102), does not contain a great deal of guidance on foreign currency cash flows, requiring only that they should be translated at the rate prevailing on the transaction date. This requirement covers both individual company and consolidated cash flows.

4092   FRS 23 "The Effects of Changes in Foreign Exchange Rates" **only applies to entities** that prepare their financial statements in accordance with FRS 26 "Financial Instruments: Measurement", to which a number of further conditions apply, as set out below and in greater detail in ¶3400. Where **FRS 26 and** hence **FRS 23 are not applied**, existing UK GAAP in the form of SSAP 20 still applies.

> MEMO POINTS   1. **FRS 23 and FRS 26** form part of a package of standards including FRS 24 "Financial Reporting in Hyperinflationary Economies", and FRS 25 "Financial Instruments: Disclosure and Presentation". FRS 23 is covered in greater detail in ¶8382.
> 2. FRS 26 applies to all listed entities. **Other entities** are free to adopt the standard with the proviso that all standards in the package (FRS 23-26) are adopted. **Unlisted entities** that have adopted fair value accounting policies must also apply the new standards.
> 3. **Most of FRS 4**, with the exception of material relating to the measurement of debt and gains and losses on the repurchase of debt, is withdrawn when an entity opts to adopt FRS 25. The remainder of FRS 4 is withdrawn on implementation of FRS 26.

Settled currency transactions

4094   For **direct transactions** in foreign currencies the entity must assess the basic components of each transaction in order to determine the relevant cash flows.

Examples of operational transactions include:
– purchase or sale of trading items, such as stock, in a foreign currency;
– settlement by a foreign currency trade debtor; or
– settlement of a foreign currency trade creditor.

The results of the foreign currency transaction are translated into the reporting currency of the company, at the rate ruling at the transaction date. **Exchange differences** arise because of differences in the exchange rate at the transaction date and settlement date.

4096   The **profit or loss arising on exchange differences**, resulting from operational foreign currency transactions, will be reflected in the profit and loss account and included in the cash flow statement as part of "Net cash flow from operating activities". No specific adjustments are required.

EXAMPLE Settled transactions
Notes to the cash flow statement
Repayment of foreign currency trade creditor

A UK-based company had only two transactions in the first financial year to July 20X3. It raised £350,000 through a share issue. The company then purchased goods for resale from Germany in August 20X2 for €300, 000 at an exchange rate of £1 = €1.20. The purchase was entered in the accounts as €300, 000/1.2 = £250,000. Under the terms of the contract, the company paid the outstanding creditor in June 20X3 when the exchange rate has moved to £1 = €1.15. The amount paid in settlement was: €300, 000/1.15 = £260,870. An exchange rate loss of £10,870 should be recorded when calculating operating profit for the year.
A simplified cash flow statement would be as follows assuming no other transactions in the year.

Cash flow statement: June 20X3

	£
Net cash flow from operating activities (payment for stock)	(260,870)
Financing	350,000
Increase in cash	89,130

Note to the accounts
Reconciliation of operating profit to net cash flow from operating activities

	£
Net operating profit/ (loss)	(10,870)
Increase in stocks	(250,000)
Net cash flow from operating activities	(260,870)

The cash flow statement will reflect the amount of sterling that has flowed in or out of the business as a result of the transaction, irrespective of how that has ultimately been recorded in the profit and loss account and balance sheet.

Unsettled currency transactions (operational)

Foreign currency transactions that remain **outstanding at the balance sheet date** can give rise to exchange differences, where the asset was recorded at the actual exchange rate prevailing at the time of the transaction and then re-translated at the rate prevailing at the balance sheet date.   **4100**

Any differences arising from the translation of **short-term working capital items** denominated in foreign currencies, such as cash and bank balances, debtors, creditors and loans, will generally be included in the profit and loss account. Therefore, **no adjustment is necessary when** preparing the cash flow statement. This is due to the fact that increases or decreases in the debtor or creditor balances will include exchange differences on their re-translation at the balance sheet date, and the total movement in debtors and creditors constitutes an adjusting item in the reconciliation of operating profit to operating cash flows.

Any **exchange differences on long-term monetary items** reported as part of profit and loss account and included in operating profit, should be eliminated in arriving at net cash flow from operating activities. This is because the actual movement on long-term monetary items, which includes the exchange difference, is not reported in the reconciliation of operating profit to operating cash flow. Any exchange difference should be reported instead in the reconciliation of net cash flow to net debt (funds) (¶4144).   **4104**

Non-operational transactions

Transactions that fall outside the scope of operations require the profit or loss arising to be matched and included as part of the cash flow arising from the related transaction. Examples include the following: **4112**
- **dividends** received from a foreign investment; and
- repayment of **foreign currency debt** (i.e. loan).

The dividend received plus any conversion profit or loss should be included under "Returns on investments and servicing of finance" or "Dividends from associates and joint ventures".

Where foreign debt is repaid the capital repayment should be included under "Financing". **Any profit or loss on conversion** should not be shown separately but included in the reconciliation of "Net cash flow from operating activities".

Hedging transactions

4116
FRS 1 (66)
Companies enter into hedging transactions as a protection from financial loss that can result from variations in price or exchange rates. This topic is introduced in this chapter in the context of cash flow statements, with greater detail given in ¶8300.

4117
The **general rule** is that where a **futures, forward, option or swap contract** is accounted for as a hedge, the cash flows of the contract should be reported under the same standard heading as the transaction that gives rise to the hedge. This treatment ensures that the cash flows resulting from the hedging instruments are paired with the cash flows arising from the items being hedged.

For example, the reporting entity may purchase a futures contract to reduce its exposure to increases in the price of planned stock purchases. Any cash flows generated by the futures contract should be reported in operating cash flows.

Another example is that an entity wishing to convert an existing fixed rate borrowing into a floating rate equivalent might enter into an interest rate swap, by which it receives fixed rates but pays floating rates. All the cash flows under this transaction should be reported under "Returns on investment and servicing of finance", because they are equivalent to interest or are hedges of interest payments.

SECTION 4

Reconciliations to other primary statements

4124
In addition to the main cash flow statement, a number of reconciliations **are required** to link the cash flow statement to the balance sheet and profit and loss account. Additional disclosures are required in the notes to the cash flow statement.

A. Compulsory reconciliations

4128
The information provided in the cash flow statement should be viewed in the context of information given in the other primary financial statements and not in isolation. In order to reconcile the cash flow statement to key components in the balance sheet and the profit and loss account, **two important reconciliations** are required, namely that between:
– the operating profit and net cash flow from operating activities; and
– the movement in cash in the period to the movement in net debt.

4130
FRS 1 (12)
The reconciliation of movement in cash to movement in net debt (¶4144) should also include an analysis of both the **changes in net debt** and **total closing net debt**. Both reconciliations should be clearly labelled to highlight the fact that they are not part of the main cash flow statement. The reason for this is that some of the reconciling amounts may not be actual cash flows, so to include them in the cash flow statement would be inappropriate.

1. Operating profit to net cash flow from operating activities

4134
A **reconciliation between** the operating profit reported in the profit and loss account and the net cash flow from operating activities, forms part of the **indirect method**. The analysis should disclose separately the movements in stocks, debtors and creditors related to operat-

ing activities and other differences between cash flows and profits. This reconciliation should either adjoin the cash flow statement or be shown by way of note. However, some companies choose to include the reconciliation at the top of the cash flow statement.

The reconciliation adjusts operating profit for **non-cash charges** (e.g. depreciation) and **credits** in the profit and loss account, in order to reconcile it with the net cash flow from operating activities. It also recognises that some transactions in the profit and loss account which will ultimately result in "cash flows", for example purchases of goods and services, may not yet have generated cash flows, so that at any given point in time there are debtors and creditors. The **cash flow information** is obtained by analysing the movement in the figures in the balance sheet that correspond to the standard headings in the cash flow statement.

Increases in work in progress, stocks, and debtor balances represent cash outflows, as does a decrease in creditor balances. Conversely, a decrease in WIP, stocks or debtors represents cash inflows, as does an increase in creditor balances. **Depreciation charges** do not represent cash flows and as such are added back to operating profits in the reconciliation, as illustrated below.

4138

EXAMPLE **XYZ Ltd**
Reconciliation of operating profit to net cash flow from operating activities
Indirect method

	20X3 £'000	20X2 £'000
Operating profit	759.5	625.0
Depreciation and amortisation	191.3	152.0
Increase in work in progress	(25.3)	(20.0)
Increase in stocks	(272.3)	(299.0)
(Increase)/ decrease in debtors	(119.6)	(99.0)
Increase/ (decrease) in creditors	326.0	250.0
Payments against provisions	(22.0)	(11.0)
Net cash inflow from operating activities	**837.6**	**598.0**

Discontinued operations

Where an entity has reported discontinued operations in the profit and loss account, it is recommended that a note is provided, showing the division of cash flows into continued and discontinued operations. The reconciliation is generally positioned directly under the cash flow statement or by way of note. The **two principal methods** of presentation are illustrated in the example below.

4140
FRS 1 (56)

EXAMPLE **Notes to the cash flow statement**

Method 1

OPERATING ACTIVITIES	£'000
Net cash inflow from operating activities	16,662
Net cash outflow in respect of discontinued operations	(990)
Net cash inflow from operating activities	15,672

Method 2

	Continuing operations £'000	Discontinued operations £'000	Total £'000
Operating profit/ (loss)	18,829	(1,616)	17,213
Depreciation charges	3,108	380	3,488
Restructuring provisions	-	(560)	(560)
Increase in stocks	(11,193)	(87)	(11,280)
Increase in debtors	(3,754)	(20)	(3,774)
Increase in creditors	9,672	913	10,585
Net cash inflow – continuing operations	16,662	–	–
Net cash outflow – discontinued operations	–	(990)	
Net cash flow from operating activities			15,672

2. Reconciliation to net debt (funds)

4144
FRS 4 (6)
FRS 1 (33)

A note reconciling the movement of cash in the period to the movement in debt should be given either adjoining the cash flow statement or in a note to the financial statements. The FRS emphasises that the reconciliation is not part of the cash flow statement and as such should be clearly labelled. The purpose of the analysis is to provide information about the **impact of changes in debt** on the liquidity of an entity.

Where cash and liquid resources exceed the borrowings of the entity, reference should be made to "net funds" rather than "net debt".

MEMO POINTS   **Net debt** is defined as the borrowings of the entity, including debt as defined in FRS 4, together with derivatives and obligations under finance leases less cash and liquid resources. Total net debt is the cumulative total of net debt for the financial period with net debt brought forward at the beginning of the financial year.

4146

The **changes in net debt** arising from both cash flows and non-cash items, should be separately analysed and then reconciled with the opening and the closing net debt balances per the balance sheet. The reconciliation **starts with the closing cash position** for the period as shown at the foot of the cash flow statement. This figure will include cash flows relating to the management of liquid resources and borrowings included in financing, which should be added back to give the total change in net debt resulting from the cash flows in the period. Non-cash movements include assets acquired under finance leases and exchange rate differences.

EXAMPLE   **XYZ Ltd**
Notes to the cash flow statement
Reconciliation of net cash flow to movement in net debt

	20X3	
	£'000	£'000
Decrease in cash in the period	(6,752)	
Increase in debt	(2,347)	
Decrease in liquid resources	(700)	
Change in net debt resulting from cash flows		(9,799)
Loans and finance leases acquired with subsidiary		(3,817)
New finance leases		(2,845)
Exchange movements		643
Increase in net debt in the period		(15,818)
Net debt at 1.1.20X3		(15,215)
Net debt at 31.12.20X3		(31,033)

Analysis of total change in net debt

4150

This analysis should contain the following information, where material:
– the general cash flows of the entity relating to net debt;
– debt movements arising as a result of the acquisition or disposal of subsidiary undertakings;
– other non-cash changes; and
– the recognition of changes in market value and exchange rate movements.

The cash flows **relating to the acquisition or disposal** of subsidiaries include borrowings acquired or transferred, as part of the sales or acquisitions, which are not included in the financing section of the standard, but impact on the closing net debt balances. **Other non-cash** charges include the acquisition of fixed assets under finance leases.

4152

Where **several balance sheet amounts** or proportions thereof **have been combined** to form the components of opening and closing net debt, sufficient detail should be shown to enable the cash and other components, to be traced back to the amounts shown under the relevant captions in the balance sheet. For example, bank loans or overdrafts included as a single figure within current liabilities should be identified separately, because overdrafts should be included within the cash component of net debt.

Examples of **two different methods** of presenting an analysis of changes in net debt (funds) are given below.

EXAMPLE **XYZ Ltd**
Notes to the cash flow statement
Analysis of changes in net debt

Method 1

	At 1 Jan. 20X3 £'000	Cash flows £'000	Other changes £'000	At 31 Dec. 20X3 £'000
Cash at bank	42	847		889
Overdraft	(1,784)	1,784		
		2,631		
Debt due within 1 year	(149)	149	(230)	(230)
Debt due after one year	(1,262)		230	(1,032)
Current asset investment	250	450		700
Total	(2,903)	3,230	-	327

Method 2

XYZ Ltd.
Notes to the cash flow statement
Detailed analysis of changes in net debt

	At 1 Jan. 20X3 £'000	Cash flows £'000	Acquisition ex.cash/ overdraft £'000	Other non-cash charges £'000	Foreign exchange movements £'000	At 31 Dec. 20X3 £'000
Cash at bank and in hand	235	(1,250)	–	–	1,392	377
Overdrafts	(2,528)	(5,502)	–	–	(1,422)	(9,452)
		(6,752)				
Debt due after 1 year	(9,640)	(2,533)	(1,749)	2,560	(792)	(12,154)
Debt due within 1 year	(352)	(1,156)	(837)	(2,560)	1,465	(3,440)
Finance leases	(4,170)	1,342	(1,231)	(2,845)	–	(6,904)
Current asset investments	1,240	(700)	–	–	–	540
Total	(15,215)	(9,799)	(3,817)	(2,845)	643	(31,033)

B. Supplementary notes

There are a number of supplementary notes required including non-cash transactions, a commentary and comparative figures, examples of which are set out below.

4160

Non-cash transactions

Material transactions **not resulting in movements of cash** should be disclosed in the notes to the cash flow statement, if the disclosure is necessary for an understanding of the underlying transactions, such as:

– finance lease arrangements;
– exchange of assets for non cash consideration; and
– shares issued for the acquisition of a subsidiary.

4162
FRS 1 (67)

4164   **A finance lease** is one of the more common non-cash transactions. The transaction is reflected in the balance sheet but not reflected in the cash flow statement, because the reporting entity neither remits or receives cash.

The **conversion of debt to equity** is the equivalent of repaying debt in cash and receiving cash for new shares, although as the transaction represents only notional cash flows it does not appear in the cash flow statement. However, this information should be disclosed by way of note. Similarly, a note detailing the value of shares issued in exchange for a controlling interest in a subsidiary should be given.

Restrictions on remitting funds

4165
FRS 1 (47)   A consolidated cash flow statement should identify and explain the circumstances and effect of the **restrictions preventing** a transfer of cash from one part of the group to meet the obligations of another. The requirement also applies to overseas branches and subsidiaries.

The note to the accounts should only include details of circumstances, where access is severely restricted by external factors beyond the control of the group, such as cash balances:
- in escrow;
- retained within employee share ownership trusts; or
- deposited with an industry regulator.

Commentary

4166   Additional information should be given in the Directors' report and cover "funds from operating activities", other sources of "cash" and current liquidity, as illustrated in the example below.

The commentary in the Directors' report should highlight the level of borrowings and whether they are seasonal, as well as the maturity profile of commitments. Although useful to the reader there is no formal requirement to disclose the following:
- borrowing facilities not utilised;
- restrictions on possible transfer of funds from one part of the group to another;
- any breaches of borrowing covenants; and
- assets and liabilities denominated in foreign currencies.

> EXAMPLE **Ameira Property Development Ltd**
> **Directors' Report** (Financial review- extract)
>
> **Cash flow and borrowings**
>
> **Net Group borrowings** at 30 June 20X3 were £20.6m (20X2 12.6m net funds), representing a negative movement of funds of £33.2m. The cash outflow was due to a reduction in turnover, reorganisation costs and the funding of losses. Assets employed by Ameira Property Developments increased by £26m but profits of £38m resulted in a positive cash flow for the property division. The cash outflows were in associated activities.
>
> In 20X2 the Group took steps to align the **maturity profile of debt facilities** to the profile of the assets employed. A private placement of US $56m of loan notes in the USA, on terms averaging seven to ten years, provided longer-term finance to match the infrastructure investment portfolio as well as a currency hedge against US housing assets. The Group also arranged medium-term debt facilities of £45m in order to fund seasonal working capital requirements and acquisition of investments.
>
> In February 20X3, the Group purchased Northwood Investments Limited. The **purchase consideration** was £60.0m, but the assets included £23m of cash, resulting in an expansion to the asset infrastructure portfolio of £40.6m. Of this £16m was deferred consideration pending third party consent to the change of ownership of certain assets.

4170   Disclosure of **segmental cash flows** that are materially out of line with segmental profits, for example as a result of capital expenditure, should also be highlighted. FRS 1 encourages the provision of segmental cash flow information, in order to expand on the segmental disclosures required by SSAP 25, but does not specify the how this should be achieved.

EXAMPLE Pub Retailing Group Ltd
Notes to the financial statements

12. Operating cash flow	20X3	20X2
	£m	£m
Hotels	134	120
Leisure retailing	89	49
Games division	23	16
Branded drinks	100	75
Miscellaneous	9	5
Totals	355	265

Comparative figures

Comparative figures **should be given for** all items reported in the cash flow statement and supporting notes, except:
– a note to the statement that analyses changes in balance sheet amounts comprising net debt; and
– the note of the material effects of acquisitions and disposal of subsidiary undertakings on each of the standard headings.

4172
FRS 1 (48)

Treatment of non-trading gains and losses

Gains or losses **that do not give rise to cash flows** should be excluded from the cash flow statement and reported in the profit or loss account or STRGL as appropriate. If gains or losses are included in arriving at operating profit, they should be adjusted (gains deducted, losses added) in the reconciliation between operating profits and net cash flow from operating activities (¶4134).

For example, a gain on the sale of plant of £10,000 included in operating profit should be excluded from cash flow from operating activities, if it forms part of the proceeds of the sale that was disclosed under the capital expenditure section of the cash flow statement.

4174

Refinancing of borrowings

Companies may decide to **renegotiate the terms** of existing borrowings. If the borrowings are renegotiated with the same lender there may not be any immediate cash flow issues. However, if a new lender is involved then there will be cash inflows and outflows that will be reflected in the increase or decrease in cash for the period.

4176

Reconciliation of net cash inflow from operating activities to free cash flow

In addition to the reconciliation provided in ¶4134 above, a reconciliation of net cash inflow from operating activities to free cash flow, as illustrated in the example below, can also be given. Free cash flow is the amount of cash that a company has left over after it has paid all of its expenses, including investments. This cash can be used for expansion, dividends, reducing debt, or other purposes.

4178

EXAMPLE ABC Ltd
Notes to the cash flow statement

Reconciliation of net cash inflow from operating activities to free cash flow

	20X3	20X2
	£'000	£'000
Net cash inflow from operating activities	423	372
Capital expenditure net of sale of tangible fixed assets	(73)	28
Dividends received from associated undertakings	9	8
Operating cash net of fixed assets	359	408
Taxation paid	(34)	21
Net interest paid	(72)	(77)
Dividends paid	(167)	–
Free cash flow	86	352

> MEMO POINTS   **Free cash flow** is defined as cash available for distribution among all the securities holders in an company (e.g. equity/debt holders, preferred stock holders etc), after having maintained or expanded its asset base.

SECTION 5

Group cash flow statements

4180   The preparation of a consolidated cash flow statement will be similar in many cases to that of single companies. However, there are some **general rules** governing this process and a requirement for a number of additional disclosures.

The group cash flow statement should be built up from the statements prepared by the individual subsidiaries, with intra-group cash flows being eliminated as part of the consolidation process. The group cash flow statement should present only cash flows between the group and the outside world.

4182   Particular care should be taken where **a subsidiary** undertaking **joins or leaves a group** during a financial year, in that the group cash flow statement should only include the cash flows of the subsidiary undertaking for the same period as that for which the subsidiary's results are included in the group's consolidated profit and loss account.

Intra group cash flows

4184   **Examples** of internal cash flows are payments and receipts of:
 – management charges;
 – dividends;
 – interest; or
 – intra-group sales.

FRS 1 (41)   Where intra-group cash flows are **denominated in a currency** other than the parent company's reporting currency, and they are separately identifiable, and the actual rate of exchange at which they took place is known, then that rate may be used to translate the cash flows in order to ensure that they cancel out on consolidation. If the rate used to translate intra-group cash flows is not the actual rate, any exchange rate differences arising should be included in exchange rate movements, as part of the reconciliation to net debt.

Minority interests (Non-controlling interests)

4186   The **group represents a sole entity** for financial reporting purposes. Cash flows relating to minority interests should be shown under the heading "Returns on investments and servicing of finance". Where minority interests in a subsidiary are consolidated as part of a group, the treatment in the consolidated cash flow statement should be consistent with the overall approach adopted in preparing the group's financial statements.

4188   Minority interests should be shown as a liability, where **a parent or fellow subsidiary undertaking** has guaranteed their dividends or redemption of shares or undertaken to purchase the minority shares, if the subsidiary fails to make expected dividend payments. In such cases the dividends should be shown as interest paid and not as dividends to minorities, but still included under the classification "Returns on investment and servicing of finance".

> EXAMPLE   **Example**
> **ABC Ltd**
> **Notes to the cash flow statement**
>
> A parent company that has a number of subsidiaries that are not wholly owned who have minority interests should present the cash flow information as follows.

Returns on investments and servicing of finance (£m)		
	20X3	**20X2**
Dividends paid by subsidiaries to minorities	(27.9)	(20.0)

Subsidiaries

Parent companies require detailed information from their subsidiaries in order that the parent company can present the correct analysis of group cash flows and to ensure that gross cash flows are not **"netted-off"**, but recorded under the correct heading. An example would be information on debtors and creditors which are vital to ensure that movements included in the "Reconciliation of operating profit to cash inflow from operating activities" relate only to operating debtors and creditors.

4200

Where a **parent company acquires or disposes** of a subsidiary undertaking, then the related cash flows are reported under acquisitions and disposal in the cash flow statement.

In addition, the **notes to the cash flow statements** should include:
– details of cash paid or received from the purchase or sale of subsidiary companies;
– an indication of how much of the consideration comprised cash; and
– a breakdown of the subsidiaries' assets and liabilities, including purchased goodwill, underlying the purchase consideration.

4204

FRS 1 (45)

Any **shares issued** as part of the consideration in exchange for the net assets acquired do not generate cash flows, and are therefore disclosed by way of a note to the cash flow statement.

The **material effects** of any reported amounts under each of the standard headings within the cash flow statement, reflecting the cash flows of the subsidiary company purchased or sold, should also be shown (as far as is practical), where the post-acquisition cash flows of the subsidiary acquired can be clearly identified and segregated.

4206

Care should be taken to **eliminate all cash flows** between the group and the subsidiary acquired or disposed of, for the period the subsidiary's results (and cash flows) are included in the consolidated figures. Any cash or overdraft balances transferred should be shown separately, as illustrated in the following example.

EXAMPLE **XYZ Ltd**
Notes to the cash flow statement
Purchase of subsidiary undertakings

	£'000
Net assets acquired:	
Tangible fixed assets	12,195
Stocks	9,384
Debtors	13,856
Investments	1,309
Cash at bank	1,439
Creditors	(21,715)
Bank overdraft	(6,955)
Loans and finance leases	(3,817)
Deferred taxation	(165)
Minority interest	(9)
Goodwill	16,702
	22,224
Shares allotted	9,519
Cash	12,705
Total	**22,224**

The subsidiary undertaking acquired during the year contributed £1,502,000 to the group's net operating cash flows, paid £1,308,000 in respect of interest, £522,000 in respect of taxation and utilised £2,208,000 for capital expenditure.

Notes to the cash statement
Purchase and sale of investments (including cash balances transferred on acquisition)

	£'000	£'000
Purchase of subsidiary	(22,224)	
Net cash acquired with subsidiary	1,439	
		(20,785)
Sale of business		120.0
Purchase of an interest in a joint venture		(75.0)
Total		**(20,830)**

Associates and other equity investments

4210
FRS 1 (44)

Where a group has investments such as associates or **unconsolidated subsidiaries** that are accounted for under the equity method, the consolidated cash flow statement should include only the cash flows between these entities and not the cash flows of those entities. Any dividends, loans and interest on loans should be shown under "Dividends from associates and joint ventures" or "Returns on investments and servicing of finance" as appropriate. Cash flows from sales or purchases between group and associated undertakings or joint ventures should, however, be included in arriving at net cash flow from operating activities.

Joint arrangements that are not entities

4212
FRS 1 (41)

The **group's share of cash flows** from joint arrangements that are not an entity (JANE) should be included in the cash flow statement and notes on a line-by-line basis. The relevant proportion of each of the "JANE's" cash flows should be aggregated with the corresponding cash flows of the group. In addition the opening and closing net debt balances will include the relevant percentage of the JANE's balances. As there is therefore effective consolidation, based on a proportion of the JANE's cash flows, adjustments are required to eliminate cash transactions between the investor and the JANE.

Foreign currency

4218

Where business is transacted through a foreign entity, such as a subsidiary, associate or branch, then the cash flows of that entity should be converted into sterling for inclusion in the group cash flow statement. The cash flows of the foreign entity are considered as a whole rather than a series of single transactions.

There are **two methods** of preparing a consolidated group cash flow statement including overseas subsidiaries; namely:
– the net investment method (closing rate); or
– the temporal method (actual rate).

Entities **are free to choose** either of the two methods although they must be consistent in the approach adopted. A brief outline of both methods is given below; for a more detailed treatment refer to the chapter on foreign currency (¶8000).

4224
SSAP 20 (54)
FRS 1 (41)

Net investment method   This method involves the following:

Stage 1. The **foreign entity** prepares a cash flow in its own currency.

Stage 2. The cash flow is then converted into sterling at either the **closing or average rate of exchange**. The exchange method chosen must be the same as that used for converting the profit and loss account. All the cash flows of the foreign subsidiary must be included in the consolidated cash flow statement at the same rate.

Stage 3. The **sterling cash flow** is then consolidated with the group cash flow statement, after eliminating any intra-group items such as dividends payments, loans, and asset sales.

Such items plus any exchange differences should be reported in the reconciliation to net debt.

This method uses the exchange rate prevailing at the balance sheet date and any exchange gain or loss on translation is taken directly to reserves. An average rate may be used if rates do not fluctuate significantly.

Temporal method The temporal method is used when the operations of the foreign entity are more dependent on the economic environment of the investing company. Under this method all non-monetary items and profit and loss account items of the foreign entity are translated at the rate of exchange prevailing at the transaction date or an average rate if the exchange movements are not material. The financial statements of the foreign enterprise should be included in the **consolidated financial statements** as if all the transactions had been entered into by the investing company itself in its own currency. With the temporal method, the **average rate** is only used when the relevant exchange rate is relatively stable and results in only minor exchange rate differences.

4228
SSAP 20 (21)

The procedure is as follows:

1. Translate the individual entity's results and balances into sterling, using the actual or an average rate.

2. Consolidate with the results of the parent company.

3. Prepare a group cash flow statement from the consolidated financial statements.

Practical example of a group cash flow statement for a small company

The example given below illustrates a group cash flow statement prepared under the indirect method, complete with reconciliations of net cash flow to movement in net debt and analysis of net debt.

4240

EXAMPLE **Cash flow statement as at 30 June 20X3**

Indirect method

	Year to 30 June 20X3 £'000	Year to 30 June 20X2 £'000
Net cash inflow from operating activities (see 1)	423	372
Dividends received from associated undertakings	9	8
Returns on investments and servicing of finance (see 2)	(76)	(81)
Taxation (see 3)	(34)	21
Capital expenditure and financial investment (see 4)	(118)	(11)
Acquisitions and disposals (see 5)	(635)	(217)
Equity dividend paid	(163)	–
Management of liquid resource	(6)	52
Financing (see 6)	488	(68)
Decrease in cash in the period	**(112)**	**76**

Reconciliation of net cash flow to movement in net debt

(Decrease)/ increase in cash this year	(112)	76
Increase/ (decrease) in liquid resources	6	(52)
(Increase)/ decrease in loan capital	(488)	68
Movement in net debt resulting from cash flows	**(594)**	**92**
Exchange adjustments	(8)	(29)
Movement in net debt during the year	**(602)**	**63**
Opening net debt	(1,252)	(1,315)
Closing net debt	**(1,854)**	**(1,252)**

Analysis of changes in net debt

	Cash at Bank	Borrowings within 1 year	Loan capital within 1 year	Loan capital within 1 year	Net debt
	£'000	£'000	£'000	£'000	£'000
At 1 July 20X2	112	(558)	–	(806)	(1,252)
(Decrease)/ increase in cash	(5)	(107)	–	–	(112)
Increase/ (decrease) in cash	6	–	–	–	6
(Increase)/ decrease in loan capital	–	–	(110)	(378)	(488)
Exchange adjustments	(2)	5	–	(11)	(8)
Balance as at 30 June 20X3	**111**	**(660)**	**(110)**	**(1,195)**	**(1,854)**

Notes to the cash flow statement

1. Reconciliation of operating profit to net cash inflow from operating activities:

	20X3	20X2
	£'000	£'000
Operating profit	547	420
Depreciation	56	51
Goodwill amortisation	12	3
Increase in stocks	(72)	(43)
Increase in trade debtors	(55)	(97)
(Decrease)/Increase in creditors	(43)	39
Expenditure against provisions for reorganisation and restructuring costs	(34)	(54)
Other costs	12	53
Net cash inflow from operating activities	**423**	**372**

2. Returns on investments and servicing of finance

	20X3	20X2
Interest received	6	4
Interest paid	(78)	(81)
Dividends paid to minority shareholders	(4)	(4)
	(76)	**(81)**

3. Taxation

	20X3	20X2
UK Taxation	15	77
Overseas taxation	(49)	(56)
	(34)	21

4. Capital expenditure and financial investment

Purchase of tangible fixed assets	(97)	(87)
Sale of tangible fixed assets	24	115
Purchase of intangible fixed assets	(19)	–
Purchase of ordinary share capital for employee trusts	(26)	(39)
	(118)	**(11)**

5. Acquisitions and disposals

Purchase of subsidiary undertakings	(442)	(103)
Borrowings acquired with subsidiary undertakings	(193)	–
Disposal of subsidiary	4	(162)
Cash and overdrafts disposed of with subsidiary undertakings	(4)	48
	635	**217**

6. Financing

Redemption of debt	(637)	–
Increase in long-term debt	944	–
Increase/ (Decrease) in other debt	181	(68)
	488	**(68)**

SECTION 6

New UK GAAP – FRS 102

Adoption of FRS 102 by small and medium-sized entities (non-FRSSE) is mandatory for accounting periods beginning on or after 1 January 2015, although earlier adoption is permitted. The new standard is based on the international financial reporting standard (IFRS) for small companies and requires a cash flow statement to be prepared in line with IAS 7 "Cash flow statements".   **4250**

There are also a **small number of differences** between current UK GAAP and FRS 102 as set out in the table below.

Differences	FRS 1	FRS 102
Cash and cash equivalents: definition	Narrow definition of cash (cash + deposits repayable on demand).	More expansive definition: cash and cash equivalents includes highly liquid investments, bank overdrafts etc., with maturities < 3 months.
Classifications	Contains 8 headings (¶4034)	Only 3 activity classifications: Operating, Financing and Investing.Operating: key revenue generating activities. Financing: activities impacting on the size/structure of contributed equity/borrowings (e.g. share issues, loans) Investing: Acquisition and disposal of assets/investments (e.g. CAPEX, disposal proceeds).
Additional information	A statement reconciling movements in cash in the period with changes in net debt. Components of net debt should be disclosed.	No separate statements required.

There are a number of categories in FRS 1 that have no corresponding heading in FRS 102; a conversion table is set out below.   **4251**

FRS 1 Headings	FRS 102 equivalent
Taxation	No specific classification: include in operating unless related to investing/financing.
Capital expenditure and financial investment	Investing activities
Acquisitions and disposals	Investing activities
Dividends paid	Operating or financing
Liquid resources: management	Cash equivalents
Returns on investments and servicing of finance	Interest paid is covered in the operating or financing sections; interest and dividends received = operating or investing cash flows.

MEMO POINTS   1. There is no requirement under FRS 102 to produce a **reconciliation to net debt**.
2. **Hedging transactions**: Cash flows relating to a hedge must be matched with the underlying cash flows flowing from the hedged transaction/item.
3. **Group cash flow statements**: No specific guidance is contained in FRS 102.
4. **Foreign currency cash flows**: FRS 102 does not cover this topic in any great detail, other than stating these should be translated at the exchange rate prevailing on the transaction date.
5. The FRC has issued a **staff education note** covering cash flow statements (SEN 01) that illustrates the format of the cash flow statement prepared in accordance with FRS 102 and highlights important areas of consideration when transitioning to FRS 102.

CHAPTER 2

Statement of total recognised gains and losses (STRGL)

A. Scope and objective

The purpose of the statement of total recognised gains and losses (STRGL) is to show the extent to which shareholders' funds have increased or decreased during the year from all **gains and losses** (whether realised or not), and is a classified as **primary statement** that is required by FRS 3, "Reporting financial performance".

4300
FRS 3 (56)
FRSSE 5.1

As not all gains and losses will have flowed through the profit and loss account, especially those arising out of movements on reserves, they should be reflected in the STRGL.

Certain **gains and losses** are specifically permitted, or are in some cases required by law or an accounting standard to be taken directly to reserves, such as unrealised gains arising on the revaluation of fixed assets. These are not reflected in the profit and loss account but are expressly required to be taken directly to the revaluation reserve.

4302

FRS 3 (27)(57)

Because the STRGL is a primary statement, it should be presented separately and with the same prominence as the other primary statements; namely the balance sheet, profit and loss account and cash flow statement. If there are **no recognised gains or losses** in both the current and prior periods, other than those already reflected in the profit and loss account, the STRGL may be omitted. However, a statement to this effect must be given at the foot of the profit and loss account.

> [EXAMPLE] PROFIT AND LOSS ACCOUNT (extract)
>
> There were no recognised gains and losses, both in the current year and in the previous year, other than the profit [or loss, *as applicable*] for the year as shown above in this profit and loss account. As a result, no statement of recognised gains and losses is presented.

In the case of a material recognised movement in the amounts attributable to **different classes of shareholders** that has no effect on **total shareholders' funds** (e.g. an appropriation of profit to accrue a premium on redemption of preference shares), an explanatory footnote to the statement may be appropriate. In respect of **consolidated financial statements**, the requirements of FRS 3 must be satisfied by presenting a consolidated STRGL.

4304

MEMO POINTS   Under **FRS 102**, which **replaces FRS 3** from January 2015, an entity can choose from one of two presentation formats for total comprehensive income for the accounting period in question; namely:
– a single statement of comprehensive income, including all income and expense items; or
– producing two statements: i) an income statement (i.e. profit and loss account for the period) and ii) a statement of comprehensive income, which includes the profit for the financial year plus gains/losses not passing through the profit and loss.

B. Content

4307   FRS 3 imposes no strict format for the STRGL. Reporting entities are therefore permitted to use their own discretion in determining the disclosure most appropriate to their circumstances. The items most commonly included are explained in ¶4310 below.

4308   The opening entry in the STRGL is usually the profit or loss for the period. The other items are the gains and losses that were taken directly to reserves and therefore not reflected in the profit and loss account. Because the STRGL, like the profit and loss account, is regarded as a performance statement, gains and losses are taken to reserves through one or the other of these statements. Consequently, any item recognised in the STRGL in one period cannot be recognised again ("recycled") in the profit and loss account in a subsequent period.

MEMO POINTS   An amount recognised in the STRGL in one period cannot subsequently be recycled in the profit and loss account, except in respect of gains and losses that FRS 23 and FRS 26 specifically require to be recycled. In these cases, to avoid mis-stating total recognised gains and losses, the STRGL must include a separate line item to reverse the amount previously recognised.

4309   If there has been a prior period adjustment, the **comparative figures** should be restated and the cumulative effect of the adjustment shown at the bottom of the STRGL of the current period. The logic behind this treatment is that the adjustments represent gains and losses recognised in the current period even though they **relate to previous periods**.

1. Items most typically included

4310   The following items typically found in the STRGL are set out in the table below.

Accounting issue	Accounting treatment
Profit or loss before dividends attributable to shareholders for the year	This figure is taken as the starting point for the STRGL.
Gains and losses on revaluation of assets during the year	FRS 15, "Tangible fixed assets" requires certain gains and losses arising on the revaluation of tangible fixed assets to be recognised in the STRGL, rather than being taken to the profit and loss account (See ¶1420).
Unrealised currency translation differences	Covers differences in net values of investments in foreign enterprises resulting from exchange rate fluctuations not reflected in the profit and loss account.
Gains arising from lapsed warrants	see discussion at ¶3625.
Impairment losses arising on fixed assets and goodwill	FRS 11, "Impairment of fixed assets and goodwill", requires certain impairment losses relating to previously revalued assets to be recognised in the STRGL. Similarly, if the impairment is reversed, and the reversal is permitted under FRS 11, it should be recognised in the STRGL.

Accounting issue	Accounting treatment
Tax attributable to gains or losses recognised in the STRGL	Under FRS 16, "Current tax", the **current taxation** for a period should be recognised in the profit and loss account – unless it is attributable to a gain or loss that has been recognised directly in the STRGL. The reasoning is that if any transaction that results in a profit or loss is recognised directly in the STRGL, the attributable tax should also be recognised there. Any tax shown in the STRGL should be analysed into UK and foreign tax, with a sub-analysis of: – tax estimated for the current period, and – tax adjustments recognised in respect of previous periods.
Deferred tax	FRS 19 requires deferred tax to be recognised in the current period's profit and loss account – unless it is attributable to a gain or loss that has been recognised directly in the STRGL. Where this is the case, the deferred tax should likewise be recognised there. The amount of **deferred tax** recognised directly in the statement of total recognised gains and losses should be disclosed and, where the amounts are material, **analysed** into: – the origination and reversal of timing differences; – changes in tax rates and laws; – adjustments to the estimated recoverable amount of deferred tax assets arising in previous periods.

MEMO POINTS   Previously, investment companies were obliged to include only **distributable profits** in their profit and loss account and any non-distributable profits (realised or unrealised), had to be shown in the STRGL. This requirement has since been withdrawn by FRS 25, with the result that investment companies are now subject to the same rules as other companies.

2. Items not included

4320

The following items **are not shown** in the STRGL:
– contributions from or distributions to shareholders; and
– goodwill written off directly to reserves or reinstated on the subsequent sale of the business.

These items are excluded because they are not elements of a company's performance. Consequently, the best place for their disclosure is in the **reconciliation of movements in shareholders' funds** (see discussion and example at ¶3795).

3. Sample statement

4330

The following is an example of the form and content of a typical STRGL.

Statement of Total Recognised Gains and Losses For the year ended 31 December 20X3		
	20X3	20X2
	£m	£m
Profit for the year attributable to shareholders of the company	320	285
Unrealised surplus[1]/ (deficit) on revaluation of properties in associate	50	(19)
Foreign exchange translation adjustments[2]	(35)	(22)
Total recognised gains and losses for the year	335	244
Prior year adjustment[3]	(10)	–
Total gains and losses recognised since last annual report	325	244

1. Amount credited to the revaluation reserve during the year.

2. Unrealised losses or gains on translation of net foreign-currency investments, translated at rate at end of year.

3. The £10m represents the cumulative adjustment to reserves in 20X3. The comparative year's profit (i.e. £285m) will have been adjusted by the amount that relates to 20X2.

PART 7

Reports and other disclosures

CHAPTER 1

Directors' report

This chapter deals with the content of the directors' report and the reporting framework that underpins the disclosure requirements. The **objective of the directors' report** is to provide details of the company's principal activities, development and future prospects, as well as the non-financial issues affecting the entity and its stakeholders.   **4500**

It is a requirement of the Companies Act, that a director's report is included in the financial statements of all companies for each financial year. **Enhanced disclosure requirements** exist for large companies and, to a lesser degree, medium-sized companies and there are also provisions covering directors' liability for statements made in the directors' report (see ¶4508). The disclosures required of listed companies are beyond the scope of this book. **Small companies** can elect to voluntarily file a directors' report with the Registrar of Companies.

> MEMO POINTS   1. SI 2008/409 (Sch 5), "The Small Companies and Groups (Accounts and Directors' Report) Regulations 2008 and Sch 7, "The Large and Medium-sized Companies and Groups (Accounts and Reports) Regulations 2008 contain some provisions covering disclosures.
> 2. Although there is **no specific accounting standard** covering the directors' report, there is interaction between a number of standards (e.g. SSAP 13 "Accounting for research and development" (¶1150) and the requirements of the Companies Act.

A **parent company that prepares group accounts** must also produce a group directors' report, covering all entities included in the consolidation. Individual directors' reports are not required for each company. In general **small and medium-sized companies** can take advantage of certain exemptions under EU Accounting Directives, including those that are part of a group.   **4501**

> MEMO POINTS   1. Small companies (including those that are part of an **ineligible group** (s415A CA 2006) are exempt from preparing the enhanced directors' report under CA 2006.
> 2. A **group is defined as ineligible if** any of its members is (s384(2) CA 2006) a public company; a body corporate other than a company whose shares are traded on a regulated market in the EEA; a person other than a small company authorised to undertake a regulated activity under FSMA 2000; a small company that is an authorised insurance company, banking company, e-money issuer, or a person who carries on insurance market activity.

The disclosures in the directors' report must be consistent with the information given in the financial statements. Most companies tend to meet only the **minimum statutory disclosure requirements**, which may also be provided at the discretion of the individual company. A copy of the directors' report must be filed with the Registrar of Companies, except for companies entitled to the **small companies exception** (¶4512) including those who elect to file abbreviated accounts.   **4503**

Penalty for non-compliance

The directors' report must be **approved by** the board of directors and signed and dated on their behalf by a director or the company secretary, before being sent to the Registrar of Companies.   **4504**
s 416 CA 2006

The name of the signatory must be clearly stated on the report. There are penalties for failure to comply with the requirements covering the preparation, content and signature of the report.

The directors **holding office at the date** the financial statements are approved, have a responsibility to produce and approve a directors' report, even if none of the directors were actually in office during the time covered by the report. This requirement cannot be avoided on the grounds that the directors were not responsible for the activities covered in the report.

In situations where the company **does not fully comply** with the requirements for the **approval and signing** of the directors' report, the company, and every director who is in default, will be guilty of an offence, punishable by a fine. Furthermore, if the directors' report does not comply with requirements for preparation and content, then any director who knew of this and failed to take reasonable steps to ensure compliance, will be guilty of an offence and liable to a fine.

4506   **Enforcement** The **legal mechanism** for enforcing the new regulations, will be the extension of the existing administrative enforcement regime, to cover directors' reports. Responsibility for **enforcement will be undertaken**:
- for small companies by the secretary of state (BIS); and
- for large and medium-sized companies by the Financial Reporting Review Panel (FRRP).

The requirements of the directors' reports, encompassing the **business review**, are set out in the Companies Act 2006. The objective will be to see if the directors' report is consistent with the financial statements and that it reflects the development and performance of the business.

Directors' liability (safe harbour)

4508   Provisions contained in the Companies Act 2006, covering directors' reports sent to shareholders, require a director to compensate the company for losses incurred arising from:
- known false or misleading pronouncements in the directors' report; or
- material omissions intended to conceal important information.

The directors are only liable to the company and not third parties wishing to make claims against them.

A "**safe harbour clause**" has been included in the Companies Act enabling directors to omit information covering current developments, including negotiations and contracts, where disclosure is deemed seriously prejudicial to the interests of the company.

A. Companies Act disclosures

4510   The **minimum disclosure requirements** in the directors' report for all companies **(irrespective of size)**, are set out in the table below.

Disclosure requirements				
Type of company	Disclosure	Chapter Reference	s 415-6 CA 2006	Sch 5 SI 2008/409 Sch 7 SI 2008/410
All companies	Names of directors	¶4514	✓	
	Principle activities of company + subsidiary undertakings	¶4520	✓	
	Political donations	¶4532		✓
	Charitable donations	¶4546		✓
	Purchase by company of "own shares"	¶4548		✓
	Statement as to disclosure of information to the auditors		✓	

Disclosure requirements				
	Additional disclosure requirements		s 416-7 CA 2006	Sch 7 SI 2008/410
Medium/ large companies	Strategic review (including key performance indicators/ replaces the Business Review)	¶4554	✓	
	Dividend payments	¶4558	✓	
	Research & development	¶4560		✓
	Post balance sheet events	¶4562		✓
	Employee policies (companies with more than 250 employees)	¶4576		✓
	Overseas branches	¶4572		✓
	Use of financial instruments	¶3000		✓
	Carbon emissions	¶4586		
			Other	
Large companies only (non-listed)	Valuation of land and buildings			✓
	Directors statement of responsibilities		SAS 600	
	Remuneration report		SAS 600	
	Audit committees		SAS 600	
	Financial instruments			✓
	Introduction of the Euro		UITF 21	
	Overview of likely future developments			✓

MEMO POINTS   1. The disclosure requires for **listed companies** are beyond the scope of this book.
2. **The Companies Act 2006 (Strategic Report and Directors' Report Regulations 2013)** came into force in October 2013 and removes some of the disclosure requirements for all companies (e.g. details of principal activities, charitable donations) and others specific to large and medium-sized companies (e.g. creditor payment policy). In addition the enhanced business review has been replaced by a strategic report, although **small companies** will be exempt from this requirement.

Small companies exemption

A company is entitled to certain exemptions regarding the directors' report, if for the financial year in question it qualifies as a small company, or would have done so if not a member of an ineligible group. The exemptions cover the content of the business review, dividend recommendations and filing obligations.

4512
s 415-417 CA 2006

If the directors have taken advantage of the disclosure exemptions available to small companies in the preparation of the directors' report, they must disclose this fact in a prominent position above the signature on the directors' report.

EXAMPLE   **ABC Ltd – Annual Report and accounts**
Directors' report (extract)

This report has been prepared in accordance with the special provisions of section 415 A Companies Act 2006 relating to small companies.

Approved by the board of directors on 5.2.2014 and signed on its behalf by

...
B. Kavanagh
Secretary

A company entitled to the **small company exemptions** outlined above, must still deliver a copy of their financial statements to the Registrar of Companies, with submission of the directors' report being optional.

1. Small companies

4513
FRSSE 18.1 – 18.15

The following disclosures are required to be made within the directors' report:
- the principal activities of the company;
- details of the company's directors;
- political donations and expenditure and charitable donations (where the aggregate of each exceeds £2,000);
- acquisitions by the company of its own shares;
- employment of disabled persons (where the average number of employees exceeds 250);
- a statement that there is no relevant audit information of which the company's auditors are unaware and that the directors have taken the necessary steps to make themselves aware of any such information and to have established that it had been made available to the auditors.

The report must be approved by the board and signed, stating the name of the person who signed it.

2. All companies

Names of the directors

4514
s 416 CA 2006

The following **statutory information** is required in the directors report; namely the names of the persons who were directors of the company at any time during the financial year.

Non-statutory or voluntary information includes the following:
- the dates of any appointments or resignations of directors during the financial year;
- details of any appointments or resignation of directors since the end of the financial year; and
- retirement of directors at the AGM and whether they offer themselves for re-election.

EXAMPLE   **Smithsony Ltd**
Annual report and accounts – December 2013
Directors' Report (extract)

Directors
Biographies of the directors of the company are shown on pages xx to xx. Lady Thornton retired as a director on 31 May 2013, Steven Spencer retired on 30 June 2013 and Paul Rodgers resigned from the board on 31 August 2013.
In accordance with Article 68 of the Articles of Association, Ian Smith (appointed May 2009); Misha Reeves, Carmen Zipata (both appointed March 2009) and Don Ferrer (appointed July 2010) **only hold office until** the AGM and, being eligible, offer themselves for re-election. In accordance with Article 70 of the Articles of Association, Jan Edberg, and Neil Smith retire by rotation at the annual general meeting and being eligible, offer themselves for re-election.
Details of directors' interests in company shares are shown on page xx. No director was materially interested in any significant contract entered into by the company. Jim Smithson is, however, a non-executive director of Superdeals Limited (a travel and leisure company) and Tangrame publishing.

4516

In the **group financial statements**, disclosure is only required of the names of the parent company's directors. It is common for a list of the directors to be placed at the beginning of the report. If the names of the directors are not listed in the directors' report then details of where these disclosures are located must be given.

Details of **non-executive directors** and the committees on which they sit (e.g. audit committee) need not be supplied in the directors' report, although a reference to where this information can be located, should be provided.

Principal activities

4520
s 416 CA 2006

The directors' report should detail the principal activities and progress of the **company and its subsidiaries** during the financial year and details of any significant changes in these activities. However, the Companies Act does not specify a format or dictate the precise content of this review.

EXAMPLE **ABC Group Ltd – Annual report and accounts**
Directors' report (extract)

Principal activities

The group trades principally as Home Improvement, Electrical and Furniture and General Merchandise retailers across the UK and Continental Europe. In addition, the group has extensive property interests in the UK.

On 30 September 2013, the group acquired DAB electronics AG, the second largest electrical retailer in Germany, which in turns owns and manages a significant distribution company. During the year the group's activities have also been expanded further by its entry into the UK double glazing market, with the purchase of Glazedover Ltd.

A **review** of the group's principal activities and its financial position at 31 December 2013 are reported in the chairman's statement and in the financial, operational and business reviews on pages xx to xx.

Principal activities are not defined in the Companies Act, but can generally be interpreted as the different **industry segments** or **classes of business** in which the entity operates. Classes of business are defined as "a separate product or service or a separate group of related products or services". No single group of characteristics is universally applicable in determining industry segments or classes of business, although there should be consistent presentation with the requirements of **segmental reporting** in the financial statements. The judgement of the directors is required to determine what business segments or classes of business are significant, although the general rule is that any segment breaching the 10% barrier (i.e. turnover) requires separate disclosure. Broad classifications such as manufacturing or wholesaling should be avoided.

4522

Political donations

The requirements of the Companies Act relating to political donations, require companies including subsidiaries, to obtain **shareholder approval** for the following:
– political donations (subject to certain de-minimis limits); and
– political expenditure in the UK and other member states.

4532

Provisions relating to political donations contained in the new Companies Act, largely restate existing provisions and are consistent with the framework established by the Political Parties, Elections and Referendums Act 2000 (Revised 2009).

There are also **special rules** for subsidiaries and for parent companies of non-UK subsidiaries.

A company is deemed to be treated as giving money for political purposes, if it provides a donation or subscription to a political party, or a division or officer thereof.

Contributions and donations to a political party are defined as follows:
– any gift of money or property;
– sponsorship;
– subscription paid for affiliation or membership of the party;
– contributions to expenses incurred either directly or indirectly by the party;
– loans to the party (except on commercial terms); and
– provisions of property or services to a political party (unless on commercial terms).

4534

Where a **payment is made by a subsidiary company**, prior approval must be obtained from the shareholders of the parent company. This requirement is designed to prevent companies from circumventing the approval provisions by channelling payments through a subsidiary. The **same rules apply** to overseas subsidiaries of a UK parent company.

4536

The directors of the company are personally liable to reimburse the company for political contributions or donations made, where prior shareholder approval has not been sought. In the case of non-compliance by a subsidiary, the directors of the holding company will also be personally liable.

Exemptions

4538

s 374-378 CA 2006

Shareholder approval is not required for the following donations:
– contributions to trade unions, including provision of facilities and services;
– membership subscriptions to EU trade associations;
– payments to all party parliamentary groups;
– political donations below the threshold disclosure limit of £5,000; and
– political donations exempted on the authority of the Secretary of State.

4540

Disclosures Separate disclosure is required in the directors' report of political donations within the EU and the rest of the world.

4542

The following disclosures are required in the directors' report, of any political donations made by both parent and subsidiary companies to **parties within the EU**:
– the name of each person or political party within the EU to whom a sum in excess of £2,000 was given;
– disclosure of the aggregate amount paid or donated to EU political parties by a company or group; and
– where prior shareholder approval was given for political donations within the EU (including aggregate donations) during the financial year.

> MEMO POINTS **1. EU political donations** are defined as any expenditure committed in respect of:
> – the preparation, publication or distribution of promotional material that is designed to generate support for any EU political party;
> – activities that can be construed as providing support for any EU political organisation; and
> – any activities that can be regarded as helping to influence voters in a national or regional election held in a EU member state.
> 2. An **EU political organisation** is any party registered under Part II of the Political Parties, Elections and Referendums Act 2000, any political party registered in another EU state, or any independent candidates standing in EU elections.

4544

Disclosure is required of the total contributions made by a company or group of companies to political parties **outside the EU**. There is **no threshold** for these disclosures. Wholly owned subsidiaries of companies incorporated in the UK are exempt from this requirement on the basis that the details will be given in the parent company's financial statements.

Charitable donations

4546

The directors' report must disclose the total amount that the company has provided for charitable concerns, during the financial year, unless the donation is less than £2,000. If a company makes a number of charitable donations that in aggregate exceed £2,000, then disclosure is still required. The **same threshold applies** to both individual companies and groups.

The **donation threshold** has been increased to £2,000 through regulations issued under the Companies Act 2006.

Companies making payments to a **company trust**, which then has discretion to donate funds to individual charities, should disclose the sums and charities involved.

> EXAMPLE **Annual report – June 2013**
> **Directors' report** (extract)
>
> **Charitable donations**
> During 2013 the company made charitable donations totalling £367,000. The annual donations budget is administered by a committee of the Board and by local site committees. The policy is predominantly directed towards assisting charities working in the educational field and other community based projects.

4547

Exemption from the disclosure requirement to disclose charitable donations is available:
– to wholly owned subsidiaries of a company incorporated in the UK, on the basis that the information will be supplied in the directors' report of the parent company;
– where payments to a charity are of a commercial nature; or

– for payments to a person ordinarily resident outside the UK at the time the donation was made.

Purchase by company of "own shares"

Where a company **acquires its own shares** through the following **methods** it is required to make certain disclosures in the directors' report:

4548

– through a share purchase;
– by forfeiture or surrender in lieu of forfeiture;
– by purchase in compliance with a court order;
– by redemption;
– through a reduction of capital;
– indirect purchases by a nominee, where the company will have a beneficial effect; and
– charges or lien on own shares for an amount that is payable in respect of those shares.

The following **disclosures** are required for own shares acquired by the company:

– the number and nominal values of the shares purchased in the financial year;
– the percentage of the called-up share capital that any purchase represents;
– the consideration paid for the shares;
– the reasons for the purchase;
– the number and nominal values of any such shares disposed of in the financial year; and
– the reasons for the disposal.

Similar disclosures are required for shares acquired by a **nominee company or a third person** on behalf of the company. Additional disclosures are required for listed companies.

> EXAMPLE   **STL Ltd**
> **Annual report and accounts – 2013**
> **Directors' report** (extract)
>
> **Interests in own shares**
> STL Group Ltd repurchased 1,325,000 of its ordinary shares of 20p each, representing a total of 0.3% of the total called-up share capital. The aggregate consideration paid was £350,000. These shares were acquired by two trusts in the open market using funds provided by the company to meet obligations under the Performance Share Plan and Long-Term Incentive Plans.

3. Large and medium-sized companies

The disclosure requirements for large and medium-sized companies are extensive and comprise an enhanced business review and research and development initiatives, as well information regarding creditor payment, employment and dividend policies and carbon emissions.

4552

> MEMO POINTS   1. For financial years ending on or after 30 September 2013, the business review section of the directors' report is to be replaced with a **new strategic report**, which fulfils largely the same function but contains additional disclosure requirements for listed companies covering the company's business model, details of its environmental impact (carbon footprint) and key policies regarding social and community projects. This new legal requirement is encoded in the Companies Act 2006 (Strategic Report and Directors' Report Regulations 2013).
> 2. However, **small companies** will continue to be **exempt** from the requirement to produce a strategic report. The FRC has published non-mandatory guidance and proposals on how to prepare the strategic report.
> 3. The coalition Government is consulting on how to improve the quality of company reporting and encourage more effective shareholder involvement, with particular focus given to the **business review** required by large and medium-sized companies.

Strategic review (Enhanced business review)

All companies, **except those classified as** small companies, must produce a strategic review (formerly the enhanced business review" of their business in the directors' report. New regulations have expanded the existing requirements, that the directors' report provide a compre-

4554
s 417 CA 2006

hensive and balanced review of how the business has developed over the course of the financial year, including that of its subsidiaries, associates and joint ventures.

Subsidiaries that qualify as medium or large must prepare a business review, even where a group report is prepared by the parent company.

4556   The **type of information** disclosed under this heading includes:
- any material changes in turnover during the financial period;
- a brief review of the results for the year;
- the overall return on assets that the company or group obtained during the year;
- any positive or negative changes in markets or products;
- details of any major restructuring or reorganisation; and
- details of any significant foreign exchange gains or losses.

4557   The **content and analysis** should be consistent with the size and complexity of the business
s 417 CA 2006   and cover selected key performance indicators (KPIs) and the principal risks and uncertainties facing the business. Key performance indicators (KPIs) are defined as factors that measure the development, performance or position of the business.

4558   **Key performance indicators (KPIs)   Selected KPI's include** those covering:
- financial results (e.g. ROCE; average revenue per user); and
- non-financial information (e.g. employee statistics; environmental performance standards).

There is no definitive list of KPIs, and the choice of KPIs included in the report is at the discretion of each individual company.

Medium-sized companies need only include financial KPIs, unless they have adopted international financial reporting standards (IFRSs), in which case they should, along with large companies, provide details of important non-financial KPIs.

4559   KPIs are factors that aid measurement of the performance, growth or position of the company or group. An entity should provide information to enable users of the financial statements to understand each KPI or other form of **performance measure** referred to in the report including:
- the definition and method of calculation method should be disclosed;
- its purpose;
- the source of the supporting data and any assumptions explained;
- quantification or commentary on future targets;
- corresponding amounts for the preceding financial year; and
- any changes to KPIs.

Dividends

4560   Although only the proposed dividend need be disclosed, details are usually given for both the interim dividend paid during the year and the proposed final dividend as illustrated in the following example.

> [EXAMPLE] **ABC Ltd**
> **Annual report and accounts – 30 June 2013**
>
> **Directors' report** (extract)
> The directors recommend a **final dividend** of £2.50 a share to be paid on 15 April 2013, to shareholders registered on 24 February 2013. This, together with the interim share payment of £1.75 a share, paid on 7 August 2013, makes a total dividend payment of £4.25 per share for the year. The total (aggregate) dividend payment for the financial year 2013 is £13.5m.

Where the directors **decline to propose** a dividend this fact should be stated in the directors' report. Details of any shareholder agreements to waive rights to dividends payable during the last year should be disclosed. This requirement applies to waivers of future dividends. **Dividend waivers** totalling less than 1% of the value of any dividend disregarded, on each class of share, need not be disclosed.

Research and development

The directors' report should contain an overview of the company's research and develop-   **4561**
ment activity during the financial year and details of the accounting policy adopted as
required by SSAP 13 "Accounting for research and development".

The disclosures should focus on the commercial direction of the research and development
expenditure, in order to provide some indication of **future revenue streams** for the benefit
of current and potential investors, as well as the impact this may have on the activities of
the company.

The **information disclosed** typically covers:
– a broad indication of the nature and level of research and development activity;
– a brief analysis of specific research and development projects; and
– an overview of any major contracts or joint research and development projects.

> EXAMPLE **ABC Ltd**
> **Report and accounts – 30 June 2013**
> **Directors' report** (extract)
>
> The group engages in research and development activities (R & D) relating to the introduction
> of new products and production processes and to the improvement of existing products and
> processes.
> The business is supported by high quality technical facilities for R & D led by group facilities in
> Liverpool, Nottingham and Norwich, supporting the group's global activities.
> The **principal research activities** include:
> – the assessment of safety and toxicology;
> – the improvement of flavour, colouring and texture;
> – the development of packaging techniques; and
> – the application of micro-technology to the process control procedures.
> The group spent £42.5m in 2013, (£23.1m 2012) on research and development. Included in this
> figure is £5m spent on a joint research project with the Science Research Council.

Post balance sheet events

The Companies Act requires that the directors' report for companies (other than small   **4562**
companies), contain important post balance sheet events which have affected the company
since the end of the financial year. In order to avoid duplication this information is often
provided in the notes to the accounts.

Valuation of land and buildings

Where the valuation of the directors of land or buildings owned by the company **materially**   **4568**
exceeds the value recorded in the balance sheet, then this difference should be disclosed.
The disclosure should be based on a recent valuation although there is no requirement for
this to be a professional valuation.

Where the value of land or buildings is less than the book value and the directors determine
that a write-down is not required, some justification for this policy should be stated in the
directors' report.

> MEMO POINTS   Where a company adopts a policy of **revaluing assets** under FRS 15 "Tangible
> fixed assets", any gains or losses should be incorporated into the accounts.

> EXAMPLE **Handel Plc**
> **Report and accounts – 30 October 2013**
> **Directors' report** (extract)
>
> **Property**
> The directors have reviewed the current value of the premises portfolio and estimate that there is
> a shortfall of £6.5m, compared to the balance sheet value. The shortfall relates to UK properties
> and the directors are of the opinion that this will not prove to be permanent; therefore no adjustment
> has been made in the balance sheet.

Overseas branches

4572 The directors' report must, unless the company is unlimited, contain details of business establishments it operates outside the United Kingdom. Overseas establishments operated by its subsidiaries should be disclosed in the directors' report of the subsidiary companies.

Employee policies

4576 Companies employing an **average of more than 250 people** throughout the year must disclose details relating to:
- the dissemination of information to employees on matters concerning them (i.e. health and safety, employee welfare policies);
- employee consultation procedures;
- employee share schemes; and
- employment of disabled persons.

If a company prepares consolidated financial statements, the director's report need only contain the employee information for the parent company.

4578 The Companies Act requires that the **average number of employees** be calculated, by first determining the number of people employed by the company in each week of the financial year, totalling the individual weekly totals before dividing by the number of weeks in the financial year.

The threshold applies to **individual companies**; there is no requirement to aggregate figures for persons employed by a group of companies. Disclosures are not required for persons wholly or primarily employed outside the UK. Therefore, where a parent company is purely a holding company with a small number of employees, then employee policy disclosures are not required in the group accounts. However, it is regarded as **best practice** to disclosure employee numbers, where the group employs in excess of 250.

4582 The **format of the disclosures** is usually in **narrative form** and may for example cover discussion of:
- the use of internal seminars and training programmes to supply information to employees;
- details of in-house newsletters;
- relationships with recognised trade unions;
- details of employee share schemes; and
- action to promote equal opportunities.

Disclosures are not required for persons wholly or primarily employed outside the UK.

EXAMPLE **PQR Ltd**
Annual report and accounts 2013
Directors' report (extract)

Employee involvement
The Board continues to place emphasis on high standards of customer care and service by each operating company. The commitment of every employee to this business requirement is considered to be critical. Accordingly, operating companies have continued to develop their arrangements for **employee information, consultation, communication and involvement**, including attitude surveys, briefing groups, internal magazines and newsletters on matters relating to business performance and objectives, community involvement and other related issues.
Training and links with the educational sector reinforce our commitment to employee involvement and development. Employees are represented on the trustee board of the Group's pension arrangements.

Equal opportunities The Group is committed to the principle of equal opportunity in employment and to ensuring that no applicant or employee receives less favourable treatment on the grounds of gender, race, age, colour, nationality, religion, HIV status, disability, sexuality, or unrelated criminal convictions or other unjustified requirements or conditions.
The Group applies employment policies that are fair and equitable and which ensure entry into, and progression within the Group, is determined solely by application of job criteria and personal ability and competency.

Disabled persons   The statutory disclosures regarding company policy, in respect of the   **4584**
employment of disabled persons, include the following:
– equal employment opportunities for disabled people;
– continued employment and training of staff becoming disabled, whilst employees of the
company; and
– general training, career development and promotion of disabled persons.
The same **threshold rules** as for general employee policies apply.

Carbon emissions

The Government plans to impose a mandatory obligation on large and medium-sized   **4586**
companies to disclose their carbon emissions in their directors' reports from 2014. In the
meantime, guidance has been published by the Department for Environment, Food and
Rural Affairs (DEFRA) (in partnership with the Department for Energy and Climate Change
(DECC)) on how companies can measure and report their greenhouse gas emissions, as well
as set targets to reduce them. The guidance is available from the DEFRA website along with
separate guidance for small companies.

> MEMO POINTS   A new system of **carbon reporting**, overseen by the FRC, came into force in Octo-
> ber 2013 and requires quoted companies to publish details of their greenhouse gas emissions in
> the directors' report. The **new disclosure requirements**, which apply to financial periods begin-
> ning on or after 30 September 2013, form part of the UK narrative reporting framework, which
> requires companies to prepare a more informative strategic report as part of their annual financial
> statements. However, the daunting challenge for companies will be to determine how to tune
> their accounting systems in order to collect this information in a cost effective and efficient
> manner.

B. Additional disclosures

Directors' statement of responsibilities   The directors' reports of companies **subject to**   **4590**
audit, must include a statement from the directors that no information has knowingly been
withheld, that would affect the auditor's opinion of the annual financial statements. The
directors' report should also include a statement of directors' responsibilities, arising out of
the International Standard on Auditing 700, "The Auditors' Report on Financial Statements".

> EXAMPLE   **LMO Ltd.**
> **Report and accounts 2013**
> **Directors' report** (extract)
>
> **Directors' statement of responsibility**
> The directors are responsible for preparing the Directors' Report and the annual financial state-
> ments in accordance with UK company legislation and generally accepted United Kingdom
> accounting practice. The directors are satisfied that the financial statements give a true and fair
> view of the state of affairs of the company and the profit or loss for the period in question. In
> preparing the financial statements the directors have:
> – selected suitable accounting policies and applied them consistently;
> – made prudent and reasonable accounting estimates;
> – have followed UK accounting standards and explained any material departures in the notes to
> the accounts;
> – prepared the financial statements on a going concern basis;
> – taken adequate measures to ensure that proper accounting records have been maintained; and
> – put in place effective safeguards to protect company assets from fraud and misappropriation.

Environmental reporting

At present the disclosure of environmental information is **currently voluntary**, although   **4592**
there is an increasing demand for information about the impact a company's trading activi-

ties have on the environment, to be included in the financial statements and in the directors' report in particular.

Some listed companies (e.g. British Petroleum) produced separate detailed reports on the impact and risks that their operations pose to the environment, whillst others such as banks, are keen to stress their involvement in the local community. It is expected that the demand for better environmental reporting will increase and this in turn will require improved methods of environmental accounting and data capture.

4593   The major elements of environmental accounting are as follows:
– assess and reduce the negative environmental effects of a company's activities;
– identify environmentally related costs and revenues within conventional accounting systems;
– devise new forms of financial and non-financial accounting and control systems (perform-ance measurement) in order to support better environmental decision making; and
– develop methods for assessing and promoting sustainability.

There are a **number of developments** in the area of environmental reporting both in the UK and within the European Commission, that are expected to lead to a significant increase in the level of environmental disclosures by large companies in their annual report, as well as increased reporting requirements for small companies. Attempts are currently being made by a number of organisations to overcome the current limitations of conventional financial reporting in this area. The problem is that a number of governmental and private sector organisations are developing criteria and standards simultaneously, which will undoubtedly need to be harmonised at some juncture.

4594   The UK Environment Agency, in co-operation with the ACCA, has published a number of papers detailing recent developments in environmental accounting practice, covering issues such as climate change, emissions trading and product disposal legislation. The Environment Agency recommends more disclosures and discussion of the possible impact of these activi-ties on the balance sheet. The Environment Agency can also **impose fines and pollution abatement costs** and can withdraw permits and operating licences from companies and their subsidiaries. The level of disclosure is expected to increase over time with more detail expected on environmental policies and quantifiable performance targets.

> MEMO POINTS   1. The Government plans to introduce mandatory reporting of **direct emission levels**, as well as usage of electricity and other forms of power. In addition, **voluntary reporting** of associate emissions is also advocated and includes items such as business travel, specific outsourced activities and the environmental costs of purchased materials and fuels. The new reporting requirements will mean that companies will have to develop methodologies and data capture systems to collect the requisite information for inclusion in the director's report. Although the proposals are **not intended to cover SMEs** it is expected that their customers will increasingly require this information, as it relates to inputs into their own production processes.
> 2. The ACCA's **Global Forum for Small and Medium-Sized Entities (SMEs)** has published a number of policy recommendations designed to encourage SMEs to adopt more sustainable business practices, as the environmental impact of this sector accounts for approximately two-thirds of all industrial pollution. The ACCA plans to develop an SME approach to sustainability that meets the needs of this complex sector, and covers micro, small and medium-sized enter-prises.

4595   At present there are **no reporting standards** dealing specifically with environmental account-ing, although a company with environmental provisions or contingent liabilities is required to disclose the amounts and circumstances surrounding them in its annual financial report. **Further disclosures**, detailing the treatment of material changes in asset values arising from environmental factors, may be appropriate under:
– FRS 10 "Goodwill and intangible assets"; and
– FRS 11 "Impairment of fixed assets and goodwill".

4596   The **EU Modernisation Directive** states that annual reports should where appropriate, include "an analysis of environmental and social aspects necessary for an understanding of the company's development, performance and position" and also that the analysis shall include both financial and non-financial KPIs, including information relating to environmental and employee matters. The **type and scale** of environmental reports are dependent on the activity of the individual entity and the industry sector to which it belongs, and should correlate with the scale of the environmental impact. For instance, a higher level of disclosure is required of resource intensive companies such as the oil and gas sectors under International Accounting Standards. A greater recognition of natural resources as natural assets in annual reports is also expected.

The **EU Trading Emissions Scheme** is also expected to give rise to environmental assets in the form of rights to emit greenhouse gases. Under this scheme, the level of environmental reporting under the accounting standards listed above will also increase over time.

Global Reporting Initiative   The **Global Reporting Initiative (GRI)**, a not for profit organisation, has also called for better integrated financial and environmental reporting through wider use of its Sustainability Reporting Framework (SFR) and guidelines, which cover social and economic information as well as environmental disclosures. The SFR provides help for organisations, regardless of size or sector, regarding the disclosure of sustainability performance using a universally-applicable, comparable reporting framework. The guidelines, including examples of standard disclosures, are available from the GRI website and are set out here in brief.

4597

GRI Guidelines	GRI requirements
1. Strategy and analysis 2. Profile of organisation 3. Reporting parameters 4. Governance 5. Management engagement and performance measurement (KPIs)	Strategic overview of organisation's approach to sustainability.Company structure – brands, locations, segmental geographical markets, etc. Reporting cycle, data capture and measurement parameters. Governance structure, stakeholder engagement. Identify and develop core performance indicators.
Key performance indicators	Categories
Economic	Performance, market share, economic impact.
Environmental	Materials, energy/natural resources usage, emissions and waste management, products, transport.
Social	1. Labour policies (employment relations, training, health and safety, equal opportunities, grievance procedures). 2. Human rights (non-discrimination, collective bargaining, security, indigenous rights). 3. Society (anti-competitive behaviour, anti-corruption, compliance, community policies). 4. Product management (customer health and safety, good product labelling, communications, customer groups).

Summary   To date developments in environmental accounting are being generated from a number of widespread sources ranging from the EU and national governments and NGOs, in addition to private organisations such as the ACCA. The current reporting landscape resembles a patchwork of competing ideologies that should over time, coalesce around a series of standardised reporting norms, as set out below.

4598

Environmental accounting	Internal management accounting tool
Objectives	Identify cost savings Improve financial performance Minimise environmental risk Measure environmental impacts (energy use, waste, sustainability, recycling policies, transportation) Stakeholder involvement (employees, suppliers, Government, etc.) Aid investment decisions
Legal framework	Companies Act European legislation UK Environment Agency

Environmental accounting	Internal management accounting tool
Environmental costs	Identify types of environmental costs (e.g. product design/engineering costs, production facilities, waste management, compliance costs, clean up costs) Key performance indicators (KPI's) – by industry sector Supply chain management Internal control systems Offsetting environmental costs through developing by products
Techniques	Cost accounting Depreciation of natural capital (resources) Risk assessments
Taxation	Environmental tax obligations Environmental taxes – levies (e.g. aggregates, climate change, landfill taxes) Tax breaks (capital allowances for plant-machinery (ECA) Tax credits Penalties
Environmental audit	Impact assessments (EIAs) required by EU regulation for major projects SWOT analysis Environmental surveys and ECO audits Eco Labelling BS 7750 – Environmental quality management

CHAPTER 2

Directors' remuneration

SECTION 1

Regulatory framework

The term "director" includes any person who occupies the **position of director** by whatever **4800**
name called. From this definition it is clear that it is an individual's functions, and their
title, that determines whether or not they are classified as a director. The **three sources** of
requirements relating to the disclosure of the remuneration paid to directors are: the
Companies Act (Statutory rules), the Listing Rules, and the UK Corporate Governance Code
(formerly the Combined Code). **Small companies** are exempt from certain requirements
concerning directors' remuneration.

> *MEMO POINTS* Where provisions in this chapter apply to small companies, references to Schedule
> 3 of SI 2008/409 are given.

The **statutory rules** relating to disclosure of directors' remuneration fall into the following **4802**
categories: s 385 CA 2006
– those applying to all companies;
– those applying to quoted companies; or
– those applying only to unquoted companies.

> *MEMO POINTS* A **quoted company** for the purposes of the above is one whose equity share capital
> has been included in the official list in accordance with the Financial Services and Markets Act
> 2000, or is officially listed in an EEA State.

This chapter is concerned only with the earnings of directors of companies that are **4803**
unquoted. Although AIM companies are treated with unquoted companies, they are nevertheless obliged to give more information in respect of **share option gains** and long-term
incentives received in shares than other unquoted companies are obliged to do.

The provision of loans or other credit, guarantees, and any other transactions entered into between companies and their directors, whether permitted or not, are dealt with in the chapter on **related party transactions** (¶5000+).

General disclosures required by the Act

4805   In general, the Act places upon companies a duty to make full disclosure in the notes to the financial statements of all amounts paid to directors in respect of their **qualifying services as directors** (¶4810). The Act further provides that, if the directors fail to disclose the required information, the company's auditors are bound by duty to include it in their own report, to the extent they are reasonably able to do so.

There are separate disclosure requirements for amounts paid to **third parties** in respect of the services of a director.

A. Remuneration for qualifying services

4810   **Qualifying services** are defined as those services rendered:

Sch 3 para 12
SI 2008/409
Sch 5 para 15
SI 2008/410

– as a director of a company or of the company's subsidiaries (while a director); and
– otherwise in connection with the management of the affairs of the company or any of its subsidiaries (while a director of the company).

Where remuneration is paid to a director for **services as a director** or otherwise in connection with the management of the company, it should be regarded as directors' remuneration, unless it can be unambiguously shown that a particular payment was made in some other capacity. For instance, if one of a company's non-executive directors who practises as a solicitor performed a professional service (or whose firm performed that service) for the company, it may be assumed that this service does not fall within the ambit of directors' remuneration. However, it is likely that the provision of legal services will be required to be disclosed as a related party transaction under the provisions of FRS 8.

The amounts to be disclosed must include **all payments made** in respect of qualifying services, not only by the **company** itself, but also by any **subsidiaries** or any other person/s.

4811   **Connected persons**   The provisions that apply to directors also apply to "connected persons". Therefore, amounts receivable by a director will include amounts receivable by a connected person (which might also be another company or body corporate). For example, where one of the spouses is a director of a company, amounts receivable by the other spouse are taken into account in the computation of director-spouse's emoluments; on the other hand, where a husband and wife are directors of the same company, they are still connected parties but their earnings are counted only once.

4812   **Remuneration disclosed**   The amount to be shown in respect of a particular financial year is the total of all sums receivable by directors during that year even if they have not yet been paid. If a payment made to a director does not relate to a particular reporting period, it should be reported in the **year** it is **approved for payment** (because that is when the liability is created).

> EXAMPLE   At the end of its financial year, 31 December 20X3, **A Ltd** proposes directors' fees payable to its board in the sum of £200,000. This payment will not become due until approved in general meeting. The company also proposes a special bonus, not in respect of any particular financial

year, payable to its Chief Executive. Because the board does not have the authority to approve such payments, the bonus will not become due until it is subsequently approved in general meeting.

In the financial statements, the directors' fees should be recorded at their proposed amount despite the fact that they will be paid in the following year. The special bonus, however, should be reported in the year ended 31 December in which the liability to pay the bonus was created.

If the financial statements cover a **period that is more/less than 12 months**, the remuneration disclosed must be in respect of that shorter or longer period.

If a director is **appointed during the year**, only that part of his remuneration earned while he was a director is regarded as being in respect of qualifying services.

EXAMPLE Mr A has been employed by C Ltd for 5 years. His salary was £100,000 p.a. Midway through the financial year, he was appointed to the board of directors and received a salary increase of £50,000 effective from that date.
In the financial statements for the year, directors' remuneration of £75,000 is shown in respect of Mr A, i.e, the amount earned during the six months since becoming director.

Group accounts   In the consolidated accounts of a parent and its subsidiaries, only payments to the directors of the parent must be reported. Amounts paid to individuals who are directors of subsidiaries only, even if the parent company makes payments to them, need not be disclosed in the group financial statements.   **4814**

EXAMPLE B Ltd has two subsidiaries, Y Ltd and Z Ltd. Ms P is a director of all three companies and receives a salary of £20,000 from each. Mr Q, a director of Z Ltd, receives director's fees of £5,000.
In the financial statements of B Ltd, only Ms P's earnings of £60,000 are required to be disclosed. Mr Q's remuneration is not shown because he is not a director of the reporting entity.

If a company is a **member of a group** but is not the parent of that group, it must disclose only the remuneration it pays to its own directors in its financial statements. Therefore, amounts of remuneration in respect of services to its parent company or fellow subsidiaries are excluded, even if the director concerned is also a director of those companies.

EXAMPLE D Ltd has a subsidiary, E Ltd. Mr X is a director of D Ltd, from which he receives a salary of £30,000. He also earns £20,000 from E Ltd. Ms Y is the general manager of D Ltd and a director of E Ltd. Her salary from D Ltd is £18,000 and from E Ltd is £4,000.

Disclosure: E Ltd
In the financial statements of E Ltd, directors' remuneration of £20,000 for Mr X is shown only if he is a director. If he is not, no amount needs to be shown. In respect of Ms Y, her salary of £4,000 must be disclosed.

Disclosure: D Ltd
In the financial statements of D Ltd, directors' remuneration to be disclosed is £50,000 for Mr X. As Ms Y is not a director of D Ltd, her earnings are not disclosed.

Remuneration relating to services to a group of companies   Where directors are paid a single amount in respect of their services to the group, the board may apportion these salary payments in any manner that is appropriate to the circumstances.   **4816**
Sch 3 para 5(6)
SI 2008/409
Sch 5 para 7(6)
SI 2008/410

If information (other than the aggregate of gains made by the directors on the exercise of share options) that is required to be disclosed is readily ascertainable from other information shown elsewhere in the financial statements, the Act's requirements are satisfied.

B. Elements of remuneration

"Remuneration" is a broad category made up of various subcategories, as set out below.   **4819**

1. Remuneration

4820
Sch 5 para 9
SI 2008/410

Companies legislation uses terms such as "emoluments" and "remuneration" rather than "earnings" as is used, for example, in tax legislation.

In general, remuneration includes:
- salaries;
- fees;
- bonuses;
- expense allowances; and
- the value of any non-cash benefits given to directors.

Excluded from remuneration are items that are disclosed under other categories – for instance, share options and pensions.

> MEMO POINTS   Remuneration does not include amounts of cash or other **advances** that a director must account for, or pay back, to the company or any of its subsidiaries. However, if a director is granted a round sum for expenses and this is then subject to income tax, then this amount is treated as part of remuneration. If any such payments **are not treated** as remuneration (and therefore not disclosed in the year they were paid) but in a subsequent accounting period are charged to tax, the relevant amount should be included under remuneration, and shown separately in the first financial statements in which it is practical to do so.

Annual bonus schemes

4822
Sch 3 para 7(1)
SI 2008/409
Sch 5 para 9(1)
SI 2008/410

Awards under annual bonus schemes are included under remuneration whether payable in cash, shares, or any other asset.

If a bonus is awarded in respect of one accounting period but is payable only in the event that the director concerned is still in employment in a future accounting period, there are two possible treatments. On the one hand, the **continuing-employment requirement** can be regarded as a criterion on which the bonus depends. In this event, the bonus should be reported in the year it is paid. On the other hand, if the bonus is regarded as having **accrued to the director** in one year but merely paid during the next, it should be reported in the year to which it relates.

Golden hellos

4824

When recruiting new directors, some companies offer **incentives** in the form of cash, shares, options, or a combination of these. Even though these so-called "golden hello" payments may not seem to relate to the individual's services as director, the Act specifically treats them as remuneration and requires their disclosure as such. Therefore, any element paid in cash will be shown together with salaries, bonuses, etc., while any element related to shares and options will be shown under the appropriate subcategory.

Benefits not paid in cash

4825

Specifically included under remuneration is the "estimated money value" of benefits not paid in cash. Because estimates of this type can be difficult to make, a company providing such benefits will have to consider the following to provide proper disclosure:
- if the company has incurred an **identifiable and direct cost**, this actual cost should be used;
- if there is no identifiable cost, such as when a director enjoys the use of a company-owned asset, an **estimate of the market value** of this benefit should be made;
- if neither of the above methods can be used, the **taxable value** of the benefit should be used (for further information, refer to *Tax Memo*);
- if there is **no reasonable method** to value the benefit, the relevant facts should be disclosed.

> MEMO POINTS   In cases where the **market value**, rather than an actual cost to the company, is used for disclosure purposes, the amounts required to be disclosed under the Act in respect of directors' emoluments will not agree with the figures in the company's accounting records.

2. Long-term incentive plans

The Act requires companies to disclose separately the aggregate amounts paid under long-term incentive schemes. Long-term incentive plans are those in terms of which cash or other assets are receivable subject to certain **qualifying conditions** that cannot be fulfilled within a single accounting period, relating to **service** or **performance**. **4826**

The **definition** of long-term incentive plans specifically **excludes** the following, as they are shown elsewhere under other categories:
– bonuses determined by reference to a single year only;
– payments for loss of office and related amounts;
– retirement benefits.

Sch 5 para 11
SI 2008/410

In general, the amount to be disclosed includes the value of both cash and non-cash assets (excluding share options, which are disclosed separately). However, in the case of **unlisted companies**, if an award is made in shares, it is not their value that must be shown but, instead, the number of directors in respect of whose qualifying services the shares were received.

3. Shares and share options

Because the Act expressly provides that share options are excluded from the definition of emoluments, they are required to be disclosed separately in the financial statements. The nature of the information that needs to be disclosed varies according to whether the company is quoted or not. **4830**

Companies that are **not listed**, and where a market price for shares is not readily available, are required to disclose:
– the number of directors who exercised share options; and
– the number of directors who became entitled to shares under long-term incentive schemes.
Neither the number of shares nor the exercise price paid needs to be disclosed.

4835
Sch 5 para 1(3)
SI 2008/410

4. Pension contributions

The Act requires companies to disclose information relating to the number of directors to whom benefits are accruing, as well as contributions paid by the company, depending on the **type of pension fund** (see ¶8400). **4838**

Companies are also required to disclose other details relating to pensions in respect of the highest-paid director.

> MEMO POINTS   **Small companies** are required to disclose information relating to the number of directors to whom benefits are accruing, as well as contributions paid by the company. They are, however, exempt from the requirements to disclose details in respect of the highest-paid director.

Types of pension schemes

There are two main types of pension schemes:
– defined contribution schemes; and
– defined benefit schemes. **4840**

Under a **defined contribution scheme** (sometimes also called a money purchase scheme), the benefits that will accrue to the director are based on the contributions made to the scheme. Under a **defined benefit scheme**, the rules specify the benefits that will be paid (these usually being based on the director's average or final pay).

Some schemes pay either money purchase benefits or defined benefits, depending on which is higher. This gives rise to a third type of scheme, which is actually a hybrid scheme. For purposes of disclosure, the Act allows companies to classify hybrid schemes according to the type of benefits that appear most likely at the financial year-end.

The following are required to be disclosed:

Money purchase/defined contribution pension schemes:	Defined benefit pension schemes:
– contributions paid on behalf of directors, and – the number of directors who are accruing retirement benefits	– the number of directors who are accruing retirement benefits

EXAMPLE H Ltd operates a company pension scheme. The scheme is funded as if it were a defined benefit scheme, paying out a maximum pension of 60% of basic salary after 20 years of service. However, the actual pension payable will be the higher of:
– the above defined benefits, and
– the pension that would have accrued had the company instead paid contributions equal to 6 percent of basic salary into a money purchase scheme that would have invested the contributions.

In respect of the financial statements for the year ended 31 December 20X3, the company must determine which benefits are likely to be higher and make appropriate disclosures.

(1) If the defined benefits are higher, the following must be disclosed:
a. the number of directors who are members of the scheme, and
b. the amount of the accrued benefit for the highest-paid director.

It is advisable, though not mandatory, to add an explanation that the scheme is a hybrid scheme and that the directors have classified it as a defined benefits scheme because the benefits on this basis appear to be higher.

(2) If the money purchase benefits are higher, the following must be disclosed:
a. the aggregate of the contributions upon which the money purchase benefits are calculated,
b. the number of directors that are members of the money purchase scheme, and
c. the amount of the contributions made in respect of the highest-paid director.

In this case again, it is advisable to explain that the scheme is a hybrid scheme and that the directors have classified it as a money purchase scheme because the benefits on this basis appear to be higher.

5. Pensions and other retirement benefits

4842
Sch 5 para 3(1)
SI 2008/410

The financial statements must disclose the amount of retirement benefits receivable by directors (including past directors) under pension schemes, to the extent that these benefits exceed the amounts such directors were entitled to, on the later of:
– when they first became eligible for benefits; and
– 31 March 1997.

Sch 5 para 3(2–4)
SI 2008/410

Retirement benefits for these purposes are far ranging and include pensions, lump sums, gratuities and other benefits, payable in cash or otherwise. The details of any benefits in kind must be given in the notes.

If a director or former director who is already receiving retirement benefits is awarded an increase in these benefits, this must be disclosed in each subsequent financial statements until these additional benefits cease to be paid. However, this disclosure need not be made if:
– the pension scheme does not require additional funding in order to make the payments; and
– additional amounts are paid or made available to all pensioner members of the scheme on the same basis.

MEMO POINTS   **Former directors**. In addition to the requirements of the Act specifically relating to director's remuneration in Schedule 3 of SI 2008/409 and Schedule 5 of SI 2008/410, companies are obliged in any event under Schedule 4 to disclose particulars of any commitments to pay pensions to past directors.

6. Compensation for loss of office

General requirements

All companies are required to disclose the aggregate amount of any compensation, including the value of any benefits in kind, to directors or past directors for loss of office.

If any non-cash benefits in kind are included in the amounts to be disclosed, they must be explained in the notes.

4844
Sch 3 para 2
SI 2008/409
Sch 5 para 4
SI 2008/410

Loss of office as a result of a takeover

Under the Companies Act, for a payment for loss of office to a director in connection with the transfer of shares in the company, or in a subsidiary of the company resulting from a takeover bid, approval is required of the holders of the shares to which the bid relates and of any other holders of shares of the same class. If a payment for loss of office is made and the payment is in connection with a takeover bid, and the required member approvals are not obtained, then the payment is held on trust for the persons who have sold their shares as a result of the offer.

4846

Loss of office as a result of breach of contract

Where payments are made to a director in respect of his retirement resulting from a **breach of contract**, any damages, settlements or compromises in respect of the breach are to be treated as compensation for loss of office and disclosed under this category.

4848
Sch 5 para 4(3)
SI 2008/410

If, as a consequence of a director's ceasing to be a director, his pension entitlement is increased, there are two possibilities as to where this should be disclosed; namely under:
– "compensation for loss of office"; or
– "pensions to directors and former directors".

Where the increase is made **as part of the director's loss of office**, the capital cost of the increase should be disclosed as compensation for loss of office. However, any increase in pension entitlement that takes place after a director has already **ceased to be a director** is disclosed as part of pensions.

7. Amounts paid to third parties

Any consideration paid to or receivable by third parties for making available the services of a director must be disclosed. This applies when the person's services have been made available:
– as a director of the company; or
– while a director, as a director of any of its subsidiaries or otherwise in connection with the management of the company or any of its subsidiaries.

4850
Sch 5 para 5
SI 2008/410

The amounts paid include **non-cash benefits**. Both the nature and value of such benefits must be disclosed.

The Act's **definition of third parties excludes**:
– the director himself;
– any person connected with him or a body corporate controlled by him; and
– the company and any of its subsidiaries.

> EXAMPLE J Ltd enters into a joint venture with K Ltd. As part of the arrangement, K Ltd appoints one of its directors to the board of J Ltd. In respect of the services of the director, J Ltd pays K Ltd £20,000 per annum.
>
> Notwithstanding that the director is remunerated separately by K Ltd and does not receive the £20,000, J Ltd must disclose the payment as sums paid to third parties in respect of directors' services.

C. Highest-paid director

4855

Sch 5 para 2
SI 2008/410

For companies **other than quoted companies**, the Act requires details of the highest-paid director's emoluments and other benefits to be given.

If the sum of the following three elements of remuneration attributable to the directors of an unquoted company, payable in any accounting period (irrespective of its length), is £200,000 or more, details relating to the highest-paid director's emoluments and other benefits must be disclosed in the financial statements:

– **emoluments** paid to or receivable by directors **in respect of qualifying services**;
– gains made by directors on **exercising their share options** (applicable to AIM-traded companies only);
– money and the net value of other assets (other than share options) paid to or receivable by directors **under long-term incentive schemes** in respect of qualifying services.

The highest-paid director is the director to whom the greatest part of the total of the items listed above is attributable. Frequently, the person who is defined as the highest-paid director in one year is not the same person who met the definition in the previous year. Where this happens, the **comparative figures** to be given for the previous year are those relating to the other director. There is no need to state the prior year earnings of the individual who is the highest paid director in the current year.

> MEMO POINTS For **unquoted companies**, gains made on the exercise of share options and the value of shares received under long-term incentive schemes are not taken into account, because these amounts are neither calculated nor disclosed by unlisted companies (¶4835).

4856 **Disclosure** Where the disclosure is needed, the following details are to be presented:
– the total emoluments, excluding pension contributions, of the highest-paid director;
– the amount of any company contributions paid to money purchase pension schemes in respect of the director's qualifying services;
– if the director is a member of a defined benefit scheme, the amount of his **accrued pension** at the end of the year as well as any **accrued lump sum**;
– whether the highest paid director exercised any share options;
– whether any shares were received or receivable by that director under a long-term incentive scheme.

4858 The **accrued pension** and **accrued lump sum** are the amounts that would be payable to the director on reaching normal retirement age (i.e. the earliest date at which the director is entitled to receive a full pension). They are calculated on the following assumptions:
– the director left the company at the end of the year;
– there is no inflation from the end of the year to the director's pension age;
– there is no commutation of the pension or inverse commutation of the lump sum; and
– any amounts attributable to voluntary contributions made by the director to the scheme and any money purchase benefits payable under the scheme were disregarded.

In determining the amounts to be shown as **accrued lump sums**, disclosure is made only where, under the pension scheme rules, the director will automatically receive a lump sum on retirement. If the lump sum is one that would arise only if the director elects commutation of rights to an annual pension, such a lump sum is not disclosed. Similarly, an accrued pension should not include any amount of inverse commutation of a lump sum (i.e., where the director might elect to reduce all or part of his entitlement to a lump sum by taking a larger annual pension).

> EXAMPLE As of the end of the reporting period, the highest-paid director of L Ltd is 10 years away from retirement age. He joined the company as a director 15 years ago. His maximum pension is 25/50 of his final salary after 25 years. (His salary for the current financial year was £100,000.) He is also entitled to a lump sum of 75/50 of final salary after 25 years. If he so elects, however, he may commute the lump sum by taking a larger annual pension.

The accrued pension to be disclosed is:
15/50 × £100,000 = £30,000.

The accrued lump sum to be disclosed is
45/50 × £100,000 = £90,000

The effects of any inverse commutation of the lump sum are ignored, even if the director has already decided to commute the entire lump sum when he retires.

D. Sample disclosure

A sample disclosure is given below.

4860

	20X3	20X2
	£	£
Directors' remuneration		
Aggregate emoluments	700,000	640,000
Amounts receivable under long-term incentive schemes (excluding shares)	80,000	60,000
Company pension contributions to money purchase schemes	17,000	12,000
Compensation for loss of office	-	125,000
Sums paid to third parties for director's services	45,000	-
Excess retirement benefits – current directors	5,000	5,000
– past directors	8,000	8,000

Three directors exercised share options during the year and one became entitled to receive shares under the company's long-term incentive scheme.
Retirement benefits are accruing to three directors under the company's money purchase pension scheme and to two directors under a defined benefit scheme.

Highest paid director		
Aggregate emoluments and benefits under long-term incentive schemes (excluding gains on share options exercised and value of shares received)	195,000	150,000
Company pension contributions to money purchase schemes	5,000	5,000
Defined benefit scheme:		
Accrued pension at end of year	55,000	45,000
Accrued lump sum at end of year	88,000	75,000

The highest-paid director, Mr A, exercised share options during the year and received shares under the executive long-term incentive scheme.

CHAPTER 3

Related party transactions

The users of financial statements assume that companies go about their business independently and without regard to any special interests of their owners, managers and other parties
who have involvement with the enterprise. Transactions are presumed to have been undertaken on an **arm's length basis**; namely on terms such as could have been obtained in a
transaction with an external party, in which each side bargained knowledgeably and freely,
unaffected by any relationship between them.

5000

However, business enterprises such as companies, trusts, partnerships and individuals, can
be related to one another in various ways. As these groups increase in both size and diversity,
transactions between the related entities are commonplace.

To ensure that readers of financial statements understand the degree to which an enterprise
is involved in transactions with such related parties, disclosure in the financial statements of
these transactions is required by company law and by FRS 8, "Related party disclosures".
There are additional requirements for **listed and AIM companies**, which are set out in the
Listing Rules and those of the London Stock Exchange.

The general **accounting and disclosure requirements** concerning related parties under **FRS
102** "The Financial Reporting Standard applicable in the UK and Ireland", that are mandatory
from January 2015, are very similar to existing UK GAAP.

5001

SECTION 1

Identifying related parties

1. General criteria

5002   According to FRS 8, a related party is a person or entity that is related to the reporting entity and can take a number of forms as set out in the table below.

Relationship	Characteristics
1. A person, or a close member of that person's family, is related to a reporting entity if that person	– has control or joint control over the reporting entity; – has significant influence over the reporting entity; or – is a member of the key management personnel of the reporting entity or its parent.
2. An entity is related to a reporting entity if any of the following applies	– the entity and the reporting entity are **members of the same group** (which means that each parent and each subsidiary are also related); – one entity is an **associate or joint venture** of the other (or an associate or joint venture of a member of a group of which the other entity is a member); – **both entities** are joint ventures of the same third party; – one entity is a joint venture of a third entity and the other entity is an associate of that third entity; – the entity is a **retirement benefit scheme** for the benefit of employees of either the reporting entity or an entity related to it; if the reporting entity is itself such a scheme, the sponsoring employers are also related to the reporting entity; – the entity is controlled, or jointly controlled, **by a person** described in a. above; – a person who has control or joint control over the reporting entity has **significant influence** over the entity or is a member of the key management personnel of the entity or its parent.

Control

5004   "Control" is **defined as** the ability to direct the financial and operating policies of an entity with a view to gaining economic benefits from its activities.

This definition seems to suggest that control will exist where a company or an individual holds more than 50% of the reporting entity's voting rights. In addition, the possibility of economic benefit for the controlling party, through this control, must be present. It is not uncommon, however, for shareholders who hold less than 50% of the voting power to actually exercise control over a company's activities. Where this is the case, the control will be recognised.

5006
FRS 8 (13)   **Common control**   Common control arises when two entities are subject to common control either by the same individual or from boards of directors having a controlling nucleus of directors in common. (see ¶5013, Scenario 4.)

Entities under common control are deemed to be related parties because the controlling entity is in a position to compel them to enter into specific transactions and set the particular terms. For either of the controlled parties, the relationship might therefore have a material effect on their operations and results.

Influence

5008   Influence is said to exist when one party (A) is able, despite a theoretical lack of control over another party, (B), to exert such power over the financial and operating policies of B, thereby restricting its ability to pursue its own separate interests.

Common influence Where two parties that enter into a transaction are subject to influence **5010** from the same source to the extent that one of them subordinates its separate interests in favour of the other, common influence is said to exist.

On the other hand, the presence of influence alone from a common source is not sufficient to justify the supposition of a related-party relationship; there has to be subordination as well. Thus, two related parties of a third entity are not necessarily related parties if transactions between them have been conducted on a basis consistent with an arm's length transaction. Every case must be judged on the facts and circumstances pertinent to it.

Establishing the presence of influence and common influence

Where a relationship between two companies results from the power or right that one is **5012** able to exert on the other (i.e., influence), transactions between them have to be disclosed whether or not this power was actually imposed.

In the case of common influence, transactions between the parties need to be disclosed only where the influence was actually exerted and, as a result, one or both of the transacting parties subordinated their separate interests. Each case must be judged on its own merits. For example, if one company sells an asset to another at a price that differs from the commercial price, this would indicate that subordination has taken place. On the other hand, the mere fact that a transaction has taken place at the commercial rate does not necessarily mean that it should not be disclosed.

The following examples illustrate whether related-party relationships exist. **5013**

EXAMPLE Scenario 1
A Ltd has a subsidiary, B Ltd, and an associate, C Ltd.

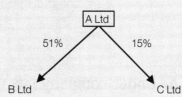

Because C Ltd is subject only to *influence* from A Ltd, while B Ltd is subject to its *control*, the relationship between B Ltd and C Ltd does not normally justify treating them as related parties.

Scenario 2
Mr X sits on the boards of D Ltd and E Ltd.
The mere fact that they have a director in common does not make D Ltd and E Ltd related parties.

Scenario 3
Two companies, F Ltd and G Ltd, are associated companies of the same investor, H Ltd.
Since both companies are subject only to the influence, rather than the control, of H Ltd, the connection is insufficient to regard them as related parties.

Scenario 4
Y Ltd, a manufacturer, purchases raw materials from Z Ltd. The composition of the companies' boards of directors is as follows:

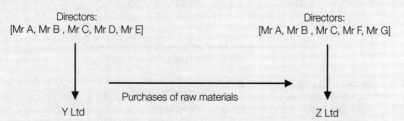

Given that there is a controlling nucleus of directors in common (Messrs A, B and C), Y Ltd and Z Ltd are related parties.

2. Parties that are not related

5015
FRS 8 (12)

The FRC has specified that the following are not regarded as related parties:
- **two entities** that happen to have a director or other member of key management in common, or where a member of key management of one entity happens to have significant influence over the other entity; and
- **two venturers** simply because they happen to share joint control over a joint venture.

5016

The following are also **not considered related** under FRS 8 and fall outside of its scope. (see ¶5073)
- providers of finance;
- trade unions;
- public utilities;
- government departments or agencies that do not control, jointly control, or significantly influence the reporting entity simply by virtue of their normal dealings with an entity (even where they may affect the decision-making or the entity's freedom of action);
- a customer, supplier, franchisor, distributor or general agent with whom an entity transacts a significant volume of business, simply by virtue of the resulting economic dependence.

SECTION 2

Identifying transactions between related parties

5025

Exactly what constitutes a related party transaction is not precisely the same under the Companies Act 2006, FRS 8 and the Listing Rules.

A. Under company law

5026

Company law is concerned primarily with relationships between the reporting entity and its directors (including other persons connected with such directors). FRS 8 is more inclusive and considers the relationships between the reporting entity and other entities.

5027

Directors have a fiduciary duty towards their companies. This means that they are obliged to avoid any circumstances in which their personal interests could conflict with the company's interests.

There are **restrictions on dealings** between companies and directors in terms of which certain transactions have to be approved by shareholders. While under the 1985 Act a range of transactions were prohibited outright, under the 2006 Act many of these transactions are no longer prohibited, though they do require approval by a company's members.

In respect of any **arrangements or transactions between the company and a third party** in which a director is interested, full disclosure must be made both to the board of directors and in the company's financial statements. The disclosure requirements apply whether or not the transactions are prohibited.

l. Definitions

5028
s 250 CA 2006

For the purposes of the Act, the term "**director**" includes any person who occupies the position of director by whatever name called. From this definition it is clear that it is the person's functions and responsibilities, and not his title, that determines whether or not he is a director.

A person can therefore be a director even if his title does not contain the word "director" and, conversely, someone whose title may contain the word "director" is not necessarily a director for purposes of the Act.

It is also possible that someone may be deemed to be a director even if not validly appointed to the post. This is known as a *de facto* director.

Shadow director   A shadow director is a person in accordance with whose directions or instructions the directors of a company are accustomed to act. However, a person is not deemed to be a shadow director by reason only that the directors act on advice given in a professional capacity. Advisers such as accountants or stockbrokers, who are not involved in the running or management of the company, are not considered shadow directors.

5029
s 251 (1), (2)
CA 2006

Alternate director   An **alternate director** is someone whose position is determined by the articles of association and who is appointed by a particular director to fulfil their functions (e.g. voting at board meetings) when they are absent. Attendance and voting at board meetings is only permitted when the appointing director is absent. If the alternate director is not already a director, the other directors must approve his appointment. If the director who appointed the alternate director ceases to be a director, the appointment of the alternate ceases simultaneously. In the interests of clarity and convenience, references to directors will include *de facto*, shadow and alternate directors.

5030

Connected persons   A **person "connected" with a director** is:
– the director's spouse or civil partner, or any other person that the director lives with in an enduring family relationship;
– the director's children or stepchildren, or any children or stepchildren of a person within the above point (who are not children of stepchildren of the director) who live with the director and are under the age of 18;
– the director's parents;
– a company with which the director is associated;
– a person acting in the capacity of trustee of any trust whose beneficiaries include the director or any of the persons described above (including a trustee of a discretionary trust that includes the persons as potential beneficiaries, but excluding a trustee under an employee's share scheme or a pension scheme); and
– a person acting in the capacity as partner of the director or anyone falling into the categories above.

5031
s 252 CA 2006

A director is said to be **connected with a company** if the director, together with the persons connected with him:
– is interested in at least 20% of its equity share capital; or
– is entitled to exercise, or control the exercise of, more than 20% of the voting power at any general meeting.

5032
s 254 CA 2006

A director of a company is said to control a company if:
a. the director, together with the persons connected with him, is interested in any part of the equity share capital of the company, or is entitled to exercise or control the exercise of any part of the voting power at any general meeting of the company;
b. the director, the persons connected with him and the other directors of the company together are interested in more than 50% of the share capital or entitled to exercise or control the exercise of more than 50% of the voting power.

s 255 CA 2006

> MEMO POINTS   For the purpose of determining whether a company is **connected with or controlled by a director**, another company with which the director is connected is not regarded as connected, unless that company is a:
> – partner of the director or of a person who is connected with him, or
> – trustee of a trust the beneficiaries of which include a body corporate with which the director is associated.

Director controls a company   A director of a company is said to control a company if:
– the director, together with the persons connected with him, is interested in any part of the equity share capital of the company, or is entitled to exercise or control the exercise of any part of the voting power at any general meeting of the company; or

5033

– the director, the persons connected with him and the other directors of the company together are interested in more than 50% of the share capital or entitled to exercise or control the exercise of more than 50% of the voting power.

5034
Sch 1 para (5)
CA 2006

Aggregated interests   A director's interests in shares must be aggregated with those of his connected persons. A person is considered to be **interested in shares** if a company is interested in them and one of the following two conditions are met:
– the person is entitled to exercise or control the exercise of more than 50% of that company's voting power at general meetings, or
– that company or its directors are accustomed to act in accordance with his directions or instructions.

5035
s 256 CA 2006

Companies are considered to be **associated** under the Companies Act 2006 if one is a subsidiary of the other or both are subsidiaries of the same company.

5036

The following examples illustrate how the rules and definitions set out above operate in practice.

EXAMPLE   Scenario 1
Mr A owns 19% of the equity share capital of Y Ltd and 21% of Z Ltd. Z Ltd owns 15% of Y Ltd.

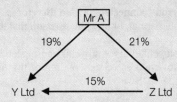

Mr A is connected with Z Ltd because his interest exceeds 20% of the equity share capital.
Before calculating Mr A's effective shareholding in Y Ltd, it must first be determined whether Mr A controls Z Ltd.
Mr A's holding is less than 50% and, because Z Ltd is neither a partner nor a trustee of Mr A, its holding in Y Ltd is not aggregated with Mr A's. Interestingly, though Mr A theoretically has an effective holding of 22.15% in Y Ltd (19 % + [21 % of 15%]) he is not connected with it.

Scenario 2
Ms B owns 7% of the equity share capital of W Ltd and 60% of X Ltd. X Ltd owns 18% of W Ltd.

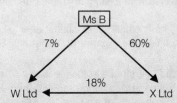

Ms B has an effective holding of 17.8% (7% + [60% of 18%]) in W Ltd, yet she is connected with it. The reason is that through her holding in X Ltd (which she controls by virtue of her shareholding being greater than 50%) she is able to control the exercise of the full 18% of X Ltd in W Ltd. This, together with her direct holding of 7%, means that her effective holding is 25%, which makes her connected with W Ltd.

Scenario 3
Mr C owns 5% of the equity share capital of U Ltd and 25% of V Ltd. V Ltd owns 22% of U Ltd.

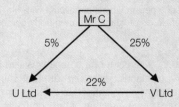

Mr C is connected with V Ltd because he owns more than 20% of the equity shares.

In determining whether he is connected with U Ltd, the interest of V Ltd should be ignored. Mr C is not assumed to be interested in the shares of U Ltd owned by V Ltd because, owning just 25% of V Ltd, he does not control that company or how it votes in U Ltd. Therefore, he is not connected with U Ltd.

The situation would be different if Mr C held more than 50% of the equity shares of V Ltd. In this event he would be able to control the vote of V Ltd in U Ltd and – because V Ltd can exercise more than 20% of the vote in U Ltd – U Ltd would be regarded as being connected with Mr C.

2. Transactions in which directors have a material interest

5040 Under the Companies Act 2006, directors are required to declare the nature and extent of any interest, direct or indirect, that they have in a proposed, or existing, transaction or arrangement entered into by the company. The declaration should be made as soon as is reasonably practicable and may be made:
– at a meeting of the directors; or
– by notice in writing; or
– by general notice.

If a director has declared his interest at the time the transaction was proposed, and before it was entered into by the company, he does not need to repeat that declaration once the transaction becomes an existing transaction.

A director **need not declare any interest** that:
– cannot reasonably be regarded as likely to give rise to a conflict of interest;
– the other directors already know about, or ought reasonably to know about; or
– concerns the terms of his service contract, considered (or to be considered) by a meeting of directors.

A director **may give a general notice** of his interests. This is a declaration that a director is interested in another company or connected with another person. If the company then enters into a contract with the company or person named in the general notice, the director does not need to declare any direct or indirect interest that arises as a result. In order to be effective, the general notice must state the nature and extent of the director's interest or connection.

3. Loans and other transactions

5050 **Rules under CA 2006**   The following transactions, which require members' approval under the Companies Act 2006, as well as exemptions applying to them, are discussed below.

5052 **Loans**   In general, all loans to directors (including the provision of a guarantee or security
s 197 CA 2006 in connection with such loans) must be **approved by a resolution** of the company's members. If the director is also a director of the company's holding company, the transaction must be approved by a resolution of the holding company's members.

Member approval may not be required in respect of small loans or transactions less than $10,000.

MEMO POINTS   The **value of a loan** is the principal amount of the loan (i.e. without interest).

5053 **Quasi-loans**   A quasi-loan is a transaction where one party (the creditor) pays an amount for another (the borrower), or reimburses expenditure incurred by another party for the borrower; where either:
– the transaction's terms are such that the borrower (or a person on his behalf) will reimburse the creditor; or
– the circumstances surrounding the transaction give rise to a liability on the borrower to reimburse the creditor.

An **example** of a quasi-loan is where a director uses a company credit card or orders goods for himself on the company's corporate account on the understanding that while the company will settle the liability the director will reimburse the company later.

A public company, or a private company associated with a public company, may only enter into a credit transaction or give a guarantee or provide security in connection with a credit transaction entered into by a third party with a director of the company, or its holding company or a person connected with such a director, if the transaction is **approved by a resolution** of the company.

5054
s 201 CA 2006

Credit transactions   As with quasi-loans, a company, or a private company associated with a public company, may only enter into a credit transaction or give a guarantee or provide security in connection with a credit transaction entered into by another third party with a director of the company, or its holding company or a person connected with such a director, if the transaction is **approved by a resolution** of the company. An **exemption** exists in respect of minor transactions.

5055

Indirect arrangements   A company may not enter into an arrangement as a result of which **another person becomes party to a transaction** that would have required member approval had the company itself entered into it, and where that other person receives a benefit of any kind from the company (or its holding company, subsidiary or fellow subsidiary) unless the arrangement in question has been approved by a resolution of the members of the company.

General exemptions from members' approval

5056

In addition to the exemptions that apply to the particular transactions discussed above, the following are also exempted:
– intra-group transactions;
– directors' business expenditure (limits apply); and
– directors' expenditure on defending proceedings or in connection with regulatory action/-investigation.

B. Under FRS 8

1. General rule

5068
FRS 8 (2.6)

The notion of related party transactions is wider, and more comprehensive, under FRS 8 than under the Act.

The standard defines a related party transaction as "the transfer of assets or liabilities or the performance of services by, to or for a related party irrespective of whether a price is charged".

Unlike the Act, FRS 8 does not exempt transactions from the requirement to disclose on the grounds of the **size of the consideration** (including where there was **no consideration**), or on the basis that the transaction took place at **arm's length**.

5069

The following are **examples of transactions** that are specified by FRS 8 to require disclosure:
– purchases or sales of goods (finished and unfinished), property and other assets,
– rendering or receiving of services;
– agency and leasing arrangements;
– transfer of research and development;
– licence agreements;

– provision of finance (e.g. loans and equity contributions – cash or non-cash), guarantees or collateral security;
– management contracts.

Note that this is not an exhaustive list.

In certain cases, the relevant transaction might not involve a consideration and, for this reason, might also not appear in a company's accounting records. Nevertheless, it is the responsibility of the reporting entity to capture this data for disclosure in the financial statements.

5070

Examples of such transactions are:
– management services provided free of charge by one company to another;
– goods manufactured under a patent granted free of charge by a fellow subsidiary;
– guarantees to third parties in respect of other group companies;
– interest-free loans;
– loans of assets at no charge (including, but not limited to, fixed property, vehicles, etc.).

2. Scope

The FRS applies to all financial statements that are intended to give a true and fair view of a reporting entity's financial position and profit or loss for a period. However, disclosure is not required by the FRS:

5072

– in consolidated financial statements of intra-group transactions that have been eliminated on consolidation;

FRS 8 (3), (16)

– of transactions entered into between two or more members of a group, provided that any subsidiary undertaking that is a party to the transaction is wholly owned by a member of that group (note, however, that this exemption applies only where all subsidiary undertakings that are party to the transaction are wholly owned, directly or indirectly, by the ultimate controlling entity of the group),
– of pension contributions paid to a pension fund;
– of emoluments in respect of services as an employee (however, the rules on disclosure of directors' emoluments apply, see ¶4800);
– where there is a legal duty of confidentiality (e.g. banks do not have to disclose transactions made in the normal course of business).

In addition, neither the **relationship** nor **transactions** between the reporting entity and the following parties that arise as a result of the **normal roles and functions** of those other parties need be disclosed:

5073
FRS 8 (4)

– providers of finance in the course of their business;
– utility companies;
– government departments and their sponsored bodies;
– customers, suppliers, franchisers, distributors or general agents with whom an entity transacts a significant volume of business.

C. Materiality

Only material items need to be disclosed. Transactions should not be excluded because they might be at arm's length or in the normal course of business. All material related party transactions, whether normal or abnormal, must be disclosed. According to FRS 8, transactions are material when their disclosure "might reasonably be expected to influence decisions made by the users of general purpose financial statements". This definition renders material almost any related party transaction that might be sensitive from the shareholders' point of view, even before the financial amount is taken into account.

5082

However, where the related party is:
– a director, key manager, or other individual in a position to influence, or accountable for stewardship of, the reporting entity; or
– a member of the close family of any individual referred to above; or
– an entity controlled by any individual referred to above;

the materiality of the transaction must be considered not only in terms of its significance to the reporting entity, but also to the other related party.

SECTION 3

Disclosures

A. Under company law

5085   This section deals with information to be disclosed in respect of **directors**.

1. General rule

5087   In the case of a company that does not prepare group accounts, details of:
s 413 CA 2006   – advances and credits granted by the company to its directors; and
– guarantees of any kind entered into by the company on behalf of its directors;

must be shown in the notes to the accounts. In the case of a parent company that prepares group accounts, this information must also be provided in relation to subsidiary undertakings.

The details required of an advance or credit are its amount, an indication of the interest rate, its main conditions and any amounts repaid. In addition, the total amount of advances or credits and the total amounts repaid must be stated.

The details required of a guarantee are:
a. its main terms;
b. the amount of the maximum liability that may be incurred by the company (or its subsidiary);
c. any amount paid and any liability incurred by the company (or its subsidiary) for the purpose of fulfilling the guarantee;
d. the totals of amounts stated in (b) and (c):
– in respect of each of the above transactions, the aggregate amounts outstanding at the end of the financial year made by the company or its subsidiaries; and
– the number of officers for whom transactions in each category were made.

2. Comparative figures

5088   Although FRS 8 is silent on the matter of comparative figures, they are required by the Act
Sch 1 para 7 (1)   in respect of related party transactions.
SI 2008/410
The **following scenarios** can arise where the related parties in the current year are not the same as those in the previous year:
a) Where a party is a related party in the **current year**, but was **not in the previous year**, there are no comparatives to be disclosed because any transactions before the parties were related did not affect the results.

b) Where a party was **related in the previous year**, but **not in the current period**, the comparative figures should be disclosed. If the presence of comparative figures with no corresponding amount for the current period might cause confusion, an explanation should be given.

B. Under FRS 8

Two separate elements of disclosure can be identified: (1) disclosure of the existence of control, and (2) disclosure of transactions and inter-party balances.

5090

1. Control

Where the reporting company is controlled by another party (¶5004), the following disclosures are required, whether or not any transactions took place between the parties:
– the related party relationship;
– the name of the controlling party; and
– the name of the ultimate controlling party; if appropriate.

5091
FRS 8 (5)

Disclosure of the existence of control by a parent company is required even where the reporting entity is a wholly owned subsidiary. The exemption in respect of 90% subsidiaries that applies to the disclosure of transactions and balances with other group members does not apply.

The controlling party need not be an individual person or other entity, but may consist of two or more parties acting in concert. Where no ultimate parent company is disclosed because the company is controlled by a trust or other unincorporated entity, it is necessary to consider whether that entity itself is controlled by a person whose identity should be disclosed as the ultimate controlling party.

If the controlling party, or ultimate controlling party, is not known, this fact must be disclosed.

Where the relationship is such that the reporting entity is a **subsidiary**, additional disclosures applicable to subsidiaries are required by Schedule 5 of the Act.

2. Transactions and balances

Transactions

The following details must be disclosed in respect of material transactions (see ¶5082) undertaken by the reporting entity and its related parties. These disclosures are to be made whether or not a price was charged:
– the names of the transacting related parties,
– the relationship between the parties;
– a description of the transactions;
– the amounts involved; and
– any other elements of the transactions necessary for an understanding of the financial statements.

5093

Further disclosures are required concerning the **year-end balances**, discussed at ¶5095.

The example given by FRS 8 to illustrate the meaning of the phrase "any other elements" is that of a transfer of a major asset at an amount materially different from the price that would have been obtainable on commercial terms.

The Act requires disclosures of certain transactions in which directors are **materially interested**. It does, however, **exempt from disclosure** those transactions entered into in the normal course of business, and at arm's length (i.e. on terms no less favourable to the reporting entity or its subsidiary than would have been reasonable if the director had not been a director). FRS 8 does not give this exemption and consequently any such transactions remain to be disclosed in the financial statements.

Related party balances

5095   The following information regarding balances between the parties must also be disclosed:
– the amounts due to or from related parties at the balance sheet date;
– the amount of any provisions for doubtful debts due at the balance sheet date; and
– any amounts written off in the period in respect of debts due to or receivable from related parties.

The requirement to disclose the balances is separate from the requirement to disclose **transactions** that take place during a given financial year. If this were not the case, and assuming that there is a material long-term loan in existence, but with no material transactions during the current year, the transaction would not be disclosed. This could potentially be to the detriment of shareholders, potential shareholders and other users.

5097
FRS 8 (6)
Aggregation of balances   To reduce the volume of information to be given if each transaction with each related party were disclosed, FRS 8 generally allows aggregation of similar transactions with similar parties. The **exception is where** the disclosure of particular transactions is required by law or is otherwise necessary for a proper understanding of the financial statements.

FRS 8 (21)
However, aggregation should not be used in such a way that significant transactions are obscured or concealed. Therefore, purchases or sales of goods with group companies should not be aggregated with purchases or sales of fixed assets.

5098

EXAMPLE   The following illustrates the disclosure of related party transactions in the notes to the financial statements.

B Ltd
Notes to the financial statements at 30 September 20X3
Related party transactions
During the year, the group purchased goods from, and sold goods to, X Ltd, a company owned by Mr X, a director of the company, as follows:

	20X3 £000	20X2 £000
Sales:		
Services supplied	401	266
Goods sold	58	27
	459	293
Purchases:		
Goods	122	69
Fixed assets	212	204
	334	273

The amounts outstanding at year-end on these purchases and sales are £95,000 and £85,000 respectively (20X2 – £57,000 and £52,000), and are shown separately under creditors and debtors due within one year respectively.

SECTION 4

FRSSE requirements for small companies

5100   If a reporting entity enters into a transaction with, or on behalf of, a related party (whether or not a price is charged) and the **transaction is material** to the reporting entity, it should be disclosed in the financial statements. The **following details** must be given:

– the names of the transacting related parties;
– details of the relationship between the parties;
– a description of the transactions;
– the amounts involved;
– any other elements of the transactions necessary for an understanding of the financial statements;
– the balances due to or from related parties at the balance sheet date including, where necessary, provisions for doubtful debts due;
– amounts in respect of debts due to or from related parties that were written off during the period.

Transactions with related parties may be **disclosed on an aggregated basis** unless separate disclosure of an individual transaction (or series of individual but connected transactions) is required by law or is necessary for a proper appreciation of the effect on the financial statements of the reporting entity.

Personal guarantees given by directors in respect of borrowings by the reporting entity should be disclosed in the notes.

Separate disclosure is required for amounts included in the profit and loss account under "Investment income" and "Other interest receivable and similar income" that were received, or are receivable from, group undertakings. Similarly, amounts included under "Interest payable and similar charges" paid (or payable) to group undertakings should be shown separately.

5102
FRSSE 15.3 – 15.5

Commitments undertaken for the benefit of a parent undertaking or fellow subsidiary, or a subsidiary undertaking of the company, must be shown separately from those commitments in respect of **pensions** or **provisions** and also from each other.

Disclosure is not required of:
a. pension contributions paid to a pension fund;
b. emoluments for services as an employee of the reporting entity;
c. transactions with the following if the transaction occurs simply as a result of their role as providers of finance in the course of their business in that regard:
– utility companies;
– government departments and their sponsored bodies; or
– a customer, supplier, franchiser, distributor or general agent.

5104
FRSSE 15.7

When the reporting entity is **controlled by** another party, there should be disclosure of the related party relationship and the name of that party and, if different, that of the ultimate controlling party. If the controlling party or ultimate controlling party of the reporting entity is not known, that fact should be disclosed. This information should be disclosed irrespective of whether any transactions have taken place between the controlling parties and the reporting entity.

5106
FRSSE 15.8

CHAPTER 4

Post-balance sheet events

Events that occur between the balance sheet date and the date on which the financial statements are approved by the board of directors, are known as post-balance sheet events. The **two categories** of post-balance sheet events are **adjusting** and **non-adjusting events**, each of which requires a different accounting treatment.

5700
FRS 21 (3)

The **main principle** is that adjusting events require changes to be made to amounts included within the financial statements whereas material non-adjusting events need only be addressed by way of a note to the accounts.

The key reporting standard is FRS 21 "Events after the Balance Sheet Date", which is **mandatory** for all reporting entities **except those** applying the Financial Reporting Standard for Smaller Entities (FRSSE). Their are no differences in accounting treatment for small companies adopting the FRSSE.

5702
FRS 21 (8)

Events occurring after the date the accounts have been signed by the directors are not covered by FRS 21.

MEMO POINTS   The FRC has published **FRS 102** "The Financial Reporting Standard applicable in the UK and Republic of Ireland" which comes into force from 1 January 2015, although earlier adoption is permitted. In terms of post balance sheet events there are no major differences between the requirements of FRS 102 (Section 32) and current UK GAAP. However, there are **small differences** in terms of terminology. For instance, the new standard refers to post balance sheet events as events after the end of the reporting period. FRS 102 is also less detailed than FRS 21.

1. Adjusting events

Adjusting events are those events that **existed at the balance sheet date**, but for which information only came to light later, thus requiring a revision of the amount recorded in the financial statements.

5706
FRS 21 (8)
FRSSE 14.1

Failure to recognise the effect of these adjusting events on the financial statements may raise doubts as to the appropriateness of the going concern assertion.

Statutory events, custom and practice

5710
FRS 21 (22)

The statutory requirements include the following:
– a declaration of dividends paid by subsidiaries and associate companies relating to periods prior to the balance sheet date;
– the effects of significant changes in rates of taxation; or
– amounts appropriated to reserves.

Non-statutory events

5712
FRS 21 (9)

It is not possible to produce a definitive list of potential non-statutory events. The following list gives some possible examples but is not intended to be exhaustive:
1. Valuations that provide evidence of an impairment (¶1550) in value e.g. property or other fixed asset investments.
2. Changes in debtor balances due to a renegotiation of the terms or insolvency of one of the debtors.
3. Discovery of fraud or material errors.
4. Subsequent determination of a purchase price or proceeds of a sale of assets purchased or sold before the year-end.
5. Incorrect (material) estimates of profits on long term contracts (¶2200).
6. Sale proceeds from stock (¶2000) after the balance sheet date differing from net realisable value.
7. Receipt of information regarding rates of taxation.
8. The determination after the balance sheet date of profit-sharing or bonus payments, relating to legal or constructive obligations to make such payments, at the balance sheet date.
9. Insurance or other legal claims not quantified at the balance sheet date. For instance, the settlement of a court case after the balance sheet date that results in the entity effectively having an obligation at the balance sheet date. As a result, any previous provision recognised under FRS 12 should be adjusted or a new provision recognised.
10. Discontinued operations.

5714
FRS 3 (4)

Discontinued operations   A decision to terminate an operation made after the end of the financial period, but before the accounts are signed, will constitute an "adjusting event", even if this indicates that applying the going concern concept to the whole or a significant part of the company is not appropriate. In this instance, **a provision for anticipated losses** arising from the closure should be made, as well as disclosure by way of note and the disclosures required by FRS 3, "Reporting financial performance", given in the profit and loss account and notes thereto.

5716
FRS 12 (75)

In accordance with FRS 12 "Provisions, contingent liabilities and contingent assets", **closure** or **reorganisation** provisions may only be included as an adjusting event where the closure was effectively in progress at the end of the year.

Taxation

5720

There are a number of areas where **tax problems can arise** in relation to post balance sheet events, including directors' emoluments and loan accounts. Directors' emoluments such as bonuses, are often determined after the year-end on the basis of draft final accounts and any provisions made will impact on the corporation tax charge for the financial year. These provisions are classified as adjusting events and are charged to the profit and loss account with the credit to the directors' loan account. A tax obligation (PAYE/NI) could arise at the time the bonus is credited and therefore only the net bonus should be credited.

The picture can be further complicated by other post balance sheet adjustments resulting from, for instance, stock valuation adjustments, provisions for warranty claims, or valuation of long term work in progress.

Disclosures

The **general rule** is that all **adjusting post-balance sheet events** must be reflected in the financial statements. Separate disclosure of adjusting events by way of note is not a specific requirement of the standard.   **5722**

However, the Companies Act requires that the **directors' report** includes particulars of materially adjusting events affecting the company which have occurred since the year-end, although the Act does not make any distinction between adjusting and non-adjusting events.

Window dressing The reversal in the post-balance sheet period of significant sales recorded prior to the balance sheet date, in order to boost turnover and debtors, is more commonly known as window dressing. This practice is discouraged.   **5723**

2. Non-adjusting events

Non-adjusting post-balance sheet events are categorised as such, if no evidence of any transaction existed at the balance sheet date but is forthcoming before the accounts are signed.   **5730**
FRS 21(3b)

If the event is material then disclosure should be made by way of a note to the accounts, in order to ensure that the financial statements are not misleading.

The **most common types** of disclosed non-adjusting events include the following:
- financial restructuring;
- the management of fixed assets; and
- operational activities.

  MEMO POINTS   The FRC (formerly the ASB) has issued guidance on the accounting treatment for **contingent fee arrangements** that are incomplete at the balance sheet date. The resolution of a contingent event in the post-balance sheet period is deemed to have occurred after the balance sheet date and, as such, the accounting treatment adopted at the financial year-end should not be adjusted. There are two generally accepted accounting treatments covering costs incurred under contingent fee contracts that straddle a period end; namely the costs can be expensed as incurred or recognised as work in progress at the balance sheet date.

Financial restructuring

Financial restructuring includes: **5732**
- mergers and acquisitions;
- reconstructions; and
- issues of shares and debentures.

EXAMPLE   **X Ltd. Report and accounts**
Non-adjusting event – acquisitions

A company prepared its balance sheet as at 31 December 20X3 which was then approved by the board of directors on 31 March 20X4. On 20 February 20X4 the company announced the acquisition of a 100% stake in BSE Energy, based in Northumberland. As the contract was signed after the financial year-end it is classified as a **non-adjusting event** with the following information being disclosed by way of note.

Notes to the accounts (extract)

The company agreed to pay £200m. As at 31 December 20X3 BSE Energy had net debt of £135m and preference shares totalling £65m. The acquisition will be wholly financed from existing internal resources and is conditional upon both groups of shareholders as well as the regulatory authorities approving the deal.

Management of fixed assets

Management of fixed assets includes the: **5734**
- purchases and sales of fixed assets and investments;
- fixed assets or stock losses resulting from a catastrophe such as fire or flooding; and
- a post-balance sheet decline in the value of fixed assets or property (verified).

An example of a non-adjusting event is a fall in the market value of investments between the balance sheet date and the date the financial statements are authorised. As the fall in value does not usually reflect conditions that existed at the balance sheet date, the value of the investments is not adjusted, although additional disclosures in the notes may be required.

Operational activities

5736 Operational activities include the following:
- exchange rate fluctuations;
- government action (i.e. nationalisation), strikes or other labour disputes;
- opening or extending new trading activities; and
- the discontinuance of a business not envisaged at the year-end.

> EXAMPLE **Exchange rate fluctuations**
>
> **Company A** has translated the results of its **overseas subsidiary** at the exchange rate prevailing at the balance sheet date. Subsequent to the financial year-end the sterling-zloty exchange rate declined turning a small moderate profit into a loss. Accordingly, the effect of the exchange rate fluctuations should not be adjusted for in the financial statements although they should be referred to in the directors' report as a post-balance sheet event.
>
> If the **fluctuations are so material** that non-disclosure might affect the true and fair view, then their financial effect should be estimated and disclosed by way of note to the financial statements as a non-adjusting post balance sheet event.

5738 **Directors' interests** Any change in directors' interests occurring between the end of the financial period and a date not more than one month prior to the date of the notice of the annual general meeting, at which the financial statements are presented, should be disclosed. Similar rules apply to **major interests** in a company's share capital.

Dividends

5739
FRS 21 (12)

Where an entity declares a dividend to holders of equity instruments **after the balance sheet date**, it is not required to recognise those dividends as a liability under FRS 12 at the balance sheet date. This is because the obligation does not meet the criteria of a present obligation in FRS 12. Details must, however, be given in the notes to the accounts. Dividends declared by a subsidiary or associate company after the balance sheet date should also be treated as a non-adjusting event.

Disclosures

5740
FRS 21 (21)

Disclosure of post-balance sheet events are required where:
- the event is a **material non-adjusting event** and where non-disclosure would impair the ability of users of financial statements to fully understand the financial position; or
- the **going concern assertion** is brought into question resulting from, for instance, a deterioration in the trading results and financial position of the entity or the withdrawal of credit facilities by the bank.

An entity **should not prepare financial statements** on a going concern basis if it intends to liquidate the entity or cease trading. If the deterioration in operating performance and financial position after the balance sheet date is very severe, and calls into question the going concern assumption, a fundamental change to the basis of accounting is required, rather than adjusting the amounts originally recognised.

5741 The **general rule** is that disclosure of non-adjusting events should be stated by way of a note to the accounts and include the nature of the event and an estimate of the financial effect. If this is not possible then a statement should be added advising that it is not possible to quantify the effect. Where applicable, any taxation implications should be separately disclosed.

EXAMPLE **Infrarail Group Plc**
Annual report and accounts 20X3
Notes to the financial statements (extract)

Non-adjusting post-balance sheet events
Non-adjusting post-balance sheet events arising from the actions of the secretary of state for transport, local government and the regions are:

Administration order
The administration order against Infrarail Plc placed it in a position of default in relation to debt of £2,963m included within creditors greater than one year, which immediately became repayable on demand. No adjustment has been made to reflect this and the debt has been classified in the summary group balance sheet consistent with the position as at 30 September 20X3.

Channel Tunnel Rail Link Railway derivatives
In 20X3 Infrarail Limited entered into a series of interest rate swaps and gilt lock transactions to hedge the financing costs associated with the purchase of section 1 of the CTRL. The bank providing these hedges required certain standard credit protection terms, which subsequently gave it the option to force termination of these hedges should Infrarail be placed in administration. To avoid unnecessary losses and an event of default within Infrarail Limited, the directors pre-emptively instructed the bank to unwind the hedges in an orderly manner. The final termination value of the hedges was a loss of £15.8m

Other non-adjusting post-balance sheet events are:

Infrarail Travel
As disclosed in Note 1, Awayday Ltd, a **joint venture** between Infrarail Travel and First Group, closed its website and ceased commercial operations on 15 November 20X3. Investments include a balance of £61,000 in respect of an investment in Awayday Ltd. No provision has been made for additional cost that may be incurred to complete the disposal or closure of the company, including an agreed settlement with the Normanton Group of £1.6m.

Date of authorisation An entity is required to disclose the date the financial statements were authorised for issue and the signatory. If the owners have the power to amend the financial statements after issue, the entity should disclose this fact.

5742

Updating disclosures Where an entity receives information after the balance sheet date concerning events that existed at the balance sheet date, the disclosures should be updated to reflect the new information. This information should be supplied even when it does not affect the amounts recognised in the financial statements. An example would be where evidence comes to light after the balance sheet date, concerning a contingent liability that existed at the balance sheet date.

5743
FRS 21 (19)

Taxation FRS 21 does not give a measurement or definition of **immateriality** as it is dependent on the size and nature of an item and the particular circumstances in which it arises. The extent to which an item of accounting information is material is determined by the fact that its omission from the financial statements could influence the decision making of its users.

5744

The planned **reduction in corporation tax rates** over a period to 2014 will have implications for **deferred tax calculations** and their disclosure. Amendments to tax legislation are usually not reflected in the amounts included in the balance sheet until the law is in force at the relevant balance sheet date. However, FRS 21, "Events after the balance sheet date", requires non-adjusting post-balance sheet events to be disclosed in relation to announced changes in tax rates, where the effect is material and where the changes have not yet been enacted.

Reclassification of non-adjusting events

In **exceptional circumstances** and in accordance with the **prudence concept**, an event previously classified as non-adjusting may need to be redefined as an adjusting event. In this instance full disclosure of the adjustment is required.

5745

5746 An example would be the disposal of a significant fixed asset after the balance sheet date that was not previously envisaged and that would normally have been classified as a non-adjusting event.

However, **if a large loss was incurred** on the disposal of an asset, this might provide evidence of an impairment requiring an adjustment to the value of fixed assets recorded in the balance sheet, as required by FRS 11. It should be noted that the standard itself does not provide any guidance as to the circumstances under which the provision should be applied. Adjusting events should not be reclassified as non-adjusting events.

Summary

5750

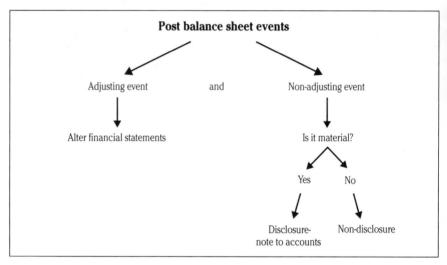

Adjusting events: Conditions exist at the balance sheet date. Separate disclosure by way of note is not specifically required by the standard, although the Companies Act requirements for the directors' report may well require disclosure.

Non-adjusting events: Conditions did not exist at the balance sheet date. Disclosures required in the notes to the accounts for material items.

CHAPTER 5

Auditors' reports

A. Audit reports on Annual Financial Statements

All companies incorporated under the Companies Act, with the exception of dormant companies, are obliged to produce annual financial statements and lodge a copy with the Registrar of Companies. Most companies are required to have their annual financial statements audited by independent accountants, although some entities meeting specific criteria can claim exemption.

5800
s 394 CA 2006

The Companies Act specifies that the accounts should consist of a balance sheet, a profit and loss account and accompanying notes. In determining whether the financial statements give a **true and fair view** of the state of affairs of the reporting entity at the close of the financial year, the auditor should consider the accounting requirements not only of the Act but also UK GAAP in general (e.g. FRSs, SORPs). Where **a company fails to comply** with the these requirements, an auditor should assess the effect on the financial statements and consider whether the audit opinion should include details of any non compliance. An **audit opinion** can be qualified (e.g. reservations) or unqualified (true and fair view).

> MEMO POINTS   An **"Unqualified Opinion"**, does not represent a clean bill of health as the Auditor can only give a reasonable assurance regarding the financial statements and the health of the company itself.

In addition, auditors are required to satisfy themselves that **proper accounting records** have been kept and that the financial statements are in agreement with them. Moreover, they must make certain that any information given in the **directors' report** is consistent with the books and records of the company.

5801

If any of these **requirements are not met,** or if the auditors have not been able to obtain all the necessary information and explanations needed to enable them to form their opinion, they are obliged to disclose this fact in their audit report.

[*MEMO POINTS*]   Information that is required to be given in the **directors' report** or elsewhere in the financial statements, such as disclosures of directors' emoluments, benefits, loans or transactions required by Schedule 3 of The Small Companies and Groups (Accounts and Directors' Report) Regulations 2008 (SI 2008/409) and Schedule 5 to the Large and Medium-sized Companies and Groups (Accounts and Reports) Regulations 2008 (SI 2008/410), should be provided by the auditors if the directors fail to provide this information.

5802   **Key sections of an audit report**   In the following paragraphs, the various **essential elements of an auditors' report** are discussed, including:
- a title identifying the persons to whom the report is addressed;
- an introduction identifying the financial statements referred to;
- a headed section dealing with both directors' and auditors' responsibilities;
- a headed section dealing with the basis of the auditors' opinion (scope paragraph);
- a headed section expressing the auditors' opinion;
- the auditors' name and signature;
- the auditors' address; and
- the date of the report.

[*MEMO POINTS*]   The **Companies Act 2006** plus strong support for a shorter audit report by institutional investors, public sector bodies and some auditing firms following the Auditing Practices Board's 2007 Discussion Paper "The Auditor's Report: A time for change?" resulted in the revision of ISA 700 in 2009.
2. Bulletin 2010/2 "Compendium of Illustrative Auditor's Reports on United Kingdom Private Sector Financial Statements for periods ended on or after 15 December 2010" was revised in February 2011, to reflect an auditor's responsibility to report on reading all financial and non-financial information in the annual report and to identify any material inconsistencies.
3. The FRC has issued **ISA (UK and Ireland) 700** "The Independent Auditor's Report on Financial Statements (Revised June 2013)". The important point to note is that the format of auditor's reports under this version may not be perfectly aligned with the format required by ISA 700 (issued by the IAASB).

---

1. Title and addressee

5804
ISA 700 (Revised) (7)   The Companies Act 2006 requires the auditor to report to the company's members because the audit is undertaken on their behalf. ISA 700 (Revised) states that the auditors' report should have an appropriate title and that it may be appropriate to use the term "Independent Auditor" to distinguish the auditors' report from reports that might be issued by others. Auditors' reports are typically addressed to either the members or shareholders of the company.

[EXAMPLE]   Sample Title and Address
INDEPENDENT AUDITORS' REPORT TO THE MEMBERS OF A LIMITED

---

2. Identification of financial statements

5805
ISA 700 (8)   The **auditors' report** should identify the financial statements that have been audited, including the date of and period covered by the financial statements.

Usually, the financial statements of larger companies contain other financial information (e.g. in the directors' report or the chairman's statement). Auditors have no responsibility for such information beyond being satisfied that it is consistent with the financial statements. It is therefore necessary that they **clearly identify** the parts of the financial statements to which their opinion does refer.

[EXAMPLE]   We have audited the annual financial statements of [*name of entity*] for the year ended [*date*], which comprise the profit and loss account, the balance sheet, the cash flow statement, the STRGL, and the related notes 1 to 22. The financial reporting framework that has been applied in their preparation is applicable law and United Kingdom Accounting Standards.

Disclaimer   It is becoming increasingly common for this introductory paragraph to include wording specifically designed to limit the parties to whom the auditor acknowledges responsibility or duty of care. This development has not taken place under the aegis of the FRC but rather as a decision by some members of the profession.

5806

[EXAMPLE]   **Sample of wording to limit the parties to whom auditors acknowledge responsibility**
This report is made solely to the company's members, as a body, in accordance with Sections 495 and 496 of the Companies Act 2006. Our audit work has been undertaken so that we might state to the company's members those matters we are required to state to them in an auditors' report and for no other purpose. To the fullest extent permitted by law, we do not accept or assume responsibility to anyone other than the company and the company's members as a body, for our audit work, for this report, or for the opinions we have formed.

[MEMO POINTS]   If the company is a **quoted company**, this disclaimer should also include a reference to the Companies Act 2006: "This report is made solely to the company's members, as a body, in accordance with Sections 495, 496 and 497 of the Companies Act 2006."

FRSSE   In the case of companies that prepare financial statements in accordance with FRSSE, the auditors should refer to this fact in the introductory paragraph of their report. They can also but need not, draw attention to such a company's exemption from the requirement to present a **cash flow statement**.

5807

[EXAMPLE]   **Extract from auditors' report of a company that prepares its financial statements in accordance with the FRSSE**
We have audited the annual financial statements of [*name of entity*] for the year ended [*date*] comprising the profit and loss account, the balance sheet, the STRGL. The financial reporting framework that has been applied in their preparation is applicable law and the Financial Reporting Standard for Smaller Entities.

---

3. Respective responsibilities of auditors and directors

The report should include a statement that distinguishes between the responsibilities of auditors, and those of directors. The distinction would be clearly expressed by including the following:
– a statement that the preparation of the financial statements is the **responsibility of the directors**;
– a **description** of these responsibilities or a reference to them if they appear elsewhere in the financial statements or accompanying information;
– a statement that the auditors' responsibility is to audit and **express an opinion** on the financial statements in accordance with an applicable legal requirements and International Standards on Auditing (UK and Ireland). The report should also state that those standards require the auditor to comply with the FRC's Ethical Standards for auditors;
– the nationality of the accounting standards and the law under which the financial statements have been prepared.

5808
ISA 700 (Revised)
(11)

[EXAMPLE]   **Extract from auditors' report**
Respective responsibilities of directors and auditors
As described in the Director's Responsibilities Statement, the company's directors are responsible for the preparation of the financial statements and for being satisfied that they give a true and fair view.
Our responsibility is to audit the financial statements in accordance with applicable law and International Standards on Auditing (UK and Ireland). Those standards require us to comply with the Auditing Practices Board's Ethical Standards for Auditors.

4. Scope of the audit of the financial statements

5809
APB Bulletin 2010/2
(2)

The auditor's report should either:
– cross refer to a "Statement of the Scope of an Audit" that is maintained on the FRC's website; or
– cross refer to a "Statement of the Scope of an Audit" that is included elsewhere in the Annual Report; or
– include a description of the scope of an audit as given in the following example.

> [EXAMPLE] An audit involves obtaining evidence about the amounts and disclosures in the financial statements sufficient to give reasonable assurance that the financial statements are free from material misstatement, whether caused by fraud or error. This includes an assessment of: whether the accounting policies are appropriate to the company's circumstances and have been consistently applied and adequately disclosed; the reasonableness of significant accounting estimates made by the directors; and the overall presentation of the financial statements. In addition, we read all the financial and non-financial information in the [describe the annual report] to identify material inconsistencies with the audited financial statements. If we become aware of any apparent material misstatements or inconsistencies we consider the implications for our report.

5. Classification of companies

5810
APB Bulletin 2010/2
(5)

Company Law (and the Listing Rules) classify companies in a number of ways, which affect the content of the auditors report. These differences are shown in the examples provided throughout the chapter.

Small companies

5811

The small companies' regime applies to the accounts of a company for a financial year during which it qualifies as small. An auditor's report in such a case must state that the financial reporting framework applied in their preparation is "applicable law and the Financial Reporting Standard for Smaller Entities".

Publicly traded and non-publicly traded companies

5812

Publicly traded companies are defined as those whose securities are admitted to trading on a regulated market in any member state in the European Union while non-publicly traded companies are those having no such securities.

> [MEMO POINTS]   If a **publicly traded company** governed by the law of a Member State is required to prepare consolidated accounts, these must follow international accounting standards (IAS). The rule does not apply where a publicly traded company is not required to prepare consolidated accounts.

Publicly traded companies are also required to include a Corporate Governance Statement in their annual report. If this statement has not been prepared, the auditors must make a statement to this effect under the heading "Matters on which we are required to report by exception."

5813

The Companies Act also classifies companies as being either **quoted or unquoted**. For the purposes of the auditor's report the implication of being a quoted company is that a directors' remuneration report is required, and the auditor has to report on certain elements of it.

6. Opinion on the financial statements

5814
ISA 700 (Revised)
(17)-(21)

The opinion paragraph of the auditor's report should clearly state the auditor's opinion as required by the relevant financial reporting framework used to prepare the financial statements and company law.

a. Unqualified opinion

An unqualified opinion on the financial statements should be expressed only when the auditor concludes that the financial statements have been prepared in accordance with the identified financial reporting framework, including the requirements of applicable law, and that the financial statements give a true and fair view.

5815

> EXAMPLE **Extract from auditors' report**
>
> **Opinion on financial statements**
> In our opinion the financial statements:
> – give a true and fair view of the state of affairs of the Company at [date], and of the company's profit (loss) for the year then ended;
> – the financial statements have been properly prepared in accordance with United Kingdom Generally Accepted Accounting Practice; and
> – have been prepared in accordance with the requirements of the Companies Act 2006.
>
> **If the company reports under FRSSE**, the opinion section will read as follows:
>
> **Opinion on financial statements**
> In our opinion the financial statements:
> – give a true and fair view of the state of the company's affairs at [date], and of its profit (loss) for the year then ended;
> – have been properly prepared in accordance with United Kingdom Generally Accepted Accounting Practice applicable to Smaller Entities; and
> – have been properly prepared in accordance with the requirements of the Companies Act 2006.

Directors' report   The auditor must state in his report on the company's annual accounts whether in his opinion the information given in the directors' report for the financial year for which the accounts are prepared, is consistent with those accounts.

5816
s 496 CA 2006

The auditor should address this additional reporting responsibility in a separate section of the auditor's report following the opinion on the financial statements.

> EXAMPLE **Extract from auditors' report**
>
> **Opinion on other matter prescribed by the Companies Act 2006**
> In our opinion the information given in the Directors' Report for the financial year for which the financial statements are prepared is consistent with the financial statements.

Investigations   An auditor, in preparing the audit report, must carry out such investigations as will enable an opinion to be formed as to:
– whether adequate accounting records have been kept by the company and returns sufficient for the audit have been received from branches not visited; and
– whether the company's individual accounts are in agreement with the accounting records and returns.

5817
s 498 CA 2006

In addition, if the auditor:
– fails to obtain all the information and explanations which are necessary for the purposes of the audit; or
– finds that disclosures of directors' remuneration required by company law have not been made,
then this should be stated in the report.

Issues such as the above should be included under a separate heading "Matters on which we are required to report by exception" and should include a suitable conclusion in respect of these matters. Where the auditors have discharged their responsibilities and have nothing to report in respect of them, the conclusion can be expressed as in the following example.

> EXAMPLE **Extract from auditors' report**
>
> **Matters on which we are required to report by exception.**
> We have nothing to report in respect of the following matters where the Companies Act 2006 requires us to report to you if, in our opinion:

– adequate accounting returns have not been kept, or returns adequate for our audit have not been received from branches not visited by us;
– the financial statements are not in agreement with the accounting records and returns;
– certain disclosures of directors' remuneration specified by law are not made; or
– we have not received all the information and explanations we require for our audit.

5818
ISA 700 (Revised)
(30)

Where auditors wish to emphasise a matter that does not affect their unqualified opinion (for instance, the possible outcome of a lawsuit), this can be expressed as follows:

EXAMPLE In forming our opinion, which is unqualified, we have considered the adequacy of the disclosures made in Note 31 to the financial statements concerning the possible outcome of a lawsuit, in which the company is the defendant, alleging infringement of certain patent rights and claiming royalties and punitive damages. The company has filed a counter action, and preliminary hearings and discovery proceedings on both actions are in progress. The ultimate outcome of the matter cannot at present be determined. No provision for any liability that may result has been made in the financial statements.

b. Other opinions

5819
ISA (Revised) 700
(57)

The auditors cannot express an unqualified opinion where:
– there is a **disagreement** with those charged with governance regarding the acceptability of the accounting policies selected, or the method of their application to the adequacy of financial statement disclosure; or
– there is a **limitation on the scope** of the auditors' work, the effect of which is or may be material to the financial statements.

Their opinion must therefore be expressed as one of the following:
– a **qualified** opinion;
– an **adverse** opinion; or
– a **disclaimer** of opinion.

5820
ISA 700 (Revised)
(61), (63)-(64)

The table below summarises the circumstances giving rise to the various opinions. Each is discussed in detail subsequently.

	Material	Material and pervasive
Disagreement	Qualified opinion ("Except for...")	Adverse opinion ("In view of the effect of...")
Scope limitation	Qualified opinion ("Except for...")	Disclaimer ("Because of the possible effect...")

Qualified opinion

5821
ISA 700 (Revised)
(61), (64)

A qualified opinion should be expressed when the auditor concludes that an unqualified opinion cannot be given but that the effect of any disagreement or limitation on scope is not so material and pervasive as to require an adverse opinion or disclaimer of opinion. A qualified opinion should be expressed as being "except for" the effects of the matter to which the qualification relates.

A clear description of all the **substantive reasons** for the qualified opinion should be included in the report and, unless impracticable, a quantification of the possible effects on the financial statements. Ordinarily this information would be set out in a separate paragraph preceding the opinion or disclaimer of opinion and may include a reference to a more extensive discussion, if any, in a note to the financial statements.

EXAMPLE **Extract from auditors' report**

Qualified opinion arising from disagreement about accounting treatment
Included in the debtors shown on the balance sheet is an amount of £XX due from a company that has ceased trading. The company has no security for this debt. In our opinion the company is unlikely to receive any payment and full provision of £XX should have been made. Accordingly, debtors should be reduced by £XX, the deferred tax liability should be reduced by £YY and profit for the year and retained earnings should be reduced by £ZZ.

Except for the financial effect of not making the provision referred to in the preceding paragraph, in our opinion the financial statements:

– give a true and fair view of the state of the company's affairs as at 31 December 20X3 and of its profit for the year then ended;

– have been properly prepared in accordance with United Kingdom Generally Accepted Accounting Practice; and

– have been prepared in accordance with the requirements of the Companies Act 2006.

Adverse opinion

An adverse opinion should be expressed when the effect of a disagreement is so material and pervasive to the financial statements that the auditor concludes that a qualification of the report is not adequate to disclose the misleading or incomplete nature of the financial statements.

5822
ISA 700 (Revised)
(63)

EXAMPLE **Extract from auditors' report**

Basis for adverse opinion on financial statements
As more fully explained in Note [x] to the financial statements, no provision has been made for losses expected to arise on certain long-term contracts currently in progress, as the directors consider that these losses should be off-set against amounts recoverable on other long-term contracts. In our opinion, provision should be made for foreseeable losses on individual contracts as required by Statement of Standard Accounting Practice 9, *Stocks and long-term contracts*. If losses had been so recognised, the effect would have been to reduce the carrying amount of contract work in progress by £X, the deferred tax liability payable by £Y, and the profit for the year and retained earnings at [*date*] by £Z.

Adverse opinion on financial statements
In our opinion, because of the significance of the matter described in the Basis for Adverse Opinion paragraph, the financial statements:

– do not give a true and fair view of the state of the company's affairs as at [*date*] and of its profit (loss) for the year then ended; and

– have not been properly prepared in accordance with United Kingdom Generally Accepted Accounting Practice.

In all other respects, in our opinion the financial statements have been properly prepared in accordance with the Companies Act 2006.

Opinion on other matters prescribed by the Companies Act 2006
Notwithstanding our adverse opinion on the financial statements, in our opinion the information given in the Directors' Report for the financial year for which the financial statements are prepared is consistent with the financial statements.

Matters on which we are required to report by exception
We have nothing to report in respect of the following matters where the Companies Act 2006 requires us to report to you if, in our opinion:

– adequate accounting records have not been kept, or returns adequate for our audit have not been received from branches not visited by us; or

– the financial statements are not in agreement with the accounting records and returns; or

– certain disclosures of directors' remuneration specified by law are not made; or

– we have not received all the information and explanations we require for our audit.

Disclaimer of opinion

A disclaimer of opinion is expressed when the possible effect of a **limitation on the scope** of the auditors' work is so material and pervasive that the auditors have not been able to obtain sufficient appropriate audit evidence to form an opinion. Their report therefore indi-

5824
ISA 700 (Revised)
(62)

cates that the scope of the examination was limited and includes a disclaimer of opinion on the financial statements arising from that limitation.

5826   A limitation on the scope of the auditor's work may sometimes be imposed by an entity (for example, when the terms of the engagement specify that the auditor will not carry out an audit procedure that the auditor believes is necessary). When the limitation in terms of a proposed engagement is such that the auditor believes the need to express a disclaimer of opinion exists, the auditor would ordinarily not accept such a limited engagement as an audit engagement, unless required to do so by statute. Also, a statutory auditor would not accept such an audit engagement when the limitation infringes on the auditor's statutory duties.

EXAMPLE   **Extract from auditors' report**

Basis of disclaimer of opinion on financial statements
The audit evidence available to us was limited because we were unable to observe the counting of physical stock having a carrying amount of £X and send confirmation letters to trade debtors having a carrying amount of £Y due to limitations placed on the scope of our work by the directors of the company. As a result of this we have been unable to obtain sufficient appropriate audit evidence concerning both stock and trade debtors.

Disclaimer of opinion on financial statements
Because of the significance of the matter described in the Basis for Disclaimer of Opinion on Financial Statements paragraph, we have not been able to obtain sufficient appropriate audit evidence to provide a basis for an audit opinion. Accordingly, we do not express an on the financial statements.

Opinion on other matter prescribed by the Companies Act 2006
Notwithstanding our disclaimer of an opinion on the view given by the financial statements, in our opinion the information given in the Directors' Report for the financial year for which the financial statements are prepared is consistent with the financial statements.

Matters on which we are required to report by exception
Arising from the limitation of our work referred to above:
– we have not obtained all the information and explanations that we considered necessary for the purpose of our audit; and
– we were unable to determine whether proper accounting records have been kept.
We have nothing to report in respect of the following matters where the Companies Act 2006 requires us to report to you if, in our opinion:
– returns adequate for our audit have not been received from branches not visited by us;
– the financial statements are not in agreement with the accounting records and returns; or
– certain disclosures of directors' remuneration specified by law are not made.

---

7. Dating and signing of auditors' report

5827   Auditors should not express an opinion on financial statements until the statements have been approved by the directors and the auditors have completed an assessment of all the evidence considered necessary for the opinion to be given in the auditors' report. Furthermore, the date of the report should be the date on which the auditors actually sign the report expressing their opinion. Auditors should not backdate an audit report.

The report should name the location of the office where the auditor is based and state the name of the auditor.

The report may be signed in the name of the auditors' firm, the personal name of auditor, or both. Where the auditor is an individual, the report is required to be signed by the individual. Where the auditor is a firm, the report is required to be signed by the senior statutory auditor in his or her own name, for and on behalf of the auditor.

---

8. Changes to wording occasioned by Companies Act 2006

5828   The Auditing and Assurance Council (formerly the Audit Practices Board) issues, from time to time, revisions to ISA 700 and also publishes Bulletins to illustrate the latest requirements.

The FRC has issued a compendium of illustrative auditor's reports contained in Bulletin **5829** 2010/2, from which the following general example has been taken. A revised version of the Bulletin was issued subsequently in order to reflect the auditor's responsibility to read all financial and non-financial information in the annual report and to identify any material inconsistencies. The added requirement is shown in the "Scope" paragraph in the example below in bold type, and is now mandatory. The Bulletin is obtainable on the FRC's website.

[EXAMPLE]   **Auditors' report on group and parent company financial statements of a non-publicly traded company**

Independent Auditors' Report to the members of XYZ Ltd
We have audited the group and company financial statements of XYZ Ltd for the period ended... which comprise [*state the primary financial statements such as the Group Profit and Loss Account, the Group and Company Balance Sheets, the Group Cash Flow Statement*] and the related notes. The financial reporting framework that has been applied in their preparation is applicable law and United Kingdom Accounting Standards (United Kingdom Generally Accepted Accounting Practice).

Respective responsibilities of directors and auditors
As explained more fully in the Directors' Responsibilities Statement [set out...], the directors are responsible for the preparation of the financial statements and for being satisfied that they give a true and fair view. Our responsibility is to audit and express an opinion on the financial statements in accordance with applicable law and International Standards on Auditing (UK and Ireland).

Scope of the audit of the financial statements
Either: A description of the scope of an audit of financial statements is [provided on the FRC's website]/[set out [on page...] of the Annual Report].
Or: An audit involves obtaining evidence about the amounts and disclosures in the financial statements sufficient to give reasonable assurance that the financial statements are free from material misstatement, whether caused by fraud or error. This includes an assessment of: whether the accounting policies are appropriate to the company's circumstances and have been consistently applied and adequately disclosed; the reasonableness of significant accounting estimates made by the directors; and the overall presentation of the financial statements. In addition, **we read all the financial and non-financial information in the** [*describe the annual report*] **to identify material inconsistencies with the audited financial statements. If we become aware of any apparent material misstatements or inconsistencies we consider the implications for our report.**

Opinion on financial statements
In our opinion the financial statements:
– give a true and fair view of the state of the company's affairs as at... and of the group's profit (loss) for the year then ended;
– have been properly prepared in accordance with United Kingdom Generally Accepted Accounting Practice; and
– have been prepared in accordance with the requirements of the Companies Act 2006.

Opinion on other matter prescribed by the Companies Act 2006
In our opinion the information given in the Directors' Report for the financial year for which the financial statements are prepared is consistent with the financial statements.

Matters on which we are required to report by exception
We have nothing to report in respect of the following matters where the Companies Act 2006 requires us to report to you if, in our opinion:
– adequate accounting records have not been kept, or returns adequate for our audit have not been received from branches not visited by us; or
– the financial statements are not in agreement with the accounting records and returns; or
– certain disclosures of directors' remuneration specified by law are not made; or
– we have not received all the information and explanations we require for our audit.

[Signature]
John Smith (Senior Statutory Auditor)
for and on behalf of ABC LLP, Statutory Auditor
[Address]
[Date]

B. Special reports required by companies' legislation

1. Abbreviated accounts

5840   Certain **small and medium-sized companies** are entitled to take advantage of various exemptions under the Act and may file abbreviated accounts with the Registrar of Companies (¶6270). These accounts must be accompanied by a copy of a **special auditors' report** in which the auditors must state that, in their opinion:
– the company is entitled to deliver abbreviated accounts; and
– the abbreviated accounts are properly prepared.
If the auditors' report on the full financial statements is **unqualified**, there is no need to reproduce it in full in the special auditors' report. If the auditors are not able to report positively in respect of both of the above, the company may not deliver abbreviated accounts to the Registrar.

5841   **Unqualified audit report** Where the full audit report is **unqualified**, but contains an **explanatory paragraph** regarding a fundamental uncertainty, such as the going concern basis, the special auditors' report should also include the explanatory paragraph, under a section entitled "other information". The auditor should also include any further information necessary for a proper understanding of the report.

5842   **Qualified audit report** Where a small company files abbreviated accounts, it is not obliged
s 449(3)(a), (b)   to file a copy of the complete audit report with the Registrar of Companies, unless the full
CA 2006   audit report:
a. was **qualified**, in which case the special auditors' report must set out that report in full together with any further information necessary to understand the qualification; and
b. contains a statement that:
– the accounts, records or returns are inadequate or that the accounts do not agree with the records and returns, or
– the auditors have failed to obtain the necessary information and explanations.

5843   The exact wording of the special report will depend upon whether the company is small or medium-sized.

> [EXAMPLE] **Example of a report on the abbreviated accounts of a small company**
>
> **Independent Auditors' Report to B Ltd under Section 449 of the Companies Act 2006**
> We have examined the abbreviated accounts set out on pages xx to xx, together with the financial statements of the company for the year ended 30 September 20XX prepared under Section 396 of the Companies Act 2006.
>
> **Respective responsibilities of directors and auditors**
> The directors are responsible for preparing the abbreviated accounts in accordance with Section 444 of the Companies Act 2006. It is our responsibility to form an independent opinion as to whether the company is entitled to deliver abbreviated accounts prepared in accordance with Section 444 of the Act to the Registrar of Companies and whether the accounts to be delivered are properly prepared in accordance with that provision and to report our opinion to you.
> We conducted our work in accordance with Bulletin 2008/4 issued by the Auditing Practices Board. In accordance with that Bulletin, we have carried out the procedures we consider necessary to confirm, by reference to the financial statements, that the company is entitled to deliver abbreviated accounts and that the abbreviated accounts to be delivered are properly prepared. The scope of our work for the purpose of this report did not include examining or dealing with events after the date of our report on the full financial statements.

Opinion
In our opinion the company is entitled to deliver abbreviated accounts prepared in accordance with Section 444(3) of the Companies Act 2006, and the abbreviated accounts are properly prepared in accordance with the regulations made under that section.

[Signature]
John Smith (Senior Statutory Auditor)
For and on behalf of ABC LLP, Statutory Auditors
[Address]
[Date]

MEMO POINTS 1. In a special report on the **abbreviated accounts** of a medium-sized company, references to sections 444 and 444(3) of the Companies Act 2006 are replaced by references to sections 445 and 445(3) respectively.
2. A **new accounting directive** issued by the **European Parliament** (2013/34/EU) aims to simplify the accounting requirements for small companies and micro-entities, and in time make it easier for various stakeholders (e.g. investors, suppliers) to compare accounts prepared in different EU jurisdictions. Under the **new accounting rules**, a small company can benefit from reduced disclosure requirements by preparing an **abbreviated balance sheet and P & L account**, with additional voluntary disclosures permitted. In addition, the **audit thresholds** for qualifying as a small company will be increased, thus exempting more of these entities from the requirement to have their accounts audited. The new regulations become mandatory in January 2015.

Medium-sized companies   The rules relating to the auditors' report on abbreviated financial statements filed by a medium-sized company are the same as those for small companies, and are discussed at ¶6075.

5845

---

2. Distributions

When a company intends to make a distribution, it must first determine the amount that is legally available for the purpose (¶3711). This is usually done by reference to the last annual financial statements before the distribution. If the audit report on those accounts was **qualified**, the company must obtain a further report from the auditors stating whether, in their opinion, the circumstances giving rise to the qualification is material in the determination the legality of the distribution.

5850
s 837 CA 2006

This statement may be made either at the time of the audit report, as an addition to the opinion section, or it can be made in a separate report.

EXAMPLE **Example of report given separately from the audit report on the last financial statements**

Independent Auditors' Report to the Members of K Ltd Pursuant to Section 837(4) of the Companies Act 2006
We have audited the financial statements of K Ltd for the year ended... in accordance with International Standards on Auditing (UK and Ireland) issued by the Auditing Practices Board and have expressed a qualified opinion thereon in our report dated...

Respective responsibilities of directors and auditors
The directors are responsible for preparing the financial statements in accordance with the applicable laws and United Kingdom Accounting Standards (United Kingdom Generally Accepted Accounting Practice).
They are also responsible for considering whether the company, subsequent to the balance sheet date, has sufficient distributable profits to make a distribution at the time the distribution if made.
Our responsibility is to report whether, in our opinion, the subject matter of the qualification of our auditors' report on the financial statements for the year ended... is material for determining whether, by reference to those financial statements, the distribution is permitted under section 830 of the Companies Act 2006. We are not required to form an opinion on whether the company has sufficient distributable reserves to make the distribution proposed at the time it is made.

Opinion

In our opinion, the subject matter of the qualification is not material for determining whether, by reference to those financial statements, the distribution of £xx,xxx proposed by the company is permitted under Section 830 of the Companies Act 2006.

Statutory Auditor
[Address]
[Date]

---

3. Reports pertaining to private companies

Share capital

5853   Where a private company either intends to:
– give financial assistance for the purchase of its own shares, e.g., by lending money to a potential shareholder (¶3617), or
– purchase or redeem its own shares out of capital (i.e., when there are no other reserves out of which the purchase could be made), it has to comply with a number of conditions.

One of these is the requirement that the directors make a declaration that the company's financial position will not be compromised as a result of the proposed transactions. The Companies Act 1985 required the auditors to report on the directors' declaration to the effect that they are not aware of anything that indicates that the opinion expressed therein is unreasonable.

The provisions of the Companies Act 2006 relating to a private company wishing to **redeem or purchase its own shares** out of capital came into effect on 1 October 2009. The APB issued Bulletin 2008/9, which provides an example of the statements required when a private company redeems or purchases its own shares out of capital under the Companies Act 2006.

> EXAMPLE **Report of the independent auditor to the directors of XYZ Limited pursuant to Section 714(6) of the Companies At 2006**
>
> We report on the attached statement of the directors dated…, prepared pursuant to the Companies Act 2006, in connection with the company's proposed [purchase]/[redemption] of… (number) [ordinary]/[preferred] shares by a payment out of capital.
>
> **Basis of opinion**
> We have inquired into the company's state of affairs in order to review the bases for the directors' statement.
>
> **Opinion**
> In our opinion the amount of £xx specified in the directors' statement as the permissible capital payment for the shares to be [purchased]/[redeemed] is properly determined in accordance with sections 710 to 712 of the Companies Act 2006. We are not aware of anything to indicate that the opinion expressed by the directors in their statement as to any of the matters mentioned in section 714(3) of the Companies Act 2006 is unreasonable in all the circumstances.

> MEMO POINTS   Audit matters now come under the direct remit of the FRC Board and its **Codes and Standards Committee**, with input and advice provided by the Audit and Assurance Council.

Re-registration as a public company

5855
s 92 CA 2006   If a **private company** intends to re-register as a public company, it must lodge with the Registrar of Companies various documents, including the company's balance sheet as at a date not more than seven months before the application to re-register. It is usual to submit the balance sheet from the last audited accounts for this purpose but, if more than seven months has elapsed since the last financial year end, a more recent balance sheet is needed. In addition, the following is required from the company's auditors:
– an unqualified audit report in relation to the balance sheet, and
– a written statement from the auditors that the balance sheet shows, in their opinion, that the company's net assets did not amount to less than the aggregate of its called up share capital and undistributable reserves.

MEMO POINTS   **APB Bulletin 2008/9** provides an example of the statements that are required if a private company wishes to re-register as a public company under the Companies Act 2006.

EXAMPLE   **Independent Auditors' Report to A Ltd for the Purpose of Section 92(1) (b) and (c) of the Companies Act 2006**

We have examined the balance sheet and related notes of A Ltd as at 31 December 20X3, which formed part of the financial statements for the year then ended which were audited by us.
Respective responsibilities of directors and auditors
The company's directors are responsible for the preparation of the balance sheet and the related notes.
It is our responsibility to:
– report on whether the balance sheet has been properly prepared in accordance with the Companies Act 2006; and
– form an independent opinion, based on our examination, concerning the relationship between the company's net assets and its called up share capital and undistributed reserves at the balance sheet date.

Opinion concerning proper preparation of balance sheet
In our opinion, the audited balance sheet at 31 December 20X3 has been properly prepared in accordance with the requirements of the Companies Act 2006.

Statement on net assets
In our opinion, at 31 December 20X3 the amount of the company's net assets (within the meaning given to that expression by Section 831(2) of the Companies Act 2006) was not less than the aggregate of its called-up share capital and undistributable reserves.

[Signed]
Statutory Auditor
[Address]
[Date]

---

4. Revised annual financial statements

If the directors discover that the annual accounts, or directors' report, contained errors or were otherwise defective, they may, at their option, prepare revised accounts (including reports). If the previous statements have already been presented to the company in general meeting or delivered to the Registrar, the revisions that may be made are confined to correcting instances of non-compliance with the Act (which, in practice, includes compliance with Accounting Standards) and the necessary consequential alterations.

5860
s 454 CA 2006

At the directors' discretion, the corrections may be made by replacing the accounts and reports in their entirety, or by issuing a supplementary note.

The **auditor's opinion** on the view given by the revised accounts is given at the date the original accounts were approved – and the opinion should not be influenced by events after that date. The following examples show how the relevant paragraphs of the auditors' report will be affected.

EXAMPLE   **1. Introduction to auditors' report of a company that revised its accounts by replacing them in their entirety:**
We have audited the revised financial statements for B Ltd for the year ended... which comprise the Profit and Loss Account, the Balance Sheet, the Cash Flow Statement and related notes. These revised financial statements have been prepared under the accounting policies set out therein and replace the original financial statements approved by the directors on [date of directors' original approval].

2. Introduction to auditors' report of a company that revised its accounts by a supplementary note:
We have audited the revised financial statements for B Ltd for the year ended... which comprise...
The revised financial statements replace the original financial statements approved by the directors on [date] and consist of the attached supplementary note together with the original financial statements that were circulated to members on [date].

3. *Opinion* **section of auditors' report on revised accounts:**

In our opinion:
– the revised financial statements give a true and fair view, seen as at the date the original financial statements were approved, of the state of the company's affairs as at... and of its profit for the year then ended;
– the revised financial statements have been properly prepared in accordance with United Kingdom Generally Accepted Accounting Practice seen as at the date the original the financial statements were approved;
– the revised financial statements have been properly prepared in accordance with the provisions of the Companies Act 2006 as they have effect under the Companies (Revision of Defective Accounts and Reports) Regulations 2008;
– the original financial statements for the year ended... failed to comply with the requirements of the Companies Act 2006 in the respects identified by the directors in the statement contained in note [x] to these revised financial statements; and
– the information given in the revised Directors' Report is consistent with the revised financial statements.

4. In the case of revision by replacement:

In our opinion the original financial statements for the year ended... failed to comply with the requirements of the Companies Act 2006 in the respects identified by the directors in the statement contained in Note x to these revised financial statements.

5. In the case of revision by supplementary note:

In our opinion the original financial statements for the year ended... failed to comply with the requirements of the Companies Act 2006 in the respects identified by the directors in the supplementary note.

MEMO POINTS   The provisions of the Companies Act are supplemented by the ability of the **Financial Review Panel** to require a listed company to revise its financial statements.

CHAPTER 6

Ratio analysis

Ratio analysis is a technique that allows investors, finance directors and analysts to gain a better understanding of how an organisation has performed by analysing the financial statements. Once the ratios have been calculated, comparisons can be made of the entity's performance versus previous years and other organisations in the same industry and trends can be analysed. With the **exception** of the ratio for earnings per share (EPS), provision of this information in the financial statements is not compulsory.   **5900**

Five groups of ratios are commonly employed; namely: liquidity, profitability, asset, investment, and debt (gearing) ratios. Within each category, there are a number of standard ratios that are generally calculated. **Individual ratios** should not be considered in isolation and a number of ratios should be calculated and reviewed in unison with the trends determined over time.

There are **a number of limitations** in using ratio analysis: **5902**
– financial statements are based partly on estimates (e.g. depreciation, revaluations, accruals, etc.) and should these be materially incorrect then this will impact on the quality of the ratio analysis;
– changes in accounting policies make comparisons over a number of years and with other entities difficult;
– ratios are based on past performance and are no guide to the future; and
– the economic climate must be taken into consideration when interpreting business trends.

A. Liquidity ratios

Management monitors liquidity in order to maintain the **solvency** of the business through managing the working capital that is tied up in debtors, stock and cash. The two principal liquidity ratios are the current ratio and acid test.   **5910**

Liquidity ratios give an insight into an entity's ability to meet its financial obligations as they fall due, through the availability of liquid assets. Liquid assets are current assets that can be converted into cash promptly and include:
– cash;
– short-term investments;
– fixed term deposits; and
– trade debtors.

It is not unusual for a business to be making a profit but at the same time experience liquidity problems. A **common problem** is that of **overtrading**, where most of the profits are used to finance expansion in the form of additional fixed assets, stocks and debtors required to sustain a growing business. This can result in a shortage of cash to meet short-term financial obligations. The liquidity and working capital ratios are useful in detecting early signs of overtrading.

Some assets are more liquid than others. Stocks of **finished goods** might be sold quickly and consumer goods held as stock can also be sold on. Other stocks are not so liquid. **Raw materials and components** in a manufacturing company are required in the production of a finished good before they can be sold on and cash generated. In this case, the degree of liquidity will depend on the speed of the stock turnover and length of the production cycle.

1. Current ratio

5912   The current ratio measures the relationship between an entity's current assets and current liabilities.

> [EXAMPLE] $\dfrac{\text{Current assets £60,000}}{\text{Current liabilities £20,000}} = 3:1$
>
> For every £1 of current liabilities the entity has £3 of current assets.

The **ideal current ratio** will depend on the type of industry and a ratio that is acceptable for one industry will not necessarily be suitable for another. For example, fast food outlets typically operate with low current ratios, resulting from minimum levels of current stock and debtor balances and the quick recycling of resources generated from cash (rather than credit) sales.

A **low ratio** could mean that a business is nearing insolvency, although the timing of the liabilities must also be considered. For instance, some liabilities such as finance lease repayments or corporation tax payments may not be due for a number of months. Alternatively, **a high ratio** could indicate that one or more categories of current assets are too high and therefore not being managed efficiently (i.e. stock levels).

2. Acid test

5916   The acid test ratio ignores the stock component of the current ratio and concentrates on assets which can be turned quickly into cash, should liquidity problems occur. Stock is excluded from this ratio because it may take longer to liquidate, especially if it is of a specialist nature.

> [EXAMPLE] $\dfrac{\text{Current assets- stock £60,000} - £30,000}{\text{Current liabilities £20,000}} = 1.5:1$

5917   Some companies may not be able to convert current assets into cash quickly. Manufacturing companies, for instance, may hold large quantities of raw materials and finished goods could also be warehoused for a considerable time or sold on generous credit terms. Where the stock turnover is slow, stocks are not deemed liquid assets as the cash cycle is relatively long.

Ideally, this ratio should be at least 1 for companies with a slow stock turnover. For companies with a quick stock turnover, a ratio could be less than 1, without necessarily indicating cash flow problems. **Remedial action** includes encouraging debtors to settle more promptly, whilst short-term investments can be sold and converted into cash.

The **reverse applies** where the ratio is bigger than it should be. This occurs when an entity has over invested its working capital in terms of stocks and debtors and so has more funds tied up in the business than required.

⌐ *MEMO POINTS* ⌐   A variation on the current ratio is the **balance sheet test** applied in prospective insolvency cases, which measure total assets against total liabilities, to determine whether a company can meet its financial obligations. For more information see our *Company Law memo*.

The **minimum safety ratio** will vary from industry to industry. Where this ratio differs markedly from other entities in the same sector, this could indicate a number of problem areas as set out in the table below.

5918

Problem	Underlying causes
A ratio significantly lower than industry average	Entity too dependant on short-term borrowings for daily funding (i.e. high levels of trade creditors, short-term loans and overdrafts).
High acid/current ratios	Indicate an entity is not utilising resources efficiently = low rates of return. **Solutions**: Excessive stock levels require better stock control High debtor balances require – better credit control-prompt payment. Cash balances should be reinvested.

B. Profitability ratios

Profitability ratios help illustrate how effective a company is in utilising the assets at their disposal to generate profits. Investors, banks and other lenders and suppliers will want to know how profitable a company is and that it is generating enough profits to meet its financial commitments.

5920

The key profitability ratios are the gross profit percentage and net profit percentage.

Expressing profit as a percentage of sales indicates how efficiently an organisation is controlling its costs.

1. Gross profit percentage

The gross profit ratio expresses the gross margin as a percentage of total sales.

5922

[EXAMPLE] $\dfrac{\text{Gross profit £150,000}}{\text{Total sales £300,000}} \times 100 = 50\%.$

For every £100 of sales the company makes a gross profit of £50.

Negative changes in gross profit margin may result from:
– lower turnover;
– increased cost of raw materials where higher costs have not been passed onto the customer;
– increased competition; or
– a change in the product mix, with the entity selling a higher proportion of goods with a lower gross product margin.

2. Net profit percentage

5924   The net profit percentage shows an organisation's net profit as a percentage of total sales.

EXAMPLE $\dfrac{\text{Net profit £25,000}}{\text{Sales £250,000}} \times 100 = \text{net profit percentage of 10%.}$

Changes in the net profit percentage may not be accompanied by a similar change in gross profit percentage. This indicates that an organisation needs to review its expenses, salary costs, etc.

C. Asset ratios

5930   There are a number of ratios that can be used to indicate how efficiently an organisation is using its assets, the most common of which are reviewed below.

1. Sales to fixed assets

5932   The sales to fixed asset ratio indicates how much of each £1 invested in fixed assets generates sales.

For example, an entity with annual sales of £250,000 and a fixed asset net book value of £100,000; the ratio will be 2.5 to 1. Every £1 invested generates £2.50 in sales.

5933   The **higher the ratio** of sales to fixed assets the more efficient the utilisation of the fixed assets. However, the ratio should be interpreted with care as it may be distorted by the following factors:
– a significant increase in fixed assets will increase the value of these fixed assets and result in a short-term lowering of the ratio; or
– alternatively, if there is little or no investment in new fixed assets, this would increase the sales to fixed asset ratios and mask the under investment reflected in the low assets values carried in the balance sheet.

2. Stock turnover

5934   The stock turnover ratio expresses the average number of days' stock is held by the entity.

EXAMPLE $\dfrac{\text{Average stock £12,000}}{\text{Cost of sales £500,000}} \times 365 = \text{approximately 9 days}$

5935   **High levels of stock** result in:
– increased storage, handling, insurance and security costs;
– risk of stock obsolescence with slow moving items; and
– valuable resources being committed.

5936   The shorter the stock turnover period the better as less resources are committed.

The **average length of time** that **stock is retained** will depend on the organisation and industry sector. For example a restaurant would not hold fresh food stocks for very long while a coal based electricity generating company would typically hold a few months supply of coal. Also, some manufacturers operate a "just-in-time" delivery system, with pressure placed on suppliers to hold stocks of spare parts on their behalf (e.g. car manufacturers).

A **low stock turnover** could result from significant quantities of obsolete or damaged stock that cannot be sold, or that stock levels are simply too high. Other reasons include poor stock control and bulk buying to obtain discounts, resulting in excess funds committed to stocks. The idea is that the entity should not burden itself with excessive levels of stock, but should retain sufficient supplies so that sales are not threatened. Good stock control/delivery systems are required to determine and then manage the optimum level of stock.

---

3. Average trade debtor collection period

The debtor collection period indicates the number of days elapsing between a credit sale and receipt of the cash.   **5937**

$$\boxed{\text{EXAMPLE}} \quad \frac{\text{Average trade debtors £50,000}}{\text{Credit sales £750,000}} \times 365 = \text{approx. 24 days}$$

The **shorter the collection period**, the better the liquidity and the lower the risk of bad debts. A good credit control system will ensure that the debtor collection period is kept as short as possible and that cash is available to meet creditors as they fall due.

Generally, normal terms of credit are 30 days, so anything in excess of this figure should be investigated. Note that debtors are quoted inclusive of VAT whilst the turnover is stated net.

---

4. Creditor turnover period

This ratio shows the average number of days an entity takes to pay its suppliers for goods purchased on credit. If a figure for credit sales is not available the annual cost of sales figure can be used.   **5938**

$$\boxed{\text{EXAMPLE}} \quad \frac{\text{Average trade creditors £25,000}}{\text{Credit purchases £350,000}} \times 365 = 27 \text{ days}$$

Although some entities view delaying payment as a form of interest free credit, there are costs involved as discounts for prompt payment are often sacrificed and business credit ratings can suffer.

D. Investment ratios

Investors seek returns on investments in the form of dividends and profits on share sales that compensate them for the risk attached to the investment. Investors also require information on share performance to aid them in their decision making process on whether to buy, sell or hold shares. Ratios are often used to assess the return on an investment, the most common of which are set out below.   **5940**

---

1. Return on capital employed (ROCE)

The ROCE ratio indicates how well an entity utilises the resources invested in it, by expressing its profit as a percentage of the total capital employed required to generate the profit.   **5942**

The ROCE measures both profitability and the efficient use of assets in generating sales, as measured by net profit margin and asset turnover. There is often a **trade-off between** these two ratios in different industry sectors. For instance, retailers usually operate on lower profit margins, while capital intensive industries such as building or engineering have higher asset turnovers.

> [EXAMPLE] $\dfrac{\text{Profit before interest and taxation £15,000}}{\text{Capital employed £150,000}} \times 100 = 10\%.$

From the investor's standpoint, the higher the ROCE the more efficient the use of the resources employed by the company.

5943   The **problem** is deciding which definition of "capital employed" to use. Some entities only include shareholders funds (share capital/reserves) while others include shareholders funds and long-term debt including creditors falling due after one year.

Whichever definition is adopted it should be applied consistently.

2. Dividend cover

5944   The dividend cover ratio indicates the proportion of available profits distributed to shareholders retained in the organization. Entities seek to strike a balance between the funding requirements of the organization and the expectations of the investors.

> [EXAMPLE] $\dfrac{\text{Profit after tax less preference share dividend £25,000}}{\text{Gross dividend on ordinary shares £10,000}} = \text{dividend cover 2.5: 1}$
>
> For every £2.50 profit made, £1 is distributed to the investors by way of a dividend, with the balance retained in the organization.

3. Dividend yield

5946   The dividend yield expresses the shareholder's dividend as a percentage of the market value of a share.

The yield **will be influenced by** the dividend policy adopted by the company and the level of funds retained (reinvested) in the business. From an investor's viewpoint, the dividend yield indicates the return that an investor earns from holding shares in a certain company, so allowing comparison with other forms of investment.

> [EXAMPLE] $\dfrac{\text{Ordinary dividend per share £0.25p}}{\text{Market price per share £4.00}} \times 100 = 6.25\%$

The dividend yield is compared with the market average. **Low dividend yields** will encourage investors to switch their money into other shares so affecting the share price and with it the ability of the entity to attract further investment.

4. Price/earnings

5948   The price/earnings ratio (PER) indicates how cheap or expensive a particular share is and is determined by dividing the market price of a company's ordinary shares by the earnings per share (EPS).

> [EXAMPLE] $\text{Price/earnings ratio} = \dfrac{\text{market price of share 550p}}{\text{Earnings per share 50p}} = 11$
>
> Eleven years earnings of 0.50p per share are being purchased.

The current market price of the share reflects the expectations of the market regarding the future profits of the company and the price/earnings ratio helps elaborate this through comparison with other entities. Companies with higher PER's, all other factors being equal, will be deemed to have the better commercial prospects. On the other hand, an entity may have a low PERs as a result of one poor trading year, or exceptional circumstances that may be short-term in nature.

The PER is therefore highly subjective, as it is primarily dependant on the opinion of investors concerning future profitability.

E. Debt ratios

Debt ratios illustrate how much a company owes in relation to its size and whether the **debt burden** is increasing or decreasing along with the resulting impact on the long-term capital structure of the company. **5950**

1. Debt ratio

The debt ratio shows the relationship between a company's total debt and its total assets. Assets consist of fixed and current assets at the balance sheet date and debts consist of all creditors, including those falling due after more than one year. Long-term provisions and liabilities are ignored. **5952**

A debt ratio of 50% is generally deemed prudent, although many companies operate with a debt ratio in excess of this. Examples include companies that have a dominant market position or companies funding takeovers with high levels of debt.

2. Gearing

The term "gearing" expresses the relationship between a company's borrowings and share-holders funds. Investors and other lenders will be interested in an entity's long-term funding arrangements. **5954**

> [EXAMPLE]
> $$\frac{\text{Long-term debt}}{\text{Long-term debt + shareholders funds}}$$
>
> $$\frac{£200,000}{£500,000} = \text{a gearing ratio of 0.4.}$$
>
> For every £100 of equity, £40 represents long-term borrowings (amounts due for repayment after one year).

The **higher the ratio of debt to equity**, the more dependent the organization is on borrowed funds and the greater the risk of defaulting on interest or dividend payments. **Poor gearing ratios** will result in these entities having to pay a premium to attract adequate funding.

There is no generally agreed norm for this ratio and many companies are highly geared. The problem is that these types of companies may have difficulty in raising future funds unless they can increase shareholders' capital either through retained profits or through a share issue.

A **number of questions** should be addressed, such as: **5956**
1. Are long-term financial commitments being financed by long-term finance?
2. Do the company's ratios for gearing levels and interest cover (see below) seem reasonable?
3. Have any significant changes in funding been highlighted by the ratios? If so what does this indicate?

3. Interest cover

5958   This ratio indicates how many times interest payments on short-term debt are covered by profit before tax and interest. The **higher the ratio**, the less the likelihood of an entity defaulting on its interest payments and hence the lower the financial risk of investing in the entity. Generally, an interest cover of 3 times is deemed suitable.

EXAMPLE $\dfrac{\text{Profit before interest and tax } £250{,}000}{\text{Interest charges } £60{,}000} = 4.17 \text{ times}$

Reporting options for smaller entities

CHAPTER 1

General criteria

In general, the financial statements of small and medium-sized businesses are seldom as complex as those of large companies and the types of business activities undertaken do not typically require the same level of disclosure, in order to give users of their financial statements a proper appreciation of their results. In order to cater for these differences, **special concessions** apply to small and medium-sized companies, which simplify certain disclosure requirements or, in some cases, even remove them entirely. Some reporting concessions are also available to **small and medium-sized groups** (see ¶6340). **6000**

The various options available to small and medium-sized companies are as follows: **6001**

Financial statements for presentation to:	Small companies	Medium-sized companies
Shareholders	• **Full** financial statements (i.e. in terms of companies legislation and current UK GAAP); **or** • **Shorter-form** financial statements (i.e. in accordance with FRSSE)	• **Full** financial statements
Registrar of Companies	• **Full** financial statements; **or** • **Abbreviated** financial statements (i.e. in terms of companies legislation) for small companies[1, 2]	• **Full** financial statements; or • **Abbreviated** financial statements (i.e. in terms of companies legislation) for medium-sized companies[2]

Notes:
1. Even if a small company files abbreviated financial statements with the Registrar of Companies, it is still required to provide full or shorter-form financial statements for its members.
2. Abbreviated financial statements for small companies are not the same as those for medium-sized companies.
3. Another concession available to small companies is whether they choose (subject to satisfying certain criteria) to have their accounts **audited** (¶6070).
4. For the general reporting options available to all sizes of company see ¶243.

The **exemptions** from producing full financial statements are **voluntary** and as a consequence some small and medium-sized companies choose to continue preparing their financial statements under the rules applying to larger companies. There can be a number of reasons for this, for instance, if they are part of a group or if, due to anticipated future growth, they do not expect to be able to take advantage of the exemptions in the immediate future. Similarly, while certain medium-sized companies are entitled to prepare **abbreviated financial statements**, they may prefer to avoid the additional expense of doing so and simply file a conventional set of accounts (such as are given to shareholders) with the Registrar, especially where no issues of confidentiality arise. **6002**

> `MEMO POINTS`   The Financial Reporting Standard for Smaller Entities (**FRSSE**) and subsequent amendments represents a single source to which smaller enterprises can refer. The FRSSE has since been amended and the changes will apply to accounting periods beginning on or after 1 January 2015. Until such time the FRSSE (version effective from April 2008) remains in force.

1. Qualification criteria

6010   There are **three stages** in establishing whether a company is entitled to the small and medium-sized company exemptions.

Stage 1	Make sure that the company is not **ineligible** by virtue of its **nature** or **activities**
Stage 2	Test whether the company falls within the **size limits**
Stage 3	Test whether the company satisfies the **reference-period conditions**

2. Nature or activities

6015   The following types of companies cannot be classified a small even if they meet the small company criteria:
- a public company;
- a parent of a group that is not a small group;
- a small company that is an authorised insurance company, a banking company, an e-money issuer, an MiFid investment firm or a UCITS management company or that carries on insurance market activity; or
- a member of an ineligible group.

The above criteria also apply to medium-sized entities.

> `MEMO POINTS`   1. Companies that would otherwise qualify as small but for the fact that they are members of ineligible groups can still take advantage of the exemption from including an enhanced **business review** in the directors' report prepared for members and from filing the directors' report at Companies House.
> 2. These exclusions do not preclude a company being treated as small or medium-sized if it is a subsidiary of a **large private company** but still meets all the other qualification criteria.

6016   A **group is ineligible** if any of its members is:
- a public company;
- a small company that is an authorised insurance company, a banking company, an e-money issuer, an MiFid investment firm or a UCITS management company or that carries on insurance market activity;
- a person who has permission under Financial Services and Markets Act 2000 (Part 4) to carry on one or more regulated activities; or
- a body corporate whose shares are admitted to trading on a regulated market in an EEA State.

3. Size limits

6017   To be treated as a small or medium-sized company under the Companies Act 2006, a company must meet any two of the following three size criteria:

Criterion	Small company	Medium-sized company
Turnover (adjusted proportionately if the period is not a full year) must not exceed	£6,500,000	£25,900,000
Gross assets (i.e. total assets before the deduction of liabilities) must not exceed	£3,260,000	£12,900,000
Average number of employees must not exceed	50	250
Notes: 1. The average number of employees is determined by adding those defined as employed for each month and dividing the total by the number of months in the period. 2. The size limits are subject to periodic review and therefore change from time to time. The amounts shown above came into effect by the Companies Act 2006 (Amendments) (Accounts and Reports) Regulations 2008.		

4. Reference period

The final stage in the determination of whether a company will qualify for the relevant exemptions is to make sure that it satisfies the reference-period conditions set out in the table below.

6020
s 247 (1)(c) CA 2006
ss 382 (2), 465 (2)
CA 2006

First financial year	A company will qualify provided that it satisfies the size conditions in that year.
Subsequent years (conditions satisfied)	A company will qualify provided that it satisfies the size conditions in both the year in question and the preceding year.
Subsequent years (conditions not satisfied)	A company that qualifies as small or medium-sized in a particular year will **continue to be treated** as one in the following year, even if it fails to satisfy the size conditions in that year. However, if it does not satisfy the qualifying conditions in the year after that, then, for the third year, it must produce its financial statements in a format appropriate to its size. On the other hand, if the company again satisfies the qualifying conditions in the third year, it may continue to take advantage of the exemptions to which it became entitled in the first year.

6024

EXAMPLE Scenario 1

A Ltd was incorporated on 1 July 20X1. The following details relate to reporting periods ending 31 December 20X1, 20X2, and 20X3. Assume the prevailing size limits applied in each of the three reporting periods.

	20X1	20X2	20X3
Turnover	£2,375,000	£5,800,000	£5,400,000
Gross assets	£2,600,000	£3,000,000	£3,000,000
Average number of employees	55	60	49

In **20X1**, its year of incorporation, A Ltd meets the size criteria of a small company on the basis of its turnover and gross assets. (Because the company was in existence for only six months, the turnover for the period is annualised to £4,750,000. However, this figure remains within the limit.) Note that even though the average number of employees exceeds 50, the company has only to meet two of the three requirements. As 20X7 is its first financial year, the company qualifies as a small company.

In **20X2**, A Ltd exceeds all the size criteria. However, it will still qualify as a small company because, in terms of section 382 (2), it fulfilled the size conditions in the previous financial year, which was its first. As a result, it is permitted to continue to prepare its financial statements as a small company.

In **20X3**, the company again satisfies the size criteria (on the basis of its turnover and number of employees falling below the respective limits). Despite the fact that it did not satisfy the size conditions in 20X2, it nonetheless qualifies as a small company in 20X3 because it had been treated as one in the previous year.

Scenario 2

B Ltd has been in existence for many years. It has consistently met the size requirements applicable to a medium-sized company since inception.

	20X1	20X2	20X3	20Y4
Turnover	£24,000,000	£26,500,000	£26,500,000	£25,100,000
Gross assets	£11,200,000	£13,800,000	£13,700,000	£12,700,000
Average number of employees	220	234	255	248

In 20X1, B Ltd meets all the size criteria for qualifying as a medium-sized company. And, because it has also fulfilled the size conditions for two consecutive years, it is entitled to the exemptions.

In 20X2, gross assets and turnover exceed the size criteria. However, B Ltd still qualifies as a medium-sized company because it fulfilled the size criteria in the two previous years.

In 20X3, the company once again exceeds the limits applicable to a medium-sized company. It therefore cannot prepare abbreviated financial statements.

In 20Y4, B Ltd meets the size criteria for a medium-sized company. However, for purposes of preparing abbreviated financial statements, it will not qualify as a medium-sized company because, in the previous two consecutive years, it did not qualify. (Note that if it meets the criteria again in 20Y5, it will be able to file abbreviated financial statements again.)

5. General accounting rules and principles

True and fair view

6040
FRSSE 2.2

The financial statements should present a true and fair view of the results for the period and of the state of affairs at the end of the period. To this end, the **substance** of any arrangement or transaction, or any series of such, into which the entity has entered should be considered.

6041
FRSSE 2.3

Departures from true and fair view   If there are circumstances in which compliance with any of the provisions of the FRSSE or of the Act does not give a true and fair view, the directors are obliged to **depart** from the relevant provision to the extent necessary to give a true and fair view (this is the so-called **true and fair override**). In this event, the following should be disclosed in the notes:
– a statement that there has been a departure from the requirements of the FRSSE or Companies Act and that the departure is necessary to give a true and fair view;
– a statement of the treatment that the FRSSE or Companies Act would normally require and a description of the treatment adopted;
– a statement of the reasons why the treatment prescribed would not give a true and fair view; and
– a description of how the position shown in the financial statements is different as a result of the departure.

6043
FRSSE 2.4

Where a departure continues in **subsequent financial statements**, the disclosures should be made in all subsequent statements and should include corresponding amounts for the previous period.

6044
FRSSE 2.5

If any **doubt exists** as to whether applying the FRSSE would be sufficient to give a true and fair view, adequate explanation should be given in the notes to the accounts of the arrangement or transaction.

Accounting policies and estimation techniques

6046
FRSSE 2.6

The financial statements should **state** that they have been "prepared in accordance with the Financial Reporting Standard for Smaller Entities (effective April 2008)". This statement may be included with the note of accounting policies or given on the balance sheet. If abbreviated accounts are also being prepared, the statement should be included with the note of accounting policies so that it is reproduced in the abbreviated accounts.

6048
FRSSE 2.9

Accounting policies and estimation techniques should be consistent with the requirements of both the FRSSE and companies legislation. Where this permits a choice, an entity should select the policies and techniques most **appropriate to its particular circumstances** for the purpose of giving a true and fair view, taking account of the objectives of relevance, reliability, comparability and understandability (¶28).

6050
FRSSE 2.10

Accounting policies should be **applied consistently** and **reviewed regularly** to ensure that they continue to give a true and fair view. However, in deciding whether a new policy is more appropriate than an existing policy, consideration should be given to the effect on comparability. Where a change in accounting policy is made, the amounts for the current and corresponding periods should be restated on the basis of the new policies.

Financial statements should include:
- a description of each material accounting policy followed;
- details of any changes to the accounting policies previously followed, including a brief explanation of why each new accounting policy is more appropriate, and an indication of the effect of the change on the current period's results; and
- if material, the effect of a change to an estimation technique, a description of the change, and where practicable, the effect on the current period's results.

6052
FRSSE 2.7

Going concern

The company should be **presumed to be operating** as a going concern. In preparing financial statements, the directors should assess whether there are significant doubts about the entity's ability to continue as a going concern. Any material uncertainties should be disclosed. Where the period considered by the directors in making this assessment has been limited to a period of less than one year from the date of approval of the financial statements, that fact should be stated. Financial statements should be prepared on the going concern basis unless the directors determine after the balance sheet date either that they intend to liquidate the entity or to cease trading, or that they have no realistic alternative but to do so.

6055
FRSSE 2.12

Prudence

The amount of any item should be determined on a prudent basis. Prudence is the inclusion of a degree of caution in the exercise of the judgements needed in making the estimates required under conditions of uncertainty, such that gains and assets are not overstated and liabilities are not understated. It is not appropriate to use prudence as a reason to knowingly understate assets or gains, or overstate liabilities or losses.

6058
FRSSE 2.13

Accruals

Except for cash flow information, financial statements are required to be prepared on the accruals basis of accounting. Therefore, all income and expenditures – whether or not actually received or paid at the end of the financial year – are brought into account.

6060
FRSSE 2.14

Prior period adjustments

Prior period adjustments should be accounted for by **restating** the comparative figures for the preceding period in the primary statements and the notes, and **adjusting** the opening balance of reserves to take account of the cumulative effect. The cumulative effect of the adjustments should also be noted at the foot of the statement of total recognised gains and losses (STRGL) in respect of the current period. The effect of prior period adjustments on the results for the preceding period should be disclosed where it is practicable to do so.

6062
FRSSE 2.15

---

6. Approval and signing of accounts

A company's annual accounts must be approved by the board of directors and signed on its behalf, on the face of the balance sheet, by one of their number. The date on which the financial statements are approved by the board must be disclosed. In addition, the balance sheet must clearly show by way of a prominent statement that the accounts have been prepared in accordance with the **special company law provisions** relating to small companies.

6063
FRSSE 2.30 – 2.36

Every copy of the balance sheet which is published by or on behalf of the board must state the name of the director who signed it on behalf of the board.

The financial statements of the balance sheet delivered to the **Registrar** must, in addition to having been signed, also prominently state the company's registration number, the name of the director who signed on behalf of the board and the registered auditors as appropriate.

7. Report of the directors

6066
FRSSE 18.1 – 18.15

The following disclosures are required to be made within the directors' report:
– the principal activities of the company;
– details of the company's directors;
– political donations and expenditure and charitable donations (where the aggregate of each exceeds £2,000);
– acquisitions by the company of its own shares;
– employment of disabled persons (where the average number of employees exceeds 250);
– a statement that there is no relevant audit information of which the company's auditors are unaware and that the directors have taken the necessary steps to make themselves aware of any such information and to have established that it had been made available to the auditors.

The report must be approved by the board and signed, stating the name of the person who signed it.

8. Audit exemption criteria

6070
s477–478 CA 2006

The criteria for claiming an exemption from auditing financial statements have been aligned with those already established for claiming small company status. Therefore a small company will now qualify for an audit exemption if it meets any two of the conditions set out in ¶6017.

> MEMO POINTS   **Subsidiary companies** can claim exemption from audit if their parent company guarantees their liabilities.

A company is **not entitled to the exemption** from audit if at any time during the financial year it was:
– a public company (unless it is dormant);
– a subsidiary company (unless its parent company guarantees its liabilities);
– an authorised insurance company or it carried out insurance market activity;
– involved in banking or issuing e-money;
– a MiFID (Markets in Financial Instruments Directive) investment firm or an Undertakings for Collective Investment in Transferable Securities (UCITS) management company;
– a corporate body and it shares have been traded on a regulated market in a European state.

6071
FRSSE 2.37

Where a company meets these conditions, and has elected not to be audited, its balance sheet must contain a **statement by the directors** to the effect that:
– for the year in question, the company was entitled to exemption under the Companies Act 2006;
– no member or members eligible to do so have deposited a notice requesting an audit within one month before the end of the financial year; and
– the directors acknowledge their responsibility for ensuring that the company keeps accounting records consistent with its duty to do so and for preparing accounts that give a true and fair view of the state of affairs of the company as at the end of the financial year and of its profit or loss for the year.

6072
FRSSE 2.37

The Act provides a safeguard to protect the **interests of external shareholders**. Where holders of at least 10% of the share capital of a company so require, an audit of the accounts will be mandatory. Where the company has taken advantage of the exemption from audit because the **company is dormant**, and the company, during the financial year, has acted as an agent for any person, that fact must be stated.

6074
FRSSE 2.39

Where **exemption from audit is not available**, or the directors have not taken advantage of the exemption, and the company has entered into a liability limitation agreement with its auditors, the notes to the accounts must disclose the principal terms of the agreement and either the date of the resolution:
– approving the agreement or the agreement's principal terms; or
– waiving the need for such approval.

9. Decision Table

Choice of financial statements available for shareholders and for filing with the Registrar of **6075** Companies.

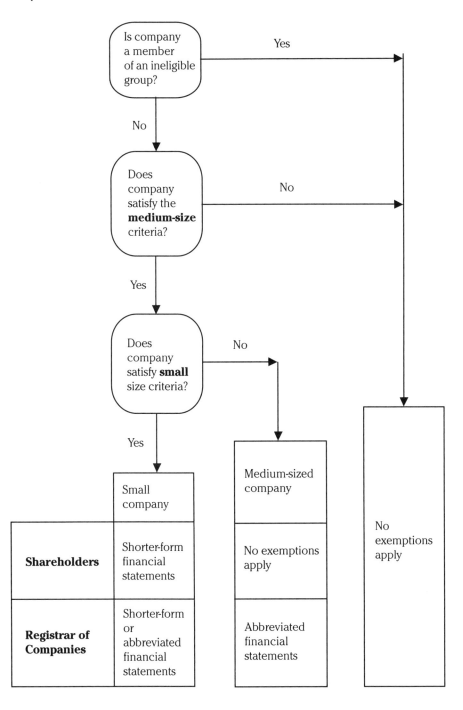

SECTION 1

Smaller companies

Companies meeting the requisite size criteria (¶6017) can **voluntary elect** to adopt the Financial Reporting Standard for Smaller Entities (FRSSE), and in so doing it is released from the requirements of the other Financial Reporting Standards (FRSs) and UITF abstracts. Where the FRSSE is adopted, this fact must be disclosed in the financial statements, either in the directors' statement or separately within the notes to the accounts. The decision by an eligible entity to abide by the FRSSE can be taken independently of any decision regarding the adoption of other accounting and disclosure exemptions offered by the Companies Act 2006. Furthermore, where an entity can, on a selective basis, comply with the additional requirements of various other Financial Reporting Standards, this should be made clear in the note on accounting policies.

6080

> MEMO POINTS   The **general accounting rules** and principles underpinning shorter-form accounts are covered in Part 8 Chapter 1. Abbreviated accounts for filing with the Registrar of Companies are covered in Part 8 Chapter 3. Both the FRSSE and other Financial Reporting Standards are **updated periodically**. There may be times, therefore, when a new FRS is implemented before the FRSSE has been revised to reflect a similar change applicable to smaller entities. In such cases, entities adopting the FRSSE are permitted to continue to apply its provisions even though they may be out of line with the provisions of the new standard.

Medium-sized companies (¶6325) are not permitted to file shorter-form financial statements prepared for shareholders. Even where they prepare abbreviated accounts (for the Registrar),

6081

the concessions that are available relate principally to the profit and loss account, leaving the normal requirements in respect of the directors' report, balance sheet and notes to the financial statements fundamentally intact.

The rules pertaining to parents of small and medium-sized groups are covered in brief in (¶6255).

A. Profit and loss account

1. Formats

6083
FRSSE 2.28–2.29
FRSSE 2.17

The format of the profit and loss account must comply **with one of the following formats**, with items listed in the order and under the headings shown in ¶6077 and ¶6079.

Small companies are required to retain the same format in preparing their accounts for subsequent financial years of the company unless in their opinion there are special reasons for a change. Particulars must be disclosed of any change in the profit and loss account format, together with the reasons for the change. Where compliance with the provisions of companies legislation as to the matters to be included in a company's individual accounts or in notes to those accounts would not be sufficient to give a true and fair view, the necessary additional information must be given in the accounts or in a note.

6084

Profit and loss account
(Format 1)
1. Turnover
2. Cost of sales*
3. Gross profit or loss
4. Distribution costs
5. Administrative expenses
6. Other operating income
7. Income from shares in group undertakings
8. Income from participating interests
9. Income from other fixed asset investments
10. Other interest receivable and similar income
11. Amounts written off investments
12. Interest payable and similar charges
12a. Profit or loss on ordinary activities before taxation
13. Tax on profit or loss on ordinary activities
14. Profit or loss on ordinary activities after taxation**
19. Other taxes not shown under the above items
20. Profit or loss for the financial year
* This figure must include provisions for depreciation and write-downs of tangible and intangible fixed assets, and must also be separately disclosed in a note to the accounts.
** Extraordinary items, which are extremely rare, would be shown separately after the profit or loss on ordinary activities after taxation.

6085

Profit and loss account (Format 2)
1. Turnover
2. Change in stocks of finished goods and in work in progress
3. Own work capitalised
4. Other operating income
5.   A.   Raw materials and consumables
B.   Other external charges
6. Staff costs:
A.   Wages and salaries
B.   Social security costs
C.   Other pension costs
7.   A.   Depreciation and other amounts written off tangible and intangible fixed assets
B.   Exceptional amounts written off current assets
8. Other operating charges
9. Income from shares in group undertakings
10. Income from participating interests
11. Income from other fixed asset investments
12. Other interest receivable and similar income
13. Amounts written off investments
14. Interest payable and similar charges
14A. Profit or loss on ordinary activities before taxation
15. Tax on profit or loss on ordinary activities
16. Profit or loss on ordinary activities after taxation*
21. Other taxes not shown under the above items
22. Profit or loss for the financial year
* Extraordinary items, which are extremely rare, would be shown separately after the profit or loss on ordinary activities after taxation.

2. Specific treatment

All **gains and losses** recognised in the financial statements for the period must be included in the profit and loss account or the STRGL. Only profits that are realised at the balance sheet date should be included in the profit and loss account. All **liabilities** that have arisen in respect of the period (or in respect of a previous period) are to be taken into account (including any that may have become apparent between the balance sheet date and the date on which it is signed). Gains and losses may be **excluded** from the profit and loss account only if they are specifically permitted or required to be **taken directly to reserves** by the FRSSE or by company law. Where an amount relating to any **preceding financial year** is included in the profit and loss account, the effect of its inclusion must be stated.

6086
FRSSE 3.1 - 3.4

If the company has supplied **markets outside the UK** during the financial year, it must disclose separately the percentage of turnover that is attributable to those markets. In analysing the source of turnover, account must be taken of the manner in which the company's activities are organised.

6087

a. Exceptional items

All exceptional items must be taken into account in arriving at the profit or loss on ordinary activities and included under the **statutory format headings** to which they relate. However,

6089
FRSSE 3.5 - 3.6

the following are **exceptions** because they are required to be shown separately in the profit and loss account:
- profits or losses on the sale or termination of an operation;
- costs of a fundamental reorganisation or restructuring having a material effect on the nature and focus of the reporting entity's operations; and
- profits or losses on the disposal of fixed assets.

The **amount** of each exceptional item, either individually or as an aggregate of items of a similar type, should be disclosed separately by way of a note, or on the face of the profit and loss account if that degree of prominence is necessary in order to give **a true and fair view**. A **description** of each exceptional item should be given to enable its nature to be understood.

b. Revenue recognition

6091
FRSSE 4.1–4.5
As a general rule, revenue is recognised by a seller when it obtains **the right to consideration** in exchange for its performance. (Typically, at the same time it would recognise a new asset, i.e. a debtor).

6092
If a seller receives **payment in advance** of performance, the amount should be recognised, and accounted for, as a liability. Later, when the seller, by its performance, obtains the right to consideration, the liability should be reduced (in part or in full, as the case may be) and the amount transferred to revenue. In cases where a seller has partially performed its contractual obligations, it should recognise revenue to the extent that it has obtained the right to consideration.

6093
Revenue must be measured at the **fair value** of the right to consideration, which is normally the price specified in the contractual arrangement, net of discounts, value added tax and similar sales taxes. However, where the effect of the time value of money is material, the present value of the amounts expected to be received should be used.

c. Turnover

6095
FRSSE 4.8–4.9
Turnover is the revenue arising from transactions under which a seller supplies goods or services to customers in the ordinary course of its business. Sellers may, of course, enter into other transactions (e.g. the sale of fixed assets) that do not give rise to turnover.

d. Profit or loss on disposal

6097
FRSSE 3.7
The profit or loss on the disposal of an asset should be accounted for in the profit and loss account of the period in which the disposal occurs. It is **computed** as the difference between the net **sale proceeds** and the net **carrying amount**, whether carried at historical cost (less any provisions made) or at a valuation. Profit or loss on disposal of **a previously acquired business** should include the attributable amount of purchased goodwill where it has previously been eliminated against reserves as a matter of accounting policy and has not previously been charged in the profit and loss account.

e. Auditors' remuneration

6099
Amounts paid to auditors by way of remuneration, including expenses, must be disclosed in the notes to the accounts. The nature and value of benefits in kind, if any, must also be given.

B. STRGL

6101 If the only recognised gains and losses are included in the profit and loss account, no separate statement to this effect needs to be made. In other cases, a **primary statement** should be presented, (i.e. with the **same prominence** as the profit and loss account), showing the total of recognised gains and losses (see ¶4307).

C. Balance sheet

1. Format

The FRSSE adopts the balance sheet formats of SI 2008 No. 409 ("The Small Companies and Groups (Accounts and Directors' Report) Regulations 2008"). These are a simplification of those in SI 2008 No. 410 ("The Large and Medium-Sized Companies and Groups (Accounts and Directors' Report) Regulations 2008"), which are prescribed for medium and larger sized companies (¶988). **6105**

Format per SI 2008 No. 409 (for small companies and groups)	
A	Called up share capital not paid
B	Fixed assets
B-I	Intangible assets
	1. Goodwill
	2. Other intangible assets
B-II	Tangible assets
	1. Land and buildings
	2. Plant and machinery, etc
B-III	Investments
	1. Shares in group undertakings and participating interests
	2. Loans to group undertakings and undertakings in which the company has a participating interest
	3. Other investments other than loans
	4. Other investments
C	Current assets
C-I	Stocks
	1. Stocks
	2. Payments on account
C-II	Debtors
	1. Trade debtors (See Note 1)
	2. Amounts owed by group undertakings and undertakings in which the company has a participating interest
	3. Other debtors

Format per SI 2008 No. 409 **(for small companies and groups)**

C-III	Investments
	1. Shares in group undertakings
	2. Other investments
C-IV	Cash at bank and in hand
D	Prepayments and accrued income
E	Creditors: amounts...within one year
	1. Bank loans and overdrafts
	2. Trade creditors
	3. Amounts owed to group undertakings and undertakings in which the company has a participating interest
	4. Other creditors
F	Net current assets (liabilities)
G	Total assets less current liabilities
H	Creditors: amounts...after one year
	1. Bank loans and overdrafts
	2. Trade creditors
	3. Amounts owed to group undertakings and undertakings in which the company has a participating interest
	4. Other creditors
I	Provisions for liabilities and charges
	(Items 1-3 need not be shown)
J	Accruals and deferred income
K	Capital and reserves
K-I	Called up share capital
K-II	Share premium account
K-III	Revaluation reserve
K-IV	Other reserves
	(Items 1-4 need not be shown)
K-V	Profit and loss account

Note 1. Small companies need not show amounts falling due after more than one year separately for each item included under debtors, if it discloses the aggregate amount of debtors falling due after more than one year in the notes.

---

2. Fixed assets and goodwill

a. Disclosure

6107
FRSSE 6.1 – 6.2
In respect of all fixed assets and goodwill, the cost or valuation at the beginning and the end of the year, together with the effect of any of the following during the year must be shown:
- revaluations;
- acquisitions;

– disposals; and
– transfers.

In respect of provisions for **depreciation** or diminutions in value, the cumulative amount of such provisions as at the beginning and end of the year must be shown, as well as the effects of the amount of any provisions or other adjustments made during the year.

b. Research and development

The **cost** of **fixed assets acquired or constructed** in order to **provide facilities** for research and development activities over a number of accounting periods should be capitalised but written off over their useful lives through the profit and loss account.

6109

Expenditure on pure and applied research should be charged to the profit and loss account in the year incurred.

Expenditure on **development** should generally be written off **in the year incurred**. Where the development expenditure may be **deferred** to future periods (to the extent that its recovery is assured), it should be amortised commencing with commercial production or application of the relevant product, service, process or system. Deferral is appropriate when:

6110

a) there is a **clearly defined project**; and
b) the related expenditure is **separately identifiable**; and
– the outcome of such a project has been assessed with reasonable certainty as to its technical feasibility and its ultimate commercial viability; and
– the aggregate of the deferred development costs, any further development costs, and related production, selling and administration costs is reasonably expected to be exceeded by related future sales or other revenues; and
– adequate resources already exist or are reasonably expected to be available to enable the project to be completed and to provide any consequential increases in working capital.

If a policy of **deferral** is adopted, it must be applied to all development projects. At the end of each accounting period, deferred development expenditure for each product should be **reviewed**. If the circumstances that originally justified the deferral of expenditure no longer apply, or are considered doubtful, the expenditure should be written off.

6111

The amount of deferred development expenditure carried forward at the beginning and end of the period should be **disclosed under intangible assets** in the balance sheet or in the notes to the balance sheet. Disclosure must also be made of the **reason for capitalising** these costs as well as the **period** over which they are being depreciated. Where development costs are not treated as a realised loss or realised revenue loss this must be stated together with an explanation of the circumstances relied upon by the directors to justify this decision.

c. Other intangible assets and goodwill

Internally generated goodwill and intangible assets should not be capitalised, while **purchased** positive goodwill and intangible assets should be.

6112
FRSSE 6.11

Intangible **assets purchased with a business** should be recognised separately from the purchased goodwill if their value can be measured reliably.

Capitalised goodwill and intangible assets should be **depreciated** on a straight-line (or more appropriate) basis over their useful economic lives, which in any event may not exceed 20 years. The period chosen, and the reason for choosing it, must be shown by way of a note.

The **residual value** assigned to goodwill should be zero. A residual value exceeding this may be assigned to an intangible asset only when this value can be established reliably (e.g. if it has been agreed contractually).

At the end of each accounting period, useful economic lives should be reviewed and, if necessary, **revised** but by no more than 20 years from the date of acquisition. At the date of revision, the carrying amount should be depreciated over the **revised estimate** of the intangible asset's remaining useful economic life. Goodwill and intangible assets are not revalued.

6113
FRSSE 6.17

If an acquisition appears to give rise to **negative goodwill**, fair value should be checked to ensure that the assets acquired have not been overstated and liabilities have not been understated. The negative goodwill up to the fair value of the non-monetary assets acquired should be released to the profit and loss account over the lives of those assets. Any additional negative goodwill should be recognised in the profit and loss account over the period expected to benefit from it. Both the amount of negative goodwill on the balance sheet and the period over which it is to be written back must be disclosed.

There are **no specific rules** on how negative goodwill should be **disclosed** in the balance sheet.

d. Tangible fixed assets – other than investment properties

6116
FRSSE 6.19–29

Tangible fixed assets should **initially be measured** at cost, then written down to recoverable amount if necessary (see ¶6138). The initial carrying amount of a tangible fixed asset received as a **gift or donation** by a charity should be its current value (i.e. the lower of **replacement cost and recoverable amount**) at the date received. If no record of the purchase price or production cost of an asset can be found (or if it cannot be obtained without unreasonable expense or delay), the value recorded should be the earliest available record of its value.

6117

Only those **costs** that are **directly attributable** to bringing the tangible fixed asset into working condition should be included in its measurement. In the case of entities that capitalise finance costs, only those that are directly attributable to the construction of tangible fixed assets should be capitalised. The total amount of finance costs capitalised during a period should not exceed the total amount of finance costs incurred during the same period. The notes should disclose the fact that finance costs have been included in determining the cost of the asset, as well as the amount concerned.

Capitalisation of directly attributable costs, including finance costs, should be **suspended** during extended periods in which active development is interrupted. Capitalisation should cease when substantially all the activities that are necessary to get the tangible fixed asset ready for use are complete, even if the asset has not yet been brought into use.

6119

Subsequent expenditure should be **capitalised** if:
– it enhances the economic benefits of a tangible fixed asset (i.e. if it is an improvement), or
– it replaces or restores a component that had been separately depreciated over its useful economic life.
In all other cases, it should be charged to the profit and loss account.

Revaluations

6121

Where an entity adopts an **accounting policy of revaluing** tangible fixed assets, the asset's carrying amount at the balance sheet date should be its **market value** (or the best estimate thereof) at the time. Where, in the directors' opinion, market value is not an appropriate basis, **current value** (i.e. the lower of replacement cost and recoverable amount) may be used instead. Where a tangible fixed asset is revalued, all tangible fixed assets of the same class should be revalued. However, a policy of revaluation does not have to be applied to all classes of tangible fixed assets.

It may be possible to establish with reasonable reliability the values of certain tangible fixed assets, other than properties, by reference to active second-hand markets or appropriate publicly available indices. In respect of other tangible fixed assets for which values are not easily determinable, including properties, an experienced valuer should **perform a valuation** at least every five years. It should be updated by an experienced valuer in the intervening years if it is likely that there has been a material change in value.

6123
FRSSE 6.25

Revaluation losses caused only by changing market prices should be recognised in the STRGL until the carrying amount of the asset reaches its depreciated historical cost. Other revaluation losses should be recognised in the profit and loss account.

Revaluation gains should be recognised in the statement of total recognised gains and losses, except to the extent (after adjusting for subsequent depreciation) that they reverse revaluation losses on the same asset that were previously recognised in the profit and loss account. These should be recognised in the profit and loss account. The adjustment for subsequent depreciation is aimed at achieving the same effect as would have prevailed if the original downward revaluation had not occurred.

6125
FRSSE 6.26

Where tangible fixed assets have been **revalued, disclosure** must be made of:
- the aggregate historical cost amount that would have been included if the assets not been revalued; or
- the differences between those amounts and the amounts actually shown.

6126
FRSSE 6.27 – 6.29

If, however, tangible fixed assets are constantly being replaced and, neither their value nor their degree of variation is material, they may be included at a fixed quantity and value.

The **year in which** assets have been **revalued** should be disclosed. Where the revaluation took place in the current year, the basis of the valuation should be disclosed together with the names of the persons performing the valuation or particulars of their qualifications.

6128

e. Depreciation – other than relating to investment properties

A tangible fixed asset's cost (or revalued amount) less its estimated residual value should be depreciated on a **systematic basis** over its **useful economic life**. The depreciation method used should fairly reflect the pattern in which the asset's economic benefits are consumed. The depreciation charge for each period should be recognised as an expense in the profit and loss account unless it is permitted to be included in the carrying amount of another asset.

6130
FRSSE 6.38 -.43

In the case of a tangible fixed asset consisting **of two or more** major **components**, with substantially different useful economic lives, depreciation on the individual components should be accounted for separately.

The useful economic lives and residual values of tangible fixed assets should be reviewed regularly and revised if necessary. The carrying amount of the tangible fixed asset at the date of revision, less the revised residual value, should be depreciated over the revised remaining useful economic life.

A **change in the method of providing depreciation** is permissible only on the grounds that the new method will render fairer presentation. Such a change does not constitute a change of accounting policy; the carrying amount of the tangible fixed asset is depreciated using the revised method over the remaining useful economic life, beginning in the period in which the change is made.

6132

The following should be **disclosed** in the financial statements for **land and buildings**, and for the **aggregate of other tangible fixed assets**:
- the depreciation methods used;
- the useful economic lives or the depreciation rates used; and
- where material, the financial effect of a change during the period in either the estimate of useful economic lives or the estimate of residual values.

6133

Where there has been a change in the depreciation method used, the effect, if material, should be disclosed in the period of change together with a brief explanation of the reason.

MEMO POINTS   Generally, **land** is regarded as having an unlimited life and therefore is not depreciated.

f. Write-downs to recoverable amount – except investment properties and financial instruments

Fixed assets and goodwill should be carried in the balance sheet at a value no higher than their recoverable amounts.

6138
FRSSE 6.44 – 6.49

6139   If the net book amount of a fixed asset or goodwill is considered not to be recoverable in full at the balance sheet date, the net book amount should be **written down** to the estimated recoverable amount. This revised amount is then written off over the remaining useful economic life of the asset.

6140   If the recoverable amount of a **tangible fixed asset** or investment subsequently increases as a result of a change in economic conditions or in the expected use of the asset, the net book amount should be **written back** to the lower of:
– recoverable amount; and
– the amount at which the asset would have been recorded had the original write-down not taken place.

If the recoverable amount of an **intangible asset or capitalised goodwill** subsequently increases, the net book amount should be written back only if the original write-down was the result of an external event and subsequent external events **clearly and demonstrably reverse the effects** of that event in a way that was not foreseen when the original write-down was calculated.

6141   Write-downs, and any reversals, to recoverable amount should be taken to the profit and loss account in the period concerned. However, write-downs of revalued tangible fixed assets that reverse previous revaluation gains simply as a result of changing market prices should instead be recognised in the **statement of total recognised gains and losses**, to the extent that the carrying amount of the asset is greater than its depreciated historical cost. Any amounts not shown in the profit and loss account must be disclosed in a note to the accounts.

6142   If fixed assets are not actually revalued in the balance sheet but their value has been considered by the directors, a note to the accounts should be given to reflect that:
– the directors have considered the value of fixed assets, without actually revaluing those assets;
– the directors are satisfied that the aggregate value of those assets at no time was less than the aggregate amount at which they are stated; and
– the assets affected are accordingly stated in the accounts on the basis that a revaluation of the company's fixed assets took place at that time.

---

g. Investments

Investment properties

6145
FRSSE 6.50 – 6.53   Investment properties should **not** be **subject to** periodic **depreciation** charges unless they are held on lease and the lease has an unexpired term of less than 20 years.

6146   Investment properties should be disclosed in the balance sheet at their **open market value**. The carrying value should be stated prominently on the face of the balance sheet or in the notes.

6147   Changes in market value should be taken to the STRGL and not the profit and loss account. Where a deficit, or its reversal, on an individual property is expected to be permanent, it should be taken to the profit and loss account.

6148   The names of the persons undertaking the valuations or particulars of their qualifications, together with their bases of valuation and, if relevant, the fact that they are an employee or officer of the company or group, should be disclosed.

Other investments

6150
FRSSE 6.30   Initially, fixed asset investments should be **measured at cost**. Alternatively, they may be measured at a market value determined as at the date of their last valuation or on any other value determined by the directors to be appropriate. In this event, the method of valuation

adopted and the reasons for adopting it should be disclosed by way of a note to the accounts. Gains and losses must be recognised in the profit and loss account or STRGL using the same basis applied to tangible fixed assets. This topic, including the accounting treatment of revalued investments and disclosure requirements, is treated in greater detail in ¶1751 to ¶1754.

h. Revaluation reserve

Any losses or gains arising on the revaluation of assets that have been recognised in the STRGL should be debited or credited to a separate revaluation reserve.

6155
FRSSE 6.34 – 6.36

Amounts may be transferred from the revaluation reserve to the profit and loss account as and when they are realised. In the case of tangible fixed assets, this will normally result in an annual transfer from the revaluation reserve to the profit and loss account over the useful economic life of the asset (i.e. in line with the depreciation charge). Realisation may also occur on disposal of the asset.

The tax treatment of amounts credited or debited to the revaluation reserve must be disclosed by way of a note.

i. Government grants

Government grants should be recognised in the profit and loss account so as to **match** them with the expenditure towards which they are intended to contribute. Even though a grant may have been received as a contribution towards expenditure on a fixed asset, company law does not allow the cost of the asset to be reduced. This type of grant should, therefore, be treated as **deferred income**.

6157
FRSSE 6.54 – 6.57

However a government grant should not be recognised in the profit and loss account until the **conditions for its receipt** have been complied with and there is reasonable assurance that the grant will be received.

6158

Potential liabilities to repay grants should be provided for only to the extent that **repayment is probable**. The repayment of a government grant should be set off against any unamortised deferred income relating to the grant. Any excess should be charged immediately to the profit and loss account.

The following information should be **disclosed** in the financial statements:
– the effects of government grants on the results for the period and/or the financial position of the entity; and
– where the results of the period are affected materially by the receipt of forms of government assistance other than grants, the nature of that assistance and, to the extent possible, an estimate of the effects.

6159

3. Leases

Hire purchase contracts that are of a financing nature should be accounted for on the same basis as **finance leases**. Other hire purchase contracts should be accounted for in the same way as **operating leases**.

6162

a. Accounting by lessees

A finance lease should be recorded in the balance sheet of a lessee both as an **asset** and as an **obligation** to pay future rentals. In other words, at inception, the fair value of the asset should be recorded both as an asset and a liability. This represents a difference to SSAP 21, which requires the value of the asset and liability to be recorded initially at the present value

6164
FRSSE 7.2 – 7.7

of the minimum lease payments. However, where the **fair value** of the asset does not give a realistic estimate of the cost of the asset and the value of the obligation entered into, a more reliable estimate should be made. For example, if the lessee has benefited from grants and capital allowances such that the minimum lease payments can be adjusted to an amount less than the fair value of the asset, discounting the lease payments at the interest rate implicit in the lease would provide a more suitable estimate. A negative finance charge should not be shown.

6166   The **total finance charge** under a finance lease should be allocated to accounting periods during the lease term so as to produce a constant periodic rate of charge on the remaining balance. The straight-line method may provide such a reasonable approximation.

6167   The **rental under an operating lease** should be charged on a straight-line basis over the lease term even if the payments are not made on that basis, unless another basis is more appropriate.

Incentives to sign a lease, in whatever form they may take, should be spread over the lease term on a straight-line basis. If these are shorter than the full lease term, they should be spread over the period to the review date on which the rent is first expected to be adjusted to the prevailing market rate.

An asset leased under a finance lease should be **depreciated** over the shorter of the lease term and its useful life. However, in the case of a hire purchase contract that has the characteristics of a finance lease, the asset should be depreciated over its useful life.

b. Accounting by lessors

6170   The amount due from a lessee under a finance lease should be recorded in the lessor's
FRSSE 7.8–7.11   balance sheet as a debtor at the amount of the **net investment** (i.e. after providing for items such as bad and doubtful rentals receivable) in the lease.

The **total gross earnings** under finance leases should be recognised on a systematic and rational basis, such as a constant periodic rate of return on the lessor's net investment.

6171   Rental income from an operating lease should be recognised on a straight-line basis over the period of the lease, even if the payments are not made on that basis, unless another basis is more representative of the time pattern in which the benefit from the leased asset is receivable.

An asset held for use in operating leases by a lessor should be recorded as a fixed asset and depreciated over its useful life.

6172   A lessor that is a manufacturer or dealer should not recognise a selling profit under an **operating lease**. Under a **finance lease**, the selling profit should be restricted to the excess of the fair value of the asset over the cost to the manufacturer/dealer less any grants towards the purchase, construction or use of the asset.

c. Sale and leaseback transactions

6175   In a sale and leaseback transaction that results in a **finance lease**, any apparent profit or
FRSSE 7.13–7.14   loss (i.e. the difference between the sale price and the previous carrying value) should be **deferred and amortised** in the financial statements of the seller/lessee over the shorter of the lease term and the useful life of the asset.

6176   In the case of an **operating lease**, any profit or loss should be **recognised immediately** provided it is clear that the transaction is established at fair value. However, if the sale price is not at fair value, two possibilities exist:
– if the sale price is **below fair value**, any profit or loss should be recognised immediately, except that if the apparent loss is compensated for by future rentals at below market price

it should to that extent be deferred and amortised over the remainder of the lease term (or, if shorter, the period during which the reduced rentals are chargeable);
– if the sale price is **above fair value**, the excess over fair value should be deferred and amortised over the shorter of the remainder of the lease term and the period to the next rent review (if any).

Disclosure by lessees

Disclosure should include the following:
– the gross amounts of **assets held under finance leases** together with the related accumulated depreciation and analysed into "land and buildings" and "other fixed assets" in aggregate; or, alternatively, leased assets may be aggregated with owned fixed assets provided that there is separate disclosure of the net amount of assets held under finance leases and the amount of depreciation for the period attributable to them;
– the amounts of **obligations related to finance leases** (net of finance charges allocated to future periods). These should be disclosed separately from other obligations and liabilities, either on the face of the balance sheet or in the notes to the accounts;
– the amount of any commitments existing at the balance sheet date in respect of finance leases entered into but whose inception occurs after the year end;
– the amount of **commitments in respect of operating leases** for the next year, analysed into those in which the commitment expires within that year, those expiring in two to five years, and those expiring more than five years after the balance sheet date. There is no requirement, as there is under SSAP 21, to analyse these commitments into those relating to land and buildings, and all other operating leases.

6178
FRSSE 7.16

Disclosure by lessors

Disclosure should include the following:
– the gross amounts of assets held for use in operating leases and the related accumulated depreciation;
– the cost of assets acquired, whether by purchase or finance lease, for the purpose of letting under finance leases;
– the net investment in finance leases and in hire purchase contracts at balance sheet date.

6180
FRSSE 7.18

---

4. Current assets

---

a. Stocks and long-term contracts

Stocks are stated in the financial statements at the lower of cost and net realisable value. This amount must be given in respect of separate items of stock or of **groups** of similar items. If there is **no record** of the purchase price or production cost of stock, the earliest available record of its value must be used (and this fact disclosed in the first year it applies).

6185
FRSSE 8.1 – 8.8

Finance costs (such as interest) that are directly attributable to the acquisition, construction or production of stock may be included as part of the cost. By way of note, the fact that finance costs are included in determining the cost of the asset, and the amount, must be disclosed.

Where **stocks are constantly being replaced** and their value is not material to assessing the company's state of affairs and their quantity, value and composition are not subject to material variation, they may be included at a fixed quantity and value.

Distribution costs may not be included in the production costs of stocks.

Long-term contracts should be assessed on a contract-by-contract basis and reflected in the profit and loss account by recording turnover and related costs as contract activity progresses. Turnover is ascertained in a manner appropriate to the stage of completion of the contract, the business, and the industry in which it operates.

6187

Where it is considered that the outcome of a long-term contract can be assessed with reasonable certainty, attributable profit should be calculated on a prudent basis and recognised in the profit and loss account as the difference between turnover and related costs for that contract.

6189   Long-term contracts should be **disclosed** in the balance sheet as follows:
– the amount by which recorded turnover is in excess of payments on account should be classified as "amounts recoverable on contracts" and disclosed separately within **debtors**;
– the balance of payments on account (in excess of the amounts matched with turnover and offset against long-term contract balances) should be classified as "payments on account" and disclosed separately within **creditors**;
– the amount of long-term contracts, at cost, net of amounts transferred to cost of sales, after deducting foreseeable losses and payments on account not matched with turnover, should be classified as "long-term contract balances" and disclosed separately within **stocks** in the balance sheet, with the following balances shown in the notes:
– net cost less foreseeable losses; and
– applicable payments on account;
– the amount by which the provision or accrual for foreseeable losses exceeds the costs incurred (after transfers to cost of sales) should be included within "provisions for liabilities and charges" or "creditors".

Consignment stock

6190
FRSSE 8.9
Where consignment stock is in substance an asset of the dealer, it should be recognised as such on the dealer's balance sheet, together with a corresponding liability to the manufacturer. Any deposit should be deducted from the liability and the excess classified as a trade creditor.

Where stock is not in substance an asset of the dealer, the stock should not be included on the dealer's balance sheet until title has transferred. Any deposit should be included under "other debtors".

b. Debt factoring

6192
FRSSE 8.10 – 8.12
Where all significant **benefits** (i.e. the future cash flows) and all significant **risks** (i.e., slow payment risk and the risk of bad debts) relating to the factored debts have been **transferred** to the factor, the debts should be removed from the entity's balance sheet and no liability should be shown in respect of the proceeds received from the factor. A profit or loss, calculated as the difference between the carrying amount of the debts and the proceeds received, should be recognised.

6193   Where the entity has **retained significant benefits and risks** relating to factored debts, but all of the following conditions are met:
– there is no doubt that the entity's exposure to loss is limited to a fixed monetary amount,
– amounts received from the factor are secured only on the debts factored,
– the debts factored are capable of being separately identified;
– the factor has no recourse to other debts or assets;
– the entity has no right to reacquire the debts in the future; and
– the factor has no right to return the debts even in the event of the cessation of the factoring agreement;
the factored debts should be shown **gross** (after providing for bad debts, credit protection charges and any accrued interest) separately on the face of the balance sheet. Any amounts received from the factor in respect of those debts, to the extent that they are not returnable, should be shown as deductions against the debts on the face of the balance sheet (i.e. a **linked presentation**).

6194   The financial statements should include a note stating that the entity is not required to support bad debts in respect of factored debts and that the factors have stated in writing that they will not seek recourse other than out of factored debts. The **interest element** of the factor's charges should be recognised as it accrues and included in the profit and loss account with other interest charges.

In all other cases, a **separate presentation** should be adopted (i.e. the gross amount of the debts should be shown on the balance sheet of the entity within assets, and a corresponding liability in respect of the proceeds received from the factor should be shown within liabilities). The interest element of the factor's charges and other factoring costs should be recognised as it accrues and included in the profit and loss account with other interest charges.   **6195**

c. Current asset investments

Current asset investments must initially be stated in the financial statements at the lower of cost and net realisable value. They may alternatively be measured at their current cost. Gains and losses must be recognised, in the profit and loss account or STRGL, using the same basis applied to tangible fixed assets (¶6123 and ¶6125).   **6198**
FRSSE 8.13 – 8.15

d. Start-up costs and pre-contract costs

Start-up costs should be accounted for on a basis consistent with the accounting treatment of similar costs incurred as part of the entity's ongoing activities. Where no such similar costs are incurred, start-up costs that do not meet the criteria for recognition as assets under any other specific requirement of the FRSSE should be recognised as an expense when they are incurred. They should not be carried forward as an asset.   **6202**
FRSSE 8.15

Pre-contract costs shall be expensed as incurred, except that directly attributable costs shall be recognised as an asset when it is virtually certain that a contract will be obtained and the contract is expected to result in future net cash inflows with a present value no less than all amounts recognised as an asset. Costs incurred before the asset recognition criteria are met shall not be recognised as an asset.   **6203**
FRSSE 8.16

5. Taxation

Tax, both current and deferred, should be **recognised in the profit and loss account**, except to the extent that any part of it is attributable to a gain or loss that has been recognised directly in the **statement of total recognised gains and losses** (STRGL). In that event, the relevant tax should be recognised directly there as well.   **6205**
FRSSE 9.1 – 9.15

The material components of the tax charge or credit for the period, as well as those of the deferred tax balance, should be disclosed separately.

Any special circumstances that affect the overall tax charge or credit for the period – or future periods – should be disclosed, and their individual effects quantified, by way of a note. The effects of a fundamental change in the basis of taxation should be included in the tax charge or credit for the period and separately disclosed on the face of the profit and loss account.

While deferred tax should be recognised in respect of all **timing differences** that have **originated but not reversed** by the balance sheet date, in the following instances it should not be recognised: **6207**
– in respect of **permanent differences**,
– on **revaluation gains and losses** unless, by the balance sheet date, the entity has entered into a binding agreement to sell the asset and has revalued it to selling price, and
– in respect of taxable gains on revaluations or sales if it is more likely than not that the gain will be rolled over into a replacement asset.

Unrelieved tax losses and other deferred tax assets should be recognised only to the extent that it is more likely than not that they will be recovered against the reversal of deferred tax liabilities or other future taxable profits.

[MEMO POINTS]   The existence of **unrelieved tax losses** serves as strong evidence that there may not be other future taxable profits against which the losses will be relieved.

Deferred tax should **be recognised** when **tax allowances** relating to the cost of a fixed asset are received either before or after the related depreciation is recognised. Only when all the conditions for retaining the tax allowances have been met should the deferred tax be reversed.

Deferred tax should be measured at the **average tax rates** expected to apply when the timing differences are due to reverse, based on tax rates and laws enacted by the balance sheet date.

6209   The discounting of deferred tax assets and liabilities is not required. However, if an entity adopts a policy of discounting, all deferred tax balances that have been measured without discounting, and for which the impact of discounting is material, should be discounted. Where discounting is used, the unwinding of the discount should be shown as a component of the tax charge and disclosed separately.

6211   The following should be **disclosed** in respect of deferred tax:
– the balance at the end of the period and its material components;
– any movement between the opening and closing net deferred tax balances;
– the material components of this movement;
– in cases where assets have been revalued (or their market values have been disclosed in a note) the amount of tax that would be payable or recoverable if the assets were sold at the values shown.

6214   **Tax on dividends**   Both incoming and outgoing dividends (and similar amounts receivable and payable) should be recognised net of any withholding tax but excluding other taxes, such as attributable tax credits. Withholding tax suffered should be shown as part of the tax charge.

6216   **Value added tax (VAT)**   Turnover shown in the profit and loss account excludes either VAT on taxable outputs or VAT imputed under the flat rate VAT scheme. **Irrecoverable VAT** allocable to fixed assets and to other items disclosed separately in the financial statements should be included in their cost where practicable and material.

6. Retirement benefits

a. Defined contribution schemes

6220
FRSSE 10.1 – 10.4   The **cost** of a defined contribution scheme is equal to the contributions payable to the scheme for the accounting period. The cost should be **recognised** within operating profit in the profit and loss account.

6221   Disclosure must be made of pension commitments – whether included under any provision shown in the balance sheet or not. Where any such commitment relates to pensions payable to past directors of the company, separate particulars must be given of that commitment.

6222   The following **disclosures** should be made:
– the nature of the scheme (i.e. defined contribution);
– the cost for the period; and
– any outstanding or prepaid contributions at the balance sheet date.

b. Defined benefit schemes

6225   Because **defined benefit schemes** have limited applicability to smaller entities (very few participate in them), the accounting requirements relating to such schemes are not contained in the FRSSE itself but set out in an Appendix (II) to the standard. They are based on FRS 17, "Retirement benefits".

7. Provisions, contingent liabilities and contingent assets

The requirements under this heading do not apply to leases, deferred tax, and retirement benefits for which there are specific requirements (dealt with above in ¶6162, ¶6207, and ¶6220 respectively).

6228

A provision should be recognised only where it is more likely than not that a present obligation exists as a result of a past event, and that it will require a transfer of economic benefits in settlement that can be estimated reliably. The amount recognised as a provision should be the best estimate of the **expenditure required to settle the obligation** at the balance sheet date. Where the effect of the time value of money is material, the amount of a provision should be the present value of the expenditures expected to be required to settle the obligation. Where discounting is used, the unwinding of the discount should be shown as "other finance costs" adjacent to interest.

6230
FRSSE 11.2

Where some or all of the expenditure required to settle a provision may be **reimbursed by another party** (for instance, resulting from an insurance claim), the reimbursement should be recognised as a separate asset only if it is virtually certain to be received. In the profit and loss account, the expense relating to the provision may be presented net of the recovery. Gains from the expected disposal of assets should be excluded from the measurement of a provision.

6232
FRSSE 11.3 - .5

Provisions should be **reviewed** at each balance sheet date and adjusted to reflect the current best estimate. They should be used only in respect of expenditures for which the provision was **originally recognised**.

For each class of provision the following must be disclosed:
- the amount of the provision at the beginning and the end of the financial year;
- amounts transferred to or from the provision during the year;
- the source and application of the amounts transferred; and
- particulars of each material provision included under "other provisions" in the company's balance sheet in any case where the amount of that provision is material.

6233
FRSSE 11.6

MEMO POINTS   The **above disclosures** are not required where the movement consists of the application of a provision for the purpose for which it was established.

Contingent liabilities and contingent assets should not be recognised in the accounts but the following should (unless, in the case of contingent liabilities, where their existence is remote) be disclosed in the notes:
- a brief description of the nature of the contingent item;
- where practicable, an estimate of its financial effect;
- its legal nature.

6235
FRSSE 11.7 - 11.11

Where any valuable security has been provided by the company in connection with a contingent liability, details must be disclosed.

6236

Where practicable, the aggregate amount, or estimated amount, of contracts for capital expenditure not provided for must be disclosed. Details of any other financial commitments not provided for, which are relevant to assessing the company's state of affairs, must also be disclosed.

Particulars must be given of any charge on the assets of the company to secure the liabilities of any other person, including where practicable, the amount secured.

8. Financial instruments

A financial instrument, or any of its components, must be classified as a financial liability, a financial asset or an equity instrument in accordance with the **substance of the contractual arrangement** rather than its legal form. Some financial instruments take the legal form of equity but are liabilities in substance. Others combine features associated with equity instruments and features associated with financial liabilities; they must, however, be classified

6238
FRSSE 12.1 - 12.8

according to the substance of the contract. For instance, a preference share that provides for mandatory redemption by the issuer for a fixed or determinable amount at a fixed or determinable future date, or gives the holder the right to require the issuer to redeem the instrument at or after a particular date for a fixed or determinable amount, is a financial liability.

6239   All **finance costs** should be charged in the profit and loss account. The finance costs of borrowings should be allocated to periods over the term of the borrowings at a constant rate on the carrying amount.

Where an **arrangement fee** is such that it represents a significant additional cost of finance when compared with the interest payable on the instrument, the same treatment should be followed. However, if the arrangement fee is not material, it should be charged to the profit and loss account at once.

Any convertible debt issued should be disclosed separately from other liabilities.

Initially, borrowings should be **stated in the balance sheet** at the fair value of consideration received. The carrying amount of borrowings should be increased by the finance cost in respect of the reporting period and reduced by payments made in respect of the borrowings in that period.

Dividends relating to a financial instrument or a component that is a financial liability must be recognised as **expense**. Distributions to holders of an equity instrument should be debited by the entity directly to equity, net of any related income tax benefit. If an entity declares dividends after the balance sheet date, the dividends are not recognised as a liability at the balance sheet date.

6240   The following is the required **disclosure of dividends** in the notes:
– the aggregate amount of dividends **paid** in the financial year (other than those for which a liability existed at the immediately preceding balance sheet date);
– the aggregate amount of dividends **liable to be paid** at the balance sheet date;
– the aggregate amount of dividends that are **proposed** before the date of approval of the accounts, and not otherwise disclosed above; and
– any fixed cumulative dividends on the company's shares that are **in arrears** (i.e. the amount of the arrears and the period for which each class of dividends is in arrears).

9. Share capital

6242
FRSSE 12.9 – 12.12
The following must be disclosed with respect to the company's share capital:
a. the number and aggregate nominal value of shares of each class allotted;
b. for any part of the allotted share capital that consists of redeemable shares:
– the earliest and latest dates on which the company has the power to redeem those shares,
– whether those shares must be redeemed in any event or are liable to be redeemed at the option of either the company or the shareholder, and
– any premium payable on redemption;
c. in respect of shares allotted during the period:
– the classes of shares allotted; and
– for each class, the number allotted, their aggregate nominal value, and the consideration received;
d. the amount of allotted share capital and of called up share capital that has been paid up;
e. the number, description and amount of shares in the company held by any of its subsidiaries.

10. Share-based payments

6243
FRSSE 12.13
If a company undertakes a share-based transaction – i.e., one in which it acquires goods or services and incurs a liability to be settled either by its own shares ("equity-settled") or by a

cash payment based on the value of its equity instruments ("cash-settled"), it must account for the transaction accordingly.

If a **cash-settled** share-based transaction:
- the goods or services should be treated as assets or expenses – as the circumstances dictate;
- the corresponding liability must reflect the best estimate of the expenditure required to settle the liability at balance sheet date;
- at each subsequent balance sheet date and at the date of settlement the liability must be remeasured;
- a description of the principal terms and conditions relating to the transaction – including its current and potential financial effect – must be disclosed by way of a note.

If an **equity-settled** share-based transaction, disclosure in the notes of:
- the principal terms and conditions – including the number of shares and the number of employees and others potentially involved;
- the grant date;
- any performance conditions, and the period over which these apply;
- any option exercise prices, if applicable.

Where the **other transacting party has the choice** of whether the entity settles in cash or equity, the transaction should be treated as a cash-settled transaction. However, if the obligation is eventually settled by the issue of equity, the previously recognised liability should be treated as the proceeds of the issue of that equity.   **6244**

Where the **entity itself has the choice** as to method of settlement, the transaction should be treated as either cash-settled or equity-settled as is felt appropriate.

---

11. Foreign currency translation

---

a. Transactions in foreign currencies

If any sums that were originally denominated in foreign currencies have been brought into account in the balance sheet or profit and loss account, the basis on which they were translated into local currency must be disclosed. Assets, liabilities, revenues and costs arising from transactions in foreign currencies should be translated into local currency at the exchange rate prevailing at the time of the transaction. An **average rate** may be used if the rates do not fluctuate significantly. However, where the transaction is to be settled at a **contracted rate**, that rate should be used and where a trading transaction is covered by a related or matching forward contract, the rate of exchange specified therein may be used.   **6245**
FRSSE 13.1 – 13.6

Once translated and recorded, no subsequent translations should be made in respect of non-monetary assets. However, for monetary assets and liabilities denominated in a foreign currency, they should each year be translated at each balance sheet date using the **closing rate** or, where appropriate, rates of exchange fixed under the terms of the relevant transactions. Where there are related or matching forward contracts in respect of trading transactions, the rates of exchange specified in those contracts may be used.   **6246**

All exchange gains or losses on settled transactions and unsettled monetary items should be reported as part of the profit or loss for the year from ordinary activities.

Subject to the conditions below, where a company has used foreign currency borrowings to finance – or to provide a hedge against – its foreign equity investments, the investments may be denominated in the foreign currency and the carrying amount translated at the end of each accounting period at **closing rates**. Where investments are treated in this way, any **exchange differences** arising should be **taken to reserves** and the exchange gains or losses on the foreign currency borrowings should then be offset, as a reserve movement, against these exchange differences. The conditions that must apply are as follows: **6247**

– in any accounting period, exchange gains or losses on the borrowings may be offset only to the extent of exchange differences arising on the equity investments;
– the foreign currency borrowings in respect of which the exchange gains or losses are used in the offset process should not exceed, in the aggregate, the total amount of cash that the investments are expected to generate, whether from profits or otherwise; and
– the accounting treatment adopted should be applied consistently from period to period.

b. Incorporating accounts of foreign entities

6248   When preparing accounts for a company and its foreign entities (including the results of associated companies or foreign branches) the closing rate/net investment method of translating the local currency financial statements should normally be used.

Exchange differences arising from the retranslation of the opening net investment in a foreign entity at the closing rate should be recorded as a movement on reserves.

The profit and loss account of a foreign entity accounted for under the closing rate/net investment method should be translated at the closing rate or at an average rate for the period. Where an average rate is used, the difference between the profit and loss account, translated at an average rate and at the closing rate, should be recorded as a movement on reserves. The average rate used should be calculated by the method considered most appropriate.

6249   Where the trade of the foreign entity is more dependent on the economic environment of the investing company's currency than that of its own reporting currency, the transactions of the foreign operation should be reported as if they had been entered into by the investing company itself in its own currency.

Unless there have been changes in financial and operational relationships between an investing company and its foreign entities, the method used for translating the financial statements should be applied consistently from period to period.

6250   Subject to the **following conditions**, where foreign currency borrowings have been used to finance, or provide a hedge against, group equity investments in foreign entities, exchange gains or losses on the borrowings (which otherwise would have been taken to the profit and loss account) may be offset as **reserve movements** against exchange differences arising on the retranslation of the net investments. The conditions that must apply are:
– the relationships between the investing company and the foreign entities concerned justify the use of the closing rate method for consolidation purposes;
– in any accounting period, the exchange gains and losses arising on foreign currency borrowings are offset only to the extent of the exchange differences arising on the net investments in foreign entities;
– the foreign currency borrowings whose exchange gains or losses are used in the offset process should not exceed the total amount of cash that the net investments are expected to generate, whether from profits or otherwise; and
– the accounting treatment is applied consistently from period to period.

12. Post balance sheet events

6251
FRSSE 14.1 – 14.4
An entity must adjust the amounts recognised in its financial statements to reflect **adjusting events** after the balance sheet date but must not make adjustments to reflect non-adjusting events after the balance sheet date. However, if non-adjusting events after the balance sheet date are **material**, non-disclosure could adversely affect users. Some form of disclosure is therefore necessary, and the FRSSE requires details of the **nature** of the event, and an **estimate** of its financial effect (or a statement that such an estimate cannot be made, if applicable) to be given. The date on which the financial statements are approved for issue and the names of those who gave that approval should be disclosed.

13. Related party transactions

If a reporting entity enters into a transaction with, or on behalf of, a related party (whether or not a price is charged) and the **transaction is material** to the reporting entity, it should be disclosed in the financial statements. The **following details** must be given:
- the names of the transacting related parties;
- details of the relationship between the parties;
- a description of the transactions;
- the amounts involved;
- any other elements of the transactions necessary for an understanding of the financial statements;
- the balances due to or from related parties at the balance sheet date including, where necessary, provisions for doubtful debts due;
- amounts in respect of debts due to or from related parties that were written off during the period.

6252
FRSSE 15.1

Transactions with related parties may be **disclosed on an aggregated basis** unless separate disclosure of an individual transaction (or series of individual but connected transactions) is required by law or is necessary for a proper appreciation of the effect on the financial statements of the reporting entity.

Personal guarantees given by directors in respect of borrowings by the reporting entity should be disclosed in the notes.

Separate disclosure is required for amounts included in the profit and loss account under **"Investment income"** and **"Other interest receivable and similar income"** that were received, or are receivable from, group undertakings. Similarly, amounts included under **"Interest payable and similar charges"** paid (or payable) to group undertakings should be shown separately.

6252–1
FRSSE 15.3 – 15.5

Commitments undertaken for the benefit of a parent undertaking or fellow subsidiary, or a subsidiary undertaking of the company, must be shown separately from those commitments in respect of **pensions** or **provisions** and also from each other.

Disclosure is not required of:
a. pension contributions paid to a pension fund;
b. emoluments for services as an employee of the reporting entity;
c. transactions with the following if the transaction occurs simply as a result of their role as providers of finance in the course of their business in that regard:
- utility companies;
- government departments and their sponsored bodies; or
- a customer, supplier, franchiser, distributor or general agent.

6252–2
FRSSE 15.7

When the reporting entity is **controlled by** another party, there should be disclosure of the related party relationship and the name of that party and, if different, that of the ultimate controlling party. If the controlling party or ultimate controlling party of the reporting entity is not known, that fact should be disclosed. This information should be disclosed irrespective of whether any transactions have taken place between the controlling parties and the reporting entity.

6253

D. Cash flow statement

Small companies are not required to provide a cash flow statement although the Board **encourages** doing so, using the indirect method, as shown by the following steps.

6254

Step 1 – The indirect method starts with operating profit (i.e. normally profit before income from shares in group undertakings) and adjusts it for non-cash charges and credits to reconcile it with cash generated from operations. Other sources and applications of cash are shown to arrive at total cash generated (or used) during the period.

Step 2 – Cash is taken as "cash at bank and in hand" less overdrafts repayable on demand, which should be reconciled to the balance sheet.

Step 3 – Cash flows are shown net of any attributable VAT or other sales tax unless the tax is irrecoverable by the reporting entity.

Step 4 – It is recommended that material transactions not resulting in movements of cash of the reporting entity are disclosed by way of note, if disclosure is necessary for an understanding of the underlying transactions.

For more detail on the accounting treatment and disclosure requirements for smaller companies see ¶4020.

SECTION 2

Parents of a group

6255
s 383(1), s 466(1)
CA 2006
A company that qualifies as a small or a medium-sized company can be the parent company of a group. However, the parent company will not be entitled to qualify for reporting exemptions in respect of a particular financial year, unless the group, during the year in question, qualifies as

– a small group, where the parent is a small company; or

– a medium-sized group, where the parent is a medium-sized company.

6256
s 383(1), s 466(1)
CA 2006
For the purposes of preparing abbreviated financial statements, a parent company may not be treated as either a small or medium-sized company in a specific year unless the group it heads **also qualifies** as a small or medium-sized group. Therefore, if the parent is a small company, it may file abbreviated financial statements if it is also the parent of a **small group**. Furthermore, if the small company is the parent of a medium-sized group, it may file abbreviated financial statements applicable to a medium-sized company only.

> ‎ MEMO POINTS ‎ It should be noted that these exemptions apply to the individual company accounts of the parent where it is eligible for, and taken advantage of, the exemption from preparing group accounts. There is no provision for **small and medium-sized groups** to file abbreviated group accounts.

6257
The rules for the parent company's individual accounts are summarised in the following table:

Exemptions based on size of company and group	Parent company is a small company	Parent company is a medium-sized company
Group is a small group	May file abbreviated accounts and prepare shorter-form accounts for shareholders	
Group is a medium-sized group	May file abbreviated accounts as a medium-sized company (i.e., exemptions are less extensive than for small companies)	May file abbreviated accounts as a medium-sized company
Group is neither small nor medium-sized	May not file shorter-form accounts	

Size limits

Under the Companies Act 2006 a group may be entitled to be treated as small or medium-sized in respect of a financial year if it satisfies any two of the following three conditions:

6258

	Small group		Medium-sized group	
Aggregate[1] turnover	Net[2]	£6,500,000	Net[2]	£25,900,000
	Gross[3]	£7,800,000	Gross[3]	£31,100,000
Aggregate[1] balance sheet total	Net[2]	£3,260,000	Net[2]	£12,900,000
	Gross[3]	£3,900,000	Gross[3]	£15,500,000
Average number of employees		50		250

Notes:
1. Aggregate figures are the sum of the relevant figures for each member of the group.
2. Net figures are stated after set-off and elimination of intra-group turnover, balances and profits/losses.
3. Gross figures are stated before set-off and elimination of intra-group turnover, balances and profits/losses.

The size limits are subject to periodic review and therefore change from time to time. The amounts shown above came into effect by the Companies Act 2006 (Amendments) (Accounts and Reports) Regulations 2008.

MEMO POINTS   The criteria do not have to be satisfied on the same basis (i.e, gross or net) from year to year. In addition, in any one year, it is permitted to use gross, net, or a combination of the two, in determining eligibility for the exemptions.

Reference period

In addition to satisfying the basic size tests referred to above, groups must also satisfy the following criteria before they qualify for the relevant exemptions:
– In respect of the parent company's **first financial year**, the group will qualify provided that it satisfies the size conditions in that year.
– In respect of **subsequent years**, the group will qualify provided that it satisfies the size conditions both in the year in question and the preceding year.
– A group that qualifies as small or medium-sized in one year will **continue to be treated** as so qualifying in the following year, even if it fails to satisfy the size conditions in the following year. However, if it does not satisfy the qualifying conditions in the year after that, then, for the **third year**, the group's financial statements must be prepared in a format appropriate to its size. On the other hand, if the group is able to satisfy the qualifying conditions in this third year, it may continue to take advantage of the exemptions.

6259

The financial years of a parent and its subsidiaries are not necessarily the same. Where this situation exists, the financial statements of the subsidiary to be used are the **most recent** available, as long as they **predate** the financial statements of the parent. However, if the subsidiary's figures cannot be ascertained without disproportionate expense or undue delay, the latest available figures may be used.

6260
s 383(7) CA 2006

Consolidated financial statements

As a general rule, parent companies are required to prepare consolidated financial statements under both the Companies Act and the accounting standards (in particular, FRS 2, "Accounting for subsidiary undertakings"). However, there are specific exemptions from this general requirement, namely that a parent company does not have to prepare consolidated financial statements if the group:
– qualifies as a small group; and
– is not an ineligible group.

6261
s 399 CA 2006

A **small company is not entitled to the exemptions** with respect to abbreviated or shorter-form financial statements **if** it is, or was at any time during the financial year, a member of an ineligible group. Similarly, the company is not entitled to the exemption from preparing consolidated financial statements if, at the year end, it is a parent of an ineligible group.

6262
s 398 CA 2006

If at the end of a financial year a company subject to the small companies' regime is a **parent company**, the directors, as well as preparing individual accounts for the year, may prepare group accounts for the year but are not obliged to do so.

> MEMO POINTS   The **exemption** given by s 248 of the Companies Act 1985 from the preparation of group accounts by parent companies heading medium-sized groups was abolished by the Companies Act 2006.

6263

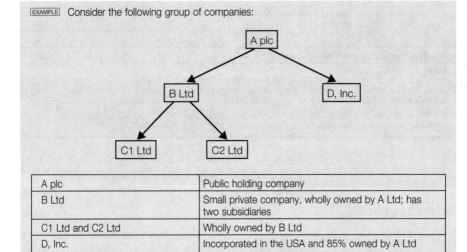

EXAMPLE   Consider the following group of companies:

A plc	Public holding company
B Ltd	Small private company, wholly owned by A Ltd; has two subsidiaries
C1 Ltd and C2 Ltd	Wholly owned by B Ltd
D, Inc.	Incorporated in the USA and 85% owned by A Ltd

B Ltd is not entitled to the exemptions relating to abbreviated financial statements as it is a member of an ineligible group (A plc is a public company).

6264
FRSSE 16.1

Where a small reporting company prepares **consolidated financial statements**, it should follow the accounting practices and disclosure requirements set out in FRSs 2, 6, 7 and, as they apply in respect of consolidated financial statements, FRSs 5, 9, 10 and 11.

6265

Where a small company has prepared **individual accounts** in accordance with the legal requirements contained in the FRSSE and is preparing group accounts in respect of the same year:
– it is bound by the legal requirements contained in the FRSSE and companies legislation;
– it must modify the balance sheet format (set out in ¶6105) in respect of item **B-III Investments** so as to contain:
1. Shares in group undertakings
2. Interests in associated undertakings
3. Other participating interests
4. Loans to group undertakings and undertakings in which a participating interest is held
5. Other investments other than loans
6. Others; and the balance sheet must state in a prominent position that they are prepared in accordance with the special regulations relating to small companies.

6266
s 409 CA 2006

Disclosures   Under the Companies Act 2006, the requirement to disclose information about related undertakings in the notes to a company's annual accounts applies whether or not the company has to produce group accounts, unless certain grounds for exemption are met. These grounds are applicable if the directors consider that disclosing information about a related undertaking would be seriously prejudicial to the business of:
– that undertaking;
– the company;
– any of the company's subsidiary undertakings; or
– any other undertaking which is included in the consolidation.

A parent undertaking making use of an exemption from preparing consolidated accounts should make a statement that its financial statements present information about it as an individual undertaking and not as a group. The statement should also give the grounds on which the parent undertaking is exempt from preparing consolidated financial statements. FRS 2(22)

A small parent company of a small group that has prepared shorter-form financial statements but is exempt from preparing consolidated financial statements may decide in favour of preparing consolidated financial statements all the same. In this case, it may adopt the **shorter format as modified for consolidated financial statements**. This modification consists of the standard exemptions available to small companies but requires the information in the balance sheet formats under Item B III to be expanded by requiring each of the following to be disclosed separately: **6267** FRSSE 16.4

– shares in group undertakings
– interests in associated undertakings
– other participating interests
– loans to group undertakings and undertakings in which a participating interest is held
– investments other than loans
– others. FRSSE 16.6

Similarly, these small companies are also entitled to take advantage of the FRSSE provisions, in terms of which consolidated financial statements prepared in accordance with the accounting practices and disclosure requirements set out in FRSs 2, 6, 7 and as they apply in respect of consolidated financial statements – FRSs 5, 9, 10 and 11. Where the reporting entity is part of a group that prepares publicly available consolidated financial statements, it is entitled to the exemptions given in FRS 8 paragraph 3(a)-(c). There is no provision, however, for a small parent company that voluntarily prepares consolidated accounts to file abbreviated accounts. **6268**

CHAPTER 3

Abbreviated accounts

In general, small companies deliver their accounts to the Registrar of Companies in the same format as those presented to shareholders. **Small and medium-sized companies** may take advantage of the exemptions offered under the Act to file abbreviated accounts. This entails the preparation of a separate set of accounts solely for this purpose, with levels of disclosure that differ according to whether the company is small or medium-sized. These disclosures are even less onerous than those required for shorter-form accounts prepared for shareholders. **6270**

Small companies do not necessarily use the exemption, especially given the fact that smaller entities are able to prepare shorter-form accounts for members and usually file these with the Registrar as well. Abbreviated accounts are often filed for reasons of business confidentiality. **6271**

Abbreviated accounts must be accompanied by a **special auditors' report** (¶5845), unless the company qualifies for and has taken advantage of the exemption not to appoint auditors. **6272**

Abbreviated accounts are not required to comply with the disclosure requirements of the accounting standards, including the FRSSE. The disclosure requirements are governed solely by the Companies Act.

Under the Companies Act 2006, a parent company that is subject to the **small companies regime** may prepare group accounts if it opts to do so. This option is not available to the parent of a medium-sized group. **6273**
s 398 CA 2006

The **statutory framework** governing the form and content of abbreviated accounts is contained in the Companies Act 2006 under Schedule 4 of SI 2008 No. 409. A number of exemptions from the disclosure requirements of Schedule 2 (information about related undertakings) and Schedule 3 (information about directors' benefits: remuneration) are available.

The following table summarises the requirements concerning abbreviated accounts for small companies: **6275**
s 444(5) CA 2006

Element of financial statements	Details of disclosure
Profit and loss account	Not required
Balance Sheet	Abbreviated balance sheet – Schedule 4 format (¶6278) Debtors and Creditors falling due after more than one year to be disclosed in the notes
Directors' report	Not required

Element of financial statements	Details of disclosure
Directors' statement (on face of balance sheet)	As required by s 414 (3) CA 2006 – see ¶6285
Cash flow statement	Voluntary disclosure encouraged
Notes to the accounts	Limited disclosures – Schedules 2, 3 and 4
Auditors' report	Special report required – unless company is exempt from requirement to appoint auditor. (See ¶5800).

1. Balance sheet

6278
SI 2008/409

A choice of two **abbreviated balance sheet formats** is permitted by Schedule 4 of SI 2008 No. 409 for a small company (see table below). These formats are adapted from the formats for large and medium-sized companies by aggregating the balance sheet headings to which an arabic number is assigned under SI 2008 No. 410. In other words, only **totals** for those balance sheet headings to which a roman numeral is assigned in Schedule 4 are required to be shown. Note that the above principle applies equally to Format 1 and Format 2.

6279
s 450(1)(2) CA 2006

The abbreviated balance sheet must be **signed on behalf of the board** of directors by a director of the company.

6281

The following table shows the requirements under Format 1.	
A	Called up share capital not paid
B	Fixed assets
I	Intangible assets
II	Tangible investments
III	Investments
C	Current assets
I	Stocks
II	Debtors [see Note]
III	Investments
IV	Cash at bank and in hand
D	Prepayments and accrued income
E	Creditors: amounts falling due within one year
F	Net current assets (liabilities)
G	Total assets less current liabilities
H	Creditors: amounts due after more than one year
I	Provisions for liabilities and charges
J	Accruals and deferred income
K	Capital and reserves
I	Called up share capital
II	Share premium account
III	Revaluation reserve
IV	Other reserves
V	Profit and loss account
Note. The aggregate amount falling due after more than one year must be shown separately, unless it is disclosed in the notes to the financial statements.	

2. Directors' statement

Abbreviated accounts must contain a statement in a prominent position on the balance sheet, above the signature of the director, that the accounts have been prepared in accordance with the special provisions relating to small companies.

6285
s 450(3) CA 2006

> [EXAMPLE] **Extract from directors' report**
> The directors' report has been prepared in accordance with the special provisions applicable to companies entitled to the small companies exemption.

Accounts that are subject to **audit exemption** are also required to attach similar statements. Where advantage is taken of the audit exemption, the directors must ensure that there is a statement on the **balance sheet** confirming:
– the company's entitlement to an audit exemption;
– that the members have not required the company to obtain an audit;
– their duty to keep accounting records and prepare accounts in accordance with companies legislation.

6286
s 475(3) CA 2006

> [EXAMPLE] For the year ending [date] the company was entitled to exemption under section 477 of the Companies Act 2006 relating to small companies.
> The members have not required the company to obtain an audit in accordance with section 476 of the Companies Act 2006.
> The directors acknowledge their responsibilities for complying with the requirements of the Act with respect to accounting records and the preparation of accounts.
> These accounts have been prepared in accordance with the provisions applicable to companies subject to the small companies regime.

3. Notes to the accounts

The notes to the abbreviated accounts must contain the disclosure requirements listed in Schedules 2, 3 and 4, as detailed below.

6288

a. Accounting policies

The accounting policies adopted in determining the amounts to be included in respect of items shown in the balance sheet and in determining the profit and loss of the small company must be disclosed in a note to the abbreviated financial statements.

6290
Sch 4 para 3
SI 2008/409

Most of the disclosures required by the FRSSE do not apply to small companies filing abbreviated accounts. However, where assets, liabilities, income or expenses have been measured in accordance with the requirements of the FRSSE, this fact should be disclosed in the note to the accounts, usually within the accounting policies.

> [EXAMPLE] The full financial statements from which these abbreviated financial statements have been extracted have been prepared in accordance with the Financial Reporting Standard for Smaller Entities (effective April 2008) under the historical cost convention.

b. Share capital

The following information must be given regarding the small company's share capital:
– the number and aggregate nominal value of shares of each class allotted,
– share allotments during the year including the type of shares allotted; their number and aggregate nominal value; the reasons for the allotment; and the consideration received by the company, and

6293
Sch 4 para 4
SI 2008/409

– for redeemable shares, the earliest and latest redemption dates, redemption premiums and details of options held.

c. Fixed assets

6295   For tangible assets, intangible assets and investments classified under the general term "fixed assets" in the balance sheet, the following information must be given:
1. The cost or valuation at the beginning and end of the financial year.
2. The impact of any of the following movements during the financial year:
– revaluations;
– acquisitions;
– disposals; or
– transfers.
3. In respect of provisions for depreciation or diminution in value:
– the cumulative amount of such provisions as at the beginning and end of the year;
– the total provision provided during the year;
– the amount of any adjustments to the provision on disposal of a fixed asset; or
– the amount of any other adjustments to the provisions during the year.

d. Creditors

6298

Sch 4 para 8 (1)
SI 2008/409

For all items shown under creditors the following **aggregate figures** must be stated:
– creditors payable **otherwise than in instalments** and falling due for payment more than five years after the balance sheet date; and
– any creditors payable **by instalments** and the amount of any instalments that fall due more than five years after the balance sheet date.

6299   In respect of each item shown under creditors in a small company's abbreviated balance sheet, the aggregate of any debts included under that item for which the company has given any security must be disclosed.

If any fixed cumulative dividends of a small company are in arrears, the following must be shown:
– the amount of the arrears; and
– the period for which the dividend or (if there is more than one class of share) for each class is in arrears.

e. Foreign currencies

6301

Sch 4 para 9
SI 2008/409

Where sums originally denominated in foreign currencies have been brought into the balance sheet or profit and loss account, the basis on which those sums were converted into sterling should be stated.

f. Comparative figures

6305

Sch 1 para 7
SI 2008/409

Comparative figures must be stated for items appearing in the notes to the financial statements. Where corresponding amounts in respect of the preceding year are not comparable, they should be adjusted and particulars and the reasons for it must be given. Comparative figures are not required for:
– directors' loans;
– shareholdings in other undertakings;
– accounting treatment of acquisitions; and
– fixed assets.

g. Subsidiaries and other investments

Disclosures are limited to the following:

a. **subsidiary undertakings**:
- details of subsidiary undertakings;
- shareholdings in subsidiary undertakings; and
- financial information about subsidiary undertakings.

b. **other investments**:
- significant holdings in undertakings other than subsidiary undertakings;
- membership of certain partnerships and unlimited partnerships;
- a parent undertaking drawing up financial statements for a larger group; and
- identification of the ultimate parent company.

6308
Sch 2 paras 1-3
SI 2008/409

Sch 2 paras 5-10
SI 2008/409

Under the provisions of the Companies Act 2006, the requirement to disclose information about related undertakings in the notes to a company's annual accounts applies irrespective of whether the company has to produce group accounts.

h. Loans and transactions involving directors and officers

The small company preparing abbreviated financial statements has to provide the disclosures required by companies legislation that deal with loans, quasi-loans and other dealings in favour of directors and particulars of transactions, arrangements and agreements with officers.

6311
s 413 CA 2006

i. Auditors' reports

Normally, abbreviated accounts filed with the Registrar of Companies must be accompanied by a copy of a special report from the auditors, stating that in their opinion:
- the company is entitled to deliver abbreviated financial statements in accordance with the relevant provisions, and
- the abbreviated financial statements have been properly prepared in accordance with the said provisions.

6314
s 247B(2) CA 2006

The special auditors' report on the abbreviated accounts should be dated on, or as soon as possible after, the date of the full audit report. This report is not required where a company is entitled to and has taken advantage of the exemption from appointing auditors.

6315

EXAMPLE **Special Auditors' Report**

In our opinion the company is entitled to deliver abbreviated financial statements prepared in accordance with Section 444 (3) of the Companies Act 2006, and the abbreviated financial statements on pages xx to xx have been properly prepared in accordance with those provisions.

Where a small company files abbreviated accounts, it is not obliged to file a copy of the complete audit report with the Registrar of Companies, unless the **full audit report**:
a. was **qualified**, in which case the special auditors' report must set out that report in full together with any further information necessary to understand the qualification; and
b. **contains a statement** that:
- the accounts, records or returns are inadequate or that the accounts do not agree with the records and returns, or
- the auditors have failed to obtain the necessary information and explanations.

6316
s 449(3)(a), (b)
CA 2006

Where the full audit report is **unqualified**, but contains an **explanatory paragraph** regarding a fundamental uncertainty, such as the going concern basis, the special auditors' report should also include the explanatory paragraph, under a section entitled "other

6318

information". The auditor should also include any further information necessary for a proper understanding of the report.

4. Medium-sized companies

6325
s 455(3) CA 2006
Medium-sized companies enjoy **no concessions** in respect of financial statements prepared for shareholders. Even where they prepare abbreviated accounts (for the Registrar), the concessions that are available relate principally to the profit and loss account, leaving the normal requirements in respect of the directors' report, balance sheet and notes to the financial statements fundamentally intact.

> *MEMO POINTS*   Under the Companies Act 2006, the Secretary of State is given the power to make regulations concerning abbreviated accounts for medium-sized companies.

Profit and loss account

6326
s 455(3)(a) CA 2006
Limited exemptions permit the following items in the profit and loss account items to be aggregated and shown as one item under "Gross profit or loss":

Format 1 and 3:	Format 2 and 4:
– Turnover; – cost of sales; – gross profit or loss; and – other operating income	– Turnover; – the change in stocks of finished goods and in work in progress; – own work capitalised; – other operating income; – raw materials and consumables; and – other external charges.

Notes to the accounts

6328
s 445(3)(b) CA 2006
Under the dispensation for medium-sized companies preparing abbreviated financial statements, the notes to the financial statements may omit the **segmental analysis** of turnover that would otherwise be required.

6330
Because the concessions applicable to medium-sized companies are limited, the cost of preparing abbreviated accounts might seem to outweigh the possible benefits of confidentiality. Where, however, the directors are of the opinion that publishing certain sensitive information may be detrimental to the company's business (e.g., under FRS 8), they will choose the option of filing abbreviated statements. In this event, as with small companies, the statements must contain a declaration – occupying a prominent position on the balance sheet – that they have been prepared in accordance with the special provisions relating to medium-sized companies.

6331
Readers will be aware that companies currently reporting under UK GAAP (excluding small companies using the FRSSE) will become subject to the **new regulatory regime** introduced by the FRC. In brief, all existing financial reporting standards and extracts are being replaced with a single new standard. The effective date is 1 January 2015, but until that time the existing rules continue to apply.

Auditors' report

6332
s 449 CA 2006
The rules relating to the auditors' report on abbreviated financial statements filed by a medium-sized company are the same as those for small companies, and are discussed at ¶6075.

5. Illustrative financial statements

In the following set of financial statements, S Ltd is the parent company of a small group **6370** that has taken advantage of the exemption in respect of producing group accounts. It has chosen to file abbreviated financial statements with the Registrar of Companies.

S Ltd
Abbreviated Accounts
30 April 20X4

INDEPENDENT AUDITORS' REPORT TO S LTD UNDER SECTION 449
OF THE COMPANIES ACT 2006

We have examined the abbreviated accounts set out on pages xx to xx, together with the financial statements of S Ltd for the year ended 30 April 20X4, prepared under section 396 of the Companies Act 2006.

Respective responsibilities of directors and auditors

The directors are responsible for preparing the abbreviated accounts in accordance with section 444 of the Companies Act 2006. It is our responsibility to form an independent opinion as to whether the company is entitled to deliver abbreviated accounts to the Registrar of Companies and whether the abbreviated accounts have been properly prepared in accordance with the regulations made under that section and to report our opinion to you.

We conducted our work in accordance guidance issued by the Auditing Practices Board (Now the Audit and Assurance Council). In accordance with that guidance we have carried out the procedures we consider necessary to confirm, by reference to the financial statements, that the company is entitled to deliver abbreviated accounts and that the abbreviated accounts are properly prepared. [See memo point 3, below]

Opinion

In our opinion the company is entitled to deliver abbreviated accounts prepared in accordance with section 444(3) of the Companies Act 2006, and the abbreviated accounts have been properly prepared in accordance with the regulations made under that section.

Other information

[*This section would be used only if other information needs to be given, e.g. any qualification the auditors deem necessary in particular circumstances.*]

...

[Signature]
A.N. Other (senior statutory auditor).
for and on behalf of: **XYZ LLP, Statutory Auditors**

[Address]   [Date]

MEMO POINTS   1. In the above, it is assumed that the company has taken advantage of sections 444 (3). This reference should be included or amended as appropriate.
2. The wording for a **Special Auditors' Report** for a medium-sized company is essentially the same as the above except that reference is made to section 445 of the Act (directors' and auditors' responsibilities, declaration and opinion) and the abbreviated accounts have been prepared in accordance with section 445 (3) of the Act.
3. The auditor dates the **special report** with the date on which it is signed. The auditor does not sign the special report until the directors have approved and signed the abbreviated accounts. Therefore, if the special report is dated after the signing of the auditor's report on the full annual accounts, add appropriate wording such as "The scope of our work for the purposes of this report does not include examining events occurring after the date of our auditor's report on the full financial statements."

S Ltd
Abbreviated Balance Sheet
30 April 20X4

	Notes	20X4	20X3
Fixed assets	2	£	£
Intangible assets		xxx	xxx
Tangible assets		xx, xxx	xx, xxx
Investments		x, xxx	x, xxx
		xx, xxx	xx, xxx
Current assets			
Stocks		xxx	xxx
Debtors	4	xxx	xxx
Cash at bank and in hand		x, xxx	x, xxx
Creditors: amounts falling due within one year	5	xxx	xxx
Net current assets		xx, xxx	xx, xxx
Total assets less current liabilities		**xx, xxx**	**xx, xxx**
Creditors: due after more than one year	5	xxx	xxx
Provisions for liabilities and charges		x, xxx	x, xxx
Net assets		xx, xxx	xx, xxx
Capital and reserves			
Share capital	6	xx, xxx	xx, xxx
Profit and loss account		xxx	xxx
Shareholders' funds		xx, xxx	xx, xxx

Directors' statement

These abbreviated accounts have been prepared in accordance with the special provisions relating to small companies contained in Part 15 of the Companies Act 2006, and are signed on behalf of the Board of Directors.

[Name]

Director

[Date]

MEMO POINTS   Where a company with an accounting period starting on or after 6 April 2008 has taken advantage of the **exemption from audit**, it must include the following statement on the balance sheet:

For the year ending... [date] the company was entitled to exemption from audit under section 477 of the Companies Act 2006 relating to small companies.

Director's responsibilities:

– The members have not required the company to obtain an audit of its accounts for the year in question in accordance with section 476,

– The directors acknowledge their responsibilities for complying with the requirements of the Act with respect to accounting records and the preparation of accounts.

These accounts have been prepared in accordance with the provisions applicable to companies subject to the small companies regime.

(Source: Companies House website)

S Ltd
Notes to the accounts at 30 April 20X4

1. Accounting policies

Basis of accounting

The accounts have been prepared under the historical cost convention and in accordance with the Financial Reporting Standard for Smaller Entities. The company and its subsidiaries comprise a small group. The company has therefore claimed the exemption provided by section 398 of the Companies Act 2006 not to prepare group accounts.

Turnover

Turnover comprises invoiced sales net of returns, trade discounts and VAT.

Goodwill

Goodwill arising on acquisition is capitalised and amortised over the useful economic life of the asset, subject to a maximum of 20 years.

Tangible fixed assets

The following depreciation rates are applied in order to write off each asset over its estimated useful life:

– Freehold land and buildings	2% on cost or revalued amounts
– Plant and machinery	20% on cost
– Fixtures/fittings	10% on cost
– Motor vehicles	25% on cost

Stocks

Stocks and work in progress are valued at the lower of cost or net realisable value, after allowing for slow-moving and obsolete items. The cost of stock comprises all direct expenditure and a proportion of fixed and variable overheads.

Research and development

Research and development expenditure is written off in the year it was incurred. Development expenditure is also written off, except where the directors are confident of the technical, commercial and financial viability of individual research projects. In these cases the development expenditure is deferred – to be amortised over the period during which the group is expected to benefit from the research.

Government grants

Government grants relating to expenditure on tangible fixed assets are treated as deferred income and released to the profit and loss account over the expected useful lives of the assets. Revenue related grants are credited to the profit and loss account as the expenditure is incurred.

Foreign currencies

Assets and liabilities in foreign currencies are translated into sterling at the rates of exchange ruling at the balance sheet date. Foreign currency transactions are translated into sterling at the rate of exchange ruling at the transaction date. Exchange gains and losses are taken to the profit and loss account or reserves as appropriate.

Pension costs

Contributions to the company's defined contribution pension scheme are charged to the profit and loss account for the year in which they are payable to the scheme. Differences between contributions payable and contributions actually paid in the year are shown as either accruals or prepayments at the year end.

Taxation

Corporation tax payable is provided for on taxable profits at the current rate.

2. Fixed Assets

Cost or valuation	£
1 May 20X3	xx, xxx
Additions	x, xxx
Disposals	
30 April 20X4	**xx, xxx**

Depreciation	
1 May 20X3	x, xxx
Disposals	x, xxx
Charge for the year	x, xxx
30 April 20X4	x, xxx

Net book value	
30 April 20X3	xx, xxx
30 April 20X4	xx, xxx

3. Subsidiary undertakings

As at 30 April 20X4 investments consist of an investment in a subsidiary undertaking totalling £xxx, which represents the acquisition cost of 100 percent of the ordinary share capital of M Ltd, which specialises in importing and distributing music. At 30 April 20X4 the aggregate share capital and reserves of M Limited totalled £xx, xxx and its profit for the year was £x, xxx.

4. Debtors

Debtors include an amount of £x, xxx (2X03: £x, xxx) falling due after more than one year.

5. Creditors

		20X4	20X3
		£	£
Bank loan	– due within 5 years	xxx	xxx
	– due after 5 years	xxx	xxx
		xxx	xxx
Bank overdraft		xxx	xxx
		xxx	xxx

6. Share capital

	20X4	20X3
	£	£
50,000 ordinary shares of £1 each		
Allotted, called up and fully paid		
30,000 ordinary shares of £1 each	xx, xxx	xx, xxx

7. Transaction with directors

Loan to director

During the course of the financial year Mr C was granted a short-term advance of £x, xxx, which is repayable on 1 January 20X6. Interest is charged at 6% per annum, payable at the end of the financial year.

CHAPTER 4

Dormant companies

A dormant company is defined as an entity that has **no significant accounting transactions** during the accounting period. Dormant companies are not exempt from the normal requirements to prepare, issue, and file financial statements, although the form and content of dormant accounts will inevitably be brief, given the absence of any significant accounting transactions.   **6400**

The directors can decide to keep a company dormant for a number of reasons, such as protecting a company name, to hold an asset or intellectual property, or as a management company set up as a vehicle to own the head lease or freehold of a property. The directors must ensure that, to **retain the company's dormant status**, no significant expenses are incurred, as these would compromise the possibility of claiming dormant status.

Agency, non-trading, and **nominee** companies are other types of entities that may claim dormant status.   **6402**

SECTION 1

Dormancy

Companies can be dormant from date of inception or they can qualify subsequently if they meet certain criteria.   **6404**

The **main benefit** of dormant status is that an entity qualifies for **exemption from audit** providing certain criteria are met, although the benefits of dormant status have been considerably ameliorated by the introduction of exemptions from audit now available to small companies.

A dormant company remains obligated to prepare accounts albeit that it has had no financial activity and can show no financial results. Accounts must be filed even if the company has been dormant for a number of years or where it has never traded.

Sample dormant company accounts are provided at the end of this section.

a. Criteria for claiming dormant status

6410   A company can be **classified** as dormant only if it has no significant accounting transactions in the financial period.

The Companies Act requires an entity's accounting records to contain entries regarding all:
– monies received or expended;
– assets and liabilities; and
– stocks purchased or sold.

The existence of these transactions would prevent a company claiming dormant status. However, such a company might still be able to avoid the audit requirement if it fulfils the requirements to be considered a small company (¶6017).

6412   When planning to make a company dormant, care must be taken to ensure that the company's **dormant status is not compromised** by incidental transactions such as:
– bank charges;
– interest received on bank and other balances;
– movement on inter-company accounts;
– sundry expenses; and
– write offs.

6414   The audit concept of **materiality** does not apply in the consideration of whether a company is dormant or not as it is the presence of a transaction, without regard to its monetary value, that affects the dormant classification. The **exception** to this rule are the transactions deemed insignificant.

Insignificant transactions

6416   The following transactions are deemed immaterial and **do not affect** a claim for dormant status:
a. The payment of a fee to the registrar of companies in relation to:
– a change of name;
– re-registration of the company;
– registration of the annual return; or
– a penalty for failing to deliver financial statements within the statutory time limits.
b. A transaction generated by a subscriber to the company's Memorandum of Association acquiring shares in the company as a result of an obligation under the memorandum.

> MEMO POINTS   In some cases a dormant company can submit **Form DCA** (Dormant Company Accounts) to Companies House, although this is **not suitable for all dormant companies**. The form has been designed for those companies seeking only to issue shares to subscribers to the Memorandum of Association. The form cannot be used for recording other transactions.

6418   A company wishing to remain dormant is **not permitted any paid employees** because the related transactions would have to be recorded in the company's accounting records and have the effect of setting aside the dormant status. Nevertheless, dormant companies are required to have at least one director, if private, or two directors, if public, as well as a company secretary.

b. Preparing and filing dormant accounts and other directors' responsibilities

6420   A dormant company is not exempt from **preparing, filing, and issuing financial statements**, although it can be eligible for certain other exemptions.

A dormant company that is a **subsidiary**, does not have to prepare or file accounts if its parent company guarantees all its liabilities as at the end of the financial year.

6422   The **directors and company secretary** for a dormant company have the same responsibilities as those of a trading company – namely to manage the company on behalf of the shareholders or members and to ensure all the required returns, accounts and other documents reach Companies House by due date. If accounts are filed late the company will be penalised as there is no special treatment for dormant companies.

Typically, a **dormant set of accounts** will include a balance sheet and related accounting **6424** policies and notes, although they will inevitably be relatively brief. However, in respect of the first year in which a company is dormant (i.e. where it had traded in the previous financial year), a profit and loss account showing the comparative figures is required.

Filing time limits

Dormant companies are required to file a **balance sheet** and any relevant notes to the **6426** accounts that must comply with the statutory requirements of the Companies Act. Annual accounts must be delivered to Companies House in accordance with the normal rules: within 9 months of a company's accounting reference date (ARD) for a private company and 6 months for a public company (see ¶9354).

c. Audit exemption

One of the most important implications for dormant companies is that the majority are **6430** exempt from the obligation to have their financial statements audited.

Certain entities enjoy automatic exemption, but others also qualify for this status if they meet **additional criteria**.

A dormant company is **automatically exempt** if it has been dormant since formation. **6432**

It may also **claim exemption** in respect of a particular financial year if it has been dormant since the end of the previous financial year and it meets the following conditions:
a. it is entitled to prepare its accounts as a **small company** (see ¶6435), or it would have been entitled to do so but for the fact that it was a public company or a member of an ineligible group; and
b. it is not required to prepare **group financial statements** for the year.

> MEMO POINTS Note that there is a **specific exclusion** in respect of a company that at any time during the financial year was a banking company, an authorised insurance company or an authorised person under Part 4 of the Financial Services and Markets Act 2000. Such a company is never exempted from the audit requirement.

Any member, or group of members, holding not less than 10% of the company's issued share **6434** capital may require the company to be audited notwithstanding any exemption it would otherwise enjoy. Thus, even if a company would be automatically exempt, this exemption would fall away if the requisite number of shareholders wished it. They would achieve their objective by lodging a notice during the financial year in question but not later than one month before the end of the year.

A further condition for the exemption is that the balance sheet must contain a **signed** **6435** **statement by the directors** that:
– the company was entitled to exemption from audit under s. 480 of the Companies Act 2006;
– no members have required the company to obtain an audit;
– the directors acknowledge their responsibilities for complying with the requirements of the Act relating to accounting records and the preparation of accounts.

> MEMO POINTS The **qualifying criteria for small companies** (dealt with in detail in ¶6017) are that at least two of the following conditions must be met:
> – the annual turnover is £6.5m or less;
> – the balance sheet total is £3.26m or less; and
> – the average number of employees is 50 or less.

Where a company **has not been dormant since formation** but subsequently seeks dormant **6438** status, it must pass the test that it was permitted to prepare small company financial statements for the previous financial year. The following examples illustrate how the test is applied.

EXAMPLE **Small company seeking dormant status**

1. If Company A was a small company with a December year end, and it became dormant during 20X2, it could elect to **dispense with an audit** in 20X3.
2. If Company B first met the criteria for classification as a small company in 20X2, it would become entitled to prepare small company financial statements in respect of 20X3. This results from the requirement to meet the small company criteria **two years in succession**. The company may dispense with the audit in 20X4.
3. If Company C was not a small company in 20X2, the **earliest date** at which it could elect to dispense with the audit would be 20X5 because it would not be able to prepare small company accounts until 20X4.

Companies not meeting small company criteria

6440 **Public company and ineligible groups** There is a relaxation of the normal "small company" rules in respect of dormant public companies and members of ineligible groups that are dormant. As long as these companies meet the size criteria to be a small company, their status as a public company or their membership of an ineligible group does not stop them taking advantage of the audit exemption available to other dormant companies.

6442 Where a dormant company files **abbreviated accounts** (¶6270) with the Registrar of Companies, it is exempt from the requirement that they be accompanied by a copy of a **special auditors' report** (¶5800).

Accounts to be filed when audit exemption is claimed

6444 Dormant companies that are **eligible** and wish **to claim audit exemption** can be distinguished as follows:
a. Private companies need only prepare and deliver to Companies House an abbreviated balance sheet and notes. A profit and loss account and directors' report are not required for filing at Companies House but a directors' report and, where a company traded in the previous financial year, a profit and loss account must be supplied to members.
b. Dormant public companies must prepare and file with Companies House:
– a balance sheet;
– directors' report;
– notes to the accounts; and
– if the company traded in the previous financial year, a profit and loss account.

6446 Where a dormant company's accounts are not audited, then the balance sheet delivered to the Registrar of Companies must also contain **a statement by the directors**, in a position above the signature or signatures of the director(s), stating that:
1. the company was dormant throughout the financial year and so entitled to claim exemption from audit under the Companies Act;
2. the **members have not requested** the company have its accounts for the respective financial period audited; and
3. the directors recognise their responsibilities for ensuring the company keeps **adequate accounting records** (s.221 CA 2006) and for preparing accounts that give a true and fair view of the company at the end of the financial period in accordance with the requirements of the Companies Act.
An example of a directors' statement is given in the sample accounts for a dormant company (see ¶6454).

---

d. Ending of dormant status

6450 In general a company may **forfeit its dormant status** either by resuming trading, engaging in "significant transactions" or failing to continue to satisfy the conditions required for any of the exemptions.

Where the company ceases to fulfil the conditions required for dormant status, the conse-quence is that audit exemptions will also cease and the entity will no longer be exempt from the obligation to appoint auditors for the financial year in which it lost its dormant status. However, the company may remain exempt from audit if it nevertheless satisfies the audit exemption criteria for small companies.

When **a company loses its dormant status** it is not required to notify the Registrar of the fact. However, if it starts trading again, it must notify HMRC and put together statutory accounts and Company Tax Returns after its year end.

The steps below should be followed:
– inform HMRC within 3 months that business has commenced;
– send accounts to Companies House within 9 months of the year end;
– pay any Corporation Tax due within 9 months and 1 day of the company's year end; and
– send a Company Tax Return, including full statutory accounts, to HMRC within 12 months of the end of the company's year end.

Appointment of auditors

Where a **company ceases to be dormant**, it is the directors' responsibility to appoint auditors (unless exemption from audit can be claimed on the grounds of being a small company).   **6452**

The directors are required under the Act to appoint the auditors either:
a. at any time before the next meeting of the company at which accounts are to be laid, or
b. where the company is a private company that has dispensed with the requirement to lay accounts in general meeting:
– at any time before the end of the period of 28 days beginning with the day on which copies of the company's annual financial statements are next sent to members; or
– at the beginning of the general meeting if notice has been given by any member or director requiring the laying of accounts.

e. Sample accounts

The following sample accounts illustrate the accounts of a company that was dormant throughout the financial year and which was exempt from the provisions relating to the audit of accounts.   **6454**

Registered number:
01568974834
England and Wales

Dormant Limited
Annual Report and Unaudited Accounts
Year ended 31 December 20X3

Report of the directors
(*Not required in abbreviated accounts*)

The directors present their annual report with the unaudited accounts of the company for the year ended 31 December 20X3. The company is dormant and has not traded during the year. The company has, however, **acted as an agent** during the year.

Mr A, Mr B, and Mr C were directors of the company throughout the accounting period. Their interests in the parent company, X Ltd, are disclosed in the report and accounts of that company.

Signed on behalf of the board of directors by

Mr A   Approved by the board on [*date*]
Director/Secretary

Profit and loss account for the year ended 31 December 20X3

The company has not traded during the year or the preceding financial year. During these years, the company received no income and incurred no expenditure and made neither a profit nor a loss. There were no other gains or losses in the year.

Balance Sheet at 31 December 20X3

	20X3	20X2
	£	£
CURRENT ASSETS		
Debtors		
Amounts due by group undertakings – parent company	xxx	xxx
Total assets less current liabilities	xxx	xxx
	xxx	xxx
CAPITAL AND RESERVES		
Called up share capital		
Allotted and fully paid		
xxx shares of £1	xxx	xxx
SHAREHOLDERS' FUNDS	xxx	xxx

For the financial year ended 31 December 20X3, the company was entitled to exemption from audit under section 480 of the Companies Act 2006 relating to dormant companies. Members have not required the company to obtain an audit of its accounts under section 476. The directors acknowledge their responsibilities under the Act in respect of maintaining accounting records and the preparation of accounts.

Signed on behalf of the board of directors by

Mr A   Approved by the
Director   board on [date]

Notes to the accounts

Agency arrangements (disclosed to third parties) The company was dormant and has not traded during the financial year. It has, however, acted in certain transactions as an agent for the parent company.

SECTION 2

Special companies that may claim dormant status

1. Agency companies

6460   A dormant company may **act as an agent** and allow its name to be used by another trading company. The trading company acting as the principal is frequently another company in the same group.

Type of agency agreement

6462   The precise details of the agreement between an agency company and its principal company determine whether the agency is dormant or not. One of the most significant details in this respect is the **type** of agency agreement and whether it is disclosed or undisclosed.

6464   **Disclosed agency agreement**   A disclosed agency arrangement is one in which the parties transacting with the agent are made aware of the identity of the principal and the fact that the company is acting as agent for that principal. Where the agency agreement is disclosed to a **third party**, the agent will be able to claim **dormant status**, subject to the relevant disclosure requirements.

Where the agent contracts on behalf of a principal whose existence is disclosed to all parties in the documentation, it is the principal who becomes a party to the contract. In this instance, the transactions are shown in the principal's accounts. The agent is not directly liable under the contract and therefore records nothing in its books of account. As a result, the agent has no significant transactions (¶6416) arising from the agency which could prevent it being regarded as a dormant company.

One potential **problem area** is that of **agency fees**. If the agency does not earn any fees or commission, there will not be any significant accounting transactions, thus allowing dormant status to be claimed. It must be made clear in the terms of trade underpinning each agreement that the company enters into that the agent is acting only in the **capacity of an agent** and not as the principal.

An **example of a disclosed agency agreement** might be a travel agent tied to a particular travel operator, who states on its booking forms, or in its terms and conditions of business, that the contractual relationship is a direct one between the travel operator and the customer.

6466

Undisclosed agency agreement   An agent acting for an undisclosed principal is deemed to be contracting on its own behalf and is liable on any contracts so entered into. As a result, the agency will have to account for any transactions in its accounting records and will not then qualify as a dormant company.

6468

An **example of an undisclosed agency agreement** is where a company leasing equipment to customers may enter into an arrangement with a finance company, who assumes the legal rights and obligations of the lease agreement. However, the documentation may also indicate that the company has entered into a direct contract with the customer and not the financier.

Another **example** is where a subsidiary transfers its business to a parent company but effectively continues to act as an agency for trading purposes.

Disclosure requirements   Where the agency does not disclose the principal, it will have to account for any transactions entered into with the principal as its own transactions through its profit and loss account. Any debtor or creditor balances with customers and the principal will also have to be reported in the balance sheet.

6470

The **profit and loss account disclosures** will depend on the terms of the agency agreement. For instance, if the principal invoices the agent for goods that the agent sells to third parties and invoices, then the gross trading figure should be recorded in the profit and loss account. Where no trading is shown through the profit and loss account, transactions are conducted through an **inter-company account** with its principal.

6472

When **claiming exemption from audit** on the grounds of being dormant under section 285 of the Companies Act 2006, any company that has acted as an agent for any person in the financial year must state this fact in their accounts. This disclosure will not jeopardise any claim for dormancy.

6474

2. Non-trading companies

The fact that a company might not currently be trading does not necessarily mean that it is dormant. For example, **incidental transactions** such as various non-trading expenses or sundry other activity in accounts (see ¶6412 for a more complete listing) can compromise a dormant company's status. Nevertheless, such non-trading companies may still be able to claim dormant status where either of the following apply:
– the accounting transactions are deemed insignificant and can be disregarded for the purpose of claiming dormant status; or
– it may be able to claim exemption under the rules for exemption from audit.

6476

Non-trading companies with significant accounting transactions passing through its books **will not qualify as dormant in a legal sense**, and will not be able to take advantage of the dormant company audit exemption.

3. Nominee companies

6478   Generally, a nominee company is one that has been nominated by another to hold shares on its behalf. Such a company does not receive an income or incur costs that need be shown in the profit and loss account. Furthermore, it is not permitted to hold assets or liabilities in its own name.

As such, it can be likened to a non-trading company. However, in its ordinary course of business, it acquires, disposes of, or transfers investments on behalf of the beneficial owners. Even though the nominee company does not have a **beneficial interest** in the transactions it records in its books, these activities can be construed as significant accounting transactions and would preclude dormant status.

SECTION 3

Impact of FRS 102

6480   The transition requirements in FRS 102 "The Financial Reporting Standard applicable in the UK and Ireland" covering dormant companies are brief, as one would expect. Basically a dormant company (meeting the Companies Act definition) can elect to retain its pre FRS 102 accounting policies, covering equity, assets and liabilities at the transition date, and continue to do so until it is involved in any new transactions.

PART 9

Group accounts

CHAPTER 1

General requirements

A group comprises a parent and its subsidiary undertakings structured for a variety of legal, tax and strategic objectives. A group company is defined as a holding company or subsidiary undertaking. **6500**

Under the Companies Act, a group is not recognised as a separate legal person, but rather as a concept for enabling one or more individual companies to report as a single entity, for the purposes of providing financial information. **Each individual undertaking** comprising a group, has its own obligation to maintain accounting records and produce individual financial statements.

MEMO POINTS   An **undertaking is defined** in the Companies Act and FRS 2 "Accounting for subsidiary undertakings" as a body corporate or partnership, or an unincorporated association carrying on a "trade" or "business" with or without a view to a profit.

Group accounts consist of the financial statements of the individual companies in the group, which are added together, before a number of consolidation adjustments are made. Group accounts must also be accompanied by a group directors' report. A group is effectively treated as if it is a separate company, with one group of shareholders. The group financial statements as such, represent the balances and profits (or losses) resulting from transactions with external third parties after eliminating all inter-company transactions. **6501**

This chapter covers the rules regulating the requirement to prepare group accounts, the exemptions available to parent undertakings, the criteria for determining whether a **parent and subsidiary relationship** actually exists and the circumstances that permit individual subsidiary undertakings exemption or exclusion from consolidation. Small and medium sized groups are covered in ¶6340 and ¶6562. **6502**

The **form and content** of consolidated accounts is covered in ¶6700.

MEMO POINTS   1. Under the Companies Act 2006, the Secretary of State has the power (through drafting new regulations) to adjust the formats of the financial statements. To-date, **two sets of**

regulations have been issued: one set specific to small companies (see ¶6000) and the other to large and medium-sized companies. These regulations effectively restate the provisions of the 1985 Act.

2. The **terms** "Consolidated accounts" and "Group accounts" are synonymous.

3. Each individual undertaking forming part of a group is responsible for its own **tax affairs** as they are dealt with as separate entities under the UK tax system. There is, however, a system of Group Loss Relief for UK Corporation Tax purposes, governed by a different set of criteria. Group aspects of taxation are covered in ¶9000.

4. As with individual accounts, **non-listed companies** can elect to prepare group accounts in accordance with the Companies Act or under international accounting standards.

5. The FRC has published **amended versions** of FRS 2 and FRS 6 "Mergers and Acquisitions". The amendments do not alter the existing requirements of the two standards, but update the references to correspond with the Companies Act 2006 and the Large and Medium-sized Companies (and Reports) Regulations 2008.

A. Overview and classification

6504   The Companies Act requires a company that is **a parent undertaking** at the end of the financial year, to produce group consolidated accounts in addition to individual accounts for the parent undertaking. **Consolidation** refers to the process of adjusting and combining the individual financial information of a parent undertaking and its subsidiary undertakings, within consolidated financial statements.

All parent companies are required to prepare group accounts, including entities that prepare financial statements intended to give a true and fair view and which have subsidiary undertakings, including charitable trusts and pension funds, that undertake trading activities or that control resources through subsidiary undertakings.

6505   The test of whether group accounts should be prepared is based on the situation pertaining at the end of the financial year.

Test	Should group accounts be prepared?
1. Where a parent company has subsidiary undertakings throughout most of the accounting period, but not at the financial year-end.	There is no requirement to prepare group accounts.
2. Where a company acquires a subsidiary undertaking on the last day of its financial year thereby creating a group.	Obliged to prepare group accounts for the year, unless it is entitled to one of the exemptions outlined in ¶6570.

Types of Group structure

6506   The most common types of group structure are set out in the diagrams below.

A. Parent with one or more direct subsidiaries

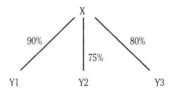

Y1-Y3 = direct subsidiaries of X which controls over 50% of the voting rights.

B. Parent with sub-subsidiaries

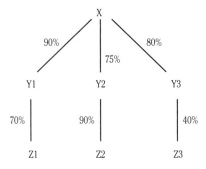

Both Z1 (63%) and Z2 (67.5%) are sub-subsidiaries of X.
X holds (indirectly) only 32% of Z3 via its holding in Y3.

C. Sub-subsidiaries (including direct holdings)

X has a controlling interest in Y1 (90%) that in turn has a controlling interest of 70% in Z, which then becomes a sub-subsidiary of X (63%). X also has a direct holding of 20% bringing its total holding in Z1 to 83%.

General framework requirements   There are a number of general requirements that are applicable to the preparation of group accounts (see also ¶6700). Group accounts should:
– comprise a consolidated balance sheet and profit and loss account covering the parent company and its subsidiary undertakings;
– comply with the Companies Act provisions regarding the **form and content** of the consolidated financial statements; and
– be prepared in accordance with the true and fair view concept. If compliance with the provisions of the Companies Act is insufficient to meet this requirement, additional information must be given in the notes to the financial statements.

6508

In addition all companies within the reporting group should:
– use **uniform accounting policies** and if this does not apply, consolidating adjustments should be made to the subsidiaries' financial statements prior to consolidation;
– select the same financial period except in the year of acquisition, and the same financial year-end date.

6509

An **exception** to this rule is where a subsidiary does not prepare co-terminus financial statements, for instance **due to legal reasons**. In this case interim financial statements for the subsidiary company should be used, made up to the same date as the parent company's year end, or where this is not possible, up to a date not more than 3 months preceding the group's year end.

Classification

6510   The **principal methods** by which entities can further their economic activities through investments in other entities is tabulated below, starting with the highest level of involvement: namely, a parent/subsidiary relationship through to associate investments, joint arrangements or simple trade investments.

Entity/arrangement	Nature of relationship	Description of the defining relationship
Subsidiary (50% +)	Investor controls the investee.	Has the ability to direct and control operational and financial policy.
Associate (20% +)	Investor holds a participating interest and exercises significant influence but does not control its investee.	A substantial minority shareholding enabling the investor to be actively involved in policy.
Joint venture (50%)	Investors hold long-term interest and shares control under a contractual arrangement.	A contractual relationship under which two or more investors control a venture as a separate venture in its own right.
Joint arrangements that are not an entity (JANE)	Entities participate in an arrangement to carry on part of their own trades or business.	Does not carry on a trade of its own. Investor extends its own trade through the joint arrangement.
Simple investment (¶1750)	Passive	The investor's interest does not qualify the investee as an associate, a joint venture or a subsidiary. The interest involves limited influence.

B. Identifying the parent-subsidiary relationship

6512
FRS 2 (14)

Whether a parent-subsidiary relationship exists is determined by the **degree of control** exercised by the parent over the "subsidiary". The **principal test** is therefore one of control, whereas previously, the emphasis of a parent and subsidiary relationship was primarily based on share ownership. This **change in emphasis** has reduced the opportunities for structuring groups in ways that enabled certain ventures or enterprises to be excluded from consolidation. "Control" may take a number of forms as discussed below. **Unincorporated undertakings** are also subject to the requirements for inclusion in group financial statements.

 MEMO POINTS 1. The term "subsidiary company" has now been replaced by "**subsidiary undertaking**" as it covers a greater range of entities such as charitable trusts and pension funds, that undertake trading activities or that control resources through subsidiary undertakings.
2. A **parent undertaking** will be treated as the parent of any subsidiary undertakings and its immediate subsidiary undertakings.

1. Evidence of a parent-subsidiary relationship

6514
FRS 2 (14)

Both the Companies Act 2006 and FRS 2 stipulate that **an undertaking is a parent undertaking** of another subsidiary where one or more of the following aspects of control apply, as set out in the table below.

Control category	Parent company – basis of control
a. Voting rights (ownership – s1162 CA 2006)	It holds a majority of **voting rights** in the subsidiary undertaking subject to a number of general rules).
b. Member of the undertaking	It has the **right to appoint or remove directors** holding a majority of the voting rights at meetings of the board on all, or substantially all, matters.
c. Dominant influence	It has the right to exercise dominant influence over the undertaking: **a.** by virtue of **provisions** contained in the undertaking's Memorandum and Articles of Association; or **b.** by virtue of a **control contract** (in writing, authorised by the Memorandum and Articles of the controlled undertaking and permitted by the law under which the undertaking is established); or **c.** It is a **member** of the undertaking and controls alone, pursuant to an agreement with other shareholders or members, a **majority of the voting rights** in the undertaking. There is no longer any reference to participating interest.

MEMO POINTS   **Shares** held by another on behalf of the parent company are treated as direct holdings of the parent in the undertaking.

a. Voting rights

"Voting rights" is taken to mean the rights conferred on shareholders in respect of their shares, or if the undertaking does not have a share capital, on its members, to vote at general meeting. Where an undertaking **does not conduct general meetings** at which matters are decided by the exercise of voting rights, references to "a majority of voting rights" mean having the right to direct its overall policy or to alter the terms of its constitution.

6515

General rules

The general rules which should be applied in determining whether an undertaking **holds a "right"** in another undertaking are as follows:

6516

Rights that are exercisable in **certain circumstances** can only be taken into account if:	– these circumstances have arisen and continue to arise; or – these events are within the control of the persons owning the rights.
Rights normally exercisable, but **temporarily incapable of being exercised**	– must continue to be taken into account.
Rights held by a person in a **fiduciary capacity**	– are to be disregarded.
Rights **held by a nominee** for another	– are to be treated as held for the other.
Rights **attached to shares held** by way of security are to be treated as held by the person holding the security:	– where the rights are exercisable only in accordance with that person's instructions, disregarding any right to exercise them in order to preserve the value of, or realise, the security; and– with regard to shares held in connection with the granting of loans as part of normal business activities, where the rights are exercisable only in that person's interests, disregarding any right to exercise them in order to preserve the value of, or realise, the security.

b. Member of another undertaking

6518 An undertaking shall be treated **as a member of another undertaking** if:
– any of the first undertaking's subsidiary undertakings is a member of the second undertaking; or
– a person acting on behalf of the first undertaking or any of its subsidiary undertakings holds any shares in the second undertaking.

These provisions confirm, that any shares held by another on behalf of the parent undertaking, are effectively **direct holdings** of the parent undertaking.

c. Dominant influence

6520 The term "dominant influence" is defined as, the influence that can be exercised to achieve the operating and financial policies desired by the holder of the influence, notwithstanding the legal rights or interests of any other party.

The recognition by the Companies Act of dominant influence, as the key factor that impacts on the obligation to prepare group accounts, supports the emphasis placed on *de facto* control, rather than legal ownership, as the basis for consolidation.

6522 Examples include identifying the following:
– the markets an undertaking should target for expansion;
– sources of finance and optimal gearing structure; and
– dividend policy.

Right to exercise dominant influence

6524
FRS 2 (7a)

The right to exercise dominant influence refers to the right of the holder to give directions, concerning the operating and financial policies of another undertaking. The **following guidance** can be used to assess whether dominant influence exists:
1. The **individual circumstances of each case** should be considered, including the effect of any formal or informal agreements between the undertakings.
2. A **power of veto**, or any other reserve power that has the necessary effect in practice, can allow an undertaking to exercise dominant influence over another.
3. The influence may actually be exercised in an **interventionist or non-interventionist manner**. For instance, this influence could take the form of setting broad performance targets or intervening only in critical matters, without being involved on a day to day basis.
4. On **evidence that one undertaking** has exercised dominant influence over another, it is assumed that this influence continues, until there is evidence to the contrary. However, for consolidated financial statement purposes, the relationship between the undertakings should be examined each year to assess any evidence of a change in status.
Commercial relationships such as that of supplier, customer or lender do not of themselves constitute dominant influence.

> ⬚ MEMO POINTS ⬚ 1. The **legal holder of a veto** may be able to exercise dominant influence over an undertaking only if the powers are held in conjunction with other rights or powers, or if they relate to the day-to-day activities of that undertaking and no similar veto is held by other, albeit unconnected, parties.

2. Problems with identifying subsidiary-parent relationships

6530 There are a number of possible problem areas in trying to identify whether a parent-subsidiary relationship exists, including where:
– there is more than one parent undertaking;
– entities are managed on a unified basis;
– control is exercised by a third party;

– the status of quasi-subsidiaries needs to be determined; and
– others (e.g. venture capital companies and limited partnerships).
Each of these is discussed below.

More than one parent undertaking

The criteria for identifying whether a parent and subsidiary relationship exists includes **some tests based on ownership** (e.g. voting rights), as well as other **tests based on control** (e.g. dominant influence). As a consequence, more than one undertaking may qualify as the parent of a particular subsidiary undertaking, such as where:
– undertaking A holds the majority of voting rights in undertaking X; or
– undertaking B holds the remaining minority of voting rights in undertaking X, but actually exercises dominant influence over undertaking X.

6532
FRS 2 (14)

In the above circumstances, both undertakings A and B would technically qualify as the parent of undertaking X.

6534

In practice, however, it will be necessary for each of the "parents" to carefully consider whether, despite its own shareholdings or its rights of control, the rights of the other parent effectively stop it exercising its own theoretical rights and if so to exclude the undertaking from its own group accounts on the grounds of severe long-term restrictions hindering the exercise of its rights.

> ☐ MEMO POINTS ☐ 1. The **scope of the term "undertaking"** is more inclusive than the term "company" and is defined as a body corporate, partnership, or unincorporated association carrying on trade or business.
> 2. **Specific guidance** is given in the Companies Act on the following:
> – for **group financial statements**, references to shares in an undertaking with a structure that has capital but no share capital, should be interpreted as the rights to share in the capital of the undertaking, as it is structured.
> – where the **undertaking does not have any capital**, the interests of the parent company relate to any right to share in the profits or liability to contribute to the losses of the undertaking, or any potential obligation to contribute to the debts or expenses of the undertaking, in the event of a winding up.

Entities managed on a unified basis

Where two or more undertakings are managed on a unified basis, because the whole of the operations of the undertakings are integrated and they are managed as a single unit, a parent-subsidiary relationship will not exist.

6535
FRS 2 (12)

However, unified management does not arise solely because one undertaking manages another, as this may not meet the condition that the operations of the undertakings are integrated. The **test for management** on a unified basis should be considered in conjunction with the test on existence of dominant influence.

Control exercised by a third party

Control is defined as the ability of an undertaking to direct the operating and financial policies of another undertaking, with a view to gaining economic benefit from its activities. Situations may arise where control flows from a common third party, which brings into question whether a parent-subsidiary relationship exists.

6539
FRS 2 (6)

Benefits of control enjoyed by other parties   In certain cases, one party exercises control over an entity, but another party obtains the benefits from the entity. This gives rise to the question whether a parent and subsidiary relationship exists.

6540

A practical example of this is the **securitisation industry**. Securitisation is the means by which the providers of finance fund a specific block of assets rather than the general business of the company. The assets that have been most commonly securitised in the United Kingdom are household mortgages, credit card balances and trade debtors. The assets to be securitised are transferred by a company (the "originator") to a special purpose vehicle (the "issuer") in return for an immediate cash payment. Additional deferred consideration may also be payable.

FRS 5 (D1)

6541   The major **financial and operating policies of the issuer** are usually predetermined by agreements that constitute the securitisation, so that neither the owner of its share capital nor the originator, has any significant discretion over how it is run. The originator is granted rights to surplus income, and where relevant, capital profits, from the assets. Under these circumstances, the originator does not enjoy an ownership interest in the issuer nor does it exercise dominant influence over it. Hence, it is not a parent undertaking within the rules of either the Companies Act or FRS 2, but could fall within the definition of a quasi-subsidiary under FRS 5, as discussed below.

The status of quasi-subsidiaries

6543   A quasi-subsidiary of a reporting entity is defined as a company, trust, partnership or other vehicle that, though not fulfilling the definition of a subsidiary, is directly or indirectly controlled by the reporting entity and gives rise to benefits, that are in substance no different from those arising from a subsidiary. The ability to direct the financial and operating policies of that entity with a view to gaining economic benefit from its activities is evidence of control, as is the ability to prevent others from also enjoying any gains.

6544   The **definition of a subsidiary undertaking** is based on the concept of control. However, it was nevertheless still possible to design organisational structures where some entities, though controlled by the reporting entity, could avoid consolidation. This was achieved by placing assets and liabilities in an entity, or "vehicle", generally called a "controlled non-subsidiary", that fell beyond the reach of the legal definition of subsidiary undertaking.

With these organisational structures, the commercial effect of the transactions from the perspective of the reporting entity, would be no different from that which would result were the "vehicle" actually a subsidiary. The reporting entity would still benefit from the overall contribution of the "vehicle". As such, FRS 5 seeks to ensure that such "vehicles" are consolidated by introducing the concept of a quasi-subsidiary.

6545
FRS 5 (32)   Evidence of which party gains the benefit from the net assets of any entity depends on which party is exposed to the risks inherent in them. Where the financial and operating policies of a "vehicle" are in substance predetermined, contractually or otherwise, then the party possessing control will be the one that gains the benefits arising from the net assets of the entity.

6546
FRS 5 (35)   **Exclusion**   Under FRS 5, quasi-subsidiaries should be included in the consolidated accounts as if they were legal subsidiaries. The only circumstance in which it is appropriate to exclude a quasi-subsidiary from consolidation, is where the interest in the quasi-subsidiary is held exclusively with a view to subsequent resale and the subsidiary has not previously been included in the reporting entity's consolidated financial statements. The general conditions for exclusion from consolidation are addressed in ¶6570.

Venture capital companies

6550
FRS 9 (50)   In the venture capital and investment trust industry, the business of the investor is to provide capital to other entities, often accompanied by advice and guidance. The stake taken by the investor and the rights attributable to that stake, vary according to circumstances.

When considering investments made by venture capital companies, care must be taken to distinguish between those investments described as short/term "trade investments", which are bought with the intention of being sold for a quick profit and where the investors' relationship to its investment tends to be that of a portfolio investor, and those which are part of the venture capitalist's long term strategic investment policy.

Limited partnerships

6553   The topic of limited partnerships is beyond the scope of this book **except the requirements** that effect group accounts, which are outlined below.

With a limited partnership, one or more of the partners has limited liability for the firm's debts. However, there must be **at least one general partner** whose liability is unlimited. A body corporate may be a limited partner. A limited partner may not bind the partnership contractually, nor take part in its management which gives rise to the following scenarios as set out in the table below.

Scenario	
A **limited partner** holds the majority of the equity interest	Limited partners do not take part in the management of the business.
A **general partner holds a minority interest** but exercises dominant influence	If the general partner is a company or an undertaking that prepares true and fair financial statements, this would make them parent undertakings (under both the Companies Act and FRS 2) and the limited partnership would be a subsidiary undertaking.
Where a **general partner** has **no equity interest**, but exercises a dominant interest	The lack of equity interest may make it harder to demonstrate that a parent-subsidiary undertaking relationship exists.

C. Exemptions from obligation to prepare group accounts

Under the Companies Act, consolidated accounts are not required for a financial year, where:
- the parent is itself a subsidiary undertaking included in the accounts of a larger group;
- the group headed by that company qualifies as small and is not an ineligible group; or
- all subsidiary companies within the group are excluded from consolidation.

6556

Parent undertakings that are exempt from the requirement to prepare group accounts may still elect to do so voluntarily.

Parents included in the accounts of a larger group

A company is exempt from the requirement to prepare group accounts, if it is itself a subsidiary undertaking that is included in the accounts of a larger group.

6558
FRS 2 (21)

The **exemption is only available where**:
1. The company claiming the exemption is a wholly owned subsidiary of that immediate parent undertaking; or
2. The parent undertaking holds more than 50% of the shares in the company claiming the exemption and a notice requesting the preparation of group accounts has not been served on the company by shareholders, holding in aggregate:
- more than half of the remaining shares of the company; or
- 5% of the total shares of the company.
Such **notice must be served** no later than six months after the end of the financial year to which it relates.

MEMO POINTS   In determining whether shares are **majority owned**, the following must be attributed to the parent undertaking; namely shares held by a wholly-owned subsidiary of the parent company or those held on behalf of the parent undertaking or a wholly-owned subsidiary.

3. The **company claiming the exemption** does not have any of its securities listed on a stock exchange in any European Union member state. This requirement is extended under FRS 2 to cover any parent undertaking, that is not in itself a wholly-owned subsidiary and its immediate parent is established under the law of a EEA member state.

The **consolidated financial statements** must also be:
- prepared to the same date, or an earlier date, in the same financial year, as the company claiming the exemption;

6560
FRS 2 (21b)
s 400 CA 2006

– drawn up and audited in accordance with the law based on the European Union 7th Directive or IFRS; and
– submitted, together with the auditor's report, to the UK Registrar of Companies, within the required filing deadline, together with the company's individual accounts. The name of the parent undertaking that prepares group accounts, its country of incorporation or if unincorporated, the address of its principal place of business, should also be included.

> ☐ *MEMO POINTS* ☐ **Intermediate parents** may now be exempt from preparing consolidated accounts, where the parent is not established under the law of an EEA state. "Equivalence" does not mean compliance with every aspect of the EU 7th Directive, as a qualitative rather than quantitative approach has been championed.

Small groups

6562
FRS 2 (21a)

A parent company **need not prepare group accounts** for a financial year in which the group headed by that company qualifies as small or medium-sized (¶6000) and is not an ineligible group. A group meeting the size criteria may still be **deemed ineligible** under certain conditions (see ¶6010).

> ☐ *MEMO POINTS* ☐ 1. All **parent companies**, except for those heading small groups, are required to prepare group accounts.

s 399 CA 2006
2. The **thresholds for qualifying as small** (under CA 2006) are as follows:
– Aggregate turnover (net) – less than £6.5m (Gross: £7.8m);
– Aggregate balance sheet total (net) – less than £3.26m (Gross: £3.9m);
– Aggregate no: of employees (net) – less than 50.
The net amounts apply after all consolidation adjustments have been made (e.g. elimination of intra-group sales and balances).

6563

The **exemption** from preparing group accounts (for small groups) is not available if any of its members are:
– a public company;
– a corporate entity with securities listed on a European Economic Area (EEA) exchange; or
– insurance companies, banks, and investment firms.

All subsidiaries are excluded from consolidation

6566
FRS 2 (21d)
s 402 CA 2006

Both the Companies Act and FRS 2 permit a parent company exemption from preparing group accounts, where all the subsidiary undertakings comprising the group are individually excluded from consolidation. Where this is the case, a number of disclosures are required in the accounts of the parent undertaking (see ¶6588).

D. Exclusion of an individual subsidiary undertaking from consolidation

6570
s 399-405 CA 2006

The **general rule is** all confirmed subsidiary undertakings of a parent undertaking must be included in the group's consolidated accounts, subject to the exemptions discussed in section C.

However, there are a number of instances where an individual subsidiary undertaking need not be included in the consolidated accounts; namely as a result of:
– immateriality:
– undue expense and delay;
– severe long-term restrictions; or
– it is a subsidiary undertaking held for subsequent resale.

Where subsidiary undertakings are excluded, **certain disclosures** are required in the parent undertakings accounts.

1. Immateriality

A subsidiary undertaking may be excluded from consolidation if its inclusion is not material for the purpose of giving a true and fair view. Two or more subsidiary undertakings may be excluded if they are not material in aggregate.

6572

2. Undue expense and delay

In terms of the Companies Act, a subsidiary undertaking may be excluded from consolidation, where the required information is only available at disproportionate expense or with undue delay. However, guidance on how "disproportionate undue expense and delay" should be determined is not given in the Act.

6574
FRS 2 (24)

In addition, this **exemption is only permitted** where the subsidiaries are immaterial, individually or collectively relative to the size of the group.

3. Severe long-term restrictions

Under the Companies Act 2006, a subsidiary undertaking may be excluded from consolidation if there are "severe long-term restrictions", that greatly impede the ability of a parent company to exercise its **rights or control over the assets or management** of that subsidiary. The rights affected include:
- voting rights attached to shares;
- the right to appoint or remove the board of directors; and
- the right to exercise dominant influence.

6576
FRS 2 (25)

There is **no formal definition** of what constitutes long term. In practice, a judgement will have to be made at each year end as to whether the severe restrictions will persist for the foreseeable future. If so, the restriction should be regarded as long term and the exclusion from consolidation should continue.

A subsidiary undertaking **should not be excluded** merely because the restrictions are threatened or the other party has the power to impose them, unless such threats or the existence of such powers has in practice, a severe and restrictive long-term impact on the rights of the parent undertaking.

6577

Examples of types of "severe long-term restrictions" include:
- a subsidiary undertaking subject to UK insolvency proceedings; and
- the existence of restrictions on cash flows from a subsidiary undertaking (e.g. an overseas subsidiary which is not permitted to remit dividends to its parent).

6578

However, both scenarios may not automatically justify the exclusion of the subsidiary undertaking from the group consolidation. For instance, a receivership or administration order may not necessarily mean severe long-term restrictions, as the subsidiary could subsequently trade its way out of receivership or administration.

Where **severe restrictions** exist, but the directors of the parent do not believe they are long term, the appropriate treatment is to make full disclosures of the facts in the notes to the financial statements, rather than opt for non-consolidation.

Accounting treatment

Where restrictions have been imposed **after control has been acquired**, the following accounting treatment is required:

6580
FRS 2 (27)

1. The subsidiary should be consolidated up to the date the restrictions came into force.

2. The subsidiary should cease to be consolidated at the date restrictions were imposed, and should be transferred to fixed asset investments at a valuation derived using the equity method.

6581   Once the **restrictions come into effect**, the ongoing accounting treatment will be dependent upon the level of influence retained by the parent.

Issue	Accounting treatment
Where **significant influence is not retained** during the period of restriction	- the subsidiary should continue to be classified as a fixed asset at the initial valuation, subject to impairment which should be charged to the consolidated profit and loss account. No further accrual should be made for the profits or losses of that subsidiary.
Where **significant influence is retained** during the period of restrictions	– the subsidiary should be accounted for as an associate under the equity method.
The **carrying amount** of subsidiary undertakings subject to severe long-term restriction	- should be reviewed each year and where appropriate written down for any diminution in value. In assessing diminution in value, each subsidiary undertaking should be considered individually.
Any **intra-group amounts** due from subsidiary undertakings excluded on these grounds	– should also be reviewed and written down if required.
Similarly, any **amounts previously charged** for diminution in value	– should be written back as a result of the restrictions ceasing, should be separately disclosed.

6582   On **termination of the restrictions**, and where significant influence has been retained, the unrecognised profit and loss that has accrued during the period of restrictions relating to that subsidiary, should be recognised in and disclosed separately in the consolidated profit and loss account.

FRS 2 (28)

4. Held for subsequent resale

6583   A subsidiary undertaking may be excluded from consolidation, where the interest of the parent company is held exclusively with a view to subsequent resale and the undertaking has not previously been included in the parent company's group accounts.

6584   **Mandatory exclusion**   FRS 2 makes exclusion of the subsidiary undertaking from consolidation mandatory rather than optional where the following conditions are satisfied:
1. A purchaser has been identified or is being sought, and there is reasonable expectation that the undertaking will be disposed of within approximately one year of its acquisition date; or
2. The interest that was acquired as a result of the enforcement of the security, unless the interest has become part of the continuing activities of the group, or the holder acts as if it intends the interest to become so.

6585   The first of these circumstances depends on the immediate intention to dispose of the subsidiary and the expectation of a sale within approximately one year. An interest for which a sale is not completed within a year of its acquisition may still fulfil the condition for mandatory exclusion if, at the balance sheet date the terms of the sale have been agreed and the process of disposing of that interest is substantially complete.

FRS 2 (78d)

Where this **condition is not met** but directors have purchased the subsidiary with a view to resale, they still have the option of excluding it from consolidation.

6586   These **exclusions apply only** to those undertakings, that have never formed a continuing part of group activities and have not previously been included in the consolidated financial statements, prepared by the parent undertaking. For example, a parent undertaking with a subsidiary undertaking that has been part of the group for several years, could not now be excluded from consolidation on the grounds that the parent has decided to dispose of the subsidiary.

Accounting treatment   Subsidiary undertakings held exclusively for resale, should be   **6587**
excluded from consolidation and the temporary nature of the parent undertaking's interest
recognised, by carrying it as a current asset (or fixed asset investment) at the lower of cost
and net realisable value.

E. Disclosures

1. Exempt groups

Parent undertakings – individual financial statements   A parent undertaking that takes   **6588**
advantage of one of the exemptions from preparing group financial statements, must disclose   FRS 2 (22)
this fact in its individual financial statements at the end of the financial year, and the reasons
for so doing. Where exemption is based on all subsidiaries being excluded from consolidation, the following information is required:
– the reasons for excluding the various subsidiaries from consolidation; and
– if they are incorporated, the address of their principle place of business or country of
incorporation if not the UK.

Intermediate parents   A **parent undertaking** may be exempt from the duty to prepare   **6589**
group accounts by virtue of it being an intermediate parent. The intermediate parent is
required to disclosure in its individual financial statements, that it is exempt from the obligation to prepare group accounts and give the name and details of incorporation of the ultimate parent undertaking.

For **subsidiary undertakings** the following information should be given in their financial   **6590**
statements, in respect of the parent undertaking of:
– the largest group of undertakings for which group accounts are drawn up and of which
the company is a member; and
– the smallest group of undertakings.
The disclosures relating to the name and incorporation of the parent company should also
be given.

2. Where individual subsidiaries are excluded

Consolidated accounts

An **individual subsidiary undertaking** may be excluded from the group financial statements   **6591**
for various reasons as outlined in ¶6570 above. The following information regarding the
subsidiary undertaking should be given in the notes to the consolidated financial statements:
1. The **name of the subsidiary and the reasons** for its exclusion from consolidation.
2. The **aggregate amount** of its capital and reserves as at the end of its relevant financial
year and its profit and loss for that year. This information need not be given if:
a. the group's investment in the undertaking is included in the financial statements by way
of the equity method of valuation; or
b. the subsidiary is not required to deliver a copy balance sheet and does not otherwise
publish that balance sheet in the UK or elsewhere, and the holding of the group is less than
50% of the nominal value of the shares in the undertaking; or
c. the information is not material.
3. Details of the **balances between** the excluded subsidiary undertakings and the rest of the
group.

4. The **nature and extent of transactions** of the excluded subsidiary undertakings with the rest of the group.

5. For an excluded subsidiary undertaking **carried other than by the equity method**, any amounts included in the consolidated financial statements in respect of:
– dividends received and receivable from the undertaking;
– any write down in the period in respect of the investment in that undertaking or amounts due from that undertaking; and
– for subsidiary undertakings excluded because of different activities the separate financial statements of those undertakings.

> ☐ *MEMO POINTS* ☐ The disclosures required are contained in Sch. 4 Large and Medium-sized Companies and Groups (Accounts and Reports) Regulations 2008 (SI2008/410).

6592   The information may be presented on an **aggregate basis**, for sub-units of subsidiary undertakings that fall within one of the afore-mentioned grounds for exclusion. However, separate disclosure is required for any individual excluded subsidiary undertaking, including its subsidiaries, that alone accounts for more than 20% of any one or more of the group's operating profits, turnover or net assets. The group amounts should be measured by including all excluded undertakings.

6593   There may be circumstances where in the opinion of the directors of the parent undertaking, the above mentioned disclosures are likely to be **seriously prejudicial** to the business of the parent or group. In such cases, where the prejudicial impact can be shown, application may be made to the Secretary of State for exemption from the specified disclosures. The **following conditions** relate to the subsidiary undertaking in question; namely:
– that it is established under a law of a country outside the United Kingdom; or
– it carries on business outside the United Kingdom.

3. Omission of parent company profit and loss account from consolidation

6595   Where a parent company is required to prepare group financial statements, its **individual profit and loss account** may be omitted from the group financial statements provided that:
– the notes to the parent company's individual balance sheet show the parent's profit and loss for the financial year;
– there is disclosure in the group financial statements that the exemption applies; and
– the parent's individual profit and loss is nevertheless prepared, approved by the board and signed by a director in accordance with the general rules for approving and signing financial statements.

Under these circumstances, the parent company's individual profit and loss account need not contain the information required by the Companies Act, namely regarding **supplementary information** to the profit and loss account, such as:
– interest and similar charges;
– particulars of taxation;
– turnover details; and
– particulars of staff.

F. New UK GAAP – requirements of FRS 102

6597   Existing UK GAAP will be replaced, from January 2015 with a more streamlined reporting standard in the form of FRS 102 "The Financial Reporting Standard applicable in the UK and Republic of Ireland". The rules relating to group financial statements are set out in Section 9 of FRS 102 and areas that differ from current UK GAAP are summarised in the table below.

Issue	Accounting treatment
Group accounts – who must prepare consolidated accounts	Parent companies must produce consolidated financial statements. Exemptions apply to parents who are themselves subsidiaries that meet certain criteria. Small groups can also claim exemption.
Group accounts: Where subsidiaries can be excluded from consolidation	1. Long-term restrictions hamper the parent's ability to control the subsidiary. 2. The subsidiary is being held for immediate resale. Control equals the power to direct the operating and financial policies of a subsidiary, and to derive the economic benefits therefrom. Existing UK GAAP also permits exclusion on these grounds as well as on grounds of immateriality and undue expense and delay.
Special purpose entities	Created for specific objectives (e.g. Research and development projects). In general these legal vehicles should be included in the parent's consolidated accounts.

CHAPTER 2

Form and content of group accounts

The companies act requires group accounts in the form of consolidated accounts, consisting   **6700**
of a consolidated balance sheet and profit and loss account, that meet the true and fair
criteria. In addition, the accounting standards also require the preparation of a consolidated
cash flow statement and consolidated statement of total recognised gains and losses
(STRGL).

The consolidated balance sheet and profit and loss account must incorporate in full, the
information contained in the individual accounts of the undertakings included in the consolidation, as if it were a single company (aggregation). This requirement is subject to the
adjustments required by the legislation and generally accepted accounting principles or
practice.

The **key adjustments required** relate to:
– the elimination of group transactions;
– uniform bases for valuing assets and liabilities in the subsidiaries and group accounts;
– acquisition and merger accounting;
– minority interests (non-controlling interests); and
– the adoption of uniform accounting policies and accounting reference dates.

<u>MEMO POINTS</u>   1. **Consolidated accounts** must be prepared under Section 404 Companies Act
2006 (SI 2008/410) or under IFRS (IAS 1). The group accounts for small companies are governed
by Schedule 6 to SI 2008/409.
2. The terms **minority interests** (UK GAAP) and **non-controlling interests** (IFRS) are interchangeable.
3. The FRC has issued FRS 102 "The Financial Reporting Standard applicable in the UK and
Republic of Ireland" which will replace existing UK GAAP from January 2015. The key differences
between existing and new UK GAAP are set out in ¶6792.

A. Accounting policies

The **general rule** is that all group companies should use uniform accounting policies. For   **6704**
practical purposes it is more efficient to apply the same accounting policies at the individual

entity level and for the group accounts as this is likely to minimise the volume of **consolidation adjustments**.

However, a departure from the requirements of the Companies Act in the preparation of group accounts is permitted under certain conditions, as discussed below.

6706   **Reasons for not adopting uniform accounting policies** A departure from the requirements of the Companies Act in the preparation of group accounts **is permitted**:
– where the directors decide that there are **special reasons** for any subsidiary undertaking departing from the group accounting policies; or
– on grounds of materiality.

Valid reasons for not adopting uniform accounting policies in the preparation of individual financial statements for each group undertaking, include:
– for tax planning purposes; or
– group policies may not be compatible with the legislation or the generally accepted accounting principles of any other countries in which a subsidiary might operate.

6708   Where uniform accounting policies are not adopted, **disclosures** to this effect are required by way of a note to the consolidated financial statements. The note should explain the actual accounting policy adopted, the reasons and the effect on the financial statements of such a departure. Furthermore, any difference between a parent's individual accounts for a financial year and its group accounts should be disclosed and explained in the notes to the group accounts.

B. Accounting periods and dates

6714
FRS 2 (42)
The **general rule** is that the financial statements for all subsidiary undertakings included in the consolidated financial statements, should be prepared to the same accounting period as that of the parent undertaking (co-terminous). This is a requirement of the Companies Act, **unless in the opinion of the directors** other considerations are paramount.

6716   **Non co-terminous year-ends** might be justifiable between certain group undertakings for the reasons set out in the table.

Scenarios	Justification
1. Different annual trading cycles	The decisions regarding the year ends of the various undertakings within a group may be driven by the respective annual trading cycles of the industries in which they operate. For example, some group undertakings may be geared to peak business activities in the summer months and others in the winter months.
2. Tax planning considerations	Tax planning issues for various group undertakings
3. Overseas subsidiaries	Difficulties in meeting a group reporting timetable
4. Legislation in different countries	Different legislation may compel, or make it more practical, to prepare financial statement of an individual group undertaking to a particular date

6718   **Remedies** FRS 2 reinforces the Companies Act preference for co-terminous year ends within a group and endorses the alternatives available where the ideal situation does not prevail. The **preferred remedy** is to use specially prepared co-terminous interim accounts for the subsidiary undertaking. Only **where this is not practical**, should the parent undertaking resort to the latest statutory accounts of the subsidiary undertaking, provided that the year end is no more than three months before that of the parent undertaking.

Easter Bunnies Limited last financial year ended on 30 April 2013 whereas its two subsidiary companies Wacky Toys Limited and Easter Chicks Limited prepared their last statutory accounts to 31 January 2013 and 31 December 2012 respectively.
Under FRS 2, both subsidiaries should ideally produce interim accounts made up to 30 April 2013. If in the case of Wacky Toys Limited this is not a practicable alternative, the directors of the parent could consider using the accounts of Wacky Toys at 31 January 2013, with appropriate **consolidation adjustments**, as the gap falls within the 3 month period allowed.
However, this option is not available in the case of Easter Chicks Limited, as the gap between its own year end and that of the group (four months) exceeds the three month limit allowed under the Act and FRS 2 and therefore, interim accounts will have to be prepared.

Where the recent financial statements of a subsidiary undertaking are included in the consolidation, then any changes that have taken place in the intervening period, that would **materially impact on** the true and fair view given by the group financial statements, should be reflected in the consolidated financial statements.

6720
FRS 2 (43)

C. Elimination of intra-group transactions

In preparing group accounts, the following material inter-group transactions between undertakings included in the consolidation, should be eliminated:

6730

a. **Sales or other types of transactions** between group undertakings that may materially inflate the figures relating to group turnover and group cost of sales, as well as distort the gross margin.

b. Intra-group **debtor and creditor** balances

c. **Dividends**

d. **Unrealised profits and losses** included in book values of assets (e.g. stock, fixed assets) transferred between group undertakings, and which at the year end remain within the group, so distorting the true profit of the group (see ¶6732).

e. Where the **acquisition method** (¶6820) of accounting is used to consolidate a subsidiary undertaking, the identifiable assets and liabilities acquired must be included in the consolidation at fair values as at the acquisition date. Where the **merger method** (¶7000) is used, the assets and liabilities of the acquired undertaking must be consolidated at their balance sheet values at the acquisition date.

---

1. Treatment of unrealised profits/losses

Most consolidation adjustments are relatively straight forward. However, **problems can arise** in trying to measure unrealised profits (or losses), such as the unrealised profit included in intra-group sales retained in closing stock. This **problem can be further exacerbated** where the intra-group items form part of, or are an ingredient in, one or several other products.

6732
FRS 2 (39)

In practice, one might be able to take advantage of **the concession** afforded by the Companies Act, where the need to eliminate unrealised profits or losses is removed, if the amounts concerned are not material for the purposes of giving a true and fair view.

Where unrealised profits or losses **are deemed material**, a number of rules should be observed as set out under the specific headings below.

Unrealised profits reflected in book value of assets

Any unrealised profit reflected in the book value of assets should be eliminated in full. For example, if an engineering company supplies a fellow subsidiary with an item of plant, the intra-group profit element included in fixed assets should be eliminated, along with the depreciation charge.

6733

Allocation of unrealised profits

6734   The unrealised profits or losses should be set off against the interests held by the group and the minority interest, in proportion to their holdings in the undertaking whose individual financial statements contain the eliminated profits or losses. The minority interests must be allocated their share of unrealised profits or losses.

Transfer of fixed assets

6735   There are occasions when group undertakings are likely to transfer fixed assets between each other. Under these circumstances, the **"group entity" principle** must be maintained and the fixed asset carried in the consolidated financial statements at cost to the group, whilst any depreciation charge must be based on the cost to the group. As a consequence, **two consolidation adjustments** will be necessary; namely:
1. The removal of any unrealised profit from the carrying value of the fixed asset in the consolidated balance sheet; and
2. An adjustment to ensure that the current year charge and opening and closing balances on the depreciation provision are based on cost to the group. **Gains and losses** on realisations of fixed assets would also have to be eliminated.

The **consequence of transferring fixed assets** around the group at above or below the cost to the vendor company is particularly complex. The consolidation adjustments referred to above will need to be made each year, and those in respect of depreciation changed each year, until the asset is finally scrapped or sold.

Constructed assets

6736   Construction or contracting companies that are members of a group, may construct assets such as an investment property or new factory, for other members of the same group. There are two possible scenarios, as follows:
1. The asset is **classified as a fixed asset** and therefore any unrealised profit must be eliminated as outlined above; or
2. The asset is to be **sold on to a third party**, for which a contract of sale exists. The asset is likely to be shown in the consolidated balance sheet as a current asset. However, in such cases, the **unrealised profit arising** on the initial intra-group sale need not be eliminated provided that the profit arising on that sale is materially the same as that which would have arisen in the books of the purchasing company (for long term contracts under SSAP 9), had it acquired the asset from its fellow group company at cost.

6737   **Interest charges**   The question that arises is whether the interest on borrowed funds as part of the cost of construction, should be eliminated on consolidation. The treatment to be adopted depends on whether the interest:
– represents interest paid on monies borrowed externally, including by another group company to finance the project; or
– is merely a notional charge.
Where the interest is clearly **a cost to the group**, the interest should not be eliminated. However, where the interest is a notional intra-group charge, it should be eliminated.

Subsidiaries held for resale or that have long-term restrictions

6739   In general, profits and losses on transactions with undertakings excluded from consolidation, because they are held with a view to subsequent resale or because of severe long-term restrictions need not be eliminated, **except where significant influence** is retained.

For more detail on subsidiaries excluded from consolidation see ¶6500.

6740   The following scenarios can arise in practice:
a. A **parent undertaking** sells an asset to a partly held subsidiary undertaking at a profit. The asset including unrealised profit is held by the subsidiary undertaking at the end of the financial year;

b. A **partly held subsidiary undertaking** sells an asset at a profit to the parent undertaking. The asset including unrealised profit is held by the parent undertaking at the end of the financial year; or

c. A **partly held subsidiary undertaking** sells an asset to a fellow partly held subsidiary undertaking at a profit. The asset whose "cost" includes an element of unrealised profit is held at end of financial year by the subsidiary that purchased the asset.

EXAMPLE **Consolidated financial statements**

Scenario A

Sale by group company to a partly held subsidiary
The **parent company** has a 75% interest in a **subsidiary company**
During the financial year, the parent company sold goods to the subsidiary company for £100,000. The cost of these goods was £60,000. All of the goods were still in stock at the end of the financial year.

Accounting treatment
Compute unrealised profit in stock: £100,000 – £60,000 = £40,000;
1. Eliminate the full £40,000 from group stock and group operating profit;
2. The consolidating "journal entry" representing the elimination of unrealised profit in closing stocks, is as follows:

Debit	Group operating profit	£40,000	
Credit	Group stock (Balance sheet)		£40,000

Under this scenario, there is **no elimination** of the unrealised profit **against the minority interest**. The full debit is made against group profits on the grounds that the stock is still sitting in the partly held subsidiary undertaking and hence should not impact upon the minority interest.

Scenario B

Sale by a partly held subsidiary to the parent
The Parent company has a 75% interest in one of its subsidiaries.
During the financial year, the subsidiary company sold goods to the parent company for £100,000. The cost of these goods was £60,000, all of which were still in stock at the end of the financial year. The **accounting treatment** is to eliminate £100,000 from group turnover and £60,000 from group cost of sales, thereby reducing group operating profit by £40,000. The effect of this would be to reduce the profit attributable to minority interests by 25% of £40,000 = £10,000.

---

2. Treatment of deferred tax

UK **corporation tax** is charged on the profit of individual companies rather than on groups. The impact of this, is that the eliminations required by the Companies Act and FRS 2 may in themselves cause timing differences, as far as the group is concerned.   **6742**

If an element of profit, or expense has been eliminated on consolidation but has been taken into account in arriving at the individual company's taxable profits, a **timing difference** arises, between when the item is recognised for tax purposes and when it is reflected in the group accounts, will arise that did not exist at the entity level. This is because **material eliminations** are likely to cause misalignment, between the income recognised for consolidated financial accounts purposes and the income recognised for taxation purposes. As a consequence, if a liability or asset is likely to crystallise in the foreseeable future, a consolidation adjustment will be required to the amount set aside for deferred taxation in the consolidated financial statements, in respect of these additional timing differences. The treatment of deferred taxation is covered in more detail in ¶9000.

D. Minority interests (Non-controlling)

Minority interests **are defined** as subsidiary profits or losses, and capital and reserves owned by external shareholders. The process of consolidation involves the aggregation of the assets   **6750**
FRS 2 (13)

and liabilities of the individual group undertakings and **where the group does not own** all the share capital of a subsidiary, an adjustment is required to account for the interests of other external (non-group) shareholders.

Despite the title "Minority interests", **there is in principle no upper limit** to the proportion of shares in a subsidiary undertaking which may be held as a minority interest. This is because the parent-subsidiary relationship is established on the basis of control rather than on majority shareholding (equity ownership).

<u>MEMO POINTS</u>   Minority interests are known as non-controlling interests under IFRS.

6751
FRS 2 (34)
A company **is deemed to be a subsidiary where** the parent exercises dominant influence. For example, a parent company could own only 45% of the equity but still exercise dominant influence, in which case the group should consolidate 100% of the assets and liabilities of the subsidiary but also show minority interests of 55%. The basis of the parent company's dominant influence must be disclosed.

6752   An **exception to this rule** is that, shares issued by subsidiaries to external shareholders should be accounted for in the consolidated financial statements as liabilities and not minority interests, where the group has an obligation to transfer economic benefits in relation to the shares. In this situation, the substance of the transaction prevails over the legal form.

---

1. Classification

6754   Minority interests should be analysed between **equity and non-equity** minority interests; this analysis is given on the face of the balance sheet. Where the minority interests are **immaterial**, an indication should still be given on the face of the balance sheet with further details provided in the notes.

Equity interests

6755   Equity shares can confer unrestricted rights to shareholders to participate in the distribution of profit in the form of dividends or in the event of a company being wound up. The **most common form** is ordinary shares.

Equity minority interests represent the net proceeds on the issue of the equity shares (proceeds less issue costs), plus the equity minority shareholders' percentage interest in the other reserves (i.e. revaluation reserve).

The calculation of equity interests is illustrated in ¶6762.

Non-equity interests

6756   Non-equity interests represent shares with any of the following characteristics:
– where **rights to receive payments** (e.g. dividends or on redemption) are restricted to a certain amount that is independent of the company's assets or profits, or the dividends on any class of equity share;
– where **rights to participate in a surplus** where a company is wound up are restricted to a certain amount, irrespective of the company's profits or assets; or
– where the **shares are redeemable** according to the terms of issue or at the bequest of the holder or any other party.

6757   **Preference shares**   Preference shares are an example of non-equity interests.

Where there are non-equity minority interests a description should be given of any rights of holders of the shares against other group companies.

The following amounts should to be **attributed to** the non-equity interests:
– the nominal value (less issue costs, dividends paid); plus
– the nominal value (less issue costs, dividends paid); plus
– the premium received; plus
– an accrual reflecting the additional premium payable on redemption.

Through the **consolidation process**, the non-equity minority interests will be apportioned part of the group's reserves, in addition to the nominal value of the non-equity shares. The group's reserves will be reduced over the term to redemption of the non-equity interests.

Directors' interests

6759

Share issues	Accounting treatment
Directors' nominee shareholdings acquired – as required under articles of association	Shareholdings generally small and do not constitute a minority interest as they are normally held on the parent company's behalf.
Where directors have a beneficial interest in the company's shares	Substance of transaction must be considered Does the shareholding constitute a minority interest? If not additional disclosures probably required covering related party transactions.

2. Calculation of minority interests

The first step in calculating the minority interests is to review the group structure, in order to determine which entities are subsidiaries of the parent. This can result in a mixture of direct and indirect holdings.

6760

Direct holdings

The **simple scenario** involves a direct holding in equity shares owned by the parent company. The minority interests in a subsidiary's profit for the year, is calculated by taking the profit after taxation and calculating the proportion of the profit attributable to the minority. The value of the minority interests in the balance sheet at the end of the financial year represents the minority interest in the capital and reserves of the subsidiary.

6762

EXAMPLE **Profit and loss**

A parent company (S) **owns 75%** of a subsidiary's (T) ordinary share capital. The subsidiary's profit and loss account is as follows:

	£'000
Operating profit	1750
Non-operating exceptional item	250
Profit on ordinary activities before taxation	2,000
Tax on ordinary activities	(245)
Profit on ordinary activities after tax	1755
Minority interests (25% × £1755)	(438.7)
Retained profit for the year	1,316.3

Balance sheet calculation

		£'000
Net assets		3605
Equity share capital		250
Share premium		500
Revaluation reserve		300
Profit and loss account	800	
Retained profits	1755	2555
Equity shareholders funds		3605
Minority interests = £3605 × 25% =		**901**

Indirect holdings

6764   Where a parent holds an indirect interest in a subsidiary, the calculation of minorities will be more complicated.

Having determined which undertakings are subsidiaries to be consolidated, one of **two methods** can be adopted to calculate the indirect minority interests in the balance sheet. Both methods will produce the same result **except where goodwill** has been capitalised, in which case the first method should be used.

6766   Under **Method A** the parent company's indirect holdings in its subsidiaries are calculated from the perspective of the parent company.

EXAMPLE **Minority interests in a group – Method A**
Summarised balance sheets – Companies A, B, and C
Company A has a 75% holding in B; MI 25% and a 55% holding in C; MI 45%.

	A 000's	B 000's	C 000's
Investment in subsidiaries	60	30	-
Net assets	140	120	175
	200	150	175
Equity share capital	100	50	100
Profit and loss account	100	100	75
	200	150	175

Minority interest in group

	£
Minorities' share of net assets of company B × direct minority interest £120,000 × 25%	30,000
Minorities' share of net assets of company C × indirect minority interest £175,000 × 45% (100 – (40% × 75% + 25%))	78,750
Total minority interest	**108,750**

6768   **Method B** of calculating minority interests involves the consolidation of the minority interests of Company C with those of Company B, before consolidating Company B with the parent company. The minority interests are as calculated in method A.

Company A has a direct holding in C which forms part of the minority interests from the perspective of Company B.

EXAMPLE **Minority interest in group – Method B**

Based on summarised balance sheet given in the above example.

Stage 1. Company C consolidated into Company B

Equity share capital of Company C (£100,000 × 60%)	60,000
Company C reserves (£75,000 × 60%)	45,000
Minority interest in Group B	**105,000**

Stage 2. Group B consolidated into Company A (parent)

Equity share capital of Company B (£50,000 × 25%)	12,500
Company B reserves (£100,000 × 25%)	25,000
Company C reserves (£100,000 – £60,000 × 25%) (Note 1).	10,000

Adjustment to eliminate 25% of Company C owned directly by Company A (Note 2)

Equity share capital of C (£100,000 × 25%)	– 25,000
Reserves of C (£75,000 × 25%)	– 18,750
Minority interest in Group A	**108,750**

Notes. 1 The minority in Group B take their proportion of the reserves of Company C that have already been consolidated with Company A's reserves.

---

2. The adjustment is required as the 60% minority interest in Company C consolidated into Company B includes the 25% held by Company A.

---

3. Accounting treatment

The requirement under the Companies Act and FRS 2 for full consolidation means that the statutory headings in the consolidated profit and loss account must include the total amount for each item of income and expenditure relating to the subsidiary. A **number of problem areas can arise** in accounting for minority interests including: **6770**

– the accounting for loss making subsidiaries;
– allocation of dividends; and
– the treatment of goodwill on acquisition.

Where the **acquisition method** (¶6820) of accounting is used to consolidate a subsidiary undertaking, the assets and liabilities of the acquired undertaking should be consolidated at their fair values at the acquisition date.

Where **merger accounting** (¶7000) is used, the assets and liabilities of the acquired entity should be consolidated at the values stated in the financial statements of the acquired company, subject to any adjustments required or permitted by the Companies Act.   **6771**

Irrespective of which treatment is adopted, the assets and liabilities attributable to the minority interests should be included on the same basis (e.g. accounting policies), as those attributable to the interests held by the parent and its other subsidiary undertakings.

The **general rule** is that **profits or losses arising** in a subsidiary undertaking should be apportioned between the controlling and minority interests, in proportion to their respective interests held over the period in which the profits or losses arose.   FRS 2 (37)

Where subsidiaries are profit making, the share attributable to the minority interests should be deducted from the consolidated profit and loss account, so reducing the group's profit attributable to shareholders' funds (see ¶6762). Where the **subsidiaries are loss making**, the minority interests are added to the consolidated profit and loss account, so reducing the loss transferred to shareholders' funds.   **6772**

The allocation of goodwill depends on whether the subsidiary is a direct or indirect acquisition.

Accounting for minorities on acquisition

Direct subsidiary   When a company acquires a subsidiary it is required to apportion to the minority interests its share of the total net assets of that subsidiary. In the consolidated balance sheet, the relevant percentage of the share capital and reserves are allocated to the minority interest.   **6774**
FRS 2 (36-38)

However, there is **no allocation of goodwill** to the minority interests on direct acquisition.

EXAMPLE   Company X acquires company Y at the end of year 1. The year-end summarised balance sheets show:

Summarised balance sheets – pre-acquisition	X	Y
Net assets	750	200
Equity share capital	300	120
Share premium account	100	-
Profit and loss reserve	350	80
Equity shareholders' funds	**750**	**200**

To help fund the acquisition company X issues 10,000 £1 equity shares to the shareholders of company Y, to acquire 80% of its issued share capital. At the acquisition date the fair value of the consideration for company Y is valued at £200,000 and the fair value of the net assets at £250,000.

The balance sheets for the two companies **after the acquisition** will be as follows:

Summarised balance sheets £'000 – post acquisition

	X	Y
Investment in subsidiary	200	
Other net assets	750	200
Fair value adjustment	-	50
	950	250
Equity share capital	310	120
Share premium	290	
Profit and loss account	350	80
Revaluation reserve		50
Equity shareholders' funds	950	250

Cost of control account

	£'000		£'000
Investment	200	Equity share capital (£120,000 × 80%)	96
		P/L reserve (£80,000 × 80%)	64
		Revaluation reserve (£50,000 × 80%)	40
			200
	200		**200**

Minority interests account

	£'000		£'000
Balance	50	Equity share capital (£120,000 × 20%)	24
		P/L reserve (£80,000 × 20%)	16
		Revaluation reserve (£50,000 × 20%)	10
	50		50

Group consolidated balance sheet

	£'000
Net assets (£750,000 + £250,000 (fair value))	1000
Equity share capital	310
Share premium	290
Profit and loss account	350
Minority interests	50
Shareholders' funds	**1000**

6775
FRS 2 (82)

Indirect subsidiaries Where a subsidiary (A) acquires a controlling interest in another sub-subsidiary (B), **any goodwill arising** on this acquisition should be accounted for in company A's consolidated financial statements. This in turn will effect the calculation of minority interests in A recognised in the consolidated financial statements of the ultimate parent company P.

Goodwill arising on acquisition **should only be recognised** with respect to the part of the subsidiary undertakings, that is attributable to the interest held by the parent and its other subsidiary undertakings.

EXAMPLE A parent company X has an 80% holding in a subsidiary company Y. Company Y later acquires a 100% holding in company Z on which goodwill of £100,000 arises.

Problem
How should this goodwill be accounted for in the consolidated financial statements of company X (parent)?
Should it be carried at 100% of the goodwill with the minority interest allocated 20% or should the goodwill be carried at 80% with no recognition for the minority?

Solution
Company Y should prepare consolidated financial statements and include 100% of the goodwill. Company X consolidated financial statements should also carry goodwill of 100% and a minority interest of 20%.

Reasoning:
The capital and reserves attributable to the shares in the subsidiary undertakings includes the goodwill of £100,000 arising on the acquisition of company Z by company Y. This would be included in the financial statements of the parent company X.
The rule that **no goodwill be attributable** to the minority interests **applies only to** direct acquisitions by a parent of a part interest in a subsidiary, because the minority is often not a party to the transaction.

Loss making subsidiaries

Where the subsidiary has net assets the minority interests will be a credit and where the subsidiary has net liabilities the minority interests will be a debit balance. **6778**

Debit minority interests require special consideration. The group should make a provision where it has a commercial or legal (formal or implied) obligation to provide finance, that may not be recoverable due to the losses attributable to the minority interests. An example would be a letter issued by the parent company confirming that it will make good any losses in its subsidiary. **6779** FRS 2 (37)

Provisions should be extended to cover not just debit balances but **the minority's share of any liability** guaranteed by the group. The group must show any guaranteed obligations that it has in respect of a minority as a liability and not as minority interests.

Any provision in respect of minority debit balances should be set against the minority interests shown in the profit and loss account and in the balance sheet.

The minority's interest shares of any losses should be treated in the following sequence in the consolidated balance sheet: **6780**
– first set against the minority's share of the subsidiary's reserves;
– then set against the minority's share of the subsidiary's capital; and
– finally, recognise as a debit balance in the consolidated balance sheet where the group does not have a legal obligation in terms of the losses attributable to the minority interest.

This **process is reversed** if and when profits attributable to the minority interests are offset against the earlier losses.

Allocation of dividends paid by a subsidiary

The group profit and loss account should only reflect the dividends paid by the parent company to its own shareholders. **If a subsidiary has paid a dividend** during the year, any part paid to the parent company should be cancelled out on consolidation, because the parent will already have accounted for a dividend receivable in its own individual accounts. An adjustment will be required for any dividend paid to minority interests. **6782**

4. Disclosure requirements

A minority interest should be disclosed from the date of acquisition. The key disclosure requirements are outlined below. **6783**

General disclosures   Where **uniform accounting policies** are not adopted, disclosures to this effect are required by way of a note to the consolidated financial statements. The note should explain the actual accounting policy adopted, the reasons and the effect on the financial statements of such a departure. Furthermore, any difference between a parent's individual accounts for a financial year and its group accounts should be disclosed and explained in the notes to the group accounts. **6784**

6785   **Segmentation rather than exclusion**   Where subsidiary undertakings engage in different activities or are subject to certain restrictions, but are still consolidated, then additional information should be given regarding the assets, liabilities and turnover and results attributable to such undertakings. The reason being that the financial implications of including them within the consolidated accounts can be fully appreciated.

6786   **Different accounting periods**   For each **material subsidiary** undertaking that is included
FRS 2 (44)   in the group's financial statements, on the basis of information prepared to a different date or for a different accounting period from that of the parent undertaking of the group, the following information must be provided:
– the name of the subsidiary undertaking;
– the accounting date or period of the subsidiary undertaking; and
– the reason for using a different accounting date or period for the subsidiary undertaking.

6787   **Minority interests**   Users of consolidated financial statements may be interested in assess-
FRS 2 (94)   ing the impact of minority interests, in certain parts of the group, on the expected returns to investors in the parent undertaking. To this end it would be useful to include information showing the amounts attributable to minority interests for different group segments.

Consolidated profit and loss account

6788   The Companies Act requires that minority interests be shown as a separate item in the
FRS 2 (36)   consolidated profit and loss account formats.

The minority interests headings in the consolidated profit and loss account, in respect of profits and losses on ordinary activities, exclude extraordinary activities and the minority's share of any extraordinary items. In Formats 1 and 2, this heading should be included after "profit or loss on ordinary activities after taxation." In Format 3 and Format 4, minority interests should be included either under "charges" or "income".

The **minority interests** in the profit and loss account should be analysed between equity and non-equity minority interests. Where there are non-equity minority interests a description should be given of any rights of holders of the shares against other group companies.

EXAMPLE   Based on Format 1

Group profit and loss account
ABC Ltd – Report and Financial Statements – 31 December 2013

	2013	2012
Profit on ordinary activities before tax	250.0	210.0
Taxation	(55,8)	(46.2)
Profit on ordinary activities after tax	194.2	163.8
Minority interests		
– Equity	(5.0)	(5.0)
– Non-equity	(20.0)	(20.0)
	(25.0)	(25.0)
Dividend on preference shares	(0.5)	(0.5)
Profit attributable to ordinary shareholders	**168.7**	**138.3**

Note- Minority interests
The capital outstanding and dividends payable are classified as non-equity minority interests in both the balance sheet and profit and loss account, where the issues do not represent a contingent obligation on the part of the parent company or another group company that guarantees the issue.

Consolidated balance sheet

6789   The capital and reserves attributable to shares in subsidiary undertakings of the parent
FRS 2 (35)   company, held by interests other than the parent company and its subsidiary undertakings, should be shown under a separate heading of "Minority Interest". These disclosures are required either after "Provisions for liabilities and charges", or after "Share capital and reser-

ves" in Format 1 and between "Capital and Reserves" and "Provisions for Liabilities and Charges" in Format 2. In some **specific cases** (e.g. stapled shares, directors' interests) minority interests must be shown in another position in the balance sheet.

EXAMPLE   **Based on Format 2**

Balance sheet (extract)
ABC Ltd – Report and Financial Statements – 31 December 2013

Capital and reserves	2013	2012
Equity share capital	150.2	150.2
Non-equity share capital	5.0	5.0
Called-up share capital	**155.2**	**155.2**
Share premium account	350.0	350.0
Revaluation reserve	227.0	163.0
Profit and loss account	135.7	248.7
Shareholders funds	**867.9**	**916.9**
Minority interests		
– equity	38.6	28.5
– non-equity	150.0	175.0
	188.6	203.5
Provision for liabilities and charges	30.0	9.0
Creditors – due within a year	330.0	185.0
Creditors – due after one year	275.0	220.0
	635.0	414.0

Notes to the accounts

Disclosures are required for any **non-equity minority interests** including details of the external shareholder rights against other group companies. Where convertible securities are involved, consideration should be given to both the carrying amount when assessing materiality and also the rights and implications on conversion.

The following disclosures in relation to the effect on minority interests are required of: FRS 3 (20)
– profits or losses on the sale or termination of an operation or disposal of a fixed asset;
– costs of a fundamental reorganisation or restructuring; and
– profits or losses on the disposal of fixed assets.

6790

E. New UK GAAP – requirements of FRS 102

The FRC has issued FRS 102 "The Financial Reporting Standard applicable in the UK and Republic of Ireland" which will replace existing UK GAAP from January 2015. There are no appreciable differences between existing and new UK GAAP save for the treatment of intercompany loans.

6792

Inter-company loans   Loans to or from other group companies are treated as financial instruments and are covered in Sections 11 and 12 of FRS 102. These types of loans should be classified as **basic financial instruments** and accounted for at amortised cost, with a finance charge allocated each financial year over the term of the loan. This treatment differs from current UK GAAP, under which companies with non-interest bearing debt have usually recorded and retained the debt at its historical (face) value in the balance sheet, until it is repaid.

Under the new rules, a company will have to apply a market interest rate for similar debt instruments and discount the carrying amount to present value. Interest charges should then be calculated and accrued that will be equal to the loan repayment value.

6793

Business combinations

A business combination is defined as the fusion of separate entities into one economic unit, as the result of one company uniting with (a merger), or obtaining control over the net assets and operations of another (acquisition).

6800
FRS 6 (2)

A business combination is accounted for as either an **acquisition or merger** depending on the substance of the underlying transaction. The majority of business combinations are accounted for as acquisitions, with the possible exception of some group reconstructions, because the criteria for recognition as a merger are very strict.

Where the acquisition takes the form of a **reverse takeover** (i.e. the acquirer is a smaller entity than the acquired entity), the determination of whether acquisition accounting is appropriate is based on the same criteria applied to other business combinations.

The rules governing merger and acquisition accounting are contained in the Companies Act, FRS 2 "Accounting for subsidiaries undertakings", FRS 6 "Acquisitions and mergers", FRS 7 "Fair values in acquisition accounting" and FRS 10 "Goodwill and intangible assets".

There are a small number of differences between existing and **new UK GAAP** which are set out in section 3.

   MEMO POINTS   The FRC has issued FRS 102 "The Financial Reporting Standard applicable in the UK and Republic of Ireland", which must be applied to accounting periods beginning on or after 1 January 2015. Earlier adoption of this standard is also permitted.

Small companies Reporting entities **applying the FRSSE** are exempt from the requirements of these standards, unless preparing consolidated financial statements, in which case they should apply the FRS's to such statements as required by the FRSSE.

6801

6802   An overview of the **principal differences** between acquisition and merger accounting are given in the table below.

	Acquisition accounting	Merger accounting
Consolidated financial statements	Only reflect the acquired company's results from the acquisition date	Results of combined entity incorporated in the consolidated financial statements as if entities had always been combined
Valuation of assets and liabilities	Requires restatement at cost (fair value)	Not restated at fair value - instead book values at merger date used
Goodwill	Goodwill recognised	Does not arise

SECTION 1

Acquisition accounting

6820   In an acquisition, **the shareholders of the acquired entity** typically sell their shareholdings for either:
– cash;
– other non-equity consideration; or
– equity shares in the new parent entity or a combination thereof.

In many cases, the shareholders of the acquired entity do not retain a continuing interest in the shares of the combined entity and even where they do, it is unlikely to be on equal terms with the shareholders of the acquiring entity. One party, usually the shareholders of the acquirer, is likely to have a greater degree of influence.

6821
FRS 6 (20)

The objective of acquisition accounting is to reflect the cost of the acquisition in the consolidated balance sheet. On acquisition of a subsidiary, the purchase consideration is allocated to the fair values of the identifiable assets and liabilities (net assets) of the acquired entity, with the residue classified as goodwill.

As it is not always possible to determine accurately the fair values at the acquisition date, adjustments to the provisional estimates, including goodwill, can be made within the following 12 months, as more information becomes available.

> ⌐MEMO POINTS⌐   **Fair value** is defined as the amount at which an asset or liability could be exchanged in an arm's length transaction between willing parties, other than in a forced sale or liquidation. Assets and liabilities are classified as identifiable when they can be disposed of separately, without disposing of an entire business or undertaking.

6822   The **general principles** of accounting for a business combination (including reverse takeovers) under the acquisition method of accounting, and the recognition and measurement principles underpinning the fair value of individual acquired assets and liabilities, are set out below.

A. Accounting treatment

1. Determining the cost of acquisition

6836
FRS 7 (76)

The cost of acquisition (purchase consideration) may take some or all of the following forms as set out in the table below.

1.	The **total cash paid** and the fair value of **other monetary considerations** given by the acquirer including the assumption of liabilities.
2.	**Capital instruments** issued by the acquirer such as shares, debentures, loans, debt instruments, share warrants and other options.
3.	**Non-monetary assets** such as the securities of another entity.
4.	**Acquisition expenses** (e.g. fees).
5.	**Contingent consideration.** Where a **purchase consideration is dependent on** one or more **future events**, the acquisition cost should include an estimate of the fair value of any future payments. The acquisition cost should then be adjusted when revised estimates have been prepared, with corresponding adjustments made to goodwill until such time as a final purchase price is determined.
6.	**Piecemeal acquisition** Where a subsidiary is acquired in stages (piecemeal acquisition), the cost of acquisition is the total costs of the interest acquired, as at each transaction date (¶6964).

Cash paid and other monetary considerations

Where the **purchase consideration** is in the form of cash or other monetary considerations, the fair value attributable to them is the amount paid or due to be paid.

6839

In situations where the **cash payable is deferred**, fair values are determined by discounting to the present value, the cash value to be paid at a future date. The appropriate discount rate is the interest rate which the acquiring company would have to pay, if it were to borrow an amount equivalent to the deferred cash consideration.

Capital instruments

It is often the case, that **part of the acquisition consideration** given by the purchaser will be capital instruments in the acquiring company. Therefore, for the purposes of calculating the purchase consideration, it will be necessary to determine the fair value of those instruments at the date they were issued.

6840

Where **an entity issues capital instruments** to raise the cash required to fund an acquisition, the fair value of the instruments issued is not the relevant factor in determining the fair value of the consideration paid, but the cash that is subsequently paid to the vendor.

The fair values of shares and other securities or capital instruments issued by the acquirer, where quoted on a readily available market, will be the market price at the acquisition date. The relevant date for valuation purposes where control is transferred through a public offer, or where there are a number of revised offers, is when the successful offer becomes unconditional.

6842

Where securities issued by the acquiring entity **are not quoted**, the fair value is estimated after considering the following:
- the fair value of similar quoted securities;
- any cash alternative to the issue of securities;
- the present value of the future cash flows of the instrument issued; and
- the value of any underlying security incorporating an option to convert.

6843

FRS 7 (79)

Non-monetary assets

Where the purchase price is settled in the form of non-cash assets, the fair values should be determined with reference to:
- market prices;
- estimated realisable values;
- independent valuations; or
- other available evidence.

6844

Acquisition expenses

6845

FRS 7 (85)

The acquisition process will usually involve expenditure on professional fees paid to:
- merchant banks;
- accountants;
- legal advisers; or
- valuers and other consultants.

The **general rule** is that these incremental costs incurred directly in making the acquisition should be included in the cost of acquisition.

However, it should be noted that the expenses of issuing shares or other capital instruments that qualify as issue costs, should not be added to the cost of acquisition, but accounted for as a reduction in the proceeds of a capital instrument.

Contingent consideration

6850

FRS 7 (81)

The **acquisition terms** may stipulate that all or part of the purchase consideration in whatever form, be payable at a later date, perhaps based on some performance criteria. The **fair value of such agreements** are often difficult to determine at the acquisition date, and as such a reasonable estimate of future considerations should be included in the acquisition price.

An example is an **"earn-out"**, where the purchase consideration includes an initial payment, with future payments based on a multiple of future profits (performance based) of the acquired entity. Other examples include consideration in the form of:
- an issue of shares;
- options to settle the consideration partly in shares, partly in cash; or
- other forms of consideration such as non-competition payments or loyalty bonuses.

Initial estimates of the contingent consideration should be revised as more information becomes available and adjustments made to the goodwill recognised.

6852   **Issue of shares**   Where contingent consideration is to be satisfied by the issue of shares, there is no obligation to transfer economic benefits. The purchase consideration is reported as part of shareholders' funds, as shares yet to be issued. This is effectively a "holding account" until it is known exactly how many shares are to be issued. Appropriate transfers would then be necessary from this "holding account" to the called-up share capital and share premium accounts.

6854   **Option to settle the consideration partly in shares, partly in cash**   There may be agreements, where the acquiring undertaking has the option to satisfy part of the purchase consideration through a share issue and partly in cash. In these cases, this element of the future consideration is not a liability because no obligation to transfer economic benefits has arisen. Consequently, the expected future consideration would be accounted for as a credit to shareholders' funds, until an irrevocable decision regarding the form of the consideration has been taken.

However, in those cases the where **the vendor has the right** to demand cash or shares, the expected future consideration is regarded as an obligation to the vendor and would be accounted for as a liability until the shares are issued or the cash is paid.

6856

FRS 7 (84)

Other forms of consideration   Acquisition agreements may require payments such as **non-competition payments** or **loyalty bonuses** to vendors, who continue to work for the acquired undertaking. In such circumstances, it is necessary to determine whether the substance of the agreement is payment for the business acquired, or an expense, such as compensation for services or profit sharing. In the first case, the expected payments would be accounted for as contingent purchase consideration; in the latter case, the payments would be treated as expenses of the period to which they relate (see ¶6944).

2. Specifically excluded acquisition costs

Post-acquisition costs All post-acquisition costs must be excluded from the fair value **6860** exercise. Examples include:
- structural/organisational changes made by the acquirer;
- impairment, or other changes resulting from post-acquisition events;
- internal costs and other expenses not directly attributable to the acquisition; or
- provisions or accruals for future operating losses or for reorganisation and expected integration costs resulting from the acquisition, relating to the acquired entity or acquirer at the acquisition date.

If the acquirer subsequently decides to **close a factory** belonging to the acquired entity, this is deemed a post-acquisition event. Similarly, where the acquirer reorganises or restructures the factory to integrate the operation or to improve its efficiency, this is also considered a post-acquisition event.

Pre-acquisition costs Costs that would have been incurred irrespective of the acquisition **6861** and other pre-acquisition costs should be expensed in the profit and loss account. Examples FRS 7 (40) include the following:
- costs of running an acquisitions department;
- due diligence costs;
- expenses incurred in raising acquisition finance (e.g. shares issue); or
- certain provisions for future costs.

Provisions for future costs Where provisions for future costs were made by an acquired **6862** entity shortly before an acquisition took place, for example, during the negotiations for sale, FRS 7 (40) it would be necessary to determine whether actual obligations had been incurred by the acquired entity before the acquisition.

If the **acquired entity was committed** to the expenditure irrespective of whether the acquisition was completed or not, it would have incurred a liability at the acquisition date, and any associated provisions would be permissible. For instance, where the acquiring entity was contractually committed to a closure or restructuring plan, prior to completion of the acquisition and was unable to withdraw without due cost, then these types of provisions would be permissible.

3. Measuring the fair value of acquired assets and liabilities

The general principles governing the initial investigation period, the recognition and valu- **6864** ation of acquired assets and liabilities and the rules for determining the fair value of specific types of assets and liabilities are set out below.

a. Recognition and measurement principles

The **identifiable assets and liabilities** of the acquired entity are recognised at their fair **6866** values as at the acquisition date, in accordance with the acquiring undertaking's accounting FRS 7 (5) policies for similar assets and liabilities. The difference between the fair value of these assets and liabilities and the acquisition cost is accounted for as goodwill.

The identifiable assets and liabilities **acquired by the purchasing entity** represent rights to future economic benefits and obligations to transfer economic benefits, including contingent rights and obligations, of the acquired entity existing at the acquisition date.

Investigation period

Usually the **acquisition transaction** does not, in itself, determine the values attributed to **6867** each asset and liability. For this reason, the Companies Act and the accounting standards FRS 7 (23) require a fair value exercise to determine the initial carrying amounts of individual assets and liabilities on acquisition.

The standard sets out the **general rules** for the investigation period, which can last up to 12 months, during which determination of the fair values should take place; namely:
– the **recognition and measurement** of acquired assets and liabilities should be completed by the date of approval by the directors of the first post-acquisition financial statements; or
– **where this is not possible**, provisional valuations should be prepared and adjusted where necessary in the next financial statements, with corresponding adjustments to purchased goodwill being made at that time.

Thereafter, **any further adjustments** to the provisional valuation, except the correction of fundamental errors which are accounted for as prior-period adjustments, should be recognised in the profit and loss account.

Valuation of acquired assets and liabilities

6870
FRS 7 (42)
Fair values should be based on the value at which an asset could be exchanged in an arm's length transaction (market price). The fair value of monetary items should also take into account amounts expected to be received or paid and their timing. Where the replacement cost is **not fully recoverable** then fair value should be based on recoverable amount.

6874
Where **similar assets are bought and sold** on a readily accessible market the market price will represent fair value. Where quoted market prices are not available, they should be estimated by:
– obtaining independent valuations;
– discounting estimated future cash flows to their present values; or
– with reference to subsequent sales of acquired assets.

Impaired assets

6878
FRS 7 (47)
Where the **replacement cost** of an acquired asset **is not fully recoverable**, due for example, to reasons of obsolescence, under-utilisation or non-profitability, the fair value is the estimated recoverable amount. The recoverable amount valuation should reflect the condition of the asset on acquisition, but not any impairment resulting from subsequent events.

6880
In some instances, the recoverable amount can be determined only by considering a **group of jointly used assets** (income generating units) as a whole, rather than by attempting to determine the recoverable amount of each identifiable asset in that group. Aggregation can facilitate the allocation of cash flows to the assets that help to generate them.

6881
Any **losses arising on the disposal** of acquired assets (e.g. as part of a post-acquisition reorganisation) that were not impaired at the acquisition date, do not affect the fair values at the acquisition date. These losses could arise from the re-organisation of the enlarged group post-acquisition and should be treated as post-acquisition losses.

Assets and liabilities not previously recognised

6883
FRS 7 (35)
The identifiable assets and liabilities may include **items not previously recognised** in the financial statements of the acquired entity (pre-acquisition), because other accounting standards prohibited their inclusion. An example is a contingent asset valued on acquisition but not recognised in the financial statements, because FRS 12 "Provisions, contingent liabilities and contingent assets" prohibits recognition until realisation is all but certain.

However, **when an entity is acquired**, it is necessary to identify all assets and liabilities acquired, where they can be properly valued. Otherwise, the reporting of post-acquisition performance will be distorted by changes in assets and liabilities not being recognised in the correct accounting period. The accounting practice of **deferring recognition** of contingent assets does not apply, as recognition of the asset represents the expectation by the acquirer that the acquisition costs will be recovered at some stage. However, provisions should be made for any expected losses.

Furthermore, particular **contingent assets and liabilities may crystallise** as a result of the acquisition. Provided that the underlying contingency was in existence before the acquisition, it would be appropriate to recognise them. For example, where the acquired entity entered into contracts containing restrictive clauses that later trigger obligations in the event of a change of ownership.

6884
FRS 7 (37)

b. Identifiable individual assets and liabilities

The table below outlines the **valuation bases** for determining the fair value of acquired assets and liabilities.

6890

Category	Basis for determining fair value
Tangible fixed assets (¶6892)	Lower of recoverable amount or depreciated replacement cost (DRC) reflecting: – the market value for similar assets readily available or – DRC for specialised assets
Intangible fixed assets	Replacement cost (estimated market value)
Stock and work-in-progress (¶6894)	1. Stocks for which an active market exists – use market price 2. Other stocks: use lower of replacement cost or net realisable value 3. Long-term maturing stocks: use historic cost or market value if traded regularly
Long-term contracts (¶6904)	Based on acquirer's accounting policy
Monetary assets and liabilities (¶6906)	Quoted investments: use market price Other monetary items: expected values to be received or paid on settlement.
Non-monetary assets (¶6910)	Market value
Contingent assets and liabilities (¶6912)	Values based on reasonable estimates
Business held exclusively For resale (¶6915)	Estimate of expected net sale proceeds. Special rules apply based on time-scale for sale of investment or part-disposal.
Pension and other retirement benefits following acquisition (¶6920)	Funded scheme: Only recognition of surpluses and liabilities expected to be realised. Unfunded scheme: recognition of valuation of accrued obligations as liabilities.
Deferred tax assets and liabilities (¶6925)	Must satisfy the recognition criteria in FRS 19. Tax losses of the acquired entity recognised as an asset if it can be recovered.

Tangible fixed assets

The fair value of tangible fixed assets should not exceed the recoverable amount of the asset and be based on:

6892
FRS 7 (9)

a. **market value** where assets are similar and reliable values are obtainable (e.g. quoted investments and certain types of property); or

b. **depreciated replacement cost (DRC)**. For many types of fixed asset, such as plant and machinery and specialist property, the fair value equals the DRC reduced by depreciation to reflect the age and condition of the asset. The DRC should not exceed the recoverable amount of an asset at the acquisition date and should reflect the acquired undertaking's normal buying process and sources of supply.

For certain assets **where it is difficult to determine the DRC**, the asset's historical cost updated with the aid of price indices, may be the most reliable method of estimating replacement cost. In situations where prices have not changed greatly, it would be acceptable to use a carrying value based on historical cost.

The topic of valuation of tangible fixed assets is dealt with in greater detail in ¶1226.

6893   **Depreciation rates** adopted should, in determining the DRC, reflect the estimated asset lives and residual amounts used by the acquirer for similar assets.

Stocks and work-in-progress

6894
FRS 7 (11)
Stocks purchased in a **readily active market** and **work-in-progress**, including commodity stocks that are traded by the acquired entity, should be valued at current market prices.

6896   **Where there is no ready market**, work-in-progress should be valued at the lower of replacement cost and net realisable value. Account should be taken of the manner in which the acquired business purchased or manufactured the stocks; namely for:
– a business buying its stocks in wholesale markets, the replacement cost should be the actual cost; whilst
– the replacement cost of finished goods of a manufacturer should be the current manufacturing cost and not the cost of buying in supplies from another manufacturer.

6898   Where stock is held during the period up to the acquisition date, it would be valid to take account of the impact of input price changes during the holding period. However, no addition should be made for any unrealised profit that normally would not be recognised in the acquired undertaking until the stocks are sold.

6899   **Long-term maturing stocks**   Replacement costs should be based on market values if stocks are regularly traded in the market. Where similar market transactions do not exist because there is no active market or trading is very thin, use of replacement cost will be difficult. Instead the historical cost of bringing the stock to its present location and condition may be appropriate.

6900
FRS 7 (57)
Slow moving or obsolete stock   Care needs to be exercised in reaching a judgement about the fair value of slow moving or redundant stocks. Any **material write-down** in the carrying value of stock in the acquired entity at the acquisition date must be justified by circumstances prevailing at that time.

Where **exceptional profits** appear to have been earned on the realisation of stocks after the date of acquisition, it will be necessary to re-examine the fair values determined on acquisition. If necessary, these values will have to be adjusted with a corresponding adjustment to goodwill. If, alternatively, the profit is attributable to post acquisition events, it should be disclosed as an exceptional item.

Long-term contracts

6904   SSAP 9 "Stocks and long-term contracts" (see ¶2200) requires **turnover and cost of sales** to be recognised as the contract progresses, and attributable profit recognised in a prudent manner. As such no adjustments to book values are required other than adjustments that would normally result from assessing the outcome of the contract under SSAP 9, or that result from a change to the acquirer's accounting policies.

6905
FRS 7 (38)
Onerous contracts   Identifiable liabilities include onerous contracts and commitments existing in existence at the acquisition date, irrespective of whether the corresponding obligations were recognised as liabilities in the financial statements of the acquired entity. When an acquisition is made, provisions for liabilities may be recognised when performing the fair value exercise, only if such commitments were made by the acquired undertaking before the date of acquisition.

Monetary assets and liabilities

6906
FRS 7 (60)
The majority of **short-term** monetary assets and liabilities, such as trade debtors and creditors, will be recognised at values expected to be received or paid on settlement. However,

the fair values of certain **long-term** monetary items may differ from their book values. An example is where an acquired entity carries material levels of long-term debt at fixed rates that are different from current interest rates on borrowing. The fair values will be greater or lower than the book value depending on the direction of changes in interest rates since the debt was issued.

The following conditions apply:

a. **Monetary items** must be stated at fair values where they differ materially from book values.

b. **Quoted investments** should be valued at market price, adjusted to reflect unusual price fluctuations or size of holding such as the higher value attached to substantial voting blocks or difficulties in disposing of small shareholdings.

c. For **other monetary items**, the fair values may be calculated after considering the current terms on which a similar monetary asset or liability could be acquired or incurred.

Discounting to present values   Another method would be to discount to present values   **6907**
of the total amounts expected to be received or paid. The interest rates selected would need to reflect the current lending rates applicable to a similar credit period, the credit rating of the acquirer and the precise nature of the security involved.

Differences between fair values determined by discounting and the actual amounts subsequently received or paid represent premiums or discounts on acquisition, that should be treated in the financial statements of the acquired group as interest income or expenses. The amounts are then allocated to accounting periods over the term of the monetary item at a constant rate based on their carrying amounts.

Debt instruments   Where debt instruments issued by the acquired company are quoted,   **6909**
market values at the acquisition date should be used instead of present values. Any pre-acquisition risk that the debt would not be repaid, which was reflected in the market value, would not be adjusted as part of the fair value exercise, if the debt is expected to be paid in full.

Non-monetary assets

The **general rule** is that the fair values of non-monetary assets should be measured at their   **6910**
market value (see also ¶6844).   FRS 7 (45)

Where this is not possible, the fair values should be based on replacement cost, but this should not exceed their recoverable amount as at the date of acquisition.

The **replacement cost** is the cost to the acquired entity of replacing the asset through its normal buying process and sources of supply. Although replacement cost takes into account the effects of input price changes during the period stocks are held.

The **recoverable amount** is the greater of the net realisable value of an asset or the value in use and reflects the condition of the assets on acquisition but nor any impairments resulting from subsequent events.

Contingent assets and liabilities

The value assigned to a contingent asset or liability should reflect the best estimates of the   **6912**
expected outcome (see also ¶6883-4).

An acquired undertaking may have contingent assets and liabilities, that would not normally be recognised in its financial statements **if no acquisition was involved**, because other accounting standards preclude their immediate recognition. For example, the acquired undertaking may have previously entered into a contract that contains a clause under which obligations are triggered in the event of a change in ownership. Such contingent assets and liabilities should be recognised, if the underlying contingency was in existence before the acquisition and can be reliably valued.

This accounting treatment is required, **otherwise the possibility of changes** in assets and liabilities not being recognised in the correct period, would distort the reporting of post-acquisition performance.

The usual accounting practice of **deferring recognition** of contingent assets, does not apply, because the recognition of an acquired asset represents the expectation that amounts expended on its acquisition will be recovered; it does not anticipate a future gain. The **recoverable amount** of such assets should however be reviewed to ensure that provision is made for any probable losses.

Business sold or held exclusively for resale (Investments)

6915

FRS 7 (16) (65-69)

Sale within one year of acquisition If a separate business within the acquired entity is sold as a single unit within the first year following acquisition, the investment should be consolidated and treated as a single asset for the purpose of determining fair values, rather than assigning fair values to individual assets and liabilities. The goodwill should be apportioned between the part of the business retained and the part disposed of.

Where the adjustment for goodwill is material, the net proceeds should be discounted to determine their present value at the acquisition date, after allowing for the distribution of profits from the business. The **operational results** during the holding period are excluded from the profit and loss account of the acquiring group.

For this accounting treatment to apply the assets and liabilities should be clearly distinguishable from the other parts of the business.

6916

Sale not completed before the first post-acquisition financial statements are approved If the sale has not been completed by the date the first post-acquisition financial statements are agreed, the fair value of the business should be based on the estimated sale proceeds, providing:
– a purchaser has been identified; and
– the disposal is expected to be completed with one year of the acquisition date.

6917

Post-acquisition profit or loss There are a **number of circumstances** where the acquirer should estimate separately, the fair value of the underlying assets/liabilities of the business, at the acquisition date of a business held for resale and to record a post-acquisition profit or loss on disposal; namely:
– where the acquirer has markedly changed the acquired business before disposal;
– specific post-acquisition events occur during the holding period that materially affect the fair values of the business, compared to the estimates; or
– the disposal is quickly concluded at a reduced price.

Pensions and other post-retirement benefits following acquisition

6920

FRS 7 (70)

Accounting for an acquisition requires recognition in the acquirer's group accounts of all assets and liabilities of the acquired entity, identified at the acquisition date. However, a **pension asset** should only be recognised insofar as the acquiring or acquired entity is able to benefit from the surplus. A distinction is drawn between funded and unfunded pension schemes.

Any **changes in pension or other post-retirement arrangements** following an acquisition should be accounted for as post-acquisition items. Such an example is the cost of improving benefits to existing members of an acquired scheme in order to harmonise remuneration packages across the enlarged group.

Pensions are treated in greater detail in Part 10 Chapter 3.

6922

Funded defined benefit scheme Where **an acquired company has a pension asset or liability** in its own balance sheet, then that asset or liability should be recognised in the consolidated financial statements of the acquiring company. Where possible, the same actuarial basis used to value the subsidiary's pension asset/liabilities should be adopted by the acquiring company.

Where an acquired company has a defined benefit scheme but has yet to recognise a pension asset or liability, a valuation of the fund is required. Any **deficiency or surplus** expected to be realised, should be recognised as assets or liabilities of the acquired undertaking.

The **fair value of a pension asset** in a funded defined benefit scheme refers to the extent it can be recovered through reduced contributions or through refunds from the scheme, and not simply the actuarial surplus in the fund.

⬚ *MEMO POINTS* ⬚   The **valuation of a pension fund surplus** depends on **several assumptions** such as: the level of interest rates, inflation rates, investment returns, the estimated turnover of staff, or future salary increases. The acquiring undertaking should apply its own judgement, in determining the impact on the valuation of the pension fund, if any, of these assumptions.

Unfunded schemes   For unfunded schemes, the fair value of accrued obligations should be recognised as liabilities of the acquiring company.   **6924**

Deferred tax

Deferred tax **on adjustments** to recorded values of assets and liabilities at their fair value should be recognised in accordance with the principles of FRS 19 "Deferred Tax".   **6925**
FRS 7 (21) (74)

The existing deferred tax assets of the acquired entity should be included in the fair value exercise.

Where a deferred tax asset arises in the financial statements of the acquirer or another of its group entities as a result of the acquisition, that asset should be taken as a credit to the tax charge of the group in the post-acquisition period. This means that the enlarged group's deferred tax provision will be calculated as a single amount at the end of the accounting period, based on assumptions applicable to the group.

For example, deferred tax assets not considered recoverable prior to acquisition by the acquired entity, such as unrelieved tax losses, may become so post-acquisition by satisfying the recognition criteria set out in FRS 19.

Furthermore, **if the losses had arisen in the acquired entity**, they would be regarded as contingent assets that had crystallised as a result of the acquisition, and would be recognised as assets in the fair value exercise. **If the losses had arisen in the acquiring group**, they would not be assets of the acquired group and hence would not be recognised.

If the **criteria for recognition of tax losses** in group financial statements are not met, within the period allowed for completing the fair value exercise, then any benefits should be recognised in post-acquisition periods if the criteria are subsequently met. In these periods, any **special circumstances** that impact on the tax charge or credit for that period, or may affect those of future periods, should be disclosed in a note to the consolidated profit and account and their individual effects quantified.   **6926**

B. Date control is transferred

An entity should be **accounted for as a subsidiary**, from the date on which control of that undertaking passes to its new parent undertaking. Control is defined as "the ability of an undertaking to direct the financial and operating policies of another undertaking with a view to gaining economic benefits from its activities".   **6942**
FRS 2 (45)

The date on which the consideration for the **transfer of control is paid** is often an important indication of the date on which the subsidiary undertaking is acquired or disposed of.

However, the **complexity of some acquisition agreements** may mean that the terms of each agreement need to be reviewed carefully, in order to determine when control actually passes. This is because the date on which the consideration is paid may not constitute conclusive evidence of the date of the actual transfer of control.

In addition, the determination of the point control passes to the acquirer may be further complicated when **different forms of purchase consideration** are utilised.

Correspondingly, the date for accounting for an undertaking that **ceases to be a subsidiary** is the date on which its former parent undertaking relinquishes control over that undertaking.

1. Different forms of purchase consideration for subsidiaries

6943
FRS 2 (85)

The purchase consideration for a subsidiary can take a number of forms as set out below.

6944

Consideration paid in instalments   Some acquisition agreements involve what is known as "**deferred consideration**", whereby part of the consideration is paid to the acquiring undertaking at the time the agreement is signed, with further instalments payable on future specified dates.

Other agreements involve "**contingent consideration**" where the profile of payments made to the acquiring undertaking depends on the outcome of future events, such as the profit performance of the acquired undertaking.

The payment of consideration by instalments or the existence of contingent or deferred consideration clauses in the purchase and sale agreement, does not necessarily delay the passing of control to the acquirer and the **relevant date** will be when actual ownership of the shares in the acquired company passes to the acquirer.

However, this may not apply in all cases and the relevant facts need to be assessed on a case by case basis, in order to determine when control actually passes to the acquiring undertaking. For example, where the deferred or contingent payments represent all of the acquired undertaking's profits up to a certain date, this suggests that control does not pass on the signing of the purchase and sale agreement, but at a later date when the acquirer becomes entitled to the profits of the acquired company.

6945
FRS 2 (85) (51)

Other forms of purchase consideration   1. Where control is transferred by public offer, the date control is transferred is the date the offer becomes unconditional, usually as a result of a sufficient number of acceptances being received.

2. For **private treaties**, the date control is transferred is generally the date an unconditional offer is accepted.

3. **Other share issues or cancellation**. Where an undertaking become a subsidiary undertaking as a result of the issue or cancellation of shares, the date control is transferred is the date of issue or cancellation. Examples include the issue of new shares to minority shareholders (non controlling interests) or the repurchase by a company of the shares held by certain existing shareholders, the result of which is that one of the remaining shareholders now has a controlling interest in the company.

2. An undertaking ceases to be a subsidiary

6952
FRS 2 (86)

A subsidiary undertaking **ceases to be part of the group** in the following scenarios:

1. The **parent undertaking loses control** of its subsidiary undertaking because of:
– changes in the rights it holds, or those held by another party, in the subsidiary undertaking; or
– changes in the arrangement that gave it control without there being any change in the former parent undertaking's holding in its former subsidiary undertaking (e.g. a change in voting rights or the way these are allocated).

2. The **parent sells all or reduces its shareholding** in the subsidiary undertaking. This may result from a direct disposal of part of the interest it holds or from a deemed disposal. Any reduction in the group's proportional interest other than by a direct disposal is a deemed disposal.

The **accounting consequences** of an entity ceasing to be a subsidiary undertaking of its parent are discussed in ¶7100.

3. Increasing a shareholding

a. Categories of interest in shares

A **change in the level of investment** will require a change in accounting treatment for that investment. The following table outlines the most common levels of investment.   **6960**

Nature of relationship	Arrangement/undertaking	Accounting treatment
Minimal or no influence	Simple or trade investment	Fixed asset investment (passive investment)
Participation in arrangement to carry on own businesses	Joint arrangement not an entity (JANE)	Own accounting for assets, liabilities, cash flows etc.
Participating interest with significant influence over operating and financial policies	Associated undertaking	Equity accounting
Long-term interest with contractual joint control	Joint venture	Gross equity accounting
Control of investee undertaking	Subsidiary	Consolidation

FRS 9 (b) (d)

In addition to the change in the accounting treatment adopted for different levels of influ-   **6962**
ence, there are **further considerations** such as:
– the recognition and measurement of fair value adjustments;
– the calculation of any goodwill; and
– the measurement of minority interests.

b. Piecemeal acquisition of a subsidiary

A group's interest in an undertaking may be **acquired in stages**, until full control over the   **6964**
operating and financial policies of an entity is eventually achieved and it becomes a subsidi-   FRS 2 (50)
ary undertaking. This is known as a piecemeal acquisition. In such circumstances, FRS 2
reinforces the provisions of the Companies Act, in requiring that the identifiable assets and
liabilities of the subsidiary undertaking be included in the consolidated financial statements
at their fair value, at the **date control passes** to the acquirer.

The piecemeal acquisition of share acquisition provides a practical means of applying acquisi-   FRS 2 (89)
tion accounting, because once the investee company becomes a subsidiary, it does not require
retrospective fair value exercises to be carried out on the identifiable assets and liabilities of
acquired undertakings, at the date the previous non-controlling interests were acquired.

However, this approach may, **in certain circumstances** (e.g. when initial purchases result in
the investee company becoming an associate of the investor), create a misleading impres-
sion of the value of goodwill, in which case goodwill should be based on the difference
between the cost of each tranche and the fair values attributable to the interest acquired at
that time.

Trade investment becomes a subsidiary undertaking

There may be situations where an undertaking has bought one or more **tranches of shares** in   **6966**
another undertaking, with the initial intention of holding it as a fixed asset trade investment,
but subsequently increased its shareholding, in order to secure a long-term controlling interest.
The accounting treatment is as follows:
1. The **identifiable assets and liabilities** of the acquired undertaking should be included in
the consolidated balance sheet, at fair value only from the date of acquisition; namely the
date it becomes a subsidiary.

2. **Goodwill is based on** the fair values of the underlying assets and liabilities and determined only at the date control passes to the acquirer.

3. When the trade investment becomes a subsidiary company, the **fair values of net assets** at the dates the earlier purchases of shares were made are not considered in calculating goodwill.

4. The assets and liabilities attributable to the **minority interest** should be included on the same basis, as those attributable to the interests held by the parent.

5. The **profits from the subsidiary** undertaking are only included in the consolidated profit and loss account from the date the increased holding in the original trade investment qualified as a subsidiary undertaking.

The accounting treatment is illustrated in the following example.

EXAMPLE   **Fixed asset investment becomes a subsidiary undertaking**

Piecemeal acquisition

Andrew Smith Limited has the following record of **acquisitions of shares** in Boscombe Industries Limited, which has an issued share capital of 1,000,000 ordinary shares:

1. 31 December 2006: 100,000 shares were purchased for a consideration of £500,000 when the fair value of Boscombe Industries Limited's identifiable net assets was £5,000,000 (cumulative shareholding 10%);

2. 31 December 2007: 75,000 shares were purchased for a consideration of £1,000,000 when the fair value of Boscombe Industries Limited's identifiable net assets was £6,000,000 (cumulative shareholding 17.5%);

3. 31 December 2013: 350,000 shares were purchased for a consideration of £6,000,000 when the fair value of Boscombe Industries Limited's identifiable net assets was £10,000,000 (cumulative shareholding 52.5%).

Under the above scenario, the initial acquisitions of 10% and 7.5% on 31 December 2006 and 31 December 2007 would not qualify, both individually and in aggregate, as **participating interests**; they should initially be treated as fixed asset "trade" investments.

Following the acquisition of a further 350,000 shares in Boscombe Industries Limited on 31 December 2013, Andrew Smith Limited's holding totalled 52.5% at which point control passed to the purchaser. Boscombe Industries Limited became a subsidiary of Andrew Smith. Only its **profits from that date onward** will be consolidated in the consolidated accounts of Andrew Smith Limited.

Calculation of goodwill
The goodwill arising when Andrew Smith Limited first consolidates Boscombe Industries Limited into its group accounts as at 31 December 2013, should be calculated as follows:

Fair value of identifiable net asset of Boscombe Limited:

£10,000,000 x 52.5%	£5,250,000

Cost of acquisition in stages:

31 December 2006	£500,000
31 December 2007	£1,000,000
31 December 2013	£6,000,000
	£7,500,000

Goodwill arising on a acquisition of a subsidiary	£2,250,000

Associated undertaking or joint venture becomes a subsidiary undertaking

6970
FRS 2 (89)

The situation may arise where an investment, prior to becoming a subsidiary undertaking, was previously accounted for as an associate or joint venture (see ¶7300). If further acquisitions of shares in the associate result in the investor acquiring control of the investee, the investment becomes a subsidiary undertaking subject to consolidation accounting.

6972   **Further share purchases resulting in a reclassification**   For further purchases of shares in an associate or joint venture, that lead to a reclassification of the investment as a subsidiary company, **two key issues arise**:

1. **Profits of the associate** previously included in the investor's profit and loss account would be part of the net assets at the date it becomes a subsidiary. As a result, the group's share of profits or losses and reserve movements of the associate or joint venture would be reclassified as goodwill.

2. The **aggregate cost of the shares** in the subsidiary undertaking, will be a combination of old and new purchases, although under the Companies Act the fair value of the net assets is calculated at the date the investment becomes a subsidiary undertaking.

In this situation, compliance with the requirements of the Companies Act would be misleading. The remedy is to invoke the "**true and fair view override**" clause and calculate goodwill on each "tranche" of shares purchased (piecemeal basis). The cost of each "tranche" of shares purchased, should be matched with the fair values of the proportion of net assets acquired. This process is illustrated in the example below.

The subsidiary's net assets will be included in the consolidated balance sheet at fair value at the acquisition date.

EXAMPLE   Associate (or joint venture) becomes an associate undertaking

Accounting treatment

Tremkost Limited has the following track record of acquisitions of shares in Visco Limited, which has an issued capital of 1,000,000 ordinary shares. Tremkost Limited has always believed that Visco Limited represented a good strategic fit for its own activities and the objective of its investments in Visco Limited have been to initially exercise significant influence and ultimately gain control.
1. 31 December 2008: 200,000 Visco Limited shares were purchased by Tremkost for a consideration of £1,600,000 when the fair value of Visco Limited's identifiable net assets was £7,000,000;
2. 31 December 2009: 150,000 Visco Limited shares were purchased by Tremkost for a consideration of £1,500,000 when the fair value of Visco Limited's identifiable net assets was £8,000,000;
3. 31 December 2013: 250,000 Visco Limited shares were purchased by Tremkost for a consideration of £3,500,000 when the fair value of Visco Limited's identifiable net assets was £10,000,000.
The 2008 and 2009 acquisitions could qualify Visco Limited as an associate of Tremkost Limited and therefore, subject to equity accounting. In terms of FRS 9 this would entail the following general approach:
a. The investment is brought into the investor undertaking's financial statements initially at cost, plus any goodwill arising;
b. The carrying amount of the investment is adjusted in each period by:
– the investor undertaking's share of results of the associated undertaking;
– any amortisation or write off for goodwill;
– the investor undertaking's share of any gains or losses; and
– any other changes in the associated undertaking's net assets;

The **investor undertaking's share of the** associated undertaking's results is recognised in the investor's profit and loss account.

Multi-stage approach
The accounting treatment applying the multi-stage approach would be as follows:

1. On acquisition of associated undertaking (200,000 shares) – 31 December 2008.
Fair value of identifiable net assets of Visco Limited:

£7,000,000 x 20%	£1,400,000
Cost of acquisition	£1,600,000
Goodwill	£200,000

2. Immediately prior to acquisition of 150,000 shares – 31 December 2009

Fair value of identifiable net assets of Visco Limited as at 31 December 2009	£8,000,000
Fair value of identifiable net assets of Visco Limited as at 31 December 2008	£7,000,000
Increase in profit and loss account	£1,000,000
Equity accounted: £1000,000 x 20%	£200,000

3. On acquisition of £150,000 shares – 31 December 2009
Fair value of identifiable net assets of Visco Limited:

£8,000,000 x 15%	£1,200,000
Cost of acquisition	£1,500,000
Goodwill	£300,000

Value of investment in Visco included in the consolidated accounts of Tremkost:
Cost [£1,600,000 + £1,500,000] + goodwill* [£200,000 + £300,000] + Attributable
post-acquisition profits of Visco [£200,000] = £3,800,000.
* In this example no amortisation has been provided on goodwill.

4. Immediately prior to acquisition 250,000 shares – December 2013

Fair value of identifiable net assets of Visco Limited as at 31 December 2013	£10,000,000
Fair value of identifiable net assets of Visco Limited as at 31 December 2009	£8,000,000
Increase in profit and loss account	£2,000,000
Equity accounted: £2,000,000 x 35%	£700,000

Value of investment in Visco included in the consolidated accounts of Tremkost:
£3,800,000 as at stage 3 above plus equity accounted profits of Visco for the year, £700,000 =
4,500,000.

5. On acquisition of third batch of 250,000 shares – 31 December 2013

Fair value of identifiable net assets of Daphne Limited:	
£10,000,000 x 25%	£2,500,000
Cost of acquisition	£3,500,000
Goodwill	£1,000,000

6. Summary

Goodwill:	31 December 2008	£200,000
	31 December 2009	£300,000
	31 December 2013	£1,000,000
Total goodwill		**£1,500,000**
Profits equity accounted	31 December 2008	£200,000
	31 December 2013	£700,000
Total recognised profits		£900,000

The investment in Visco would now no longer appear as a separate item in the consolidated
balance sheet of Tremkost.

Parent undertaking increases stake in a subsidiary undertaking

6974
FRS 2 (51)
FRS 2 (90)

A group may increase its stake in an undertaking that is already a subsidiary undertaking, in
which case the identifiable assets and liabilities of the subsidiary undertaking should be
revalued to fair value and any goodwill arising on the increase in interest, should be calculated by reference to those fair values.

This **revaluation is not required**, where the difference between the fair values and the
carrying amounts of the share of identifiable net assets, attributable to the increased stake,
is not material. It should be noted that this exercise does not result in any change to the
goodwill calculated when the entity first became a subsidiary of the parent.

C. Treatment of post-acquisition dividends

6978

Where **a recently acquired subsidiary undertaking** pays a dividend shortly after the date of
acquisition, a question arises as to how the dividend should be treated, in the individual
financial statements of the recipient and the group financial statements

Where a dividend is paid to an acquirer out of **pre-combination profits**, it need not be
applied as a reduction in the carrying value of the investment in the subsidiary undertaking
but can be treated as a realised profit by the parent undertaking. On **consolidation**, a dividend so treated will be eliminated.

However, where the payment of a such a dividend by a subsidiary results in the **permanent
diminution in value** of that subsidiary, a different accounting treatment is required. For
example when, following the acquisition, the assets and trade of the subsidiary were transfer-

red up to the parent and the subsidiary became dormant, then the dividend received should be used to reduce the carrying value of the investment to its new lower value. When this **accounting treatment is adopted**, consideration should be given as to whether this dividend, in practice, represents a return to the parent of part of the purchase consideration and also whether any associated goodwill arising on consolidation, should be reduced.

D. Disclosure requirements

Mandatory disclosures

The key disclosure requirements in consolidated financial statements covering business combinations accounted for using acquisition or merger accounting are found in SI 2008/410 Schedule 6.

6984

The following disclosures must be made by the acquiring entity, or in the case of a merger, the entity issuing the shares:
- the names of the combining entities;
- the method used to account for the business combination (acquisition or merger); and
- the date of the acquisition or merger.

Additional disclosures for material acquisitions

The disclosures set out in the table below must be made in the financial statements for **each material (substantial) acquisition** and for all other acquisitions, if material when aggregated, unless exempted (as specified below). The test of materiality, is whether the information relating to the acquisition might reasonably be expected to influence decisions made by investors and other stakeholders.

6986
FRS 6 (23-35)

Disclosure requirements – individual material acquisitions
1   **Purchase consideration** a. The **composition and fair value** of the consideration given by the acquiring company and its subsidiary undertakings b. The nature of any **deferred or contingent purchase consideration** and the range of possible outcomes and principle factors that impact on the outcome c. Where the **fair values** of the acquired entity's assets or liabilities or **purchase consideration** can only be determined provisionally at the end of the accounting period in which the acquisition took place, this fact should be stated and the reasons given. Any subsequent adjustments relating to these values, with corresponding adjustments to goodwill, should be disclosed and explained in the relevant financial year.
2   **Assets and liabilities acquired** A table showing, for **each class of** assets and liabilities of the acquired entity: a. The book values, as recorded in the acquired entity's books immediately before the acquisition and before any fair value adjustments b. The fair value adjustments, giving the reasons therefore, analysed into: – revaluations; – adjustments to achieve consistency of accounting policies; and – any other significant adjustments c. The fair values at date of acquisition d. A statement of the amount of purchased goodwill or negative goodwill arising on consolidation.
3   **Pre-acquisition results** The **profit after taxation and minority interests** of the acquired entity should be given for: a. the period from the beginning of the acquired entity's financial year to the date of acquisition, giving the date on which this period began; and b. the previous financial year. This information is only required either individually or in aggregate for material acquisitions.

Disclosure requirements – individual material acquisitions
4   **Post-acquisition results.** The post-acquisition results of each acquired entity should be shown as a component of continuing operations in the consolidated profit and loss account, except discontinued operations in the same period. In addition, where the acquisition of an entity has a material impact on a major business segment, this should be disclosed. **Where it is not practical** to determine the post-acquisition results of an operation to the end of the period in which the acquisition took place, then an indication should be given of the contribution of the acquired entity to turnover and operating profit of continuing operations.
5   **Exceptional profits or losses** Examples of exceptional profits or losses arising from the use of fair values recognised on acquisition referred to in 3b above, are: – disposal of stocks at abnormal trading margins after acquisition; – release of provisions in respect of an acquired long-term contract that the acquiring entity is able to make profitable; and – realisation of contingent assets or liabilities at amounts materially different from their attributed fair values.
6   **Costs of reorganising or restructuring** The costs of reorganising, restructuring and integrating an acquired entity may extend over more than one accounting period. For major acquisitions, management may wish to disclose in the notes to the consolidated financial statements, the nature and value of the costs expected to be incurred in relation to the acquisition. The notes should also state the extent to which these costs have been charged to the profit and loss account. If part of these costs relate to asset write downs, beyond any impairment recognised in adjusting to fair values on acquisition, it may be useful to distinguish these from cash expenditure (FRS 6 (31).

6994   Substantial acquisitions – pre-acquisition results For substantial acquisitions, the following additional information should be disclosed in the consolidated financial statements of the combined entity, for the period in which the acquisition took place.

1. The **summarised profit and loss account** and **STRGL** of the acquired entity, from the start of its financial year to the effective acquisition date. The summarised profit and loss account should show as a minimum:
– profit after taxation;
– the turnover;
– operating profit and any exceptional items falling within FRS 3 (20);
– taxation; and
– minority interests

2. The **profit after tax** and **minority interests** for the acquired entity's previous financial year.

FRS 6 (36)

The disclosures set out above are required for entities that meet the following conditions:

Type of entity	Disclosures
Other entities	Additional disclosures are required where either: **a.** the **net assets or operating profits** of the acquired entity exceed 15% of those of the acquiring entity; or **b.** the **fair value of the consideration** exceeds 15% of the net assets of the acquiring entity
Other exceptional cases	Where the acquisition is of **such significance** that the additional disclosures are necessary to ensure a true and fair view is given by the group financial statements
Listed companies	*When the combination is a Class 1 transaction in terms of the Listing Rules*

Consolidated cash flow statement

6996
FRS 6 (34)
FRS 1 (45)
The consolidated cash flow statement should show the amounts of cash and cash equivalents paid for each acquisition, net of any cash or cash equivalents transferred as part of each acquisition. In addition, the notes to the cash flow statement should also provide a

summary of the cash flow effects resulting from the acquisitions, including how much of the consideration comprised cash and cash equivalents.

The **notes to the cash flow statement** should also, where practicable, contain information on any material effects that the cash flows of the acquired undertakings had on each of the standard headings in the consolidated cash flow statement. This information could be given by dividing cash flows between continuing and discontinued operations and acquisitions and need be given only for the period in which the acquisition occurs.

SECTION 2

Merger accounting

A **"true" merger is defined as** a business combination that creates a new reporting entity, formed from two or more combining parties, whose shareholders join together to share the risks and benefits of the combined entity. The results of the merging entities are combined as if they had always been part of the same reporting entity, even where the merger is completed part way through a financial year.

7000
FRS 6 (41) (44)

The **rationale for merger accounting** is that no one party to the combination gains control over the other, or is otherwise seen to be dominant, as a result of either shareholders' rights in the combined entity, or through directoral influence.

For both "true" mergers and group reorganisations, merger accounting **can only be applied** when strict criteria are met. **Goodwill** does not arise in merger accounting as the assets and liabilities need not be adjusted to reflect their fair values at the merger date. However, **merger relief is available where** a difference arises between the consideration received and the identifiable assets and liabilities.

MEMO POINTS   The OFT (replaced from March 2014 by the **Competition and Markets Authority (CMA)**) has published **merger guidance** providing information and advice to companies on the procedures involved when reviewing merger cases.
The guidance highlights:
– the different types of transactions and arrangements, and the different levels of control being acquired, that could trigger a reviewable merger;
– when parties should consider voluntarily notifying the OFT of mergers that could generate competition concerns;
– the process the OFT follows in carrying out its competitive assessment; and
– how the OFT will exercise its powers and preserve the possibility of remedial action in completed mergers.

---

1. Criteria for a "true" merger

Before a business combination can be accounted for as a merger, a number of criteria must be met under both the Companies Act and FRS 6. **Failure to meet any of these criteria** will mean that a merger has not taken place and that acquisition accounting should be applied.

7002
FRS 6 (54)

---

a. Key criteria

Shares acquired   At least 90% of the nominal value of the **relevant equity shares with unrestricted rights**, in the undertaking acquired, must be held by or on behalf of the parent. Furthermore, the shares acquired must have been attained, pursuant to an agreement allowing the issue of equity shares by the parent company or one or more of its subsidiary undertakings.

7003

MEMO POINTS   1. The reference to "**relevant shares**" in an undertaking acquired, relates to those shares carrying unrestricted rights to participate both in distributions and in the assets of the undertaking upon liquidation.

2. **Equity share capital** means, in relation to a company, its issued share capital excluding any part of that capital which, neither in respect of dividends or capital, carries a right to participate (beyond a specified amount) in any distribution.

7004 The **fair value of any consideration** (other than the issue of equity shares) given pursuant to the arrangement by the parent company or subsidiary, must not exceed 10% of the nominal value of the equity shares issued.

7005
FRS 6 (55)

Substance and form of the transaction The substance and not just the form of the merger arrangements must be analysed, including any related arrangements that are connected to the business combination, such as:
– the method by which the combination was achieved;
– the plans for the combined entity's future operations (e.g. whether any closures or disposal will impact more on one party than the other); and
– the proposed corporate image (e.g. name, logo and location of the headquarters) and principal operations.

---

b. Additional criteria

7006 Other information relevant to the combination must be taken into account, such as:
– the management structure and personnel;
– relative size of the parties to the combination;
– details of any non-equity consideration given;
– post merger performance arrangements;
– divestment; and
– combinations achieved by using a new parent company.

Each of these subject areas is considered below.

Management structure and personal

7007
FRS 6 (63-65)

All the parties to the combination, as represented by the board of directors or their appointees, must participate in establishing the management structure for the combined entity and selecting the management personnel.

Such decisions must be made on the basis of consensus between the parties to the combination, rather than purely by exercise of the respective voting rights.

Where **one party clearly dominates** the process of setting up the management structure and selection of management personnel, this would indicate that the combination is not a genuine pooling of interests. However, all the parties may agree that the management team of the combined entity should come from only one of the parties. In order for merger accounting to apply in this situation, it must be clear that all the parties to the merger genuinely participated in the decision making process that led to this structure.

7008

FRS 6 (64)

In addition to the **formal management structure** of the combined entity, the following must also be considered:
– the identity of all the persons involved in the main financial and operating decisions; and
– the way in which the decision making process is expected to operate in practice.

Relative sizes of the combining parties

7009
FRS 6 (8) (67)

The relative sizes of the combining entities **must not be so disparate** that one party dominates the combined entity by virtue of its relative size. Where one party is substantially larger than the others, it will be presumed that the larger party can or will dominate the combined enterprise.

FRS 6 (59) (68)

The **guidance on relative size**, is that a party would be presumed to dominate if it is 50% larger than each of the other parties to the combination. This is judged by reference to ownership interests; namely, by considering the proportion of equity of the combined entity attributable to the shareholders of each of the combining parties.

However, **this presumption may be rebutted**, if it can be clearly demonstrated that there is no such dominance. Factors that may indicate that a party to the combination has more influence, or less influence, than is indicated by it relative size, are as follows:
– voting or share agreements; or
– blocking powers or other arrangements.
Circumstances that rebut the presumption of dominant influence based on relative size should be disclosed.

Non-equity consideration

There may be combinations where the equity shareholders of the combining entities receive some consideration in a form other than equity shares (e.g. in cash, loan stock, or preference shares) or equity shares carrying substantially reduced voting or distribution rights.

7010
FRS 6 (9) (69)

The rules governing non-equity consideration are as follows:

7011

1. The **fair value** of any consideration other than equity shares must not exceed 10% of the nominal value of the equity shares issued (see ¶7003).

2. Any **non-equity consideration** (or equity shares carrying substantially reduced voting or distribution rights), must represent only an immaterial proportion of the fair value of the consideration received by that party. In addition, where one party to the combination acquired equity shares in another of the combining parties for up to two years prior to the merger, the consideration for this acquisition must be taken into account, when determining whether this criterion has been met.

Consideration in form of cash Equity shareholders will be deemed to have disposed of their shareholdings for cash, where any arrangement is made as part of the merger, to exchange or redeem the shares received in the combination for cash or other non-equity consideration. Cash received by the shareholders should be regarded as the consideration for the sale of their original shares when determining whether the criteria for non-equity consideration have been met.

7012
FRS 6 (71)

Normal market selling transactions, or privately arranged sale, entered into by a shareholder and not made in conjunction with the combination will not prevent the criterion being met.

Consideration in form of shares with rights In general, where a material part of the consideration offered by the issuing entity to the equity shareholders in the other parties, is in the form of shares with substantially reduced rights, the combination will fail to meet the merger criteria. In determining whether **equity shares with reduced rights** have been issued, the voting rights, as well as the rights to distributions, would need to be taken into account.

7014
FRS 6 (72)

However, some of the adjustments attaching to the shares held by the non-issuing entities' shareholders could be deemed compatible with the combination being a merger. This is because business combinations result from a negotiating process where **different pre-existing rights** have to be reconciled. Whether any changes in the rights of one group of shareholders is sufficient to prevent a particular business combination being treated as a merger, will depend on the facts of each individual case.

7015

Factors for consideration include:
– the original rights of the shareholders;
– the overall arrangement negotiated;
– time limits; and
– whether any new restrictions apply equally to all classes of shareholders.

Post-merger performance arrangements

There may be business combinations, where the share of the equity in the combined entity allocated to one of the parties, depends on the post-combination performance of only a part of the combined entity. This runs counter to the concept of a merger, whereby the participants enter into a mutual sharing of the risks and rewards of the combined entity, including the pooled future results. As such, equity shareholders of any combining entities may not retain a material interest in the future performance of only part of the combined entity.

7020
FRS 6 (11)

FRS 6 (76)   Similarly, "**earn-outs**" or similar **performance related schemes** included in the arrangements to achieve a combination, would run counter to this criterion and thereby preclude the use of merger accounting for the combination.

7021   If there is a **material minority** of shareholders in one of the combining parties that have not accepted the terms of the combination offer, the arrangement will not qualify as a merger. However, **the merger approach** would not necessarily be invalidated by an arrangement, in which the allocation of consideration between the shareholders of the combining parties depended on the future determination of the value of a specific asset or liability contributed by one of the parties. An example would be the eventual outcome of a claim against one of the parties, or the eventual sales value of a specific asset owned by one of the parties.

Divestment

7022
FRS 6 (58)   There may be instances where one of the parties to a business combination is the product of recent divestment by a larger entity. In these circumstances, merger accounting would not be appropriate for the combination, because the divested business will not have been independent for a sufficient time to establish itself as being a party separate from its previous owner. Once the divested business has established a track record of its own it can be considered as a party to a merger.

Combinations achieved by using a newly formed parent company

7024
FRS 6 (14)   One of the ways of creating a merger is to use a newly formed parent company to hold the shares of each of the other parties to the combination. In such circumstances, the accounting treatment depends on the **substance of the business combination** under consideration; namely, whether the combination of the entities involved, other than the new parent company, would have been an acquisition or merger.

Two different scenarios are envisaged:

1. A **genuine merger** exists between the parties to the combination. In such circumstances, the new parent and the other parties should be combined by using merger accounting; or

2. **Where one party can be identified** as the acquirer. In these circumstances, the acquirer and the new parent company should first be combined using merger accounting. Then the other parties to the combination should be treated as acquired by the new parent company by using the acquisition method of accounting.

---

2. Accounting treatment

7030
FRS 6 (43)   When considering a business combination it is important to understand how merger relief can affect the accounting treatment. **Merger relief** can take one of two forms; namely: merger relief or group reconstruction relief and is given under section 611 and 612 of the Companies Act 2006. Merger relief is distinct from merger accounting

Merger relief (¶7032)	A company need not recognise a share premium paid on acquisition of another company, and its application is compulsory when certain criteria have been met. Merger relief applies to business combinations accounting for as mergers and some acquisitions accounted for using acquisition accounting techniques. Merger relief can be claimed where a group wishes to distribute pre-acquisition profits that would otherwise be retained in the subsidiary acquired (see ¶7032).
Group reconstruction relief	With the minimum share premium must be recorded in the share premium account. This relief could be utilised in certain situations where assets are transferred within a group involving wholly-owned subsidiaries. The rules for calculating the minimum share premium are complex and are reviewed in outline in paragraphs ¶7040-7054.
Merger accounting	A method of accounting for a business combination.

Merger accounting

Merger accounting is applied in business combinations where acquisition accounting is not suitable, such as where a new entity is formed from the merged companies in which there is no dominant party with overall control. The key elements of merger accounting are outlined in the table below.

7031
s 612 CA 2006

Accounting Issue	Current UK GAAP
Merger expenses	Merger expenses should be charged to the profit and loss account of the combined entity at the effective date of the mergers, as a reorganisation or restructuring expense in accordance with FRS 3 "Reporting Financial Performance".
Valuation of assets and liabilities	The assets and liabilities of the acquired undertaking are included in the group financial statements at book value (nominal value), subject to the adjustments authorised or required by the Companies Act, or that arise from the adoption by the subsidiary of group accounting policies different from those previously followed.
Pre-acquisition profits and cash flows	The results and the cash flows of the acquired undertaking, should be included in the group financial statements for the entire financial year in which the combination occurred, including the period before the merger, adjusted so as to achieve uniformity of accounting policies.
Adjustment to consolidated reserves	The nominal value of the issued share capital of the acquired undertaking, held by the parent undertaking and its subsidiary undertakings, is set off against the aggregate of: – the nominal value of qualifying shares issued by the parent undertaking or its subsidiary undertakings as part of the purchase consideration; and – the fair value of any other consideration for the acquisition of shares in the acquired undertaking, determined as at the date those shares were acquired.

Merger relief Merger relief means that an entity does not have to recognise a share premium arising on the acquisition of another company, providing **certain criteria** are met. A share premium represents **a difference** between the nominal value of shares issued, plus the fair value of other forms of consideration and the aggregate value of the nominal shares received in exchange and normally treated as a movement on consolidated reserves. Any share premium accounts and capital redemption reserves of the new subsidiary undertaking are not preserved in the consolidated financial statements.

7032

Relief from recording a share premium account – criteria.
Merger Relief is only available where all of the following conditions are met; namely:
– the equity shares are issued as part of the acquisition agreement;
– the issuer increases its equity holding in another entity to 90% or over (in aggregate); and
– the consideration for the shares allocated represents either the issue or transfer of equity shares in the acquired company to the issuing company, or the cancellation of those equity shares in the acquired company that the issuing company does not currently own.
Where the acquired entity has **more than one class of equity share**, the criteria must be satisfied for all classes of equity share and the shares acquired must not have been transferred from a wholly-owned entity already claiming merger relief.

7033
s 612 CA 2006

EXAMPLE 1. Company M issues equity shares and acquires 95% of Company P's equity shares in a straight share-for-share exchange. This transaction meets the qualifying criteria for merger relief.

> 2. Company S owns 65% of Company T's equity shares. The shareholders of T agree to cancel the remaining 35% of shares which S does not hold in exchange for shares in Company S. Company S is entitled to merger relief as the cancellation of shares by T takes its holding over the threshold of 90%. The consideration for the allotment of shares by Company S is the cancellation of the shares by T.

7034   This relief **applies to**:
– the entity issuing the shares;
– equity shares issued to acquire other equity shares, including part consideration where all the conditions set out above have been met; or
– the acquisition of non-equity shares in another entity, in which case the relief covers both equity and non-equity shares issued.

3. Group reconstructions

7040   A group reconstruction is represented by any of the following arrangements:
FRS 6 (2), (78)   – the transfer of a shareholding in a subsidiary undertaking from one group company to another;
– the addition of a new parent company to a group;
– the transfer of shares in one or more subsidiary undertakings of a group to a new company that is not a group company but whose shareholders are the same as those of the group's parent;
– the combination into a group of two or more companies that before the combination had the same shareholders; or
– the splitting off of one or more subsidiary undertakings, as in some de-mergers, where a separate group is formed.

7041   Group reconstructions often include the transfer of various combinations of assets as well as non-share considerations such as intra-group debt. The **objective of accounting** for a group reconstruction **as a merger** is to avoid:
– the recognition of unrealised gains or losses arising from the fair value of a share consideration; and
– the fair valuation of transferred assets and liabilities and recognition of goodwill.
This is achieved by applying a **special relief** available under the Companies Act (s 611 CA 2006).

Merger accounting for group reconstructions

7042   Group reconstructions may be accounted for by using merger accounting, provided:
FRS 6 (13)   – the use of merger accounting is not prohibited by companies legislation;
– the ultimate shareholders remain the same;
– the rights of each such shareholder, relative to the others, are unchanged; and
– the transfer does not alter the minority's interest in the net assets of the group, such as the transfer of a subsidiary undertaking within a sub-group that has an existing minority shareholder.

> MEMO POINTS   In terms of **minority (non controlling) interests**, merger accounting **will not apply where**:
> 1. A subsidiary undertaking that is transferred out of, or into, a sub-group that has a minority shareholder would require the use of acquisition accounting; or
> 2. A minority has effectively acquired, or disposed of, rights to part of the net assets of the group. In both these scenarios, acquisition accounting should be applied to the group reorganisation.

Group reconstruction relief

7044   Shares issued as part of the group reconstruction arrangement at a premium, would, were it
s 611 CA 2006   not for the provisions of the Companies Act, normally be transferred in full to the share premium account. However, the Act allows the issuing company to restrict the amount of

share premium arising to the "**minimum premium value**", which is defined as the amount by which the base value of the consideration for the shares allotted, exceeds the aggregate nominal value of those shares. Share consideration in excess of the minimum premium value is not transferred to a share premium account.

MEMO POINTS   1. The **base value of the consideration for the shares allotted**, is the amount by which the base value of the assets transferred exceeds the base value of any liabilities of the transfer or company, assumed by the issuing company as part of the consideration for the assets transferred.

2. The **base value of the assets transferred is the lower of**:
– the carrying amount of the assets transferred as recorded in the accounting records of the transferor company immediately before the transfer; and
– the cost of the assets transferred.

3. The **base value of liabilities assumed** is the amount at which they are stated in the transferor company's accounting records immediately before the transfer.

EXAMPLE   Calculation of minimum premium amount

1. Carrying amount of assets transferred, as per accounting records of transferor, immediately prior to transfer	5,000
2. Cost of assets transferred	9,000
Base value of assets transferred, being lower of (1) and (2) above	5,000
Less: Base value of liabilities assumed	– 4,500
Base value of consideration for shares allotted	500
Less: Aggregate nominal value of shares allotted	- 400
Minimum premium value	100

Criteria for use of group reconstruction relief   The Companies Act sets out the criteria **7046** **that must be satisfied** for a combination to be eligible for group reconstruction relief; namely where the company issuing the shares:
– is a wholly owned subsidiary of a parent company, and allots shares to its parent company or any fellow subsidiary of the issuing company; and
– in exchange, receives assets other than cash, from the parent company or any fellow subsidiary of the issuing company.
Use of the **relief is not compulsory** and only applies to the transfer of "non-cash" assets. If the assets transferred include an element of cash, the issuing company must determine how many allotted shares this represents and the relevant share premium recognised for these shares.

Options Where the criteria are fulfilled, **three accounting options** are available.   **7047**
1. Assets can be transferred within a wholly owned group at nominal (book) value, so avoiding the recognition of unrealised gains or losses.
2. Assets can be revalued at fair value, with the additional premium recognised as a share premium or other reserve such as the merger reserve.
3. The investment can be recorded at its previous carrying value in the transferor company (nominal value of shares issued) and the shares then subsequently revalued, with any increase credited to the revaluation reserve.

Where fair value is used, the additional credit arising is taken not to a share premium   **7054** account but to another reserve, usually referred to as either a merger reserve or merger relief reserve.

EXAMPLE   Tate Haulage Limited owns 100 per cent of Dingle Limited and Woolpack Limited, which both have an issued share capital of £100,000 comprising 100,000 ordinary shares of £1 each. Tate Haulage decides that it would like to convert the current horizontal group structure into a vertical structure. The intended outcome is for Tate Haulage Limited to wholly own Dingle Limited which will in turn wholly own Woolpack Limited.
Dingle Limited is to **issue 40,000 shares** to Tate Haulage Limited in **consideration for the transfer** of its holding of shares in Woolpack Limited to Dingle Limited.
Tate Haulage Limited's investment in Woolpack Limited is carried in its balance sheet at its original cost of £45,000. Relevant details relating to Woolpack Limited are as follows:

Woolpack Limited	Original cost	Carrying value	Fair value
Assets transferred	£100,000	£170,000	£250,000
Liabilities assumed	£55,000	£55,000	£55,000
Net	£45,000	£115,000	£195,000

Accounting treatment	
Tate Haulage Limited	**£**
1. Carrying amount of assets in Woolpack Limited transferred, as per accounting records of transferor, immediately prior to transfer	170,000
2. Cost of assets of Woolpack Limited transferred	100,000
Base value of assets transferred, being lower of (1) and (2) above	100,000
Less: Base value of liabilities assumed	– 55,000
Base value of consideration for shares allotted	45,000
Less: Aggregate nominal value of shares allotted	-40,000
Minimum premium amount	5,000

Dingle Limited	£ Dr.	£ Cr.
a. Minimum premium amount Accounting for the investment in Woolpack Limited at **base value**		
Investment in subsidiary undertaking	45,000	
Share capital		40,000
Share premium account		5,000
Or an optional alternative treatment		
b. Recorded at fair value Accounting for the investment in Woolpack Limited at **fair value of net assets** and creation of merger relief reserve.		
Investment in subsidiary undertaking	195,000	
Share capital		40,000
Share premium account		5,000
Merger reserve		150,000

4. Disclosure requirements

7060
FRS 6 (22)

For each business combination accounted for as a merger, the following information should be disclosed in the financial statements of the combined entity for the period in which the merger took place.

An **analysis of the principal components** should be given as follows:

1. The current (and previous) year's **profit and loss account** (e.g. turnover, operating profit and exceptional items, split between continuing operations, discontinued operations and acquisitions; profit before taxation; taxation and minority interests; and extraordinary items) split into:
– amounts relating to the merged entity for the period after the date of the merger; and
– for each party to the merger, amounts relating to that party for the period up to the date of the merger;

2. A breakdown of the **principal components** of the current and previous period's **STRGL**, divided into:
- amounts relating to the merged entity for the period after the date of the merger;
- for each party to the merger, amounts relating to that party for the period up to the date of the merger.

Additional information   **7062**

1. The composition and fair value of the consideration given by the issuing company and its subsidiary undertakings.

2. The aggregate book value of the net assets of each party to the merger at the date of the merger.

3. The nature and amount of significant accounting adjustments made to the net assets of any party to the merger designed to achieve consistency of accounting policies, and an explanation of any other significant adjustments made to the net assets of any party to the merger, as a consequence of the merger.

4. A statement of adjustments to consolidated reserves resulting from the merger.

5. Corresponding figures (Comparatives) should be restated, by including the results for all the combining entities and their balance sheets, for the previous period, adjusted where necessary to achieve uniformity of accounting policies.

SECTION 3

New UK GAAP – requirements of FRS 102

There are **no key differences** between existing UK GAAP and the FRS 102 "Financial Report-   **7065**
ing Standard applicable in the UK and Republic of Ireland", the adoption of which is mandatory for accounting periods beginning on or after 1 January 2015.

Issue	Accounting treatment under FRS 102 (Section 19)
Terminology and principles	Acquisitions (existing UK GAAP) renamed as business combinations in FRS 102. Acquisition method reclassified as the purchase method. General accounting principles same as in current UK GAAP.
Subsequent recognition	Under FRS 102 adjustments to the initial accounting entries can be made up to 12 months after the acquisition date. This differs from current requirements that permit adjustments up to the second balance sheet date following acquisition.
Intangible assets acquired as part of a business combination	Existing UK GAAP: often included within goodwill as they are deemed inseparable. Under FRS 102: More intangible assets can be individually recognised on the balance sheet distinct from goodwill.
Merger accounting	Existing UK GAAP: Merger accounting permitted if strict criteria are met. Under FRS 102: Only permitted for group reconstructions and some business combinations concerning public benefit entities.
General	Less detailed application guidance given in FRS 102 (e.g. on reverse acquisitions, group reconstructions).

MEMO POINTS   The FRC has issued a **staff education note (SEN 15)** covering acquisitions and disposals of subsidiaries that highlights some key areas of consideration when transitioning to FRS 102. This Staff Education Note compares the accounting treatment for acquisitions and disposals of subsidiaries under current UK accounting standards: FRS 2 Accounting for subsidiary undertakings; FRS 6 Acquisitions and mergers; and FRS 10 Goodwill and intangible assets; with the requirements of FRS 102, principally: Section 9 Consolidated and Separate Financial Statements; Section 19 Business Combinations and Goodwill; and Section 22 Liabilities and Equity. The SEN looks at a number of **acquisition scenarios**, including control achieved in stages and increasing a controlling interest in a subsidiary.

CHAPTER 4

Disposals

1. Accounting treatment

The **sale or reduction of interests** by a parent undertaking in a subsidiary undertaking will take the form of one of the scenarios set out in the table below.

7100
FRS 2 (47)

Degree of control disposed of	Reduction of parent company interest in a subsidiary undertaking
Complete disposal (¶7102)	The parent undertaking **retains no interest** in the subsidiary undertaking.
Partial reduction in holding (¶7128)	The parent undertaking **reduces its interest partially**, but not enough to undermine its control and so retains its parent status. However, a minority interest is created or an existing minority interest is increased.
Significant reduction in holding (¶7133)	The parent undertaking **significantly reduces its interests** in the subsidiary, to the extent that it ceases to be a subsidiary and becomes an associated undertaking.
Considerable reduction in holding (¶7140)	The parent undertaking **divests its controlling interest** in the subsidiary, but holds on to a small interest- accounted for as a fixed asset investment.

a. Complete disposal of a subsidiary

An undertaking **may cease to be a subsidiary** as a result of the sale of a holding for cash or where the parent loses control over voting rights.

7102

Sale of shares for cash

7104

[EXAMPLE] Robust Technical Services Limited acquired and then later disposed of shares in Shillelagh Limited, which has an issued share capital of 1,000,000 ordinary shares, as follows:
A. 31 December 2006: **Acquired 1,000,000 shares** for a consideration of £9,000,000 when the fair value of Shillelagh Limited's identifiable net assets was £6,000,000
B. 31 December 2013: **Disposed of 1,000,000 shares** for proceeds of £14,000,000 when the fair value of Shillelagh Limited's identifiable net assets was £7,000,000, its post-tax profits for the year being £1,000,000.

A. On initial acquisition of 100% of subsidiary undertaking in 2006

The **parent company** Robust Technical Services Limited accounts for its investment in the subsidiary undertaking, Shillelagh Limited, at the acquisition cost of £9,000,000. On consolidation goodwill would be determined as follows:

	£
Purchase consideration paid	9,000,000
Fair value of identifiable net assets acquired	6,000,000
Goodwill arising on consolidation	**3,000,000**

B. On subsequent disposal of 100% of subsidiary undertaking – 31 December 2013 Parent company

	£	£
Proceeds received on disposal of entire holding		14,000,000
Less: Original purchase consideration paid		9,000,000
Gain arising on disposal of subsidiary undertaking		**5,000,000**

Consolidation entries

1. Set-off of investment in subsidiary undertaking against identifiable net assets on consolidation

Net assets of Shillelagh Limited	6,000,000	
Goodwill on consolidation	3,000,000	
Investment in Shillelagh Limited		9,000,000

2. Post-acquisition profits of a subsidiary

Net assets of Shillelagh Limited	1,000,000	
Profit and loss account		1,000,000

3. Determination of gain arising on disposal of subsidiary undertaking

Proceeds of disposal of shares in Shillelagh Limited	14,000,000	
Net assets of Shillelagh Limited		7,000,000
Goodwill on consolidation		3,000,000
Gain on disposal of Shillelagh Limited		4,000,000

C. Reconciliation to gain shown in accounting records of parent undertaking

Net gain on disposal of subsidiary per group financial statements	4,000,000
Post-acquisition/pre-disposal profits of Shillelagh included in the consolidated profit and loss account of Robust Technical Services Limited	1,000,000
Net gain as per parent undertaking accounting records	**5,000,000**

7106

Issue	Accounting treatment
In the accounting records of the parent undertaking that disposes of the subsidiary undertaking	Any proceeds of the sale should be credited against the carrying value of the investment. This will determine the gain or loss generated from the sale of the subsidiary undertaking.
In the consolidated financial statements	1. The **proceeds of the disposal** should be set off against the carrying amount of the identifiable net assets of the subsidiary, attributable to the group's interest at the date of disposal, together with any goodwill arising on the original acquisition of the subsidiary undertaking. 2. The **gain or loss** should be shown as an exceptional item after operating profit and before interest in the consolidated profit and loss account. 3. The consolidated financial statements should include the results of that subsidiary undertaking, up to the date that it ceases to be a subsidiary.
Where any of the subsidiary's assets have been revalued	The relevant balance on the group revaluation reserve should be transferred, at the disposal date, to the profit and loss account reserve.

7109
FRS 2 (47)

Goodwill There may be goodwill **related to the shares** that have been sold, that has not previously been either written off through the profit and loss account or attributed to prior period amortisation or impairment. Such goodwill should be added to the carrying amount of the net assets of the subsidiary for the purpose of the calculation of the gain or loss on disposal.

Change in voting rights

The parent undertaking may lose control over the subsidiary, because of changes in the voting rights it holds or in those held by another party in that subsidiary. Control may pass where there is a change:
– in voting rights given to different classes of shares issued by the subsidiary; or
– the method for allocating rights between different classes of shares.

7110

Deemed disposals

The **parent may forfeit control** without actually disposing of any of its shares (referred to as a deemed disposal), as the group's interest in a subsidiary undertaking is reduced, because:
– the parent undertaking and its group do not take up their full allocation of rights in a rights issue;
– the parent undertaking and its group do not take up their full share of scrip dividends while other equity holders in that subsidiary undertaking take up some, or all, of their share;
– another party has exercised options or warrants it holds; or
– the subsidiary undertaking has issued shares to parties other than the parent undertaking and its group.

7112

Demergers

Under a demerger, an undertaking ceases to be a subsidiary undertaking, as all or a majority of the shares in the subsidiary undertaking are re-distributed "in-specie" to members of the parent.

7120

Any **shareholding retained by the parent** will represent either an associate undertaking (equity method) or a trade investment accounted for on a cost basis.

---

b. Partial disposal of an interest in a subsidiary

A group reduces its interest in a subsidiary

A parent undertaking may dispose of part of its interest in a subsidiary undertaking **but retain sufficient interest** for the investment to remain a subsidiary undertaking. The accounting treatment in this case is similar to that applicable to a subsidiary leaving the group (see ¶7106). **Any gain or loss arising** should be calculated as the difference between:
– the carrying amount of the net assets of that subsidiary undertaking attributable to the group's interest before the reduction; and
– the carrying amount attributable to the group's interest after the reduction, together with any proceeds received.

7128
FRS 2 (52)

The net assets compared should include any related goodwill not previously written off through the profit and loss account.

Treatment of non-controlling interests (minority interests)   The non-controlling interests should be introduced, or if already in existence, increased by the carrying amount of the net identifiable assets now attributable to the minority interest, as a result of the decrease in the group's interest.

7130

In the accounting records of the parent undertaking disposing of part of its interest in a subsidiary undertaking, the relevant portion of the **carrying value of the investment** should be transferred to a disposals account. The proceeds from the sale of the shares should be credited to the disposals account and the gain or loss determined.

7132   Consolidated balance sheet Although the status of the investment is unaltered as it remains a subsidiary undertaking, **adjustments should be made** to any goodwill and interests held by non-controlling interests.

Although there is no change in the carrying amount of the net assets of the subsidiary undertaking included in the consolidation, the percentage attributable to the **non-controlling interests** increases accordingly to the level of their holding at the end of the financial year. **Goodwill** that arose on acquisition of the group's interest should not be attributed to the minority interests. However, goodwill originally recognised on acquisition should be adjusted to reflect the percentage holding disposed of.

In the **consolidated profit and loss account**, the minority share of profits is increased according to the additional level of interest held by the minority shareholders.

Significant reduction – investment becomes an associate

7133   A parent undertaking may dispose of part of its interest in a subsidiary undertaking **but retain sufficient interest** for the investment to be classified as an associated undertaking.

7134   In the **accounting records of the parent undertaking**, disposing of its controlling interest in the subsidiary undertaking, the relevant portion of the carrying value of the investment should be debited to a disposals account.

The proceeds from the sale of the shares should be credited to the disposals account and the gain or loss determined. The **residual carrying value** of the shares should then be transferred and reclassified as an "investment in an associated undertaking".

7135   Consolidation process   The consolidation process will need to reflect the **change in status** of the investment to an associated undertaking during the accounting period, as follows:

a. The **subsidiary undertaking** should be accounted for and consolidated up to the date of disposal of the controlling interest;

b. A **gain or loss on disposal** should be calculated in the same way as for a partial disposal and recognised in the consolidated profit and loss account;

c. The **investment in the associate** should be shown as a one line item within Fixed Asset Investments, valued at the investing company's share of the net assets of the associate; and

d. The **parent company's share** of net profits or losses and changes in net investment in the associated undertaking, should be accounted for under the equity method (see ¶7460).

EXAMPLE   Pike Limited acquired and disposed of shares in Salmon Limited, which has an issued share capital of 1,000,000 ordinary shares:
A. 31 December 2012: **Acquired 1,000,000 shares** for a consideration of £9,000,000 when the fair value of Salmon Limited's identifiable net assets was £6,000,000.
B. 31 December 2013: **Disposed of 800,000 shares** for proceeds of £14,000,000 when the fair value of Salmon Limited's identifiable net assets was £7,000,000, including £1,000,000 post-acquisition profits.
C. The residual investment held by Pike in Salmon satisfies the criteria to be treated as an associate.

A. On initial acquisition of 100% of subsidiary undertaking – Dec. 2012
In the accounting records of the parent company Pike Limited, its investment in subsidiary undertaking, Salmon Limited would be carried at the acquisition cost of £9,000,000.
On consolidation, **goodwill would be determined** as follows:

	£
Reconciliation	
Purchase consideration paid	9,000,000
Fair value of identifiable net assets acquired	6,000,000
Goodwill arising on consolidation	**3,000,000**

B. On subsequent disposal of 80% of subsidiary undertaking – 31 December 2013
In the accounting records of Pike Limited, the disposal of Salmon Limited would be dealt with as follows:

	£
Investment in subsidiary undertaking, at cost	9,000,000
Less: Transferred to disposals account – 80%	7,200,000
Investment in associated undertaking, at cost	**1,800,000**

	£
Proceeds received on disposal of 80% of Salmon Limited	14,000,000
Less: Purchase consideration paid – 80% of £9,000,000	7,200,000
Gain arising on disposal of shares in subsidiary undertaking	**6,800,000**

Consolidated financial statements
On consolidation, the **realisation of 80%** of Salmon Limited would
be dealt with as follows:

Exceptional item	£	£
Proceeds received on disposal of 80% of holding		14,000,000
Less: Fair value of identifiable net assets disposed (80 % of		
£7,000,000)	5,600,000	
Goodwill arising on acquisition (80 % of £3,000,000)	2,400,000	8,000,000
Net gain on disposal of 80% of subsidiary undertaking		**6,000,000**

**Reconciliation to gain shown in accounting records of parent
undertaking**

Net gain on disposal of 80% of shares in subsidiary	6,000,000
Increase in identifiable net assets included in profit and loss account – relating to the 80% shareholding sold	800,000
Net gain as per parent undertaking accounting records	**6,800,000**

Goodwill

Goodwill on acquisition of subsidiary undertaking	3,000,000
Less: Transferred on disposal of 80% of subsidiary undertaking	2,400,000
Balance of goodwill transferred to the carrying value of the associate	**600,000**

Investment in associated undertaking

Net assets £7,000,000 × 20%	**1,400,000**
Goodwill arising at the date of original purchase (not yet amortised)	600,000
Carrying value of associate	**2,000,000**

Reconciliation
Reconciliation to net assets shown on records of parent undertaking

Cost per accounting records of parent undertaking, £9,000,000 × 20%	1,800,000
Add: Post-acquisition profits attributable to remaining shares in Salmon held by Pike (equity accounted) £1,000,000 x 20%	200,000
Carrying value per consolidated financial statements	**2,000,000**

Consolidation entries
The consolidation entries would be as follows
1. Set off of investment in subsidiary undertaking on consolidation

	£	£
Net assets of Salmon Limited	6,000,000	
Goodwill on consolidation	3,000,000	
Investment in Salmon Limited		9,000,000

2. Post-acquisition profits of subsidiary undertaking

Net assets of Salmon Limited	1,000,000	
Profit and loss account		1,000,000

3. Determination of gain arising on disposal of subsidiary undertaking

Proceeds of disposal of shares in Salmon Limited	14,000,000	
Net assets of Salmon Limited		5,600,000
Goodwill on consolidation		2,400,000
Gain on disposal of Salmon Limited		6,000,000

Investment in subsidiary undertaking becomes a fixed asset investment

7140   A parent undertaking **may dispose of part of its interest** in a subsidiary undertaking but retain sufficient interest for the investment to be classified as a trade investment.

7142   **Parent undertaking** In the accounting records of the parent undertaking disposing of its controlling interest in the subsidiary undertaking, the relevant portion of the carrying value of the investment should be transferred to a disposals account.

The **proceeds from the sale** of the shares should be credited to the disposals account and the gain or loss determined. The residual carrying value of the shares should be accounted for as a trade investment.

Consolidated financial statements	Accounting treatment
1. Proceeds of the shares disposed	1. Proceeds should be set off against the carrying amount of the identifiable net assets of the subsidiary attributable to the group's interest at the date of disposal, together with any relevant part of goodwill arising on the original acquisition of the subsidiary undertaking. 2. The net gain or loss should be shown as an exceptional item after operating profit and before interest in the consolidated profit and loss account.
2. Results of the subsidiary undertaking	Results attributable to the group up till the date of disposal must be recognised in the profit and loss account.
3. Disposal reducing investment from subsidiary to that of a fixed asset investment	Only dividends received or receivable would be recognised.
4. Carrying value of investment	The investment should be carried at the same amount it is shown in the balance sheet of the parent undertaking.

EXAMPLE   **Considerable disposal of an investment in a subsidiary – becomes a trade investment**
Evergreen Limited has recently made both an acquisition and disposals of shares in Sole Limited, which has an issued share capital of 1,000,000 ordinary shares:
A. 31 December 2011: **Acquired 1,000,000 shares** for a consideration of £9,000,000 when the fair value of Sole Limited's identifiable net assets was £6,000,000.
B. 31 December 2013: **Disposed of 900,000 shares** for £16,000,000 when the fair value of Sole Limited's identifiable net assets was £7,000,000, its profit for the year being £1,000,000.

A. Original acquisition of shares
In the accounting records of the parent company Evergreen Limited, the investment in its subsidiary undertaking, Sole Limited, would be carried at the cost of acquisition of £9,000,000
On consolidation goodwill would be determined as follows:
No provision for amortisation of goodwill has been made.

	£
Purchase consideration paid	9,000,000
Fair value of identifiable net assets acquired	6,000,000
Goodwill arising on consolidation	3,000,000

B. Subsequent disposal of 90% of subsidiary undertaking – 31 December 2013
In the accounting records of the parent company Evergreen Limited, the disposal of Sole Limited would be dealt with as follows:

	£
1. Investment in subsidiary undertaking, at cost	9,000,000
Less: Transferred to disposals account – 90%	8,100,000
Trade investment, at cost, included in fixed asset investments	**900,000**

2. Exceptional item

	£
Proceeds received on disposal of 90% of Sole Limited	16,000,000
Less: Purchase consideration paid – 90% of £9,000,000	8,100,000
Gain arising on disposal of shares in subsidiary undertaking	**7,900,000**

Consolidation
On consolidation, the realisation of 90% of Sole Limited would be dealt with as follows:

1. Exceptional item	£	£
Proceeds received on disposal of 90% of holding		16,000.000
Less: Fair value of identifiable net assets of Sole at date of disposal*	7,000,000	
Goodwill arising on acquisition of Sole not amortised at date of disposal*	3,000,000	(10,000,000)
Residual value of trade interest remaining in books of Evergreen.		900,000
Net gain on disposal of 90% of subsidiary undertaking		**6,900,000**

* Although only a 90% holding has been sold as far as the group accounts are concerned, the entire subsidiary is de-consolidated and replaced with a trade investment at cost, a treatment which does not permit the inclusion of any goodwill.

2. Reconciliation to gain shown in accounting records of parent undertaking

Net gain on disposal of 90 per cent of shares in the subsidiary	6,900,000
Post-acquisition profits of Sole consolidated in the Evergreen group accounts	1,000,000
Net gain as per parent undertaking accounting records	**7,900,000**

3. Fixed assets: Trade investment
Instead of consolidating the assets and liabilities of Sole, the group accounts will show (as will the parent undertaking's own accounts) a trade investment in Sole at cost.

At cost, £9,000,00 x 10%	900,000

Consolidation entries
As Sole Limited is not a subsidiary of Evergreen at the period end it will not be included in the consolidation of the balance sheet.
The profit and loss account of Sole will be consolidated up to the date of the 90% disposal; namely, the date it ceases to be a subsidiary. In this instance, the group profits of Evergreen will include £1,000,000 of the profits relating to Sole.

---

2. Disclosure requirements

Companies Act requirements

The Companies Act stipulates, that if during the financial year, there has been a disposal of   **7170**
an undertaking or group, which **significantly impacts** on the figures shown in the group financial statements, the notes to these financial statements should include the following information:
– the name of that subsidiary undertaking, or parent of the group disposed of;
– the extent to which the profit or loss of the group is attributable to the disposed subsidiary undertaking or group; and
– comparative figures in respect of the proceeding year must be provided. Where the preceding year figure is not comparable, it should be adjusted and shown on a comparable basis. In addition, the notes should also give the particulars of the adjustment and the reasons for it.

7172   **Exemptions**   Exemption from the above mentioned disclosure requirements may be available provided the following conditions are met:
– where in the opinion of the directors of the parent company, the disclosures would be seriously prejudicial to the business of the parent company or any of its subsidiary undertakings;
– the Secretary of State agrees that the information should not be disclosed; and
– where the undertaking involved is established under the law of a country outside of the United Kingdom or carries on business outside the United Kingdom.

Additional disclosure requirements

7174
FRS 2 (48)   The consolidated financial statements should provide the following financial information for any **material undertaking**, that has ceased to be a subsidiary undertaking during the financial period; namely:
– the name of the undertaking;
– any ownership interests retained; and
– where it has ceased to be a subsidiary undertaking, without disposing of at least the interest held by the group, the circumstances should be explained.

7176   The **notes to the cash flow statement** should provide:
– a summary of the cash flows resulting from the disposal of subsidiary undertakings, indicating how much of the consideration comprised cash; and
– details of any material effects that the cash flows of the disposed undertakings had on the consolidated cash flow position. This information for example, could be given for continuing and discontinued operations and acquisitions.

---

3. New UK GAAP – requirements of FRS 102

7180   There are **no significant differences** between existing UK GAAP and the FRS 102 "Financial Reporting Standard applicable in the UK and Republic of Ireland", the adoption of which is mandatory for accounting periods beginning on or after 1 January 2015.

Issue	Accounting treatment under FRS 102
Disposal of interests	Accounting treatment depends on whether control is maintained.
Control maintained after reducing shareholding	Accounting for as a transaction between shareholders – **no gain or loss** recorded
Control forfeited	Where control over the subsidiary/associate is effectively lost, a **gain or loss** on disposal is recognised, representing the difference between the disposal proceeds and the proportion of the net assets disposed of. This may also include an element of goodwill.

☐ *MEMO POINTS* ☐   The FRC has issued a staff education note (SEN 15) covering acquisitions and disposals of subsidiaries which highlights some key areas of consideration when transitioning to FRS 102.

CHAPTER 5

Associates and joint arrangements

There are a **number of criteria** for determining whether an investment should be classified   **7300**
as an associate, a joint venture, a joint arrangement that is not an entity (JANEs) or a joint
venture in form but not substance. The accounting rules for associates and joint arrangements apply to all companies regardless of size. The key reporting standard is FRS 9 "Associates and joint ventures".

Entities **applying the FRSSE** are exempt from the requirements of FRS 9, unless preparing consolidated financial statements. In this case, the entity should apply the reporting standard to such
statements as required by the FRSSE. In addition to the statutory disclosure requirements for
associates and joint arrangements, **additional disclosures** are triggered at particular thresholds.

SECTION 1

Classification

Determining the relationship

The **principal methods** by which entities can further their economic activities through   **7304**
investments in other entities is tabulated below, starting with the highest level of involvement:

namely, a parent/subsidiary relationship through to associate investments, joint arrangements or simple trade investments.

7305 The **primary difference** between an associate or joint arrangement and a subsidiary interest, is the degree of investor control. Initially, on acquiring an investment, which is of the nature of an associate or joint venture, an assessment of its status should be made.

1. The **first stage** is to assess the relationship between the investor and the investee and to determine the actual interests owned by the investor and the attached voting rights (participating interest).

2. The **second stage involves assessing** the degree of the reporting entity's direct involvement in the management and operations of the investee (significant influence ¶7338) and the long-term intentions of the investor. An investor may have overall control, in which case a parent/subsidiary relationship exists. However, if its influence over the investee is not so dominant, then an associate or joint venture relationship may exist.

7306 Once an investee has qualified as an associate or joint venture, **minor or temporary changes in the relationship** between investor and investee should not affect its status.

7308

Entity/arrangement	Nature of relationship	Description of the defining relationship	Investor's treatment of the investment in the consolidated financial statements
Subsidiary (50% +)	Investor controls the investee	Has the ability to direct and control operational and financial policy	Consolidate assets, liabilities, results and cash flows of its subsidiaries
Associate (20% +)	Investor holds a participating interest and exercises significant influence but does not control its investee	A substantial minority shareholding enabling the investor to be actively involved in policy	Net equity method (¶7366)
Joint venture (50%)	Investors hold long-term interest and shares control under a contractual arrangement	A contractual relationship under which two or more investors control a venture as a separate venture in its own right	Gross equity method (¶7438)
Joint arrangements that are not an entity (JANE)	Entities participate in an arrangement to carry on part of their own trades or business.	Does not carry on a trade of its own. Investor extends its own trade through the joint arrangement.	Each investor accounts directly for its own share of the assets, liabilities, results and cash flows, and its shared items as set out in contractual agreement
Simple investment	Passive	The investor's interest does not qualify the investee as an associate, a joint venture or a subsidiary. The interest involves limited influence.	Investors include their interest as investments at cost or valuation

SECTION 2

Associate companies

A. Determining associate status

Regulation	Definition of associate
Companies Act	An entity other than a subsidiary or joint venture, in which another entity (the investor): – has a **participating interest**; and – over whose operating and financial policies the investor exercises **significant influence**.
FRS 9	A **stricter qualifying regime** has been introduced under FRS 9. The investor must also show that its investment qualifies as an associate, because it is retained: – on a **long-term basis** without a view to resale; and – that it contributes to the investor's activities resulting from the **exercise of control** or **significant influence**.

7320
FRS 9 (14)

MEMO POINTS 1. An undertaking is **defined in FRS 9** as a body corporate, partnership or unincorporated association carrying on a trade, with or without a view to profit. This extends the definition of an associate to include non-profit making organisations or unincorporated associations. The definition of an associate is contained in the Companies Act and replicated in para. 19, Sch 6 of the Large and Medium-sized Companies and Groups (Accounts and Reports) Regulations 2008 (SI 2008/410) and para. 19, Sch 6 SI 2008/409 (Small companies and groups).
2. An interest is held on a **long-term basis**, when it is not expected to be disposed of within one year of the acquisition date and where it is intended that the acquisition will become part of the continuing activities of the group.

Participating interest

A holding of 20% or more of the shares (but less than 50%) of an entity is deemed to be a participating interest. This **presumption is rebutted if** the interest is neither long-term nor beneficial to the investor.

7326
FRS 9 (4)

A **combination of direct and indirect holdings** through a group structure may also give rise to a participating interest (see ¶7490).

Even if an investor holds less than 20% of the share capital in an entity, it can still be classified as an associate, if the investor can exercise significant influence (¶7338) or it enjoys equivalent rights.

Equivalent rights A participating interest in the shares of another entity could take the form of equivalent rights; namely:
– an option to acquire shares; or
– an interest convertible into a shareholding (i.e. a type of management contract).

7330

"Equivalent rights" refers to any **conversion rights or options** held by investors, which if taken up would mean the 20% threshold being breached. However, this does not mean an associate relationship automatically comes into existence when the options can be exercised.

Where the 20% rule is rebutted (i.e. where it can be demonstrated, that irrespective of the level of shareholding, an associate relationship does not exist), then the equivalent rights (in the form of "interests" or shares) need not be taken into account.

Management contracts Participating interests could also take the form of control exercised through a management contract, with a performance based fee, in which the recipient is deemed to be more than a manager. In another scenario, an investor could be deemed to hold a participating interest, even if his equity holding is less than 20%. This type of investment is common in internet companies.

7334

Significant interest

7338   The Companies Act dictates that for an investment to be classified as an associate, its investor must exercise significant influence over the investee's operating and financial policies, based on the voting rights controlled. Once significant influence has been established, it should be regarded as continuing to do so until an event or transaction alters this state of affairs.

The **requirements of FRS 9 are more stringent** and state that significant interest should be determined with reference to the degree of direct control and the level of active participation exercised by the investor.

7339   **Direct control**   Direct involvement in the entity's operating and financial policies is taken to mean, that over a period of time, the associate will generally implement policies that are consistent with the strategy of the investor. If an associate persistently implements policies that are inconsistent with its investor's strategy, that investor would not be exercising significant influence over the management of the entity.

FRS 9 (16)   The investor's **direct involvement** in its associate is **commonly achieved through**:
– nomination to the board of directors, or its equivalent; or
– an arrangement that allows the investor to actively participate in policy making decisions.

7340   **Level of active participation**   Significant interest is present where the investor influences
FRS 9 (14)   the direction of its associate through active participation in policy decisions, including strategic issues such as:
– the expansion or contraction of the business;
– participation in other entities;
– changing its products, markets and activities; and
– determining the balance between dividend and reinvestment.

7348   **Voting rights**   Where an undertaking holds a participating influence (of 20% or more of the voting rights in another undertaking), it shall be presumed to exercise significant influence over that entity, unless the contrary can be shown. Any shares held by a parent and its subsidiaries in that entity should be aggregated for this purpose. **Rights held by other associates** of the investor should be excluded.

> ⬛ MEMO POINTS   Voting rights effectively mean those rights conferred on shareholders in respect of their shares or in the case of an undertaking not having a share capital, on members who can vote at general meetings on substantially all matters.

FRS 9 (17)   In practice, **it can be difficult to determine** whether the relationship constitutes that of an associate. When assessing whether significant influence exists, the distribution of the remaining voting rights must be considered as other large shareholders may prevent a 20% shareholder from exercising any real influence. This is illustrated in the following example.

> ⬛EXAMPLE   **Brown plc – Annual Report & Accounts 2013**
> Brown plc has a 22.5% interest in ABC plc. There are two other shareholders, Smith who holds 30% and Jones who has 47.5% of the shares. Brown is entitled to nominate two directors to the board which has 10 members in total. Smith nominates three directors and Jones, five. The Chairman of the board is a nominee of Jones and he has the casting vote.
> Although it might initially appear that Brown's relationship with ABC is that of an investment in an associate (as it exceeds the 20% threshold), the much stronger position of Jones, in particular, will in practice prevent Brown exercising any significant influence. Therefore, Brown should not classify ABC as an associate.

7352   **Subsequent re-classifcation**   The actual relationship might develop differently from that assumed from the arrangements on acquisition. There may be instances where the **information available to the investor** is extremely limited. In this case, the investor's relationship with its investee will need to be reassessed as post-acquisition evidence emerges, as there may be doubts as to whether the investor's influence is significant or whether it jointly controls its investment. In such circumstances, it may be necessary to modify the treatment originally adopted in the financial statements. For more detail on this topic see ¶7474.

EXAMPLE   Group A held a 25% investment in a company at the beginning of the financial year, having accounted for it as an associate in the consolidated financial statements. However, another investor subsequently acquired a 60% shareholding in the associate. Group A subsequently concluded, that it no longer exercised significant influence over the associate and downgraded it to a trade investment.

B. Accounting for associates

The treatment of an investment in an associate will depend upon whether or not the investor is preparing consolidated group accounts.

7360

1. Individual company financial statements

Where an investor prepares consolidated financial statements the interest in an associate should be accounted for using the equity method. In the investor's individual financial statements, the interest in an associate should be shown as a **fixed asset investment** and shown either at cost, less any amounts written off, or at valuation. Any goodwill arising should be separately identified.

7362
FRS 9 (26)

Where an **investor does not prepare** consolidated financial statements, it should prepare a set of individual financial statements including the relevant amounts for its associates (and joint arrangements), or disclose the relevant amounts in the notes to its own financial statements. Investing entities that **are exempt** from preparing consolidated financial statements, or who would be exempt if they had subsidiaries, are exempt from this requirement.

FRS 9 (48)

2. Consolidated financial statements

The Companies Act requires that associated undertakings be included in group accounts using the equity method of accounting (with detailed guidance set out in FRS 9), except where the amounts involved are not material.

7366

The equity method **is defined** as a method of accounting, that brings an investment into its investor's financial statements initially at cost, with any goodwill identified separately. The ongoing process is as follows:

FRS 9 (4)

1. The **carrying amount** of the investment must be adjusted in each accounting period for the investor's share of the results of its investee, less:
– any amortisation or write-off for goodwill;
– the investor's share of any gains or losses; and
– any other changes in the investee's net assets including distributions to owners, such as dividends.
2. The **investor's share** of its investee's results is recognised in the profit and loss account.
3. The **investor's cash flow statement** includes the cash flows between the investor and its investee such as dividends or loans.

The **objective of the equity method** is to reflect the actual relationship between the investor and the associate in the:
– profit and loss account, by reporting profits or losses attributable to the investor rather than dividends; and
– balance sheet, by including information based on net assets of the investee, rather than the cost or market value of the investment in shares.

7368

Profit and loss account

The information detailed in the table below should, where appropriate, be included in the investor's consolidated profit and loss account. A sample profit and loss account based on the equity method is also given below.

7374
FRS 9 (27)

Consolidated profit and loss account	Investor's share in the results of the associates
Turnover	**1.** A total combining the investor's share of its **associates' turnover** with group turnover may be shown as a memorandum item in the profit and loss account. **2.** The investor's share of its associates' turnover should be clearly distinguished from group turnover.
Operating results – investors share of	The investor's share of the **operating results** of the associate(s) should be included immediately after the group operating result, but after the investor's share of the results of any joint ventures
Goodwill write-off or amortisation	Such items arising on the **acquisition of associates** should be charged immediately after the associates' operating results and disclosed
Exceptional items	Any **exceptional items** included after operating profit in the associates' own financial statements, or interest should be shown separately from the amounts for the group. Examples include profits or losses on sale or termination of an operation, costs of reorganisation or restructuring or profits or losses on disposal of fixed assets.
Profit before tax	**1.** The investor's share of the relevant **figures for associates** should be included within the amounts for the group (including minority interests in subsidiaries held by associates). **2.** For items below this level, such as interest and taxation, the amounts relating to associates should be separately disclosed.
Segmental analysis	**Turnover and operating profit**, if given, should clearly distinguish between that of the group and that of any associate companies

More detail on the disclosure requirements outlined in the table above is given in Section 5.

FRS 9 (Appendix IV)

EXAMPLE Equity method of accounting
Consolidated profit and loss account
Year to 31 December 2013

	£m	£m
Turnover: group and share of associates	400	
Less: share of associates' turnover	(200)	
Group turnover		200
Cost of sales		(120)
Gross profit		80
Administrative expenses		(40)
Group operating profit		40
Share of operating profit in:		
Joint ventures	30	
Associates	24	
Amortisation of goodwill on associates	(7)	
Exceptional items-reorganisation costs of associate	(4)	
		43
		83
Interest receivable (group)		6
Interest payable:		
Group	(26)	
Joint ventures	(10)	
Associates	(12)	
		(48)
Profit on ordinary activities before tax		41
Tax on profit on ordinary activities		(12)
Profit on ordinary activities after tax		29
Minority interests		(6)
Profit on ordinary activities after tax and minority interests		23
Equity dividends		(10)
Retained profit for group and its share of associates and joint ventures		13

* Tax relates to the following:
  Parent and subsidiaries   (5)
  Joint ventures   (5)
  Associates   (2)

Dividends and retained profit or loss The group's share of dividends paid by associates **7376** should contra the dividends received, accounted for in the investor's consolidated accounts, with neither payments or receipts included in the group profit and loss account.

Elimination of profit and losses on associate transactions The investor's share of any **7378** profit or loss on transactions between an investor and an associate, should be eliminated from the consolidated accounts. Balances between the group and its subsidiaries and associates are not eliminated, so any **unsettled trading balances** should be shown as current assets or liabilities in the consolidated balance sheet.

The amounts shown for "Associates" are subdivisions of the item for which the statutory prescribed heading is "Income from interests in associated undertakings". The subdivisions may also be shown in a note rather than on the face of the profit and loss account.

EXAMPLE **Notes to the accounts**
Investor's share of operating results of an associate

Y. Ltd has a share capital of 10,000 ordinary shares of £1, each carrying one vote. Z. Ltd holds 2,000 of Y's shares and is represented on the board of Y. Ltd.
Z. Ltd accounts for Y. Ltd as an associate in its group accounts. Both companies have a financial year-end of 31 December 20XX and Y's profit and loss for the year was £120,000. The consolidated profit and loss account for Z. Ltd includes £24,000 in respect of Y's operating profit (£120,000 x 20%).

Balance sheet

At the date of acquisition, the investment in an associate should be shown as the aggregate **7384** of the investor's share of the associates' net assets, plus any goodwill arising on the acqui- FRS 9 (29) sition.

In **subsequent years**, the carrying value of the associate in the consolidated balance sheet is adjusted in each period in respect of the investor's share:
– of the results of its associate less any amortisation or write-off for goodwill;
– of any relevant gains or losses; and
– any other changes in the investee's net assets including distributions to its owners (e.g. dividends).

In this way, the carrying value is maintained at the investor's share of the associates' net assets plus the unamortised goodwill.

Although **goodwill arising** on an investor's acquisition of an associate, less amortisation or write-offs should be included in the carrying amount of the associate, it should be separately disclosed.

Where **an associate itself has associates** (or subsidiaries), that generate goodwill in its own **7386** consolidated accounts, this goodwill should be excluded from the fair value of the associate's net assets used to calculate the goodwill arising on the acquisition of the associate. However, **separate disclosure** is not required for the components of goodwill arising from an acquisition and in particular any goodwill arising on past acquisitions made by the associate itself.

Loans to associates that constitute part of their long-term funding should be included in **7388** the carrying value of the associate within fixed asset investments, although the loans should still be separately disclosed. Where a loan is short-term in nature, it can be included in debtors.

Any **dividends remitted** by the associate effectively converts part of the investment into cash (or if not yet paid, debtors) and therefore, should be excluded from the carrying value of the associate in the balance sheet.

FRS 9 (Appendix IV)   The following balance sheet reflects the normal presentation using the equity method.

EXAMPLE   Consolidated balance sheet
As at 31 December 2013

	£m	£m	£m
Fixed assets			
Tangible assets		480	
Investments			
Investments in joint ventures			
Share of gross assets	130		
Share of gross liabilities	(80)		
Goodwill re associates		50	
Investments in associates (See 1)		20	
			550
Current assets			
Stock		15	
Debtors		75	
Cash at bank and in hand		10	
		100	
Creditors		(50)	
Net current assets			50
Total assets less current liabilities			600
Creditors (due after more than one year)			(250)
Provision for liabilities and charges			(10)
Equity minority interests			(40)
			300
Capital and reserves			
Called up share capital			50
Share premium account			150
Profit and loss account			100
Shareholders' funds (all equity)			300

Notes to the consolidated balance sheet
1. Investments in associates:

	£m
Share of net assets	10
Loans to associates	5
Goodwill arising on acquisition (less amortisation)	5
Total	**20**

7392   **Accounting for acquisition of an associate**   On purchase of an associate, the fair values (less goodwill) of the underlying net assets and liabilities should be identified, using the accounting policies adopted by the investor. The difference between the investor's share of the fair values and the consideration paid is attributed to goodwill on acquisition. For more information on the fair values see ¶6864.

7394   **Associate with subsidiaries**   Where an associate itself **has subsidiary undertakings**, the amounts to be included in the investor's accounts are the consolidated figures for the associated undertaking and its subsidiaries. **Annual changes in value of the associate** will reflect:
– the share of profits or losses of the associate and the proportion of any other gains or losses as reflected in the STRGL, less any dividends remitted to the group by the associate; and
– any amortisation of goodwill.

Investor's consolidated cash flow statement

The requirements of FRS 9 covering the investor's consolidated cash flow statement are as follows:

7400
FRS 9 (30)

1. Only actual cash flows **between associates and the group** should be included in the consolidated cash flow statement.
2. The consolidated cash flow statement (¶4180) should include dividends received from associates, as a separate item between operating activities and returns on investments and servicing of finance.
3. Any **other cash flows** between the investor and its associates such as loans, should be included under the appropriate cash flow heading for the activity giving rise to the cash flow.

The following items should be excluded from the consolidated cash flow statement:
– amortisation of goodwill on acquisition of an associate; and
– the group share of any items included on an equity basis such as operating profit, exceptional items, interest payable, and tax.

STRGL

In the consolidated STRGL, the investor's share of the total recognised gains and losses of its associates should be included (shown separately under each heading), if the amounts included are material, either in the statement itself or in a note that is referred to in the statement.

7402
FRS 9 (28)

EXAMPLE	Statement of total recognised gains and losses		
Year to 31 December 2013			
		2013	2012
		£'000	£'000
Profit/ (loss) for year – Group		480.3	425.6
Joint ventures – revaluation losses		(10.2)	-
Associates		**25.6**	**11.2**
Exchange adjustments		(2.6)	(3.2)
Total recognised gains and losses for the year		**493.1**	**433.6**

SECTION 3

Joint arrangements

"Joint arrangements" is **an umbrella term** covering joint ventures, joint arrangements that are not entities and arrangements that are joint ventures in form but not substance. The different types of joint arrangement and the respective accounting treatments are set out below.

7404

Joint arrangements **are governed by** a formal agreement and comprise two or more investors, even though they are no more than agents for the principle investors. The **level of detail required** of investors in joint ventures, in their consolidated financial statements, is greater than for investments in associates; so investors must take considerable care to correctly categorise their investments.

The **general criteria** for determining the exact nature of a joint arrangement is outlined below, although in reality it can be difficult distinguishing a joint venture from other types of joint arrangement. In addition, the nature of the joint arrangement may change over time.

FRS 9 makes a clear distinction between joint ventures which are equity accounted and other joint arrangements which are not.

Types of joint arrangement

7406   There are in essence, three types of joint arrangement, each of which has a separate accounting treatment.
1. A joint arrangement that has its own trade or business is potentially a **joint venture**.
2. A joint arrangement **that is not an entity** (JANE) is a joint activity entered into by two or
more investors, that does not represent an extension of their own trade or business.
3. A structure with the **form, but not substance** of a joint venture.

A. Joint ventures

7410
FRS 9 (4)   FRS 9 defines a joint venture as an entity in which the reporting undertaking holds an
interest:
– on a long-term basis; and
– is jointly controlled by the reporting entity and one or more other venturers under a
contractual arrangement.

> ⬚ MEMO POINTS   The Companies Act defines a joint venture, as an undertaking managed jointly
> with one or more undertakings that are not included in the consolidation. The legal references
> for joint ventures are para. 18 Sch 6 SI 2008/409 (small companies and groups) and para. 18 Sch
> 6 SI 2008/410 (large and medium-sized companies and groups).

7412   The **simplest form** of joint venture involves two investors each with an equal share of control
and ownership. As the number of investors increases, so the ability of each to participate in
the process of joint control will diminish.

FRS 9 (10)   An entity is a joint venture only with respect to an investor that shares control in it. This
must be distinguished from an investor, who has an interest in an entity that is a joint venture
for some of its other investors. Where **an investor does not share control** of the entity, it is
merely an investment and should be accounted for as such.

1. Long term interest

7414   A long-term interest is defined as an interest held other than exclusively for subsequent
resale, and where the business is reasonably expected to be retained for more than one year
from the date of its acquisition.

A long-term interest can also be an investment acquired as a result of the enforcement of a
security, in which the interest has become part of the continuing activities of the group or
the holder acts as if it intends the interest to become so.

Joint control

7416
FRS 9 (4)   A reporting entity jointly controls a venture with one or more other entities, if no one particular entity alone can assume overall control of that entity. Decisions on financial and operating policy essential to the activities, economic performance and financial position of the
venture require the consent of each venturer.

2. Joint venture agreement

7418
FRS 9 (11)   The investors usually **exercise joint control** through a joint venture agreement with each
participant. Each conducts its part of the contractual arrangement with a view to its own

benefit. Each venturer that shares control should play an active role in setting the operating and financial policies of the joint venture, at least in terms of general strategy. This does not preclude one investor managing the joint venture under a separate agreement, provided that the **principal operating and financial policies** are collectively agreed by all the venturers, each of whom has the resources to ensure compliance.

The requirement for each venturer's consent to strategic decisions does not have to be set out in the joint venture agreement, provided that the joint venture works in practice on the basis of securing such consent.

A joint venture agreement can override the rights normally conferred by ownership interests. **7420**
There is also usually a procedure for settling disputes between venturers and, possibly for terminating the joint venture, after a predetermined period of time or on completion of a particular task.

Unequal shareholdings It is possible to have a joint venture between investors where the **7421**
venturers do not possess equal shares in the entity, for instance where the investor's holdings are split: 20: 35: 30: 15 or 30: 35: 35. As long as joint control is applied with all parties having the power of veto, then the actual percentage holding does not preclude the investment's classification as a joint venture.

Powers of veto The requirement in the definition for consent to strategic decisions of joint **7422**
control, effectively gives each venturer a veto on such decisions. This veto distinguishes a FRS 9 (12)
joint venture from a minority holder of the shares in a joint stock company, because the latter, having no veto, is subject to majority rule, except for the limited statutory protection for the minority.

Subsidiary interests An investor may qualify as the parent of an entity, under the defini- **7424**
tion of a subsidiary in FRS 2 "Accounting for subsidiaries", by holding a majority of the FRS 9 (11)
voting rights in that entity. However, contractual arrangements with the other shareholders could in practice mean the shareholders share control over their investment.

For example, a company may control over 50% of the entity's voting rights, but the joint venture agreement might significantly restrict this control, as it may require unanimous agreement before it can commit to the following strategic decisions:
– commit capital expenditure;
– alter operating or financial policies; or
– pay a dividend.

In such a case, the **interests of the minority shareholders** amount to severe long-term restrictions, that would substantially hinder the exercise of the rights of the parent undertaking over the assets or management of the subsidiary undertaking. The subsidiary therefore, should not be consolidated but should instead be treated as a joint venture according to the requirements of FRS 9.

3. Accounting treatment

The **general rule** is that a reporting entity that prepares consolidated financial statements **7436**
should include its joint ventures in those statements using the **gross equity method** in all its FRS 9 (20)
primary statements. The accounting treatment is similar to that adopted by the equity method, except that the gross equity basis incorporates additional information on the face of the primary statements.

Individual financial statements As with the equity method, in the investor's own financial **7438**
statements, the joint ventures should be treated as fixed asset investments at cost less any amounts written off, or at a valuation.

Accounting for joint ventures – gross equity basis	
Consolidated financial statements	Investor's share in the results of the joint venture
Profit and loss account	The investor's share of its joint ventures: 1. **Turnover** should also be shown separately as a memorandum item (as well as in the segmental analysis) and not as part of group turnover. 2. **Operating results** should be shown after group operating result. 3. **Separate disclosable items** (under FRS 3) – exceptional items – interest – taxation 4. **Goodwill** charged on investments in joint ventures should also be disclosed.
Balance sheet	1. The investor's share of the **gross assets and liabilities** underlying the net amount included for joint ventures should each be shown under the caption "investment in joint ventures", which in turn comes under fixed assets. 2. Any goodwill on acquisition less amounts amortised or written-off should be included in carrying value but disclosed separately.
STRGL	**Share of joint venture** items should be disclosed separately if material, under each heading in the statement or in the notes to the accounts
Cash flow statements	**Dividends received** should be shown separately between operating activities and returns on investments. **Other cash flows** between investor and investee to be shown under the appropriate cash flow heading i.e. interest on loans. No other associate cash flows should be included.

More detail on the disclosure requirements outlined in the table above is given in ¶7494.

Supplementary information

7440

The provision of supplementary information is **subject to the following guidance**:

a. Except for items below profit before tax in the profit and loss account, any supplementary information given for joint ventures, either in the balance sheet or in the profit and loss account, must be shown separately from amounts for the group and must not be included in the group totals.

b. Because an investor's joint control of its joint venture is a more direct form of influence than the **significant influence** exercised over associates, a reporting entity that conducts a major part of its business through joint ventures should give more detailed supplementary information about them.

One option for including supplementary information on joint ventures is to use the columnar presentation, based on the gross equity method shown in the following examples of a consolidated profit and loss account and balance sheet.

Alternatively, the subdivisions may also be shown in the notes to the accounts rather than on the face of the profit and loss account.

EXAMPLE Gross equity method
Consolidated profit and loss account
For the year to 31 December 2013

	£m	£m Group	£m Interests in joint ventures	£m Total
Turnover		200	120	320
Cost of sales		(120)	(85)	(205)
Gross profit		80	35	115
Administrative expenses		(40)	(5)	(45)
Operating profit		40	30	70

	£m	£m Group
Share of operating profit in:		
Joint ventures		30
Associates		24
Total operating profit in: group and share of joint ventures and associates		94
Interest receivable (group)		6
Interest payable:		
Group	(26)	
Joint ventures	(10)	
Associates	(12)	
		(48)
Profit on ordinary activities before tax		52
Tax on profit on ordinary activities *		(12)
Profit on ordinary activities after tax		40
Minority interests		(6)
Profit on ordinary activities after taxation and minority interest		34
Equity dividend		(10)
Retained profit for group and its share of associates and joint ventures		24
* Tax relates to the following:		
Parent and subsidiaries		(5)
Joint ventures		(5)
Associates		(2)

Consolidated balance sheet
For the year to 31 December 2013

	£m Group	£m Interests in joint ventures	£m Total
Fixed assets			
Tangible assets	480	100	580
Investments			
Investments in joint ventures	50	(50)	
Investments in associates	20		20
	550		600
Current assets			
Stock	15	5	20
Debtors	75	23	98
Cash at bank and in hand	10	2	12
	100	30	130
Creditors	(50)	(20)	(70)
Net current assets	50	10	60
Total assets less current liabilities	600	120	670
Creditors (due after more than one year)	(250)	(70)	(320)
Provision for liabilities and charges	(10)		(10)
Net assets	340		340
Equity minority interests	(40)		
Total net assets	**300**		
Capital and reserves			
Called up share capital	50		
Share premium account	150		
Profit and loss account	100		
Shareholders' funds (all equity)	**300**		

B. Joint arrangements that are not entities (JANEs)

7444
FRS 9 (4)

A reporting entity may enter a variety of commercial arrangements, some of which result in the creation of entities. Where a joint arrangement is set up to carry out a **specific project** with no planned activity after its completion, this usually implies there is no separate trade or business and, therefore, cannot be classified as a joint venture under FRS 9. Even if the participants have a **long-term interest** and have **joint control** within an arrangement, this would not necessarily represent a joint venture, unless it constitutes a legal entity.

A JANE represents a **contractual arrangement** under which the constituent parties engage in joint business activities. A JANE **does not carry on a trade or business of its own** and is simply an extension of the separate businesses of its investors.

A contractual agreement where all significant matters of operating and financial policy are predetermined, does not in itself, create a legal entity as the policies are those of its participants and not those of a separate undertaking.

7445
FRS 9 (8)

Criteria   In practice, a joint arrangement **is not an entity (JANE) if**:
– its activities do not amount to its carrying on a trade or business of its own;
– it is no more than a cost or risk sharing device for carrying out a process in the participants' trades or businesses;

– the participants derive their benefit from products or services taken in kind rather than by receiving a share in the results of trading; or
– each participant's share of the output or result of the joint activity is determined by its supply of key inputs to the process producing that output or result.

Although a JANE **may give the legal appearance** of a joint venture, in substance the arrangement may not amount to an entity, as there may be little commonality of interest between the partners.

7446
FRS 9 (9)

Examples of joint arrangements include:
– joint marketing;
– joint distribution; and
– shared production facilities.

> [EXAMPLE] **Scenario A – Joint marketing**
> A typical example is a joint marketing or distribution network or a shared production facility. Therefore, a joint arrangement carrying out a single project as, for example, often occurs in the construction industry, is unlikely to meet the criteria of carrying on a trade or business of its own. Instead this is likely to be a facility or agent in its participants' trades or businesses and a cost or risk-sharing device.
>
> **Scenario B – Joint distribution**
> In another example, the investor's reward may involve taking products or services in kind. A joint arrangement may be formed to cover a research project where the investor's gain from the benefits of the research undertaken without being charged for its use by the research institution, such as a university, in return for funding.
>
> **Scenario C – Shared production facilities**
> Investing entities may share in the profits of any joint arrangements, determined by their supply of inputs to the venture. This arrangement can only apply where it is possible to segregate clearly the activities of the joint arrangement. This type of agreement is similar to the type of joint arrangement that has the form but not the substance of a joint venture (see ¶7454).

Joint arrangements that appear to be no more than agents for the interest of the respective ventures should be accounted for as a JANE.

Accounting treatment

The **general rule** is that participants in a JANE should account for their own assets, liabilities and cash flows, measured according to the terms of the agreement governing the arrangement. Some assets, liabilities and cash flows may be wholly attributable to one participant or shared in which case, they must be accounted for proportionally in the individual entity accounts of the participants.

7450
FRS 9 (18)

> [EXAMPLE] **Accounting for joint arrangements that are not entities**
>
> **Scenario A**
> Two construction companies, X and Y, set up two joint ventures to build a hospital and access roads. **Joint venture 1 (JV1)** is recognised as an entity under FRS 9 as it will build and maintain the hospital for 30 years under a PFI contract. **Joint venture 2 (JV2)** is accounted for as a JANE as it will construct the access roads (but will not maintain them), under a separate contract with JV1.
> The **accounting treatment** of Joint venture 1 – both company X and Y should account for the joint interest under the gross equity method, after eliminating their respective share of unrealised profit Joint venture 2 should be accounted for as a JANE, as follows:
>
> **Separate assets, liabilities, cash flows**: Construction equipment, materials, resources
> **Shared assets, liabilities, cash flows**: Construction equipment, project management expenses, maintenance expenses.

Changing nature of a joint arrangement

The nature of a joint arrangement may change over time and should be reflected in the accounting treatment. For example, a pipeline operated as a joint arrangement that initially provided a service only, directly to the participants, may develop into a pipeline business providing services to others (i.e. joint venture), in which access to the pipeline is sold on the open market. The stocks of oil running through the pipeline are separate assets. In this

7452

scenario, the pipeline itself is a shared asset, along with any revenue from third party sales; shared liabilities include running and financing costs.

C. Joint venture in form not substance

7454
FRS 9 (24)

There may be circumstances where a reporting entity operates through a structure that has the appearance of a joint venture, in so much that the participants hold a long-term interest in an entity and exercise joint management. However, a joint venture does not exist where there is an extremely **limited commonality of interest** between the venturers, each of which, in effect, operates its own business independently of the others within that structure. This form of joint venture differs from a JANE in that there are no shared assets, liabilities or cash flows.

7456

Accounting treatment   The nature of such a structure, means that the framework entity acts merely as an agent for the venturers, with each venturer able to identify and control its share of the assets, liabilities and cash flows within that framework. Therefore, in order to **reflect the substance** of its operations, **each venturer should account directly** for its share of the assets, liabilities and cash flows arising within the entity, as predetermined by the agreement governing the venture.

Some **special purpose vehicles** operate in this manner. An example is an arrangement whereby mortgages or loans are secured through a special venture. Each of the participants in the arrangement is able to segregate the assets that each has contributed to the venture, as well as any associated benefits and risks. **Where such an arrangement exists** and is conducted through the medium of a limited company, the undertaking will only be a joint arrangement if it acts as an agent for its principals. The accounting treatment required for arrangements that resemble joint ventures in form not substance, is the same as that outlined for JANEs.

> EXAMPLE   Four investors form a company X, to supply IT services to a customer. Two investors supply the hardware and the other two the software which are then sold on to the customer. The sole purpose of the arrangement is to meet the customer's requirement for a single source supplier. Each investor is only entitled to the profits from the venture which are generated from the sale of items that they supplied to company X. The determination of the profit and the treatment of company X's own operating costs, are set out in a shareholders' agreement entered into by each of the venturers.

SECTION 4

Principles and rules of equity accounting

7460
FRS 9 (31)

When calculating the values to be included in the investor's consolidated financial accounts, using the equity method for associates and the gross equity method for joint arrangements, the same **accounting principles and policies** used in the consolidation of subsidiaries by the investor, should be applied.

Fair values and goodwill

7462
FRS 9 (31)

1. **On acquisition**, fair values should be attributed to the associates' underlying assets and liabilities, which provides the basis for subsequent amortisation.

2. Both the **consideration paid** for the acquisition and the goodwill arising should be calculated in the same way as on the acquisition of a subsidiary.

3. The associates' assets used in calculating the goodwill arising on its acquisition should not include any goodwill carried in the balance sheet of the associate.

4. Subject to the presentation requirement in FRS 9, the **goodwill balance** should be treated in accordance with the provisions of FRS 10 "Goodwill and Intangible Assets" (¶1000).

5. Where there has been **impairment in any goodwill attributable** to an associate or joint venture, the goodwill should be written down and the amount written off in the accounting period should be separately disclosed.   FRS 9 (38)

6. Thereafter, **any impairment in the underlying net assets** of an associate or joint venture, would normally be reflected at the level of the entity itself and no further provision against the investor's share of these net assets, would usually be necessary. Fair value is discussed in greater detail in ¶6864.

Period-end

Where the period-end of an associate or joint venture **differs from that of the investor**, the entity should be included on the basis of financial statements prepared to the investor's year end. **Where this is not practicable**, the entity should be included on the basis of financial statements, prepared for a period ending not more than three months before the investor's period end.   **7464** FRS 9 (31d)

Price sensitive information In certain cases, the publication of the financial statements might release restricted, price-sensitive information relating to the associate or joint venture. In these circumstances, financial statements prepared for a period that ended not more than six months before the investor's period-end may be used. **Any changes after the period end** of the associate or joint venture and before that of its investor that would materially affect the view given by the investor's financial statements, should be disclosed.   **7465**

Inter group transactions

Where **profits and losses resulting from** transactions between the investor and its associate or joint venture are included in the carrying amount of assets in either entity, the part relating to the investor's share should be eliminated. This required adjustment applies only in the investor's consolidated financial statements, to transfers of assets or liabilities to set up a joint venture or to acquire an initial stake in an associate.   **7466** FRS 9 (31b)

> EXAMPLE A sale made from **an associate to an investor** will result in an asset that appears in the consolidated balance sheet, whilst any profit will be included in the associate's profit and loss account. The **double entry on consolidation** is as follows:
>
> dr   Share of associate/joint venture profit
> cr   Stocks or other asset – with the investor's share of the unrealised profit or loss.
>
> If a sale is made from **an investor to an associate**, the asset will appear within net assets of the investee and the profit will be included within the group's profit or loss. The entries needed to account for the investor's share of the unrealised profit or loss are as follows:
>
> dr   Consolidated profit and loss account
> cr   Share of associate net assets or joint venture gross assets.
>
> An example of a transaction requiring this treatment would be where assets representing an investor's contribution to a joint venture are transferred at a gain.

Where associates and joint ventures are **not part of the investor's group**, balances between the investor and its associates or joint ventures are not eliminated and therefore unsettled normal trading transactions should be included as current assets or liabilities.

Beginning or cessation of relationship

The **general rules** for determining when an associate or joint venture relationship begins or ends are as follows: **7468** FRS 9 (40)
a. An investment **becomes an associate**, on the date which the investor meets the two essential requirements for defining an associated undertaking; namely that the investor holds a participating interest and exercises significant influence. An investment ceases to be an associate on the date it no longer fulfils either of the above elements.

b. An investment **becomes a joint venture** on the date the investor begins to control an entity jointly with other venturers, provided that it has a long-term interest. An investment ceases to be a joint venture on the date which the investor no longer enjoys joint control.

7470 **Disposal of interest** When an interest in an associate or joint venture is disposed of, the profit or loss arising on disposal should be calculated, after taking into account any related goodwill that has not previously been written off.

7471 **Piecemeal disposals** Where an investment in an associate or joint venture is disposed (or
FRS 9 (41) acquired) of in stages, processes similar to those set out for subsidiaries in FRS 2 "Subsidiary undertakings" should be followed (see also ¶7100).

Retained interest

7474 There may be instances where an entity ceases to be either an associate or joint venture,
FRS 9 (42) but the investor nevertheless retains an interest in the investee. Then the **initial carrying amount** of any interest retained in the entity, is based on the percentage retained of the final carrying amount for the former associate or joint venture, at the date the entity ceased to qualify as such (including the investor's share of associates profits or losses up to that sale date).

The initial carrying amount should include any related goodwill in terms of FRS 10, "Goodwill and Intangible Assets" and if calculated on this basis, then the carrying amount should be reviewed and written down, to its recoverable amount.

7475 **Former associates or joint ventures** When an entity ceases to be either an associate or
FRS 9 (43) joint venture, the investor may retain all or some of its interest in that entity as a simple investment.

The initial carrying amount of any **interest retained** in a former associate or joint venture is a surrogate cost derived from the former carrying amount rather than any consideration paid. In applying the requirement to review and write down that initial amount, to its recoverable amount, it should be noted that the recoverable amount could be affected by the amount that has been paid in dividends or through other distributions to owners.

An interest in another entity that ceases to be a joint venture may still qualify as an associate. Once an interest qualifies as long-term it should continue to be treated as long-term, irrespective of whether the investor intends to keep its interest or dispose of it.

7476 An **investment may be increased** so that it becomes an associate where:
– the group acquires a further shareholding that takes it over the 20% barrier; or
– the group acquires significant influence.

In the former case, the consideration paid by the investor plus cost of additional shareholdings should be compared with the fair value of the underlying net assets and liabilities of the associate, at the date the shareholding exceeded 20%.

In the latter case, the relevant valuation date is when significant interest influence was acquired, with the differences between the price paid and the fair value of underlying assets and liabilities representing goodwill.

7478 **Subsidiary that becomes an associate** A parent company could dispose of part of its shareholding in a subsidiary but retain an investment exceeding 20% plus significant influence; the subsidiary then becomes an associate.

The **accounting treatment** is as follows:
– the subsidiary's results are consolidated up to the date it ceased to be a subsidiary;
– the profit or loss on disposal is calculated by comparing the sale proceeds with the group's share of the subsidiary's net assets at the disposal date;
– the results of the associate are included in group accounts on an equity basis from the date the former subsidiary became an associate; and
– in the group balance sheet, the investment in the associate is shown at cost, plus share of associate's retained profit or loss since acquisition (less goodwill written-off).

Treatment of losses and interests in net liabilities

The investor should record changes in the carrying amount for each associate and joint venture, even if application of the equity method or gross equity method results in an interest in net liabilities rather than net assets.

7480
FRS 9 (44)

The **only exception**, is where there is sufficient evidence that an event has irrevocably changed the relationship between the investor and its investee, in that the investor downgrades its investment in an associate or joint venture to that of a passive investment.

Evidence that the necessary irrevocable change has taken place, includes a public statement from the investor that it is withdrawing, or confirmation that the direction of the operating and financing policies of the investee is to become the responsibility of the investee's creditors (e.g. bankers), rather than its equity shareholders.

Where an interest in net liabilities arises, the amount recorded should be shown as a provision or liability.

Group interests

Where the **investee is a group**, the investor's share is the aggregate of the parent's interest and the interests of its subsidiaries in the investee. The group's aggregate interest in that entity provides the basis of its entitlement to dividends and other distributions.

7486
FRS 9 (32)

Percentage shareholding The most straightforward example is where the investors hold only an interest in the equity share capital of an associate or joint venture. In this case the number of shares held is divided by the total number of shares in issue to ascertain the percentage shareholding.

7488

Complications arise when the investor holds **different types of shares** or where the entitlements to dividends and other distributions are different. In this case the actual rights and substance attached to each class of share must be considered in order to determine the appropriate percentage held, and the level of group interest.

> EXAMPLE A group owns 30% of the **equity shares in an associate** that has remitted £75,000 in dividends, and all 200,000 of the 4% cumulative preference shares in issue. The **investor's (the group) share of net assets** is determined by adding together its entitlement to dividends on the preference shares with the dividends from the equity shareholding.
> In this instance the total dividends were:
>
> Equity dividends.   £75,000 x 30% = £22,500
> Preference dividends   £200,000 x 4% = £8,000 Preference dividends.
>
> Whether the 30% equity shareholding in addition to the preference shares could be deemed to be a **participating interest**, depends on the substance of the specific rights attached to the preference shares.

Economic interest Although entities X and Y may have an equal shareholding in a joint venture 50:50, they may have an agreement whereby one company is entitled to a greater share of the profits, say 55:45. In this instance it would be more appropriate to equity account for the economic interest rather than the equity shareholding.

7489

Calculating group interests An associate may itself have subsidiaries, associates or joint ventures. These are known as **direct interests**.

7490

1. In such cases, the results and net assets to be taken into account by the equity method are those reported in the investee's consolidated financial statements. This includes the investor's share of the results and net assets of its associates and joint ventures, after any adjustment necessary to support the investor's accounting policies.

2. Where an investing group holds an **indirect interest** in an associate or joint venture through a subsidiary undertaking, or another associate or joint venture, then the investor's share of the results and net assets should be based on the aggregate holdings of the investor and its subsidiaries. Interests held by associates and joint ventures of the group should be disregarded, as the parent has little or no control over these shareholdings.

The **following example** illustrates how Company A calculates both its direct and indirect holdings in company D.

7492

EXAMPLE Calculating Company A's direct and indirect interests in Company D.

Classification	Share	Note
Direct holding in D	25%	
Indirect holding in D via B	20%	1
Indirect holding in D via C	0%	2
Total share	45%	

1. A holds a controlling interest in B and is therefore able to control all of B's 20% stake in D, which should be aggregated in full.
2. A does not hold a controlling interest in C and is not able to control any of C's 25% stake in D, which is disregarded in determining whether D is an associate of A.

Accounting treatment
A's consolidated statements:
The share of the associate's results (operating profit to tax line) and net assets:
– 45% share of D
– 20% share of C (to include C's 25% share of D).

Minority interests
The share of the associate results attributable to minority interests.
– 6% share of D (equal to the minority interest in B (20% -14 % (70% x 20% = 14 %)).

SECTION 5

Disclosures

7494   The **general disclosures** for associates and joint ventures are contained in the Companies Act, FRS 9, and SSAP 25 "Segmental Reporting".

The general disclosures required for both the equity and the gross equity method must be given separately. Certain information is required to be given on the face of the primary financial statements for all associates and joint ventures, with other supplementary information given by way of note. The **level of disclosure** is also dependent upon the extent of the investor's interest in the associate or joint venture.

1. Small companies adopting FRSSE

7495   Associates and Joint ventures are not specifically addressed in the FRSSE so the requirements of the Companies Act and FRS 9 apply. Small companies benefit from reduced disclosure requirements.

Where a group has investments in associates or joint ventures these should be disclosed in the **balance sheet** as follows:

B.III Investments (per Companies Act formats)

1. Shares in group undertakings

2. Interests in associated undertakings

3. Other participating interests

4. Loans to group undertakings and undertakings in which a participating interest is held

5. Investments other than loans

6. Others.

The **profit and loss format** set out in ¶361 needs to be modified for small companies. The category "Income from participating interests" should be replaced by two items: "Income from interests in associated undertakings" and "Income from other participating interests".

2. Companies Act disclosures

Associates and joint ventures (arrangements)

The Companies Act requires the following disclosures where, at the end of a financial year, **7496** a company has a significant holding in an undertaking which is not a subsidiary of the company:
- the name of the undertaking;
- if the undertaking is incorporated outside the UK, the country in which it was incorporated;
- the identity of each class of shares held separately in the undertaking by the parent and other group companies;
- the proportion of the nominal value of the shares of that class represented by those shares, separately for parent and other group companies;
- the aggregate amount of the capital and reserves of the undertaking as at the end of its relevant financial year; and
- the profit and loss for that year.

If the holding is less than 50% and the undertaking is not required to deliver or publish financial statements, then the disclosures required by the Companies Act do not apply.

Joint ventures

Where a joint venture is dealt with in consolidated financial statements by use of the **7498** **proportional consolidation method**, the following disclosures are required in respect of the undertaking:
- its name;
- the address of the principle place of business;
- the factors on which the joint management is based; and
- the proportion of the capital of the joint venture held by undertakings included in the consolidation.

Where the financial year of the joint venture did not end with that of the company, the date of its most recent year-end must be disclosed.

Where an undertaking included in the consolidation **manages another undertaking jointly** with one or more other entities, which are not included in the consolidation, then the other undertaking ("the joint venture") may be dealt with in the group accounts by the proportional consolidation method, **provided it is not**:
- a body corporate; or
- a subsidiary undertaking of the parent company.

Although, the use of proportional consolidation is permitted by the Companies Act it does not fit with the requirements of FRS 9; as such this method is not greatly used.

Disclosure exemptions

There are a number of available reliefs from the disclosure requirements of the Companies **7504** Acts, such as prejudicial or excessive information.

There may be circumstances where in the opinion of the directors, the disclosures required **7506** would be **seriously prejudicial** to the business of that entity, or any of its subsidiary undertakings. The fact of the non-disclosure must be stated.

In these cases, the Secretary of State may approve non-disclosure if the undertaking:
- is established under the law of a country outside the United Kingdom; or
- carries on business outside the United Kingdom.

7508   **Excessive information**   The directors of the company may be of the opinion, that the number of entities requiring disclosure is such, that compliance with the provision would result in information of excessive length being given.

In such a case, the information need only be given for those undertakings:
– whose results or financial position, in the opinion of the directors, principally affected the figures shown in the company's annual financial statements; or
– they are excluded from consolidation under the Companies Act.

Where advantage is taken of the above relief from disclosure:
– a statement that the information is given only regarding significant undertakings must be given in the notes accompanying the company's annual financial statements; and
– detailed information not disclosed in the notes to the financial statements, must be annexed to the company's next annual return. This provision is reinforced with a penalty regime.

3. FRS 9 disclosures

7510   FRS 9 disclosures supplement those required by the Act. There are however, **no exemptions** from the detailed disclosure requirements under FRS 9 for associated undertakings, preparing either shorter-form accounts or abbreviated accounts for small or medium-sized companies.

Principal investments

7512
FRS 9 (52)

The names of the principal associates and joint ventures should be disclosed in the financial statements of the investing group, showing:
– for each class of issued shares the proportion held by the investing group, indicating any special rights or constraints attaching to them;
– the accounting period or date of the financial statements, where these differ from those of the investing group; and
– an indication of the type of its business.

EXAMPLE   **Notes to the accounts**
Principle associates and joint ventures as at 31 December 2013

Company	Country of incorporation	Group equity holding %	Total issued capital £m
Hamish Kilpatrick	Scotland	35.6	1.5
BICC Finance	Holland	46.5	2.0
Capital Projects	England	25.6	8.5
Metrorail	England	50.0	15.2
Environmental Services ltd	England	50.0	7.6

Associates or joint ventures whose results did not, in the opinion of the Directors, materially affect the results or the assets of the Group are not shown.

7514
FRS 9 (53)

Contingent liabilities and commitments   Any information relating to the financial statements of associates and joint ventures, that should have been noted had the investor's accounting policies been applied, and that are material to understanding the effect on the investor of its investments should be disclosed, in particular the **investor's share of**:
– contingent liabilities incurred jointly with other venturers; or
– the capital commitments of the associates and joint ventures themselves.

7516
FRS 9 (54)

Restrictions on distributable reserves   There may be circumstances where there are significant statutory, contractual or exchange control restrictions on the ability of an associate or joint venture to distribute its reserves, other than those shown as non-distributable. In such cases, the extent of the restrictions should be indicated.

Balances between investor, associate and joint venture   The amounts owing and owed between an investor and its associates or its joint ventures, should be analysed into amounts relating to loans and trading balances.

7518
FRS 9 (55)

Rebuttal of the 20% rule   There may be instances where the 20% rule that implies that the investor has a participating interest or exercises significant influence over its investee (through either share ownership or voting rights), is rebutted. In such instances, a note should explain why the facts rebut the assumption.

7520
FRS 9 (56)

An investor not preparing consolidated financial statements   If the investor does not prepare consolidated financial statements, it should present the relevant figures for associates and joint ventures, as appropriate, by either:
– preparing a separate set of financial statements; or
– by showing the relevant amounts, together with the effects of including them in the entity's own financial statements, as additional information to its own financial statements.

7522
FRS 9 (48)

Threshold disclosures

The **general rule** is that disclosures required for all associates and joint ventures should be supplemented if **two key threshold limits** are exceeded. The thresholds are applied by comparing the investor's share, for either its associates or joint ventures in aggregate or its individual associates or joint ventures, with the corresponding amounts for the investor group (excluding amounts included under the equity method for associates and the gross equity method for joint ventures) of:
– gross assets;
– gross liabilities;
– turnover; and
– operating results (on a three year average).

7524
FRS 9 (57)

If any of the relevant amounts for the investor's share exceed the specified proportion of the same amounts for the investor group, the threshold has been exceeded and the additional disclosures outlined below, should be made.

Where the **investor's share** in any **individual associate or joint venture exceeds** a 25% threshold with respect to the investor group, the associate or joint venture should be disclosed in a note to the accounts, along with its share of the relevant categories as listed in the table below.

Disclosures Associates and joint ventures	Aggregate disclosure 15% threshold	Aggregate disclosure 25% threshold
Name		Yes
Share of:		
Turnover	Yes (Associates only)	Yes
Profit before tax		Yes
Taxation		Yes
Profit after tax		Yes
Fixed assets	Yes	Yes
Current assets	Yes	Yes
Liabilities within one year	Yes	Yes
Liabilities due after one year or more	Yes	Yes

If **one individual associate or joint venture** accounts for primarily all of the amounts included for that class of investment, only the aggregate, not the individual information need be given, provided that this is explained and the associate or joint venture identified, as illustrated in the following example.

7525

In addition to the disclosures required, as outlined in the table above, **further information should be given** where necessary to aid comprehension of the nature of the amounts disclosed. In deciding the most relevant balance sheet headings to use in the analysis, regard should be given to:
- the nature of the business; and
- provide an indication of the size and maturity profile of the liabilities held.

EXAMPLE **Notes to the accounts – Joint ventures**
The group has investments in joint ventures established to provide long-term services to the government as part of the Private Finance Initiative (PFI). The aggregate share of the net assets of all joint ventures are noted below.

Share of joint venture balance sheets (extract)

	£	£
	2013	2012
Fixed assets	115,367	99,655
Current assets	11,286	8,756
Liabilities due within one year	(6,789)	(5,897)
Liabilities due after one year	(98,756)	(82,633)
Net assets	**21,108**	**19,881**
Net loans to joint ventures	2,010	1,655
Total investment in joint ventures	**23,118**	**21,536**

Included within the aggregated figures above is the Group's share of AMC Group Ltd, the details of which are separately shown below.

Group's share of AMC Group's:
Profit and loss account

	£	£
	2013	2012
Turnover	9,578	8,569
Operating profit	5,456	4,689
Interest	(4,568)	(3,897)
Profit before tax	888	792
Tax	(267)	(253)
Profit after tax	**621**	**539**

Balance sheet

Fixed assets	77,850	79,865
Current assets	8,622	7,387
Liabilities due within one year	(5,895)	(2,758)
Liabilities due after one year	(70570)	(75,384)
Net assets	**10,007**	**9,110**

---

3. SSAP 25 disclosures

7526   If an associate accounts for at least 20% of the total results or net assets of the reporting entity (investor), the following disclosures are required under SSAP 25 "Segmental Reporting"; namely, the entity's share of associates' results before tax, minority interests and extraordinary results and net assets. –

SECTION 6

New UK GAAP – requirements of FRS 102

7530   Existing UK GAAP will be replaced by FRS 102 "The Financial Reporting Standard applicable in the UK and Republic of Ireland" from January 2015, although earlier adoption is permitted. A brief overview of the accounting requirements for associates and joint ventures contained in FRS 102 are set out below.

Accounting for associates under FRS 102	
Recognition	1. Parent company records investment in Group accounts using equity accounting as with current UK GAAP. 2. If the investor is not the parent company, the investment can be recognised at cost or fair value. For the latter option changes in value are taken to profit or shown in other comprehensive income.
Where investment is held as part of investment portfolio	Recorded at fair value with changes taken to profit

7532

Accounting for joint ventures under FRS 102	
Classification	Based on IAS 31 "Interests in joint ventures"; namely: jointly controlled operations, jointly controlled entities and jointly controlled assets.
Jointly controlled operations (JCO)	Similar to a joint arrangement that is not an entity (JANE) under existing UK GAAP.
Jointly controlled assets (JCA)	Group financial statements of venturer must show share of jointly controlled assets and liabilities, expenses and income.
Jointly controlled entities (JCE)	Parent companies must account for a JCE using the equity method, except where held as pure investments. Accounting treatment = measure at fair value, with changes in value taken to profit and loss. Non-parent companies – choice of cost model or fair value.

PART 10

Miscellaneous

CHAPTER 1

Government grants

Government grants are broadly defined as assistance in the form of cash to a company, in return for past or future compliance with certain conditions relating to the operations of the enterprise. Government assistance may also take the form of subsidised loans or non-cash loans such as guarantees, consultancy, or leasing of government property. Government grants are generally provided to persuade or assist companies in pursuing courses of action that are deemed socially or economically desirable. The **range of grants** is often flexible and diverse, reflecting changes in the priorities and direction of government policy.

7900
SSAP 4 (22)

The **classification of** government grants as either revenue, capital or non-cash grants, will determine its recognition and accounting treatment. **Capital grants** are generally specific and fund purchases of fixed assets for continuing use in the business. **Revenue grants** on the other hand, can be general (discretionary) or awarded for a specific project.

7902

SSAP 4, "Accounting for government grants", contains the **general principles** that should be applied to different types of government grants. Reporting **entities applying the FRSSE** have fewer disclosure requirements than entities adopting SSAP 4, although the accounting treatment is similar. The Companies Act does not deal explicitly with the issue of government grants, although some of its provisions do affect how they are recorded in the financial statements.

7904

The FRSSE requirements regarding **small companies** are covered as are the requirements for **non FRSSE entities** electing to adopt FRS 102 "The Financial Reporting Standard applicable in the UK and Republic of Ireland", which are mandatory from January 2015. **Charities** are subject to the additional requirements of the SORP "Accounting for Charities".

Definition of government

In respect of government grants, the term "government" is defined as the various tiers of local, regional, and national government, as well as:
– government agencies and quangos;
– the European Commission and other EC agencies; and
– other international agencies and bodies.

7910

SSAP 4 (21)

Government **grants can be awarded** for the following purposes:
– research and development;
– technical support;
– acquisition of fixed assets;
– reimbursement of costs already incurred;

7912

– financing the activities of a company over a specified period of time; or
– compensation to a company for loss of income.

A. Accounting treatment

7916

SSAP 4 (4)

The **main accounting issue** is how to treat revenue or capital grant income.
The accounting treatment adopted for both capital and revenue grants is determined by the application of the matching and prudence concepts. Under the matching principle, **capital grants** intended to subsidise the cost of fixed assets are credited to revenue over the life of the assets involved, whilst **revenue grants** (including discretionary grants) are matched to related expenditure.

1. Revenue grants

7922

The **key principles** are that **revenue grants** should be recognised in the profit and loss account over the same period as the related expenditure, be it revenue expenditure or amortisation of capital expenditure. The **grants should only be recorded** as income, when the conditions that give rise to the grant have been met and there is a reasonable assurance that the grant will be received.

7924

SSAP 4 (8)

The **terms and conditions** attached to each grant will vary. The determination of the relationship between grants received and related expenditure is simple, where the grant is a straightforward contribution towards agreed expenditures.

The following **general rules** should be applied:
a. Grants received in respect of expenditure which has already been incurred, should be recorded as income earned and taken immediately to the profit and loss account.
b. If the grant has been received but the expenditure has not been incurred, then it will be necessary to defer a part of the grant in deferred income.

For this purpose, expenditure incurred includes the amortisation of capital expenditure, whilst the unamortised element of the capital expenditure should be regarded as not having been incurred.

Difficulties in matching grant income and expenditures

7928

There may be difficulties in matching the grant to the related expenditure, especially when the reason for the grant is not clear, as illustrated in the following scenarios.

7930

SSAP 4 (9)

a. Where the terms of the grant do not specify precisely the expenditure it is intended to meet. Examples include grants for capital expenditure that are linked to research and development targets or the general costs of relocating production facilities to government sponsored enterprise zones. In these instances, it is appropriate to consider the circumstances that give rise to the payment of instalments of the grant in determining its recognition.

b. The award of a grant may also **rely on more than one criterion** being met or not tied to any particular expenditure. For instance, a grant may be linked to both capital expenditure and the number of jobs created in a certain time period or by project, or the grant awarded may form part of a package of government assistance with different costs and terms, each requiring a different treatment.

c. The grant might be paid on the **achievement of a non-financial objective**. In these circumstances, the grant should be matched with the identifiable costs of creating and maintaining the jobs for an agreed time period. The costs in these instances may be higher at the start of the project, therefore a higher proportion of the grant should be recognised in the earliest periods.

Matching process   There are a **number of rules** that cover the matching process: **7932**
a. If an instalment payment of the grant is dependent on evidence of expenditure being produced, then the income should be treated in the same accounting period as the expenditure incurred.
b. If the grant payment is dependent on another basis, such as the number of jobs created, then income should be matched to the projected costs of reaching that objective.
c. If a grant is designed to reimburse a company for a range of separate expenditures, it should be allocated to each form of expenditure in proportion to the total cost of that type of expenditure, as illustrated in the following example.

EXAMPLE   **Capital and revenue grant combined**

A company was awarded a **mixed grant** of £60,000 up front towards the cost of a project lasting two years to develop new accountancy software. The **revenue portion** of the grant totalled £40k and the **fixed asset** element £20k. Total project costs of £100,000 are to be split evenly over the two years of the project.
The grant is to be apportioned over the life of the project against the following costs:

	Total Cost		Total Grant
– Fixed assets	£20,000	100%	£20,000
– Staff costs	£30,000	50%	£15,000
– Materials	£50,000	50%	£25,000
	£100,000		£60,000

Year 1.
At the end of the financial year 20X3, fixed assets costs of £20,000 were matched by a capital grant. Staff and material costs of £30,000 were incurred, 50% of which were met by a revenue grant. Additional costs of £50,000 are expected in 20X4, 50% of which will be met by a revenue grant of £25,000 carried forward.

Discretionary grants

The government may authorise discretionary grants to be awarded as a **revenue**   **7934**
contribution to certain costs, such as training or the provision of working capital. However, where the relationship between the grant and related expenditure is not clearly defined, a number of accounting treatments are possible.

Depending on the **precise terms** under which a government grant relating to training costs   **7936**
was awarded, it could be treated in the following manner, namely:
– matched directly against training costs;
– deferred and matched with salary costs over the period staff are expected to benefit from the training (i.e. duration of the project);
– simply matched against total project costs; or
– recognised as income when received.

Summary

7938

Purpose of the grant	Recognition in the profit and loss account
Reimburse related expenditure	Record in profit and loss in same period
Immediate financial assistance	Recognise income in period as cash received
Compensation for loss of revenue	Account for income when cash received
Finance general activities of the enterprise	Recognise income when cash received
Contribution to the purchase of fixed assets (capital grants)	Income recognised over the useful economic life of the asset

2. Capital grants

In some instances, all or part of the grant may not be immediately recognised in the profit and   **7944**
loss account, in which case it should be classified as deferred income in the balance sheet.   SSAP 4 (15)

7946   Where a capital grant is made towards the cost of fixed assets, there are theoretically **two possible treatments**, namely:

a. The fixed asset is initially recorded at cost and depreciated over its useful economic life. The grant should be treated as **deferred income** and credited to the profit and loss account in instalments over the same period, and on the same basis as the depreciation charge.

b. The grant is deducted from the purchase price or production cost of the relevant asset, reducing the annual depreciation charge accordingly. This is known as the "**netting method**".

Whilst both methods are permitted under SSAP 4, the deferred income method is generally adopted.

Deferred income method

7948   Capital grants should be recorded as deferred income and credited to the profit and loss account over the estimated useful life of the asset.

EXAMPLE   A company purchased a fixed asset at the start of 20X0 at a cost of £250,000. The asset is deemed to have a useful economic life of 10 years, and is depreciated on a straight-line basis. The company has been awarded a grant of £75,000 towards the cost of the asset. The net charge represents the depreciation charge of £25,000 less the grant income of £7,500.

Year	Asset book value £	Deferred income £	Depreciation £	Grant income £	Net Charge (P & L) £
20X0	225,000	67,500	25,000	(7,500)	17,500
20X1	200,000	60,000	25,000	(7,500)	17,500
20X2	175,000	52,500	25,000	(7,500)	17,500
20X3	150,000	45,000	25,000	(7,500)	17,500
20X4	125,000	37,500	25,000	(7,500)	17,500
20X5	100,000	30,000	25,000	(7,500)	17,500
20X6	75,000	22,500	25,000	(7,500)	17,500
20X7	50,000	15,000	25,000	(7,500)	17,500
20X8	25,000	7,500	25,000	(7,500)	17,500
20X9	0	0	25,000	(7,500)	17,500
			250,000	**(75,000)**	**175,000**

Netting method

7952
SSAP 4 (25)

Grants may be given as a contribution to assets, which are not depreciated on the basis that they do not have a finite life. Such a policy of non-depreciation is used by the utility companies concerning **infrastructure assets** (¶1472). Grants awarded to cover part of the infrastructure costs are not carried indefinitely in the balance sheet as deferred income but "netted-off" against the expenditure concerned, even though this represents a departure from the Companies Acts.

EXAMPLE   Alpha Plc
Annual report and accounts
Non-depreciating assets
Accounting policies (extract)

1. Basis of policy
The financial statements have been prepared under the historical cost convention and, except for the treatment of certain grants, comply with both the Accounting Standards and the Companies Act. A departure from the requirements of the Act is given in the policy note on grants below.

15. Grants
Grants and contributions received in respect of **new infrastructure assets** are treated as **deferred income** and are recognised in the profit and loss account over the useful economic life of those assets. Grants and contributions relating to infrastructure assets have been deducted from the original cost of the fixed assets, contrary to the requirements of Companies Act, which requires assets to be shown at their purchase price or production cost and grants presented as deferred income.
The departure from the requirements of the Act is, in the opinion of the Directors, necessary to give a **true and fair view** as, while a provision is made for the depreciation of infrastructure assets,

these assets do not have determinable finite lives and therefore, no basis exists by which to recognise the grants as deferred income. The effect of this departure from the Act is that the cost of fixed assets is £35.7m lower than it would otherwise have been.

Those grants relating specifically to maintaining the operating capability of the infrastructure network, are taken into account in determining the depreciation charged for infrastructure assets.

Non-cash grants

Grants can sometimes be given in the form of non-cash assets. For instance, in local enterprise zones, a local authority may lease a factory or land to a company at a peppercorn rent. These assets should be accounted for in the balance sheet at fair value, with the "grant" recorded as deferred income and taken to income over the same period as the useful economic life of the asset.

7956
SSAP 4 (16)

Government assistance in the form of consultancy or advice is now a more popular form of government aid, although it is unlikely that the benefits associated with the non-financial assistance can be quantified for inclusion in the financial statements.

---

3. Post-income recognition issues

There are a number of post-grant income recognition issues including repayment of grants, asset disposal, taxation and impairment, which are discussed below.

7960

Repayment of grants

Grant covenants There are usually conditions attached to the receipt of a government grant, in order to ensure that the grants are utilised for the purpose for which they were awarded. The criteria may relate to a specific period of time, such as the retention of an asset for a contracted period, or to a particular event.

7964

Failure to comply with the grant covenants may mean that the grant has to be repaid. If a breach of the terms of the grant is expected to occur, then provision should be made for the repayment of grants already accrued as required by FRS 12 "Provisions, Contingent Liabilities and Contingent Assets", unless the possibility of repayment is remote. For disclosure requirements relating to contingent liabilities arising on grants, see ¶7990.

SSAP 4 (27)

Full or partial repayment Where a company is required to repay a government grant, either in full or part, the amount to be repaid, after allowing for any excess deferred income relating to the grant, should be charged to the profit and loss account as it becomes payable. This treatment is also in accordance with FRS 3 "Reporting financial performance".

7966
SSAP 4 (14)

The **qualifying conditions** that must be complied with are not always linked to the financial period that benefits from the grant income. Certain types of grant may be repayable if assets cease to be used for a qualifying purpose within an agreed time period.

7968

Asset disposal

In a situation where the company disposes of an asset on which a **deferred income balance** remains, and where the grant has to be repaid, this should be accounted for by first reducing the balance on the deferred income account, with any additional charge being direct to the profit and loss account.

7970

Where the grant itself does not need to be repaid, then the balance on the deferred income account should be considered in calculating the profit or loss on disposal.

EXAMPLE   A company sells an asset originally purchased for £45,000, on which depreciation of £30,000 has been charged. A government grant for £22,500 was awarded to help fund the purchase, which is being released to the profit and loss account over the useful economic life of the asset (15 years). The asset was subsequently sold for £8,000 after year 10 and the company was not required to repay the outstanding grant.

The profit or loss on disposal can be calculated as follows:

	£	
Cost	45,000	
Accumulated depreciation	(30,000)	(£45,000/15 × 10 yrs)
Net book value	**15,000**	
Less deferred income remaining	(7,500)	(£22,500/15 × 5 yrs)
Net amount transferred to P & L	**7,500**	
Sale proceeds	8,000	
Profit	**500**	

Taxation

7974
SSAP 4 (7)

The accounting treatment for taxation purposes will vary according to the terms attached to each grant and the statute or regulation under which it was made. Some grants will be tax-free (capital) whilst others are taxed as income upon receipt.

7976

The **tax treatment** of an item does not necessarily determine its accounting treatment and a grant may be taxed in a different period, from that in which it is recognised in the profit and loss account. Any **timing differences** that may arise between the tax charge and the recognition of the corresponding credit in the profit and loss account, should be dealt with in accordance with FRS 19 "Deferred tax" (¶9000).

7978
SSAP 21 (41)

Leased assets Tax-free grants that are available to lessors to be set against the purchase price of the assets should be spread over the period of the lease. The grant should be treated as non-taxable income. Grants relating to leased assets should be accounted for in the financial statements of the lessor in accordance with SSAP 21 "Accounting for leases and hire purchase contracts" (¶3400).

Impairment

7980

Where an asset funded through a government grant has become impaired, then the release of the grant to the profit and loss account should match the impairment write-down.

B. Disclosures

7982

There are a number of disclosures required in the financial statements relating to government grants, which are set out briefly below.

7984

Balance sheet The Companies Act balance sheet formats require that accruals and deferred income be shown under the heading "Creditors" or separately as "Accruals and deferred income". Where the deferred income will be released to profit and loss account over several years, the balance at the year-end should be split between creditors due within one year and due after more than one year as appropriate.

EXAMPLE **ABC Ltd. – Annual report and accounts**
Notes to the accounts
Creditors: amounts falling due within one year

	20X3 £m	20X2 £m
Trade creditors	478.2	378.5
Amounts owed to subsidiary undertakings	15.2	12.3
Taxation	25.3	13.6
Dividends	–	5.0
Accruals and deferred income	**245.7**	**137.6**
	764.4	**547.0**

Notes to the accounts   The following information concerning government grants should   **7986**
be disclosed in the financial statements.

SSAP 4 (28)

Disclosure requirements under SSAP 4	Disclosure requirements under FRSSE
The effects of government grants on the results for the period and/or the financial position of the company	as for SSAP 4
Where the results for the period are materially affected by the receipt of government assistance, the nature of that assistance and its impact on the financial statements;	as for SSAP 4
The accounting policy re. government grants adopted	Not required
Type and value of government grants reflected in the financial statements;	Not required
Any balances on deferred grants should be analysed between its major components, such as building grants or plant and machinery	Not required
Details should also be given of material revenue grants deducted from the cost of an asset as opposed to being treated as deferred income.	Not required

The **accounting policy** selected and the periods over which the grants are credited to the   **7988**
profit and loss should be disclosed, where practical. This may not be the situation, if a large   SSAP 4 (17)
number of different types of grant are given. If this is the case, a broad indication of future
periods expected to benefit from the grants already received and recognised in the profit
and loss account should also, where practical, be disclosed.

Where there is some doubt over how the grant is to be recognised in the accounts, and it
is a material sum, the entity should disclose the accounting treatment adopted.

The first part of the following example is of a general accounting policy note for government
grants. The second part illustrates the accounting treatment for the two elements of the grant;
namely a deferred grant and a grant related to the upgrading of the rail network.

EXAMPLE   **Railnet Group Ltd**
Notes to the accounts
Accounting policies (extract)

2. Grants
Capital grants and other contributions received towards the cost of tangible fixed assets are
included in creditors as deferred income and credited to the profit and loss account over the life
of the asset. **Revenue grants** are credited to the profit and loss account so as to match them with
the expenditure to which they relate.

5. Turnover

	20X3 £m	20X2 £m
Passenger revenue	742	1024
Revenue grant	635	
Freight revenue	26	17
Property rental income	15	13
Other income	21	20
Total	**1439**	**1074**

Revenue grants comprise the following:
– **Deferred income grant**. The Government agreed to release revenues due for settlement in 20X3.
The first payment of £215m was received in August 20X3.
– **Network grant**. The grant replaces the loss of track access charges forfeited in line with the
upgrading of the network and the disruption caused to the train operating companies.
In accordance with SSAP 4, and on the basis that the Directors at the time of the interim statements
had reasonable assurance that future payments will be received from the Government, the

grants due in respect of services provided in the year have been credited to revenue and amount to £420m.

7990   **Contingent liabilities**   Where the possibility exists of **repayment of a government grant**, a contingent liability should be created, and the following information disclosed:
SSAP 4 (35)
– the amount or estimated liability;
– the legal nature of the liability; and
– whether any security has been provided by the company in connection with the liability and if so, what security.

C. Small companies adopting the FRSSE

7992   Government grants should be recognised in the profit and loss account so as to **match** them
FRSSE 6.54 – 6.57   with the expenditure towards which they are intended to contribute. Even though a grant may have been received as a contribution towards expenditure on a fixed asset, company law does not allow the cost of the asset to be reduced – the grant, therefore, should be treated as **deferred income**.

7993   A government grant should not be recognised in the profit and loss account until the **conditions for its receipt** have been complied with and there is reasonable assurance that the grant will be received.

Potential liabilities to repay grants should be provided for only to the extent that **repayment is probable**. The repayment of a government grant should be set off against any unamortised deferred income relating to the grant. Any excess should be charged immediately to the profit and loss account.

7994   The following information should be **disclosed** in the financial statements:
– the effects of government grants on the results for the period and/or the financial position of the entity; and
– where the results of the period are affected materially by the receipt of forms of government assistance other than grants, the nature of that assistance and, to the extent possible, an estimate of the effects.

D. New UK GAAP – requirements of FRS 102

7998   FRS 102 "The Financial Reporting Standard applicable in the UK and Republic of Ireland", has now been issued and its requirements are mandatory from January 2015, although earlier adoption is permitted. The new standard is based on the international financial reporting standard for SMEs and the accounting requirements are similar to existing UK GAAP.

FRS 102 distinguishes between a **performance model**, where income is only recognised when the conditions attached to the loan have been fulfilled and an **accruals model**, where grant income is matched against related costs. FRS 102 makes no distinction between capital and revenue grants.

7999   The **disclosure requirements** of FRS 102 cover details of the accounting policies adopted, details of amounts and specific conditions (including contingencies yet to be met) attached to grants and other forms of government assistance received.

　　　MEMO POINTS   The FRC has issued a **staff education note** (SEN08) that compares the accounting treatment for government grants under SSAP 4 and FRS 102 (Section 24) and highlights key issues concerning the transition to the new standard.

CHAPTER 2

Foreign currency transactions

This chapter reviews the accounting treatment and disclosures required for foreign currency transactions, covering individual companies and the preparation of consolidated financial statements, including foreign branches. Exchange rate gains and losses, the hedging of foreign currency transactions and the financing of foreign equity investments from foreign currency borrowings are also covered.   **8000**

A company can directly enter into foreign currency transactions before translating them into the presentation currency used in its financial statements (Individual company stage). Alternatively, a company can conduct currency operations through ownership or control of a foreign enterprise, whose financial statements are then translated into the currency of the investing company for consolidation. For the purposes of this chapter, a **foreign enterprise is defined** as a company or branch, whose operations are based in a country other than that of the investing company or whose assets and liabilities, are mainly denominated in a currency other than the reporting currency of the investing company.   **8002**   SSAP 20 (1)

8003   **Accounting framework**   The accounting framework covering foreign currency transactions is now governed by **three different sets of standards**, depending on the size of the entity and the accounting policies adopted. In general, most small and medium sized companies continue to adopt UK GAAP as set out in the table below.

Entity	Standards
Small entities (FRSSE)	Can adopt the FRSSE + exempt from applying standards listed below.
Small and medium entities adopting historical cost accounting (non- FRSSE)	SSAP 20 "Foreign currency translation" and UITF 9 "Accounting for operations in hyperinflationary economies".
	The FRC has published **FRS 102** for non-listed entities not adopting the FRSSE. Although early adoption of the new standard is permitted it only becomes mandatory from 1 January 2015.
Companies applying fair value accounting	FRS 23 "The effects of changes in foreign exchange rates" and FRS 24 "Financial Reporting in Hyperinflationary Economies" + FRS 26 "Financial instruments: measurement and the disclosure requirements of FRS 29 "Financial instruments: disclosures" (see point 1 below).

⌐ MEMO POINTS ⌐   1. **FRS 23 and FRS 24** only apply to those entities which have adopted FRS 26, which covers the accounting treatment of all financial instruments, including those involving foreign exchange. FRS 26 is mandatory for the small number of companies who have opted to apply fair value accounting. Most companies will probably continue to adopt SSAP 20 for the foreseeable future.
2. The **exchange rates** used in the examples in this chapter may not correspond to the current exchange rate and are for illustrative purposes only.
3. **Listed companies** must apply IFRS.

SECTION 1

Definitions of currency

8004   All these **terms/definitions** are regarded as being interchangeable.
SSAP 20 (39)

Definitions	
"Local currency"	Defined in SSAP 20 as the currency of the primary economic area in which the enterprise operates and generates cash flows.
"Functional currency"	The term is used more widely in FRS 13 "Derivatives and other financial instruments" and in US GAAP, and in practice is equivalent in meaning to "local currency".
"Reporting currency"	Used in the international accounting standards to describe the currency in which the financial statements are actually prepared. This term is not defined in the UK accounting standard.

⌐ MEMO POINTS ⌐   Under UK company law, there is no requirement for a company to prepare the financial statements it files with the Registrar of Companies in **sterling**. Other currencies, such as US Dollars or the Euro may be used. A company may elect to do this, for example, where most of its transactions are denominated in a currency other than sterling. In such cases the functional or reporting currency would be different from the local currency.

Translation process

8010   Translation is the process by which the transactions, balances and indeed complete financial statements denominated in one currency, are converted into the local currency of the individual or parent company. Translation should be distinguished from currency conversion which represents the physical exchange of currency.

The **purpose of the translation** of foreign currency transactions and financial statements is to:
- reflect the transactions and balances in a foreign currency in the company's reporting currency;
and
- highlight the effects of exchange rate changes on a company's profits, cash flow and its equity.

8012
SSAP 20 (2)

Exchange gains and losses arise primarily on the translation of monetary assets and liabilities and are recorded separately from the original transaction. This is because these transactions result from an event that is unrelated to the original purchase or sale transaction; namely exchange rate movements.

Translation rates

8014

Translation rates for recording transactions in foreign currencies	Description
Historical rate	The exchange rate ruling on the transaction date.
Average rate	An approximation of the actual exchange rates prevailing over a given time period (i.e. month, quarter).
Contract rate	Where a trading transaction is covered by a related or matching forward contract, the rate of exchange specified in the contract should be used.
Closing rate	The exchange rate ruling at the balance sheet date.

SECTION 2

Companies adopting the FRSSE

The FRSSE contains the accounting treatment for simple foreign currency transactions. In essence, assets or liabilities originally denominated in foreign currencies must be accounted for in the profit and loss or balance sheet and the conversion basis used for their translation into sterling must be disclosed. The **general rule** is that conversion should be at the exchange rate prevailing on the transaction date, although an **average rate** can be used where the exchange rates do not fluctuate significantly during the financial year. An exception is permitted for transactions that must be settled using a **contracted rate**, including transactions covered by a forward exchange contract, more commonly known as hedging. Once translated, there are a number of accounting rules that must be observed as set out in the table below. The accounting requirements for consolidating the accounts of foreign entities are set out in the second table.

8016
FRSSE 13.1-13.12

Transactions in foreign currencies

8017

Accounting issues	Accounting treatment
Non-monetary assets	Once translated and recorded in the accounts no subsequent adjustments are permitted.
Monetary assets & liabilities denominated in foreign currencies	Translate at exchange rate prevailing at the balance sheet date (closing rate) or where appropriate the contract rate (e.g. related or matching forward contracts covering trading activities).
Exchange rate gains and losses	On settled transactions or unsettled monetary items should be recorded in the profit and loss account as arising from ordinary activities.

Accounting issues	Accounting treatment
Where foreign currency borrowings used to finance or hedge investments in foreign equities	The FRSSE requirements are similar to those contained in SSAP 20 (see ¶8224); namely: Where certain criteria apply, the equity investments can be denominated in the relevant foreign currencies and the carrying amounts translated at the closing rate (financial year end) for inclusion in the investing entities financial statements. The criteria are as follows: – exchange rate gains and losses arising on borrowings to finance the purchase of equity investments, should only be offset to cover any exchange differences arising on the said investments; – foreign currency borrowings generating the exchange rate gains or losses, should not exceed, in aggregate, the total cash expected to be generated by these investments; and – the accounting treatment selected should be applied consistently from one accounting period to the next.
Hyperinflation	Not treated in the FRSSE. Where a small company has operations in a hyperinflationary economy UITF 19 should apply (see ¶8200).
Disclosures	Amounts originally denominated in foreign currencies and subsequently accounted for in the balance sheet or profit and loss account must be supported by disclosure of the basis (exchange rate) on which these amounts have been translated into the local currency.

8018 **Consolidating the accounts of foreign entities**   There are a number of accounting issues to be addressed when consolidating the accounts of foreign entities, as set out in the table below.

Accounting issues	Accounting treatment
Which exchange rate classification should be used?	When consolidating the local currency accounts of foreign entities (e.g. associates, branches) the closing rate/net investment method should normally be used.
How does one treat exchange rate differences?	Exchange rate differences arising from the retranslation of the opening net investment in a foreign entity at the closing rate = treat as a movement on reserves.
How should the foreign entity's profit and loss account be translated?	If accounted for under the closing rate/net investment method then the foreign entity's results should also be translated using either the closing rate or average rate (¶8074). If the average rate is used then the difference between the P & L account translated using this rate and the closing rate should be recorded as a movement on reserves. No firm guidance is given on how to determine the average rate.
What if the key economic environment of the foreign entity happens to be that of the investing company?	Where foreign entity trade is more dependent on the economic environment of the investing company, than its local markets then it should report its operations/transactions in the currency of the investing company.
Translation method – issue of consistent application	Method used for translating foreign entity's financial statements should be consistently applied from one accounting period to the next.
What happens if foreign currency borrowings have been used to finance, or provide a hedge against, group equity investments in foreign entities?	Any exchange rate gains or losses should be offset as reserve movements (and not taken to the P&L) arising on the retranslation of net investments if certain criteria are met; namely: – the relationship between the investor and the foreign entity support use of the closing rate method for consolidation purposes; – in any one accounting period, the exchange rate gains or losses arising on foreign currency borrowings are offset only to cover any exchange differences that have arisen on net investments in foreign entities; – foreign currency borrowings generating the exchange rate gains or losses, should not exceed, in aggregate, the total cash expected to be generated by these investments; and – the accounting treatment selected should be applied consistently from one accounting period to the next.

SECTION 3

Companies adopting SSAP 20

The first stage is the preparation of the financial statements for an **individual company**, including those that are part of a group, prior to the preparation of the consolidated financial statements.

8019

A. The individual company stage

This section covers the procedures to be followed by an individual company accounting for foreign currency transactions. This involves the initial recording of the individual transactions concluded during the financial year, where a distinction first needs to be drawn between non-monetary assets and monetary assets and liabilities.

8020
SSAP 20 (46)

The accounting treatment for **exchange rate gains and losses** arising on unsettled transactions giving rise to monetary assets and liabilities at the balance sheet date is also discussed.

Individual companies		
Translation date	**Non-monetary assets** (e.g. Stocks, properties, plant and machinery).	**Monetary assets & liabilities** (e.g. Cash and bank balances, foreign currency loans, debtors and creditors).
Transactions during the financial year	All companies have a choice between: 1. Historical rate 2. Contract rate 3. Average rate **Exemption**: applies to foreign equity investments (¶8220)	When initially recording the transaction companies have a choice between: 1. Historical rate 2. Contract rate 3. Average rate Exchange gains or losses **on settled transactions** are recognised in the profit and loss account (on settlement date).
Balance sheet date	No re-translation	**Unsettled transactions are re-translated using:** 1. Short-term – closing rate (¶8050) 2. Long-term – closing rate (¶8054) (Use of average rate permitted) Exchange gains or losses recognised in the profit and loss account.

1. Transaction recording during the financial year (settled)

The **accounting process** is straightforward for companies undertaking a one-off or small number of individual transactions in a foreign currency. Irrespective of whether the transaction relates to a non-monetary asset or a monetary asset and liability, it should be translated at the historical rate prevailing on the transaction date or a contracted rate where applicable.

8024
SSAP 20 (46)

For **larger non-listed companies**, the translation process is the same, except greater use is usually made of the average rate of exchange for a given time period (e.g. month, quarter), which may be used as an approximation if rates do not fluctuate greatly.

Where a trading transaction is covered by a related or matching forward contract, the rate of exchange specified in the contract may be used.

Non-monetary assets

8028
SSAP 20 (47)

Once a **non-monetary asset** denominated in a foreign currency has been recorded in the balance sheet, its value is set. The transaction is not re-translated and as such no subsequent gains or losses on translation are generated.

However, where for example, the purchase of a non-monetary asset is settled at a date subsequent to that on which the transaction was initially recorded, the actual amount paid in sterling may differ from the amount recorded in the company's ledgers. This difference is treated as a foreign currency gain or loss.

The **one exception to this rule** applies to foreign equity investments hedged by foreign currency borrowings, where the net realisable value of equity investments should, where certain conditions are satisfied, be re-translated at the closing rate at the end of the period. The conditions to be met are specified in ¶8220.

Monetary assets and liabilities

8032

A **settled transaction** is defined as one that is completed by the balance sheet date. Where settled transactions generate exchange gains or losses, the effects of fluctuating exchange rates on settled transactions are automatically reflected in the cash flows of an individual company's operations, as the movement in the exchange rate either increases or decreases the local currency equivalent paid or received in cash settlements.

SSAP 20 (49)

All exchange gains or losses on settled transactions should be reported as part of the profit or loss for the year from ordinary activities. The distinction between trading and non-trading transactions is primarily an issue of disclosure, as the accounting treatment is the same. A distinction would normally only be made for material trading or non-trading activities.

8034
SSAP 20 (8)

Trading activities **Exchange gains and losses** arising from normal trading operations should be recognised in the profit and loss account in arriving at the profit or loss on ordinary activities. In practice they are included under "other operating income or charges". This accounting treatment should be adopted for all exchange rate differences arising from monetary items.

> EXAMPLE   **Treatment of an exchange loss on trading activity.**
>
> In June 2013, a British company purchased for immediate delivery, plant and equipment from a Dutch company for €255,000. The sterling exchange rate was £1 = €1.20. The company's financial year end was October 2013.
> The purchase price was due for settlement two months hence and was recorded as a liability in the accounts at £212,500 (€255,000/1.20). In August 2013, the Euro exchange rate had moved to £1 = €1.10 resulting in a liability of £231,818 and an exchange loss of £19,318, which was recorded in the profit or loss account under other operating charges.

8036

Non-trading activities Exchange rate gains and losses from non-trading activities, such as finance arrangements, will usually be included for the purposes of the year-end financial statements, within "Other interest receivable and similar income" or "Interest payable and other charges". **Exchange gains or losses on extraordinary items**, in the unlikely event that there should be such an item, should be accounted for as part of that item.

2. Unsettled transactions at the balance sheet date

8040

Unsettled transactions are monetary transactions outstanding at the balance sheet date, and can be **classified as short or long-term**. The accounting treatment for exchange gains and losses arising on unsettled (unrealised) transactions is the same as for settled transactions (translated at the closing rate). An average rate may only be used where this provides a close approximation to the closing rate.

Special attention should be paid to the treatment of **unrealised exchange rate gains** on long-term monetary items.

Where there is **a related or matching forward contract** in respect of the underlying transac- **8042** tion, giving rise to the balance, the rate specified in the contract may be used instead of the closing rate.

Also, it is necessary to consider in terms of **prudence**, whether the exchange gain (or the amount by which such a gain exceeds past exchange losses on the same items), recognised in the profit and loss account should be restricted, where there are doubts over the convertibility or marketability of the currency concerned.

Short-term monetary items

Short-term monetary assets and liabilities are items that are realised within one year of the **8050** balance sheet date.

Where the **exchange rate differences relate** to short-term monetary items they will be reported in arriving at the profit and loss for the year from ordinary activities, even though the cash has not been physically realised at that instant.

The following examples illustrate the accounting treatment for unrealised exchange rate gains and losses on short-term monetary items calculated at the balance sheet date.

EXAMPLE **Scenario 1**

Unsettled short-term monetary item
Exchange gains or losses
In March 20X3, a UK company brought telecommunications equipment from a company in the US for $550,000, due for settlement on 30 June 20X3. The $/£ exchange rate on the date of delivery was $1.65 = £1 and the asset and liability initially therefore recorded in the company's books at £333,333. The balance sheet date was 30 May 20X3.

At the **balance sheet date** of 30 May 20X3, the **creditor** was still outstanding. No further translation of the rate at which the purchased equipment was recorded is necessary. The creditor however, should be re-translated at the rate of exchange at the balance sheet date; namely £1 = $1.52 = £361,842. The **loss on exchange** of £28,509 (£361,842 – 333,333) should be taken to the profit and loss account.

Similarly, if the rate of exchange at the balance sheet date was £1 = $1.75, the creditor balance would be re-translated at £314,286 resulting in the recognition of an unrealised exchange rate gain of £19,047.

Scenario 2
Unsettled short-term monetary item
Exchange gain
Portland Stone Ltd., purchases some goods from Voller AG in Germany on 30 September 20X3 for €40,000 due for settlement in equal instalments on 30 November 20X3 and 31 January 20X4. The balance sheet date is 31 December 20X3. The exchange rate moved as follows:

	£ = €
30 September	1 = 1.15
30 November	1 = 1.18
31 December	**1 = 1.22**
31 January	1 = 1.25

The accounting treatment for the following entries is as follows:

A. 30 September 20X3 – equipment ordered/purchased
Purchase price (€40,000/ 1.15)

Debit:	Purchases (historical rate)	£34,783	
Credit:	Trade creditors		£34,783

B. 30 November 20X3 – (first instalment)
The first instalment of €20,000 falls due. This will now cost €20,000 at €1.18/£1 = £16,949 as the exchange rate has moved from €1.15 to €1.18 versus the pound. The company has made an exchange gain of £422 (£17,391 – £16,949).

Debit:	Trade creditors	£17,391	
Credit:	Exchange gains: P & L account		£442
	Cash		£16,949

C. 31 December 20X3 – the balance sheet date.
The outstanding liability at the year end will be recalculated using the rate applicable on that date €20,000 at €1,22/£1 = £16,393.
A further exchange gain of £998 (17,391–16,393),has been made and should be accounted for as follows:

Debit: Trade creditors	£998	(closing rate)
Credit: Exchange gains: Profit & loss account		£998

At the year end the remaining creditor of €20,000 is now stated at £16,393 [£17,391 – £16,393 = £998].
The **total exchange gain** of £1,440 (£998 + £442) will be included in the operating profit for the year 2013.

D. 31 January 20X4 – (the second instalment)
Portland Stone Ltd. must settle the second instalment of €20,000 at a cost of £16,000 (€20,000/€1.25). As the pound has strengthened further against the Euro, an additional exchange gain has materialised.

Debit: Trade creditors	£16,393
Credit: Exchange gains	£393
Credit: Cash	£16,000

Reconciliation

		£	
Total cash paid (1 st + 2 nd instalments) =	32,949	(£16,949 + 16,000)
Trade Creditor initially recorded in the accounts	34,783	
Total exchange gain	**1,834**	(£442 + £998+393)

Long-term monetary items

8054 Long-term monetary items are items realised more than one year after the balance sheet date.

Exchange rate gains and losses arising from the **re-translation** of long-term monetary items should be recognised in the profit and loss account, even though they may not be reflected in cash flows for some considerable time.

8055 Predicting the exchange rate at which long-term monetary assets or liabilities mature is a subjective process. However, it is necessary, when stating the liability or asset in the reporting currency, to make the best assessment in the light of the information available. In general, **translation at the closing rate** will provide the best estimate, particularly where the currency concerned is traded on the spot and forward exchange markets (¶8310). There is an important exception to this rule (see ¶8057).

8056 When dealing with long-term monetary items, **additional factors** must be considered. A **possible conflict** may arise between the requirements of the Companies Act, that only profits realised at the balance sheet date be included in the profit and loss account and SSAP 20, where unrealised gains on long-term monetary items should be recognised in the profit and loss account. The problem is that recognising losses whilst deferring gains, would be inconsistent, as it does not allow for any favourable movements in exchange rates.

SSAP 20 (10) The requirement to give **a true and fair view** provides the basis for the departure from the Companies Act. Disclosure of this departure and the reasons for it is required in the notes to the accounts.

EXAMPLE Departure from the Companies Act
Nightingale Services – Annual report and accounts 2013

Notes to the accounts
Accounting policies (extract)

Foreign currencies – long-term monetary items

All **transactions** denominated in foreign currencies are translated into sterling at the actual rate of exchange ruling on the date of the transaction.
Assets and liabilities in foreign currencies including **long-term liabilities** are translated into sterling at the rates of exchange prevailing at the balance sheet date.
All **exchange differences** are processed through the profit and loss account. This treatment is required by SSAP 20 "Foreign currency transactions" in order to give a true and fair view of the company's results. **Compliance with SSAP 20** overrides the Companies Act, which states that only realised profits at the balance sheet date should be included in the profit and loss account.
The effect of currency revaluation is disclosed in note 5

5. Operating costs (extract)	2013	2012
Foreign currency (gains)/ losses	(£1.4m)	(£0.8m)

Exception There is one exception to the general rule that long-term monetary items should be translated at the closing rate; namely that an exchange gain (including gains that exceed past exchange losses on the same items) recorded in the profit and loss account should be restricted, where there is uncertainty as to the convertibility or marketability of the currency involved.

8057
SSAP 20 (50)

EXAMPLE Taschenrechners Ltd. – Annual Report and Accounts – 2013
Notes to the accounts (extract)

Taschenrechners Ltd. has doubts over the **convertibility** of a long-term monetary loan of £3m made to an overseas supplier, on which foreign exchange control restrictions have been imposed prior to repayment. Given the current circumstances, the realisable value of the loan has been assessed and the exchange gains that would arise on re-translation should be withheld.

B. Consolidated financial statements

The **consolidation process** involves the preparation of group accounts for a company and its foreign enterprises including overseas branches. The accounting treatment for consolidating branch accounts and the **choice of translation methods** and allocation of any resulting exchange gains or losses are also considered.

8060

1. Translation methods

When preparing consolidated financial accounts the financial statements of any overseas operations must be translated into the reporting currency of the parent company, using a recognised translation method.

8064
SSAP 20 (15)

There are three methods that could be applied; namely the **closing rate, average rate** and the **temporal method**.

8066
SSAP 20 (17)

The **method used** for translating financial statements for consolidation purposes **depends on** the financial and other operational relationships, that exist between an investing company and its foreign entities. However, **once a method is adopted** it should be applied consistently from period to period.

8070 In the **majority of circumstances** the closing rate or average rate method is used. In general when the closing rate is used, the currency of the country in which the foreign company operates will be its reporting currency. The **temporal method** is adopted, primarily where the foreign enterprise trades as a direct extension of the investing company and not as a separate entity and the reporting currency of the investing company will usually be the local currency.

Translation method	Relationship with foreign enterprise	Treatment of gains or losses on retranslation of opening net investment
Closing rate method	Independent of parent company (i.e. subsidiary, associate)	Reserves
Average rate method	As above	Reserves
Temporal method (historical rate)	Extension of parent company (i.e. branch)	Profit and loss account

a. Closing rate method

8074 The closing rate method is also known as the net investment method and it is based on the assumption that a foreign entity operates as a largely independent entity.

8076
SSAP 20 (15) This method recognises that the investment in an overseas company is its net worth, rather than a direct investment in the individual assets and liabilities of the company. Where the **net current assets** and **fixed assets** of the foreign enterprise are primarily financed through borrowings in the local currency, the daily operations of the foreign company will not be fully dependent on parent company finance. In this instance, the foreign enterprise will be managed normally with the aim of providing a stream of dividends to the parent company and as such, use of the closing rate method is more appropriate. The **net investment** in a foreign enterprise owned by the parent company represents its equity stake. The closing rate is more likely to help achieve the objective of translation; namely to reflect the financial results and relationships, as measured in the foreign currency financial statements prior to translation.

8077
SSAP 20 (20) **Equity investments** in foreign enterprises normally take the form of:
  – share purchases;
  – long-term loans; and
  – inter-company deferred trading balances (¶8176).

Translation process

8080
SSAP 20 (17)

	Treatment
Profit and loss account	The values in P&L of the foreign entity should be translated at the closing rate for the accounting period.
Balance sheet	The assets and liabilities in the balance sheet of a foreign enterprise should be translated into the reporting currency of the parent company, using the closing rate of exchange ruling at the balance sheet date.
Exchange rate differences	Can arise under the closing rate, if the exchange rate used for translating the balance sheet differs from the rate in force at the previous balance sheet date or at the date of any future capital injection or reduction. Exchange rate gains or losses are taken to reserves.

8082 In the following example, the profit and loss account items of Company B are translated into the currency of the parent company. A similar process is adopted for the assets and liabilities in the balance sheet. A **reconciliation** between the Parent Company and the consolidated profit and loss accounts is also included.

EXAMPLE **Closing rate method – translation process**

Company A purchased 100% of the share capital of Company B, a US subsidiary on 30 September 20X3, when the exchange rate was £ = $1.48. The net assets of Company B on this date were £87,330 and Company A paid £117,112 including goodwill of £29,782. Company A used the **closing rate** method for the balance sheet, with the average exchange rate being used for the translation of the profit and loss account.
During 20X3, the **average exchange rate** was £1 = $1.50, whilst the closing rate was £1 = $1.47 at the end of 20X2 and £1 = $1.52 at the end of 20X3. Goodwill will be amortised over a period of 15 years, with a full year's charge in the year of acquisition.

Profit and loss account 20X3

	A	B	@ $1.50	Total
	£	$	B in £	£
Turnover	845,313	355,750	237,167	1,082,480
Cost of sales	557,000	200,800	133,867	690,867
Gross profit	**288,313**	**154,950**	**103,300**	**391,613**
Overheads	202,800	92,400	61,600	266,707
Profit before tax	**85,513**	**62,550**	**41,700**	**124,906**
Taxation	45,000	21,700	14,467	59,467
Profit after tax	**40,513**	**40,850**	**27,233**	**65,289**
Dividends	25,000	4,000	2,667	27,667
Retained profit	**15,363**	**36,850**	**24,566**	**37,622**
Profit b/f	244,152	65,243	43,495	-
Profit c/f	**259,515**	**102,093**	**68,061**	-

MEMO POINTS   1. Total overheads include goodwill amortisation of £2,307.
2. The total column comprises Company A plus Company B translated at the average rate (including goodwill of £2,307).

Balance sheet 20X3

	A	B	B @ $1.47	Total
	£	&	£	£
Tangible fixed assets	348,241	136,000	92,517	440,758
Investments	87,330			-
Goodwill				25,168
	435,571	**136,000**	**92,517**	**465,926**
Current assets	167,694	70,623	48,042	215,736
Current liabilities	116,050	43,760	29,768	145,818
Net current assets	**51,644**	**26,863**	**18,274**	**69,918**
Long-term liabilities	27,700	15,770	10,727	38,427
	459,515	**147,093**	**100,064**	**497,417**
Share capital	200,000	45,000	-	200,000
Profit and loss account	259,515	102,093	-	297,417
	459,515	**147,093**	-	**497,417**

MEMO POINTS   1. The investment in Company B is replaced by the goodwill arising in consolidation.
2. The share capital is that of Company A.
3. The goodwill on consolidation is £34,615/15 years = £2,307 p.a (x 2 yrs. = £4,614)
A higher goodwill charge was taken in years 1 & 2. £29,782 – £2,307 × 2 = £25,168).
Under FRS 10 "Goodwill and intangible assets" purchased goodwill must be capitalised.

Reconciliation – Calculation of consolidated profit and loss account
1. The balance b/fwd. at beginning of 20X3.

	£	£
A Ltd. from profit & loss account		244,152
B Ltd – the increase in profit/loss reserve from acquisition to beginning of 2011		
Beginning of 20X3 – Profit & loss $65,243/ £1 = $1.47	44,382	
On acquisition of 30 September 20X3 – Net assets of £87,330 less share capital £45,000 = £42,330/ $1.48 =	28,601	
		15,781
B Ltd – The change in shares from acquisition to the beginning of 20X4 = $45,000/ 1.52 = £29,605 – $45,000/1.48 = £30,405		(800)
Goodwill amortisation		(2,307)
		256,826

2. Movements during 20X3

	£
A Ltd – retained profit from profit/loss account	15,363
B Ltd – Retained profit of $36,850 translated at Average rate of $1.50	24,566
Goodwill amortisation	(2,307)
Exchange differences on translated **retained profit** at the year end rate of $1.47 in the balance sheet & $1.50 in the Profit and loss account. $36,850/$1.50/47 = £25,068-£24,566	502
Exchange differences on translation of **opening net assets** for B Ltd at the year end rate of $1.47 in 20X2 & $1.52 for the previous year $110,242/ 1.47 – $110,242/ 1.52	2,467

Opening net assets derived for B Ltd as follows:

– Closing net assets	$147,093
– Less retained profit 20X3	($36,850)
	$110,243
Balance sheet – profit and loss account 20X3	**297,417**

8084 A criticism of the closing rate method is that where it is only applied to some assets this leads to a mixture of items stated at historical rate and others at the closing rate.

---

b. Average rate method

8086
SSAP 20 (17)

SSAP 20 recognises that the use of the average rate may more fairly reflect the profit and losses, of a foreign entity, than the closing rate as they arise throughout an accounting period. It therefore permits the use of this method as an **alternative to the closing rate**, for the translation of profit and loss account items. If the subsidiary's profit and loss account is translated at an average rate, this should be determined over the accounting period of the individual company and not the group.

The average rate method can also be used by **individual companies** with high volumes of foreign currency transactions during the year.

Calculating the average rate

8088
SSAP 20 (18)

There is no one particular method of calculating the average rate as this will vary from group to group, and between individual companies within a group. For instance, the average rate could be **calculated weekly, monthly or quarterly**. If monthly, the rate could be the closing rate on either the last day or the middle day of each month. A system of weights could also be applied.

Whichever method is applied it should be used consistently.

The **average rate is** in practice **determined by**:
– the nature and size of a company's accounting systems;
– the materiality of the transactions;

– the period to which the rate should apply;
– the volume of transactions; and
– the frequency of transactions.

Exchange gains or losses

Where the average rate is used for profit and loss account items any differences between the **average rate** and the **closing rate** should be accounted for in reserves.   **8092**

If exchange differences arising from the re-translation of a company's net investment in its foreign enterprise, were included in the profit and loss account, the results from the trading operations, as shown in the local currency financial statements would be distorted. Any such **differences may arise from** factors unrelated to the trading performance of the foreign enterprise and, therefore, it would not be prudent to regard them as profits or losses.   SSAP 20 (19)

Translation differences arising on the re-translation of the opening net investment in a foreign enterprise should therefore be processed directly through reserves.

c. Temporal method

Use of the temporal method is recommended in the situations outlined in ¶8070.   **8094**

Under the temporal method, foreign currency transactions are translated at the exchange rate ruling on the transaction date (historical or contract rate). The **mechanics of the temporal method** are similar to the procedures adopted, in the preparation of individual company financial statements. The **problem** is that applying this method requires detailed additional record keeping and it is more complicated to use than the closing rate method.

Under the temporal method, all the transactions and balances of the foreign enterprise are accounted for, as if they had been entered into by the investing company in its own currency.   **8096**

Any **exchange rate gain or loss** is taken to the profit and loss account. This contrasts with the closing rate or net investment method where exchange rate differences are taken to reserves.

Application

Application of the temporal method **may be more appropriate**, where the activities of a foreign enterprise are closely linked with those of the investing company and it is more dependent upon the economic environment of that entity than its own reporting currency.   **8100**   SSAP 20 (22)

The **factors that should be considered** in adopting the temporal method include determining: **8102**
a. The currency in which the majority of trading transactions are denominated, such as the invoicing and payment of expenses, or whether the transactions are predominately based in the currency of the investing company;
b. The principal currency to which the financial structure of the foreign entity is exposed;
c. The extent to which the cash flows of the enterprise have a direct impact upon those of the investing company, such as the frequency of cash movements between the group companies or just periodic remittances such as dividends; and
d. The extent to which the operations of the foreign entity directly depend upon the investing company; namely, is the management locally or head office based.

The **temporal method can be used where** the overseas entity: **8104**
– acts as a selling agency receiving stocks from and remitting the proceeds to the investing company;   SSAP 20 (24)

– produces raw materials, parts or sub-assemblies for shipment to the investing company for inclusion in its own products; or
– is located overseas for tax, exchange control or other reasons that support the raising of finance for other companies in the group.

Translation process

8106

Classification	Treatment
Non-monetary items (stock, fixed assets)	Initially measured at historical cost, translated at the rate ruling on the transaction date and not re-translated at the balance sheet date.
Monetary items (debtors, creditors, loans)	Both short and long-term are translated using the closing rate at the balance sheet date.
Profit and loss account items (sales, expenses)	Translated at the historic rate. An average rate may also be used except for depreciation and stock. 1.Depreciation should be translated at same rate as for fixed assets. 2. Dividends proposed are translated at the closing rate and dividends paid at the payment date.
Exchange gains and losses on the net monetary assets or liabilities	Should be taken to profit and loss account for the year from operating activities.

This example follows on from the one used for the closing rate method with the following **additional assumptions**. All fixed assets where acquired when the exchange rate was £1 = €1.45. Depreciation totals 40% of the overheads excluding goodwill amortisation and opening and closing stocks were purchased when the exchange rates were €1.49 and €1.52 respectively.

EXAMPLE   **Profit and loss account**

	A		B	Ex. Rate	B		Total
	£	£			£	£	£
Turnover		845,313	355,750	1.5		237,167	1,082,480
Opening stock	98,650		16,500	1.49	11,073		
Purchases	547,500		200,000	1.5	133,333		
Closing stock	(89,150)		(15,700)	1.5	(10,466)		
Cost of sales		(557,000)	(200,800)			(133,940)	690,940
Gross profit		**288,313**	**154,950**			**103,227**	**391,540**
Depreciation		(81,120)					(81,120)
Goodwill amortisation		(2307)					(2,307)
Other overheads		(121,680)	(92,400)	1.5		(61,600)	(183,280)
Profit before tax		**83,206**	**62,550**			**41,627**	**124,833**
Taxation		(45,150)	(21,700)	1.5		(14,467)	(59,617)
Profit after tax		**38,056**	**40,850**			**27,160**	**65,216**
Dividends		(25,000)	(4,000)	1.5		(2,667)	(27,667)
Retained profit		**13,056**	**36,850**			**24,493**	**37,549**

Balance sheet

	A	B	Ex. Rate	B	Total
	£	euro	euro/£.	£	£
Tangible fixed assets	348,241	136,000	1.45	93,793	442,034
Investments	87,330				-
Goodwill					25,168
	435,571	136,000		93,793	467,202
Stocks	89,150	15,700	1.52	10,329	99,479
Other current assets	78,544	54,923	1.52	36,133	114,677
Current liabilities	(116,050)	(43,760)	1.52	(28,789)	(147,471)
Net current assets	51,644	26,863		15,041	66,685
Long-term liabilities	(27,700)	(15,770)	1.52	(10,375)	(38,075)
	459,515	147,093		4,666	495,812
Share capital	200,000	45,000			200,000
Profit and loss account	259,515	102,093			295,812
	459,515	147,093			495,812

| MEMO POINTS | Exchange rate differences on monetary assets and liabilities taken to consolidated profit and loss account.

---

d. Change of method

A company can **in certain circumstances** change the method used for translating the finan-   **8108**
cial statements of a foreign enterprise, from the temporal to the closing rate and vice-versa.
Circumstances where this might happen, include **changes to the operational or financial
relationships** that exist between a parent and its foreign subsidiary, that render the initial
basis inappropriate. A change of method does not constitute a change in accounting policy.
No guidance is given in SSAP 20 on this topic but the following is regarded as an appropriate
accounting treatment.

Closing rate to the temporal method

This practice might be adopted where the operations of the foreign subsidiary have become   **8110**
significantly dependent on the parents reporting currency. The translated values for non-
monetary assets at the end of the prior year end, form the accounting basis for those assets
in the period of change and subsequent periods.

There is no requirement to restate non-monetary assets at rates applicable when those assets
were originally acquired by the foreign enterprise. Any **cumulative exchange adjustments**
for prior periods already taken to reserves, remain there and are not reflected in the profit
and loss account in the period of change.

---

2. Foreign enterprises

The accounting treatment for foreign currency transactions involving foreign branches,   **8114**
associates and joint ventures are outlined in this section.

Foreign branches

A foreign branch is either a legally constituted enterprise located overseas or a group of   **8116**
assets and liabilities which are accounted for in foreign currencies. This **broad definition**   SSAP 20 (37)
allows, a company owning for instance, a fleet of aircraft or ships to account for each as a
separate branch.

Where a UK company undertakes foreign operations through the legal form of an overseas
branch, **the translation method adopted** will either be the closing rate or temporal method,

depending on the type of operation or activities involved; each branch should be assessed individually.

8118
SSAP 20 (25)

The **closing rate method should be used** where the foreign branch operates as a separate business complete with local finance, or as the owner of international assets that earn revenues in a foreign currency and are financed by **borrowings in the same currency**. This rule applies to both the financial statements of individual companies as well as to consolidated financial statements.

> EXAMPLE A **branch** operating in Florida has borrowed dollars to finance the construction of a marina on the Florida coastline, generating revenues and expenses in dollars. In this instance the branch clearly operates as a separate distinct business complete with local finance. The **net investment** in the US branch can be accounted for through a Head Office Account, with the closing rate method used to translate transactions. Any **exchange differences** should be taken to reserves.

8120

The **temporal method should be used** when the foreign branch simply operates as an extension of the company's trade and its cash flows directly impact on the parent company's cash flows. If in the above example, the finance for the construction of the marina was raised in sterling, it could be argued that the project is merely an extension of the company's trade, in which case the temporal method would be more suitable.

8122

Translation process The translation process is essentially the same irrespective of the translation method adopted and involves **the following stages**:
1. The branch trial balance should be translated into sterling using the closing rate or temporal method as appropriate.
2. Include any year end adjustments for depreciation, closing stocks, accruals in the foreign currency concerned and then translate values into sterling using the translation method selected.
3. Treat the difference on the branch sterling trial balance as the profit and loss on exchange.
4. The profit or loss on exchange is shown as follows:
– as a movement on reserves if the closing rate used (see example below); or
– in the profit and loss account if the temporal method is used.
5. Combine the sterling branch results with other group companies in the consolidation process.

Foreign associates and joint ventures

8124

The provisions in the accounting standard covering consolidated statements cover the incorporation of the results of overseas associates and joint ventures, through the adoption of the closing rate method. However, where the investing company does not exercise **significant influence** (¶7300) over an associate or joint venture, use of the temporal method may be more appropriate.

3. Treatment of exchange gains or losses

8130

There are a number of other important accounting issues related to the treatment of exchange gains or losses, generated by foreign currency transactions for both **individual companies** and in the **consolidation process**. The topics covered include the accounting treatment of foreign currency exchange gains or losses arising from:
– taxation;
– dividends;
– intra-group trading;
– intra-group loans;
– goodwill arising on translation; and
– the issue of hyperinflation.

Taxation

The gains or losses arising on the translation of financial statements of overseas subsidiaries **8132** and associates do not create timing differences for tax purposes. However, gains or losses arising on translation of an entity's overseas assets and liabilities could give rise to timing differences. In addition, exchange gains arising on foreign currency borrowings used by a company to finance or hedge its investment in a foreign enterprise, may be taxable. Determining whether exchange gains or losses are taxable as they arise for accounting purposes or are taxable when the gain or loss is crystalised at a later date, will depend on the election made under the appropriate tax legislation.

The tax rules regarding treatment of exchange gains or losses are highly complex and **specialist tax advice** should be sought.

The **circumstances where** a **tax charge** could arise are where:

a. a matching election for tax purposes is not made;

b. the foreign investment and borrowings are located in different companies in a group, and where a matching election is not available; or

c. the offset restriction applies to a matching election under which exchange gains or losses should be reported in the profit and loss account.

Exchange gains and losses should be accounted for by using either the method of matching assets with liabilities or by deferring the recognition of unrealised exchange gains.

> ⌐MEMO POINTS⌐ **Special taxation rules** that apply to currency contracts are beyond the scope of this book.

Matching election The matching rules allow a company, in certain circumstances, to **8136** match by election a liability to particular types of asset. When a matching election is made, exchange gains and losses on the liability or currency contract are held over and matched with the asset when it is disposed of. It is at this point, the **aggregate exchange rate gain or loss** is brought into the accounts as a chargeable gain or loss. A matching election is voluntary and may only be made where the foreign investment and the related currency borrowings are held with the same company.

The **currency in which a given liability is denominated** need not be the same currency as that of the underlying asset; although it much be such that it could reasonably be expected to eliminate the currency risk of holding the asset. For instance, many Caribbean countries peg their currencies to the US dollar, so an asset purchased with Barbadian dollars for example, could be matched to a US dollar loan.

The **matching rules permit** a company to eliminate a mismatch that might occur when a **8138** company hedges its balance sheet transaction exposure. Where an election for matching is not permitted or made, then the resulting gains and losses should be reported in the STRGL.

⌐EXAMPLE⌐ **Matching election**

Beta Ltd, a UK company, raised a $500,000 in June 20X3 to finance the purchase of a controlling stake in a US company. The financial year end is August, UK tax rates are 21% and the relevant exchange rates are:
– August 20X3 £1 = $1.50
– August 20X2 £1 = $1.60

What are the tax consequences of making or not making a matching election, given that the company adopts the **offset procedure** under SSAP 20 taking any exchange difference on the $ borrowing to reserves?
– August 20X3 – $500,000/ 1.5 = £333,333
– August 20X2 – $500,000/ 1.6 = £312,500

Exchange gain on loan   **£20,833**

Matching election requested
If the company makes a matching election there will be no tax consequences, as the sterling value of the liability (loan) at the year end matches fully the sterling value of the asset. The exchange gain of £20,833 matches the exchange loss on the asset taken to reserves.

No matching election requested
The company will have the following tax liability.
£20,833 x 21% = £4,375
£20,833 – £4,375 = £16,458 represents the net exchange gain on the borrowing against the exchange loss of £20,833 carried in reserves. Disclosure is required of both the exchange gain and related tax charge.

8139   **Reserves**   The **tax effects of an exchange gain or loss** already posted to reserves under the offset procedure should continue to be recognised in reserves, in accordance with UITF 19, and SSAP 20, and be reported in the STRGL.

UITF 19 "Tax on gains and losses on foreign currency borrowings that hedge an investment in a foreign enterprise", states that where exchange differences on foreign currency borrowings have been used to finance, or provide a hedge against equity investments in foreign enterprises, these should be taken to reserves and reported in the STRGL, as should the **associated tax charges or credits**. This treatment is in accordance with SSAP 20 and FRS 3 "Reporting financial performance".

The **restriction on the amount** of the gains or losses arising on the borrowings that should be dealt with in the STRGL, should, apply after taking account of tax charges or credits attributable to the borrowings. Consideration should also be given to the total cash, the related investments are expected to generate and the exposure created by the borrowings in after-tax terms.

8140   **Deferral**   In recognition of cash flow difficulties that can arise by taxing unrealised gains, companies can defer (for tax purposes) the **recognition of unrealised exchange gains** on long-term capital assets and liabilities; this concession does not extent to currency contracts.

A deferred gain is treated as being realised when the company ceases to hold the asset or carry the liability.

Multi-currency share capital

8156   A UK company can issue shares in a currency other than sterling. The accounting treatment and reporting requirements for foreign currency share capital are not covered in SSAP 20. Multi-currency share capital can either be:
– recorded initially at the historical rate when issued; or
– the shares could be re-translated at the end of each financial year using the closing rate, with any exchange differences taken to reserves.

Inter-company dividends

8160   The accounting treatment of dividends will depend on whether the temporal or closing rate method of translation is used. An **exchange rate gain or loss** will arise if the rate of exchange changes between the date the dividend is declared and the date paid, which is reported in the parent's profit and loss account as an inter-company transaction.

8162   Under the **temporal method** the dividend payment should be translated at the exchange rate ruling on the date the dividend is declared; therefore an exchange rate difference will not arise. The payment and receipt of the dividend will be eliminated on consolidation.

8163   Under the **closing rate method** it is usual that the dividend, declared and accounted for by the foreign subsidiary, will be translated at the closing rate or at an average rate. In the **consolidated accounts**, an exchange rate difference will be generated where the rate used to account for the dividend in the overseas subsidiaries, differs from the rate used to translate and record the dividend in the parent's profit and loss account.

8166   **Dividend declared but still outstanding at year end**   Where a dividend has been declared but is still outstanding at the end of the financial year, the following accounting treatment is necessary.

For the **purposes of consolidation**, the dividend payable in the subsidiary's profit and loss account, will be translated at the exchange rate prevailing on the transaction date, with the year end debtor posted at the closing rate. Any resulting exchange difference should be taken to reserves using the closing rate method.

The parent company should account for the **dividend receivable** at the closing rate in both the profit and loss account and in the balance sheet. The inter-company accounts will cancel each other out on consolidation. However, the dividends will not cancel each other out in the consolidated profit and loss account with the difference accounted for as an exchange loss.

Intra-group trading

Transactions between group companies   Exchange rate differences will arise on transactions between group companies located in different countries, which will not be eliminated on consolidation. Where transactions are recorded in the local currency of the subsidiary concerned, the exchange difference should be reported in the profit and loss account of the enterprise, in the same way as transactions with third parties.

8170
SSAP 20 (12)

The same **accounting principle** applies to an unsettled inter-company account comprising non-trading transactions, such as where the parent finances the purchase of fixed assets by a foreign subsidiary via the mechanism of the inter-company account.

8172

On **consolidation**, the net exchange rate gain or loss will have been reflected in the group cash flow, and should be included in the consolidated accounts to reflect the currency risk attached to transactions with overseas companies, albeit group companies. This is illustrated in the example below. Where the **same exchange rate is used by both companies**, one recording a gain and the other a loss, any exchange rate differences will cancel each other out on consolidation.

EXAMPLE   A **UK Company** with a wholly-owned subsidiary in Poland, who purchased plant and raw materials from the UK parent, had the following transactions during the year. The financial year end is 30 November 20X3

Polish subsidiary

Transaction 1
Purchased plant at £275,000 on 31 July 20X3   £1 = Zlty 5.0
Paid for plant – 30 September 20X3   £1 = Zlty 5.05

Transaction 2
Purchased raw materials at £400,000 – 20 Oct. 20X3   £1 = Ztly 5.20
Balance of £400,000 30 November 20X3   £1 = Ztly 5.15
Average rate for the year   £1 = Ztly 5.10

The **exchange rate** differences will be recorded in the **profit and loss account** of the Polish subsidiary for the year ending 20X3.

Transaction 1	Zlty
Plant costing £275,000 @ 5.0	1,375,000
Paid for plant @ 5.05	1,388,750
Exchange loss	**(13,750)**

Transaction 2	
Raw materials at £400,000 @ 5.20	2,080,000
Outstanding £400,000 at the year end @ 5.15	2,060,000
Exchange gain	**20,000**

Accounting treatment

The net gain recorded in the profit and loss account was 6,250 zloty. The inter-company creditor of Zl.2,060,000 in the Polish subsidiary's balance sheet, will be translated into sterling at the closing rate (£400,000). The net exchange gain of Zloty 6,250 should be translated at the average rate or

> the closing rate. The sterling exchange gains will not be eliminated on consolidation and will be reported as part of the consolidated results of the group.

8174 **Transfer of assets** The **general rule** is **intra-group profits** arising on the transfer of assets between group companies should be eliminated in full on consolidation, as this does not represent profit generated by the group, where the assets are still held by the company at the balance sheet date.

SSAP 20 does not offer any guidance on the exchange rate to be used in eliminating profit, although the average rate for translating the results of foreign operations under the net investment/closing rate method would be appropriate.

Long-term sterling loans and deferred trading balances

8176 A parent company can decide to finance an overseas entity through equity or monetary items such as long-term loans and deferred trading balances. The **choice of financing** will depend on a number of factors including taxation.

8178 **Equity finance** Where financing is intended to be permanent, any such loans or deferred
SSAP 20 (20) trading balances should be treated as part of the investing company's net investment in the foreign enterprise. Any **exchange rate differences** arising on such loans and inter-company balances should be dealt with as an adjustment to reserves.

8179 The inclusion of long-term loans and deferred trading balances as part of the net investment in an overseas subsidiary is only permitted, when the parent company considers the investment to be as permanent as there is no foreseeable intention to repay such balances. **Short-term loans** that are continuously rolled over may also be regarded as permanent.

8180 The same principle also applies to inter-company balances generated through **normal trading transactions**, where settlement in cash is not envisaged for some considerable time. In these situations the trading balances should be treated as part of the equity stake in the overseas enterprise.

8182 **Monetary items** There are a number of accounting implications where a parent company provides loans to a foreign subsidiary or vice versa. The **accounting treatment** should reflect the substance of the loan.

Intra-group loans made by the parent company to an overseas group company and denominated in the parent company's functional currency, should initially be recorded by the borrower at the exchange rate ruling on the transaction date. At the balance sheet date thereafter, until it is repaid, the loan should be re-translated into sterling at the closing rate with any exchange differences reported in the consolidated profit and loss account.

8184 On consolidation, the **intra-group loan accounts** will cancel each other out, whilst the exchange difference accounted for in the borrowers profit and loss account, will show through in the consolidated profit and loss account (or reserves if deemed an equity stake).

EXAMPLE Monetary item
Parent company's sterling loan to an overseas subsidiary.

A UK parent company has an outstanding loan of £650,000 with a Swedish subsidiary as at 31 December 2011 The relevant exchange rates are:
Opening rate Jan. 20X3 £1 = Kr 11
Closing rate Dec. 20X2 £1 = Kr 10
In the **financial statements** of both the parent and the subsidiary, the following exchange differences arise if the closing rate is used (balance sheet date).

Parent company
There is **no exchange rate difference** as the loan balance is denominated in sterling.

Swedish subsidiary

Jan. 20X3 – Loan balance of £650,000 x 11 Kr = Kr 7,150,000
Dec. 20X3 – Loan balance of £650,000 x 10 Kr = Kr 6,500,000

Exchange gain   **Kr 650,000**

Exchange gain translated at the closing rate @ 10 Kr = £65,000.

Accounting treatment.
Debit: Inter-group loan a/c   Kr 650,000
Credit: Profit and loss account   Kr 650,000

The **rational** for taking the exchange rate gain to the profit and loss account is that the loan was provided in the reporting currency of the parent company, whilst the exchange rate risk was borne by the subsidiary company.
On **consolidation**, the exchange gain in the subsidiary profit and loss account will be translated into sterling at the closing rate, and should be included in the consolidated profit and loss account. Where the loan is regarded as **long-term** and part of the **equity stake** in the foreign enterprise, the exchange gain should instead be taken to the reserves in the consolidated financial statements. There will be a corresponding exchange rate loss included in reserves that will arise from the re-translation of the net assets of the Swedish subsidiary; there is no impact on group cash flows.

Long-term loan by parent company to a foreign subsidiary   The accounting treatment   **8186**
for a long-term loan by a parent company to a foreign subsidiary in its local currency, is different from that of a sterling loan from the parent company to the foreign subsidiary. In the **consolidated financial statements**, the long-term loan will form part of the net investment in the foreign subsidiary and the related exchange gains or losses will be accounted for in reserves using the closing rate method.

In the **parent company's financial statements**, the following accounting treatment is requi-   **8188**
red for long-term loans to a foreign subsidiary:
a. If the long-term loan is accounted for in the financial statements of the parent company as a **monetary item**, any exchange differences should be charged to the profit and loss account.
b. Where the long-term loan can be considered a **permanent investment on consolidation** it should not be re-translated in the parent company's books, but retained at the historical rate of exchange. As such no exchange differences arise so reflecting the substance of the loan.
c. Where the long-term loan is **financed by foreign borrowings** by the parent company, the loan should be re-translated to offset currency differences.

Loans from foreign subsidiaries   Where a parent company receives a currency loan from   **8190**
its foreign subsidiary that it converted into sterling, the accounting treatment of foreign exchange differences in the consolidated financial statements will reflect the treatment in the parent company's financial statements.

These types of loan are sometimes regarded as **hedging transactions** as they reduce the net   **8191**
foreign currency investment in the foreign subsidiary. Where the loan is accounted for in   SSAP 20 (51)
the parent's financial statements, as a hedge against the equity investment under the SSAP 20 offset rules (see ¶8226), any exchange differences on the borrowings should be accounted for in reserves. This will offset any exchange differences on the investment being hedged. A similar treatment applies to the consolidated accounts.

MEMO POINTS   The issue of loan repayments is covered in ¶8240.

Goodwill on consolidation

Goodwill may arise on consolidation where a company **acquires the equity share capital**   **8194**
of an overseas subsidiary. If the foreign investment is accounted for using the closing rate method, the issue is whether the goodwill calculated at acquisition should be re-translated at the end of each financial year.

8196   Following the publication of FRS 10 "Goodwill and intangible assets", goodwill should be **capitalised as an intangible asset** and amortised through the profit and loss account over its useful economic life. FRS 11 "Impairment of fixed assets and goodwill" requires capitalised goodwill to be attributed to income generating units in order to facilitate annual impairment reviews. The combination of FRS 10 and FRS 11 support the notion that goodwill should be regarded as part of the net assets in the foreign investment.

8198   Where goodwill arising on consolidation is **not translated but regarded as a currency asset**, any exchange differences arising on foreign currency borrowings, used to either finance or provide a hedge against an investment in a foreign subsidiary would be taken to the profit and loss account. However, **exchange differences** on the currency borrowings are available for offset against the exchange difference arising on re-translated goodwill, which is added to the opening net investment and taken to consolidated reserves.

EXAMPLE **Neckerman Holdings – Financial Statements 30 June 20X3**

Accounting policies (extract)

16. Foreign exchange

Foreign currency assets and liabilities of Group companies are translated into sterling using the closing rate of exchange at the balance sheet date. The trading results of overseas subsidiaries and associated undertakings are translated at average rates of exchange ruling during the year, with any exchange rate differences taken to reserves.

The exchange difference arising on the **restatement of the opening net investment**, including goodwill, to overseas subsidiary and associated undertakings, and of matching foreign currency loans and foreign currency swap facilities, are dealt with as adjustments to other reserves. All other exchange differences are taken to the profit and loss account.

Notes to the financial statements

	Group £'000
25. Other reserves	
As at 30 June 20X2	(115,675)
Goodwill written off in year (note 34)	(18,100)
Goodwill of associates transferred to profit & loss	15,600
Exchange adjustments:	
– goodwill	4,300
– hedging arrangements	(7,350)
As at 30 June 20X3	**(121,225)**

34. Goodwill	Cost of goodwill eliminated £'000	Exchange Adjustment £'000	Total £'000
Eliminated to 30 June 20X2	239,600	11,235	250,835
Acquisitions during year			
– Associated undertakings	15,800		15,800
– Other businesses acquired	2,300		2,300
	18,100		18,100
Transferred to P & L a/c	(15,600)		(15,600)
Exchange adjustments		(4,300)	(4,300)
Eliminated to 30 June 20X3	**242,100**	**6,935**	**249,035**

For a more detailed treatment of goodwill in relation to intangible fixed assets see ¶1000.

Hyperinflation

8200
SSAP 20 (26)   The **historical cost** accounts of a foreign enterprises operating in a country suffering from high inflation, will probably be misleading when translated into the **local currency** of the parent company. In this instance, the local currency financial statements of the foreign enter-

prise should be adjusted prior to inflation, in order to reflect current price levels, as assets acquired in a foreign currency would be worth less in sterling terms, if the local currency has weakened against sterling.

SSAP 20 does not provide a definition of hyperinflation. The subject has since been addres-   **8202**
sed by UITF 9 "Accounting for operations in hyperinflationary economies", which **requires adjustments** to be made to financial statements in the following circumstances, where:
– the distortions resulting from hyperinflation effect the true and fair view of financial statements;
– the cumulative inflation rate is approximately 100% over a three-year period; and
– the investing company's operations in hyperinflationary economies are material.

Other factors that indicate hyperinflation, are where the general population prefers to main-   **8204**
tain its wealth in non-monetary assets or in a stable foreign currency and where interest rates, wages and general prices are linked to a price index.

The assessment of cumulative inflation rates should be determined following one of the **two**   UITF 9 (6)
alternative methods, suggested in UTF 9 as being consistent with SSAP 20 as follows:
a. adjust the local currency to reflect current price levels prior to the translation process for incorporation in the group accounts, taking net monetary gains and losses to the profit and loss account.
b. use of a third (stable) currency for measuring the results of the foreign operations.
Where the financial statements are **initially prepared in the local currency** they must be translated into the stable currency by use of the temporal method, before conversion to sterling for incorporation in the group accounts. In some Latin America economies, the dollar is the predominant business currency or "local currency".

SECTION 4

Foreign equity investments financed by foreign borrowings

Specific criteria apply to the treatment of foreign equity investments financed from foreign   **8220**
borrowings, in the financial statements of **individual companies** and **groups**. The subject of financing a foreign equity investment as a hedge against a particular currency risk is dealt with in section 4.

1. Individual company financial statements

The **rule that non-monetary items** (¶8020) must be carried at historical cost and not re-   **8224**
translated at the closing rate, does not apply where foreign equity investments are financed through foreign currency borrowings. In these circumstances, an individual company may record its foreign equity investments in the relevant foreign currencies and translate the carrying amounts at the end of each financial year at the closing rates of exchange.

Offset method

Exchange gains or losses on **equity investments** financed through foreign borrowings,   **8226**
should be taken to reserves (and not the profit or loss account), as should any exchange differences on the related foreign borrowings. This is often known as the "offset method".

The offset method is **generally applied to** individual investments or borrowings, except   **8228**
where an investment or a number of investments have been financed by a particular loan. This means that the offset method can also be applied where investments are managed on a pool basis and financed by a basket of different currency loans.

8230

SSAP 20 (51)

The **criteria that must be applied** for offset to apply to individual companies are principally the same as that to be applied to groups preparing consolidated financial statements.
1. Any exchange gains or losses in any accounting period, that arise on borrowings, may be **offset only to the extent** of the total exchange differences on the equity investments.
2. The foreign currency borrowings whose gains and losses are used in the offset process, should not exceed, in aggregate, the total net realisable value of the investments.
3. There must be **consistent application** of the accounting treatment adopted over time.

Only that part of total exchange gains or losses that are matched by the opposite movement in the value of the investment can be taken to reserves for offset purposes. Any excess gains or losses should be taken to the profit and loss account in the period concerned.

The examples below illustrate how exchange rate gains and losses on foreign currency investments and borrowings can be offset against each other and the treatment of any surpluses.

EXAMPLE   Exchange gain (loss) on equity investments

A UK company has prepared its financial statements to August 20X3. In March 20X4 the company raised a **dollar loan of $2m** to finance two equity investments; one in Italy costing €1million and one in Switzerland costing SFR 2,5million.

The relevant exchange rates are as follows:

March 20X4 £1 = US$1.50 = €1.60 = SFR 2.0
August 20X3 £1 = US$1.55 = €1.58 = SFR 2.2

	Exchange Difference £	P & L Account £	Reserves £
A. Exchange differences on investments.			
Italian company			
March 20X4 €1,000,000/ 1.60	625,000		
August 20X3 €1,000,000/ 1.58	632,911		
Exchange gain	7,911		
Swiss company			
March 20X4 SFR 2,500,000/2.0	1,250,000		
August 20X3 SFR 2,500,000/2.2	1,136,363		
Exchange loss	(113,637)		
Net exchange gain (loss) equity investments	(105,726)		(105,726)
B. Exchange difference on $borrowings			
March 20X4 $2m/£1.50	1,333,333		
August 20X3 $2m/ 1.55	1,290,032		
Exchange gain	43,301		43,301

The exchange rate gain of £43,301 on the dollar loan can be used to partially offset the exchange loss of £105,726 incurred on the foreign currency investments.
If there had been an exchange rate loss on the dollar loan this would have been taken to the profit and loss account.

EXAMPLE   If in the above example, the UK parent company suffered a net exchange loss on investments of £35,000, which was exceeded by the net exchange gains on the foreign currency borrowings of £43,301, the offset procedure would be applicable as follows:

	Total	Offset loss on Investments in reserves	Difference to P & L
Exchange gain on borrowings	£43,301	£35,000	£8,301

Consistency   A company should not change its accounting treatment simply to accommo-   **8234**
date movements in exchange rates, but should adopt a consistent policy as stipulated in FRS
18 "Accounting policies".

Where a company **uses the offset process** to match exchange losses on borrowings to gains
on the underlying investment, it should continue to adopt this policy in subsequent periods,
even if the opposite situation as regards movements on exchange rates should apply and
exchange gains realised on the currency loan. These gains should be taken to reserves and
not the profit or loss account.

Repayment of loan or sale of foreign equity investment

The **consistency principle** should be applied where a currency loan is repaid or the invest-   **8240**
ment in the foreign enterprise is sold. In both situations the offset procedure should be
applied up to the repayment or sale date.

For instance, a company adopting an accounting policy of matching in reserves, exchange
differences on borrowings with exchange differences on equity investments in reserves,
should continue this policy up to the date of sale or loan repayment. Where the "offset" is
limited, the balance should be taken to the profit and loss account.

Where the foreign enterprise is sold but the **loan remains outstanding**, the parent company   **8242**
must apply the offset procedure up to the date of sale; the loan ceases to be a hedge and
any **exchange gains or losses** arising thereafter should be accounted for in the profit and
loss account.

Valuation of a foreign equity investment

The **carrying value** of an investment (individual company's accounts) in a foreign equity   **8246**
investment is normally based on historical cost less any provisions (or recoverable amount
if impaired).

Alternatively, a foreign equity investment may be **carried at a valuation**, such as net asset
value or the directors' valuation based on an estimate of the market value or cost plus
retained post-acquisition profits, could be used. A valuation based on **net asset values** may
be appropriate where a subsidiary company was acquired a considerable time before or
was set up by the parent company.

Whichever **valuation policy is adopted** must be **applied consistently** from year to year. Any   **8248**
change in accounting policy must be justified on the grounds that it provides a more accu-   FRS 3 (62)
rate representation of the reporting entity's financial position.

Where the foreign equity investment is carried at a valuation, it will be necessary to separately account for the effects of exchange rate movements on the opening value of the investment and the effect of any revaluation of the foreign currency carrying value.

Currency borrowing restrictions

The **general rule** is that the sum borrowed should not exceed the total amount of cash that   **8254**
the business is expected to generate. SSAP 20 does not give guidance on how cash generation is to be measured or the relevant time period for making profits. In practice, it may be
difficult to calculate the cash generated by a particular foreign investment over time, given
the number of variables that must be factored into the estimate. A number of restrictions
apply.

For a more detailed review of impairment reviews and permanent diminutions in the value
of fixed asset investments see ¶1550.

Restrictions

Problems may occur when the borrowing is related to a foreign enterprise that is either   **8256**
unprofitable or earns negligible profits to meet the loan repayments. If this is the case, the
expected cash generation will be reflected in the **net realisable value (NRV)** of the invest-

ment as stated at the balance sheet date. Where the book value of the investment exceeds the NRV, the borrowing used for offset should be reduced accordingly.

Restrictions may also apply where a foreign investment is subject to exchange control restrictions that limit the finance repatriated for repayment of the initial borrowings.

---

2. Consolidated financial statements

8270   Group companies may finance investments in foreign entities through currency borrowings, or use these borrowings to provide a hedge against exchange risks associated with similar existing investments.

Any increase or decrease in the level of outstanding borrowings arising from exchange rate movements, will probably be covered by changes in the carrying amount of the net assets underpinning the net investment, which would be reflected in reserves. The group is therefore, protected against movements in the exchange rate, and as such it would not be prudent to record an accounting profit or loss when exchange rates fluctuate.

Offset method

8272
SSAP 20 (31)   Exchange differences on currency borrowings can be offset as a movement on **consolidated reserves**, against exchange differences that arise when the opening net investment in a foreign investment is re-translated for consolidation purposes. Although use of the offset method in the consolidation process is optional, certain criteria must still be met.

8274   **Criteria**   The offset criteria requirements are principally the same as those demanded for individual companies (¶8226), with an **additional requirement** that the relationship between the investing company and the foreign enterprise should justify the use of the **closing rate method** for the purpose of consolidation.

A company could meet the criteria for offset but still opt not to adopt it, as it must be consistently applied in subsequent years. This may mean forsaking the opportunity to take any larger exchange gains that may arise to the profit and loss account.

8276   **Consolidation process**   Despite the similar criteria that apply to the use of the offset method in both individual company financial statements and on consolidation, it will usually be necessary to reverse the entries made at the entity level and recalculate the adjustments on a consolidation basis. This process is required at the **entity level** because:

a. The **offset applies to** all foreign equity investments, whereas on consolidation, foreign enterprises accounted for under the temporal method, are excluded. Exchange differences on foreign borrowings taken to reserves in the individual company financial statements should be reversed and recalculated for the consolidated results for the year.

b. The **exchange difference arising each year** on the carrying value of the investment translated at the closing rate is used for offset purposes, whereas on consolidation the exchange difference on retranslation of the opening investment is used.

Where the **offset procedure is not applied** the following process should be adopted:
– any exchange differences on the net equity investment should be taken to reserves; whilst
– those generated by the borrowings used to finance the investment are taken to the profit and loss account.

8278   **Restrictions**   The offset rules **cannot be applied** to a foreign investment accounted for under the **temporal method** on consolidation, where all exchange gains or losses on foreign borrowings must be taken to the profit and loss account. Even where the offset procedure does apply there are still restrictions.

Exchange rate gains on borrowings can only partially be taken to reserves, to offset any exchange losses on foreign equity investments, with the balance taken to the profit and loss account as it is regarded as speculative.

Exception   The **entries for individual companies** should be reversed on consolidation   **8280**
where the foreign entity takes a legal form other than that a subsidiary or an associate. In
these instances, the same **offset procedure** applied in the individual company financial
statements may be used in the consolidated accounts. This rationale is that a genuine
currency hedge at the entity level does not cease to exist at the consolidated level.

SECTION 5

Hedging foreign currency transactions

Hedging is a generic term given to a range of **financial instruments** used by companies to   **8300**
reduce the risks associated with movements in currency exchange rates. In the context of
foreign exchange transactions, the most common hedging instruments (also known as
"derivative products") are forward exchange contracts and currency options.

The **purpose of hedging** is to reduce or eliminate some of the risk which is inherent in most   **8302**
financial instruments. The issue of currency risk, as well as market (or price) risk and interest
rate risk are covered in the chapter on financial derivatives (¶3000).

The **benefit of hedging** must be offset against the cost of holding the financial instrument.   **8304**
When a company has identified a position that is exposed to risk or loss as a result of
possible adverse price changes in foreign exchange markets, it can use a "hedge" to mitigate
the risk of loss of holding particular currencies. A hedge is arranged by taking a second
position that is exposed to a price risk, that moves inversely and is highly co-related with the
effects of price risks attached to an existing position.

A **hedge instrument can be designed** to match a particular exposure (i.e. price risk) or form   **8306**
part of a general portfolio of financial instruments, designed to protect a company's position
in the foreign exchange markets. It is not currently a requirement that specific hedge instruments be matched with individual items being hedged, although as different assets and
liabilities have different exposures to potential gains or losses, the item constituting a group
of financial instruments must be similar in content to the particular risk component being
insured.

1. Determination of spot and forward exchange rates

A currency exchange rate is determined by the number of units of one currency that may   **8310**
be purchased or sold for one unit of another currency. **Movements in exchange rates** reflect
the relative strength of currencies. For example, if the \$/£ exchange rate moves from
US\$1.56/£ to US\$1.63/£, sterling will have strengthened against the dollar, as each pound will
now buy more dollars. Exchange rates are quoted "**spot**" and "**forward**", and at offer and
bid prices.

Definitions	
"Spot rate"	The exchange rate for immediate delivery
"Forward rate"	The exchange rate quoted today for delivery at some agreed future date. It should be noted that on any one given day there will be several forward rates quoted by a bank – each for a different future transaction date. These rates will change from day to day and sometimes during the course of a single day.
"Offer price"	The price at which the "market-maker" offers the currency for sale
"Bid price"	The price at which the "market-maker" offers to purchase the currency

> EXAMPLE **Spot rates**
> The **$/£ spot rate** may be quoted as follows:
> 1.475 – 1.485.
>
> The lower figure represents the "**offer price**" and the higher figure the "**bid price**"
> **Company A** sells $147,500 to the bank at the current offer rate of $1.475 = $1.485, thus receiving
> £99,327 from the bank.
> · **Company B** then decides to buy the same amount of dollars from the bank at their offer price of
> $1.485 to £1. The sum of £100,000 is paid by B to the bank.
> The **difference** represents the bank's profit [£100,000 – £99,327 = £673] resulting from the spread
> in rates between the bid and offer price.

The spread between the offer and bid prices reflects the stability of the market at the time of the transaction and the depth of the market, as determined by the volume of transactions. **When currency movements are volatile**, the spread between the bid and offer prices will be wider than when exchange rates are more stable.

---

2. Forward exchange contracts

8312   A forward exchange contract is a **form of legal agreement** under which a company agrees to buy or sell an agreed sum of foreign currency at a specific rate of exchange, for delivery and settlement at a specified future date. Forward exchange contracts are normally obtained from one of the big commercial banks and are available in all major currencies.

Whilst some dealers speculate in currency markets using forward contracts, in the commercial and industrial world, the need to take out a forward exchange contract normally arises, because there is a **commercial or trading contract** anticipated by a company, that will be denominated in a currency other than that in which the company normally operates.

A typical situation in which a company [the contractor] might consider taking out a forward exchange contract is illustrated below.

> EXAMPLE Company X agreed on 15 October 20X3, to purchase some new plant and equipment
> from the USA at a fixed price of $1,600,000 payable on 1 January 20X4. The company does not
> normally trade in US dollars and so will have to buy dollars from the bank to settle the transaction.
> In recent months the exchange rate has moved from between $1.575 and $1.63 to £1. The current
> exchange rate is $1.62: £1. Whilst the pound is currently quite strong, Company X does not want
> to be exposed to the potential risk of the exchange rate falling to the previous level again so takes
> out a forward contract to buy $1,600,000 on 1 January 20X4 at a forward rate (15.10) of £1.60 to
> £1.
> Company X has therefore effectively guaranteed the sterling price of the new plant and equipment
> at £1,000.000 and has eliminated the risk that in sterling terms the price might go up should the
> pound weaken against the dollar.

8314   The **key features** of a forward exchange contract are that:
– the exchange (contract) rate is agreed when the contract is arranged;
– the currencies are exchanged in the future on a specified date at the rate agreed today; and
– the contract must be completed.

8315   Forward exchange contracts are **utilised principally by companies** wishing to protect existing currency positions against exchange losses (or gains) on both existing and anticipated transactions. Forward foreign exchange contracts are traded on an **over the counter market (OTC)**, which can be defined as a purchase of securities from, or sale of securities to, a dealer other than those on a recognised stock exchange.

8316   Apart from eliminating the exposure of the contractor to movement in exchange rates, the **other advantages of forward exchange contracts are** that there is usually:
– no deposit to pay;
– settlement is on the maturity date; and
– they can be tailored to meet the specific requirements of the company, including the amount, currency and maturity date, which are typically agreed for any time period up to a year.

Disadvantage The disadvantage is that the company forfeits the right to benefit from any **8318** favourable movements in the exchange rate. The decision as to whether to take out a forward contract will therefore depend, upon how risk averse the contractor is and their perception of which way exchange rates will move between the current date and the date on which the underlying trading contract will crystallise.

The **contracts normally mature** on standard month end dates; where this is not the case the costs of arranging the contract are higher. The market for forward exchange contracts in excess of one year is generally small as is the market for the currencies of less developed countries.

Mechanics of forward exchange rates

One of the parties to the contracts assumes a **long-position** by agreeing to buy the specified **8320** currency at an agreed future date at the forward rate. The other party assumes a **short position** and contracts to sell the currency on the same date at the same forward rate. The forward rate is quoted at a **premium or discount to the spot rate** based on:
– current market conditions;
– the interest rate differentials between the relevant currencies; and
– the duration of the forward contract.

Accounting treatment

The subject of forward exchange currency contracts is dealt with only briefly in SSAP 20. **8324**

The specific accounting treatment of forward exchange contracts will depend on whether the contract is for speculative or for hedging purposes.

The **general principle** is that forward exchange contracts are treated as a single transaction; namely a commitment to buy or sell the currency necessary to settle a foreign currency payable or receivable, as part of the purchase or sale transaction. The transaction is recorded under the rate specified in the contract.

Under existing rules there are no accounting entries made in respect of the contract itself until it crystallises. It is simply a question of disclosing the future commitment in the notes to the financial statements.

However, the **terms of a forward contract** may, as discussed below, influence the value at which a transaction hedged by the forward contract is recorded. The accounting treatment for a number of typical situations where a company enters into a forward exchange contract are outlined in examples that follow.

Forward Contracts taken out at the transaction date Under SSAP 20, the contract rate **8326** can be used to translate monetary assets and liabilities denominated in a foreign currency, where they are covered by a matching or related forward exchange rate contract. The adoption of the contract rate recognises the purpose of the contract is to hedge any exchange risk and that no economic gain or loss will materialise. The **premium** or **discount** on a forward contract is recognised in the profit and loss account when the contract is taken out.

EXAMPLE A British company prepares its financial statements to 31 Sept. 20X3. In June 20X3, the company sells merchandise to a company in Hong Kong for HK$300,000. The Hong Kong company is due to settle the account in December 20X3.

When the transaction was signed the £/HK$ rate was HK 12.7, and at the balance sheet date the rate had moved to £1 = HK$13.0. The UK company has however arranged a forward exchange contract to sell the HK$300,000 it is to receive in December 20X3 on the same day as they are due. The exchange rate specified in the forward contract was £1 = HK$ 12.6.

June 20X3	HK$300,000/12.7 =	£23,622	
Sept. 20X3	HK$300,000/ 13.0 =	£23,077	(balance sheet date)
Dec. 20X3	HK$300,000/ 12.6 =	£23,809	

SSAP 20

The UK company should account for the sale as follows:
The **sale and debtor** to be recorded at the contract rate of £1 = HK$12.6 as £23,809

In December 20X3, HK$300,000 will be due from the debtor, which is sold for £23,809.
The contract rate is used because the British company knows the rate it will be applying at the date the payment is received. This is consistent with the provisions of SSAP 20.
No aggregate exchange gain/loss arises.

8330   **Hedging a foreign currency obligation** Companies may use forward foreign exchange contracts to hedge future transactions, such as a foreign currency payable or receivable or a commitment such as an agreement to buy or sell goods to a foreign company at some time in the future. The **correct accounting treatment** is to defer any gain or loss arising on the forward contract, until the actual date the obligation is fulfilled, as both the transaction and the forward contract arranged to hedge it are future commitments.

> [EXAMPLE] A UK Company with a financial year ending on 31 December 20X3, contracts on 30 September of the same year to buy from a Canadian supplier, equipment worth $400,000. The equipment is due for delivery on 31 March 20X4 and due for settlement on 30th June 20X4.
> The UK Company wishes to hedge the commitment to pay $400,000 on 30th June 20X4 at a forward rate of £1 = C$2.
> Under SSAP 20, the transaction should be recorded at the forward contract rate: namely the asset and the liability to the creditor should be recorded at £200,000 (£1 = C$2).
> The company will record the asset and the future liability in its balance sheet.

Where the forward exchange contract is of a speculative nature, then it may generate a profit or loss, depending on the movement in the exchange rate during the period to maturity. At the end of the financial year the profit and loss on any outstanding contracts should be determined. There are **two generally accepted methods**:
1. Compare the forward rate specified in the contract with the actual forward rate to maturity at the end of the financial year; and
2. Compare the "spot rate" at the date the contract is agreed with the spot rate at the balance sheet date. The contracted forward discount or premium should be amortised over the period of the contract.
The "spot rate" is the exchange rate for immediate delivery.

> [EXAMPLE] A company took out a forward exchange contract on 1 July 20X3 to sell €2,500,00, 153 days forward at £1: €1.20. On 30 November 20X3, the company must supply €2,500,000 in exchange for £2,083,333.
> The financial year end was 31 October 20X3 and the 30 day forward rate £1 = €1.25 (£2,000,000).
>
> | Method | £ |
> |---|---|
> | Contracted price for delivery of €2,500,000 on 30 November 20X3 (£1= €1.20) | 2,083,333 |
> | Cost of €2,500,000 at 31 October 20X3 -30 day forward rate at £1 = €1.25 | 2,000,000 |
> | **Profit earned to 30 November 20X3** | **83,333** |

3. Foreign currency options

8340   A foreign currency option is a **right but not an obligation**, to buy or sell an amount of currency at a fixed price. The right to buy is known as a "call option" and the right to sell a "put option"; the agreed price is known as the "strike" or "exercise price".

8342   An **important difference** between a foreign currency option and a forward currency contract, is that the buyer of the currency is able to take advantage of any favourable currency movements, in that it will not exercise the options unless the exchange rates have moved to its advantage. Accounting for options is not dealt with by SSAP 20.

8343   In return for the right to place a call or put option with an option seller (i.e. bank) a company will have to pay a commission or non-refundable option premium, which represents the market value of the option. An **option consists of two parts**; namely its intrinsic value and its time value.

The **intrinsic value** represents the benefit to the holder of the option if exercised imme- **8344** diately and for a call option, it equals the excess of market price of the underlying option over the options strike price.

The **time value** represents the difference between the price of the option (premium) and **8346** the intrinsic value and dependent on:
– the time remaining to maturity of the option;
– the value placed on the possible increase in the option's intrinsic value prior to the matur-ity date, as a result of the volatility of the underlying financial item; as well as
– reflecting the income foregone by not holding the underlying item.

Exercising the option If the spot exchange rate is lower than the strike rate, the option **8348** holder will not exercise the option as it is said to be "**out of the money**". If the opposite is the case, the option will be exercised as it is aid to be "**in the money**". Where the strike rate is equal to the spot rate the option is considered to be "at the rate".

Disclosure requirements

Where the monies involved in the forward contracts **are material** the method adopted **8350** should be detailed in the accounting policies note. The particulars of significant forward contracts with should be disclosed in order to comply with the Companies Act requirements. Whether a contract is a matched/hedge type or open speculative type it still represents a discussable commitment for the purposes of the Act.

SECTION 6

Disclosure framework

The **reporting framework** relating to the disclosure of foreign currency transactions for both **8360** individual companies and consolidated accounts is dictated by the disclosure requirements of the Companies Act, SSAP 20, UITF 9, UITF 19 and the Business Review. The FRSSE does not contain any of the disclosure requirements of SSAP 20. The disclosure requirements for the new rules included in FRS 23 are covered in ¶8388 and for FRS 24 in ¶8396.

Companies Act requirements

The disclosure requirements of the Companies Act are limited. The Act does not include **8361** any provisions that deal with the translation of either foreign currency transactions or foreign currency financial statements. The **information that must be disclosed** in the notes to the accounts, is the basis or accounting policy adopted for the translation process and details of any material financial obligations, to the extent that they are relevant to a proper under-standing of the company's financial position, such as any amounts due under existing forward exchange contracts.

EXAMPLE Bonington Group Ltd – Annual report and accounts
31 December 20X3

Accounting Policies (extract)

A. Basis adopted for foreign currency translation
Assets and liabilities denominated in foreign currencies are principally translated into sterling at the rates ruling at the end of the financial year, **except when covered by** an **open foreign exchange contract**, in which case the rate of exchange specified in the contract is used.

B. Treatment of exchange differences arising from the translation of both the opening balance sheets of overseas subsidiary undertakings (date of control in case of acquisition during the year) and foreign currency borrowings used to finance or hedge long-term foreign investments are taken directly to reserves. All other profits and losses on exchange are credited or charged to operating profit.

The **results of specific overseas undertakings** are translated into sterling at average rates. The exchange differences arising as a result of re-stating net assets to closing rates are dealt with as movements on reserves.

SSAP 20

8362

SSAP 20 (59)

The disclosure requirements under SSAP 20 are as follows:

a. The method of translating the financial statements of foreign enterprises.

b. The accounting treatment or exchange differences.

c. The net amounts of exchange of exchange gains or losses on financial currency borrowings, less deposits, showing separately:

– any amounts offset against reserves (net movement), including as a hedge or finance for foreign equity investments; and

– the net amount charged or credited to the profit and loss account.

d. For all companies or groups of companies the **net movement on reserve** arising from exchange differences.

An example of exchange differences offset against reserves is shown in the example below.

8363

EXAMPLE   **Polonia Ltd Annual Report and Accounts – 20X3**
Notes to the accounts (extract)
Other reserves

	Group £m	Subsidiaries £m	Parent £m
Reserves b/fwd.	xxx	xxx	xxx
Movements during the year			
Profit for the year	xxx	xxx	xxx
Dividends			
Net exchange gains on currency loans	xxx		xxx
Exchange differences on translation of net investments in overseas subsidiaries	(xxx)	(xx)	(xxx)
Total	xxx	xxx	xxx

In the Group accounts £0.7m of net exchange gains on foreign currency loans have been **offset in reserves** against exchange losses on net investment in overseas subsidiaries.

Directors' report

8366

The disclosure requirements of the Business Review covering foreign currency transactions include details of the following:

– the currency profile of any borrowings;

– the use of financial instruments for hedging purposes; and

– exposure to exchange rate fluctuations and possible impact on reported results.

EXAMPLE   **Standard Group Plc**
Annual report and accounts: June 20XX
Business Review (extract)

Currency exposure

The Group engages in business activity in 15 countries accounting for some 65% of Group revenues and expenses. The Group generates a surplus in the majority of these currencies. The principal exceptions are the US dollar in which the Group has its deficit arising from capital expenditure and expenditure on fuel, and sterling covering central overhead and management costs.

Risk However, the Group is **exposed to a broad spread of currencies** through businesses linked to the dollar and sterling, which provides a measure of protection against exchange rate fluctuations.

It should be noted that there would be an adverse effect on the Group's result were sterling to weaken against the US dollar but strengthen against either the Euro or the Yen, with the reverse producing a beneficial effect.

SECTION 7

Companies adopting fair value accounting

The key aspect of this measurement system is that entities is that certain financial instruments   **8370**
may be measured at fair value, with changes in value flowing through the profit and loss account. The relevant reporting requirements are contained in FRS 23 "The Effects Of Changes In Foreign Exchange Rates" and FRS 24 "Financial Reporting In Hyperinflationary Economies".

1. FRS 23

FRS 23 covers the presentation of an entity's financial statements in a foreign currency and   **8372**
applies to unlisted entities that choose to adopt accounting policies consistent with the fair value measurement rules contained in the Companies Act, and hence, FRS 26 "Financial Instruments: Measurement".

FRS 23 does not apply to financial statements **where FRS 26 has not been applied** as SSAP 20 remains in force, as well as to entities that apply the FRSSE.

FRS 23 should be applied: FRS 23 (3)
– when accounting for transactions and balances in foreign currencies, except derivative transactions and balances falling within the scope of FRS 26;
– in translating the results of the foreign operation included in the entity's financial statements, by way of consolidation, or by the equity method; and
– in translating an entity's results into a "presentation currency".

> ⌐MEMO POINTS⌐   The **"presentation currency"** is defined as the currency in which the financial statements are presented. The **"functional currency"** (local currency), is defined as the currency of the primary economic environment in which an entity operates. Once determined, the functional currency is not changed unless the underlying transactions, events and conditions that determine this choice also change.

Disclosure requirements

The key disclosures required under FRS 23 are as follows: **8388**
1. The total of the exchange differences recognised in the profit and loss account, minus   FRS 23 (52) – (57)
those arising on financial instruments measured at fair value through profit or loss in accordance with FRS 26.
2. The net exchange differences recognised through the STRGL, including a reconciliation of such exchange differences at the beginning and end of the financial period.
3. Details of the functional currency where it differs from the presentation currency, including reasons for the use of a different presentation currency.
4. Where the functional currency of either the reporting entity or significant foreign operation changes, the reason for the change should be disclosed.
5. Where an entity adopts a currency in its financial statements that differs from either its functional currency or its presentation currency, it should:
– disclose the currency in which the supplementary information is presented; and
– disclose the entity's functional currency and translation method used to determine the supplementary information.

2. FRS 24

8392 The **criteria for adopting** FRS 24 (Financial Reporting in Inflationary Economies" is the same as that applies to FRS 23 as outlined above.

FRS 24 is in the main identical to IAS 29 "Financial reporting in hyperinflationary economies". The restatement of financial statements based on FRS 24, may generate differences between the carrying amount of individual assets and liabilities in the balance sheet and their tax bases. These **timing differences** should be accounted for in accordance with FRS 19 "Deferred Tax".

8393 **Key disclosures** A number of important disclosures are required by FRS 24 in order to clarify the basis for dealing with the effects of inflation in the financial statements and the resulting amounts; namely:

– where financial statements and comparatives have been restated to reflect changes in the general purchasing power of the functional currency and reflected in the presentation currency at the balance sheet date;

– whether financial statements are based on historical cost or a current cost approach; and

– the identity and level of price index at the balance sheet date and the movement in the index over the current and previous accounting period.

SECTION 8

New UK GAAP – requirements of FRS 102

8394 The FRC has published FRS 102 "The Financial Reporting Standard applicable in the UK and Republic of Ireland" which will replace existing UK GAAP (primarily SSAP 20) from January 2014. The key differences between current UK GAAP and new UK GAAP are set out below. The FRSSE will still be available to smaller entities.

Topic	Existing UK GAAP (SSAP 20)/ UITF 9	FRS 102
Presentation	Concentrates on local currency (see ¶8004) corresponds to functional currency in FRS 102.	Focuses on functional currency (also adopted in FRS 13) – area of primary economic activity + presentation currency (free choice).
Hedging of future transactions	Use of forward exchange rate permitted if matched by a forward currency contract.	This option is not permitted.
Net investment in a foreign entity	1. Loans recorded at historical rate (transaction date) in individual company's accounts. 2. In group accounts, loans are retranslated with exchange rate movements (gains or losses) recorded in the STRGL.	1. Loans can be retranslated. 2. Exchange gains/losses recorded in comprehensive income.
Group consolidation	1. Goodwill not specifically treated. 2. Choice of closing rate and temporal method(¶8070).	1. Goodwill = asset of foreign operation and translated at the closing rate. 2. Balance sheet translated at closing rate and statement of comprehensive income at exchange rate prevailing at the transaction date.

Topic	Existing UK GAAP (SSAP 20)/ UITF 9	FRS 102
Hyperinflation	The definitions of hyperinflation are similar in both FRS 102 and UITF 9 but there are some small differences in accounting treatment. For instance, UITF 9 allows an entity to adopt a stable currency (functional currency) other than its local currency for recording transactions.	

MEMO POINTS   The FRC has issued a **staff education note** entitled "Foreign exchange contracts" (SEN 11) to address some of the issues involved when transitioning from current UK GAAP to FRS 102. For example, for entities that currently apply SSAP 20 there will be a change of accounting treatment under FRS 102, which does not permit the application of a contracted forward rate at the transaction or balance sheet date. The forward contract rate is recognised in the balance sheet under other financial instruments at fair value, and the corresponding debtor/creditor retranslated at the year end rate. A copy of the SEN can be downloaded from the FRC website.

CHAPTER 3

Pensions and other retirement benefits

SECTION 1

Introduction

Retirement benefits include all types of remuneration received (typically a pension) in return for the services rendered by the employee. Because of the nature of these benefits, uncertainties relating to valuation and timing in turn affect the accounting treatment. This chapter considers the accounting requirements for pension schemes generally, in addition to other retirement benefits. **Small companies** typically adopt the accounting requirements of the FRSSE whilst medium and larger entities must adhere to FRS 17 "Retirement benefits", which will in turn be replaced by the requirements of FRS 102 "The Financial Reporting Standard applicable in the UK and Republic of Ireland" from January 2015.

8400

There are **two main types** of occupational pension schemes provided by employers as set out in the table below.

8401
FRS 17 (1)

Type of pension scheme	Characteristics
Defined benefit scheme ("final salary scheme")	The employer guarantees a pension based on a specific fraction of the employee's salary in turn based on the number of years of service. The **employer bears the risk** of making up any shortfall in the fund when the benefits are paid out. This type of pension is being phased out by many employers.

Type of pension scheme	Characteristics
Defined contribution scheme ("money purchase scheme")	The benefits under the scheme ultimately depend on the fund amount that has accumulated, and the level of contributions paid into it. Consequently, there is no set promise or guarantee about the level of benefits that the **employee** will receive on retirement, who **bears the ultimate risk** that benefits may be inadequate.

Key definitions

8403

Retirement benefits	All forms of consideration payable by an employer after the completion of the employment and in exchange for services of the employee, excluding: – termination payments paid before the normal retirement date; or – voluntary redundancy paid in respect of the right to future pension benefits. Examples include pensions, healthcare, and continuing use of a car during retirement.
Pension	A regular payment made to an employee above a specified age, after employment has ceased, as a result of arrangements made by the employer.
Defined contribution scheme	A pension or other retirement benefit scheme into which an employer pays regular contributions, either fixed as an amount, or as a percentage of pay.
Defined benefit scheme	A pension scheme that is not a defined contribution scheme, which broadly means the scheme rules specify the benefits to be paid, requiring it to be financed accordingly. Actuarial methods are used to determine the amounts that are to be recognised for accounting purposes, because there is great uncertainty as to the ultimate cost of the scheme. Where a scheme has features of both defined contribution and defined benefit schemes, and the employer has a potential liability to pay further contributions, it should be accounted for as a defined benefit scheme.

> MEMO POINTS   Where **death-in-service benefits** are provided by a defined contribution scheme, these do not change its classification for accounting purposes.

SECTION 2

Small companies adopting the FRSSE

8405   **Defined contribution scheme**   The cost of a **defined contribution scheme** is equal to the contributions payable to the scheme for the accounting period. The cost should be recognised within operating profit in the profit and loss account.

8406   Disclosure must be made of pension commitments, whether included under any provision shown in the balance sheet or not. Where any such commitment relates to pensions payable to past directors of the company, separate particulars must be given of that commitment.

The following **disclosures** should be made:
– the nature of the scheme (i.e. defined contribution);
– the cost for the period; and
– any outstanding or prepaid contributions at the balance sheet date.

8407   **Defined benefit scheme**   Because defined benefit schemes have **limited applicability to smaller entities** (very few participate in them), the accounting requirements relating to such schemes are not contained in the FRSSE itself but set out in Appendix II. They are based on FRS 17, "Retirement benefits".

SECTION 3

Defined benefit schemes

In this type of scheme, the **benefits** are determined by the scheme rules, and the fund must be sufficiently financed so that the necessary benefits can be paid as promised. There are two main types of scheme:
1. **Funded schemes**, where the scheme assets are held apart from the company, in a separate legal vehicle. These assets are ringfenced for the purposes of pension provision, and the scheme is usually managed by independent trustees.
2. **Unfunded schemes**, where the employer manages the assets that have been set aside to fund future employee benefits. The assets are not ringfenced for this purpose. In effect, the employer is meeting the cost of the pension benefits from its own resources.

When **accounting for the cost** of providing a defined benefit scheme, the employer looks through the pension structure, to consider the underlying assets and liabilities within the scheme itself. The same accounting principles apply to both funded and unfunded schemes.

8410

The requirements of FRS 17 are onerous and **annual actuarial advice** (a full valuation every three years with annual updates) is an essential requirement of compliance with its rules. This obviously has cost implications for the employer when preparing the accounts. In addition, the production of actuarial based information can also take some time and therefore employers should plan well ahead in order to ensure that they are able to publish their accounts within applicable deadlines. A **key requirement** under FRS 17 is the inclusion of the actuarially assessed pension asset or liability in the employer's own balance sheet.

8420

MEMO POINTS   1. Often a pension scheme will have a **different year end** to the employer, and so the actuary may need to update a valuation to the employer's year end.
2. Two full **actuarial valuations** may be required on a triennial basis, because different assumptions may be used depending on whether the valuation is prepared for the purposes of inclusion in the accounts, or for the trustees making future funding and investment decisions.

---

1. Objectives of FRS 17

The **objectives** of FRS 17 are as follows:
– assets and liabilities arising from the employer's retirement benefit obligations are to be reflected at fair value;
– operating costs of providing retirement benefits are to be recognised in the accounting periods in which the benefits are earned by the employees;
– related financing costs and other changes in the value of assets and liabilities are to be recognised in the accounting period in which they arise; and
– adequate disclosures are required in respect of the above.
The standard applies to all types of retirement benefits including post-retirement **healthcare costs**, arising from schemes both in the UK and overseas. When the standard is **first applied in full**, a prior period adjustment will need to be made to reflect the restatement of reserves in respect of the defined benefit pension asset or liability (¶488).

8430
FRS 17 (1)

Multi-employer schemes

Each employer covered by the scheme should **normally account** for it on a fair and reasonable basis, and pro rate the components required for the accounts (as detailed in the remainder of this section).

8438
FRS 17 (9)

There is an **exception** when the employer is liable only for amounts in respect of the current period, and the employer contributions are not affected by any surplus or deficit of the scheme relating to past service of the members. In this case the contributions should be accounted for as if the scheme were a defined contribution scheme. This treatment also removes the problem relating to distributable reserves.

8440   It is also possible that the employer is **unable to identify** its share of the underlying assets and liabilities in a multi-employer scheme. Again the employer would account for the scheme as if it were a **defined contribution scheme** with the following additional disclosures:
- the fact that the scheme is a defined benefit scheme;
- the reason that the employer does not have sufficient information to account for the scheme as a defined benefit scheme;
- any available information about that surplus or deficit – and the basis used in its determination; and
- any implications for the employer.

In this case, the **consolidated accounts** (¶6500) themselves will still reflect the pension scheme as a defined benefit scheme, requiring a consolidation adjustment to remove each individual company's pension accounting entries.

---

2. Measurement

8442   The **accounting entries** rely to a large extent on the calculations performed, and the information supplied, by the scheme's actuary. The **persons** who remain ultimately **responsible**, for both the actuarial assumptions and related accounting adjustments, are the directors. In addition, they will need to provide some estimates based on their knowledge of the business.

Pension scheme assets

8444
FRS 17 (14)

These assets, net of all liabilities (except the liability to pay future pensions), should be measured at their fair value at the balance sheet date.

Generally, **fair value** is the amount at which an asset or liability could be exchanged in an arm's length transaction between informed and willing parties in an unforced sale. The table provides a definition of fair value for certain common assets.

Type of asset	Definition of fair value
Quoted securities	Current bid price
Unquoted securities	Estimate
Unitised securities (such as unit trusts)	Current bid price/Average of bid and offer prices [1]
Property	Open market value or RICS approved valuation
Insurance policies	Best approximation

The estimate of fair value for **unquoted securities** is necessarily subjective, although the problem is diminished for most pension schemes as it is likely that this type of investment will form only a small part of the scheme's overall investment portfolio.

Insurance policies which exactly match the amount and timing of some scheme liabilities (i.e. the benefits payable under the scheme) should be measured at the same amount as those liabilities.

Liabilities to pay future benefits

8446
FRS 17 (20)

These **pension scheme liabilities** should also be measured at an estimate of fair value. Scheme liabilities are **defined** as:
- benefits to members stated under the scheme terms; and
- other benefits where the employer has created a valid expectation amongst the scheme members that such benefits will arise.

As there are many long-term uncertainties impacting on the scheme liabilities (such as employee turnover, salary rates, and inflation), an actuarial calculation of the fair value is required.

8447   **Reduction in pension scheme liabilities**   The Government now uses the Consumer Price Index (CPI), instead of the retail price index (RPI) as an inflation measure for determining the minimum pension increases to be applied to statutory index linked retirement benefits. Because annual CPI increases have in general been lower than general RPI increases, this change has the potential to cause a reduction in pension scheme liabilities.

UITF Abstract 48 considers three issues:
- whether there is an reduction in scheme liabilities;
- how the effect should be presented (accounting treatment); and
- when the effect should be recognised (i.e. in which accounting period).

The **accounting treatment** based on the UITF is as follows: **8448**
- if there is an obligation to pay benefit increases based on RPI, this is regarded as a change in benefit and is recognised in the profit and loss account;
- if there is no obligation to pay benefit increases based on RPI then a change to CPI reflects a different assumption and is part of
actuarial gains and losses (¶8486), which are recognised in the STRGL.

Entities must provide **disclosures** that explain the effect of changes in scheme liabilities arising from the replacement of RPI with CPI.

The question of **when to recognise** a reduction in scheme liabilities, as a result of whether there is an obligation to pay increased benefits based on RPI, is as follows:
- where there is such an obligation, the past service cost should be recognised in the accounting period when any necessary consultations have been concluded or employees' valid expectations have been changed;
- where there is no such obligation, the entity should use financial assumptions to measure scheme liabilities that reflect market expectations at the balance sheet date.

Actuarial considerations

The **overriding principle** is that the assumptions used to measure the liabilities of the   **8449**
scheme should be mutually compatible, and lead to the best estimate of the cashflows that   FRS 17 (23)
will arise in future. The actuarial assumptions relating to future economic conditions take
account of market expectations at the balance sheet date.

The **assumptions** should also take into account any future events, and any commitments   **8450**
made by the employer which have been communicated to the members of the pension
scheme, such as expected:
- early retirement;
- salary increases; and
- cost of living increases.

A **future event** in this context would not include redundancies, which are dealt with separately and are not to be anticipated. Similarly any curtailment, where the scheme is terminated or the scheme terms amended, should not be anticipated before the final decision to take action has been made (and indeed communicated to the members).

Actuarial method   The **method** to be used by the actuary in his calculations is the   **8452**
projected unit method, which takes account of future increases in salaries, and considers
that the cost of providing benefits becomes more expensive as an individual approaches
retirement. The time value of money is accounted for on the basis that the age profile of the
employees will remain consistent.

The pension benefits are normally allocated to periods of employee service in accordance with the scheme rules. An exception arises when the rules attribute a disproportionate share of the total benefits to later years of service, when a straight-line allocation should be used instead.

In order to obtain the **present value** of the scheme liability, it must be discounted to reflect   **8454**
the time value of money. The rate of discount is prescribed as the current rate of return on   FRS 17 (32)
a high quality corporate bond, which should mirror the currency and term of the scheme
liabilities (such as an AA status bond). For **overseas schemes**, the discount rate should be
based on government bonds with a small premium over the risk-free rate.

Actuarial information will be required on an annual basis due to the information required   **8456**
for appropriate disclosure in the accounts, although a **full valuation** will only need to be   FRS 17 (35)
undertaken **every three years**. In the intervening years, the actuary will need to update the
valuation to take account of current conditions at each balance sheet date, such as:

– fair value of scheme assets; and
– changes in financial assumptions.

3. Recognition

Scheme surplus

8460
FRS 17 (37), (41)

A scheme surplus is the excess of the value of the scheme assets over the present value of the scheme liabilities. An **asset** should be recognised in the employer's balance sheet in relation to the scheme surplus where it can be recovered through:
– reduced future contributions by the employer; or
– a refund from the scheme.

In determining the amount of the asset, the actuarial assumptions used for accounting purposes should be used. No growth in the number of active members should be assumed, although a declining membership can be reflected.

Where part of the surplus will be used to **improve the benefits** available to members (such as spousal benefits), this part should not be recognised as an asset. This includes situations where the past actions of the employer have created an expectation amongst the scheme members that the surplus will be used to improve benefits. A **refund of contributions** should be recognised only if the amount has been agreed with the pension scheme trustees at the balance sheet date.

Scheme deficit

8462
FRS 17 (37)

A scheme deficit is the shortfall of the value of the scheme assets compared to the present value of the scheme liabilities. A **liability** should be recognised to the extent that it represents an obligation of the employer. Where employees can be required to pay additional contributions, the liability should only recognise the net amount payable by the employer.

For an **unfunded scheme**, the employer's liability is the obligation to pay future retirement benefits, and only this amount is carried in the balance sheet.

Effect on performance statements

8465

A simple example will show the **movement** in the performance statements dictated by the scheme surplus or deficit.

EXAMPLE   A Ltd's pension scheme had a surplus of £20m at the beginning of the year. The charge to the profit and loss account is £15m, and the contribution paid is £10m. The surplus at the end of the year is £12m.
The following entries are made in A Ltd's accounts:

	Dr £	Cr £	Pension surplus asset £
Brought forward			20m
Dr pension charge in P & L	15m		
Cr pension surplus asset		15m	(15m)
Dr pension surplus asset	10m		10m
Cr bank		10m	
Dr actuarial loss in STRGL	3m		
Cr pension surplus asset		3m	(3m)
Closing pension asset			12m

4. Balance sheet presentation

8466

Contributions payable to the pension scheme but unpaid at the balance sheet date should be disclosed in "creditors: amounts due within one year".

The presentation of the pension scheme **surplus or deficit** in the balance sheet depends on   **8468**
the format of the balance sheet adopted (¶984). In any event, the amount of the surplus or
deficit should be stated net of deferred tax, on the face of the balance sheet.

Format 1 balance sheet

The scheme **surplus or deficit** should be reflected directly on the balance sheet of the   **8470**
employer, in a separate caption, after accruals and deferred income. It is likely that the   FRS 17 (47)
employer will opt to also include a new subtotal on the face of the balance sheet and make
the disclosure as follows:

Net assets excluding pension assets and liabilities	X
Pension asset/(liability)	X/(X)
Net assets including pension assets and liabilities	X

Format 2 balance sheet

The scheme **surplus** should be reflected directly on the balance sheet of the employer, in a   **8472**
separate caption, with an optional new subtotal, as follows:

Assets excluding pension asset	X
Pension asset	X
Assets including pension asset	X

Similarly, the scheme **deficit** should be reflected as follows:

Liabilities excluding pension liability	X
Pension liability	X
Liabilities including pension liability	X

If the company has **more than one pension scheme**, the assets and liabilities for all those schemes   **8474**
should not be netted off, but should be shown separately on the face of the balance sheet.   FRS 17 (47)

---

5. Presentation in the performance statements

There are a number of **different elements** which must be disclosed in the performance   **8476**
statements, which relate to the movement in the scheme asset or liability in each accounting   FRS 17 (50)
period. The calculation of these components is performed by the scheme actuary. The
elements are **classified** as either:
– periodic costs, which will be relevant to every accounting period; or
– non-periodic costs, which will arise from one-off transactions only.

Once these **basic aspects** have been dealt with, the following issues must also be considered:
– restricted scheme surpluses (¶8494);
– increase to scheme surpluses (¶8496);
– current tax (¶8498); and
– deferred tax (¶8500).

---

a. Periodic costs

The following table explains the various components that make up periodic costs.   **8478**

Component	Explanation	Recognised in	¶¶
Current service cost	Increase in the present value of the scheme liabilities expected to arise from employee service in the current period.	P&L – operating profit[1]	¶8480
Interest cost	Expected increase in the present value of scheme liabilities during the accounting period because the benefits are one period closer to settlement.	P&L – other finance costs/income	¶8482

Component	Explanation	Recognised in	¶¶
Expected return on assets	An estimate of the long-term expected return on the scheme assets.	P&L – other finance costs/income	¶8484
Actuarial gains and losses	Gains or losses arising from: – changes in actuarial assumptions; or – discrepancies between past assumptions and reality.	STRGL	¶8486

Note:
1. If capitalised, current service cost should be included in the cost of the asset on the balance sheet.

Current service cost

8480
FRS 17 (51)

This cost is **based** on the most recent actuarial valuation at the beginning of the period, with the financial assumptions updated to reflect conditions at that date. The amount should be stated net of any employee contributions, in the same statutory accounts heading as other salary costs.

Interest cost

8482
FRS 17 (53), (56)

This cost is **calculated** by applying the discount rate to the present value of the scheme liabilities at the beginning of the accounting period. The interest cost should be netted off against the expected return on assets, and shown in "other finance costs (or income)" adjacent to interest.

> MEMO POINTS   "Other finance costs (or income)" is a new format heading, separate from "interest payable and similar charges".

> EXAMPLE   A Ltd has a defined benefit scheme with the following liabilities at the beginning of each year:
>
> | | 20X3
£m | 20X2
£m |
> |---|---|---|
> | Pension scheme liabilities | 4 | 3 |
>
> The discount rate at the beginning of the year is 8.0% and 9.0% for 20X2 and 20X1 respectively. The computed interest cost will be:
>
> | | 20X3
£m | 20X2
£m |
> |---|---|---|
> | Interest cost: (£4m @ 8%: £3m @ 9%) | 0.32 | 0.27 |

Expected return on assets

8484
FRS 17 (54)

This amount is credited to the profit and loss account, by offset against the interest cost. The expected return should be stable, although ultimately subjective. The following table summarises the **required calculations**, which are based on amounts applying at the beginning of the accounting period.

Type of asset	Calculation
Quoted government or corporate bonds	Current redemption yield x market value of bonds
Other assets including equities	Expected long-term rate x fair value

This is an area that requires careful judgement by the directors, based on advice from the actuary.

Actuarial gains and losses

8486
FRS 17 (57)

The **main instances** where such a gain or loss may arise are:
– differences between the actual and expected return on scheme assets;
– differences between the actual and expected change in liabilities in the period;

– the effect of changes in the actuarial assumptions concerning liabilities; and
– where a pension surplus has not been previously recognised as an asset in the company balance sheet.

All actuarial gains and losses are to be included only within the STRGL.

b. Non-periodic costs

The following table explains the various components which make up non-periodic costs.   **8488**

Component	Explanation	Recognised in	¶¶
Past service costs	Employees become entitled to improved benefits, and previous years of service count towards these improved benefits. For example, the employer may make a commitment to grant earlier retirement with extra years added on to the length of service.	P&L – operating profit[1]	¶8490
Gains and losses on settlements and curtailments	Settlements and curtailment are one-off events which are unlikely to have been included in the actuarial assumptions.	P&L – operating profit, unless exceptional item	¶8492
If capitalised, current service cost should be included in the cost of the asset on the balance sheet.			

Past service costs

These costs should be **recognised** on a straight-line basis over the period when members become entitled to the improved benefits. Often the entitlement arises immediately, in which case the past service cost should be recognised in the current accounting period when the decision to improve the benefits is made.   **8490**
FRS 17 (60)

Past service costs should normally be included within the same statutory accounts heading as other salary costs.

An **exception** arises when part of the scheme surplus is not recognised as an asset in the accounts. In this situation, the past service costs may be extinguished by the unrecognised surplus, in which case there will be no entries in the accounts relating to the costs, although disclosure is required (¶8512).

Gains and losses on settlements and curtailments

The following table gives details of when these events might arise: **8492**
FRS 17 (1), (64)

Event	Explanation	Examples
Settlement	An irrevocable action which relieves the employer of the responsibility to provide a pension in the future.	– lump sum cash payment in exchange for members' rights to pension benefits; – purchase of an irrevocable annuity contract to cover all accrued benefits.
Curtailment	An event which leads to a reduction in the expected future years of service, or reduction in the defined benefits relating to future service for some employees.	– early termination of employee services, such as the closure of an operation; – amendments to the terms of the scheme, such that the future service of the employees leads to reduced benefits.

The **accounting treatment** for both these types of events depends on whether a loss or gain (basically the movement in the scheme surplus or deficit) results from the decision to settle or curtail.

1. **Losses** should be recognised in the profit and loss account (within operating profit unless the item is exceptional) measured at the date when the employer is demonstrably committed to the transaction. An **exception** arises when part of the scheme surplus is not recognised as an asset in the accounts. In this situation, the loss may be extinguished by the unrecognised surplus and so there will be no entries in the accounts relating to the loss, although disclosure of the extinguished amounts is required.

2. **Gains** should be recognised only when all involved parties are irrevocably committed to the transaction giving rise to the gain, and included in the profit and loss account (again within operating profit unless the item is exceptional).

---

c. Other issues

Restriction of surpluses

8494
FRS 17 (67)

A scheme surplus will not always be recognised as an asset, as discussed at ¶8460. When part of the surplus **becomes irrecoverable**, the accounting process should follow these steps:

1. The normal entries should be made, which will result in the full surplus being shown as an asset in the accounts.

2. The following adjustment is then made to reduce the asset to its recoverable amount:

a. the unrecognised surplus is used to extinguish the following costs which would otherwise be charged in the profit and loss account in the period, and this has the effect of increasing the balance sheet asset:
– past service costs;
– losses on settlements; and
– losses on curtailments;

b. a debit entry is made in the profit and loss account to reduce the expected return on assets to no more than the total of all the cost elements of the pension i.e., current service cost, interest cost, past service costs, and settlement and curtailment losses not covered by an unrecognised surplus; and

c. the balance of the unrecognised surplus is reflected as an actuarial loss in the STRGL.

[EXAMPLE] C Ltd has a defined benefit pension scheme with a surplus of £20m, although only £15m is to be recognised as an asset in the company's accounts.

The movement in the surplus in the year, before taking account of the unrecognised surplus of £5m, is as follows:

	£m
Surplus in scheme at beginning of the year	14
Movement in year:	
Current service cost	(4)
Contributions	2
Past service costs	(2)
Expected return on assets	13
Interest cost	(4)
Actuarial gain	1
Surplus in scheme at end of the year	20

The asset relating to the scheme surplus then needs to be reduced to £15m, and the following steps must be taken:

1. The past service costs of £2m are extinguished by part of the unrecognised surplus. The journal required would be:

	Dr	Cr
Dr recoverable surplus (asset)	£2m	
Cr past service costs (P & L)		£2m

2. The limit of the credit to the profit and loss account is £1m (being the £15m recoverable surplus less the opening balance of £14m).
The total profit and loss items excluding the expected return on assets are:

	£m
Current service cost	4
Past service cost (after step 1)	0
Interest cost	4
Total	8

The expected return on assets cannot exceed £9m, calculated as:

	£m
Total costs in profit and loss account	8
Overall increase in recognised surplus in the year	1
Total	9

3. The expected return on assets is reduced from £13m to £9m by the following journal:

	Dr	Cr
Dr expected return on assets (P&L)	£4m	
Cr recoverable surplus (asset)		£4m

4. The remaining £3m adjustment required is debited against the actuarial gain to create a £2m actuarial loss:

	Dr	Cr
Dr actuarial gain (STRGL)	£3m	
Cr recoverable surplus (asset)		£3m

So the asset has now been reduced to £15m, and the amended movement to the surplus is as follows:

	£m
Surplus in scheme at beginning of the year	14
Movement in year:	
Current service cost	(4)
Contributions	2
Past service costs	0
Expected return on assets	9
Interest cost	(4)
Actuarial loss	(2)
Surplus in scheme at end of the year	15

Increase to surplus

Occasionally a situation will arise where a surplus **previously not recognised** is now deemed to be recoverable in the current accounting period, and this should be included in the accounts as follows:

8496
FRS 17 (67)-(68)

1. If a **refund is received** in respect of a surplus which has not previously been recognised, the refund should be shown as other financial income and separately disclosed in the notes to the financial statements. If the surplus has already been recognised as an asset in the accounts, the receipt of the cash refund will be a pure balance sheet entry.
2. If an **increase in the active membership** results in the recoverable surplus, it should be treated as an operating gain. This might arise as a result of an acquisition of a business.

Current tax

Tax **relief on pension contributions** should be regarded as relating to the items reported in the profit and loss account first, before the actuarial losses reported in the STRGL. Any **excess tax relief** should normally be allocated to the profit and loss account.

8498
FRS 17 (71)

EXAMPLE   B Ltd pays corporate tax at the rate of 30% and makes a contribution of £100,000 to its defined benefit scheme in the year, resulting in related tax relief of £30,000. The pension charges in the performance statements are as follows:

	£
Profit and loss account charge	45,000
STRGL- loss	25,000
Total	70,000

The related tax entries would be:

	Pension charge £	Current tax entry £	Net charge after tax relief £
Profit and loss account	45,000	(13,500)	31,500
STRGL	25,000	(7,500)	17,500
Total	70,000	(21,000)	49,000
Excess tax relief		(9,000)	
Total tax relief		(30,000)	

The excess tax relief of £9,000 should be included as a credit to the profit and loss account unless it clearly relates to an item in the STRGL.
The total profit and loss tax credit entry will therefore be £22,500.

Deferred tax

8500
FRS 19 (34)

Full **provision** should be made in respect of deferred tax on the pension scheme deficit or surplus, using the appropriate tax rates. The related deferred tax balance is netted against the pension asset or liability. The presentation of the pension related deferred tax charge/credit should follow the usual rules (¶9122), and be allocated to the profit and loss account, unless it relates to items included in the STRGL.

EXAMPLE   Continuing the example in ¶8498, the movement on the pension scheme asset can be analysed as follows:

	£
Profit and loss account charge	(45,000)
Loss in STRGL	(25,000)
Contribution	100,000
Overall movement in scheme asset	30,000

The overall movement results in a deferred tax charge of £9,000, assuming a tax rate of 30%.
1. **One possible option** is to pro rate the deferred tax charge and show it in the performance statements as follows:

	Pension charge £	Deferred tax charge £
Profit and loss account (45,000/70,000 x £9,000)	45,000	5,786
STRGL (25,000/70,000 x £9,000)	25,000	3,214
Total	70,000	9,000

2. **Alternatively**, the charge can be allocated to the profit and loss account to counteract the effect of the excess current tax relief, as follows:

	Pension charge £	Current tax £	Deferred tax £	Total tax charge £
Profit and loss account	40,000	(22,500)	9,000	(13,500)
STRGL	30,000	(7,500)	0	(7,500)
Total	70,000	(30,000)	9,000	(21,000)

Recognising the deferred tax charge in the profit and loss account gives an overall tax entry which is 30% of the pension charge of £45,000, reflecting the correlation between the overall tax charge of £21,000 and pension charge of £70,000.

6. Disclosure

The following disclosures should be made in respect of a **defined contribution scheme**:
- the nature of the scheme (i.e. defined contribution);
- the cost for the period; and
- any outstanding or prepaid contributions at balance sheet date.

8505
FRS 17 (75)

According to FRS 17, employers are obliged to disclose, in respect of their **defined benefit schemes**, information that enables users of financial statements to evaluate the nature of the schemes as well as the financial effects of changes in those schemes during the period. The prior rules form the basis of the remainder of this section. The changes required in subsequent years are summarised from ¶8516.

8506
FRS 17 (76)

Compulsory disclosures   The following disclosures should be made:
- information that will enable users to evaluate the nature of a company's participation in defined benefit schemes and the **financial effects of changes** in those schemes;
- the **principal actuarial assumptions** used as at the balance sheet date. Previously, only information regarding the main financial assumptions was required. The most significant change this is likely to bring is the requirement to disclose mortality rates (where this is considered to be a material assumption);
- the **contribution made** in respect of the current accounting period, and any agreed contribution rates for future years;
- an **analysis of** the opening and closing scheme liabilities and scheme assets showing separately the movements in scheme assets and scheme liabilities;
- an **analysis of** scheme liabilities into amounts arising from schemes that are (1) wholly or partly funded and (2) wholly unfunded; and
- information about **contingent liabilities** arising from retirement benefit obligations as well as the nature of contingent assets, where an inflow of the economic benefits is probable. In addition, in accordance with the provisions of FRS 12, "Provisions, contingent liabilities and contingent assets", companies should in any event disclose contingent assets and contingent liabilities, including guarantees, arising from retirement benefit obligations.

8507

Assumptions

Each of the main financial assumptions used at the **balance sheet date** should be disclosed as separate figures, and not combined or netted off. The main assumptions would include:
- inflation assumption;
- the rate of increase in salaries;
- the rate of increase for pensions in payment and deferred pensions; and
- the rate used to discount scheme liabilities.

8509
FRS 17 (78)

Components of the pension cost

1. The following amounts, which are included in **operating profit**, should be disclosed in the notes to the financial statements:
- the current service cost;
- any past service costs;
- any previously unrecognised surplus deducted from past service costs;
- gains and losses on any settlements or curtailments; and
- any previously recognised surplus deducted from the settlement or curtailment losses.

2. Any gains and losses on **settlements or curtailments** (and any previously unrecognised surplus deducted from the losses) included within a separate item after operating profit should be disclosed in a note.

3. The following amounts included as **other finance costs or income**:
- interest cost; and
- expected return on assets in the scheme.

8512
FRS 17 (82)

4. The following amounts included within the **STRGL**:
– difference between the expected and actual return on assets;
– experience gains and losses arising on the scheme liabilities; and
– effects of changes in the demographic and financial assumptions underlying the present value of the scheme liabilities.

History of amounts recognised in the STRGL

8513
FRS 17 (86)

For the **accounting period and previous four periods** (this disclosure is not required to be created retrospectively and will be built up over time):
– the difference between the expected and actual return on assets expressed both as an amount and as a percentage of the scheme assets at the balance sheet date;
– the experience gains and losses arising on the scheme liabilities expressed both as an amount and as a percentage of the present value of the scheme liabilities at the balance sheet date; and
– the total actuarial gain or loss expressed both as an amount and as a percentage of the present value of the scheme liabilities at the balance sheet date.

Reconciliation to the balance sheet

8514
FRS 17 (88)

1. The fair value of the scheme assets, the present value of the scheme liabilities based on the accounting assumptions, and the resulting surplus or deficit.
2. An explanation of any difference between the asset or liability on the balance sheet and the surplus and deficit of the scheme. Examples of such differences would be deferred tax and any restriction in the recognition of the surplus.
3. An analysis of the movements in the surplus or deficit in the scheme during the period.

Analysis of reserves

8515
FRS 17 (90)

The analysis of reserves in the notes to the financial statements should **distinguish** the amount relating to the defined benefit asset or liability net of the related deferred tax.

EXAMPLE **Balance sheet presentation**

	20X3 £m	20X2 £m
Net assets excluding pension asset	800	700
Pension asset	380	335
Net assets including pension asset	1,180	1,035

Reserves note

Profit and loss reserve excluding pension asset	500	400
Pension reserve	380	335
Profit and loss reserve	880	735

Pension cost note
Composition of the scheme

The group operates a defined benefit scheme in the UK. A full actuarial valuation was carried out at 31 December 20X3 and updated to 31 December 20X2 by a qualified independent actuary. The major assumptions used by the actuary were:

	At 31.12.20X3	At 31.12.20X2	At 31.12.20X1
Rate of increase in salaries	5.0%	4.0%	5.5%
Rate of increase in pensions in payment	2.5%	2.0%	3.0%
Discount rate	6.5%	4.5%	7.0%
Inflation assumption	3.0%	2.5%	4.0%

The assets in the scheme and the expected rate of return were:

	Long-term rate of return expected at 31.12.20X3	Value at 31.12.20X3 £m	Long-term rate of return expected at 31.12.20X2	Value at 31.12.20X2 £m	Long-term rate of return expected at 31.12.20X1	Value at 31.12.20X1 £m
Equities	6.9%	1,235	7.3%	1,116	8.0%	721
Bonds	6.0%	357	5.5%	298	6.0%	192
Property	4.5%	94	6.0%	74	6.1%	49
Total market value of assets		1,686		1,488		962
Present value of scheme liabilities		(1,143)		(1,009)		
Surplus in scheme		543		479		
Related deferred tax liability		(163)		(144)		
Net pension asset		380		335		

Analysis of the amount charged to operating profit

	20X3 £m	20X2 £m
Current service cost	42	34
Past service cost	15	12
Total operating charge	57	46

Analysis of the amount credited to other finance income

	20X3 £m	20X2 £m
Expected return on pension scheme assets	81	73
Interest on pension scheme liabilities	(48)	(53)
Net return	33	20

Analysis of the amount recognised in STRGL

	20X3 £m	20X2 £m
Actual return less expected return on pension scheme assets	324	480
Experience gains and losses arising on the scheme liabilities	(45)	(58)
Changes in assumptions underlying the present value of the scheme liabilities	(206)	(146)
Actuarial gain recognised in STRGL	73	276

Movement in surplus during the year

	20X3 £m	20X2 £m
Surplus in scheme at beginning of the year	479	204
Movement in year:		
Current service cost	(42)	(34)
Contributions	15	25
Past service costs	(15)	(12)
Other finance income	33	20
Actuarial gain	73	276
Surplus in scheme at end of the year	543	479

The full actuarial valuation at 31 December 20X2 showed an increase in the surplus from £204m to £479m. Improvements in benefits costing £15m were made in 20X3 and contributions reduced to £15m (4% of pensionable pay). It has been agreed with the pension trustees that contributions for the next three years will remain at that level.

History of experience gains and losses

	20X3	20X2	20X1	20X0
Difference between the expected and actual return on scheme assets:				
– amount (£m)	324	480	138	(6)
– percentage of scheme assets	25%	32%	14%	(1%)
Experience gains and losses on scheme liabilities:				
– amount (£m)	(45)	(58)	(6)	34
– percentage of scheme assets	(5%)	(6%)	(1%)	5%
Total amount recognised in statement of total recognised gains and losses:				
– amount (£m)	73	276	91	1
– percentage of scheme assets	6%	27%	12%	0%

7. The December 2006 amendment

8516 A few years ago, the ASB (now abolished) published an amendment to FRS 17, requiring certain additional disclosures whilst dispensing with others previously required. Although the changes have been incorporated into the preceding text, they are repeated here for ease of comparison.

8517 The significant **additional disclosures** include:
– information to enable users to evaluate the nature of a company's participation in defined benefit schemes and the financial effects of changes in those schemes. Previously, FRS 17 required only the nature of schemes to be disclosed.
– the principal actuarial assumptions used as at the balance sheet date. Previously, only information regarding the main financial assumptions was required. The most significant change this is likely to bring is the requirement to disclose mortality rates – where it is considered to be a material assumption.
– an analysis of the opening and closing scheme liabilities and scheme assets showing separately the movements in scheme assets and scheme liabilities.
– an analysis of scheme liabilities into amounts arising from schemes that are funded and those that are not.
– information about contingent liabilities arising from retirement benefit obligations as well as the nature of contingent assets, where an inflow of the economic benefits is probable.

> MEMO POINTS   At the same time as the amendment to FRS 17 was issued, the Audit Practices Board (now the Audit and Assurance Council) also published a Reporting Statement (RS), **"Retirement benefits"**, intended as a formulation of **best practice**. Aimed at larger companies, it does not have mandatory force. However, it sets out the following **six principles** to be considered when providing disclosures for defined benefit schemes:
> – the relationship between the entity and trustees (managers) of the defined benefit scheme;
> – the principal assumptions used to measure scheme liabilities;
> – the sensitivity of scheme liabilities to changes in the principal assumptions used to measure the scheme liabilities;
> – how the liabilities arising from defined benefit schemes are measured;
> – the future funding requirements to the defined benefit scheme; and
> – the nature and extent of the risks arising from the assets held by the defined benefit scheme.

SECTION 4

Other types of scheme

A. Defined contribution schemes

Under this type of scheme, also known as a "money purchase scheme", the employer does not guarantee a particular level of pension benefit and so there is **no obligation** upon it to pay extra contributions into the fund. **8600**

The benefits are based on the amount of contributions paid into the scheme as amplified by investment return on those contributions. These funds may also provide death-in-service benefits.

Under a defined contribution scheme, the risk is borne by the employee, and not the employer-company, and the final pension the employee will receive depends upon the performance of the scheme itself. **8601**

The **charge against profits** should be the actual amount of the employer's contributions paid, or payable, to the pension scheme in respect of the accounting period in question. A balance sheet asset or liability may result from the application of the normal matching concept, if payments do not equal the contributions falling due.

The following **disclosures** should be made: **8604**
- the nature of the scheme; FRS 17 (75)
- accounting policy;
- the pension cost charge for the period;
- any outstanding or prepaid contributions at the balance sheet date.

> [EXAMPLE] D Ltd operates a defined contribution pension scheme. The assets of the scheme are held separately from those of the company in an independently administered fund. The pension cost charge represents contributions payable by the company and amounted to £500,000 (20X4 £450,000). Contributions totalling £40,000 (20X4 £37,000) were payable to the fund at the year end and are included in creditors.

The cost relating to a defined contribution scheme should be recognised within operating profit in the profit and loss account.

B. Other retirement benefits

Other retirement benefits, such as continuing medical cover, are often provided to employees who have retired. The related cost of these benefits should be **measured and recognised** in accordance with the rules for defined benefit schemes. **8610**

Estimating the **future changes** in the cost of retirement healthcare is particularly difficult due to: **8612**
- advances in medical skills and technologies; FRS 17 (30)
- the rise in the expectations of patients; and
- the reduction in future benefits in light of the above.

It is **not appropriate** to anticipate the reduction of any benefits or assume that the employer may curtail the scheme at some time in the future. An actuary will need to be appointed by the scheme managers to enable the cost of providing the benefit offered under the scheme to be estimated, and to enable the appropriate accounting entries to be made.

Death-in-service and incapacity benefits

8614

FRS 17 (73)

UITF 35

The **expected cost** of these benefits should be recognised in the profit and loss account as part of the operating profit. The cost will depend on whether the benefits are insured.

Type of scheme	Applicable cost	Accounting treatment
Insured	Insurance premium	Profit and loss charge
Not insured	Estimated expected cost	Profit and loss charge
	Difference between actual and expected cost	Gain or loss in STRGL

The difference between the expected cost and the actual cost should be treated as an actuarial gain or loss. In practice such a difference is usually insured against, and is therefore unlikely to arise.

Uninsured benefits should be measured using the projected unit method (¶8452).

SECTION 5

New UK GAAP – requirements of FRS 102

8620   The introduction of FRS 102 "The Financial Reporting Standard applicable in the UK and Republic of Ireland", which becomes mandatory from January 2015, contains some differences from current UK GAAP in relation to **defined benefit schemes**. These are set out in the table below.

There are no appreciable differences between FRS 17 and FRS 102 involving **defined contribution schemes**.

Defined benefit scheme	FRS 17	FRS 102
General accounting treatment	Net liability: Costs recognised in the P & L, except actuarial gains and losses which should be taken to the STRGL. Disclosures: Net surplus/deficits are shown on face of the balance sheet.	Net liability: As for FRS 17 except actuarial gains and losses which are taken to other comprehensive income. Disclosures: No guidance given.
Multi-employer plans	1. Accounted for as a defined benefit scheme unless the entity's contributions relate only to the current service period (financial year), or it has difficulty identifying its share of the plan's assets and liabilities, in which case it is a defined contribution scheme. 2. Each entity recognises its contributions to fund deficits only in financial period they fall due.	Terms and conditions of plan determine its classification as a defined benefit or contribution scheme.
Group plans	Not explicitly covered. Not differentiated from multi-employer plans	Contractual agreements between group companies under common control for sharing costs: Each entity recognises its share in its individual financial statements. If no such policy/agreement exists then the Group entity that administers the pension plan accounts for assets, liabilities, administration costs while the other participating group entities account for their contributions.

Defined benefit scheme	FRS 17	FRS 102
Short term employee benefits	Not explicitly covered	Short term absences such as holiday or sick leave: accruals required for unused leave c/fwd. Profit share/bonus schemes: Where constructive obligations exist these should be provided for.

MEMO POINTS   1. The FRC has issued two staff education notes (SEN 09, SEN 10) in order to highlight key areas of consideration when transitioning to FRS 102.

2. **Staff Education Note 9**: "Short-term employee benefits and termination benefits" compares the accounting requirements for short term employee benefits under FRS 102 and existing UK GAAP, which is less detailed when accounting for short-term benefits. For instance, many companies do not currently provide for holiday pay (short-term compensated absences); this position will need reconsideration when applying FRS 102 for the first time.

3 . **Staff Education Note 10**: "Employee benefits – Defined benefit plans" compares the accounting treatment for defined benefit plans as set out in FRS 17 "Retirement Benefits" and Section 28 "Employee Benefits" of FRS 102 and focuses on multi-employer and group schemes.

CHAPTER 4

Share-based payment

FRS 20 "Share-based payment", provides guidance on all forms of payment that are made in shares or on the basis of the value of shares (or other equity instrument) and requires companies to recognise in their profit or loss and financial position, the effects of share-based payment transactions in which **share options** are granted to employees.   **8850**

More specifically, a company is obliged to reflect an expense (or, if applicable, an asset) measured at fair value in respect of its employee share option schemes, share purchase plans, and any other share-based payments (i.e. payments made in shares or other equity instruments, or by way of a cash amount based on the value of those instruments).

There are a number of important differences between the requirements of FRS 20 and the **FRSSE** (see ¶8855).

The **transactions** to which FRS 20 might apply can take many forms, though the following table represent the three main types it identifies, each of which discussed in detail in the sections that follow.   **8851**
FRS 20 (2)

CONDITIONS APPLYING
1. **Equity-settled** share-based payment transactions in which the entity receives goods or services as consideration for equity instruments of the entity.
2. **Cash-settled** share-based payment transactions in which the entity acquires goods or services by incurring liabilities to the supplier or amounts that are based on the price (or value) of the entity's equity instruments.
3. **Choice of cash or equity settlement** (i.e. where the entity receives or acquires goods or services and the terms of the arrangement provide one or other of the parties to the transaction to choose whether the settlement should be made in cash (or other assets) or by issuing equity instruments).

Exemptions

Certain business combinations and arrangements **do not fall within the scope** of FRS 20. The following table provides a summary.   **8852**

EXAMPLES OF SHARE-BASED TRANSACTIONS		
Form of transaction		**Covered by FRS 20?**
Entity receives services from employees	Pays by way of share issue	Yes
Entity receives goods or services from persons other than employees	• Pays by way of share option (or other equity instrument), or • Settles amount owing by cash (or other assets) based on the value of the entity's shares or other equity instruments, or • Equity instruments are transferred by shareholders, parent/s or other group members to supplier of these goods or services.	Yes
Business combinations (e.g., acquisitions, mergers, etc.)	Issues shares or other equity instruments directly as part of transaction.	No
Arrangement affected by a business combination but not arising from it	Shares to be issued to employees in terms of existing contract are altered as a result of business combination.	Yes
Contracts to buy or sell non-financial items	Settlement to be made in cash or other financial instruments as if they are financial instruments (including exchange of financial instruments).	No
Transactions with employees in their capacity as shareholder (e.g., where an employee receives a rights issue because he owns a particular class of share).		No

A. Small companies adopting FRSSE

8855

FRS 12.13

A share-based transaction is defined as a transaction in which an entity acquires goods or services and incurs a liability to be settled either by its own shares (**"equity-settled"**) or by a cash payment based on the value of its equity instruments (**"cash-settled"**). These types of transactions should be accounted for as set out in the table below.

TRANSACTION TYPE	ACCOUNTING TREATMENT
If a **cash-settled** share-based transaction:	– the goods or services should be treated as assets or expenses as the circumstances dictate; – the corresponding liability must reflect the best estimate of the expenditure required to settle the liability at balance sheet date; – at each subsequent balance sheet date and at the date of settlement the liability must be remeasured; – a description of the principal terms and conditions relating to the transaction, including its current and potential financial effect must be disclosed by way of a note.
If an **equity-settled** share-based transaction:	Disclosure is required in the motes detailing: the principal terms and conditions – including the number of shares and the number of employees and others potentially involved; – the grant date; – any performance conditions, and the period over which these apply; and – if applicable, any option prices.

TRANSACTION TYPE	ACCOUNTING TREATMENT
Where the **other transacting party has the choice** of whether the entity settles in cash or equity	The transaction should be treated as a cash-settled transaction. However, if the obligation is eventually settled by the issue of equity, the previously recognised liability should be treated as the proceeds of the issue of that equity.
Where the **entity itself has the choice** as to method of settlement	The transaction should be treated as either cash-settled or equity-settled as is felt appropriate

B. Transactions settled by payments of equity

This discussion deals with transactions an entity settles by issuing equity instruments rather than settling with cash.

8860

In respect of such transactions settled by issuing equity instruments, the entity is required to measure the subject of a transaction (i.e. the goods and/or services acquired) at its **fair value**, except where it cannot be determined reliably, in which case the entity must then measure the value of the goods or services by reference to the fair value of the **underlying equity** instruments granted. The value so determined will be the amount at which the transaction is recorded (i.e. by which equity is increased in the balance sheet).

FRS 20 (10)

> EXAMPLE A company receives goods worth £20,000 from a supplier. Instead of payment in cash, the supplier would prefer to receive shares in the enterprise. The share issue is deemed to take place at a value of £20,000 with the book entry being a debit to current assets and the credit to share capital.

1. Employees

In the majority of cases, transactions with employees are concerned with **services**, rather than goods. Payments in respect of services received are recorded in the profit and loss account as expenses. The **timing** in respect of which the expense is recognised is the same as it would have been had the transaction been cash-based.

8864

a. Valuation

In practice, where services are received from employees, it is generally not possible to estimate reliably the fair value of the services received. This can be for many reasons; the most usual being that equity instruments are granted to employees as part of a remuneration package consisting of various components (cash, benefits, etc.). In addition, these grants may be linked to specific bonus or incentive arrangements, in other words, the employee's future services are involved. The value of all these elements is difficult to measure.

8867

Therefore, the transaction must be valued at the fair value of the equity instruments granted. The valuation should be made at the measurement date based on **available market prices**, and taking into account any terms and conditions of the grant.

8869

Often, **market prices are not available** as, for instance, it is generally not the case that options granted to employees are the same as publicly traded options for which there is a market price. Therefore, the valuation will be based on an estimate of the fair value of the equity instruments in an arm's length transaction. The **valuation technique** should be consistent with commonly used valuation methodologies for pricing financial statements and take account of all factors that arm's length participants would normally take into account in calculating a fair price.

8871

8872   For transactions with employees, valuation of the payment should be at the date the equity instruments are granted.

---

b. Conditions attaching

8873
FRS 20 (14)   With respect to share-based payments for services, **two possibilities** exist: the instruments can **vest immediately** (i.e. the employee becomes unconditionally entitled to the equity instruments), or they may vest at some future time when certain conditions have been met. In the former case (immediate vesting), the company should account for the instruments at the grant date.

8874   Depending on the specific nature of the vesting conditions in cases where the instruments do **not vest immediately**, the services are presumed to be received during the period ending on the date that vesting takes place and the company therefore accounts for the instrument at vesting date. Various vesting conditions are discussed below.

Continuity of employment

8875
FRS 20 (15)   A vesting condition might relate purely to the requirement that an employee remains in employment for a specific period. If an employee is granted share options conditional upon completing three years' service, then the entity should presume that the services to be rendered by the employee as consideration for the share options will be received in the future, over the three-year vesting period.

Performance targets

8876   An employee may be granted share options conditional upon the achievement of a performance target. If the time of vesting depends on a **market-related condition**, any assumptions made at the grant date about the likely length of the vesting period (e.g., an assumption about when the market value of the instrument might reach a certain level) must be consistent with those used to estimate the fair value of the instrument granted.

The estimates are not adjusted subsequently, even if it transpires that the assumptions were not reliable or had been revised.

8877   Where the condition is **not market related** (e.g. where it is dependent on reaching an **internal target** such as a sales volume), then estimates of the length of the vesting period should be adjusted in later accounting periods if it becomes clear that the vesting period is likely to differ from previous estimates.

8879
FRS 20 (19)   Vesting conditions other than market conditions should not be taken into account in estimating the fair value of the shares or share options. Instead, their effect is taken into account by adjusting the number of equity instruments to be issued. Ultimately, the amount recognised for the services received will be based on the number of equity instruments that eventually vest.

In the meantime, the entity should recognise an amount for the goods or services received during the vesting period based on the best available estimate of the number of equity instruments expected to vest. On the vesting date, if the estimate does not equal the number of instruments that actually vested, an adjustment should be made.

8881   **Market conditions** (e.g. a target share price that triggers vesting) must be taken into account in estimating fair value. Therefore, the entity should recognise the goods or services received from the other party that satisfies all other vesting conditions (e.g., services received from an employee who has remained in service for the specified period) irrespective of whether the market condition is actually satisfied.

8883
FRS 20 (22)   If options have a **reload feature**, this should not be taken into account when estimating fair value. A reload feature provides for the automatic re-granting of additional options to option-holders who exercise their options using the entity's shares instead of cash. Instead, a reload option should be accounted for as a separate option grant if and when it takes place.

In those cases where it is **impossible to make a reliable estimate** of the fair value of the **8885**
instruments issued, the entity should:
– initially, measure the equity instruments at their **intrinsic value** (i.e., the difference
between the fair value of the underlying shares and the price required to be paid);
– at subsequent reporting dates, including after the final settlement, recognise any **change**
in intrinsic value in the profit and loss account; and
– recognise the goods or services received based on the **number of instruments** that ultimately vest.

If the instruments **are settled during the vesting period**, the company should immediately **8887**
recognise the amount that would otherwise have accrued over the remainder of the vesting
period. In addition, where payments are made on settlement, they are treated as a repurchase of equity (i.e. as a deduction from equity) but only up to the intrinsic value. Any
excess over the intrinsic value must be recognised via the profit and loss account as an
expense.

---

c. Modifications to terms and conditions

An entity might modify the terms and conditions on which the equity instruments were **8889**
granted (e.g. by re-pricing the share options). Where transactions are measured at values FRS 20 (26)
determined by reference to the equity instruments underlying them – whether with
employees or otherwise – the entity must take into account the **nature** of the change and
account for its effect.

At a minimum, the entity must recognise the **fair value** of the equity instruments granted at **8891**
the measurement date, except in instances where the equity instruments do not vest because
a non-market-related vesting condition was not met. Where there have been changes that
benefit the other party (i.e. changes that increase the fair value of the instruments concerned), the effect must also be recognised.

Cancellation or settlement of a grant of equity   If the entity **cancels or settles** a grant of **8895**
equity during the vesting period (other than by failing to meet the vesting conditions), it FRS 20 (28)
must:
a. account for it as an acceleration of vesting and recognise immediately the amount that
otherwise would have been recognised over the remainder of the vesting period;
b. treat as a repurchase of equity any payment made on cancellation, up to the fair value
of the equity instrument (with any excess being accounted for as an expense); and
c. treat any new instruments granted at the same time in one of two ways:
– where they are **regarded as a replacement** for the old instruments, the issue is accounted
for in the same way as a modification to the conditions. The incremental fair value granted
(the value granted as a result of the change) is the difference between the fair value of the
new instruments (at date of replacement) and the fair value of the old, less any amounts
previously treated as a deduction from equity;
– where they **are not regarded as replacement** instruments, the transactions are accounted
for separately.
Where an entity repurchases vested equity instruments, the payment made to the employee
must be treated as a deduction from equity. To the extent that the **payment exceeds the fair
value** at the repurchase date, any excess is to be recognised as an expense.

Where an option is unable to be exercised because vesting conditions are not met (e.g. if **8896**
the employee leaves the employment or a performance target is not achieved), the cost of
the options is reversed. However, if the **employer cancels** the options, the full value of the
options is charged to the profit and loss account. Where the **employee cancels** the options
(other than on leaving employment), the treatment should be the same as that for cancella-
tions by the employer.

2. Non-employees

8898
FRS 20 (13)

Where **services** are received from **parties other than employees** and it is not possible to value these services fairly, the entity must base the value of these services on the value of the equity instruments granted.

Where the subject of the transaction is **goods**, the payment should be recorded as an asset.

Measurement of the payment should be at the date on which the entity obtains the goods or the counterparty renders the services.

8899

Under the amendments to FRS 20, where the identifiable consideration received appears to be less than the fair value of the equity instruments granted or liability incurred, this situation indicates that **unidentifiable** goods or services have been (or have yet to be) received by the entity. These unidentifiable goods or services must be measured as the difference between the fair value of the share-based payment and the fair value of any **identifiable** goods or services.

The entity must measure the unidentifiable goods or services received at the grant date. In the case of **cash-settled transactions**, the entity must re-measure the liability at the end of each reporting period until it has been settled.

C. Transactions settled by payments in cash

8900

Some transactions are settled by an entity in cash (or other assets) but the amount is determined by reference to the value of its shares (or other equity instruments). For example, a company might grant **share appreciation rights** to employees as part of their remuneration package, whereby employees will become entitled to a future cash payment (rather than an equity instrument) based on an increase in the share price from a specified level over a specified period. Or, an employer might grant the right to employees to receive a future cash payment by granting them a **redeemable right to shares** that is either mandatory (such as on cessation of employment) or at their own option.

FRS 20 (30)

In respect of such transactions, the entity is required to measure the value of the goods or services acquired – and the liability incurred – at the fair value of the liability. All terms and conditions, and the extent to which the service has been rendered, are taken into account.

Until such time as the liability is settled, the entity must, at each reporting date, re-measure the fair value of the liability. Any changes should be recognised in the profit and loss account during the period concerned.

8902

Where the rights are **granted retrospectively**, e.g. where a bonus to be paid is based on the share price during a preceding period and there is no future service requirement, the services are presumed to have been received and a liability is recognised immediately.

8904

On the other hand, where the conditions relate to a **future period** (e.g., a continuing period of service), the liability is recognised over the period concerned.

D. Transactions settled by payments either of equity or in cash

8907

It is also possible for the terms of an arrangement to give the **choice** to both parties to a transaction as to whether the entity must settle the transaction by way of cash (or other assets) or by issuing equity. In other words, either the entity or the other party may make this election.

In these cases, the transaction must be accounted for as a cash-settled transaction if, and to the extent that, the entity has incurred a **liability to settle** in cash or other assets. It must account for the transaction as an equity-settled transaction if, and to the extent that, no liability has been incurred.

8908
FRS 20 (34)

The accounting treatment therefore depends both on the basis of valuing the transaction as well as the party that has the right to elect how it will be settled.

In the case of the **employees in a subsidiary** company being granted **rights to equity instruments of the parent**, two possibilities exist: the rights can be granted either by the subsidiary or by the parent itself. The problem that arises is that the accounting treatment is different. If granted by the parent, the transaction is regarded as **equity-settled**. If granted by the subsidiary, the transaction is treated as **cash-settled in the subsidiary's** accounts but as **equity-settled in the group** accounts.

8909

a. Entity grants right to elect choice of settlement to the other party

If the entity has granted the right to the other party to choose how the transaction is to be settled, it has in fact granted a **compound financial instrument** consisting of a debt component (i.e. the other party's right to receive payment in cash) and an equity component (i.e., its right to demand settlement in equity).

8910
FRS 20 (35)

For transactions with parties **other than employees**, in which the fair value of the goods or services is measured directly, the entity must measure the equity component of the compound financial instrument as follows:

8911

Fair value of goods or services received	£ xxx
Less: Fair value of debt component	xxx
Fair value of equity component	£ xxx

For other transactions – including those **with employees** – the entity must measure the fair value of the compound financial instrument as follows:

8912

Fair value of debt component	£ xxx
Add: Fair value of equity component [1]	xxx
Fair value of compound instrument	£ xxx
1. Note that the other party must forfeit the right to receive cash in order to receive the equity instrument.	

Transactions in which **the other party has the choice of settlement** are usually structured so that the fair value of one alternative is the same as the value of the other. For instance, the counterparty may have the choice of receiving share options or cash-settled share appreciation rights. In this case, the fair value of the equity component is zero, therefore the fair value of the compound instrument is equal to the fair value of the debt component. Similarly, where the fair values of the settlement options differ, the fair value of the equity component is usually higher than zero, so that the fair value of the compound instrument is greater than the value of the debt component. If the entity makes **a cash payment instead of issuing equity**, the payment is applied to settle the liability in full. By electing to receive cash, the other party forfeits the right to receive equity.

8914

b. Entity has right to elect choice of settlement

Where the entity has the choice of whether to settle in cash or by issuing equity, it must first determine whether it has a present obligation to settle in cash.

8918
FRS 20 (41)

If a **present obligation** exists, the company is obliged to treat the transaction as cash-settled. The following are the circumstances in which a present obligation is deemed to exist:
- the choice of settlement in equity has no commercial substance (e.g. the entity has no legal authority to issue shares);
- the entity has a past history or stated policy of settling in cash;
- the entity generally settles in cash when requested to do so by the other party.

8920
FRS 20 (42)

Where the entity has **no such present obligation**, it must account for the transaction as an equity-settled share-based transaction (as described from ¶8860, above).

On **settlement**, the entity will account for the transaction in one of the following ways, as circumstances dictate:

FRS 20 (43)

CONDITIONS APPLYING	TREATMENT
1 Entity elects to settle in cash.	Cash payment treated as repurchase of an equity interest (i.e. a deduction from equity, except as stated in (3), below).
2 Entity elects to settle by issuing equity.	Transfer from one component of equity to another.
3 Entity elects the settlement alternative with the higher fair value.	Amount of excess value given to be recognised as expense (e.g., the difference between cash paid and the value of the equity that would otherwise have been issued is transferred to expense).

8921

Groups – additional requirements   An amendment to FRS 20 sets out additional requirements relating to share-based payment transactions among group entities.

In its separate or individual financial statements, the **entity receiving goods or services** must measure the goods or services received as either an equity-settled or a cash-settled share-based payment transaction by assessing the nature of the awards granted and its own rights and obligations. Where the awards granted are the entity's own equity instruments or the entity has no obligation to settle the share-based payment transaction, the goods or services received should be measured as an equity-settled share-based transaction. In all other circumstances, the entity should measure the goods or services received as a cash-settled share-based payment transaction. The entity settling a share-based payment transaction when **another entity in the group** receives the goods or services should recognise the transaction as an equity-settled share-based payment transaction only if it is settled in the entity's own equity instruments. If it is not, the transaction should be measured as a cash-settled share-based payment transaction.

E. Disclosure

8925

FRS 20 requires entities to make such disclosures as are necessary to enable users of financial statements to understand:
- the nature and extent of share-based payment arrangements during the period under review,
- how the fair value of goods and services received – or the fair value of equity instruments granted, was calculated, and
- the effect of share-based transactions on both its profit and loss for the period and its financial position at the reporting date.

The above requirements will be satisfied if the entity supplies the following information:

1. **Description** of each type of share-based payment arrangement during the period.
2. Number and weighted average **exercise price** of share options outstanding at the beginning and end of the period, exercisable at the end of the period, and granted, forfeited, exercised or expired during the period.
3. Weighted average share price **at the date of exercise** for those share options exercised during the period – or, where options were regularly exercised throughout the period, the weighted average share price for the period.
4. The range of exercise prices and weighted average **remaining contractual life** for options outstanding at the end of the period.
5. Where goods and/or services received were valued by reference to the value of equity granted, in the case of **new options**, their weighted average fair value at the measurement date including information on how the value was ascertained; in the case of **new equity instruments other than options**, the number and their weighted average fair value at the measurement date including information on how the value was ascertained; and in the case of **equity instruments changed during the period**, an explanation of the changes, the incremental fair value granted and information on how these were ascertained.
6. Where goods and services have been measured directly, details of how this was done.
7. Where the company **rebuts the presumption** that the fair value of goods and services received can be measured reliably, a statement of this fact together with an explanation of how the presumption was rebutted.
8. Where goods and services did not qualify for recognition as assets, the total **expense** of share-based payment transactions in the period.
9. Total **carrying amount** of liabilities at the reporting date that arose as a result of share-based payment transactions, and the total **intrinsic value** at the end of the period for liabilities where the other party's rights had already vested by that date.

F. New UK GAAP – requirements of FRS 102

In terms of definitions, recognition and measurement of both equity based and cash based transactions, there are **no key differences** between existing UK GAAP and the new financial reporting standard FRS 102 "The Financial Reporting Standard applicable in the UK and Republic of Ireland". There are, however, some small differences in relation to determining fair value and arrangements where a choice exists between cash or equity settlement and group issues, as set out in the table below.

8930

ACCOUNTING ISSUE	ACCOUNTING TREATMENT UNDER FRS 102
1 Fair value (FV)	FV of shares should be assessed in the following order: – is there a benchmark market price? and – available comparable market data in which entity operates (e.g. recent share transactions in company's shares or an independent valuation.
2 Choice of cash or equity based transactions	Regardless of whether the transaction is **cash or equity** based it is accounted for as the former where the transaction is deemed devoid of commercial substance.
3 Group issues	Where share options are given to employees of a subsidiary the parent has one of two options: – account for the transaction on the basis it is paying the cash or offering shares itself, (following section 26 FRS 102); or – include a charge based on a realistic assessment of the group expense.

CHAPTER 5

Taxation

The calculation and presentation of the tax entries in the financial statements is dictated by the status of the company, the types and sources of income included within the accounting profits, and the nature of the costs incurred. **9000**

At the most basic level, corporate tax is an expense, related to profit on income, levied by national governments and borne by businesses. In the UK there are two rates of corporation tax charged on taxable profits; namely the mainstream rate and the small profits rate. Which rate is applied depends on the level of taxable profits in an accounting period. Further details of all tax issues can be found in *Tax Memo* and also *Corporation Tax Memo*.

There are two elements to the tax charge included in the financial statements:
– current tax; and
– deferred tax.

In addition, VAT affects most businesses, while in the context of **groups** there may also be specific tax implications.

A. Current tax

The rules relating to how current tax should be disclosed in the financial statements are contained in FRS 16, "Current Tax",and covers the following issues from a reporting perspective: **9005**
– recognition, measurement and disclosure of the current (corporation) tax charge; and
– other taxes relating to dividends and interest (e.g. tax credits, withholding tax and underlying tax).

The **objective of tax accounting** is to recognise taxation in a consistent and transparent manner.

MEMO POINTS From 1 April 2015 the main corporation tax rate will be the same as the small profits rate.

1. Common terms

9007
FRS 16 (2)

The term "current tax" includes the amount of tax estimated to be payable or recoverable relating to a company's profit or loss for a period, excluding the effects of deferred tax. Providing for current tax is an application of the matching concept. As the **tax liability**, calculated for the purposes of the financial statements, is often subject to refinement and possibly negotiation with HMRC, an adjustment is also usually required to the estimates used for previous periods. It is important to note that such adjustments should be treated as part of the current year's tax charge or credit, and not as a prior period adjustment.

9010

Dividends and **interest**, both payable and receivable, are often affected by the requirement to withhold tax at source.

The most common types of deducted taxes are:

1. **Withholding tax**, which is the tax paid over to the tax authorities by the payer of the income on behalf of the recipient. The table below gives examples of income from which withholding tax may be deducted, depending on the nature and location of the parties to the transaction.

Payer	Recipient	Types of income
UK	UK	Interest (unless between UK companies) Patent royalties
UK	Overseas	Interest Royalties Rent Dividends
Overseas	UK	As above, subject to rules of overseas jurisdiction

The amount chargeable to corporate tax is the gross amount of income, including withholding tax. When a UK company receives taxed income from overseas, double tax relief is often claimed (¶9029). This may be sufficient to extinguish the UK corporation tax liability on that source of profit where the rate of deduction is high enough.

2. **Underlying tax** is the tax levied by the local jurisdiction on the overseas entity's profits. As dividends are paid out of taxed profits, the recipient of the dividend is indirectly suffering this tax, and double tax relief is available in some circumstances.

3. **Tax credits** are given to the **non-corporate recipient** of a dividend from a UK company, which can result in the dividend being tax free (unless the recipient is a higher or additional rate taxpayer). Under this imputation system, a company's profits are taxed only once, and individuals receiving a distribution of profits (usually dividends) are given credit for tax already suffered by the company.

> ⌐MEMO POINTS⌐ The **tax credit rate** (currently 10% for 2013–14) is subject to periodical change and can be checked via the HMRC website.

2. Measurement

9018
FRS 16 (14)

Current tax is measured by applying the **tax rates**, which the UK authorities specify in advance. The tax rates for the coming financial year are set out in a Finance Bill that is approved by the House of Commons.

a. Overview of corporation tax

9020

Corporation tax is charged on taxable profits of companies under Corporation Tax Self Assessment. Under this system, the company **calculates** the corporation tax due, and completes a CT600 Tax Return, which is submitted to HMRC, together with a computation of the tax liability and a copy of the statutory accounts. Various factors affect the calculation of the tax charge.

Residence

The company's residence status is crucial to determining the liability to UK corporation tax: **9022**
– **UK companies** are liable to UK corporation tax on their worldwide profits and gains, arising from any source; and
– **other companies** may be liable to UK corporation tax, depending on the nature of their activities.

Period

Tax is levied on the results of the **accounting period**, which is usually the same as the period **9024** covered by the statutory accounts, although it cannot exceed 12 months. A **longer** period of account will be split into two accounting periods, the first being 12 months long.

Taxable profits

Corporation tax is **chargeable** on the aggregated profits from all sources, after adjustments **9025** have been made for:
– non-taxable income (e.g. dividends that enjoy the dividend exemption);
– disallowable items (e.g. business entertaining);
– deductions (e.g. charitable donations); and
– any allowable losses.

Taxable profits are seldom the same as the accounting profits, and this issue is addressed in the accounts by the use of deferred tax (¶9060).

Income and expenses subject to non-standard rates of tax

Income and expenses should be included in the financial statements on the basis of the **9026** amount **actually receivable or payable**, ignoring any notional tax effects of the individual FRS 16 (11) items. For example, certain types of leasing transactions can result in a pre-tax loss but a post-tax profit, because certain items are allowable for tax in an amount that exceeds the accounting expense. Only the pre-tax loss should be included in the financial statements, however.

Where a company's accounts are **materially affected** by items that are subject to non-standard rates of tax, appropriate disclosure should be made.

Computation

Income from **different sources** is dealt with by various tax rules in order to calculate the tax **9027** due. A tax computation shows the profits chargeable to corporation tax and the calculation of the corporation tax charge, using the corporation tax rates applicable for the period, and is the main supporting document for the company tax return.

The **basic format of the computation** is as follows: **9028**

	£
Trading income	X
Loan relationship gains	X
Overseas income	X
Miscellaneous income	X
Income from land and property	X
Income received under deduction of tax and taxable distributions	X
Chargeable gains	X
Less: Qualifying charitable donations	(X)
Profits chargeable to corporation tax (PCTCT)	X
Corporation tax thereon @ x%	X
Less: Income tax suffered at source	(X)
Net corporation tax payable	X

Overseas issues

9029   The **basis of taxation** for overseas income depends on the nature of the income. For example, dividends received from overseas are taxed (if not considered to be exempt) when received, while overseas trading income is taxed on an accrued basis.

If **tax has already been suffered** (such as withholding or underlying tax) in the overseas country, double tax relief may be claimed under the terms of the relevant treaty or unilaterally under the applicable UK rules. Relief is limited to the amount of UK corporation tax levied on the overseas income.

Rates

9030   The rates of corporation tax are **dependent** on the **level of taxable profits** in a 12-month period, and are subject to periodic change. The financial year commences on 1 April and is denoted by the year in which it starts. For the years beginning 1 April 2013 (FY2013) and 2014 (FY2014) the rates of tax are summarised in the following table.

Taxable profits	Corporation tax rate FY2013	Corporation tax rate FY2014
0 to £300,000	20%	20%
£300,001 to £1,500,000	23% less marginal relief [1]	21% less marginal relief [1]
Over £1,500,000	23%	21%
Notes: 1. The relief is calculated as £1,500,000 less the amount of profits, multiplied by a standard fraction (for FY2013, 3/400 and FY2014 1/400 (Marginal rate 21.25%)). See *Corporation Tax Memo* for full details.		

If the accounting period is **shorter than 12 months**, the profit limits are pro-rated.

MEMO POINTS   1. In the case of **associated companies**, the profit levels in the table above may be reduced. In broad terms, a company is an associate of another where one company controls the other, or both are controlled by a third party. A dormant company is not counted as an associated company for these purposes. See *Corporation Tax Memo* for further details.
2. The **marginal fraction** depends on the financial year in question and when a company's accounting period spans two financial years, the profits must be time apportioned.

9032   **Marginal relief calculation**   Marginal relief is calculated according to the following formula:

(Upper limit – profits) × basic profits/profits × fraction.

Basic profits are defined as the company's profits whilst profits includes the basic profits plus franked investment income. Upper and lower limits are reduced for short periods of account and where there are associate companies. The first £300,000 of profits are taxed at the small profits rate of 20% with the rest (where profits are below £1.5m) taxed at the marginal rate (i.e. 21.25% for FY 2014).

Payment

9036   **Most companies** must pay corporation tax by nine months and one day after the end of the accounting period. Exceptionally, **larger companies** (broadly, those with taxable profits exceeding £1,500,000 per annum, as adjusted for shorter periods and associated companies) must pay **quarterly instalments**. These instalments, which are payable in months 7, 10, 13 and 16 of a 12-month accounting period, require the company to estimate its current tax liability and to make payments accordingly.

---

b. Other taxes

Income tax

9038   Income tax affects companies in the following ways:
a. Companies must **deduct** income tax at source from certain payments and submit a form CT61 under a quarterly system. Examples of such items are annuities, interest paid to individ-

uals and patent royalties. The **rate** of tax depends on the type of payment, with basic rate tax usually being deducted.

b. Companies can **claim relief** for income tax suffered at source by set off against:
– any income tax deducted at source on payments which are disclosed on that quarter's CT61;
– the following quarter's return if in the same accounting period; or
– where there is a surplus at the year end, the company's corporation tax liability shown in the tax computation.

3. Recognition

The **general rule** is that the current tax charge should be recognised in the same perform-ance statement as the item to which it relates, which is normally the profit and loss account. If a particular item has been recognised in the statement of recognised gains and losses **(STRGL)**, related current tax should be recognised in that statement. Examples of such items would be:
– foreign currency differences; and
– the disposal of an asset that had been previously revalued.

9048
FRS 16 (5)

The amount of **dividends** payable or receivable, and **interest** payable or receivable should be stated excluding tax credits and other taxes, but including withholding taxes. For UK dividends payable or receivable, only the cash amount is included in the accounts. Overseas dividends and interest may be subject to withholding tax.

9054
FRS 16 (8–9)

EXAMPLE D Ltd has a 1% shareholding in an overseas company, from which it receives a net dividend that is not eligible for the dividend exemption. The rate of withholding tax is 10%, and the company is liable to UK corporation tax at 23%.
The dividend income shown in the accounts will be £200, and the tax note to the profit and loss account would show the following:

	£	£
UK corporation tax		
Current tax on income for the period (200 x 23%)	46	
Double tax relief (200 × 10%)	(20)	
		26
Foreign tax		
Current tax on income for the period		20
Tax charge		46

B. Deferred tax

1. Purpose

Taxable profits are rarely the same as accounting profits, because the criteria for recognising items of income and expense differ. Such items are often taxable or tax deductible at a different time to when they are recognised for accounting purposes, or in some cases may not be recognised or allowed at all, and the tax adjustments made to the accounting profit distort the resulting tax charge shown in the accounts.

9060
FRS 19 (2)

At the most basic level, deferred tax is the estimated amount of tax that will arise resulting from the **timing difference** between accounting and taxable profits.

MEMO POINTS Accounting for deferred tax is dealt with by **FRS 19 "Deferred Tax."** The standard reflects the need to harmonise the way in which deferred tax is accounted for under UK GAAP with the way in which it is accounted for in other countries. Therefore, the requirements of the FRS are broadly similar to those of the equivalent IAS 12 in that both require deferred tax to be provided for in full on most timing differences.

9062
FRS 19 (7)

Applying the **accruals concept**, the tax charge shown in the accounts should take account of all tax consequences of income and expenses disclosed in the current period, even though those consequences may only be recognised in a later period.

A **distinction** must however be made between differences in the accounting and tax treatment which are permanent, and those which purely relate to timing issues.

Permanent differences arise when items recognised in the financial statements will never be charged to tax, or allowed as a tax deductible expense (e.g. certain entertainment expenses). No adjustment for deferred tax is required.

Timing differences arise when an item is taxable or deductible in a different period to that in which it is recognised in the accounts. They are said to "originate" when they first arise, and "reverse" when they resolve in a later period. As such an **adjustment for deferred tax purposes** is required.

The rationale adopted by FRS 19 is to apply the liability method, which broadly means that tax is provided for on timing differences only, representing an estimated tax liability payable at some point in the future. In order to help remove the distortions to the tax charge, a provision for a deferred tax liability or a deferred tax asset is created.

9064
FRS 19 (2)

The following table summarises the deferred tax treatment of certain common items:

Item	Reference	Type of difference	Adjust for deferred tax purposes
Disallowable expenditure	¶9062	Permanent	No
Accelerated capital allowances	¶9066	Timing	Yes
Unrelieved tax loss	¶9074	Timing	Yes
Revaluation gain	¶9076	Timing	Yes
Deferred expenditure	¶9080	Timing	Yes
Pension liabilities	¶9082	Timing	Yes
Intra-group profits on stock reversed on consolidation	¶9154	Timing	Yes
Unremitted income from group undertakings	¶9158	Timing	Yes

Accelerated capital allowances

9066
FRS 19 (9)

Deferred tax is often relevant in respect of capital allowances, which are the tax deductible equivalent of depreciation (which is not tax deductible). An asset is commonly **depreciated at a slower rate** in the financial statements (i.e., over a longer period) than is allowed for tax purposes (in other words, the capital allowances claimed in the tax computation have the effect of "writing off" the asset faster). This gives rise to an initial tax advantage; however, this timing difference will slowly erode over time, and ultimately resolve when the asset is sold, because an adjustment will be made in the tax computation to reverse the excess capital allowances previously given.

EXAMPLE A Ltd purchases plant for £10,000 on 1 January 20X3 which qualifies for capital allowances on a 20% reducing balance basis, and is depreciated at 15% per annum on a straight-line basis. The company has a 31 December year end.
The following timing differences will arise up to 31 December 20X3:

	20X1 £	20X2 £	20X3 £	Total £
Depreciation charge	1,500	1,500	1,500	4,500
Capital allowances	2,000	1,600	1,280	4,880
Timing differences: Originating/(reversing)	500	100	(220)	380

In 20X4, A Ltd sells the plant for £6,000, when the net book value is £5,500, giving an accounting profit on disposal of £500. For tax purposes, the maximum capital allowances which should have been given are only £4,000 (£10,000 – £6,000), so a balancing charge of £880 is required.

	20X4
	£
Profit on disposal	(500)
Balancing charge	880
Timing differences: Originating/(reversing)	(380)

With the **effluxion of time**, as the accumulated depreciation charge converges with the   **9068**
cumulative capital allowances claimed, the deferred tax liability will be released.

EXAMPLE   A company purchases an asset for £10,000 and depreciates it over three years. The asset
qualifies for the annual investment allowance at 100%. The company uses the asset for four years
before scrapping it.

	Year 1	Year 2	Year 3	Year 4
	£	£	£	£
Depreciation charge	3,333	3,333	3,333	0
Capital allowances	10,000	0	0	0
Timing differences: Originating/(reversing)	6,666	(3,333)	(3,333)	0

The timing differences have reversed by Year 4, because in that time the asset has been fully
depreciated and all possible capital allowances have been claimed.

MEMO POINTS   The **annual investment allowance** for 2014/15 has been increased, for companies
investing more that £25,000 in plant and machinery. The maximum amount of the annual investment allowance (AIA) has risen from £25,000 to £500,000 for a temporary period running from
1 April 2014 to December 2015.
In January 2013 the AIA was increased from X¿‰25,000 to X¿‰250,000 before being increased
again in the 2014 budget to X¿‰500,000.

Even where an asset is **not depreciated**, deferred tax should still be provided on the timing   **9070**
difference that arises when capital allowances are claimed. An example of such an asset is
plant included within an investment property.

Certain types of capital **allowances are retained** by the company even when the asset is sold   **9072**
for a profit, depending on the length of time the asset has been held. For example, business
property renovation allowances cannot be withdrawn once a set period of ownership has
elapsed (currently 7 years). From acquisition, deferred tax should still be recognised on such
an asset, as the company should not anticipate holding the asset for the requisite period. After
the period has expired, however, the allowances claimed become a permanent difference
and the deferred tax that has previously been recognised should be reversed.

EXAMPLE   B Ltd acquires an investment property (which is not depreciated) on 1 January 20X1 for
£800,000, and it qualifies for business property renovation allowances, being used as an office for
the 7 year period. By 31 December 20X7, allowances of £800,000 have been claimed in the tax
computation. Deferred tax has been provided for this timing difference, and is now reversed at 31
December as the allowances can no longer be clawed back.

Unrelieved tax losses

Trading losses can be used in the following ways: **9074**
– set off in the current year against other profits and chargeable gains;
– carried back to set against the profits of the prior accounting period; or
– carried forward to set against profits of the same trade.

Where **set off** can occur in the current year or by way of carryback, the appropriate reduction is made to the current tax charge. Where set off is not available, and the losses are
carried forward, deferred tax comes into play, because the losses, when utilised, may lead
to an eventual tax reduction or even refund. This constitutes a timing difference.

The use of **capital losses** is more restricted, so deferred tax is rarely provided as a consequence (¶9100).

Revaluation gain

9076
FRS 19 (12), (14)

Normally revaluation gains **do not give rise** to a deferred tax adjustment. However, by **exception** deferred tax is provided if:
– the revaluation gain is recognised in the profit and loss account (such as for marked-to-market gains revalued to fair value); or
– there is a binding agreement to sell the asset at the balance sheet date and the resulting profit or loss has been recognised.

> MEMO POINTS   Very often **marked-to-market** items are taxed at the same time as they are recognised in the accounts; as a result no timing difference arises.

9078

Rollover relief, which is available only for certain types of assets, defers the tax charge resulting from a sale when the proceeds are reinvested in a replacement asset. When rollover relief is expected to be obtained, no deferred tax should be recognised, although related disclosure is required.

> MEMO POINTS   The rolled over **tax charge will crystallise** when the replacement asset is sold, although it is possible for another rollover claim to be made, which could then defer the resulting tax charge again.

Deferred expenditure

9080

Where expenditure is allowed for tax in the year that it is incurred, but for accounting purposes there is a delay in recognition, a deferred tax liability will arise. Examples include capitalised interest costs, and expense prepayments.

Pension liabilities

9082

For **accounting purposes**, contributions to pension schemes are recognised on the accruals basis while the **rule for tax purposes** is that contributions paid wholly and exclusively for the purposes of the business to registered schemes are allowed in the period in which they are made (i.e. cash basis).

Where there have been **special payments** to a pension fund (such as lump sum payments to make up a shortfall), tax relief may be spread according to specific rules that will not necessarily be the same as for accounting purposes. This will have deferred tax implications. For more information on this topic see *Tax Memo*.

---

2. Measurement

9085
FRS 19 (37)

Deferred tax is measured using the average tax rates that are expected to apply when the timing differences reverse, based on the tax rates that have been enacted, or substantively enacted, by the balance sheet. **In practice** current tax rates are often used, as they are invariably the only rates that have been enacted.

If future profits are expected to increase, it is prudent to use the standard rate of corporation tax.

> EXAMPLE   Continuing the example at ¶9066, an average tax rate of 23% applies throughout the period. The associated deferred tax balances would be:
>
> | | 20X1 £ | 20X2 £ | 20X3 £ | 20X4 £ |
> |---|---|---|---|---|
> | Timing difference | 500 | 100 | (220) | (380) |
> | Tax rate | 23% | 23% | 23% | 23% |
> | Deferred tax liability increase/(decrease) | 115 | 23 | (51) | (87) |
> | Deferred tax balance | 115 | 138 | 87 | 0 |

Discounting

To reflect the **time value of money**, it is possible to discount a deferred tax liability, although this is not usually undertaken due to the increased complexity of calculation.

9087
FRS 19 (42)

In making the decision whether to discount the deferred tax liability, the **following factors** should be considered:
– materiality;
– whether transparency outweighs the costs of performing the discounting calculations; and
– whether there is established industry practice which may influence the comparability of the accounts with those of other industry incumbents.

Discounting should be applied consistently, although care should be taken not to discount deferred tax provisions relating to timing differences that have already been discounted, such as defined benefit pension balances. The **discount period** should run until the timing differences completely reverse. For example, the relevant period for accelerated capital allowances is the time taken for the depreciation charge to catch up with the cumulative capital allowances.

3. Recognition

The deferred tax charge or credit is usually recognised in the profit and loss account, unless it relates to an item that has been recognised in the STRGL (¶4300). As with current tax, a reasonable allocation between the two performance statements may be appropriate in certain circumstances.

9096
FRS 19 (34)

Any deferred tax liabilities or assets which arise from **timing differences** should be provided for in full, subject to certain criteria.

9098

Deferred tax assets

The **basic rule** is that a deferred tax asset may only be recognised if there is sufficient evidence that it is likely to be recoverable at the balance sheet date.

9100

Where both a **deferred tax liability and asset exist** at the balance sheet date, arising on different items, it can be assumed that the asset is recoverable, as the reversal of the deferred tax liability will give rise to eventual taxable profits.

Where the **deferred tax asset cannot be fully set off** against a deferred tax liability, other evidence should be considered in deciding whether to recognise an asset, and this would include profits:
– that arise within the same entity and jurisdiction as the income or expenditure giving rise to the deferred tax asset;
– generated in the same period as the deferred tax asset is expected to reverse; and
– against which the tax loss will be set in a loss carry back or carry forward claim.

> MEMO POINTS   1. If there are any doubts about the company's **going concern** status, a deferred tax asset should not be recognised.
> 2. The recovery of a deferred tax asset arising from a **capital loss** is restricted because there must be plans to sell an asset which will result in a capital gain, to offset the loss.

> EXAMPLE   C Ltd believes that it will make taxable profits of £100,000 in the foreseeable future. At the balance sheet date, a deferred tax asset of £40,000 exists.
> Assuming an average tax rate of 25%, the deferred tax asset provided in the accounts should be £25,000 (£100,000 x 25%), and so £15,000 is unrecognised.

Overall, the **existence of unrelieved tax losses** at the balance sheet date normally indicates a doubtful future profit position, and a deferred tax asset would not therefore normally be recognised. An exception arises if the losses result from an identifiable and non-recurring cause, such as an arson attack, when profits are expected to resume in future periods, and the deferred tax asset may well be recoverable.

9102

> MEMO POINTS   When considering **suitable profits**, tax planning can used to restrict future capital allowances claims to utilise tax losses.

9104
FRS 19 (23)

The **recognised amount** of the deferred tax asset at each balance sheet date should be assessed annually, and where circumstances have changed, the recoverability of the asset should be reconsidered. Where future profitability is less than expected, the asset may be impaired. Alternatively, a previously unrecognised asset may be assessed as recoverable, and require inclusion in the current year's accounts as a change in accounting estimate.

> EXAMPLE D Ltd made a **trading loss** of £200,000 in 20X1, and due to continuing production problems, no deferred tax asset was recognised in 20X1. D Ltd made further losses of £40,000 in 20X2.
>
> In 20X3, the company started to reap the benefits of a capital reinvestment programme, and profits of £90,000 were made. Similar profits are expected in future years.
>
> Assuming £150,000 of the trading loss is still carried forward at the end of 20X3, after offset against the current year profits, D Ltd recognises a deferred tax asset of £34,500 (£150,000 x 23%) in 20X3.
>
> The credit to the profit and loss account is recognised as a current item relating to 20X3.

C. Disclosure and presentation

1. Current tax

9110
FRS 18 (55)

Any particular accounting policy adopted in relation to current tax should be disclosed.

9112

The following items must be included in the **note accompanying the tax charge** in the performance statements:

a. details of special circumstances that affect the tax liability for the current year or following year; and

b. the following amounts should be stated in "tax on profit on ordinary activities" allocated between UK corporation tax and foreign tax:

– the charge for UK corporation tax (with and without double tax relief);

– the charge for UK income tax;

– amount of overseas tax;

– tax attributable to the group share of profits from associated companies and joint ventures; and

– adjustments required in respect of prior periods.

9116

The **corporation tax balance** due to or from HMRC is disclosed within either:

– social security and other taxes; or

– other debtors, if the tax is recoverable.

Many companies choose to disclose corporation tax in the balance sheet as a separate subcategory of creditors.

Any corporation tax **payable more than 12 months** after the balance sheet date should be disclosed within "creditors: amounts falling due after more than one year".

2. Deferred tax

a. Profit and loss account

9120
FRS 19 (59)

In the profit and loss account the deferred tax charge should be included within the heading "tax on profit or loss on ordinary activities".

Notes to the profit and loss or STRGL   1. Tax on ordinary activities in the **profit and**   **9121**
loss account, identifying the following components, where material:
a. changes in deferred tax balances (before discounting where applicable) arising from:
– the origination and reversal of timing differences;
– changes in tax rates and laws; and
– adjustments to the estimated recoverable amount of deferred tax assets arising in previous
periods; and
b. where applicable, changes in the amounts of discount deducted in arriving at the deferred
tax balance.
2. Tax charged or credited directly in the **STRGL** for the period, separately disclosing the
main components including those in 1.a. above.

---

b. Balance sheet

Deferred tax balance

This balance (except deferred tax relating to defined benefit pensions) is **usually disclosed**   **9122**
separately in the balance sheet within either: FRS 19 (55–56)
– provisions for liabilities and charges (for a net deferred tax liability); or
– debtors (for a net deferred tax asset).

Deferred tax **debit and credit balances** should be offset within the above headings only if
they relate to taxes levied by the same authority, and arise in the same company or group.
Otherwise a separate presentation is required.

Separate disclosure **on the face of the balance sheet** is required if the amounts are so
material that readers may misinterpret the financial statements in the absence of such disclosure. For example, the balance sheet shows net current assets of £10,000, of which £20,000
relates to a deferred tax asset.

> MEMO POINTS   For **defined benefit pension schemes**, FRS 17 requires the deferred tax relating to
> the defined benefit asset or liability to be offset against the defined benefit asset or liability
> (¶8468).

Accounting policy

The accounting policy adopted in relation to deferred tax should **specifically** mention the   **9124**
following: FRS 18 (55)
– the basis of recognition for deferred tax, taking account of timing differences which have
originated and not reversed by the balance sheet date; and
– whether discounting has been used.

> EXAMPLE   **B Ltd**
> **Accounting policies**
> **Deferred taxation**
>
> The payment of taxation is deferred or accelerated because of timing differences between the
> treatment of certain items for accounting and taxation purposes. Full provision for deferred taxation
> is made under the liability method, on all timing differences that have arisen, but not reversed by
> the balance sheet date, unless such provision is not permitted by FRS 19.
> Deferred tax is measured at the rates that are expected to apply in the periods when the timing
> differences are expected to reverse, based on the tax rates and law enacted at the balance sheet
> date.
> Where gains or losses are recognised in the statement of total recognised gains and losses, the
> related taxation is also taken directly to that statement.
> In accordance with FRS 19, deferred taxation is not provided for:
> – revaluation gains on land and buildings, unless there is a binding contract to sell them at the
> balance sheet date; and
> – gains on the sale of non-monetary assets, where on the basis of all available evidence it is more
> likely than not that the taxable gain will be rolled over into the replacement assets.

Detailed disclosures

9128   The type of disclosures required in the taxation note to the financial statements are set out below.

General
a. the total deferred tax balance (before discounting, where applicable) showing the amount recognised for each significant timing difference separately;   **b.** the impact of discounting on, and the discounted amount of, deferred tax balance; and   **c.** the movement between the opening and closing net deferred tax balance, analysing separately: – the amount charged or credited in the profit and loss account for the period;   – the amount charged or credited directly in the STRGL for the period; and   – movements arising from the acquisition or disposal of businesses.
Deferred tax asset
In relation to a deferred tax asset, the amount of the asset should be disclosed, and the nature of the evidence supporting its recognition if: **a.** the recoverability of the deferred tax asset is dependent on future taxable profits in excess of those arising from the reversal of deferred tax liabilities; and   **b.** the reporting entity has suffered a loss in either the current or preceding period in the tax jurisdiction to which the deferred tax asset relates.
Circumstances affecting current and future tax charges
The notes to the financial statements should highlight circumstances that affect the current and total tax charges or credits in future periods, to include: **a.** a reconciliation of the current tax charge (or credit) on ordinary activities to the current tax charge that would result from applying a standard rate of tax to the profit on ordinary activities before tax;   **b.** for assets which have been revalued (including where the market value has only been disclosed in the accounts), and assuming these were sold at the values shown: – an estimate of the tax that could be payable or recoverable;   – an explanation of the circumstances in which the tax would crystallise; and   – an indication of the amount of tax that may become payable or recoverable in the foreseeable future;   **c.** for an asset which has been sold, or is the subject of a binding agreement to sell, and rollover relief is expected to be claimed: – the conditions which will need to be met for rollover relief to be available; and   – an estimate of the tax which would crystallise if those conditions were not met;   **d.** the amount of any unrecognised deferred tax asset and the circumstances in which the asset would be recovered; and   **e.** for any other deferred tax which has not been recognised: – the nature of the unrecognised amounts;   – the circumstances in which the tax would become payable or recoverable; and   – an indication of the amount that may become payable or recoverable in the foreseeable future.

MEMO POINTS   The **standard rate of tax** for an overseas group of companies may not be the usual UK rate.

9129   A **common way** of setting out the tax note to support the entry in the performance state-
FRS 16 (Appendix. I)   ments, which also complies with statutory requirements, is shown in the following pro forma.

	£	£
Current tax		
UK corporation tax		
Current tax on income for the period	X	
Adjustments in respect of prior periods	X	
	X	
Double tax relief	(X)	
		X
Foreign tax		
Current tax on income for the period	X	
Adjustments in respect of prior periods	X	
		X
Tax on profit on ordinary activities		X

The **interaction of the current tax and deferred tax** disclosures are best illustrated by the following example. Discounting has been ignored.

EXAMPLE **1. Tax on profit on ordinary activities (profit and loss note) (illustrative purposes only).**
a. Analysis of charge in period

	£'000	£'000
Current tax:		
UK corporation tax on profits of the period	25	
Adjustments in respect of previous periods	4	
		29
Foreign tax		11
Total current tax (note 1.b.)		40
Deferred tax:		
Origination and reversal of timing differences	57	
Total deferred tax (note 2.)		57
Tax on profit on ordinary activities		97

b. Factors affecting tax charge for the period

Profit on ordinary activities before tax	275
Profit on ordinary activities multiplied by standard rate of corporation tax in the UK of 20%	69
Effects of:	
Expenses not deductible for tax purposes	11
Capital allowances in excess of depreciation	(25)
Utilisation of tax losses	(7)
Rollover relief on profit on disposal of property	(10)
Adjustments to tax charge in respect of previous periods	2
Current tax charge for period	26

c. Factors that may affect future tax charges
Based on current capital investment plans, the company expects to continue to be able to claim capital allowances in excess of depreciation in future years but at a slightly lower level than in the current year. The company has now used all brought forward tax losses, which have significantly reduced tax payments in recent years.

No provision has been made for deferred tax on gains recognised on revaluing property to its market value, or on the sale of properties where potentially taxable gains have been rolled over into replacement assets. Such tax would become payable only if the property were sold without it being possible to claim rollover relief. The total amount unprovided for is £20,000, and at present it is not considered likely that any tax will become payable in the foreseeable future.

2. Provision for deferred tax (balance sheet note) (illustrative purposes only)

	£'000
Accelerated capital allowances	294
Pensions contributions accrued	(10)
Provision for deferred tax	284
Provision at start of period	227
Deferred tax charge in profit and loss account for period (note 1.a.)	57
Provision at end of period	284

MEMO POINTS The small company corporation tax rate for FY2013 has been used in the example; namely 20%.

Disclosures relating to the STRGL

The material components of the tax charged or credited directly to the STRGL should be disclosed in the same manner as for the profit and loss account (¶4319).

EXAMPLE **Statement of recognised gains and losses**

	£'000
Profit earned for ordinary shareholders for the year	340
Currency translation differences on foreign current investments	(23)
Taxation on translation differences	(12)
Total recognised gains and losses for the year	305

Provision for deferred tax (balance sheet note)

	£'000
Provision at start of period	200
Currency translation adjustment	(3)
Deferred tax charge in profit and loss account for period	80
Other movements	5
Provision at end of period	282

D. Value Added Tax

General principles

9140
SSAP 5 (1–4)
Income and expenditure should be stated net of VAT as the accounts should reflect the role of the company as a collector of VAT only. By **exception**, VAT is included within expenditure because it cannot be reclaimed in the following situations:
– the company is not registered for VAT;
– some or all of the activities of the company may be exempt for VAT purposes, which affects the recoverability of input VAT; and
– certain types of expenditure, such as business entertaining, incur VAT which cannot be recovered.

Turnover should always be stated net of VAT. If a company wishes to show turnover inclusive of VAT, then the VAT element must be shown as a deduction to arrive at the turnover figure net of VAT charged.

9141
SSAP 5 (5–6)
The balance of **VAT due** to be paid or recovered from HMRC should be included as a creditor or debtor in the financial statements as appropriate, and does not require separate disclosure.

If the company is **committed** to certain expenditure, such as the acquisition of a building, and will not be able to recover the related VAT, an appropriate disclosure should be made within a note on capital commitments.

Irrecoverable VAT relating to fixed assets should be included within each particular asset's cost.

Use of small business VAT schemes

9144
A small company may choose to use cash accounting, annual accounting or the flat rate scheme, all of which have implications for the financial statements.

9145
Cash accounting Under the cash accounting scheme, VAT is not payable or refundable until income is received and expenses are paid. This means that the **balance** shown as due to/from HMRC **in the accounts** will not agree to the amount shown on the relevant VAT return, even if the financial year end and VAT year end coincide.

9146
Annual accounting The annual accounting scheme requires only one VAT return a year to be submitted, and VAT payments can be made in instalments based on the previous year's liability. Again this means that the **balance** shown as due to/from HMRC **in the accounts** will not agree with the amount shown on the VAT return. This scheme is available to entities with an estimated VAT taxable turnover during the next tax year of less than £1.35 million.

Flat rate scheme This scheme allows a very small business (with turnover of up to £150,000) to remove the complexity of the usual VAT rules, and apply a set percentage (dependent on trade sector) to turnover which becomes the amount due to HMRC. The **amount payable** is the only entry in the balance sheet VAT account, and is deducted from turnover. All expenses are shown gross, with the exception of capital assets costing more than £2,000, when input VAT can still be recovered.

9147

EXAMPLE Mr A is using the flat rate scheme, and his flat rate percentage is 10%.
He has net VATable turnover of £60,000 in a VAT quarter, and incurs expenses of £40,000 (including VAT).
Mr A's gross turnover is £72,000 (60,000 x 1.200)
The amount due to HMRC is £7,200 (72,000 x 10%)
On a very simple level, Mr A's profit and loss is as follows:

Turnover	72,000 – 7,200	64,800
Expenses		(40,000)
Profit		£24,800

MEMO POINTS For a full discussion of VAT matters refer to our *VAT Memo*.

E. Group considerations

Corporation tax reliefs

There are four important levels of **group relationship** for corporation tax – these being 51% groups, 75% groups, 75% capital gains groups, 90% groups and consortia. The table summarises the broad requirements and the tax consequences of each type of group:

9150

Type of group	Definition	Tax consequences
51% Group	A company owns more than 50% of the share capital of another company.	– affects the rate of tax payable (¶9030); – instalment payments will be due on lower profits;
75% Group	A company holds, or is entitled to, at least 75% of all of the following: – ordinary share capital; – distributable profits; and – assets on a winding up. Ultimate parent must be entitled to at least 75% of sub-subsidiary.	– trading losses and certain other amounts may be group relieved; – tax refunds can be surrendered between group members.
75% (CG) Group	As above, with ultimate parent beneficially entitled to at least 50% of sub-subsidiary	– assets can be passed around the group without creating a tax charge; – rollover relief can be claimed on a group basis.
Consortia	20 or fewer companies each own at least 5%, and jointly at least 75%, of the ordinary share capital of another company.	– surrender of certain losses between the consortium company and the members.

Loss relief

The most common timing difference to affect groups is loss relief. Where **losses are group relieved**, the claimant company may pay an amount up to the amount of loss to the loss-making company, with no tax consequences. For a wholly owned subsidiary, payment for group losses is probably optional, but where minority interests are involved, payment is almost certainly required.

9152

9153   The **amount of payment** may vary between nil and the full amount of the loss surrendered. In any event, sufficient information should be clearly disclosed in the accounts of both the surrendering company and claimant company as shown in the table below.

Amount of payment made for group relief	Claimant company	Surrendering company
No payment	Full explanation of the loss received and its effect on the tax charge.	Surrendered losses are not taken into account for the purposes of deferred tax. Disclose full financial impact.
Amount of tax saved	Included in tax charge in profit and loss account as "amount payable in respect of tax saved by group relief".	Credited to profit and loss account. Disclose full financial impact.
Amount of loss surrendered	Reduce profit before tax by amount paid as "amount payable in respect of group relief".	Increase profit before tax by amount received as "contribution receivable from group".

EXAMPLE   E Ltd surrenders its trading loss of £150,000 to its 100% parent company, F Ltd. E Ltd's accounting loss is £130,000, and £20,000 of tax adjustments are made. F Ltd makes an accounting profit of £500,000, and the tax charge after claiming group relief is £93,000. F Ltd has timing differences of £40,000 upon which deferred tax is provided. The main corporation tax rate is 23%.

1. If F Ltd makes a **payment of £45,000** to E Ltd, the following **disclosures** will be made:

E Ltd (illustrative purposes only)	£
Loss on ordinary activities before taxation	(130,000)
Taxation:	
UK corporation tax @ 23%	0
Amount received from group company in respect of group relief	45,000
Deferred tax (20,000 x 20%)	(4,000)
Loss for the financial period	(89,000)

Taxation note
Losses have been surrendered to a group company in return for consideration of £45,000. There are no tax losses available to carry forward, and deferred tax of £6,000 has been provided in respect of timing differences included in the surrendered losses.

F Ltd	£
Profit on ordinary activities before taxation	500,000
Taxation:	
UK corporation tax @ 23% (£115,000 minus £47,500 (marginal relief £200,000 @ 23.75%)	(67,500)
Amount payable to group company in respect of tax saved by group relief	(45,000)
Deferred tax (40,000 x 20%)	(8,000)
Profit for the financial period	379,500

A payment of **£45,000** has been made in respect of the corporation tax saving resulting from a **group relief claim**.

Consolidated accounts

9154   On consolidation, the group's position must be viewed as a whole. While the **individual tax charges** of each group member will be aggregated in the group accounts, the tax effect of consolidation adjustments must also be included. Such **adjustments** give rise to timing differences for the group which must be recognised by deferred tax. Examples would include:
– alignment of accounting policies; and
– elimination of intra-group transactions.

EXAMPLE   A Ltd sells stock to B Ltd, a subsidiary, for £100,000. The profit included in this price is £20,000, which must be eliminated on consolidation. Assuming a corporation tax rate of 23%, A Ltd would have accounted for current tax of £4,600 in relation to the profit from this stock.

In the group accounts, a deferred tax asset of £4,600 should be recognised to cancel out A Ltd's current tax charge.

When a **fair value adjustment** is made for an acquisition, it is treated as if it is a timing difference in the acquired company's accounts. The most common type of fair value adjustment is on property, and as this would be treated as a revaluation (¶9076), in most instances no deferred tax provision is required.

9156

Unremitted earnings from group undertakings

Where tax could be payable on the **future receipt** of past earnings of a subsidiary, associate or joint venture (taking account of any double taxation relief), deferred tax should be recognised to the extent that:
– dividends have been accrued as receivable; or
– a binding agreement has been entered into so that past earnings will be distributed in the future.

9158

VAT

Groups of companies where **common control** exists may apply to be treated as a single taxable person for VAT. Only companies with a fixed establishment in the UK can be included within a **group registration**. The representative company in the group will deal with all the VAT administration, and only this company needs to include a VAT liability or debtor in the balance sheet.

9160

F. Taxation for small companies adopting the FRSSE

Tax, both current and deferred, should be **recognised in the profit and loss account**, except to the extent that any part of it is attributable to a gain or loss that has been recognised directly in the **statement of total recognised gains and losses** (STRGL). In that event, the relevant tax should be recognised directly there as well.

9170
FRSSE 9.1 – 9.3

The material components of the tax charge or credit for the period, as well as those of the deferred tax balance, should be disclosed separately.

Any special circumstances that affect the overall tax charge or credit for the period – or future periods – should be disclosed, and their individual effects quantified, by way of a note. The effects of a fundamental change in the basis of taxation should be included in the tax charge or credit for the period and separately disclosed on the face of the profit and loss account.

Deferred tax While deferred tax should be recognised in respect of all **timing differences** that have **originated but not reversed** by the balance sheet date, in the following instances it should not be recognised:
– in respect of **permanent differences**,
– on **revaluation gains and losses** unless, by the balance sheet date, the entity has entered into a binding agreement to sell the asset and has revalued it to selling price, and
– in respect of taxable gains on revaluations or sales if it is more likely than not that the gain will be rolled over into a replacement asset.

9171

Unrelieved tax losses and other deferred tax assets should be recognised only to the extent that it is more likely than not that they will be recovered against the reversal of deferred tax liabilities or other future taxable profits.

Deferred tax should be recognised when **tax allowances** relating to the cost of a fixed asset are received either before or after the related depreciation is recognised. Only when all the conditions for retaining the tax allowances have been met should the deferred tax be reversed.

Deferred tax should be measured at the **average tax rates** expected to apply when the timing differences are due to reverse, based on tax rates and laws enacted by the balance sheet date.

> ⌐ MEMO POINTS ⌐   The existence of **unrelieved tax losses** serves as strong evidence that there may not be other future taxable profits against which the losses will be relieved.

9173   The discounting of deferred tax assets and liabilities is not required. However, if an entity adopts a policy of discounting, all deferred tax balances that have been measured without discounting, and for which the impact of discounting is material, should be discounted. Where discounting is used, the unwinding of the discount should be shown as a component of the tax charge and disclosed separately.

9174   The following should be **disclosed** in respect of deferred tax:
- the balance at the end of the period and its material components,
- any movement between the opening and closing net deferred tax balances,
- the material components of this movement,
- in cases where assets have been revalued (or their market values have been disclosed in a note) the amount of tax that would be payable or recoverable if the assets were sold at the values shown.

Tax on dividends

9175
FRSSE 9.13   Both incoming and outgoing dividends (and similar amounts receivable and payable) should be recognised net of any withholding tax but excluding other taxes, such as attributable tax credits. Withholding tax suffered should be shown as part of the tax charge.

Value added tax (VAT)

9178
FRSSE 9.15   Turnover shown in the profit and loss account excludes either VAT on taxable outputs or VAT imputed under the flat rate VAT scheme. **Irrecoverable VAT** allocated to fixed assets and to other items disclosed separately in the financial statements should, where material, be included in their cost.

G. New UK GAAP – FRS 102 provisions

9180   There are no significant differences between existing UK GAAP and the FRS 102 "Financial Reporting Standard applicable in the UK and Republic of Ireland", the adoption of which is mandatory for accounting periods beginning on or after 1 January 2015.

Issue	Accounting treatment under FRS 102 (Section 29)
Basis of Section 29	Based on timing differences approach adopted in FRS 19 "Deferred tax" modified to a "Timing differences plus" approach. Impact: Additional deferred tax may be recognised on investment properties + revaluations of property, plant and equipment.
Discounting	Deferred tax assets/liabilities cannot be discounted contrary to FRS 19.

CHAPTER 6

Preparation and filing of financial statements

This chapter sets out the general principles for keeping accounting records and the **general rules** for the preparation, filing and publication of financial statements. The filing exemptions available to small, medium and large entities, as well as specific types of company such as unlimited or overseas companies are also covered.

9300

In general, the Companies Act 2006 incorporates the provisions and powers pertaining to the preparation and filing of financial statements, with one set of provisions designed specifically for **small companies** and another for large and **medium-sized entities**. For more detail on the legal requirements underpinning the preparation, publishing and filing of financial statements see *Company Law Memo*.

> ⌐MEMO POINTS⌐ 1. The terms "**Accounts**" **and** "**Financial Statements**" can be used interchangeably, despite these terms having specific meanings under the Companies Act and Accounting Standards. In practice, "Accounts" are considered to include the balance sheet and profit and loss account, as well as the other "primary statements" required by the accounting standards (e.g. cash flow statement).
> 2. "**Financial statements**" is the terminology adopted by the FRC (formerly the ASB) in its "Statements of Accounting Standards", and represents a complete set of documents, including the annual accounts and other specified explanatory material, such as the notes to the accounts and the directors' report.
> 3. The Government has issued a number of important **financial reporting regulations** under the Companies Act 2006:
> i. Companies Act (Amendment) (Accounts and Reports) Regulations 2008, which increased the financial thresholds for small and medium-sized companies, and the audit exemption thresholds.
> ii. Large and Medium-Sized Companies and Groups (Accounts and Reports) Regulations 2008; and
> iii. Small Companies and Groups (Accounts and Directors' Reports) Regulations. These regulations cover the form and content of a company's accounts and reports under Schedule 15 of CA 2006.

A. Preparation of annual financial statements

9301 In general companies are required to prepare annual financial statements, the form and content of which are underpinned by a comprehensive regulatory framework, comprising mandatory and advisory elements, collectively referred to as GAAP (Generally Accepted Accounting Practice). **Mandatory sources** (¶202) include the requirements of the Companies Act 2006, the Financial Reporting Standards (FRSs), Statements of Standard Accounting Practice (SSAPs), Statements of Recommended Practice (SORPs) and UITF Abstracts. **Advisory sources** include Financial Reporting Exposure Drafts (FREDs) and Technical Releases from professional bodies such as the ICAEW and the ACCA.

Listed companies must now meet the accounting and disclosure requirements of IFRS. For **other entities**, special legislation may apply, governing the nature of their accounting records (e.g. charities, banks, insurance companies). For parent companies at the financial year-end the directors must prepare consolidated financial statements unless subject to the **small company regime**, under which consolidated accounts are optional. Special exemptions are currently being developed for **micro-entities**.

> MEMO POINTS   **Group accounts** are prepared under Section 404 Companies Act (Group accounts) 2006, Schedule 6 SI 2008/409 or IFRS (IAS 1).

1. General legal & accounting framework

9302 This section contains an overview of the general legal framework governing the preparation of accounts, including determination of the accounting reference date and the general composition of accounting records.

Overview of form and content of accounts

9303 **Companies, whether trading or not**, must prepare in addition to the underlying accounting records, for each financial year:
– a balance sheet (choice of two formats);
– a profit and loss account (unless dormant; choice of four formats);
– a statement of recognised gains and losses (STRGL) where applicable;
– a cash flow statement, (unless exempted by FRS 1);
– a statement of directors' responsibilities; and
– notes to the accounts.

These elements form the "accounts" or financial statements, which should be accompanied by a **directors' report** (including an enhanced business review) and, unless the company is exempt, an auditor's report. Statutory accounts must be approved by the board of directors and circulated to the shareholders, before being filed at Companies House.

9304 The form and content of the balance sheet, profit and loss account and accompanying notes must comply with the provisions of the Companies Act. Once the directors have adopted a particular format, it should be consistently applied in subsequent years, unless there are special reasons for a change. Particulars of any change should be disclosed and the underlying reasons explained in a note to the accounts. Details on the **choice of profit and loss and balance sheet formats** are shown in ¶350 and ¶984 respectively.

The financial statements must show a **true and fair view** of the company's financial affairs at the balance sheet date. Where the directors have departed from the accounting or disclosure requirements of the Companies Act or an FRS and invoked the true and fair view override, details of the circumstances involved should be given in the notes to the accounts.

Accounting period (ARP)

The Accounting Reference Period (ARP) for a **new company** represents the period between **9305**
the date of incorporation (not the first day of trading) and the first anniversary, adjusted to
the last day of the month the company was incorporated. For example, if the company was
incorporated on 15 September 2012, its Accounting Reference Date (ARD) would be set at
30 September, and the first accounts would cover the period from this date to 30 September
2013.

> MEMO POINTS   An **accounting reference period** (ARP) is a more precise term for financial year
> and ends on the accounting reference date or up to seven days either side of the ARD, if this is
> more convenient. For **new companies**, accounts must be prepared for a period of at least 6
> months, with a maximum of 18.

Accounting reference date (ARD)

After incorporation, a company will select a accounting reference date (ARD) that is usually **9306**
the last day of the month in which the anniversary of its incorporation falls. It marks the end   s391 (2-3) CA 2006
of the annual accounting period and is also known as the balance sheet date. Directors can
change the ARD by filing an appropriate form with the Registrar of Companies. Every
company has an **accounting reference date** which represents its financial year-end and
determines when accounts are due for delivery to Companies House.

All companies must prepare annual accounts that report on the performance and activities
of the company during the financial year, which starts on the day after the end of the
previous financial year, or in the case of a new company, on the day of incorporation.

Changing the ARD   Even though the ARD is set on incorporation it can be changed, as **9307**
can subsequent accounting periods. An ARD can be obtained notifying the Registrar
of Companies, by completing the relevant form available from Companies House.
However, the change can only be made to the current or previous ARD and the new ARD
must be registered before the filing deadline for the accounts has passed. If the **filing
deadline has been missed**, a company cannot then apply to the Registrar to change the
ARD.

Restrictions on changing the ARD   A company may change its ARD by **shortening the** **9308**
ARP as often as they like, and by as many months. However, there are restrictions on
extending ARPs, as follows:
1. An ARD cannot be extended beyond 18 months from the start of the accounting
period.
2. A company may not extend the ARD more than once every 5 years, unless either of the
following apply:
– the company is subject to an administration order; or
– the Secretary of State has ordered the extension; or
– the company is aligning its reference date with that of a subsidiary or parent company
established within the European Economic Area (EEA).

> MEMO POINTS   1. The European Economic Area (EEA) comprises the 28 countries that make up
> the European Union plus 3 EFTA states: Iceland, Norway and Liechtenstein. 2. In addition to
> meeting the requirements of the Companies Act, a **listed company** must also notify a Regulated
> Information Service of any change in its ARD.

Underlying accounting records

All companies are required to keep accounting records sufficient to show and explain **9310**
the company's transactions. The records must disclose with reasonable accuracy, the   s386 CA 2006
financial position of the company at any one time and enable the directors to ensure that
the balance sheet and profit and loss account comply with the requirements of the
Companies Act.

9312 The **books of prime entry** in which a business records its transactions normally comprise:
- Sales day book;
- Sales returns book;
- Purchase day book;
- Purchase returns book;
- Cash books;
- Sales ledger control account;
- Purchase ledger control account;
- Journals;
- Asset registers; and
- General ledger.

9314 The **accounting records must contain** the following information:
s386(3) CA 2006
- the daily transactions involving monies received and expended by the company and the supporting reasons thereof; and
- a record of the assets and liabilities of the company (including transaction dates).

For **companies trading goods** additional records are required:
- details of the stock held by the company at the financial year-end;
- details of capital expenditure and major contracts; and
- statements of all goods sold and purchased, detailing the buyers in sufficient detail to enable their identification.

Retention of accounting records

9316 Accounting records must be retained from the date they are prepared, this being 3 years for
sec 388(4) CA 2006 a **private company** and 6 years for a **public company**. This is subject to any provision contained in the rules made under the Insolvency Act 1986, or the requirements of other statutes such as the VAT legislation. For instance, companies that are **registered for VAT** must retain their records and accounts for six years, unless a shorter period has been agreed with Customs and Excise.

In practice, many companies will keep their accounting records for a longer period to cover the possibility of any retrospective revenue enquiries.

> MEMO POINTS   Companies subject to the **money laundering regulations** are required to retain accounting records relating to the relevant customers for the duration of the client relationship + 5 years.

9317 **Registered office**   A company's accounting records should be kept at its registered office or such other place as the directors see fit, and should be available at all times for inspection by the company's authorised officers. This requirement also applies to overseas subsidiaries of UK companies. If a company registered in the UK keeps its accounting records overseas, then certain accounts and returns are required to be sent to a place in the UK and be open for inspection.

If a company **fails to comply** with any of the provisions for retaining accounts, then a director or officer of the company guilty of such an offence is liable to imprisonment or a fine, or both (¶9370).

9318 The Companies Act also requires of companies, the **retention of certain statutory books and records** at the registered office, including:
- the register of directors and secretaries;
- the register of charges;
- register of directors' share and debenture interests of group companies;
- memorandum and articles of association;
- the minute books detailing general meetings of the company; and
- the register of members, debenture holders.

Accounting records **may be stored** on microfilm or **digital formats** which are acceptable to HMRC, except that prior approval should be sought.

2. Approval of financial statements

The board of directors must approve the annual financial statements, which must carry the signature of one director on the face of the balance sheet and state the name of the signatory. The directors' report must also be signed by a director or the company secretary. The copy of the **directors' report** and the balance sheet filed with the Registrar of Companies must bear an original signature and any copies laid before the company at the annual general meeting must also state the name of the signatory. **Group financial statements** should also be signed by the same director.

9320
s414 CA 2006

The date on which the financial statements are approved should be disclosed in the financial statements and represents the date, up to which the directors are responsible for disclosing material post-balance sheet events (¶5700).

MEMO POINTS   **Small companies** are no longer required to have a company secretary.

3. Requirements for micro entities, groups and subsidiaries

Micro entities

The European Parliament (EP) has in principle agreed changes to European Union (EU) accounting rules that could **exempt micro-companies** in the UK from preparing annual accounts. These amendments still have to be ratified by the EU Council of Ministers and would only apply if the UK regulatory authorities agreed to grant the exemption. Micro-companies will still need to **maintain proper accounting records** and prepare financial reports for shareholders and HMRC.

9322

Micro entities are defined as a business that meets two of the following three **criteria**:
– a turnover not exceeding £632,000;
– a balance sheet value not exceeding £316,000;
– an average of fewer than 10 employees during the financial year.

9323

MEMO POINTS   1. The FRC has issued **new proposals** for amending the Financial Reporting Standard for Smaller Entities (FRSSE) in order to incorporate recent legislation covering micro-entities, introduced by BIS in November 2013. The 1.5m plus micro-entities registered in the UK can now prepare simplified financial statements within the regulatory framework of the FRSSE, including the option to provide fewer disclosures. The closing date for commenting on the proposals contained in **FRED 52** "Draft Amendments to the Financial Reporting Standard for Smaller Entities – Micro-entities", was 12 February 2014.
2. Entities **excluded from registering as micro-entities** include, in addition to those is excluded from the small companies regime, charities, LLPs, investment undertakings, financial holding and insurance undertakings, credit institutions, qualifying partnerships, overseas companies, and unregistered companies.
3. The **turnover limit** is adjusted proportionately if the financial year is longer or shorter than twelve months.

Reporting requirements   The Department for Business, Innovation and Skills (BIS) has issued a discussion paper entitled "Simpler Reporting for the Smallest Businesses" covering the accounting and reporting requirements for micro-entities. The objective is to create a **lighter regulation regime** for small companies by simplifying the preparation and filing of financial statements and reduce the administrative costs of regulatory compliance. The current system is deemed to impose disproportionate costs on micro-entities. BIS is proposing that the smallest businesses should no longer produce true and fair view accounts, but instead prepare the following:
– a simplified trading statement using cash accounting (i.e. no accruals or prepayments) to replace the profit and loss account; and
– a statement of position, including shareholders' funds, debtors, creditors, cash, loans and major assets, to replace the balance sheet.

9324

Annual returns would also be simplified and only require disclosure of a company's ultimate owners, average employee numbers and key financial information. It is estimated that approximately 1.7m UK-incorporated companies meet at least two of three classification criteria for a micro entity whilst a further 3.5 million unincorporated businesses should also benefit. The BIS is currently reviewing the responses to this discussion paper and any further proposals will have to be aligned with the EU's recommendations regarding micro entities, as set out above.

> *MEMO POINTS*   1. Under a **simplified financial reporting regime**, micro-entities can prepare and publish simplified financial statements (a simplified balance sheet (Statement of Position), profit and loss account (Trading Statement) and an Annual Return) for financial years ending on or after 30 September 2013. From December 2013 micro-entity accounts can be filed at Companies House.
> 2. The FRC has also outlined plans to develop an **integrated software package** to help small businesses prepare financial information and help business forecasting and planning.
> 3. The FRC has now issued **proposed amendments to the FRSSE** 2008 (FRED 52) that will permit entities to prepare accounts in compliance with the FRSSE. However, until these amendments have been agreed, companies will not be able to state that their micro entity accounts have been prepared in accordance with the FRSSE.

Groups

9327
sec 400 CA 2006

A company that is **a parent company** at the end of a financial year, should prepare consolidated financial statements for the group, unless it qualifies for one of the exemptions from preparing group accounts given in the Companies Act.

A parent company's individual profit and loss account can be omitted from the consolidated accounts in certain situations, although it must be approved by the board of directors or signed on behalf of the board by a director. This topic is covered in greater detail in ¶6556. **All companies in the group** should have the same financial year as the parent company. Should the **reporting dates differ**, then the parent company must consolidate accounts for accounting periods that end before its own, as long as the time difference does not exceed three months. Where this is the case the subsidiary must prepare interim accounts for the required accounting period.

9328

A **small parent company** that has prepared individual accounts for its members, using the special provisions of the Companies Act relating to shorter-form accounts, can also elect to prepare group accounts. These accounts must contain a statement above the signature on the balance sheet, stating that they have been prepared in accordance with the special provisions of Part 15 Companies Act 2006, applicable to small companies.

A **small group** cannot file abbreviated accounts. Where a **medium-sized company** prepares group accounts, they must be full group accounts. The formats of accounts must follow the relevant Schedules of the Companies Act.

9329

Exemption from preparing group accounts   A parent company need not prepare group accounts (or send them to the Registrar), where the group of which it is the parent, is small and is not an ineligible group.

> *MEMO POINTS*   The qualifying **criteria for classification** as a small or medium-sized group is contained in ¶6340.

The **exemption is not available if the parent company** was at any time during the financial year, one of the following:
– a public company;
– a banking or insurance company;
– an authorised person under the Financial Services and Market Act 2000; or
– a member of an ineligible group.

> *MEMO POINTS*   1. A **group qualifies as ineligible** if any of its members is one of the following:
> – a public company or body corporate lawfully able to issues shares or debentures to the public on a regulated market in an EEA State;

– a banking institution authorised under the Banking Act;
– an e-money issuer, a MiFID investment firm or a UCITS management company;
– an insurance company authorised under the Insurance Companies Act 1982; or
– a person (other than a small company) permitted under the Financial Services and Market Act 2000 (revised 2012) to carry on a regulated activity under that Act.

2. The **Financial Conduct Authority ("FCA")** has largely taken over functions previously performed by the FSA. The FCA is the UK regulator responsible for the business conduct of all firms previously regulated by the FSA, including insurance intermediaries, personal investment firms, mortgage intermediaries etc. The FCA also regulates firms providing market services, such as recognised investment exchanges and providers of multilateral trading facilities.

Subsidiary companies

Subsidiary companies incorporated in the UK are subject to the requirements to prepare, file and publish annual financial statements as other companies, although there are special rules that govern the disclosures required.   **9331**

Additional disclosures   Subsidiary companies are required to provide additional disclosures relating to the following: **9332**
a. guarantees and financial commitments undertaken for group undertakings (i.e. parent undertaking, fellow subsidiary or one of its own subsidiaries);
b. details of where **copies of the group accounts** referred to above can be obtained and if unincorporated, the principal place of business;
c. information on **parent undertakings** covering:
– the name and country of incorporation of the ultimate parent company;
– the parent undertaking of the largest group of companies for which group accounts are prepared, of which the reporting company is a member; or
– the parent undertaking of the smallest group of which the company is a member, for which accounts are prepared.

The disclosures required under (a) above cover any charge on the assets of the business, contingent liabilities, pension commitments and other significant commitments not provided for, such as capital expenditure.

B. Publication of financial statements

The Companies Act sets out the requirements covering the publication of financial statements, including the deadlines for laying of the accounts. Smaller companies have the option of publishing shorter-form accounts for shareholders (¶6030).   **9340**
s423 CA 2006

Shorter-form financial statements for shareholders   If a company prepares shorter-form financial statements for shareholders instead of a full set of accounts, they must be authorised by the board of directors and laid before the company in general meeting (AGM). Shorter form accounts may not be filed with the Registrar of Companies although small companies can elect to submit **abbreviated financial statements** (¶6270) instead. The formats for shorter-form accounts do not differ greatly from the full financial statements.   **9341**

MEMO POINTS   The accounting requirements for small companies preparing **shorter-form financial statements** are considered in Part 8 Chapter 1.

Persons entitled to receive financial statements   A copy of the financial statements, directors' report and audit report, must be dispatched to **every member and debenture holder** of the company, although some companies are not required to deliver an audit report (e.g. dormant companies).   **9342**

The financial statements sent to members are usually the same as those filed with the Registrar of Companies, except for **small and medium-sized companies** who are entitled to certain disclosure exemptions in the accounts filed with Companies House.

> MEMO POINTS   **Listed companies** need not send copies of financial statements to those members who elect not to receive them. Summary financial statements may be sent instead.

9343   **Laying of financial statements at the AGM**   The directors **must present copies of** the annual report and accounts, together with the audit report and directors' report before the annual general meeting (AGM) of the members of the company. This is known as laying the accounts before members. Copies of the annual report should be sent to the members not less than 21 days before the date of the AGM. The time period for laying financial statements is the same as for filing accounts at Companies House (see ¶9350). Where directors fail in their obligation to lay accounts may be guilty of an offence subject to penalty.

Under the Companies Act 2006 **private companies** are no longer obligated to hold an AGM or lay financial statements before a general meeting, unless this requirement is specified in the company's articles of association.

9344   **Members of a private company** may elect not to lay accounts and reports before shareholders at the AGM. Where this is the case, a company must send:
– a copy of the accounts and reports to members, not less than 28 days before the end of the period allowed for laying and delivering financial statements. This is normally 9 months after the last day of the relevant accounting reference period; and
– a notice informing the members of their right to request the laying of accounts and reports at the AGM. This option is not available to public companies.

Companies may **electronically dispatch** accounts and reports to members who elect to receive them. Accounts published on a website are also deemed to be dispatched electronically, provided the members have been notified of the publication.

9347   **Electronic communications**   Under the Companies Act 2006 companies are being encouraged to improve electronic communications with shareholders. With shareholder permission, entities can now distribute annual reports, interim financial statements and AGM notices electronically. **Quoted companies** are expected to publish financial information of their website. Electronic communications must be dispatched to the address supplied by the member. Failure to comply with the regulations covering electronic communication of financial statements will leave the company (and its officers) liable for an offence under section 425 of the Companies Act 2006. A company must make its financial statements available at least 21 days before the AGM.

> MEMO POINTS   Electronic communications includes Fax, CD-ROM, E-Mail, and websites.

9348   **Summary**   The choice of financial statements available for shareholders and for filing are set out in the flowchart below.

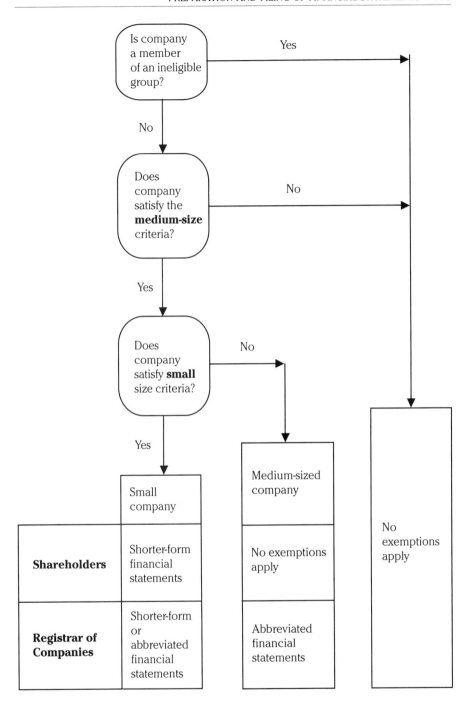

C. Filing of financial statements

9350   The **directors of all companies** have obligations to file annual financial statements, including where appropriate a directors' report (¶4500) and auditor's report, with the Registrar of Companies within certain time limits. **Small or medium-sized companies** qualify for reduced disclosure requirements and have the option of filing abbreviated accounts (see ¶6005 and ¶6270). **Special provisions** apply to entities that shorten their accounting reference period (¶9305).

The balance sheet and directors' report must be signed by a director on behalf of the board and the auditors' report must contain the name of the auditors, and where this is an audit firm, the name of the senior auditor.

The Registrar can enforce the filing requirements through a set of **filing deadlines** backed up by a **penalty regime**. An overview of the filing exemptions available to specific types of company is also given below.

> ⌐MEMO POINTS⌐   1. In order to comply with the **self-assessment rules** contained in the Finance Act a company must submit to HMRC, along with its corporation tax return, a full set of financial statements, including a directors' report.
> 2. HMRC have decreed that all company **tax returns and financial statements** must be **filed online**, using the iXBRL format. This ruling is independent of the filing requirements of Companies House.
> 3. **Companies House** is delaying the **mandatory use of iXBRL** for submitting company accounts, until after the moratorium on new regulation for small businesses has ended. Financial statements should continue to be submitted by post or electronically using a PDF file. HMRC, on the other hand, is proceeding with its compulsory requirement for electronic submission of accounts (iXBRL).
> 4. Provisions contained in the Legal Aid, Sentencing and Punishment of Offenders Act 2012 (LASPO), which passed into law on 1 May 2012, mean that judges will have powers to **levy unlimited fines** on companies in England and Wales that fail to file annual accounts, returns and reports or omit to lay accounts and reports before a general meeting. The current maximum statutory fine for such an offence is £5,000.
> 5. The requirements covering the preparation and filing of accounts for **dormant companies** are covered in ¶6400.
> 6. Filing requirements for **quoted companies**: The annual financial statements filed with the Registrar should include a copy of the company's individual financial statements and consolidated financial statements where appropriate, a signed copy of the directors' report, a copy of the directors' remuneration report and a copy of the auditors' report on the financial statements including the directors' remuneration report.

Obligations for small companies

9351
secs. 445-6
CA 2006

The annual financial statements filed with the Registrar must include the following minimum requirements:
– a copy of the company's balance sheet and notes to the financial statements sent to members; and
– a copy of the auditors' report on the financial statements, unless exempt from audit and the directors have taken advantage of this exemption under s.444 of the Companies Act 2006.

Where the directors take advantage of the **exemption** from delivering a copy of the company's profit and loss account or the directors' report, the balance sheet must contain a statement that the company's accounts have been prepared in accordance with the provisions covering entities subject to the small companies regime.

9352   **Abbreviated accounts**   Where a company submits abbreviated accounts to the Registrar of Companies these must include a balance sheet, profit and loss account, auditors' report (except where the company is exempt from audit under section 449 (3) CA 2006) and notes prepared in line with SI 2008/409 Sch. 4 and Regulation 6. A statement must be included in the balance sheet to the effect that the accounts have been prepared in accordance with the **small companies regime**. An entity qualified to adopt the small companies regime, or that would be were it not an ineligible group, is permitted to claim the small companies exemption covering the **directors' report** (s415 CA 2006).

The filing requirements for **medium sized companies** are the same as for large companies with the exception of the directors' remuneration report. Where medium sized entities submit abbreviated accounts these must be prepared in accordance with SI 2008/410 Reg. 4 "The Large and Medium sized Companies and Groups (Reports and Accounts) Regulations 2008 along with a special auditors' report (unless the company is exempt from audit).

1. Filing requirements

The financial statements are required to show the **registered number** of the company, in a prominent position, usually on the first page. If any of these documents are in a language other than English then the directors should annex a certified translation.

9353
secs. 441-2
CA 2006

Financial statements may be submitted in a foreign currency; namely, the local currency of the economic environment in which the company operates and generates cash flows.

Time limits

There are general time limits that apply to the majority of companies for the filing of their financial statements:
- **private companies** – 9 months from the ARD; or
- **public companies** – 6 months from the ARD.

9354
sec. 453 CA 2006

The table illustrates the dates by which accounts must be delivered to the Registrar of Companies, although December and March are generally speaking the most popular dates.

End of relevant accounting period (ARP)	Delivery deadline- Private companies	Delivery deadline- Public companies
Jan 31	Oct 31	Jul 31
Feb 28	Nov 28	Aug 28
Mar 31	Dec 31	Sep 30

If the company's accounting period does not end on the last day of a month, then the period allowed for filing the financial statements ends on the corresponding day in the appropriate month. For example, a public company with an accounting reference date of 15 August has until 15 February following, to file its accounts. If a filing deadline expires on a Sunday or Bank Holiday the law still requires accounts to be filed by that date.

⌐MEMO POINTS¬   The FRC has signalled that it will allow the **electronic filing** of financial statements based on the new financial reporting standards (FRS 100, FRS 101, FRS 102), although their adoption is not mandatory before January 2015. The FRC plans to update the **XBRL taxonomy** (electronic tagging conventions/coding of accounts) in the coming months in order to accommodate the new standards. At present only HMRC requires compulsory filing of financial statements using this electronic format.

Initial registration

For a newly formed company whose initial ARP is **longer than twelve months**, the maximum time period allowed for filing the accounts, is the later of:
- **private companies** – 21 months from the date of incorporation or 3 months from the ARD, whichever is longer;
- **public companies** – 18 months from the date of incorporation or 3 months from the ARD, whichever is longer.

9356

The accounts must be delivered to the Registrar of Companies.

Event	Private Ltd	Public plc
First accounting reference period	1 January 2012 to 30 June 2013	1 January 2012 to 30 June 2013
21 months from the date of incorporation	30 September 2013	N/A
18 months from the date of incorporation	N/A	30 June 2013
3 Months from end of accounting reference date	30 September 2013	30 September 2013

9358   A company that has **shortened its ARP** during its initial accounting period, is still subject to the normal 6 and 9 month time periods for public and private companies, with an alternative filing date (if later) being three months from the date the Registrar receives notice, to shorten the ARP.

Example – shortening the ARD Event	Private Limited	Public (Plc)
Original accounting reference date	31 December 2012	31 December 2012
Date of notice to Registrar requesting shortening of accounting reference period	31 March 2013	31 March 2013
Shortened accounting reference period	1 January 2012 to 31 October 2012	1 January 2012 to 31 October 2012
9 months from end of amended accounting reference date	31 July 2013	N/A
6 months from end of amended accounting reference date	N/A	30 April 2013
3 months from date of notice to Registrar	30 June 2013	30 June 2013

Extensions to the time limits

9360   The Secretary of State can extend the filing period, if deemed appropriate on the basis of an application made prior to the expiry of the period. The need to finalise significant **legal disputes** or the **loss of accounting records**, are examples of the type of extenuating circumstances for which the registrar may grant an extension. An application must be made, detailing the reasons for the required extension and the additional time needed. The period may be extended for as long as the Registrar so decides and specifies in the notice.

> MEMO POINTS   For companies incorporated in **England and Wales**, an application should be made to the Secretary of State for Trade and Industry at the companies' administration section at Companies House (Cardiff). In **Scotland**, the application should be to the Secretary of State for Trade and Industry at Companies House (Edinburgh).

Rejected accounts

9362   Documents and forms sent to Companies House are scanned and stored in electronic form and the original documents archived. There are a number of quality guidelines for the delivery of documents which are set out below.

Documents rejected by the Registrar will be returned to the company for **amendment in the following instances**:
– the accounts fail to comply with the accounting or disclosure requirements of the Companies Act;
– the documents are incomplete (e.g. not signed by a director or name of signatory not stated, company registration number or pages missing, typographical errors etc); or

– the accounts do not meet the submission guidelines stipulated by the Registrar of Companies.

Where the Registrar rejects financial statements, because they are **defective** in respect of the accounting or disclosure requirements of the Act, the directors must follow the revision of defective accounts rules, which are discussed below.

Rejection of accounts is not a valid **excuse for the late filing** of the corrected accounts, which must be delivered to the registrar before the normal filing deadline. Failure to do so will result in a late filing penalty.

> ⬚ MEMO POINTS   The **submission guidelines** are available on the Companies House website.

Revision of defective accounts

Liability for approving defective financial statements lies with every director of the company who approved them, unless a director can prove that they have taken reasonable steps to prevent their approval.

9365

Under the Companies Act, the are **two remedies** for the revision of defective accounts; namely:
– voluntary revision by the directors; and
– an appointee of the Secretary of State making an application to the courts, requiring the directors to revise the accounts.

Revision of defective financial statements (both voluntary and involuntary) should take place within the statutory time limits, otherwise the normal penalty rules apply.

Voluntary revision   Where the directors of a company have prepared financial statements that do not appear to comply with the requirements of the Companies Act, they may prepare revised financial statements. If the accounts or reports have already been laid before the company at the AGM or delivered to the Registrar of Companies, the revisions should be confined to the correction of those parts of the financial statements that do not comply with the Act.

9366

The directors **can elect to either**:
– prepare a set of new financial statements; or
– opt for a partial revision requiring only a supplementary note to the original financial statements.

Voluntary revision is permitted under SI 2008/373 "The Companies (Revision of Defective Accounts and Reports) Regulations 2008". The revised financial statements must be approved by the board and signed by a director. Where supplementary notes are prepared these should also be authorised by a director.

Where the **original accounts** have already been **sent to the members**, laid before the company in general meeting or sent to the Registrar of Companies, the revised accounts must include a note of the following:
– that the revised financial statements replace the original financial statements;
– that the accounts have been prepared to the same date as the original accounts;
– the reasons for the revision;
– details of any significant changes to the original financial statements submitted.

Where the original financial statements have been **revised by supplementary note**, the following information is required:
– a note confirming that the accounts have been revised and where the revisions apply; and
– confirmation that the revised financial statements have been made up to the same date as the original and not the revision date.

> ⬚ MEMO POINTS   Companies House has introduced a procedure for **amending incorrect information** given on certain forms which have formally been registered at Companies House. The so-called **"second filing" scheme** only covers certain areas such as the appointment, termination or change in the registered particulars of company officers, the allotment of new shares or amendments to an annual return. The records at Companies House will be updated whilst the original form registered will still be kept on file.

9367   **Involuntary revision** The Secretary of State has empowered the Financial Reporting Review Panel (FRRP) to request directors to revise their accounts where appropriate.

Penalty regime

9370   The penalty regime consists of a system of late filing penalties and default fines for company directors. If the accounts are delivered late, the Registrar will impose an **automatic filing penalty** which will not be waived, even if the accounts are delayed in the post.

Late filing penalties are imposed under civil law whereas a **failure to file accounts** is a criminal offence. The penalty regime is designed to encourage directors to file accounts on time, as they must provide statutory information for the public record. It is possible that a civil penalty and a default fine could be payable if a set of accounts are not filed on time. The penalties are set out in SI 2008/497 "The Companies (Late Filing Penalties) Regulations 2008 and are based on a sliding scale that reflects the delay from the statutory filing date and the actual date the accounts are delivered to the Registrar.

> MEMO POINTS   The penalty regime for **public companies** is more draconian, with fines effectively doubled for late filing in consecutive years. In addition, the penalty periods have been shortened in order to encourage more effective compliance.

9372   **Civil law filing penalties** There is an **automatic civil penalty** for late filing.
sec. 441 CA 2006   The severity of the penalty will be determined by reference to whether the company is public or private, as well as to the delay between the actual filing date and the required filing deadline. It is the date of receipt by the Registrar which is important, not the date of posting. The scales of automatic fixed civil penalties are as set out in the table below.

Length of period (months)	Private company	Public company
1 month or less	£150	£750
More than 1 month but less than 3 months	£375	£1500
More than 3 months but less than 6 months	£750	£3000
More than 6 months	£1500	£7500

These penalties are similar to those imposed on directors, for failing to lay accounts and reports before the company in a general meeting, within the legal time limits outlined in ¶9354.

If the accounts are delivered late, an invoice is issued automatically to the company's registered office address. If the penalty is not paid, it will be referred to collection agents and if the fine remains unpaid, **legal action** may be taken in the form of a County Court Judgement or a Sheriff Court decree against the company.

9374   In the example below, the statutory filing date for a private company falls on a bank holiday. However as the registrar will not take delivery of the accounts until the following day, the first of September, an automatic late filing penalty will be triggered. The Registrar can waive the late filing penalty but only in exceptional circumstances.

Event	Private Company (9 months)	Pubic Company (6 months)
Accounting reference date (ARD)	31 October 2012	31 December 2012
Statutory filing deadline	30 July 2013	30 June 2013
Actual filing date	3 August 2013	3 July 2013
Filing penalty	**£150**	**£750**

9375   **Neglecting to file accounts is a criminal offence** which can result in directors being fined personally in the criminal courts. In addition, the Registrar may take steps to strike the company off the register of companies. Where a **filing deadline has been missed**, the registrar will serve notice on the directors of the company, requiring compliance with the filing requirements within 14 days. Where the directors fail to respond to the Registrar's new deadline, the Registrar may take the matter further by instituting legal proceedings (as may a member or creditor), in order to enforce compliance by a date which will be specified in the court order. All the costs relating to the application shall be borne by the directors. Directors that consistently breach the filing deadlines can be disqualified under the Company Directors (Disqualification) Act 1986 (e.g. three defaults over a five year period).

Where **directors are persistently in default** of their obligations to file accounts and other returns with the Registrar, they may be disqualified from being a company director. The directors are also liable to receive a criminal record and a fine for each offence to be determined by the court.

9376

If a **company is restored to the register** after being struck-off and dissolved, then it is regarded as having continued to exist as though it had never been struck off. Accounts filed, including those covering periods while the company was dissolved, will be subject to late filing penalties.

In cases of non-compliance, every partner in a qualifying partnership or every director of a company that is a partner, may be prosecuted and fined up to £5,000.

2. Permissible filing (disclosure) exemptions

There are a number of filing exemptions covering SMEs, groups, intermediate parents, and unincorporated companies.

9380

Small and medium-sized companies

Eligible small and medium-sized companies may qualify for some, or all of the exemptions allowing them to file **abbreviated accounts**. In addition, **dormant companies** and certain categories of small company are not required to appoint an auditor or obtain a directors' report. In these cases, an auditor's report is not required.

9382

It should be noted that abbreviated accounts are not the same as "shorter-form" accounts, which small companies may prepare for their shareholders. If a small company chooses not to prepare abbreviated accounts, it may however file "shorter-form" accounts. However, if a small or medium-sized company files abbreviated accounts, a complete set of accounts or shorter-form accounts must still be presented to members.

> MEMO POINTS   1. Under the Companies Act 2006, the **abbreviated balance sheet** must be accompanied by a statement confirming it has been prepared under the small companies regime.
> 2. For **medium-sized companies**, the exemption from disclosing turnover in abbreviated profit and loss accounts delivered to the Registrar of Companies, has been removed.

Group companies

A parent company must prepare **consolidated accounts** (group accounts) and file them with the registrar, except if a group qualifies as a small group or is an ineligible group (see ¶9327).

9384

Subsidiary companies that are also parent companies

A subsidiary company that is itself a parent company, is in **certain circumstances exempt** under the Companies Act from preparing and filing consolidated financial statements. The exemption does not apply, if the subsidiary company is listed on a stock exchange in the European Union. However, a copy of the consolidated financial statements of the **ultimate parent company** must be attached to the company's individual financial statements delivered to the Registrar.

9385

9386 The **above exemption** from filing group accounts **applies in the following situations**:
1. The company must be a wholly-owned subsidiary of a parent undertaking registered in the EU.
2. Where such a parent holds more than 50% of the shares in the company, and no notice has been served on the subsidiary company by minority interests, to prepare consolidated financial statements.
3. The subsidiary is included in the consolidated financial statements of a larger group compiled by an EU parent to the same date, or an earlier date in the same financial year and those financial statements are drawn up and audited. In addition, the parent's annual report must be compiled in compliance with the EU 7th Directive.
4. Where the subsidiary files the following copies with the Registrar of Companies:
– the group financial statements; or
– the group's annual report and auditor's report. These submissions must be within the time period permitted for the subsidiary to file its individual accounts. If the parent company accounts are not in English, a copy translated into English must also be filed.
5. Where the subsidiary discloses the following in its financial statements:
– the fact that it has taken advantage of the above filing exemption;
– the identity of the EU parent company preparing the group accounts;
– the country of incorporation of the parent undertaking, if not the UK and where the parent does not have a business establishment the UK; or
– where the parent is an unincorporated undertaking, the address of the parent company's principal place of business.

Unlimited companies

9388 The **directors** of an unlimited company **are not required to file a copy** of the company's
SI 220/589 financial statements with the Registrar of Companies, where it was not at any time during the relevant accounting reference period:
– a subsidiary of a limited undertaking;
– a parent of a limited undertaking;
– a banking or insurance company or the parent company of such;
– subject to rights exercisable by or on behalf of two or more limited undertakings which, if exercised by one of them would make the company its subsidiary; or
– a qualifying company within the meaning of the meaning of the SI 2008/569 "The Partnerships (Accounts) Regulations 2008".

If an unlimited company **publishes non-statutory financial statements**, they must include a statement that the company is exempt from the requirement to deliver statutory financial statements. Where an unlimited company is exempt from filing its financial statements under s.448 of the Companies Act 2006, the accounts will have been prepared under Part 15 of the same act and approved by the board.

CHAPTER 7

Not for Profit Organisations

Not for profit organisations is an umbrella term covering general charities and other organisa-   **9500**
tions such as clubs and associations, community interest companies or higher education
institutes. This chapter **focuses primarily on charities** and in particular the requirements of
the Statement of Recommended Practice (SORP) and the Charities Acts. The SORP is
compatible with the requirements of company law and accounting standards and is the key
source of accounting guidance for charities, although its adoption is not compulsory.

Charities choosing **not to adopt the SORP** must continue to comply with the specific require-   **9501**
ments of the Companies Acts, the Charities Act and accounting standards, as discussed in
this book. Where a separate SORP exists for a particular class of charity (e.g. Higher Education Institutions), the trustees should apply the recommendations of that SORP. International
Accounting Standards (IFRS) do not apply to **charitable companies**, although the Charity
SORP will be continually reviewed to reflect changes to UK accounting standards, including
those amendments arising out of the convergence process. **Smaller charities** meeting certain
threshold criteria have the option of preparing cash-based accounts, or adopting the reporting frameworks (FRSSE) available to small or medium-sized companies.

   MEMO POINTS   1. A **new Charity SORP** is being developed by the Charity Commission and the
Charities SORP Committee, which updates the accounting and reporting guidance for charities

under the new accounting framework contained in FRS 102 "The Financial Reporting Standard applicable in the UK and Republic of Ireland". The exposure draft is also aimed at smaller charities who choose to continue preparing their accounts using the FRSSE. The consultation process expired in November 2013, during which the Commission canvassed opinions from charities, auditors, trustees, employees and other stakeholders (e.g. donors).

2. The FRC has issued a **staff education note** (SEN 12) to aid the transtion to FRS 102 "The Financial Reporting Standard applicable in the UK and Republic of Ireland", whose adoption is mandatory for accounting periods beginning on or after 1 January 2015 (¶9532).

SECTION 1

Charities – registration

9502 This section covers the registration and reporting thresholds for charities in **England and Wales**.

A "charity" **is defined as** an institution created exclusively for charitable purposes and may be unincorporated and administered by trustees or take the form of a charitable company run by its directors. Currently there are over 160,000 registered charities in the United Kingdom, the majority of which are unincorporated.

Some **special charities**, such as religious organisations, are now required under the Charities Act 2006 to register when income exceeds the registration threshold. The Charities Act has also created a legal framework for new legal formats such as Charitable Incorporated Organisations (CIOs) and Community Interest Companies. The key regulatory authority is the Charity Commission.

> MEMO POINTS   1. **The Charities Act 2011** was granted Royal Assent came into force in March 2012. The new Act repeals and replaces the Recreational Charities Act 1958, the Charities Act 1993 and many of the provisions of the Charities Act 2006.
> 2. A **public benefit entity** has been defined as an entity whose primary objective is to provide goods or services for the general public, community or social benefit and where any equity is provided with a view to supporting the entity's primary objectives, rather than with a view to providing a financial return to equity providers, shareholders or members.
> 3. **Registration process.** A charity must attach certain documents (e.g. governing documents, trustee declaration, bank statements and other supporting documents) when submitting an online registration application.

9503 **All charities** in England and Wales are required by law to produce an annual report and accounts and to make them available on request. The requirement to file annual accounts and a **Trustees' Annual Report** with the Charity Commission applies to all registered charities with a gross annual income exceeding £25,000. Furthermore, charities whose gross income exceeds £10,000 in the financial year, must also send an **annual return** to the Charity Commission. All the above documents must be filed within 10 months of the end of the financial year. An **audit or independent examination** is required by charities whose gross income exceeds £25,000 in the full financial year, unless stipulated by the charity's governing document.

Charity Commission – registration thresholds

9504 Charities in **England and Wales** with an annual income exceeding £5,000 must register with the Charity Commission, although charities with an annual income of less than this can still register voluntarily. The threshold is designed to reduce the administrative burden on small charities. Charities in Scotland and Northern Ireland must register with their own charity regulators. Charities that are part of a larger organisation are only required to register if they are an independent local branch that control its own funds.

9505 Previously, certain charities were not required to register with the Charity Commission, because they were regulated by other public sector bodies known as the "**Principal Regulator**" (e.g. The Financial Conduct Authority (FCA). Now, if **a suitable regulator is not available** the charity will now have to register with the commission, although initially only those charities with an annual income exceeding £100,000 will be affected. The income threshold is expected to apply for at least five years, after which it will be reviewed.

MEMO POINTS   1. The **principal regulators in England are** the Department for Culture, Media and Sport and the Higher Education and Funding Council.
2. Charities in Scotland must register with The Office of the Scottish Charity Regulator, based in Dundee
3. Charities in Northern Ireland must register with The Charity Commission for Northern Ireland based in Belfast.

Special charities such as religious organisations or armed forces charities were previously exempt from registering with the Commission. These excepted charities as they are termed, will now come under the jurisdiction of the Commission although only those entities with an annual income exceeding £100,000 will be required to formally register. **Voluntary registration** is also permitted.   **9506**

MEMO POINTS   1. Although **excepted charities** do not need to register with the Charity Commission they do come under its jurisdiction, and their charitable activities can be investigated if there is cause for concern. Charities may be excepted by Order or Regulation or a registered place of worship. Examples include churches and charitable service funds of the armed forces.
2. Excepted charities differ from **exempt charities** which are not regulated by the Charity Commission but are supervised by another organisation or body such as the Higher Education Funding Council. Examples include universities, museums and foundation schools.
3. **Registration process**. A charity must attach certain documents (e.g. governing documents, trustee declaration, bank statements and other supporting documents) when submitting an on-line registration application.

Reporting options – thresholds

The current income thresholds are set out in the table below.   **9507**

Income thresholds	Accounts	Reporting options
Charities (non-companies) whose gross income is less than £250,000	Choice of preparing either:	
	a. Cash-based accounts (see ¶9509); or	Use format developed by Charity Commission (see ¶9940)
	b. Accrual accounts	Adoption of SORP required
Charities (non-companies) whose gross income exceeds £250,000	Preparation of accrual accounts is compulsory	Choice of FRSSE, SORP or GAAP
Charitable companies	Must prepare accrual accounts irrespective of the gross income threshold	Choice of FRSSE, SORP or GAAP – depending on whether the charity qualifies as a small or medium-sized company

MEMO POINTS   1. The **thresholds** are subject to periodic review.
2. Where accounting periods **are shorter or longer than 12 months**, the thresholds should be adjusted accordingly.
3. Charities often undertake **trading activities** through companies that they control and as such a parent charity is legally required to prepare own entity accounts.

SECTION 2

Small charities

Charities meeting the threshold requirements set out in ¶9507 can elect to produce cash-based receipts and payments accounts, instead of applying the Charity SORP. This option is not available to **charitable companies** who must prepare accruals accounts. Smaller charities may also take advantage of a number of reporting concessions (including adoption of the FRSSE for accruals based accounts) when preparing financial reports.   **9508**

9509 **Cash-based receipts and payments accounts** For **very small charities** with simple organisational structures and no principal assets except cash and deposit accounts, cash-based receipts and payments accounts will suffice, containing a summary of monies received and expended during the year and a list of assets at the end of the year. The issue of recognition is confined only to physical cash receipts and payments.

> ⌐MEMO POINTS⌐ The Charity Commission has produced a **standard format** for preparing cash-based accounts which is set out in the Appendix.

9510 **FRSSE** Charities meeting the threshold requirements for small companies and producing accrual accounts are free to adopt the FRSSE, except in the following areas:
- investments including properties must be stated at market value;
- the profit and loss account and STRGL are replaced by the Statement of Financial Affairs (SOFA);
- foreign exchange gains or losses must be shown in the gains or losses section of the SOFA as the FRSSE permits these differences to be taken to reserves.

A charity should apply the accounting practice and disclosure requirements required by the accounting standards and the charity SORP in relation to consolidated accounts.

SECTION 3

Application of the Charity SORP

9512 The charity SORP has been developed within the framework of the UK financial reporting system, in order to provide clarification for the charity sector on the applicability of the accounting standards and enhance the quality of charity accounts.

This section covers the structure of charity accounts and a detailed review of the accounting treatment required under the SORP. The **accounting recommendations** of the SORP apply to accounts prepared on an accruals basis, which is the case for the majority of charities.

Structure of charity accounts

9514 Charities differ greatly in structure. However, the accounts should detail how money and assets entrusted to the charity have been utilised during the year and the balance on each type of fund at the end of the accounting period. The structure of charity financial statements are summarised in the table below and considered in detail in the sections that follow.

Report	Content	Ref
I. A Statement of Financial Activities (SOFA)	Highlights incoming resources and resources committed, reconciled to changes in funds. The SOFA is based on a columnar format if more than one fund is involved.	¶9514
Ia. Income and Expenditure Account	Where legally required (certain charitable companies)	¶9694
II. Balance Sheet	Highlights assets, liabilities and different fund categories used by the charity	¶9570
III. Notes to the Accounts	Detailing accounting policies and explanation of material items	¶9624
IV. Cash Flow Statement	Where required in accordance with the accounting standards	¶9660
V. Trustees' Annual Report	Supplements information in the primary statements – reflects impact of material transactions and commitments. Provides information on structure, corporate governance, and details of charity's objectives and key performance indicators not measurable in monetary terms.	¶9664

A. Statement of Financial Activities

The Statement of Financial Activities (SOFA) provides information on the **sources and application of revenues** utilised by the charity, to meet its stated objectives and shows whether there has been a net inflow or outflow of resources. The SOFA should also contain a reconciliation of movements in the charity's funds.   **9515**

The SOFA is designed to include all the gains and losses of a charity that would normally be found in the profit and loss account and STRGL, as required under FRS 3.

Format

The format and activity categories of the SOFA are set out in the example below and expanded on in the following section.   **9516**

Statement of Financial Activities (SOFA)	Aggregate of Unrestricted funds	Aggregate of Restricted funds	Aggregate of Endowment funds	Total funds	Prior year-total funds
1. Incoming resources					
Incoming resources from generated funds					
- Voluntary income					
- Activities for generating funds					
- Investment income					
Incoming resources from charitable activities					
Other incoming resources					
Total incoming resources					
2. Resources expended					
Costs of generating funds (fundraising)					
- Costs of generating voluntary income					
- Fundraising trading: cost of goods sold and other costs					
– Investment					
Management costs					
Cost of undertaking charitable activities					
Governance costs					
Other resources expended					
Total resources expended					
Net incoming/ outgoing resources before transfers					

Statement of Financial Activities (SOFA)	Aggregate of Unrestricted funds	Aggregate of Restricted funds	Aggregate of Endowment funds	Total funds	Prior year-total funds
3. Transfers					
- Gross transfers between funds					
Net incoming resources before other recognised gains and losses					
4. Other recognised gains/losses					
- Gains on revaluation of fixed assets for charity's own use					
- Gains/losses on investment assets					
- Actuarial gains/losses on defined benefit pension schemes					
Net movement in funds					
5. Reconciliation of funds					
Total funds brought forward					
Total funds carried forward					

MEMO POINTS   Where a charity has **discontinued (or undertaken new) operations**, the accounts should distinguish between continuing, discontinued and acquired operations by activity. This requirement does not apply to the development or termination of projects within a specific activity.

Type of funds

9518   A charity will often have **several individual funds** comprising a particular category. Where material, more detail can be given in the notes to the accounts or additional columns can be added to the SOFA.

9519   **Endowment funds**   Capital funds that cannot be converted into income by the trustees are known as endowment funds and must generally be held indefinitely, although the underlying assets can be exchanged or may be subject to depreciation or impairment. An exchange of assets can include simply a change of investment or the replacing of one asset with a similar asset.

Where trustees have the power to convert endowment funds into expendable income, these funds are termed **"expendable endowments"**. The fund must be invested to produce income used to further the objectives of the charity. **Certain expenses** can be deducted from endowment funds such as related investment management fees, valuation fees etc.

9520   **Restricted funds**   Restricted funds can only be used for a particular purpose and must be accounted for separately. These funds may be set up by a donor, or through public appeals or a legal process. Restricted funds can be income funds expendable at the discretion of the trustees or capital funds, where the assets are retained by the charity. The terms and conditions attached to the restricted funds will vary according to the individual charity.

9521   **Unrestricted funds (General funds)**   Unrestricted funds can be used at the discretion of the trustees to further the objectives of the charity. A part of the fund may still be designated for specific purposes, although this is an administrative classification only, or to make up any shortfall on a restricted fund. Where funds are used to construct or improve a building on land classified as an endowment asset, this expenditure should be classified as part of the permanent endowment.

---

1. Incoming resources

Incoming resources arise from **different types of transactions** ranging from the provision of goods or services to the receipt of unrestricted grants or donations. Guidance on how the different types of incoming resources in the charity sector should be recognised and recorded in the financial statements and how accounting principles and standards should be applied, is given in the following section.

9522
Charity SORP (96)-(97)

The main **disclosure requirements** are covered in ¶9624.

---

a. Type of incoming resources from generated funds

The **principal types** of incoming resources can broadly be classified as voluntary income, fundraising activities and investment income, each of which is considered below.

9524

Voluntary income

Voluntary income is defined as gifts that do not generate a financial return for the donor, such as legacies, gifts in kind and donated services. Disclosure should be made of activities representing voluntary income, linked where possible to an analysis of the supporting costs incurred. This information should be provided either on the face of the SOFA or in the notes to the accounts.

9526

Legacies 1. Legacies that are **not payable immediately** should not be classified as receivable until all the criteria attached to the payment of the particular legacy have been met (e.g. death of a life tenant). The value of the incoming resource is then determined and recognised at that date.
2. Where **entitlement** to the legacy **is in doubt** due to legal disputes, then the resource should not be recognised until such time as the legal situation is resolved.
3. **Payments on account** from a legacy are treated as receivable. When payments on account have been agreed prior to the end of the financial year, but actually received after the balance sheet date, they should be accrued in the SOFA and the balance sheet.

9528

Gifts in kind Gifts in kind can be classified as per the following table.

9529

The **general rule** is that the amount at which gifts in kind are recognised in the SOFA should either be a reasonable estimate of their gross value on the open market or, in the case of second-hand goods donated for resale, the amount actually realised.

Type	Recognition
1. Stock given to a charity for distribution	Recognise as an incoming resource (under voluntary income), when an equivalent amount has been included under resources expended, to reflect the distribution of the stock
2. Assets given to a charity for its own use (e.g. property)	Recognise as an incoming resource in the SOFA – plus within the relevant fixed asset category in the balance sheet
3. Gift made on trust for later conversion into cash – for subsequent expenditure by the charity	Two possible accounting treatments: **a.** Gift should be recognised when received and value adjusted on subsequent realisation **b.** Where option (a) is not practical, a gift is recognised only in accounting period when the asset is sold (e.g. second-hand items donated for resale).

9530 **Donated services** A charity could receive aid through donated resources such as services or favourable loan arrangements. Examples of donated services include services provided free by individuals such as accountants, lawyers or tradesmen.

Type	Recognition
Donations	Should **only be recognised** in the SOFA when the benefits to the charity are quantifiable, and are based on prices the charity would expect to pay in the open market for an equivalent service.
When donated services are recognised	Then **an equivalent amount** must also be included as expenditure in the SOFA. However, a distinction must be drawn between this and time given by volunteers which should not be included in the SOFA.
Disclosure requirements	The notes to the SOFA should cover an analysis of donated services or facilities such as loaned assets and the valuation bases adopted. Donated services (e.g. type, value) relating to **volunteer services** not included in SOFA, should be disclosed in the Trustees' Annual Report.

Activities for generating funds (trading and fundraising)

9532 The category "activities for generating funds" (non-donated funds) includes the trading and income generating activities of the charity such as:
– fundraising events (e.g. appeals, jumble sales, concerts);
– sponsorships, lotteries;
– income from letting property temporarily surplus to operational requirements; and
– income from charity shops through selling donated goods.

> ☐ MEMO POINTS ☐ 1. The income from selling donated goods legally, represents the realisation of a donation and is recognised under this category as it is similar to a trading activity. **Recognition is based on** an assessment of the balance of activities. For instance, where a charity shop sells primarily donated goods but also a small amount of goods produced in-house, it would be acceptable to recognise all as "shop income" under "activities for generating funds".
> 2. **New UK GAAP.** The FRC has issued a **staff education note** 12 "Incoming resources from non-exchange transactions" (SEN 12), to aid the transtion to FRS 102 "The Financial Reporting Standard applicable in the UK and Republic of Ireland", whose adoption is mandatory for accounting periods beginning on or after 1 January 2015. The SEN covers incoming resources from non-exchange transactions specific to public benefit entities and include donations of cash, goods and services, and legacies.

b. Incoming resources from direct charitable activities

9534 This category covers incoming resources representing payment for goods and services, provided for the benefit of the charity's beneficiaries and includes trading activities and conditional grants that are similar in nature to income from trading and fundraising.

An analysis of the main incoming resources from charitable activities should be given in the notes to the SOFA. This analysis should be linked to resources expended on charitable activities.

Charity SORP (145) **Examples** of incoming resources from charitable activities **include**:
– sale of goods or services as part of direct charitable activities;
– sale of goods or services provided by beneficiaries of the charity (e.g. paintings by disabled artists);
– letting of non-investment property;
– specific grants for activities provided by the charity; and
– contractual payments from local authorities or government for the provision of services (e.g. fees for respite care).

c. Recognition criteria

All incoming resources must meet the general criteria in order to be recognised in the financial statements. The trustees may also need to consider additional factors specific to each type of funding as set out in the tables below.   **9540**

Incoming resources earned by the charity and its agents and volunteers, should be reported gross.

General criteria   Incoming resources **can only be recognised** in the SOFA, when the effect of a transaction or other event is to increase the assets of the charity. This in turn is dependant on whether: **9541**
Charity SORP (94)
– there is an entitlement arising from control over rights (e.g. legal arrangements, terms, jurisdiction, trust or contract law) to an incoming resource;
– it is certain the incoming resource will be received;
– it can be reliably measured in monetary terms; and
– the funding is dependent on specific contractual or performance related conditions or use is restricted.

2. Resources expended

The SOFA provides the framework for the recognition and analysis of the resources expended by the charity. Additionally, **where material**, an analysis should be provided of sub-activities, programmes, projects and other initiatives that support the principal activities of the charity.   **9546**
Charity SORP (149)

Charities expend resources in a variety of ways including meeting contractual liabilities and payment of grants or donations. The SORP provides guidance on how these **different types of transactions** should be recognised in **accruals based accounts** and how the accounting standards and principles should be applied. In cash based accounts, the recognition of resources expended is based on the actual physical outflow of cash resources from the charity.

a. Type of resources expended

This section considers the recognition and accounting treatment of the costs of generating funds from different sources.   **9550**

Cost by type	Definition/examples	Additional requirements
A. Cost of generating funds	The costs of generating funds **should exclude** trading costs related to the provision of goods and services, and any subsequent negotiation or monitoring required under the terms of a performance related grant or contract.	Where the costs **are material**, additional information should be given in the notes to the SOFA, and where possible matched to the analysis of income.
- Voluntary income	Represents the costs incurred in generating monetary gifts made to the charity. **Examples include**: – producing advertising, marketing and direct mail; – maintaining a database; – door to door collections; – generating sponsorship; – legacy development; and – start-up costs for new fundraising activities.	

Cost by type	Definition/examples	Additional requirements
- Fundraising	Covers expenses incurred through selling for charitable purposes, either donated or purchased goods, or the provision of non-charitable services intended to generate income. **Examples include:** – the direct costs of goods sold or services provided; – other related trading costs (e.g. staff costs, premises, support costs); or – licensing (e.g. charity logos).	
- Investment management costs	Includes the costs of: – portfolio management; – investment advice; – administration of investments; and – property repairs and maintenance charges; and – rent collection.	1. Where management fees have been deducted by external investment managers, the charity should show the investment income gross with fees charged to the appropriate cost category (e.g. the costs associated with endowment fund investments should be charged to the respective endowment fund in the SOFA). 2. The cost of disposing of investments are excluded from this category and usually netted-off against the disposal proceeds.
B. Costs of undertaking charitable activities	Covers the resources expended by charities conducting their charitable activities (e.g. delivery of goods and services) as opposed to the costs of the initial fundraising.	Resources expended by charities in undertaking their charitable activities should be analysed on the face of the SOFA or in the notes to the accounts (see example below).
- Grant funding	Includes grants made to individuals (e.g. educational, bursaries) as well as institutional grants (e.g. research projects).	The costs associated with grant funding activities include: – costs resulting from the decision to award a grant; – subsequent monitoring costs; or – related general management and administration costs (e.g. budgeting, payroll, IT).
- Support costs	Include the costs of supporting income generation and supporting the governance of the charity. **Examples include** the costs of general management accounting and administration and information technology support.	1. Details of the total support costs incurred and cost allocation should be given in the notes to the accounts. 2. Where the support costs are material, information on the apportionment bases adopted should also be given.
- Governance costs	Defined as costs incurred by the charity in meeting its statutory reporting requirements including: – internal or external audits; – legal advice for trustees; – trustee meetings; or – preparation of statutory accounts.	

9554 **Support costs** In charging support costs to different activities the **following principles** should be applied; namely that expenditure should where possible, be allocated direct to a specific activity and shared costs (e.g. staff costs, depreciation) should be apportioned on a justifiable and consistent basis.

b. Recognition criteria

Liabilities are recognised as resources expended when there is a "legal or constructive obligation" (see the note below), committing the charity to the expenditure. The criteria for recognising resources expended by type are set out below.

9556
Charity SORP (148)

Contract for supply   Where a charity enters into a contract for the supply of goods or services, expenditure is recognised once the supplier has delivered the goods or provided the service.

9558
Charity SORP (150)-
(156)

Grants   **a.** Expenditure on **performance related grants** should be classified as resources expended, to the extent that the grant recipient has provided the contracted level of services or goods, and satisfied all other conditions that are linked to the grant (e.g. number of meals provided or a time-based service).
b. Grants related to a specific purpose are known as **restricted grants** (e.g. two-year research programme) and should be recognised as a liability when a constructive obligation is incurred to make a grant payment.
c. Under **non-performance related grants** and other expenditure relating directly to charitable activities, an "exchange for consideration" does not arise, as a contractual relationship with the grant beneficiary is not created. However, the charity may still have a liability which should be recognised, arising from a legal or constructive obligation.

9559

3. Transfers between funds

Transfers **between different types of funds** should be shown here in the SOFA, including:
– capital funds moved from an endowment fund to an income fund;
– restricted assets released and reallocated to unrestricted income funds;
– assets transferred to cover a deficit on a restricted fund; or
– the value of a fixed asset transferred from a restricted to an unrestricted fund, when the asset has been purchased from a restricted fund donation.

9560
Charity SORP (214)

Material transfers should not be netted-off but shown gross on the face of the SOFA and details of material transfers between funds should be provided in the notes to the accounts.

9561

4. Other recognised gains and losses

Gains or losses arising on the disposal, revaluation or impairment of fixed assets, held for investment purposes or for the own use of the charity, should form part of the particular fund in which the asset is held, at the time the profit or loss is determined.

9562

Category of gain or loss	Recognition	Accounting treatment
Gains or losses on fixed assets (charity's own use, non-investment)	1. Revaluation	Include in gains and losses on revaluations of fixed assets.
	2. Disposal	Gains on disposal – include under "Other incoming resources". Losses on disposal – treat as additional depreciation and charge to resources expended section in the SOFA.
	3. Impairment	Impairment losses – same treatment as for losses on disposal.
Gains or losses on investment assets (including property)		Recognised under gains or losses on the revaluation and disposal of fixed assets – single row in the SOFA
Actuarial gains or losses on defined benefit pension schemes		Disclose separately in the gains or losses section of the SOFA

B. Balance sheet

9570   The balance sheet provides a summary of the charity's assets at the end of the financial year and how the assets are divided between different funds. The balance sheet should also highlight which resources have **legal restrictions** attached to their use or that have been designated for a specific use.

Structure

9572   The format of the asset, liability and fund headings are set out in the table below. Charities may adopt a columnar presentation in the balance sheet, analysed between each fund group. **Where the columnar method** of presentation **is not adopted** then the assets and liabilities constituting each fund should be analysed in the notes to the accounts.

The order in which the categories of funds are presented will vary according to the preference of the individual charity.

Balance Sheet	Total Funds	Prior Year Funds
1. Fixed assets:		
Intangible assets		
Tangible assets		
Heritage assets		
Investment assets		
Programme related investments		
Total fixed assets		
2. Current assets:		
- Stocks and work-in-progress		
- Debtors		
- Investments		
- Cash at bank and in hand		
Total current assets		
3. Liabilities		
Creditors: Amounts falling due within one year		
Net current assets and liabilities		
Total assets less current liabilities		
Creditors: Amounts falling due after more than one year		
Provisions for liabilities and charges		
4. Defined benefit pension scheme asset or liability		
5. The funds of the charity:		
- Endowment funds		
- Restricted income funds		
- Unrestricted income funds		
- Share capital		
- Revaluation reserve		
- Pension reserve		
Total unrestricted funds		
Total charity funds		

1. Assets and liabilities

The accounting requirements for intangible and tangible fixed assets, heritage assets and investment assets are covered in this section.   **9580**

a. Fixed assets

Intangible fixed assets

Where a charity has an intangible fixed asset (e.g. licence, brand) which does not meet the recognition criteria under FRS 10 (see ¶1018), it should not be included in the primary statements but details of the asset should be given in the notes to the accounts.   **9581**

Tangible fixed assets

Tangible fixed assets should be capitalised on initial acquisition at cost or valuation. Subsequent expenditure which enhances the performance of tangible fixed assets should also be capitalised. Tangible fixed assets are treated in greater detail in ¶1200 with charity specific issues covered below.   **9582**

Tangible fixed assets (other than investments)	Accounting treatment
General rules	1. Cost of acquisition including directly attributable costs 2. Fixed assets acquired in full or part from grant proceeds – should be included at acquisition cost and not netted off 3. Donated assets – include at value at date of donation. Also included in the SOFA under incoming resources.
Depreciation	See ¶1444.
Revaluation	The **general rule** is that where a revaluation policy is adopted it must be applied to all assets in a particular classification (see also ¶1352). The **exception to the rule** is that where assets **are donated or capitalised** as a result of a change in accounting policy, the initial valuation is not deemed a revaluation. This means that other assets in this group/class need not be revalued. Where a charity adopts a policy of revaluation – revaluation must be updated regularly (see ¶1374-¶1440).
Impairment	Impairment is measured according to the process outlined in ¶1562-¶1568. 1. **Impairment losses** should be recognised in accordance with FRS 11 – treat as additional depreciation and include in the SOFA. Asset then depreciated over revised UEL. 2. **Valuation measures** based on service delivery or replacement cost may be appropriate as charities often hold assets for other reasons than generating cash flows. "Value in use" based on future cash flows would be an inappropriate valuation measure.

Heritage assets

Heritage assets are defined as assets of historical, artistic or scientific importance held to further the preservation, conservation and educational activities of charities. These assets include land, buildings, collections, exhibits or artefacts and are often central to the objectives of the charity such as supporting education in the arts (galleries) and sciences (museums).   **9586**

Assets **used by the charity as administrative offices** or as part of a property investment portfolio or works of art and antiques retained as a store of wealth, should not be classified as heritage assets (see also ¶1330).

EXAMPLE
1. The Woodland Trust holds land relating to the preservation and enhancement of forests through-out the UK, including many areas of natural beauty and scientific interest.

2. The National Trust for England, Wales and Northern Ireland seeks to preserve and protect the coastline, countryside and specific historical buildings, for future generations through active management and conservation.

9588

Heritage assets	Accounting issues/recognition/measurement
1. Newly purchased	**Initially recognised** at cost in accordance with FRS 15 (¶1226).
2. Valuation issues	Heritage buildings, structures or sites **present different valuation issues**, such as: 1. Determining the service potential of a unique building or structure, in terms of its heritage value (e.g. medieval castles, archaeological sites, monuments). 2. Valuing donated heritage assets where rarely sold on the open market. 3. Assets that are part purchased/part donated and that are capable of reliable measurement as should gifts and lifetime transfers which are usually valued for inheritance tax purposes. 4. Specialised buildings – use depreciated replacement cost (¶1400).

9590
FRS 30 (11)

Disclosures   A separate line for heritage assets is required on the balance sheet, with addi-tional information given in the notes to the accounts, including:
– an analysis or description of the age, scale and nature of heritage assets;
– details of cost, additions, and disposals during the year;
– where assets are not capitalised, a description of the assets; and
– the accounting policy note covering measurement bases and capitalisation policy.

MEMO POINTS   **FRS 30 "Heritage assets"** (see ¶1330) is designed to improve the consistency and trans-parency of the financial reporting of heritage assets, covering entities such as museums and organisa-tions that own and manage landscapes or buildings for their environmental and historical qualities. FRS 30 includes **enhanced disclosure requirements** for heritage assets, whether reported in the balance sheet or not. The detailed disclosure requirements cover the nature and value of heritage assets held, as well as the stewardship policies adopted, including development, preservation and disposal of assets and also includes guidance regarding the requirement for regular impairment reviews.

b. Current assets

9604   Current assets should normally be recognised at lower of cost or net realisable value. The headings may be adapted to meet the requirements of individual charities. For instance, debtors can be further classified as follows:
– trade debtors;
– amounts due from subsidiary and associated undertakings;
– other debtors; and
– prepayments and accrued income.
Where **long-term debtors are material** in terms of total net current assets, they should be listed separately in the balance sheet.

c. Current liabilities and long-term creditors

9606   Current liabilities are recorded at settlement value. The balance sheet headings may be expanded or adapted to meet the requirements of the individual charity or reflect the type of creditor. The totals for short-term and long-term creditors should be separately analysed in the notes to the accounts for:
– loans and overdrafts;
– trade creditors;
– amounts due to subsidiary and associated undertakings;

– other creditors; and
– accruals and deferred income.

Where the charity **acts as an agent** for another charity or organisation, then any assets held   **9607**
(and associated liabilities) should be separately identified in the notes to the accounts but
not included in the balance sheet. Sufficient detail should be given in order that the exact
relationship and nature of the transactions between the funding partner, the intermediary
and the funding recipient is clear.

Where the charity is **the intermediary and principal**, then assets and associated liabilities
should be included in the balance sheet.

Provisions for Liabilities

Provisions for liabilities are defined as the best estimate of the expenditure required to   **9608**
discharge the present obligation at the balance sheet date. The debit entry is to the SOFA in   Charity SORP (321)
line with the recognition criteria set out in ¶9550.

Due consideration should be given to any further uncertainties that could affect the total obligation,
and in addition provisions should be regularly reviewed and adjusted where appropriate.

2. Defined benefit pension schemes

An asset or liability derived from a surplus or deficit in a defined pension scheme is included   **9612**
in this category and disclosed on the face of the balance sheet.

A charity must create a **pension reserve** when there is a surplus (asset) or deficit (liability)
on a defined pension scheme. Where the pension reserve relates only to unrestricted funds
then the reserve itself forms part of the unrestricted funds. Likewise, where the pension asset
or liability forms part of a restricted fund, then the pension reserve will also form part of the
restricted fund, subject to certain criteria being met.

A detailed treatment of this topic relating to charities is beyond the scope of this chapter.
The application of FRS 17 "Retirement Benefits" in general and the required accounting
treatment and disclosures are set out in ¶8410.

3. Types of charity fund

The definitions of endowment funds and restricted and unrestricted funds are given in ¶9518   **9614**
and the main disclosure requirements are covered in ¶9630. Other types of fund include
share capital and the revaluation reserve.

Share capital   Some charities are constituted with a share capital such as Industrial and   **9618**
Provident Societies or incorporated as companies under the Companies Act. Typically, the
share capital is for a nominal amount. Furthermore, as owners are prevented from benefiting
from share ownership, any capital contributed effectively forms part of the unrestricted funds
of the charity. Share capital must be shown separately on the balance sheet.

Revaluation Reserve   Charities incorporated as companies must detail in the revaluation   **9619**
reserve, in terms of unrestricted funds, any differences between the historic cost of fixed
assets and the revalued amounts.

C. Notes to the accounts

The trustees are obliged to prepare accounts that give a true and fair view of the resources   **9624**
and financial commitments of the charity at the end of the financial year, which could result

in more detailed disclosures than those recommended by the Charity SORP. This section outlines the disclosure requirements covering accounting policies, individual funds and other key disclosures not already covered in Section 2.

1. Accounting policies

9626
FRS 18 (17)

The notes to the financial statements should detail the accounting policies selected and confirm that they are consistent with the Charity SORP, the accounting standards, and the Companies Acts.

The **notes should state** the following, where applicable:
1. That the historic cost basis of accounting has been adopted except for investments which are included at market value.
2. Where a branch has been omitted from the accounts (see ¶9720), the reasons justifying this policy.
3. Details of changes to policies that result in material adjustments to prior-periods.
4. The reasons for any material departures from the accounting standards.
5. The reasons for any material departures from the Charity SORP, including:
– how the accounting treatment differs from the SORP;
– the reasons why the trustees adopted this accounting treatment; and
– an estimate of the financial effect on the accounts of the policy adopted.

9628
Charity SORP (361)

Additional disclosures are also required of accounting policies relevant to **material amounts** in the financial statements, as set out in the table below.

Accounting policy	Policy disclosures required
Incoming resources	Policy for each individual type of incoming resource, for example: – basis of recognition of gifts in kind and donated services + methods of valuation; – recognition criteria for grants receivable including for fixed assets; – whether endowment funds are restricted or unrestricted; – whether incoming resources are deferred and the reasons why; – details of legacies deemed receivable; and – whether incoming resources have been included in the SOFA net of expenditure.
Resources expended	– Policy for recognition of liabilities including constructive obligations; – Provisions – and the point at which a provision is deemed binding (e.g. grants); – Policy for including costs within certain activity categories in resources expended; – Methods and principles of allocating or apportioning costs to different activity categories (i.e. based on staff time, salaries).
Asset policy	Capitalisation policy for fixed assets including: – for each class of asset, whether they are included at cost, valuation or revaluation; – the valuation (revaluation) methods and bases used; – the value below which assets not capitalised; – depreciation methods and rates; – details of impaired assets (e.g. reviews); and – any differences between carrying value and market value of assets (non-investments).
Investments	Policy of inclusion at market value except where: – investments are not listed on a recognised stock exchange; – investment properties; or – investments in subsidiary undertakings. Policy on dealing with investment gains or losses in the SOFA.

2. Details of individual funds

Information on the structure of the charity's funds should be given in the notes to the accounts, differentiating between:
- unrestricted income funds (general and designated);
- restricted income funds;
- permanent endowment; and
- expendable endowments.

9630

The trustees must decide on the most appropriate presentation for the charity depending on **the complexity of the funds** and their structure.

Additional disclosures include:
- an analysis of assets and liabilities representing each type of fund where a columnar balance sheet is not adopted;
- details of the purpose of each fund and any restrictions imposed on its use;
- separate disclosure of funds in deficit, material transfers between funds; and
- allocations to designated funds with the accompanying reasons.

9631

D. Cash flow statement

Charities **that do not qualify** as a small company (see ¶9507) are required to prepare a cash flow statement. Cash flow statements should comply with the requirements of FRS 1, which is covered in greater detail in ¶4000. The **specific requirements** in relation to charities are dealt with below.
1. The **analysis of cash movements** should reflect the charity's operations as reported in the SOFA. The starting point is normally, the "net incoming/outgoing resources before other recognised gains or losses" (see ¶9515).
2. **Movements in endowments** should not be included in "cash flows from operating activities" but treated as increases or decreases in the financing section as follows:
a. cash donations to endowment funds should be treated as additions to endowments; and
b. the receipts and payments from the acquisition and disposal of investments should be shown gross under "capital expenditure and financial investments". A single line should be included in this section showing the net movement in cash flows relating to endowment investments. A corresponding row showing the same should be included in the financing section, reflecting the cash movements in and out of the endowment fund.

9660

The **disclosure requirements** of FRS 1 apply to charities with the most common being as follows:
1. Cash movements should be reconciled to the appropriate opening and closing balance sheet amounts; and
2. A reconciliation of "cash flows from operating activities" within the cash flow statement to the "net incoming resources/expenditure" row in the SOFA.

9661

E. Trustees' Annual Report

The Trustees' Annual Report (TAR) must provide a review of the management structure of the charity as well as its objectives, activities, funding requirements and performance over the financial year. A TAR must be filed by all registered charities whose gross income or total expenditure exceeds £25,000. Charities not subject to a statutory audit can produce an abbreviated TAR, the framework for which is set out in ¶9670. Additional disclosures are required by **larger charities** whose gross income exceeds £250,000 as they are subject to a statutory audit.

9664

9665 The **legal requirement** for a TAR and its contents differ, according to the different charity reporting frameworks that apply within the separate legal jurisdictions in the UK (see appendix 1). Legal requirements and the Charity SORP do not limit the inclusion of other information within the TAR, such as a chairman's report. The TAR should be attached to the financial statements. The deadline for filing the TAR with the Charities Commission is 10 months after the end of the financial year. **Charitable companies** must prepare a Directors' Report. A separate TAR is not required as long as the statutory Directors' Report contains all the information required in the TAR.

> ☐MEMO POINTS☐ The TAR can now be **submitted online** via the Charities Commission Website.

9666 **Purpose** The purpose of the TAR is to discharge the charity's trustees' duty of public accountability and stewardship through the provision of information concerning:
- the progress made by the charity against its stated objectives;
- its financial position at the end of the financial year; and
- a review of its plans for the future.

Public benefit reporting

9670 The Charity Commission has published guidance for charity trustees, covering disclosures in the TAR, and in particular, the new requirements for **public benefit reporting**. The TAR must include a statement by the trustees confirming their compliance with section 4 of the Charities Act 2006, regarding the public benefit guidance published by the charity commission.

> ☐MEMO POINTS☐ Two **key principles** underpin the notion of public benefit; namely that there must be an identifiable benefit and this must accrue to the public or section of the public.

Small charities that are **not subject to a statutory audit**, may limit the disclosures to a summary of the main achievements of the charity during the year. The public benefit reporting requirements are also less stringent.

The disclosure requirements for **larger charities** have been expanded to include a more detailed review of significant activities and strategy, including how the aims and objectives of the charity have been met. Additional disclosures are required for larger charities (depending on the size and complexity) as set out in the following table. **All charities** must confirm that they have considered the latest guidance on public benefit reporting.

The **key disclosure requirements** cover the following:
- Administrative details (e.g. name, registration, principal address etc);
- Governance structure and management (e.g. operating policies, key risks etc);
- Objectives and activities (e.g. governing document, strategic review);
- Performance review (summary of main activities); and
- Financial review (sources of funding, investments etc).

For smaller charities the level of disclosures is reduced.

SECTION 4

Charitable companies and groups

A. Charitable companies

9690 In adopting the SORP, charitable companies meet most but not all of the requirements of the Companies Act and accounting standards, as they are not replicated in full. Charitable companies, irrespective of size, must prepare accrual based accounts. One of the best known examples of a charitable company is Cancer Research UK. A new legal form of charitable company known as a Charitable Incorporated Organisation has also been introduced.

There are a number of **additional requirements** for charitable companies; namely that they must:
1. Comply with the Companies Acts concerning the form and content of accounts, plus directors' report.
2. Apply the Companies Act financial statement formats and adapt headings and sub-headings where the special nature of the company's business so requires.
3. Include the names of its directors in the annual report as no exemption is permitted.
4. Give details of any material departures from the Charity SORP.
5. Disclose specific information relating to the revaluation reserve.
6. Where required, provide a summary income and expenditure account.

9692

Summary income and expenditure account In a **minority of cases**, a charity may be required to prepare a summary income and expenditure account in addition to the SOFA; namely where:
– the income and expenditure account cannot be identified within the SOFA due to the structure and headings adopted; or
– certain items are subject to challenge such as movements on endowment funds during the year.

9694

Where a summary income and expenditure account is required, it should be derived from and cross-referenced to the corresponding figures in the SOFA. A distinction need not be drawn between unrestricted and restricted funds, but the accounting basis adopted must be the same as that for the SOFA, with a separate analysis of continuing operations, acquisitions and discontinued operations covering:
– gross income from all sources;
– transfers from endowment funds to income expendable;
– total income;
– total expenditure from the charity's income funds; and
– net income or expenditure for the year.

Revaluation reserve Charitable companies must give details of the revaluation reserve in respect of their unrestricted funds, on the face of the balance sheet. Where permitted under FRS 11 and FRS 15 (¶1348), impairment losses and downward revaluations can be off-set against the revaluation reserve.

9695

Accounting records Charitable companies are required to keep accounting records (e.g. cash books, invoices, receipts, Gift Aid records etc.) for at least 3 years. Charitable companies must prepare annual accounts and make them available to the public on request. This is important for public accountability, and must be complied with in all cases, although the trustees can make a reasonable charge to cover the costs of complying with the request (e.g. photocopying and postage).

9696

Charitable companies must prepare an Annual Report and make it available to the public on request.

> ◻ MEMO POINTS All registered charities will receive an **Annual Information Update form**, and larger charities will also receive an Annual Return from the Commission. Although trustees of charities with an income of £10,000 or less do not have to complete and return the update form, by doing so they will meet their legal obligation to keep the Commission informed of any changes to the Register. Charities with a total income exceeding £10,000 have a legal duty to complete and return the Annual Return form to the Commission.

Charitable incorporated organisations (CIO)

Charities **opting for a corporate structure** have to register both as charities and companies and are subject to the regulatory requirements of both Companies House and the Charities Commission.

9697

The Charities Act 2006 created a new vehicle for these charities called "The Charitable Incorporated Organisation" (CIO), which retains the advantages of a corporate structure such as reduced personal liability for trustees, whilst dispensing with the burden of dual recognition. This corporate form is now available to new charities wishing to register in England and Wales and to existing charities wishing to convert to this format. The Charity Commission is currently developing a model constitution for CIOs, following consultation and parliamentary approval.

9698   CIOs have a number of **special features** that differentiate them from other forms of Not For Profit Organisations.

Category	Special features
Single registration	CIOs report directly to the Charities Commission (and not Companies House, or the FSA). Recognised as separate legal entities and their members enjoy limited liability.
Accounting requirements	Less onerous than for companies – small CIOs can prepare receipts and payments accounts.
Filing requirements	Accounting and reporting and filing requirements are less onerous than those for companies in general.
Constitution and governance	Governance reporting requirements less extensive than for companies. CIOs have simpler constitutional forms and there is a choice of formats and administration, available to suit organisations of all sizes.

9699   **Conversion to a CIO**   Existing companies, already registered as charities or community interest companies, will be allowed to convert to CIOs through a **special conversion process**. Other types of charity (not incorporated) will also be able to convert to a CIO by setting up a new entity that subsequently acquires the existing charity's assets.

However, charitable companies or regulated societies with a share capital, including partly paid shares, will not be able to apply for conversion to a CIO. Whilst the Charities Act 2006 established a legal framework for CIOs, the detailed provisions will be developed by the Office of the Third Sector, in the form of regulations. However, it is expected that the thresholds that apply to non-company charities will also apply to CIOs.

B. Group accounting

9700   The SORP contains **additional requirements** for charities that may result from the specific nature of the legal or operating structures adopted, such as the consolidation of subsidiary undertakings and accounting for associates and joint ventures. Charities often undertake trading activities through companies that they control and as such, a parent charity is legally required to prepare own entity accounts. The preparation and publication of group accounts is designed to improve transparency concerning the full range of activities performed by the charity and the resources it controls.

1. Consolidation of subsidiaries

9702
Charity SORP (384)
A parent charity should prepare consolidated accounts for all its subsidiaries, **except where** one of a small number of **exemptions apply** as follows:
1. The gross income of the group, after consolidation adjustments, does not exceed the threshold for a statutory charity audit (£250,000).
2. The results of the subsidiary are immaterial relative to the size of the group.
3. A subsidiary is incorporated but subject to winding-up proceedings.

The majority of **unincorporated charitable subsidiaries** are aggregated within the accounts of the parent charity, as they are normally either restricted funds or endowment funds. However, **where a charity controls another charitable entity** whose remit is wider than that of the parent charity, then consolidation will depend on the ability of the parent to control ("tests for control") the subsidiary.

The **principles and methods** of consolidation are covered in more detail in ¶6570, and are applicable irrespective of whether the parent charity and its subsidiaries are incorporated or not. Although charities use subsidiaries for both profit and non-profit activities (e.g. non-trading or investment purposes), the distinction does not in itself determine whether or not consolidation is appropriate.

9703

In general, the following **consolidation rules apply**:
– consolidation should be on a line-by-line basis (similar items matched);
– resources, whether incoming and expended should be shown gross; and
– all intra-group transactions should be cancelled.

Tests for control

Subsidiary undertakings can be identified by the measure of control enjoyed by one party over another, in the context of voting rights, participating interests and the exercise of dominant influence.

9706

Control arises in the following instances:
– the charity trustees, members or employees of the parent charity have the right to appoint or remove, the majority of the trustees of the charity; or
– the governing document of the subsidiary charity gives the parent charity's trustees or employees the right to direct or control the subsidiary charity.

Condition	Applying the test
Where the **parent is able to direct and benefit** from the activities of the subsidiary	Tests of control are met and the charitable subsidiary should be consolidated.
Where the **objectives** of the subsidiary charity are **narrower** than those of the parent	Tests of control are met and the charitable subsidiary should be consolidated and accounted for in the restricted fund columns in the consolidated accounts.
Where the **objectives** of the subsidiary charity are **substantially different** to those of the parent.	"Tests of control" will not be met – and the subsidiary should not be consolidated.

Dominant influence may also be less formal. For instance, charities may be formed to support an established charity, and although they may remain a separate legal entity, they may be heavily influenced as to the timing and nature of this support. Where evidence of dominant influence exists, the criteria for consolidation should be deemed as having been met.

9708

A **similar type of relationship** to that of a parent and subsidiary undertaking arises where a parent charity transacting with another undertaking, retains the **risks and rewards** of the transaction. An example is a quasi-subsidiary, where assets are transferred to another entity, but the parent continues to use them and bears the costs of maintaining them. These undertakings should be accounted for in accordance with FRS 5 "Reporting the Substance of Transactions".

9710

Investment income

Where a parent charity receives investment income from **subsidiary undertakings**, the following accounting treatment is required:
1. Payments to a charity by its subsidiary undertakings and dividend entitlements (other than amounts receivable by the charity for provision of goods and services) should be treated as incoming resources under investment income in the parent charity's accounts; and

9712

2. Material gift aid payments from subsidiary undertakings must be separately disclosed in investment income in the SOFA.

Filing of accounts

9714   In England and Wales it is a **statutory requirement** under the Charities Act 2006, that individual charity accounts be filed with the Charity Commission. Therefore, where the group and parent charity's accounts are consolidated, separate balance sheets and SOFAs should be provided for both the parent and the group.

Where consolidated accounts are filed without a **Statement of Financial Affairs (SOFA)** for the parent charity, details should be provided in the notes to the financial statements of gross income/turnover and the results of the parent charity. Furthermore, the group accounts should still contain the balance sheet for the parent charity.

Disclosures

9716   The key disclosure requirements **for subsidiary undertakings** should be given in the notes to the consolidated financial statements as follows:
– segmental information on the activities of material subsidiaries, including name, shareholding, aggregate amount of assets, liabilities and funds and a summary of turnover and profit or loss for the year;
– policy note covering the method of consolidation;
– details of excluded subsidiaries;
– aggregate amount of total investment in subsidiary undertakings;
– details of minority interests held in subsidiaries and restrictions placed on group activities;
– information regarding any subsidiary undertakings excluded from consolidation; and
– details of funds and reserves retained by subsidiaries other than funds available for use in supporting a charity's objectives.

2. Branches

9720   A charity can operate and raise funds through branches, which are defined as entities or administrative bodies set up to undertake a particular aspect of the charity's work (e.g. geographical, specific type of fundraising). The branch may also:
– form part of the administrative structure of a reporting charity;
– represent a restricted fund or an endowment fund; or
– be a legal entity separate from the reporting charity.

9722   The most **common characteristics** of a branch are that it:
– uses the name of the reporting charity in its title;
– raises funds exclusively for the reporting charity and its own local needs;
– is covered by the reporting charity's registration number for tax purposes (i.e. tax relief);
– acts as a local representative for the reporting charity; and
– receives marketing and other support from the reporting charity (i.e. staff, funding).

9724   **Consolidation rules**   The following rules also apply:
1. Branches should be consolidated with the accounts of the parent charity.
2. Where both the reporting charity and individual branches are companies, each entity must prep are financial statements. Consolidated accounts should be prepared in accordance with the rules outlined in ¶9690.
3. Where a branch is **not a separate legal entity**, its accounts must be consolidated with those of the parent charity.
4. Some charities may be termed branches within a particular organisational structure or network. However, where the branch has a considerable degree of**administrative autonomy** from the reporting charity, as set out in its founding document, it should not be consolidated and separate accounts should be prepared for submission to the regulatory authorities.

Accounting treatment

1. **Inter-branch** transactions and **parent-branch** transactions should be eliminated on consolidation.

9728

2. All **assets and liabilities** of a branch should be incorporated into the parent charity's balance sheet.

3. Funds raised by the branch for **the general charitable purposes** of the reporting charity, are accounted for as unrestricted funds in the parent charity's accounts.

4. Funds raised by the branch for **specific charitable purposes** of the reporting charity, are accounted for as restricted funds in the parent charity's accounts.

5. Where **a branch is a separate charity** and retains funds for general branch purposes, these should be accounted for as restricted funds in the reporting charity's accounts.

3. Associates and joint ventures (arrangements)

For the purposes of consolidated accounts, there are a number of additional accounting requirements where a charity has associates, joint ventures and joint arrangements. The **rules governing classification** of an entity or arrangement are covered in ¶7300, as is the accounting treatment and disclosure requirements for associates and joint arrangements.

9730

Associates

A definition of "associates" is given in ¶7320.

9732

Where a charity has a long-term **participating interest** (see ¶7326) in another undertaking and exercises **significant influence** (see ¶7338) over its operating and financial policies, it should be classified as an associate. Participating interest and significant influence are presumed where a charity holds 20% + of the voting rights in an entity, unless proved to the contrary.

> EXAMPLE   A large charity provided grants and advice and expertise to a small charity operating in a related area. The charity also nominated a trustee to sit on the board of the recipient charity, under a formal agreement to help formulate strategy and objectives. In this example, **should the recipient charity be classified as an associate**?
> Yes. The recipient charity should be consolidated as it is small relative to the donor charity and the provision of expertise is linked to a formal agreement to exercise significant influence, through directing or influencing its financial and operating policies. If the donor charity had only provided expertise without attempting to influence policy, then associate status would not be appropriate.

Accounting treatment   Associates are accounted for using the **net equity method**. The following rules also apply:

9734

1. The consolidated SOFA of the charity should show the net interest in the results for the year in the associates, as a separate row after "the net incoming/ (resources expended) before transfers".

2. In the balance sheet, the net interest in associates should be shown as a separate row within fixed asset investments.

3. If a charity's rights to the associate's assets are restricted, this should be accounted for in the valuation.

Joint ventures (arrangements)

A definition of "joint ventures" is given in ¶7410.

9736

Where a charity holds 20% + of the voting rights in another legal undertaking, but where control is shared with other partners, the investment should be classified as a joint venture. Charities may also undertake joint arrangements covering shared activities without a separate legal entity being established.

Joint ventures should be accounted for using the **gross equity method** (see ¶7438). The charity should also declare:
– its share of the gross incoming resources for joint ventures on the face of the SOFA, on a line by line basis;
– the net interest in the results of joint ventures as a separate row after "net incoming resources/resources expended"; and
– in the balance sheet, the share of gross assets and liabilities should be shown with a linked presentation within fixed asset investments.

9738   **Joint arrangements**   For joint arrangements, the charity's share of the incoming resources and resources expended should be included in the financial statements. In general, the accounting treatment is the same as for branches. Where the charity is liable for an obligation, it should accrue that part of the obligation for which it is responsible (contingent liability), with the remainder to be met by the other parties to the arrangement.

Disclosures

9739   The general disclosure requirements for associates and joint arrangements are covered in ¶7494.

The following **additional disclosures** are required for charities:
– name of organisation;
– the parent charity's shareholding and other interests;
– details of associate or joint venture activity;
– parent charity's share of results covering gross income resources by type, cost of generating funds;
– expenditure on charitable activities, and expenses on governance;
– gains or losses on investments;
– types of funds managed by the charity;
– contingent liabilities and other commitments, including those made by the charity to a joint arrangement; and
– its share of pre and post-tax results.

For **joint arrangements**, details should be given of the obligations/commitments made by the charity to the arrangement.

C. Audit and independent examination thresholds

9744   The thresholds at which an external professional audit is required are set out in the table below. Charitable companies that were exempt from audit under the Companies Act will now be covered by the Charities Act.

Gross annual income thresholds	
1. Non-charitable companies	**Audit/examination requirements**
Less than £25,000	Independent examination not required
Between £25,000 and £500,000	Independent examination required. If income is above 250k, the examiner must be qualified.
£500,000 + or total net assets in excess of 3.26m + gross annual income of £250,000 +	Full audit required
2. Charitable companies	**Audit/examination requirements**
Gross income less than £500,000 + net assets less than £3.26m	Independent examination by a qualified person
£500,000 + or B/S total (3.26m +)	Full audit required

Clubs and associations

In general, clubs and associations can be defined as a number of persons who voluntarily join together to promote a common social or economic purpose. Working men's clubs in particular, have played an important role in local society from the late 19th century onwards. Although there is no legal obligation to incorporate, the majority of these organisations choose this option.

9920

> *MEMO POINTS* There is **no legal definition** of a club, association or society and as such the terms are used interchangeably in this chapter. The accounting requirements for building societies and credit unions are outside the scope of this book.

A. Type of clubs and associations

Clubs and societies comprise many different types and may or may not be incorporated, as either as a limited company under the Companies Act, a Community Interest Company (CIC), an Industrial and Provident or Friendly Society. In comparison, proprietary clubs, such as night clubs and casinos, must incorporate under the Companies Act.

9921

Incorporated	Clubs & associations	Legal framework
Industrial and provident societies	Working men's clubs, political associations – the Royal British Legion, sports clubs, social clubs, agricultural societies, retail and wholesale cooperatives (e.g. workers cooperatives), Friendly societies (new registrations only).	Industrial and Provident Societies Act 1965-78.
Friendly societies	Savings, insurance, private healthcare services, critical illness cover.	Friendly Society Act 1974 (No new registrations permitted).
Community interest companies (¶9926)	Profit for public good – community theatre groups – educational support for disadvantaged children.	The Companies (Audit, Investigations & Community Enterprise) Act 2004 + Community Interest Company Regulations 2005.
Unincorporated – Private members clubs	Social groups-small scale, shared interests, trade associations, political clubs, allotment societies, sports clubs and literary societies.	Not recognised as a legal entity. Register with the Charities Commission.

> *MEMO POINTS* **Clubs run for profit** such as proprietary clubs (e.g. night clubs and casinos) are registered under the following legislation: The Companies Act, The Gambling Act 2005 and the Licensing Act 2003.

Industrial and provident societies

Industrial and provident societies are mutual, incorporated societies and must register under the Industrial and Provident Societies Act 1965 (IPSA Act 1965). At present there are in excess of 8,000 societies and 3,000 clubs registered under this Act, categorised according to the nature of their activity, as set out in the table below. Societies run for the benefit of a community, must provide services for people other than their members and reinvest any surplus profit in the organisation.

9922

MEMO POINTS   The Co-operative and Community Benefit and Societies and Credit Union Act 2010 represents the latest in a series of measures designed to reform and modernise the regulatory position of NFP organisations providing financial services; namely those organisations with **mutual status** and whose classifications reflect their industrial origins, such as industrial and provident societies and credit unions.

Friendly societies

9925   A friendly society, otherwise known as a **mutual society or benevolent society**, typically provides insurance, pensions, savings and loan facilities, or cooperative banking services. Friendly societies are composed of people who join together for a common financial or social purpose, providing financial and social services to individuals, often according to their religious or political affiliations. Historically, these types of societies have played a very important role and although many of these societies still exist today, their numbers are in decline.

Registrations are now normally made under the Industrial and Provident Societies Act 1965 as no new registrations are permitted under the Friendly Societies Act 1974. Other friendly societies have developed as large mutually-run financial institutions (e.g. insurance companies), and have lost any social and ceremonial aspect they may have had; whilst others have taken on a more charitable or social aspect.

Community interest companies (CICs)

9926   A Community Interest Company (CIC) was introduced under the Companies (Audit, Investigations and Community Enterprise) Act 2004, and is **designed for social enterprises** that plan to utilise their profits and assets for a designated public good. CICs are relatively easy to set up, with all the flexibility and certainty of the company form, but with some **special features** to ensure they operate for the benefit of the community, rather than the need to maximise profit for shareholders.

CICs cover a wide range of social and environmental activities, operate in all parts of the economy, are diverse in character and include local community enterprises, social firms, and mutual organisations (e.g. co-operatives).

A CIC is not permitted to register as a charity but a charity can own a CIC, in which the profits are then directed into the charity. **Existing entities**, including charities, can convert to a CIC, by passing a special resolution amending their memorandum and articles of association. Charities can convert to a CIC, but will lose their charitable status in so doing.

CICs are subject to a **community interest test** and an **asset lock**, and must be approved by and continuously monitored by a special regulator.

9927   **Registration**   A CIC must register under one of the following **legal regimes**:
– a company limited by guarantee;
– a private limited company; or
– a public limited company.

The CIC format appeals to charities that want to separate their trading activities and pursuit of profit for the social good, from their philanthropic activities. Charities can run **trading operations**, although there is no guarantee that profits can be sheltered from tax. New charities may prefer to register as CICs where they intend to trade and hold property, although they must balance the advantages of a flexible corporate structure against the loss of tax concessions available to registered charities.

On registration, the company must submit a **Community Interest Statement** signed by all the directors, setting out the scope of its activities and how these will benefit the community.

Unincorporated clubs and associations

9929   Although **the majority of clubs are legally incorporated** there is still a significant number of smaller clubs that are not. Unregistered clubs have no separate legal status, but must still operate within a legal framework. Some clubs are registered under the Industrial Societies

Acts (e.g. employees' social clubs and canteens), whilst others, if selling alcohol, must be registered under the Licensing Act. Examples of such clubs include political associations, theatre clubs and sports clubs.

Each club must decide on its own set of rules and governance procedures. All the members are jointly entitled to a share of the club's property. The clubs have unlimited liability and the members are liable for any debts incurred in equal shares. Club members need to ensure that they are aware of their obligations in the event the club or association is wound up. Unincorporated clubs and associations generally elect a management committee, that is authorised to enter into contracts on the members' behalf and legal actions can be brought in the name of the club by the committee. The authority for signing contracts and division of powers, should be set out in the rules governing the club.

B. Accounting requirements

The accounting and audit requirements for the majority of clubs and associations can be found in the Industrial and Provident Societies Act 1965 and the Friendly Societies Act 1974. Whilst these Acts do not specify the exact form and content of the accounts, clubs are required to prepare a profit and loss account and balance sheet that comply with the requirements of UK GAAP. The majority of clubs and societies meet the size criteria for reporting under the FRSSE.   **9930**

In addition, the FSA has issued guidance on the preparation of accounting statements. Where the accounts do not comply with these guidance notes, an annual return obtainable from the Registrar of Companies must be completed. Where accounts are prepared for a period less or more than 12 months, the turnover should be pro-rated after deducting any discounts or VAT. The accounts must be signed by the secretary of the society and two other committee members.

Accounting records

All societies and clubs must maintain proper accounting records. The majority of clubs and associations are cash businesses that keep manual or simple computer records, for recording income and expenditure. A number of **accounting controls** should be in place to ensure the protection of the clubs assets. Each club must be able to demonstrate that its accounting records are detailed and accurately present a true picture of the club's financial activities.   **9931**

Accounting records	Basic information required
Cash book	Show different types of income, with zero rated or exempt VAT items clearly identified. Income from non-members (e.g. rental income from conferences, functions etc) should also be analysed separately, to demonstrate compliance with the rules for mutuality. A summary of general income controls is given in the table below.
Fixed asset register	Details of categories of asset, residual values, depreciation, NBV
Wages/Salaries	P11 for each staff member, Tax paid + NI Other PAYE forms (P46)
Goods received	Records of deliveries, bar stocks, invoices etc.

9932

Income by type	Controls
Subscription/membership fees	Joining fees, annual subscriptions, life membership fees reconciled to register of members.
Bar income	Records of bar takings should be retained, including till rolls, till readings etc. Regular cash reconciliations should be the norm, with variances between receipts and cash banked examined. Till records should be scrutinised and any amendments checked and authorised.

Income by type	Controls
Fruit (gaming) machines	Controls should cover readings, cash collected. Machines should be emptied by an officer or club member as required by the Gambling Act. Unusual patterns (high number of jackpots etc.) should be investigated.
Ticket income	Ticket sales (e.g. fundraising events) reconciled to income received.
Raffles, bingo, lotteries	Records of prize monies, ticket sales must be kept.
Other income	Room hire, sponsorship jukebox, cigarette machines etc. Same controls needed as for fruit machines.

9933   **Taxation**   There are a number of taxation issues affecting clubs and associations, with perhaps the most complex involving VAT.

The principal VAT issue concerning clubs and associations is whether they are involved in a business activity, and if so, what is the exact nature of the income they receive. This will in turn dictate the VAT arrangements. A business activity is principally one involving a supply made in return for a consideration (although not necessarily a profit).

A club is deemed to undertake a business activity when it provides services to:
– members including: benefits, in return for subscriptions or a separate charge (e.g. admission fees); or
– non-members, in return for a charge (e.g. catering, social etc.)

Lobbying for a political or public/charitable cause or receipt of donations for which no benefits/services are supplied in return, does not constitute a business activity.

> *MEMO POINTS*   1. The **statutory definition** of a business activity has developed via case law and HMRC opinion.
> 2. Small clubs and associations may use one of the **VAT schemes** designed for small businesses such as cash accounting, the flat rate scheme or annual accounting.
> 3. If there is a **mixture of taxable and non-taxable supplies**. VAT registration may be an option under which the club would be partially exempt and able to recover some of its input tax. Non-taxable supplies could include club subscriptions which might be classified as a donation, and therefore outside the scope of VAT. In other cases, there might be a package of benefits, some of which are deemed a supply, thereby resulting in a mixed supply. However, this area can be complex and so specialist advice should be sought. For **a more detailed assessment** of the type of VAT issues facing clubs and association see *VAT Memo*.

Audit requirements

9934   Every society must be audited by a qualified auditor, unless it can claim exemption under the Deregulation (Industrial and Provident Society) Order 1996. The income and expenditure account should not be published until an audit has been conducted, and it should be accompanied by an audit report, except where the society has taken advantage of the exemptions available, as set out below.

If any of the above requirements have not been complied with this should be mentioned in the audit report, which should be drawn up in accordance with SAS 600.

9935   **Audit objective**   The auditor is required to report whether the accounts give a true and fair view of the society's affairs at the balance sheet date and that:
– the accounts comply with the requirements of the relevant legislation;
– the society has kept proper records and books of accounts;
– a system of internal controls is in place to cover transactions and prevent fraud and misuse of assets; and
– the accounts tally with the underlying accounting records.

Appendix

Sample format – Cash based receipts and payments accounts

9940

Receipts and payments accounts

Name of charity: ... The Equal/Unequal Pay Trust...
Registered number: ...2223334...
Financial year ending on: ...31 December 2013...

A. Unrestricted funds
See ¶9521 for a definition.
All figures to the nearest £.

A1	Receipts	Unrestricted funds	Restricted funds	Endowment funds	Total funds	Last year
A1a	Donations, legacies and other similar receipts (e.g. donations, legacies)					
A1b	Operating activities to further charity's objectives (e.g. local authority grants)					
A1c	Operating activities to generate funds (e.g. fundraising events)					
A1d	Investment income receipts (e.g. deposit interest)					
	Sub total (A1a-A1d)					
A2	Asset sales					
	Total receipts					

A3	Payments	Unrestricted funds	Restricted funds	Endowment funds	Total funds	Last year
	For generating funds(e.g. fetes, concerts, fundraising)					
	Grants					
	Charitable activities (staff costs)					
	Support costs (volunteers)					
	Management and administration (overheads, trustee meetings)					

A3	Payments	Unrestricted funds	Restricted funds	Endowment funds	Total funds	Last year
	Sub total					
A4	Asset & investment purchases					
	Total payments					
	Net of receipts/(payments)					
A5	Transfers between funds					
A6	Cash funds last year end					
	Cash funds this year end					

Statement of Assets and Liabilities at the end of the period

B1	Cash funds	Details	Unrestricted funds	Restricted funds	Endowment funds
		Current account			
		Deposit account			
	Total cash funds	(agree balances with receipts/payments account(s)			

B2	Other monetary assets	Details	Unrestricted funds	Restricted funds	Endowment funds
		Income tax rebate			
		Local authority grants			

B3	Investment assets	Details	Fund to which asset belongs	Cost (optional)	Current value (optional)
		Common investment funds	Endowment		

B4	Assets retained by the charity's own use	Details	Fund to which asset belongs	Cost (optional)	Current value (optional)
		Furniture – day centre	Endowment		
		Computer equipment	Unrestricted		
		Mini-bus	Restricted		

B5	Liabilities	Details	Fund to which liability relates	Amount due (optional)	When due(optional)
		Alarm call system	Unrestricted		
		PAYE + NIC	Unrestricted		

Signed by one or two trustees on behalf of all the trustees (Optional – see section...of notes)

1...   Name (Print)...

2...   Name (Print)...

Date of approval...

PART 11

General information

General information

I. Model Financial Statements

The following is a model Annual Report for a hypothetical company, The Example Company Limited.   **9945**

The annual report has been prepared for illustrative purposes only and shows typical disclosures and formats. While it serves as a guide to layout and style, a single example obviously cannot cater to all situations (and therefore it should not be used as a checklist). Similarly, the suggested disclosures do not necessarily apply to all companies.

Please note that the dates used in these model statements (years ending in **2X11** and **2X10**) are not intended to correspond with the actual calendar years 2011 and 2010; they merely reflect a current year and a previous year.

The Example Company Limited does not apply fair value accounting rules (and does not apply FRS 23, or relevant sections of FRS 25, FRS 26, and FRS 29).   **9946**

THE EXAMPLE COMPANY LIMITED

ANNUAL REPORT
AND ACCOUNTS
2X11

Directors
Mr A (Chairman)
Ms B (Managing Director)
Mr C
Mr D

Secretary
Mr E

Registered Office
125 Any Street
Anytown
AN1 0WN
England

Registered Number
012345678900
England and Wales

Auditors
True, Fair and Partners
125 Accountancy Square
Anytown
AN5 8YZ

THE EXAMPLE COMPANY LIMITED

REPORT OF THE DIRECTORS

The Directors present their Annual Report on the affairs of the Company, together with the accounts and the auditors' report for the year ended 5 April 2X11.

Principal activity

The principal activity of the company during the year under review was the manufacture and distribution of electronic components.

Business review

Sales turnover in the year under review was £xxxx compared with £xxxx in the previous year. Sales turnover reflected the continued demand for the company's products and services. Trading margins were xx.x% (2X10 – xx.x%) reflecting more competitive market conditions experienced during the financial year than previously.

[The above is an example of a review in the simplest of circumstances. The review should cover the following:
- *a fair review of the company's business, and*
- *a description of the principal risks and uncertainties facing the company.*

The review required is a balanced and comprehensive analysis of:
- *the development and performance of the company's business during the financial year; and*
- *the company's position at the end of that year, consistent with the size of the business and its complexity.*

The review must, to the extent necessary for an understanding of the development, performance or position of the business, include:
- *analysis using financial key performance indicators; and*
- *where appropriate, analysis using other key performance indicators, including information relating to environmental and employee matters.*]

Future developments

[An indication should be given of the likely future developments in the company's business.]

Financial risk management

The company's operations expose it to a variety of financial risks that include the effects of changes in debt market prices, credit risk, liquidity risk and interest rate risk. The company has in place a risk management programme that seeks to limit the adverse effects on the financial performance of the company by monitoring levels of debt finance and the related finance costs.

In order to ensure stability of cash out flows and hence manage interest rate risk, the company has a policy of maintaining 90% of its debt (2X10 – 90%) at fixed rates. The company seeks to minimise the risk of uncertain funding in its operations by borrowing within a spread of maturity periods. Given the size and nature of operations, the company's policy is to operate with 50% of its debt being repayable within one year. At the year end, 53% (2X10 – 49%) of debt was repayable within one year. The company does not use derivative financial instruments to manage interest rate costs and no hedge accounting is applied.

Given the size of the company, the directors have not delegated the responsibility of monitoring financial risk management to a sub-committee. The policies set by the board of directors are implemented by the company's finance department. The department has a policy and procedures manual that sets out specific guidelines to manage interest rate risk, credit risk, and circumstances in which it would be appropriate to use financial instruments to manage these.

Price risk

The company is exposed to commodity price risk as a result of its operations. However, given their size, the costs of managing exposure to commodity price risk exceed any potential benefits. The directors will revisit this policy should the company's operations change in size or nature. The company has no exposure to equity securities price risk, as it holds no listed or other equity investments.

Credit risk

The company has implemented policies that require appropriate credit checks on potential customers before sales are made. Where debt finance is used, this is subject to pre-approval by the board of directors, and such approval is limited to financial institutions with an AA rating or better. The amount of exposure to any individual counterparty is subject to a limit, which is reassessed annually by the board.

Liquidity risk

The company actively maintains a mixture of long-term and short-term debt finance that is designed to ensure that the company has sufficient available funds for operations and planned expansions.

Interest rate cash flow risk

The company has both interest-bearing assets and interest-bearing liabilities. Interest-bearing assets include only government securities and cash balances, all of which earn interest at fixed rates. The company has a policy of maintaining debt at fixed rate to ensure certainty of future interest cash flows. The directors will revisit this policy should the company's operations change in size or nature.

[Note: This disclosure is not required where the information is not material for the assessment of the company's assets, liabilities, financial position and profit or loss. In addition, there is an exemption for small companies from making these disclosures.]

Results and dividends

Turnover for the year was £xxx (2X10 – £xxx). Profit before taxation and goodwill was £xxx (2X10 – £xxx). Profit before taxation was £xxx (2X10 – £xxx).

The Directors have proposed a final ordinary dividend of x pence per share, which, together with the interim dividend of x pence, make a total for the year of x pence (2X10 – x pence). The Company will pay the final ordinary dividend on 30 April 2X11 to shareholders on the register at the close of business on 22 March 2X11.

Directors

The directors in office during the year, and their interests in the company's issued ordinary share capital, were as follows:

	Number of Ordinary shares of £1	
	2X11	2X10
Mr A	xxx	xxx
Ms B	xxx	xxx
Mr C	xxx	xxx
Mr D	xxx	xxx
Ms E	-	xxx

Ms E retired as a director on 15 January 2X11.

Ms B and Mr D retire by rotation at the Annual General Meeting, and, being eligible, offer themselves for re-election. Their service contracts can be terminated by either party's giving not less than twelve months' notice in writing.

Statement of directors' responsibilities   The directors are responsible for preparing the directors' report and the financial statements in accordance with applicable law and regulations.

Company law requires the directors to prepare financial statements for each financial year. Under that law, the directors have elected to prepare the financial statements in accordance with United Kingdom Generally Accepted Accounting Practice. Under company law, the directors must not approve the financial statements unless they give a true and fair view of the state of affairs of the company and of the profit or loss of the company for that period. In preparing those financial statements, the directors are required to:
• select suitable accounting policies and then apply them consistently;
• make judgements and estimates that are reasonable and prudent;
• state whether applicable UK accounting standards have been followed, subject to any material departures disclosed and explained in the financial statements; and
• prepare the financial statements on the going concern basis unless it is inappropriate to presume that the company will continue in business.

The directors are responsible for keeping proper accounting records which disclose with reasonable accuracy at any time the financial position of the company and enable them to ensure that the financial statements comply with the Companies Act 2006. They are also responsible for safeguarding the assets of the company and hence for taking reasonable steps for the prevention and detection of fraud and other irregularities.

Political and charitable contributions

During the year, the company made a political contribution to the X Party of £xx and various charitable contributions totalling £xx.

Events since the balance sheet date

There have been no significant events since 5 April 2X11.

Differences between market and balance sheet value of land

In the opinion of the directors, the difference between the market value and balance sheet value of land is not significant.

Supplier payment policy

Company policy is to set terms of payment when agreeing each transaction with suppliers, clearly explain payment procedures, consistently settle bills within contract terms and extend terms only with prior agreement. The Company operates systems for promptly advising suppliers of, and resolving, queried and contested items.

Trade creditors of the Company at 5 April 2X11 were equivalent to 35 days' purchases (2X10 – 45 days'), based on average daily amount invoiced by suppliers during the year.

Employee involvement

Quarterly meetings are held between senior management and employee representatives to discuss matters of concern. Employees are kept well informed about the progress and position of the Company by means of regular departmental meetings, newsletters, journals and, as part of an initiative introduced during the year, the intranet.

An employee share scheme, which is open to all full-time employees, is operated.

Equal opportunities   The Company is committed to the principle of equal opportunity in employment and to ensuring that no applicant or employee receives less favourable treatment on the grounds of gender, race, age, colour, nationality, religion or belief, HIV status, disability, sexuality, pregnancy or maternity or unrelated criminal convictions or other unjustified requirements or conditions.

The Company applies employment policies that are fair and equitable and that ensure entry into, and progression within, the Company is determined solely by application of job criteria, personal ability and competency.

Disabled persons   The Company gives full consideration to applications for employment from disabled persons where the requirements of the job can be adequately fulfilled by a disabled person. Where existing employees become disabled, it is the Company's policy to provide continuing employment under normal terms and conditions.

Disclosure of information to auditors

[*The report must contain a statement that – in the case of each of the directors who are directors at the date of the approval of the report – the following applies:*
• *so far as the director is aware, there is no relevant audit information of which the company's auditor is unaware; and*
• *he has taken all the steps that he ought to have taken as a director in order to make himself aware of any relevant audit information and to establish that the company's auditor is aware of that information.*]

Auditors

The auditors, True, Fair and Partners, have signified their willingness to continue in office and a resolution to re-appoint them as auditors will be proposed at the Annual General Meeting.

125 Any Street	**By order of the Board**
Anytown	[*Name of signatory & Signature*]
AN1 0WN	...
England	**Director**
(registered office)	[*Date*]

THE EXAMPLE COMPANY LIMITED

INDEPENDENT AUDITORS' REPORT TO THE MEMBERS OF THE EXAMPLE COMPANY LIMITED

We have audited the financial statements of The Example Company Limited for the year ended 5 April 2X11, comprising the Profit and Loss Account, the Balance Sheet, the Cash Flow Statement, the Statement of Total Recognised Gains and Losses and the related notes numbered 1 to 18. The financial reporting framework that has been applied in their preparation is applicable law and United Kingdom accounting standards (United Kingdom Generally Accepted Accounting Practice).

Respective responsibilities of directors and auditors

As explained more fully in the Directors' Responsibilities Statement set out on page x, the directors are responsible for the preparation of the financial statements and for being satisfied that they give a true and fair view. Our responsibility is to audit the financial statements in accordance with applicable law and International Standards on Auditing (UK and Ireland). Those standards require us to comply with the Auditing Practices Board's Ethical Standards for Auditors.

Scope of the audit of the financial statements

An audit involves obtaining evidence about the amounts and disclosures in the financial statements sufficient to give reasonable assurance that the financial statements are free from material misstatement, whether caused by fraud or error. This includes an assessment of: whether the accounting policies are appropriate to the company's circumstances and have been consistently applied and adequately disclosed; the reasonableness of significant accounting estimates made by the directors; and the overall presentation of the financial statements. In addition, we read all the financial and non-financial information in the annual report and financial statements 2X11 to identify material inconsistencies with the audited financial statements. If we become aware of any apparent material misstatements or inconsistencies we consider the implications for our report.

Opinion on financial statements

In our opinion the financial statements:
– give a true and fair view of the company's affairs as at 5 April 2X11 and of the profit for the year then ended;
– have been properly prepared in accordance with United Kingdom Generally Accepted Accounting Practice; and
– have been prepared in accordance with the requirements of the Companies Act 2006.

Opinion on other matter prescribed by the Companies Act 2006

In our opinion the information given in the Directors' Report for the financial year for which the financial statements are prepared is consistent with the financial statements.

Matters on which we are required to report by exception

We have nothing to report in respect of the following matters where the Companies Act 2006 requires us to report to you if, in our opinion:
– adequate accounting records have not been kept, or returns adequate for our audit have not been received from branches not visited by us; or
– the financial statements are not in agreement with the accounting records and returns; or
– certain disclosures of directors' remuneration specified by law are not made; or
– we have not received all the information and explanations we require for our audit.

[Signature]
John Smith (Senior Statutory Auditor)
For and on behalf of True, Fair and Partners
Chartered Accountants and Statutory Auditors
Anytown
[Date]

THE EXAMPLE COMPANY LIMITED

PROFIT AND LOSS ACCOUNT
FOR THE YEAR ENDED 5 APRIL 2X11

	Notes	2X11 £	2X10 £
Turnover	2	xxx, xxx	xxx, xxx
Cost of sales		xxx, xxx	xxx, xxx
Gross profit		xxx, xxx	xxx, xxx
Distribution costs		xxx, xxx	xxx, xxx
Administrative expenses		xxx, xxx	xxx, xxx
Operating profit (loss)	3	xxx, xxx	(xxx, xxx)
Loss on disposal of fixed assets		xxx, xxx	xxx, xxx
Income from investments		xxx, xxx	xxx, xxx
Interest payable		xxx, xxx	xxx, xxx
Profit (loss) on ordinary activities before taxation		xxx, xxx	(xx, xxx)
Taxation		xx, xxx	x, xxx
Profit (loss) for the financial year after taxation		xxx, xxx	(xxx, xxx)
Dividends	4	xx, xxx	xx, xxx
Retained profit (loss) for the financial year		xxx, xxx	(xx, xxx)
Retained profit at 6 April 2X10 (2X09)		xxx, xxx	xxx, xxx
Retained profit at 5 April 2X11 (2X10)		£xxx, xxx	£xxx, xxx

The Company's turnover and expenses all relate to continuing operations for both the current and the prior year.

THE EXAMPLE COMPANY LIMITED

BALANCE SHEET AT 5 APRIL 2X11

	Notes	2X11 £	2X10 £
Fixed assets			
Intangible fixed assets	5	xxx, xxx	xxx, xxx
Tangible fixed assets	6	xxx, xxx	xxx, xxx
Listed investments	7	xxx, xxx	xxx, xxx
		xxx, xxx	xxx, xxx
Current assets			
Stocks	8	xxx, xxx	xxx, xxx
Debtors	9	xxx, xxx	xxx, xxx
Cash at bank and in hand		xxx, xxx	xxx, xxx
		xxx, xxx	xxx, xxx
Creditors – amounts falling due within one year	10	(xxx, xxx)	(xxx, xxx)
Net current assets		xxx, xxx	xxx, xxx
Total assets less current liabilities		xxx, xxx	xxx, xxx
Creditors – amounts falling due after one year	11	(xxx, xxx)	(xxx, xxx)
Net assets		£xxx, xxx	£xxx, xxx
Capital and reserves			
Called-up share capital	12	xxx, xxx	xxx, xxx
Share premium account	13	xxx, xxx	xxx, xxx
Revaluation reserve	13	xxx, xxx	xxx, xxx
Profit and loss account	13	xxx, xxx	xxx, xxx
Total shareholders' funds	14	£xxx, xxx	£xxx, xxx

THE EXAMPLE COMPANY LIMITED

STATEMENT OF TOTAL RECOGNISED GAINS AND LOSSES
FOR THE YEAR ENDED 5 APRIL 2X11

	2X11 £	2X10 £
Profit for the year after taxation	xxx, xxx	xxx, xxx
Unrealised surplus on revaluation of property	xxx, xxx	xxx, xxx
Total recognised gains relating to the year	£xxx, xxx	£xxx, xxx

There are no material differences between the profit on ordinary activities before taxation and the retained profit for the financial year stated above and their historical cost equivalents.

[The Statement of Total Recognised Gains and Losses should be shown as a primary statement with the same prominence as other primary statements. However, it could also be shown underneath – and on the same page as – the profit and loss account.]

THE EXAMPLE COMPANY LIMITED

CASH FLOW STATEMENT
FOR THE YEAR ENDED 5 APRIL 2X11

	2X11 £	2X10 £
Net cash inflow from operating activities	xxx, xxx	xxx, xxx
Returns on investments and servicing of finance:		
Interest paid	(x, xxx)	(x, xxx)
Interest received	x, xxx	x, xxx
Taxation	(xx, xxx)	(xx, xxx)
Capital expenditure:		
Payments to acquire intangible fixed assets	(xx, xxx)	(xx, xxx)
Payments to acquire tangible fixed assets	(xx, xxx)	(xx, xxx)
Receipts from sale of tangible fixed assets	(xx, xxx)	(xx, xxx)
Capital expenditure	(xx, xxx)	(xx, xxx)
Equity dividends paid	(xx, xxx)	(xx, xxx)
Cash outflow before use of liquid resources and financing	xxx, xxx	xxx, xxx
Management of liquid resources	(xx, xxx)	(xx, xxx)
Financing:		
Issue of ordinary share capital	xx, xxx	xx, xxx
Expenses paid in connection with share issue	(x, xxx)	(x, xxx)
Increase in cash in the financial year	£xx, xxx	£xx, xxx

THE EXAMPLE COMPANY LIMITED

NOTES TO THE ACCOUNTS AT 5 APRIL 2X11

1 Accounting policies

Basis of accounting

The accounts have been prepared on a going concern basis, under the historical cost convention as modified by the revaluation of certain tangible fixed assets and in accordance with the Companies Act 2006 and applicable accounting standards in the United Kingdom. The principal accounting policies are set out below.

Turnover

Turnover represents net invoiced sales of goods, excluding VAT.

Tangible fixed assets

Depreciation is provided, after taking account of any grants receivable, at the following annual rates in order to write off each asset over its estimated useful life:

Freehold buildings – 2% on cost or revalued amounts

Plant and machinery – 15% on cost

Fixtures and fittings – 10% on cost

Motor vehicles – 25% on cost

No depreciation is provided on freehold land.

Stocks

Stocks and work in progress are valued at the lower of cost and net realisable value, after allowing for obsolete and slow-moving items. Cost includes all direct expenditure and an appropriate proportion of fixed and variable overheads.

Deferred taxation

Deferred tax arises as a result of including items of income and expenditure in taxation computations in periods different from those in which they are included in the company's accounts. Deferred tax is provided in full on timing differences which result in an obligation to pay more, or less, tax at a future date, at the average tax rates that are expected to apply when the timing differences reverse, based on current tax rates and laws.

Deferred tax is not provided on timing differences arising from the revaluation of fixed assets where there is no commitment to sell the asset.

Research and development

Expenditure on research and development is written off in the year in which it is incurred.

Foreign currencies

Assets and liabilities in foreign currencies are translated into sterling at the rates of exchange ruling at the balance sheet date. Transactions in foreign currencies are translated into sterling at the rate of exchange ruling at the date of the transaction. Exchange differences are taken into account in arriving at the operating profit.

Leased assets

Rentals applicable to operating leases where substantially all of the benefits and risks of ownership remain with the lessor are charged against profit as incurred.

Assets held under finance leases and hire purchase contracts are capitalised and depreciated over their useful lives. The corresponding lease or hire purchase obligation is treated in the balance sheet as a liability. The interest element of rental obligations is charged to the profit and loss account over the period of the lease at a constant proportion of the outstanding balance of capital repayments.

Pension costs

Contributions in respect of the company's defined contribution pension scheme are charged to the profit and loss account for the year in which they are payable to the scheme. Differences between contributions payable and contributions actually paid in the year are shown as either accruals or prepayments at the year end.

2 Turnover

Turnover, all of which originates in the United Kingdom, comprises retail and wholesale sales, net of returns, and is shown exclusive of value added tax and discounts allowed.

3 Operating profit (loss)

The operating profit (2X10 – loss) is stated after charging:

	2X11 £	2X10 £
Amortisation of intangible fixed assets	xxx, xxx	xxx, xxx
Auditors' remuneration	xxx, xxx	xxx, xxx
Depreciation of tangible fixed assets	xxx, xxx	xxx, xxx
Directors' emoluments	xxx, xxx	xxx, xxx
Pension costs	xxx, xxx	xxx, xxx

4 Dividends

	2X11 £	2X10 £
Non-equity preference dividend	xx, xxx	xx, xxx
Ordinary shares	xx, xxx	xx, xxx

5 Intangible fixed assets

	Goodwill £	Other £	Total £
Cost			
At beginning of year	xxx, xxx	xxx, xxx	xxx, xxx
Additions	-	xxx, xxx	xxx, xxx
(Disposals)	-	(xx, xxx)	(xx, xxx)
At end of year	xxx, xxx	xxx, xxx	xxx, xxx
Amortisation			
At beginning of year	xxx, xxx	xxx, xxx	xxx, xxx
Charge for the year	x, xxx	x, xxx	xx, xxx
(On disposals – written back)	-	(x, xxx)	(x, xxx)
At end of year	xxx, xxx	xxx, xxx	xxx, xxx
Net book values			
At end of year	xxx, xxx	xxx, xxx	xxx, xxx
At end of previous year	xxx, xxx	xxx, xxx	xxx, xxx

6 Tangible fixed assets

	Freehold land and buildings	Motor vehicles	Fixtures and equipment	Total
	£	£	£	£
Cost				
At beginning of year	xxx, xxx	xxx, xxx	xxx, xxx	xxx, xxx
Additions	xxx, xxx	xxx, xxx	xxx, xxx	xxx, xxx
(Disposals)	(xx, xxx)	(xx, xxx)	(xx, xxx)	(xx, xxx)
At end of year	xxx, xxx	xxx, xxx	xxx, xxx	xxx, xxx
Depreciation				
At beginning of year	xxx, xxx	xxx, xxx	xxx, xxx	xxx, xxx
Charge for the year	xxx, xxx	xxx, xxx	xxx, xxx	xxx, xxx
(On disposals – written back)	(xx, xxx)	(xx, xxx)	(xx, xxx)	(xx, xxx)
At end of year	xxx, xxx	xxx, xxx	xxx, xxx	xxx, xxx
Net book values				
At end of year	xxx, xxx	xxx, xxx	xxx, xxx	xxx, xxx
At end of previous year	xxx, xxx	xxx, xxx	xxx, xxx	xxx, xxx

The net book value of fixtures and equipment includes £xxx (2X10 – £xxx) in respect of assets held under finance leases. The amount of depreciation in respect of these assets was £xxx for the year (2X10 – £xxx).

7 Listed investments

Listed investments consist of investments listed on the London Stock Exchange.

	2X11 £	2X10 £
Cost		
At beginning of year	xxx, xxx	xxx, xxx
Additions/(disposals)	xx, xxx	(xx, xxx)
At end of year	xxx, xxx	xxx, xxx

8 Stocks

	2X11 £	2X10 £
Work in progress	xxx, xxx	xxx, xxx
Finished goods and goods for resale	xx, xxx	xx, xxx
	xxx, xxx	xxx, xxx

9 Debtors

	2X11 £	2X10 £
Trade debtors	xxx, xxx	xxx, xxx
Prepayments and accrued income	xx, xxx	xx, xxx
Other	xx, xxx	xx, xxx
	xxx, xxx	xxx, xxx

Other debtors include an amount of £xxx (2X10 – £xxx) falling due after more than one year.

10 Creditors – amounts falling due within one year

	2X11 £	2X10 £
Obligations under finance leases and hire purchase contracts	xxx, xxx	xxx, xxx
Bank loans	xxx, xxx	xxx, xxx
Other loans	xxx, xxx	xxx, xxx
Trade creditors	xxx, xxx	xxx, xxx
Corporation tax	xxx, xxx	xxx, xxx
Value added tax	xxx, xxx	xxx, xxx
Payroll taxes and social security	xxx, xxx	xxx, xxx
Accruals	xxx, xxx	xxx, xxx
Proposed dividend	xxx, xxx	xxx, xxx
	xxx, xxx	xxx, xxx

Finance leases are secured against specific assets.
Bank loans are secured by fixed and floating charges over the company's assets.
Other loans of £xxx comprise guaranteed loan notes, which attract interest of 2.85%. All loan notes are redeemable at par and are repayable in December 2X11.

11 Creditors – amounts falling due after one year

	2X11 £	2X10 £
Obligations under finance leases and hire purchase contracts	xxx, xxx	xxx, xxx
Other loans	xxx, xxx	xxx, xxx
Secured bank loans	xxx, xxx	xxx, xxx
	xxx, xxx	xxx, xxx

The Company's borrowings are repayable as follows:

On demand or within one year
Hire purchase and finance leases £xxx (2X10 – £xxx)
Loans and overdrafts £xxx (2X10 – £xxx)

Between one and two years
Hire purchase and finance leases £xxx (2X10 – £xxx)
Other loans £xxx (2X10 – £xxx)

Between two and five years
Hire purchase and finance leases £xxx (2X10- £xxx)
Loans £xxx (2X10 – £xxx)

12 Called-up share capital

	2X11 £	2X10 £
Allotted, called-up and fully paid		
60,000 (2X10 – 50,000) ordinary "A" shares of £x each	xx, xxx	xx, xxx
6,000 ordinary non-voting "B" shares of £x each	xx, xxx	xx, xxx
	xxx, xxx	xxx, xxx

During the year, 10,000 ordinary "A" shares of £x were allotted and fully paid at a premium of £x per share.

13 Reserves

	Share Premium	Revaluation Reserve	Profit and Loss
	£	£	£
At beginning of year	xx, xxx	xx, xxx	xx, xxx
Share issue during year	x, xxx	-	-
Retained profit for the year	-	-	xx, xx
	xx, xxx	xx, xxx	xx, xxx

14 Shareholders' funds

Analysis of shareholders' funds

	2X11 £	2X10 £
Equity	xx, xxx	xx, xxx
Total shareholders' funds	xx, xxx	xx, xxx

[*In this example, the company has only ordinary shares in issue. However, had there been non-equity shares in addition, e.g., preference shares, the non-equity element of shareholders' funds would be shown here, together with a description of the underlying shares. Such a disclosure might take the following form*:

Shareholders' funds attributable to non-equity interests comprise 25,000 5% preference shares of £1 each at par value. Dividends, which are cumulative, are payable annually at 5% net of tax credit. The shares are redeemable at par, solely at the company's option. In the event of winding up, these shares have a priority over ordinary shares to the extent of their par value and any arrears in respect of dividends. Except when dividends are in arrears, these shares carry no vote.]

Reconciliation of movements on shareholders' funds

	2X11 £	2X10 £
Profit for the year after tax	xx, xxx	xx, xxx
Less: Dividends	xx, xxx	xx, xxx
	xx, xxx	xx, xxx
Other recognised gains for the year	xx, xx	xx, xx
Share capital issued	xx, xx	-
	xx, xx	xx, xx
Opening shareholders' funds at beginning of year	xx, xx	xx, xx
Shareholders' funds at end of year	xx, xx	xx, xx

15 Contingent liability

A claim for damages amounting to £xx, xxx has been served on the company in respect of a road traffic accident involving one of the company's delivery vehicles. The directors have sought legal advice on the basis on which the other company is contesting the case, which is considered to be without foundation. Consequently, no provision has been made in the accounts.

16 Commitments

Capital commitments

At 5 April 2X11, capital expenditure commitments were as follows:

	2X11 £	2X10 £
Contracted but not provided for	xx, xxx	xx, xxx

Pension commitments

The company operates a defined contribution pension scheme on behalf of its directors and certain employees. The assets of the scheme and those of the company are held separately. The scheme is administered in an independent fund. The annual commitment under this scheme is for contributions of £xx, xxx (2X10 – £xx, xxx).

Lease commitments – operating leases

At year end, the company had annual commitments of £xx, xxx (2X10 – £x, xxx) under non-cancellable operating leases.

17 Related party transactions

Loan to director

During the year Mr D was granted a short-term loan in respect of the purchase of a residence. Indebtedness on the loan was as follows:

Liability at beginning of year	£ Nil	
Maximum liability during the year		£xx, xxx
Liability at end of year		£xx, xxx

The loan is repayable on 5 June 2X13. Interest, at the rate of x% per annum, is payable upon repayment. At 5 April 2X11 no interest was due and unpaid.

Material interests of directors

During the year the company purchased goods to the value of £xx, xxx (2X10 – £xx, xxx) from A.N. Other Company Limited, a company in which Mr A is materially interested as a shareholder. The purchases were made on a normal trading basis.

Controlling party

Ms B, a director, together with members of her close family, control the company by virtue of a controlling interest (directly or indirectly) of 58.5% of the issued ordinary share capital.

18 Post balance sheet events

On 18 July 2X10 the company acquired the net assets of Competitor Limited, for a consideration of £xx, xxx, which has been financed by a secured loan, repayable over six years.

II. Lists

9950

Financial Reporting Standards		¶¶
FRS 1	Cash flow statements	4000
FRS 2	Accounting for subsidiary undertakings	6558+
FRS 3	Reporting financial performance	4300
FRS 4	Capital instruments	3001
FRS 5	Reporting the substance of transactions	110
FRS 6	Acquisitions and mergers	6800
FRS 7	Fair values in acquisition accounting	6866
FRS 8	Related party disclosures	5000
FRS 9	Associates and joint ventures	7300
FRS 10	Goodwill and intangible assets	1000
FRS 11	Impairment of fixed assets and goodwill	1550
FRS 12	Provisions, contingent liabilities and contingent assets	3250
FRS 13	Derivatives and other financial instruments: disclosures	3000
FRS 14	*Earnings per share (superseded by FRS 22)*	
FRS 15	Tangible fixed assets	1210
FRS 16	Current tax	9005
FRS 17	Retirement benefits	8400
FRS 18	Accounting policies	7
FRS 19	Deferred tax	9120
FRS 20	Share-based payment	8850
FRS 21	Events after the balance sheet date	5700
FRS 22	Earnings per share (replacing FRS 14)	
FRS 23	The effects of changes in foreign exchange rates	8373
FRS 24	Financial reporting in hyperinflationary economies	8392
FRS 25	Financial instruments: disclosure and presentation	3000
FRS 26	Financial instruments: measurement	3000
FRS 27	*Life assurance (to be withdrawn in favour of FRS 102)*	
FRS 28	Corresponding amounts	
FRS 29	Financial instruments: disclosures	3000
FRS 30	Heritage assets	9586
FRSSE	Financial Reporting Standard for Smaller Entities	6000+
	Improvements to Financial Reporting Standards (2010)	Various
FRS 100	Application of Financial Reporting Requirements	Various
FRS 101	Reduced Disclosure Framework	Various
FRS 102	The Financial Reporting Standard applicable in the UK and Republic of Ireland	Various
FRS 103	Insurance contracts (FRED 49)	

9960

Statements of Standard Accounting Practice	
SSAP 4	Accounting for government grants
SSAP 5	Accounting for value added tax
SSAP 9	Stocks and long-term contracts
SSAP 13	Accounting for research and development
SSAP 19	Accounting for investment properties
SSAP 20	Foreign currency translation
SSAP 21	Accounting for leases and hire purchase contracts
	Guidance notes on SSAP 21
SSAP 25	Segmental reporting

9970

Urgent Issue Task Force Abstracts	
UITF Abstract 4	Presentation of long-term debtors in current assets
UITF Abstract 5	Transfers from current assets to fixed assets
UITF Abstract 9	Accounting for operations in hyper-inflationary economies
UITF Abstract 11	Capital instruments: issuer call options
UITF Abstract 15	Disclosure of substantial acquisitions
UITF Abstract 19	Tax on gains and losses on foreign currency borrowings that hedge an investment in a foreign enterprise
UITF Abstract 21	Accounting issues arising from the proposed introduction of the euro
UITF Abstract 22	The acquisition of a Lloyd's business
UITF Abstract 23	Application of the transitional rules in FRS 15
UITF Abstract 24	Accounting for start-up costs
UITF Abstract 25	National Insurance contributions on share option gains
UITF Abstract 26	Barter transactions for advertising
UITF Abstract 27	Revision to estimates of the useful economic life of goodwill and intangible assets
UITF Abstract 28	Operating lease incentives
UITF Abstract 29	Website development costs
UITF Abstract 31	Exchanges of businesses or other non-monetary assets for an interest in a subsidiary, joint venture or associate
UITF Abstract 32	Employee benefit trusts and other intermediate payment arrangements
UITF Abstract 34	Pre-contract costs
UITF Abstract 35	Death-in-service and incapacity benefits
UITF Abstract 36	Contracts for sales of capacity
UITF Abstract 38	Accounting for ESOP trusts
UITF Abstract 39	(IRFIC Interpretation 2) Members' shares in co-operative entities and similar instruments
UITF Abstract 40	Revenue Recognition and service contracts
UITF Abstract 41	Scope of FRS 20 (IFRS 2)
UITF Abstract 42	Reassessment of embedded derivatives
UITF Abstract 43	The interpretation of equivalence for the purposes of section 228A of the Companies Act 1985
UITF Abstract 44	(IFRIC Interpretation 11) FRS 20 (IFRS 2) – Group and Treasury Share Transactions
UITF Abstract 45	(IFRIC Interpretation 6) Liabilities arising from Participating in a Specific Market – Waste Electrical and Electronic Equipment
UITF Abstract 46	(IFRIC Interpretation 16) Hedges of a Net Investment in a Foreign Operation
UITF Abstract 47	(IFRIC Interpretation 19) Extinguishing Financial Liabilities with Equity Instruments
UITF Abstract 48	Accounting implications of the replacement of the retail prices index with the consumer prices index for retirement benefits

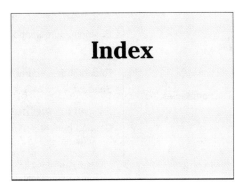

Index

Using the index

Numbers refer to paragraphs.

Entries that duplicate the Outline at the head of each chapter are not repeated in the index; refer instead to the main entry in respect of individual subjects.

The symbol + following a paragraph number indicates that the subject is dealt with in the series of paragraphs beginning with that number.

The following abbreviations are used in the index.

Govt	Government	**PBS**	Post balance sheet events
IGUs	Income generating units	**P&L a/c**	Profit and loss/profit and loss account
L/T contracts	Long term contracts	**R&D**	Research and development
		SMEs	Small and/or medium-sized entities
JVs	Joint ventures	**TFAs**	Tangible fixed assets

A

Abbreviated accounts:
Main entry: 6270+
Auditors' report: 5845
Reporting options for smaller companies: 6001

Abnormal costs:
Of stock: 2044

Actuarial Council:
Main entry: 224

Accounting conventions:
Main entry: 185
Current cost accounting: 196
Current purchasing power: 196
Historical cost convention: 195
Modified historical cost convention: 196

Accounting Council:
Regulatory framework financial reporting: 220

Accounting periods:
Group accounts: 6714
Non-coterminous year-ends for subsidiaries: 6716

Accounting policies:
Abbreviated statements by small companies: 6290
Change in: 491
Finance costs capitalised:
SMEs under FRSSE: 6116+
Leasing and hire purchase contracts: 3514
SMEs:
Choice, revision etc: 6046
Revaluations: 6121+
See also specific subject heading – e.g. Stock, etc.

Accounting principles: 3+

Accounting records:
Requirements to keep: 9310

Accounting reference date (ARD): 9306

Accounting reference period (ARP):
Restrictions on changing: 9305
Shortening of: 9358

Accruals basis:
Accounting principle: 35
Accruals: 3218

Accrued income disclosure:
Debtors: 2454

Acquisition accounting:
Business combinations: 6820

ACT:
Recognition of current tax: 9056
Shadow ACT: 9040

Actuarial method:
Defined benefit scheme: under FRS 17:
Actuarial loss: 8494
Assumptions: 8449+
Gains and losses: 8486
Information: 8456

Adaptation works:
Tangible fixed assets: 1398

Adjusting events:
Post balance sheet – recognition: 5706

Administration costs:
Tangible fixed assets: 1270
Overhead costs: 380

Agency agreements:
Disclosed:
Implications for dormant status: 6464
Undisclosed:
Implications for dormant status: 6468

Agency companies:
For dormant companies: 6460

Accountancy Investigation and Discipline Board (AIDB): 236

Allocation:
Of lease rentals: 3421
Of assets to income-generating units (IGUs): 1594

Alternative accounting rules:
Current asset investments: 2730
Fixed assets: 1358
Fixed asset investments: 1795
Stock: 2109
Tangible fixed assets: 1230

Amortisation:
Goodwill for associates: 7374
Methods of: 1086
Of intangible fixed assets: 1122
Of issue costs: 412

Annual revaluations:
Updated valuation of tangible fixed assets: 1358

Donated services:
Charities: 9530

Donations:
Charitable: 4546, 6116 (SMEs), 9530
Political: 4532
Services: 9530

Dormant companies:
Main entry: 6400+
Filing requirements: 6444

Dormant status:
Criteria for claiming: 6410
Ending of: 6450

E

Early repayment of debentures: 3042

Earnings, unremitted: 9158, 9158

Emissions allowances:
Intangible assets: 1012

Employee:
Policies – directors' report: 4576
Services (share based payment): 8867

Endowment funds: 9519
Charities: 9519

Environmental accounting/reporting: 4592

Equities:
Defined benefit scheme under FRS 17:
Expected return on assets: 8494

Equity instrument (share based payment): 8860

Equity method of accounting:
Accounting for associates & JVs: 7460

Equivalent rights (Associates): 7330

ESOPs/ESOP Trusts:
Type of fixed asset investment: 1784
See also Employee share plans

Estimates:
On long-term contracts: 2252

Estimation techniques:
Choice by SMEs: 6046

Euro:
Changeover:
In general: 476
Tangible fixed assets: 1499
Impact on accounting systems: 8146

Exceptional items:
Associates: 7374
Cash flows: 4085
SMEs: 6089
Tangible assets: 1244
Types of: 474

Exchange differences (or gains and losses):
SMEs: 6248

Exchange rates:
Differences – tangible fixed assets: 1290
Forward rate: 8312
Methods of accounting: 8130
Spot rate: 8310

Excluded costs:
Existing use value: 1390

Exclusion from consolidation:
Of subsidiaries:
Grounds for: 6570
Mandatory: 6570
Segmental reporting: 6790

Executive committee:
Regulatory framework: 216

Exemptions:
Associates and joint ventures (disclosures): 7506
Cash flow statement: 4010
Filing of accounts: 9380
From Companies Act and Accounting Standards – SMEs: 6000+
Group accounts: 6520

Existing use value (EUV):
Valuation basis: 1390

Expenses:
Administrative: 380

Extension:
For filing financial statements: 9360

External review:
Valuing property: 1377

Tax-free grants: 3461

Taxation:

Main entry: 9000+

Cash flow statements: 4052

Debtor balances (VAT, Recoverable Corporation Tax): 2454

Exchange gains: 8132

Grants: 7974

P&L disclosure requirements: 426

R&D: 1176

Relief on finance costs: 1290

SMEs: 9170

Intangible assets: 1063

Temporal method:

Cash flows from foreign subsidiaries: 4228

Foreign currency translation method: 8094

Termination:

Early termination of a lease: 3410

Profit or loss: 385

Tests for control:

Not for profit organisations: 9706

Third party:

Control exercised by: 6539

Development contracts: 1178

Threshold disclosures:

For associates and joint ventures: 7524

Time limits:

For filing financial statements: 9354

Timing differences: 1438

Trade debtors: See Debtors

Trade discounts:

Deduction from turnover: 368

Exclusion from stock valuation: 2025

Trademarks:

Intangible assets: 1012

Trading assets (unsold): 2085

Trading stock: 2005

Training costs:

Government grants for training: 7936

Transactions:

Currency:
Settled: 8032
Unsettled: 8040

Transactions *(continued)*

Group: 6732

Sale and leaseback: 3485

Significant accounting transactions: 6410

With directors:
Main entry: 5027+

Translation rates:

Re: Foreign currency: methods of: 8010

Treasury shares:

Disclosure: 3085

Legal procedures: 3689

True and fair view:

Main entry: 4+

Application to smaller companies: 6040

STRGL: 4302

Trustee annual report: 9664

Turnover:

Associates – accounting for share of turnover: 7374

Components of: 368

SMEs: 6095

Limit on SME exemptions: 6017

Long-term contracts: 2260

U

Uncleared banking items: 2626

Underlying accounting records:

Books of prime entry: 9312

Understandability:

Accounting policies: 27

Unified basis:

Identifying a parent-subsidiary relationship: 6535

Uniform accounting policies:

Re: group accounts: 6708

Unit costs: See Batch costing: 2055

Unit production cost method:

Method of valuing closing stock: 2076

Unlimited companies:

Filing exemptions: 9388

Unlisted investments/securities: 4077, 8444

Typeset by NORD COMPO
Printed April 2014 by L.E.G.O. S.p.A, Lavis (TN)